PROSPERITY
AND UPHEAVAL
THE WORLD ECONOMY
1945–1980

Herman Van der Wee

Translated by
Robin Hogg and Max R. Hall

UNIVERSITY OF CALIFORNIA PRESS
Berkeley · Los Angeles

University of California Press
Berkeley and Los Angeles, California

LIBRARY OF CONGRESS CATALOGING IN PUBLICATION DATA

Wee, Herman Van der.
    Prosperity and upheaval.
    (History of the world economy in the twentieth
century; v. 6)
    Translation of: De gebroken welvaartscirkel.
    Bibliography: p.
    Includes index.
    1. Economic history——1945—   I. Title.
II. Series.
HC59.W38513 1986——330.9′04——85–22282
ISBN 0–520–05709–0 (alk. paper)
ISBN 0–520–05819–4 (pbk.)

Printed in Great Britain

For Monique, Miek, and Babs: with love

CONTENTS

LIST OF TABLES

LIST OF GRAPHS

PREFACE

World economic development since the Second World War has traced a fascinating course. In global terms, the balance can undoubtedly be seen as a positive one. Over much of the world, material well-being increased significantly and in many other countries the industrialization process was begun or there were signs of economic development. Naturally there have also been countless disappointments; the distribution of wealth and income around the world has been far from ideal.

To write a book that summarizes the main developments of the post-war world economy was a major challenge, to put it mildly. The material was so complex that not all issues could be adequately covered, and the documentation and literature were so abundant that a selection had to be made. The subject itself had to be redefined in order to give the book a coherent framework. The term 'world economy' is thus used only in respect of those countries which can be said to have formed part of a world economy in its fullest sense, that is the Western industrialized nations, especially in Western Europe and North America, together with Japan. As a further form of shorthand, Japan, despite its geographical position, is treated as part of the 'Western' economy. Other countries have been covered only in so far as they came into contact with the West. From the end of the 1960s onwards, the Eastern bloc and the Third World have been studied more fully, since from that time they became more actively integrated into the world economy.

The book is in two parts. In Part One, the achievements of the world economy between 1945 and 1980 are examined. First there was the rapid transition by the United States from wartime to peacetime economy and, for the rest of the world, the powerful recovery from the ruins of the Second World War. Later came the spectacular expansion of world production and international trade, the smoothing of cyclical fluctuations in the economy, and the attainment of higher living standards, particularly in the industrialized nations of the West. A final achievement was the industrialization of a number of developing countries, unmistakable indications of this appearing in the 1970s. Naturally there was also much disillusion, the most bitter examples undeniably being the stagflation and the high unemployment of the late 1970s in the West, and the continued underdevelopment and poverty in many Third World countries.

Part One is not confined to a description of events – an explanatory framework has been added. This is reflected in the structure of the book, so that from Chapter III the approach is systematic rather than chronological. Malthusian explanations are treated first. What effect has the demographic explosion in the second half of the twentieth century had on agricultural development in the West and elsewhere? What effect has the Western mass consumer economy had on the world's production of raw materials and energy, and how has it faced the difficulties encountered in both those fields? A second series of questions concerns supply. To what extent has the supply of economic resources, notably labour, capital, and entrepreneurship, contributed to the growth achieved in the 1950s, 1960s, and early 1970s? Similarly, to what extent can it be regarded as responsible for the economic crisis of the late 1970s and the early 1980s? A third and final series of explanations concerns demand. To what extent have social activity and the internationalizing of social life and trade widened the demand for modern consumer goods? How far can these same factors explain the recent slackening of demand?

The second part of the book is about the institutional structure of the world economy. The central question of Part Two is as follows: did new institutions and new social systems make the construction of the post-war modern consumer economy possible, and must they also bear some responsibility for the stagflation of the late 1970s and early 1980s and the consequent decline in prosperity? To tackle this problem three separate sub-themes are outlined. The first concerns the 'mixed economy'. To what extent has this new form of economic system contributed to the establishment of the post-war affluent society and what, if any, long-term negative effects has it had? The same questions are asked in respect of the organization of world trade after the Second World War and finally of the international monetary system after the Bretton Woods Agreement.

Although in both parts this book adopts a systematic approach, the chronology of events is not wholly neglected and in fact is often used as a point of reference for the sub-themes. The choice of a systematic treatment obviously brings with it the danger of over-lapping, and indeed there are repetitions despite my endeavours to avoid them as much as possible. But the advantages of a systematic approach seemed so overwhelming that they more than made up for the drawback of having some repetition here and there.

One final remark. This book was written for a wide readership in the hope that it could give the interested layman an insight into the complex economic events which have taken place since the war. The use of graphs and tables has been restricted as much as possible in order to make the book more readable.

This book would not have been written without the help of many people, and I must express my sincere gratitude to all of them. First I would like to thank various academic institutions. The Katholieke Universiteit te Leuven and its President Professor Dr Pieter de Somer gave me the opportunity to make time available for research. The Nationaal Fonds voor Wetenschappelijk Onderzoek van België and its Deputy-Secretary-General José Traest greatly supported my research project and provided many other invaluable services. The Woodrow Wilson International Center for Scholars in Washington DC, and its Director J. H. Billington and Deputy-Director P. Gifford, granted me a fellowship for the academic year 1975–6 which made it possible for me to do the groundwork for this book. The Institute for Advanced Study in Princeton and its Director Professor Dr Harry Woolf, the School of Historical Studies, also in Princeton, and in particular Professor Dr John H. Elliott, granted me a fellowship as well, so that I could spend the academic year 1981–2 in the United States and complete the book. I received on two occasions a Fulbright-Hayes Award from the Commission for Educational Exchange between the United States of America, Belgium and Luxemburg in connection with my stays in Washington and Princeton.

I am no less grateful to those who gave me assistance in the preparatory research, Geert Dancet, Guy Hendrix, Jan Piet Ureel, and above all Frank Vandenbroucke. Many colleagues and friends have helped me with comments or advice, François R. Crouzet, Paul de Grauwe, Johan de Vries, Jan de Vries, William Fellner, Wolfram Fisher, Rainer Fremdling, Gottfried Haberler, Max M. R. Hall, Peter Mathias, Hugo Paemen, William N. Parker, R. W. Rasmussen, Robert Triffin, Dominique Van der Wee, Leo Van Houtven. I am also much obliged to those who helped to prepare the text for the printers, Erik Aerts, Jenny Overton, Stefaan Peeters, Martine Goossens, Chris Schroeven, and the staff of the Centrum voor Economische Studiën at Leuven. Finally I wish to express my heartfelt thanks to my wife for all the dedication, patience, and wit she put into the finishing of this book.

Herman Van der Wee

De Hettinghe, 27 February 1985

PART ONE

ECONOMIC GROWTH:
SUCCESSES AND PROBLEMS

CHAPTER I

WAR AND RECOVERY, 1945–50

The Second World War greatly exceeded the First in losses of men, destruction of buildings and equipment, and slumping of morale. This was as true for the winners as for the losers, and recovery was therefore a major undertaking for all. The fight against inflation required strenuous exertion. Overcoming the problem of the dollar shortage in Europe appeared impossible without American help. A whole new economic ideology was necessary in order to provide a firm foundation for future society.

1. WAR LOSSES

It is a remarkable paradox that the prosperity achieved by the West during the third quarter of the twentieth century was preceded by a disastrous world depression and a bloody, destructive war. As a result of these misfortunes Europe, and Japan and some other Asiatic countries, could well have entered a period of fundamental decline. Initially this was indeed the case. Everywhere production for the war effort had ceased, and except in the United States the transition to a peacetime economy met with serious difficulties.

Human losses had been enormous. Estimates vary between 45 and 50 million dead. According to Angus Maddison, in Europe (including the Soviet Union) there were about 42 million dead, four times the number during the First World War. In the Soviet Union alone, 20 million died.[1] If one adds the severely wounded, sick and disabled (in Japan, for example, these numbered 4 million as against 2 million dead), the losses appear even more apocalyptic.[2]

The material losses, too, were not restricted to Europe but occurred also in North Africa and in East and South-East Asia. Capital infrastructure in Europe and the Far East was seriously damaged.[3] The transport system had almost collapsed. Everywhere, demolished bridges paralysed the railway network and hindered traffic along rivers and canals. The railways also suffered from a woeful shortage of rolling stock. In pre-war France, for instance, there were about 17,000 locomotives, but only 3,000 were serviceable in 1945. The German submarine offensive had dealt a heavy blow to European merchant shipping. In Japan only 10 per cent of the merchant navy survived intact.[4] Numerous ports in Europe (notable exceptions being Antwerp and Bordeaux) were unusable or only partly usable, and the same was true in East Asia. Private motor vehicles in Europe and in Asia had almost disappeared.

The destruction of houses and other buildings was just as considerable. In Germany 10 million dwellings, 40 per cent of the total, were wiped out or badly damaged. In Britain the number was 4 million, or 30 per cent; and in France it was 2 million, or 20 per cent. In Japan one-quarter of all dwellings were destroyed and 2 million people were without shelter. In Nagasaki and Hiroshima there was, in addition to the material devastation, the terrible psychological trauma of nuclear warfare.

The human losses, the physical and mental exhaustion of the surviving population, and the damaged capital infrastructure, all contributed to the initial slowness of recovery in Europe and in East Asia. Agricultural production was disrupted by lack of manpower, the reduction in livestock, the shortage of fertilizer, and the devastation of a large amount of farmland, either by flooding or in other ways. The resumption of industrial production in Europe was retarded by the extremely low level of stocks of raw materials and semi-finished goods, and by transport difficulties. At that time coal was an important source of energy, and so disorder in the coal industry was another brake on recovery. For years machines for non-military production had been neither replaced nor modernized and were generally in need of attention. Whole factories had been crippled or blown off the earth, and others were dismantled either during or after the war by occupying powers.

Germany lost all the territory it had annexed before and during the war. The transfer of the Saar to France was only temporary, but East Prussia and the lands east of the Oder-Neisse were lost for good. Some Eastern and Central European countries received portions of these lands, but in turn they had to cede territory to the Soviet Union. Among the areas coming under Russian sovereignty were the Baltic States, Eastern Prussia, Eastern Poland, Bessarabia, the Transcarpathian Ukraine, the Kuril Islands, South Sakhalin, and part of Finland. Japan had to give up its colonies, notably Manchuria, Korea, and Formosa (now Taiwan), losing nearly one-half of the Japanese Empire as it had existed in 1930. Furthermore, these territories were ones in which Japan had made large industrial investments. The large-scale ceding of territory and redrawing of frontiers caused migrations involving millions of people. In Japan about 5 million civilians and troops were repatriated, causing serious problems of reintegration. In Eastern, Central, and South-Eastern Europe, migration assumed still larger proportions, for vast numbers of people abandoned or were driven from their homelands. Thus arose the tragic problem of displaced persons who could not readily fit themselves into a totally new environment.

The effect of all this was overwhelming. In Japan famine was so acute and appalling that the American authorities decided to grant direct aid. In 1946 Japanese industrial production fell to one-fifth of the average recorded between 1939 and 1944.[5] In Germany too, the situation was traumatic, 1945 being regarded as *das Jahr Nul* (the Year Zero).[6] Many Germans had to be satisfied with a daily food ration of less than 1,000 calories, and during the bad winter of 1946–7 there was a serious shortage of coal for both industrial and domestic purposes. In the rest of Europe too, the situation was critical. During the war living standards had fallen below subsistence levels and many had already died from undernourishment. The end of the war naturally brought an improvement in many countries, but the greatly reduced productivity of labour, land, and capital caused poverty to remain widespread. Moreover, the dislocation of the transport network generally increased the tendency towards autarky. Central and Eastern Europe, which before the war had exported a large amount of food to Western Europe, now had barely enough to satisfy the area's own needs – a situation made worse by the ceding of land to the Soviet Union. During these years, the United States, either directly or via the United Nations Relief and Rehabilitation Administration (UNRRA), provided considerable help in feeding the populations of Western and Central Europe, the Soviet Union, and many other famine-affected areas.

In contrast to reduced, stagnating, or barely increasing production stood a huge rise in the amount of paper money. During hostilities, the combatant nations had already financed their war effort by increasing the issue of bank notes and floating state loans. Occupied countries had also financed both the obligatory deliverance of goods and the payment of war taxes imposed on them by the occupying power through an increase in note issue and the national debt. Immediately after the war, the situation deteriorated further. Liberated countries financed reconstruction and recovery by further use of the printing press and still more borrowing. France provides a good example of post-war developments. Between 1938 and 1945, the national debt quadrupled and the money supply quintupled.[7] Further stimulus to this headlong movement came after liberation when the government, for psychological reasons, decided to relax price controls. The imbalance between swollen purchasing power and the serious shortage of consumer goods instantly led to steep price inflation. Inflation was even worse for the defeated powers, since they had to use note issue to finance occupation costs and reparations, while at the same time their scarcity of goods was even greater.[8]

In Britain the difficulties were of a different nature. Price controls and rationing were continued after the war and were also much stiffer than elsewhere. Moreover, the post-war recovery was financed by a sharp increase in taxation, sales of foreign assets, and enormous loans raised in the United States and in Commonwealth nations. In consequence, there was little difference in consumption per head between the war period and immediately afterwards, and post-war inflation was comparatively moderate (Table 1). On the other hand,

Table 1 *Index of Wholesale and Consumer Prices*

	Index of wholesale prices in 1949 (1945 = 100)	Index of consumer prices in 1948 (1937 = 100)
France	511	1,900
United Kingdom	122	180
Belgium	290	400
United States	146	166

Source: P. LEON (ed.) *Guerres et crises 1914–1947*, p. 519, p. 522

the so-called sterling balances held by other countries piled up and Britain became very greatly indebted to the United States. In the long term the huge debt would weigh heavily on Britain and compromise post-war economic development.

2. POSITIVE EFFECTS OF THE WAR

The war did not have an exclusively negative influence. In this matter the Soviet Union provides the clearest example. Although human and material losses were much greater than elsewhere, at the same time the Soviet Union was able to increase its territory by annexation. In addition, during the war the transfer of factories from Soviet Europe to areas east of the Urals laid the foundation for industrial development in Soviet Asia. The post-war dismantling and transfer to the Soviet Union of German and other factories had a similar expansive effect. Finally, the Russians gained the opportunity to exercise political and economic controls over countries in Eastern and South-Eastern Europe. These controls were the start of a successful policy for the western extension of Soviet hegemony.[9]

The United States also emerged from the war considerably strengthened.[10] Human losses were substantial, but material destruction was minimal. Industry grew spectacularly because of a massive transition from peacetime to wartime economy, an expansion in the stock of capital goods, a notable increase in employed labour, and rising productivity. Despite the entry of 12 million Americans into the armed forces, the employed labour force grew by 20 per cent, specifically from 54 million in 1940 to 64 million in 1945. This miracle could only be achieved because of the existence of an unemployed labour reserve of 9 to 10 million at the start of the war. Other factors were an increase in the working population and the greater number of economically active women. The considerable rise in production per worker came largely from longer working hours (in manufacturing the average working week rose from 37.7 hours to 45.2), from patriotic motives, and from co-operation by the unions.

Immediately after the war, the United States carried out a fast and successful transition to a peacetime economy. Although at one time half of industrial capacity had been geared for war production, the transition appeared practically complete by the middle of 1947 and a high level of employment could still be maintained. The chief explanations for the achievement were: good government planning, programmes to retrain army veterans, a rapid expansion of personal consumption, a similar expansion of investment in inventories and equipment, and, finally, the government-organized export of goods and services. In the period from 1938 to 1948 the index number for Gross National Product (GNP), at constant prices, rose from 100

Table 2 *Index of Gross National Product at Constant Prices after the Second World War: Western Europe, United States, Japan, and the Soviet Union* (*1938 = 100*)

	1938	1948	1950
Belgium	100	115	124
France	100	100	121
West Germany	100	45	64
Italy	100	92	104
Netherlands	100	114	127
Norway	100	122	131
Sweden	100	133	148
Switzerland	100	125	131
United Kingdom	100	106	114
Western Europe	100	87	102
United States	100	165	179
Japan	100	63	72
Soviet Union	100	105	128

Sources: A. MADDISON, *Growth in Japan and the USSR*, p. 154, p. 155
W. W. ROSTOW, *World Economy*, p. 234

to 165 (Table 2). During the same period, the index figure for Western Europe fell from 100 to 87.[11] For the Soviet Union the figures were slightly better than in Western Europe but in Japan they were considerably worse.[12]

This strengthening of economic might helped to support the American post-war policy of leadership of the Western world. This new American attitude was a complete reversal of the inter-war position. In reality, as far back as the turn of the century, the United States had already emerged as the strongest nation on earth; and the United States should have taken over the role of leading nation from Britain after the Treaty of Versailles in 1919. The dollar had become the strongest currency and New York the most important international money and capital market. American industry was now the most powerful and innovative in the world, and already the first outlines of the modern consumer society were taking shape there. Yet still the United States refused to accept the role commensurate with its economic power, preferring instead to maintain its isolationist tradition. A high point of American isolationism was reached at the start of the Great Depression when the government implicitly rejected a role of 'stabilizing leadership' in the world economy. According to Charles Kindleberger, this rejection had a disastrous influence on the course of the Depression because it led to the increasing break-up of international trade and capital flows.[13] This attitude continued right up to the Second World War, an unwelcome event which nevertheless brought the Depression to an end.

The American elite retained a vague feeling of guilt for these twentieth-century developments, and the historical context facilitated the post-war reversal of earlier policy as the Americans adopted a more 'international' approach. The United States consciously took over the reins of world leadership, capitalized on the enlarged economic lead it had gained over the rest of the world during the war and sought to realize the dream of a *Pax Americana*, that is, a liberal world order under American leadership.[14]

The United States and the Soviet Union were not the only countries to derive positive benefits from the war. Other examples were Sweden and Switzerland, which had both remained neutral. In the 1938–48 period Sweden raised its GNP (at constant prices) from 100 to 133, Switzerland from 100 to 125. For many colonies and developing countries, the increase in the price of foodstuffs and raw materials in relation to that of industrial products was also a considerable advantage. This alteration in the terms of trade had been going on as early as 1936. The trend continued during the war and went on to reach a high point at the time of the Korean conflict.[15] The favourable income position which resulted was reflected in the imposing sterling balances which many Commonwealth nations and others were able to build up against Britain during and after the Second World War.

Some economists, including Sima Lieberman, have contended that in respect to stocks of capital goods the whole world benefited from the war. Although capacity in Germany, Japan, the Soviet Union, France, Britain, and Italy was certainly seriously damaged, the transport system and the stock of housing and other buildings were more affected than machinery. There was a considerable world-wide increase in investment for war production. Furthermore this growth was accompanied by much scientific and technological progress in the arms industry, and this in turn stimulated the training of technical and administrative people. Finally, most war investment and a number of military inventions could be speedily adapted to peacetime needs.[16] Walt W. Rostow found that in world production of a large number of the most important products, such as electricity, oil, natural gas, aluminium, rubber, and motor vehicles, the annual growth rate between 1938 and 1948 was greater than 5 per cent, and in some cases greater than 10 per cent.[17] This extension of the world's ability to produce, combined with the rather limited damage to capital equipment, largely explain the strength of economic growth in the industrialized nations of West and East during the 1950s.

3. THE NEW ECONOMIC IDEOLOGY

Growth and development were central objectives in the post-war economic policies of governments in the West, and this represented a fundamental revision of attitudes.

The revision had its origins in the disillusionment of previous decades. After the First World War, Europe had faithfully tried to re-establish the liberal capitalism of the nineteenth century. But the old paradigm soon appeared totally unsuited to the new economic circumstances of the inter-war period. The orthodox recipes of classical economics failed to bring about any self-correcting economic mechanism, either nationally or internationally. Fixed exchange rates and the gold standard no longer guaranteed stable world prices, because countries did not all follow identical policies designed to ensure equilibrium in the balance of payments. Countries found that the tragic problem of unemployment could no longer be solved by balanced budgets and deflation, because the union movement was able to restrict the downward flexibility of wages. During the disastrous crisis years of the 1930s, belief in the liberal economy evaporated and its instruments were increasingly regarded as irrelevant and even irrational.[18] In contrast, the successes of Nazi Germany, with its extensive state intervention, and the progress of the Soviet Union, due to its five-year plans, made a great impression. '*Laissez faire, laissez passer*' as guiding doctrine was dead.

The British economist John Maynard Keynes provided a theoretical framework for the new developments in his book *The General Theory of Employment, Interest and Money* (1936). By means of a subtle, careful analysis of the prevailing economic uncertainty and the behaviour of entrepreneurs, he gave an explanation for the stubborn persistence of low economic activity. According to his analysis, the economic mechanism did not automatically guarantee full employment. Moreover, government deflationary policies would bring no benefit but in fact the reverse. Instead, a government had to introduce active counter-cyclical policies in order to raise demand to a level that ensured full employment. Keynes was not, however, against the principle of the market economy and free competition. He merely wanted to make sure that the system operated at a higher equilibrium of demand and employment rather than a lower one.

As well as generating new theories, the crisis of the 1930s also promoted new departures in the study of economic statistics. Institutes were set up to chart the course of economic development in quantitative terms. The Dutchman Jan Tinbergen took a pioneering role in this. During the war, the methods of collection and study of economic statistics made further strides. Many new techniques for economic measurement were invented in order to improve the planning of the war economy. From that moment, all-inclusive systematic national accounts were compiled, and these were used as points of economic plans.

Thus the war completed a change of mentality in the West. Traditional liberalism was seen to have caused the Great Depression, which in turn was only ended by the catastrophe of world war. The post-war economy had to start anew. The former priority for balance-of-payments equilibrium had to make way for the domestic interests of the national economy. Social objectives of the economic system were now given precedence, based on the idea of the right to work, set out by Lord Beveridge in his *Full Employment in a Free Society*. Keynesian doctrine provided the theoretical framework for the new economic order. Only active government intervention designed to maintain full employment could bring a socially just stability to the free-market economy. At the same time the Keynesian school elaborated a whole series of new instruments and techniques for government intervention, especially with respect to income redistribution by means of fiscal policy, and with respect to counter-cyclical budgetary policies. The 'Keynesian Revolution' in consequence played a decisive role in the development of the mixed economy after the Second World War.

Naturally there were also other forces at work. Some countries in continental Europe, including France and Germany, had a long tradition of state intervention. Germany had even introduced a system of central planning of production during the First World War. In some cases the socialist-inspired plans to meet the crisis of the 1930s were also influential.

The mixed economy found its first application in a series of legislative measures framed to promote full employment in Britain, Sweden, the United States and elsewhere.[19] Large-scale nationalizations, especially in France, Italy, and Britain, gave it further impetus. This nationalizing ensured that the state would become the largest employer in the land and at the same time gave the government total control over key sectors of the national economy.

Full employment was only one aspect of the social objectives which characterized the mixed economy. No less important was income redistribution, which had to be organized and guaranteed by the state. In many countries, examples being Britain, the Netherlands, France, and Belgium, plans for an all-embracing system of social security, supported and guaranteed by the government or the government-in-exile, or by the resistance movements, had been worked out during the war. These plans were gradually implemented when peace was established.

Other methods of redistributing income were also given attention. A final aspect of the social objectives was the creation of an economic democracy in which both workers and employers, possibly guided or controlled by the state, would participate in industrial decision-making. Important initiatives were taken in this field in Europe. The United States lagged behind. Indeed the Taft-Hartley Act of 1947 went back on some of the concessions gained by American workers in the 1930s. In Europe, at the company level, attempts to further co-operation between the two sides of industry came to fruition with the creation of industrial councils. In some of these councils, workers were brought into closer contact with company affairs through share-holdings and profit-sharing. At the national level, bipartite councils operated for various industrial sectors. And on an even larger scale there was a national consultative structure, bringing together representatives of workers, management, and government to discuss socio-economic policy. This desire to promote co-operation in industry as a means of attaining the social objectives of the mixed economy was as new as the mixed economy itself and would make a decisive contribution to its success. Moreover, the spirit of co-operation was not limited to national politics but was clearly evident in the area of international trade and monetary relations.[20]

Once the social objectives of the mixed economy were reached, the prospect of the modern welfare state came into view. A policy of full employment, social security, income redistribution, and mutual co-operation held out the possibility of a share in prosperity for all. Yet there was more. Keynesian doctrine was initially concerned only with the reduction of cyclical unemployment. It was a theory designed to tackle the problem of domestic economic recovery – in other words, for short-term application only. Nevertheless the essence of the Keynesian lesson, that is, the idea of active government intervention, could also be applied to a theory of economic growth. The post-war policy of full employment and the construction of the modern welfare state quickly gave way to vigorous government policies to expand national production by increasing investment in men and machines. The welfare state thus transformed itself into the consumer society.

So the post-war years were characterized not only by impressive growth but also by the social and political consensus which supported it. Economic growth became a goal in itself and formed a central plank in post-war government programmes. Growth became a *frontier*, even an obsession. Moreover, the aim was not just to grow but to grow *fast*, faster than the historical average of the Western economies.[21] Governments announced minimum target growth figures which had to be reached. Many countries even went over to economic planning in order to be able to specify extra-high growth rates and ensure they were achieved. Some economists made a special study of refining the analysis of economic growth. They broke it down into its constituent parts in order to examine how it could be stimulated more systematically. At the same time many economists had become so convinced of the dynamism of economic growth that they believed that counter-cyclical policies could be limited to a few indicative measures.[22] These new ways of thinking and acting, which began to take hold in the West during the late 1940s, rose to dominance in the 1950s and 1960s. Thus economic growth as the mainspring of government policy will require a chapter of its own – Chapter II. But first there is more to tell about the momentous years before 1950, including the grim march of inflation, the shortage of dollars, and the Marshall Plan.

4. THE FIGHT AGAINST POST-WAR INFLATION

In the United States the rapid 'return to normality' convinced the general public and its elected representatives in Congress that the measures which had been introduced during the war to control the economy should be discontinued as soon as possible.[23] On 9 November 1946, President Harry Truman abolished all price controls except those on rents, sugar, and rice.[24] But considerable imbalance between demand and supply remained for all foodstuffs, as well as in the housing sector and motor car industry. There were various causes of this. After the general scarcity of consumer goods during the war, there was inevitably much pent-up demand, augmented by the growth in population, the return of 12 million servicemen, and the new-found business optimism. The increased money supply was also an important factor. Considerable savings had been made during the war and could now be drawn on. In addition the commercial banks were keen to make their abundant reserves available to the public, and there was still an inflow of gold from abroad. The large balance-of-payments surpluses contributed to this. To make matters worse, each effort by the government to freeze a part of the money supply by increasing taxes was hindered by a Congress distrustful of any measures restricting the free flow of economic forces. In total the amount of immediate short-term financial resources to which the public had access rose to $222.5 billion in mid 1946, as against $65 billion at the end of 1939.

In these circumstances inflation was unavoidable. With 1938–9 as a base period (equalling 100), the US wholesale price index between June 1946 and February 1948 rose from 147 to 210 and retail prices for the same dates rose from 150 to 192.[25] Wages rose too but did not keep step with prices and the consequent fall in real incomes came as a blow.[26] During the war, on the advice of their unions, workers had made great exertions to raise labour productivity and had settled for hourly wage increases which only kept pace with the cost of living. Nevertheless the overtime worked in war production had greatly increased the workers' 'take-home pay' and when peace brought overtime to an end they thought they were entitled to hourly increases sufficient to preserve the take-home levels to which they had become accustomed. Their disillusionment was so profound that in 1946 a major strike wave broke out, and there were additional strikes in 1947 and 1948. In 1946 alone there were 4,700 work stoppages in the United States, directly involving nearly 5 million workers.[27] Wages went up quickly and so did the pace of inflation. Public opinion held the workers and unions fully responsible for the high rate of inflation and the consequent economic disruption.

At the same time, there was a growth of prestige for the businessman, who, after the failures of the 1930s, had begun to play a more positive role and by increasing investment was laying down the foundations for a new period of prosperity. A conservative backlash was reflected in the legislation passed by Congress, which after the 1946 elections was dominated by the Republicans. The Labor-Management Relations Act of 1947, better known as the Taft-Hartley Act, was designed to curtail the powers granted to the unions under the old National Labor Relations Act of 1935. Labour union practices regarded as unfair were specifically listed and forbidden. The consensus in Congress over this was so great that President Truman's veto was overruled by a two-thirds majority.

The immediate effects of the Taft-Hartley Act were considerable. The new legislation helped to check rising production costs and gradually slow down the pace of American inflation. In turn, this stabilized the transition to peacetime economy and established American leadership over world industry. The technological lead and better labour productivity which the United States had built up during the war were thus not undermined by steep wage increases. Rising costs were curbed and extra-high profits were made, which in turn could be employed for new investment at home and abroad.[28] Industrial expansion during the war and the rapid return to normality and stabilization afterwards were important factors underpinning the change in American foreign policy. Isolationism could be abandoned and responsibility for political and economic leadership of the world assumed. The Americans could also begin to set up the means of achieving world-wide economic domination.

In Western and North-Western Europe, economic recovery was not so smooth a process. Price inflation was a serious problem which hindered rapid reconstruction and implied fundamental changes

for the future. The imbalance between the increased money supply
and the still limited supply of consumer goods was so enormous
that all countries were faced with strong inflationary tendencies.
Currency reforms followed, but these were not all equally prompt
or effective.

Belgium took the lead.[29] In October 1944, even before the country
was fully liberated, Finance Minister Camille Gutt implemented a
drastic currency reform. By means of organizing an obligatory
exchange of bank notes and blocking bank deposit accounts, the
amount of money in circulation was reduced from 140 billion Belgian
francs to 25 billion in bank notes and 6 billion in short-term
government bonds.[30] As production increased, part of the blocked
currency was freed accordingly. The rest was converted into long-
term government bonds which could be used for the payment of
taxes. The banks were subject to strict controls. At the same time,
in order to reduce the scarcity of goods in the country, Gutt relaxed
import controls. This enabled him to make use of the substantial
dollar reserves which Belgium had built up in the war as a result of
earnings, first by deliveries of uranium and copper from its African
colony to the United States and, secondly, from September 1944
onwards, by the intensive military use of the undamaged port of
Antwerp. Gutt's stabilization policy was very successful and was an
important element in the rapid post-war recovery of the Belgian
economy. Other countries tried to emulate the Belgian currency
reform, with varying degrees of success.

The Netherlands put the Lieftinck Reform into effect in September 1945. The reform itself was less drastic than in Belgium but
it was supplemented by a more interventionist policy of price
controls, subsidies, and continued rationing.

In France Pierre Mendès-France, then Minister of Economic
Affairs, proposed a currency reform closely based on the Belgian
example, but this was rejected by Charles de Gaulle. The deflationary policy which was to accompany the reform envisaged a drastic
decrease in military expenditure for at least two years and this
proved unacceptable to de Gaulle. Instead he chose a reform worked
out by the Finance Minister René J. Pleven, which started from a
totally different premise. Pleven wanted to postpone deflation until
the recovery of agricultural and industrial production had brought
a normal supply of goods. Bank notes were to be exchanged but
there was to be no partial blocking of currency in circulation. On

the other hand, a special tax would have the effect of taking excess money out of circulation. In reality, the proceeds of this tax were immediately used up in financing day-to-day expenditure, and any shortfall was made good by the creation of still more paper money. Consequently, despite attempts to stabilize the situation with price controls, inflation soared. Since wage increases lagged behind prices, social tension served to foster pessimism about France's future, and this led to a heavy outflow of capital. In the autumn of 1947 the new Finance Minister, René Mayer, launched a plan which broke with the system of rigid price controls and introduced multiple exchange rates. This liberalizing policy was a success and in 1948 was supplemented by a devaluation which reduced the official value of the French franc to 20 per cent of its 1944 value, expressed in gold and dollars.[31] Although the Mayer Plan did not dismantle completely the network of price cartels, it did represent an important step forward in the fight against inflation.

Britain tackled inflation with a specific policy, the main objective of which was to finance the costs of the war as much as possible from foreign sources.[32] This had already been done during the war, via the sale of foreign assets, the Lend-Lease agreements with the United States, and the increase in sterling balances abroad. The same policy was used to finance post-war reconstruction. Once again the United States and Canada provided large long-term loans, and the colonies and dominions continued to exchange their dollar holdings for sterling balances. Naturally, domestic measures were also taken to counter the threat of inflation. The Labour government which came to power in July 1945 further strengthened these measures. The Chancellor of the Exchequer, Stafford Cripps, announced in 1947 a new Austerity Policy which froze wages and profits and continued to restrict consumption by rationing. In addition, direct taxation, which during the war had almost equalized British incomes, remained high. The taxes and, even more, the strict rationing curbed prices in a very satisfactory way. The rationing, however, remaining in effect until 1954, kept the British standard of living at a low level. Cripps's policy was, furthermore, unable to restore equilibrium in the balance of payments. Direct import controls and a major export drive (many industrial sectors were obliged to export a specific proportion of their output) were obviously positive factors for the balance of payments. But these were totally insufficient to withstand the shock which came on 15 July 1947. On this date, under American pressure, Britain reintroduced full sterling convertibility, and the subsequent rush to exchange sterling into dollars was so great that after only two weeks convertibility had to be discontinued.[33] Britain's highly vulnerable balance of payments was to prove a major restraint on its post-war growth.

Switzerland and other neutral countries also had to face inflationary tendencies. Money which had been hoarded during the war suddenly reappeared, and government debts had increased considerably. Moreover, foreign capital sought refuge in Switzerland, and at the same time trade surpluses caused an inflow of yet more gold and foreign currency. Finally, the scarcity of goods throughout the world also served to push up Swiss prices. But inflation was curbed by a combination of measures, including gradual reductions in government expenditure and government subsidies to counteract some especially high prices. As a result, it was possible to stabilize the Swiss currency at its pre-war dollar parity, which was a major benefit to the financial sector. Similar steps to restrain inflation were taken in Austria, Sweden, Norway, and Denmark, among others.[34]

Those countries defeated in the war had still greater difficulties, at least in the short term, when it came to currency reform. During the initial post-war years most of them experienced alarming rates of hyperinflation. In Germany, where a repetition of the monetary catastrophe of the early 1920s was feared, almost nothing could be bought for money, and items such as cigarettes became an important medium of exchange. Japan had large budget deficits, and to finance them the government issued more paper money. This led to runaway rates of inflation in 1946 and 1947. Japanese wholesale prices increased almost 100-fold between 1945 and 1951. In Italy during the same years prices rose 26-fold and in Greece 110-fold.[35] Rumania and Hungary also suffered hyperinflation.

In 1946 the American authorities had submitted a detailed plan for German currency reform to the Control Council in Berlin, but nothing came of it owing to Russian objections. On 20 June 1948 the controllers of the three Western occupied zones went ahead with a currency reform of their own.[36] The objective was to reduce the amount of money in circulation and in bank deposits from 130 billion Reichsmarks (RM) to 12–13 billion Deutsche Marks (DM). The exchange of the old currency unit for the new was not done at a fixed rate but at a variable one. Every civilian was allowed to exchange directly a maximum of RM 40 for DM 40, that is at a rate of R M 1 = D M 1. The remaining notes in circulation and all bank deposits were converted at a rate of R M 10 = D M 1, and paid into new bank accounts, 30 per cent of each account being temporarily frozen.[37] During the first few days, businesses were permitted to exchange additional sums at the R M 1 = D M 1 rate, but only if this money was used to pay wages. One final measure was that all government debt was cancelled.

Although the German currency reform drastically curtailed hyperinflation, it was later subject to much criticism, especially in respect to its effect on bank credit. The cancellation of government debt hit the commercial banks very hard. Therefore steps were taken to increase their liquid assets by means of claims on the separate *Länder* (states). These steps, taken at the time that personal and company bank accounts were still partly frozen, stimulated *too much* bank credit. A 10 per cent inflation rate in the second half of 1948 was seen as a direct result. In November of that year new moves were made explicitly to reduce bank credit. These were apparently successful, in that prices stabilized during the following month.[38]

In Italy the Minister of Finance, Luigi Einaudi, attempted to stabilize the lira with a stringent deflationary policy. From the autumn of 1947, lending by the commercial banks was severely restricted. Advances by the Banca d'Italia to the government were also subject to strict limits. Finally the general price level was frozen, though at a level fifty times higher than it had been in 1938. Einaudi's policy was successful, and it ensured monetary stability in Italy for the next ten years.[39]

In Japan the Economic Stabilization Programme devised by Dodge, financial adviser to the Supreme Commander for the Allied Powers (SCAP), brought the post-war inflation to a standstill. A more nearly balanced budget, higher taxes, wage controls, drastic restrictions on bank lending, and a hefty currency devaluation, all contributed to a gradual improvement in Japanese finances from 1948 onwards. These measures, known as the 'Dodge Line', were an important factor in the recovery of the Japanese economy.[40]

In September 1949 most of the European countries devalued their currencies, establishing new exchange rates with the dollar. The effect was to bolster all the various currency reforms which had gone before. The somewhat arbitrary rates of 1944 were replaced by rates based on economic reality. Consequently parities in purchasing power became clearer and expectations about the future economic development of the countries found securer footing. The 1949 devaluations contributed substantially to economic recovery. Integration of the various national economies of the West into a new world system was now possible.

5. THE DOLLAR SHORTAGE AND THE MARSHALL PLAN

Meanwhile another serious obstacle to economic recovery outside the United States was being attacked with heroic measures. This was the acute shortage of dollars. Mainly because of this dollar gap, European reconstruction clanked to a halt in 1947.

The gap was largely caused by Europe's heavy reliance on imports. A sufficient supply of the new capital goods necessary to re-equip European infrastructure and industry was available in the United States only. That part of European capacity which had not been destroyed in the war was in any case considerably outdated and in need of replacement. In addition, European producers wanted to increase their investment, for two main reasons. First, they expected that demand in Europe for consumer goods would leap forward after the years of restraint. Secondly, they wanted to prepare for the confrontation with American producers, now that the United States had plumped for a liberal world trading system. There was not only demand for capital goods. American foodstuffs, industrial products, and energy were also needed. The demand for energy resulted from sluggishness in restoring coal production in Western Europe – delays caused by disruption of the industrial complex in the Ruhr, the general shortage of miners, and the scarcity of mining equipment. Europe's dependence on coal at that time made the problem a serious one.[41] Hence it was decided to import American coal.

Of course the time finally came when it was necessary for the European allies to pay back the colossal sums they had borrowed from the United States under the wartime Lend-Lease Act. Moreover, they also had to pay off other war debts they owed, including debts to their dominions and colonies. These payments had to be made in either dollars or goods. To make matters worse, the terms of trade after the war continued to move in favour of raw material producers.[42] Since economic recovery and the settlement of war debts required an early influx of raw materials Europe's trade balance suffered severely.

At the very time when Europe needed additional dollars to pay for the revival of industry and to reduce debts, its customary supply of dollars from exports and reserves took a bad tumble.[43] Exports of European goods were not only low but offered no expectation of immediate improvement. The United States' technological lead was too great. Despite higher wage costs, American industry with its better productivity was more competitive. Europe's performance in invisible trade – shipping services, tourism, and the like – was no more satisfactory. The German submarine offensive had largely destroyed merchant fleets in Europe. The London money and capital market was barely functioning, owing to lack of resources. Countries such as Switzerland, Sweden, and Belgium, which did have a trade surplus with the United States, could not pass their dollar balances on to other European countries since they would only receive weak, unconvertible currencies in exchange. Another factor was the considerable flight of capital out of Europe to the United States.

Initially, the American government thought that it could relieve these difficulties through long-term loans, such as the one made to Britain in order to restore sterling convertibility.[44] Such loans were to be used immediately to reduce Europe's huge balance-of-payments deficit. The long period of repayment would give European countries, in the mean time, the opportunity to complete their economic recovery and so enable them eventually to pay back the loans via trade surpluses.[45]

In fact things worked out differently. Inflation in the United States made the prices of the necessary European imports much higher than had been expected. A further blow was the total failure of the European harvest in 1947, forcing a request for American grain. Those two factors – US inflation and European weather – rendered the dollar shortage so acute that European countries had to slash their imports of American capital goods, thus prejudicing reconstruction and recovery.

In the mean time the Cold War had broken out and the United States came to see an economically strong Europe as a crucial bulwark against Russian expansionism.

A solution to the impasse, later known as the Marshall Plan, was presented in a speech by General George Marshall, the American

Secretary of State, at Harvard University on 5 June 1947. He proposed a large-scale aid programme to help complete European recovery. At the same time, American imports from Europe would be promoted by special measures. A final point was that Marshall aid was to be organized on a basis of economic co-operation among *all* European countries including the Soviet Union.[46] The Soviet Union, however, instructed the Eastern bloc countries to refuse to participate.

Apart from this, the Marshall Plan was a great success. It gave a new impetus to reconstruction in Western Europe and made a decisive contribution to the renewal of the transport system, the modernization of industrial and agricultural equipment, the resumption of normal production, the raising of productivity, and the facilitating of intra-European trade. Marshall aid also played a crucial role in the revival of the London money and capital market and financed indirectly the expansion of world trade. The index of GNP in Western Europe (1938 = 100) rebounded from 87 in 1948 to a level of 102 in 1950 (in constant prices), and the rapid increase continued thereafter.[47] In tonnage terms, Western European exports reached 123 in 1950 (1938 = 100).[48]

As important as the Marshall Plan was for the immediate recovery of the Western European economy, its effects were much more far-reaching than that.[49] The recovery permitted significant progress towards the attainment of a welfare state. In addition, the Marshall Plan consolidated the new world system of two dominant spheres of influence, East and West. Western Europe definitively chose the United States camp. Finally, the Marshall Plan and the Cold War were vital factors in the eventual recovery of West Germany and its rapid integration into the Western European economy.

West German economic recovery had been delayed because of an earlier conscious policy of the Allies to reduce German industrial capacity to a low level and instead give agriculture a greater priority. The 1945 Potsdam Conference and the inter-Allied agreement of March 1946 formulated concrete decisions to this end.[50] In order to eliminate the German economy's capacity to wage war, it was decided to implement a total ban on the German output of strategic products such as aluminium, synthetic rubber, and synthetic benzene. Furthermore, Germany would be obliged to reduce its steel capacity to 50 per cent of its 1929 level, and the superfluous equipment would be dismantled and transported to the victorious countries of both East and West. Nevertheless, contrary to the demands of the Soviet Union, the Western Allies, bearing in mind the lessons of the 1919 Versailles Treaty, decided not to set reparation payments at too high a level. One final important decision was that the economic unity of Germany would be restored.

Once again, things worked out differently. The destruction, the political chaos, and the millions of refugees from the eastern zone led to a dramatic dislocation of the German economy immediately after the war. Famine and misery were so great that the United States felt obliged to organize the free delivery of foodstuffs and raw materials (Government Appropriation for Relief in Occupied Areas). And, most important of all, the Cold War caused a radical change in the Western Allies' policy towards Germany. According to the framework of this new strategy, it became vital to strengthen the economy of West Germany. The creation of specific West German institutions was the first step towards complete recovery. The former policy of industrial dismantling was abandoned and replaced by a conscious American effort to revive economic activity in West Germany. Spectacular results, however, were not immediately achieved. For instance, in the Anglo-American occupied zones, industrial production in 1947 reached only 38 per cent of the 1936 level, and during the first half of 1948 it was still only 47 per cent.[51] Not until later that year, when both Britain and France fell fully in line with American policy and the International Control Authority for the Ruhr had been established, could West German industrial recovery really get under way. The currency reform of June 1948, already mentioned, was the starting-point. Under the new conditions of monetary stability, economic controls could be lifted. In order to give extra stimulus to investment, Ludwig Erhard, the Minister of Economic Affairs, relaxed price controls faster than wage controls. This served to increase social tension and a strike wave broke out at the end of 1948. But the government and employers were easily able to offer concessions in view of the prospective American aid. The path was now clear for the West German economic miracle.[52] Industrial production, which for the year 1948 reached only 63 (1936 = 100), by 1950 had risen to 113.7 and by 1951 to 136.

Recovery in Japan was much more slow and difficult. Agricultural production grew slightly but remained insufficient to feed the population, which had increased during the war. So the United

States had to step in and supply foodstuffs. The industrial situation was even worse, with industrial production in 1946 only 20 per cent of the annual average between 1939 and 1944. From 1947, production improved but only very slowly. It was not until 1954 that Japanese GNP reached pre-war levels; indeed on a per capita basis it was not until 1957.[53] Clearly, on these terms, West Germany had established a considerable lead in comparison to Japan. There were two main causes for this.

First, unlike Germany, Japan was not ringed by countries which themselves were recovering quickly and thus offered rapidly increasing sales markets. On the contrary, 40 per cent of Japan's pre-war trade had been with China, Korea, and Formosa (Taiwan), all of which were themselves struggling with economic and political difficulties in the post-war years.

A second explanation was that Japan for years was caught up in radical alterations to its institutional structure. American-style democracy was introduced. General Douglas MacArthur, using his position as Supreme Commander for the Allied Powers, set about completely reorganizing Japan in agricultural, financial, social and military terms.[54] An agricultural reform of October 1946 dispossessed non-resident, large-scale landowners and reduced the size of all extensive holdings, even when farmed by the owner. Many tenant farmers were granted their own land. Where tenancy remained, rents paid in kind were replaced by money rents. The small number of huge family fortunes (*Zaibatsu*) which had formerly controlled heavy industry and banking were broken up. The property rights of the families involved were expropriated and their representatives in industry removed from their positions of influence. The *Zaibatsu* banks were nevertheless permitted to continue to exercise control over their respective groups. The union movement, which had been very weak before the war, was encouraged to develop. Finally, Japan was forbidden an army. For a country that over many decades had spent vast sums on the military, this too entailed a radical change in economic structure – even more so than in Germany. In the long term, though, the disappearance of the military gave great impetus to recovery, for Japan could plough extra investment into its cherished export industries.

The onset of the Cold War marked a turning-point for Japan as it did for Germany. The United States could no more allow a power vacuum in Asia than in Europe. At the end of 1948 the Supreme

Command decided on a drastic policy to stimulate economic recovery.[55] As already mentioned, monetary stabilization was achieved on the basis of the Dodge Line. An impressive aid programme was built on this firm foundation. Many financial measures which dated from the period of democratization were abrogated so that the *Zaibatsu* concerns could gradually regain their former influence. The development of the union movement was once again restricted. The Korean War, in the early 1950s, offered Japan an outstanding opportunity to accelerate its economic growth. Military operations in the area created extra sales possibilities for goods and services, and Japan thus became important for storing arms, maintaining equipment, and providing general services for the United Nations troops. When armistice was agreed in July 1953, the Japanese recovery was already fully under way.

Thus the two main defeated powers of the Second World War, whose economies, according to the Allies' original policy, were to have been based largely on agriculture with some light industry, were soon on the way to regaining all their former industrial might. Indeed, this was not simply industrial recovery, for both West Germany and Japan began to realize their old dreams of industrial *supremacy*. What for them had proved unattainable through aggression could be achieved by means of peaceful conquest.

CHAPTER II

ECONOMIC GROWTH AS THE MAINSPRING OF GOVERNMENT POLICY

The memory of the Great Depression of the 1930s and the aftermath of the Second World War shaped the post-war economic policies of the Western governments. Full employment was to be attained by expanding investment, with the government ready to step in and make good any shortfalls in the private sector. As mentioned in the preceding chapter, all post-war governments gave priority to economic expansion, by which they hoped to achieve their main objectives of increasing economic growth and improving the general welfare. For this task they chose the mixed economy as their institutional framework. The results during the 1950s and 1960s were spectacular. Afterwards, however, difficulties arose: the expansion policy generated inflation and overinvestment in particular sectors of the economy. Consequently, during the 1970s, governments were faced with serious stagflation.

1. THE 'SILVER FIFTIES' AND THE 'GOLDEN SIXTIES'

THE ACCELERATION OF GROWTH RATES

Never before in history had there been such annual growth rates for world industrial production. During the eighteenth century, when Britain's Industrial Revolution had begun, world industrial production grew on average at an annual rate of about 1.5 per cent;

and during the nineteenth century, when the Industrial Revolution spread through Europe and across to the United States, the annual average rate of growth was about 3 per cent. During the first half of the twentieth century, growth was unfavourably influenced by two world wars and by the Great Depression, but after 1948 there was a remarkable new upward surge. From 1948 to 1971 the annual average rate of growth for world industrial production reached a new high of 5.6 per cent, and even in the longer period 1948–80 it was not to be much lower. In part, the acceleration was undoubtedly due to the favourable growth figures recorded by the Eastern bloc and the successful industrializing policies of some developing countries. But the main factor was the dynamism of the Western economies.

When these growth rates are broken down on a national basis and the 1950–70 performance is compared with that of the preceding eighty years, the extent of the acceleration in Western Europe and Japan is vividly clear (Table 3). The general picture is the same when the growth rates are worked out on a per capita basis. Indeed, in some cases the acceleration in per capita growth is still very marked.

In Western Europe the acceleration of growth was not evenly spread. During the initial phase of post-war recovery the neutral countries, Sweden and Switzerland, and the older industrial nations, Britain and Belgium, led the pack. Around 1950, West Germany, Austria, Italy, and France established themselves as the leading group of fast growers, with Britain and Belgium falling behind them. During the 1960s, growth was more nearly even. Inflationary pressures caused France, Italy, and West Germany all to moderate their growth, while the smaller countries, notably Belgium, greatly increased their average rates. In general, growth in the 1960s was not only more uniform but also faster. Only Britain lagged, and even in this case post-war growth was still faster than at any time between 1870 and 1960.

The United States, too, was able to increase its rate of growth, but not as fast as Western Europe and Japan. American growth was clearly faster in the 1960s than in the 1950s; yet between 1950 and 1960 growth on a per capita basis was lower than for the period 1913–50. The reason for this probably lies in the increase in American production during the First World War and even more during the Second World War. However, growth per capita in the 1950s

Table 3 *Average Annual Rate of Growth of Total Output in Western Europe, the United States, Canada, and Japan, 1870–1979 (percentages) (in brackets: per capita)*

	1870–1913	1913–50	1950–9	1960–9	1970–9
Austria	n.a.	n.a.	5.8	4.7	3.7
Belgium	2.7 (1.7)	1.0 (0.7)	2.9 (2.3)	4.9	3.3
Denmark	3.2 (2.1)	2.1 (1.1)	3.3 (2.6)	4.8	2.4
Finland	n.a.	n.a.	5.0	5.1	3.6
France	1.6 (1.4)	0.7 (0.7)	4.6 (3.5)	5.8	3.7
West Germany	2.9 (1.8)	1.2 (0.4)	7.8 (6.5)	4.8	2.8
Italy	1.4 (0.7)	1.3 (0.6)	5.8 (5.3)	5.7	3.2
Netherlands	2.2 (0.8)	2.1 (0.7)	4.7 (3.6)	5.1	2.9
Norway	2.2 (1.4)	2.7 (1.9)	3.2 (2.6)	5.0	4.7
Spain	n.a.	n.a.	5.2	7.5	3.8
Sweden	3.0 (2.3)	2.2 (1.6)	3.4 (2.6)	4.6	2.0
Switzerland	2.4 (1.3)	2.0 (1.5)	4.4 (3.7)	4.5	1.3
United Kingdom	2.2 (1.3)	1.7 (1.3)	2.7 (2.2)	2.8	1.8
Portugal	n.a.	n.a.	3.9	6.2	4.9
Greece	n.a.	n.a.	5.9	7.5	4.8
Republic of Ireland	n.a.	n.a.	1.7	3.9	4.3
Japan	2.4 (1.3)	1.8	9.5	10.5	4.9
United States	4.3 (2.2)	2.9 (1.7)	3.2 (1.6)	4.3	3.0
Canada	3.8 (2.0)	2.8 (1.3)	3.9 (1.2)	5.6	4.2

Sources: A. MADDISON, 'Performance in Europe', pp. 502ff
A. MADDISON, *Growth in the West*, p. 28, p. 30
A. MADDISON, *Growth in Japan and the USSR*, p. 30, p. 35, p. 36
OECD, *Historical Statistics*, 1960–82

compares even less favourably when measured against the period 1870–1913. In part, this simply underlines the significance of crucial economic developments in nineteenth-century America: the opening up of the country's Midwest and Far West, the industrialization of the East Coast, and the export-based growth of the South. Nevertheless it also suggests that special factors were responsible for the dynamism of growth in Western Europe and Japan after the Second World War.

THE 'CATCHING-UP' DYNAMIC AND ITS COMPONENTS

The most powerful of these special factors was the so-called 'catching-up' phenomenon (Table 4). Western Europe was making up ground lost during both world wars and the intervening depression. Japan had less ground to cover, but the disasters of the Second World War and the crisis of the 1930s had both had considerable impact.[1] In

Table 4 *International Comparison of National Product and of Consumption per capita, 1950–70*
(national product: gross, per capita, per unit of active population)
(percentages) (United States = 100)

	GNP		GNP/ per capita		GNP/ employment	Consumption per capita
	1950	1970	1950	1970	1970	1970
United States	100	100	100	100	100	100
France	13.2	18.6	45	74	72.1	68.1
West Germany	12.0	21.2	36	74	67.2	61.5
United Kingdom	19.2	17.1	56	62	55.6	63.6
Italy	7.9	12.7	23	48	55.1	48.1
Total	52.3	69.6	n.a.	n.a.	n.a.	n.a.
Japan	8.5*	30.8	n.a.	61.0	49.5	47.4
General Total	60.8	100.4	n.a.	n.a.	n.a.	n.a.

Note: * Own estimates extrapolated on the basis of the 1970 index and the growth rates of the United States and Japan.
Sources: For GNP 1950: I. B. KRAVIS, *National Products*, p. 24
      For GNP 1970: E. F. DENISON, W. K. CHUNG, *How Japan's Economy Grew*, p. 5
      For GNP/employment and for consumption per capita: I. B. KRAVIS, *A System of International Comparison*, p. 11
      For GNP/per capita 1950 and 1970: ibid.

the United States a catching-up process had some effect, but it was less strong than elsewhere in the West. The slowdown in American growth during the 1930s was, as already stated, offset by the flourishing production during the Second World War.

Ingmar Svennilson laid great stress on the sizeable but unrealized possibilities to accelerate growth in Western Europe and reduce the economic gap with the United States,[2] an idea which Erik Lundberg and, especially, Ferenc Jánossy took over and developed in their studies of the post-war period.[3] According to Lundberg and Jánossy, Western Europe and Japan then grew faster than the United States mainly because there were greater vacuums to fill, giving those countries a chance to whittle down the lead which the United States had established over them during the first half of the twentieth century. Jánossy held that in addition to this, the catching-up dynamic did not merely mean the reattainment of former levels of production. It also entailed the attainment of levels which would have been achieved had such events as the Great Depression and the two world wars not disrupted the 'normal' development of the economy.[4] The catching-up hypothesis of Lundberg and Jánossy underlines an important aspect of the post-war growth. It supposes that the long-term stagnation which resulted from depression and world war created extra opportunities for growth, both on the demand side and the supply side.

On the demand side, it should be understood that Western Europe and Japan had lagged behind the United States in the level of modern consumption. In the United States, from the end of the nineteenth century, labour scarcity and rising labour productivity, together with a vast agricultural expansion, had pushed wages up a good deal higher than in the rest of the world. This, in turn, made possible the mass consumption of industrial and luxury products. In Europe, although the unions pressed for higher wages their demands were undermined by general surplus of labour. This labour surplus also held back the replacement of labour with capital and thereby restricted increases in both labour productivity and wages. During both world wars and their aftermath, and in the 1930s, circumstances were not favourable to change, and it was only after 1950 that attempts could be made to attain American consumption levels. Moreover, union wage demands were now backed up by a relative labour scarcity.[5] Rises in European wages and salaries were further stimulated by the international co-operation between industrialized nations which came about after the Second World War. Europe was thus able to expand its market in a way that the United States, because of its internal structure, had been able to do before 1930. Since exports provided the motor for the development of the fastest-growing European countries, the expansion of foreign markets cannot be overstressed.

For Japan, although foreign demand for its products was important, the domestic market provided the main springboard. Modern industry was controlled by a few influential financial groups (*Zaibatsu*) and made great use of modern technology and large-scale production, but at the same time it was closely linked to a network of small and semi-mechanized concerns. The resulting dual economy covered a widely differentiated wage structure. Although wages in general did rise, the weakness of the unions prevented the rise from being uniform, even after the Second World War. Nevertheless domestic demand for consumer durables grew, and this demand was not confined to workers employed in large-scale industry. Workers who had left the agricultural and artisan sectors in favour of small-scale industry also contributed to the increase in demand. They made up for their lower wage rates by working longer hours. The system of yearly or half-yearly bonuses paid to all employees was also an important factor, for these sizeable amounts of money could be used to purchase durable consumer goods.[6] In these ways Japan, like the Western European economies, was able to assimilate fully the American model of modern mass consumption.

The supply side likewise contained specific factors that favoured a catching-up process after the war. This was especially evident with respect to labour. In Western Europe and Japan, stagnation in the 1930s and uncertainty during the two world wars had kept an artificially high percentage of workers in obsolete sectors, where incomes and living standards were low and prospects bleak. Typical examples were small farms, traditional retail outlets, and artisan workshops.[7] The economic unit here was usually the family and there was much disguised unemployment. A number of family members employed in the production process could leave without any fall in output, even when production methods remained unchanged. This disguised unemployment, together with the number of people employed in relatively unproductive industrial sectors, constituted an important labour reserve which could be used for economic growth. All Western economies took advantage of this slack in order to increase their growth rates but in Western Europe and Japan the slack was particularly great, and it had a highly positive effect on growth.

In the area of technology too, there was potential for making up lost ground. The Second World War had done much to stimulate technological advance, but applications of the new knowledge had remained limited to the military sector and to industries directly concerned with the war effort. After the war, these innovations could be systematically integrated into the general economic expansion. Moreover, they formed a basis for yet further technological progress. This held good for all the industrial nations of the world and the advance became known as the new Industrial Revolution, during which mechanized production was increasingly replaced by automatized production. The faster post-war growth of Western Europe and Japan, in comparison to the United States, is usually seen purely as a consequence of higher rates of investment; but an important additional factor was the technological backwardness of Western

Europe and Japan in comparison to the United States.[8] High investment in areas of technological backwardness often leads to increased rates of productivity and economic growth.[9]

THE DYNAMICS OF POST-WAR GROWTH IN THE WEST

The acceleration of growth in the West after the war cannot be ascribed solely to a catching-up process. There was clearly more to it than that. The mixed economy itself, run on Keynesian economic principles, generated dynamic growth.

The mixed economy worked on a basis of a balanced interplay between government, unions, and management. On the government side there was considerable preoccupation with the creation of full employment and the furthering of the equality of income and wealth. Governments developed various transfer mechanisms to redistribute and equalize incomes. On the economic front, they elaborated counter-cyclical measures of both a fiscal and a monetary nature in order either to boost or restrain demand, whenever the economy appeared to be either stalling or running out of control. Public services provided by the state swelled government expenditure. The general effect was to stimulate demand. It is widely accepted that in this respect, Western European governments were more active than those in the United States during the post-war years. On the supply side as well, post-war government measures did much to stimulate growth. Everywhere education systems were greatly extended both in width and depth. The objective here was not only to offer equal chances to all but in addition to raise the quality of the labour force. New approaches to education, such as the Open University and retraining programmes, received special attention. The governments supported pure and applied research in academic institutions and subsidized the research carried out by private industry. In many countries governments also introduced a system of economic planning designed to co-ordinate their own growth policies with those of the unions and management. Within the framework of this planning system they stimulated investment in the private sector and themselves invested in nationalized industry as well as in capital infrastructure.

For unions and management in Western Europe, the development of an economy based on consultation and mutual co-operation was a very important new factor. In this spirit of co-operation, management accepted the modern welfare policies of the various workers' organizations, and these organizations consented to the investment policies followed by management. The interests of both groups converged into one joint growth policy. Management was thus presented with large and secure opportunities for business expansion, and this quickly led to a massive increase in investment, following three separate channels.

The first channel comprised that group of industrial sectors which was closely affected by the expansion of the modern consumption society, especially those producing consumer durables such as motor cars. In this group the housing, petrochemical and electronic sectors (so-called 'leading' sectors) also attracted significant investment.[10]

Secondly there was heavy investment in the development of the private and public service sectors since the provision of services was also an important element in the creation of the affluent society.

Thirdly there was a noticeable trend towards investing in industrially underdeveloped regions of each country. The expansion of the prosperity-based industrial sectors, as well as that of the closely related machine industry, was not only capital intensive but labour intensive too. Consequently, entrepreneurs sought low-wage areas within their own countries where there were still adequate labour reserves. Investment here would not have the immediate effect of forcing up wage levels. Besides, some sectors, such as petrochemicals, needed vast amounts of land, easily accessible by water, and lying outside the residential areas. Thus in industrialized countries particular regions which had lagged behind the areas of initial industrial development were able to benefit. Governments also supported this form of investment in its general drive to increase employment levels. In some countries governments even adopted specific expansive regional policies involving a system of direct and indirect subsidies to encourage private investment in development areas. There are numerous examples after the Second World War: for instance, the development of the south-eastern United States; the Mezzogiorno in Italy; eastern Scotland; the Flanders region of Belgium; and the various new decentralized growth-poles in France.

Management also increased its investments abroad, taking advantage of the economic-growth consensus and the support from unions and government. Organizational advances at this international level generated a managerial revolution and paved the way for the emergence of the multinational corporation. Thus technological progress and investment programmes assumed international dimensions. The production of raw materials, energy, and foodstuffs overseas offered tremendous potential for expansion once it could be linked with Western technological progress. The multinational corporation was able to achieve this with great effect. Unhindered by any international authority and virtually free from union control overseas, it could introduce large-scale mechanization and innovation, producing spectacular gains in productivity. So economic growth was not solely a function of the affluent society in the West. The Third World was also caught up in the general expansion.

Although the demand for primary products – raw materials and foodstuffs – rose considerably, their prices, in relation to those of industrial products, fell. In other words, the terms of trade in the period 1951 to 1972 favoured the industrialized countries.[11] Thomas Robert Malthus and David Ricardo were thus, in the short term, proved wrong. Rising population and increasing living standards did not outpace the production of foodstuffs and raw materials. Multinational corporations played a vital role in this respect by channelling considerable investment and technological advances into less-developed areas. By doing so they could achieve a large increase in production and in the productivity of land, labour and capital. Another important element is that the growth in the productivity of labour and land in the Third World did not lead to a proportional rise in wages. Naturally wage levels in the primary sector overseas did rise to some extent and the expansion in production created many new jobs. There was, therefore, an increase in income for the Third World as a whole, but a large part of the benefit was transferred to the industrialized nations via the relative decline in the prices of primary products. Increased primary production, combined with favourable terms of trade, contributed significantly to higher consumption levels in the West during the 1950s and 1960s.

GROWTH IN THE EASTERN BLOC AND THE THIRD WORLD

Economic growth was not the sole preserve of the Western world during the post-war period. It was a world-wide phenomenon. Nevertheless actual rates of growth differed markedly from country to country.

In the Soviet Union this growth was based on the industrialization model which Joseph Stalin had implemented from 1929 onwards, according to the principles of 'primitive accumulation'. By means of an authoritarian and centralized planning apparatus and the total rejection of the private-profit incentive, the surplus value yielded by agriculture was mostly ploughed into industry, with basic industrial sectors enjoying absolute priority in the drive for complete industrial autarky. As a result, GNP between 1928 and 1938 showed a growth rate of 3.3 per cent annually.[12] After the Second World War the Stalinist growth model was further developed, but from the mid 1950s consumption was gradually given more attention. During the 1950s the growth rate averaged 6.6 per cent annually, and in the 1960s 5.3 per cent. These are high rates, but, in contrast to trends in the West, growth was clearly slowing down. Eastern and Central European countries which came under Soviet domination after the war followed a similar development pattern. They were initially forced to adopt the hard-line Stalinist growth model in which attention was concentrated on the development of basic industries. GNP in these countries grew impressively during the 1950s but, again, this growth slowed during the course of the next decade – from an annual average of 5.6 per cent for 1950–60 to 4.9 per cent for 1961–70.[13]

The powerful growth in Eastern Europe during the 1950s was not wholly due to the Stalinist growth model. A catching-up process also played a role. Not only in production levels, but also in technology and productivity, there was much ground to be made up, and these catching-up movements enabled the planned increases in investments to be translated into dramatically accelerated growth rates.[14]

The slowing of growth during the 1960s had to be ascribed to structural factors which are regarded as inherent in the socialist, centralized, planned economy. Under the Stalinist model, the priority given to heavy industry became so strongly institutionalized and consolidated that it hindered the development of an affluent society based on mass consumption.

To a large extent, financial and technological resources were reserved for the military sector. In addition, the systematic neglect of agriculture kept farm productivity at such a low level that a high input of land and labour remained necessary. Organizing the supply of raw materials from progressively further-flung parts of the country required an efficient transport system. Transport technology, how-

Prosperity and Upheaval

ever, hardly improved and there was no great exertion to construct a modern transport network.

In the end, the Eastern bloc, the Soviet Union included, began to move away gradually from the strict Stalinist growth model, and by the 1960s a certain diversification in socialist growth models and planned economies was noticeable. Some socialist countries, including Yugoslavia, East Germany, and Hungary, were successful in this, but others, including Czechoslovakia and the People's Republic of China, had greater difficulty. Czechoslovakia was invaded in 1968 by the Soviet Union; and China, from 1966 onwards, underwent the ideological radicalization called the Cultural Revolution, which had a disastrous economic impact.

It is tempting to compare the growth rates recorded by the planned economies of Eastern Europe with those recorded by the mixed economies of the West. But the difficulties are insuperable. The definitions of economic categories differ considerably. The relative growth rates have been too greatly aggregated to be strictly comparable. The figures themselves are usually at best only annual averages. In any case the growth rates give no indication of the qualitative aspects of prosperity levels in East and West. Attention must be paid to the differences in productivity levels which existed at the start of any period of comparison. The differences in savings and investment must also be taken into account. For example, a higher level of investment implies automatically that a smaller amount is available for consumption, and this, in the short term at least, leads to lower standards of living than would have existed if investment had not been so high. A final aspect is the difference in military expenditure. In the face of this, all that can be safely said is that after the war both economic systems showed an impressive capacity for growth.

The developing countries – the Third World – also performed better than one might expect. Although in 1979 one-third of the population of these lands still lived in poverty, with income below subsistence level, the fact remains that agricultural and industrial production increased considerably in the Third World after the war. As a consequence, according to an estimate by the World Bank, income per head in the developing countries increased at an annual rate of 3 per cent between 1950 and 1975. This growth implied an acceleration from 2 per cent in the 1950s to 3.4 per cent in the 1960s. [15] These figures conceal wide national differences, of course.

For the poorest countries, those with a yearly income below $250 per head, the rate of growth was much lower. Most of these countries, so poor that they were barely developing, were in Africa, south of the Sahara, and in Asia. At the other end of the spectrum, by the 1960s, two sorts of developing countries had attained growth figures far in excess of the general average: (1) the oil-exporting nations, and (2) the rapidly industrializing ones, notably South Korea, Taiwan, Singapore, Hong Kong, Brazil, and Mexico.

From an analysis of the development policy in Third World countries, several surprising characteristics come to light. In these countries, aggregates of saving, investment, and stock of capital goods are, as a percentage of GNP, at levels comparatively higher than those that existed in Europe during the Industrial Revolution in the eighteenth and nineteenth centuries.[16] Seen in historical perspective, the transition to industrial society appears to be speeding up. This hypothesis receives further support after an analysis of government expenditure. In all the countries of the Third World, the share of government expenditure in total GNP increased during the post-war period. It grew at the same rate as the increase in income per head, in accordance with the law formulated by Adolph Wagner in 1883. Moreover, this ratio of government spending to GNP was higher than that regarded as normal in industrializing Europe during the nineteenth century. It can thus be argued that from the very earliest stage of development the Third World population clearly expects more from government than was the case in Europe. From the very beginning, governments must take measures to increase social welfare and economic expansion, to develop a modern capital infrastructure, to promote better education and to provide other social services. The fact that governments are expected to play a considerable role in economic and social life at an early point in the development process is precisely the reason why authoritarian regimes seem attractive to developing countries. Such a regime greatly facilitates the transfer of resources from the productive sector into investment in infrastructure and social services.[17]

Economic development in the Third World also entails significant structural changes. Urbanization increases rapidly. The agricultural sector declines (in terms of its share of national production and numbers employed) while the industrial sector expands. In the service sector some areas, such as domestic service, decline while others, such as banking, insurance, garages and petrol stations, expand rapidly. In many Third World countries one considerable difference from the nineteenth-century European pattern is the extreme development of a dual economic structure – farming and handicraft production versus modern industry.[18] Farming remains so primitive and, in some areas, even so autarkic that the agricultural sector continues to have extremely low productivity and wage levels, structural rigidities, and concealed unemployment. Simultaneously, although on a very small scale, as in an enclave, some modern, progressive industrial sectors also develop, making use of advanced capital goods, with high labour productivity and high wage levels. The gap between the two sectors is so enormous that development does not spread outside the small enclave. As a result, income distribution in these countries is very uneven, with a modern middle class monopolizing the income benefits from modern industry at the expense of low-income groups and even traditionally high-income categories.

Among the fast developers in the Third World, the oil-exporting countries of the Middle East hold a particularly important place.[19] Their incomes from nationalized oil concerns have been so great that not all could be invested in the domestic economy. They have thus invested large sums in Western industrial nations, as well as subsidizing some governments of which they approved politically. Of course, they have also embarked on large-scale capital infrastructure programmes at home, but too often these have had more to do with prestige than with increasing production efficiency. Finally, they have spent massive amounts on armaments, buying from both East and West.

Other Third World countries which developed fast, without having lucrative oil exports, relied more directly on the process of industrialization. They also made extensive use of the model of export-led growth.[20] Exports of raw materials and foodstuffs, which had previously dominated, were replaced by exports of manufactures. These countries concentrated their industrializing on labour-intensive sectors such as textiles, clothing, and electronics. Such an approach demanded relatively little capital and exploited their main comparative advantage, namely abundant cheap labour. Governments also played a very active role in providing loans, subsidies, and other fiscal advantages to the export industries, also in attracting foreign capital and manipulating exchange rates to further the process of economic growth.

Developing countries which applied the model of export-led growth did better than those which attempted to stimulate industrialization by erecting tariff barriers and substituting domestic production for imports ('import substitution'). In the export countries, employment increased, with a favourable effect on absolute and real wages. The countries aiming at industrialization through import substitution did not obtain the results they hoped for. Originally they had made their choice out of fear that export-led growth involved a certain amount of workers' exploitation. The use of cheap labour, it was argued, benefited consumers in importing countries rather than workers in exporting ones. A further contention made between 1951 and 1971 was that primary producers were being exploited via unfavourable terms of trade. Difficulties arose when domestic demand for consumer durables – the first goods being substituted – failed to expand significantly. As a reaction, the governments involved then began a policy of import substitution even in the sectors of capital goods and intermediate goods. In these cases the advantages of specialization and mass production did not apply to the same extent so that the cost of production rose and extra tariff walls had to be erected to keep out cheaper imports. In such circumstances there was no longer any question of exporting and consequent balance-of-payments difficulties led to currency depreciation and the continuation of low wages.

Even in developing countries which had successfully tried export-led growth, there remained substantial problems. From the mid 1960s they came under pressure from the World Bank and the International Monetary Fund (IMF) to reduce gradually their protective barriers against imports of industrial products from the West. Attempts to move in this direction met with little, if any, success, since the economy of these countries was still too primitive to be able to absorb the shock. In addition, the evolution of the world economy in the 1970s was so unfavourable that their exports began to get squeezed. Even rich industrial countries turned to protectionist measures in retaliation. The introduction of the proposed liberalization programmes in the export-orientated developing nations led to internal economic difficulties, which served to accentuate the authoritarian nature of their political regimes and sharpen still further income inequalities by the familiar pattern of devaluation and continued low wages. However favourable the 1950s and 1960s may have been for economic growth in the Third World, the difficulties of the 1970s raised question marks against both development models, so that new formulas have become necessary.

FROM BUSINESS CYCLE TO GROWTH CYCLE IN EUROPE

For the West, growth in the 1950s and 1960s was not only faster when compared with preceding periods, but also more stable. Dramatic crises, like those between 1875 and 1893, or during the

Table 5 *Cyclical Setbacks in Annual GNP and in Industrial Production, 1890–1978*

(maximum percentage decline from peak to trough)

	1890–1913		1920–38		1948–70		1970–8	
	GNP	Ind. prod.	GNP	Ind. prod.	GNP	Ind. prod.	GNP	Ind. prod.
Belgium	—	—	7.9	27.1	1.8	6.4	—	9.2
Denmark	—	—	11.8	22.2	0.2	4.0	—	—
France	—	—	19.3	25.6	0.0	1.0	—	8.1
West Germany	4.0	—	16.1	40.8	0.2	2.0	—	5.4
Italy	5.2	—	5.4	22.7	0.0	0.0	—	9.2
Netherlands	2.1	—	12.1	16.9	0.0	0.0	—	4.8
Norway	1.8	—	8.0	21.3	0.2	1.1	—	0.0
Sweden	3.3	—	13.3	21.4	0.4	2.0	—	2.6
Switzerland	2.4	—	8.0	37.7	1.8	—	—	3.6
United Kingdom	4.1	—	13.2	32.4	0.5	3.1	—	5.5
Canada	13.2	—	29.3	32.3	2.9	1.3	—	4.7
United States	8.3	—	28.9	44.7	1.6	7.7	—	9.2
Japan	—	—	2.7*	—	0.0	0.0	—	9.8

Note: * 1928–38
Sources: E. LUNDBERG, *Instability*, p. 29
         A. MADDISON, *Growth in the West*, p. 47
         Supplemented with my own calculations from OECD, *Historical Statistics* and *Economic Outlook*

1930s, no longer interrupted the growth process (Table 5). In the United States, GNP, worked out on a yearly basis, fell only three times between 1948 and 1973 and the greatest fall was only 1.6 per cent. During the 1930s, by contrast, GNP had fallen by no less than 40 per cent. For Western Europe, stability was even more striking. Combined European GNP, again worked out on a yearly basis for the period 1948 to 1973, did not fall once. It was only in some countries and in some years – for example, Britain (1952), Belgium (1958), and Switzerland (1949 and 1958) – that GNP actually declined.[21] Nor, over the same period of 1948 to 1973, did Japan experience any fall in GNP. Even when one singles out industrial production rather than GNP, the period consists exclusively of yearly increases. Moreover, world trade was very expansive and until 1973, at least, operated within the framework of a relatively stable international monetary system.

Thus, in regard to stability, the economic evolution of the West during the quarter-century after the war was remarkable.[22] So remarkable in fact that contemporary economists have devised a new terminology. The term 'crisis' has been replaced with the term 'recession', the classical term 'business cycle' with the new concept of 'growth cycle', and the term 'crisis policy' with that of 'fine tuning'.[23] Nevertheless, even with this new terminology, most economists did not seek to cast doubts on the business cycle as such. Specific economic indicators such as employment, stocks, capital goods, investment, interest rates, profits, and so on, continued to fluctuate.[24] However, the cycles had taken on a new form, becoming growth cycles in which absolute falls in GNP were largely replaced with decreases in the rate of growth. Thus, in the mixed economies of the West, instability in economic evolution was reduced to consecutive phases of faster and slower growth.

Quarterly figures for industrial production throw light on postwar fluctuations. The first European faltering in 1948–9 was too slight, short-lived, and localized to be regarded as a recession. On the other hand the 1951–2 weakening of industrial production was more serious. It even preceded the downturn in the United States and it hit all European countries. It was closely linked to the inventory cycle and to the results of restrictive measures taken by governments to restore equilibrium in the balance of payments. In essence this recession was a reaction to the speculative fever which had broken out in 1950 as a result of the Korean War and the consequent fears of renewed world military conflict. The prices of goods and especially raw materials rose sharply, and this upward movement was reinforced by a sudden increase in hoarding by consumers and producers alike, both in Europe and the United States. The speculative build-up of stocks entailed a considerable increase in European imports of raw materials at a time when most European governments were wrestling with serious balance-of-payments problems as well as the dollar shortage. Numerous European countries introduced measures to limit imports and some even restored a general policy of economic restrictions.[25] Such steps slowed the rise in prices and then actually caused a fall. The falling prices were accentuated by the downturn in the inventory cycle as consumers and producers began to run down stocks rather than buy more. The recession had by now become a general one and only ended when stocks were exhausted and when Europe, via the North Atlantic Treaty Organization (NATO), was brought into the American rearmament programme with the start of the Cold War. It should not be overlooked, however, that some specific government measures had a stimulating effect on the economy.

A second European recession came during 1957–8. Once again, it affected all Western European countries but it was altogether milder and shorter than the one in 1951–2. On the other hand it did involve the American and Japanese economies. The origin of the 1957–8 recession is to be found in the economic expansion of the years 1953 to 1955 and in the fears about wage inflation. In the course of the 1953–5 boom, demand for industrial products grew to such an extent that in all Western European countries except Italy full employment was virtually achieved and some countries even experienced a significant labour shortage. Wages increased considerably and higher imports of raw materials and semi-finished goods put additional pressure on the balance of payments at a time when the demand for exports of industrial finished products began to waver. Here and there in 1955, and especially in 1956, Western European governments already began to take restrictive economic measures. Yet these remained very tentative efforts to slow down the overheating of the economy, so that the transition from an expansive to a restrictive economic policy took place only gradually. An exogenous factor, the Suez Crisis at the end of 1956, had the effect of disrupting government attempts to restrain the economy. As in 1950, although to a much lesser extent, the climate of war stimulated an unusual build-up of stocks, which in turn raised demand and prices. According to business-cycle analysts, the impact of the Suez Crisis was such as to delay the recession in Europe by one year so that the low point was reached in 1958 rather than 1957.[26]

Europe got out of this recession by means of specific government measures to prod the economy. In most countries public works were expanded, taxes lowered, and hire-purchase restrictions relaxed. Simultaneously in 1958 an important new psychological factor made its appearance. The Treaty of Rome established the European Economic Community (EEC), and the signing created a favourable climate for investment. The rapid success of the EEC stimulated a growth cycle in Europe which neutralized a threat of recession in 1963.

Western Europe thus maintained a high level of economic activity until the middle of 1966. At this point, full employment and the consequent wage inflation, combined with the further upward pressure on prices following a new build-up in inventory levels, gradually led governments, especially the West German, to impose a new round of economic restraint. Recession followed, the low point of which occurred in the first quarter of 1967. In France the course of events was somewhat different. Within the framework of the Giscard d'Estaing Plan, restrictive economic measures were brought in as early as 1964. The consequent economic slump in turn made possible the restoration of an expansionary policy during 1965–6. This French upturn was still too recent in 1966–7 to cause a new series of restrictions, and so the effect of the general European recession on France was less pronounced and somewhat delayed.[27]

The European recession of 1966–7 and the subsequent recovery have to be seen in the context of European integration. Partly because of obstruction by the French, the success in the field of customs union was not matched by similar progress in general economic, monetary and political integration, even though the Treaty of Rome had been very explicit in these areas. The euphoria surrounding the first years of the Common Market gave way to feelings of disillusion and growing uncertainty. These were reflected in a new, less favourable climate of investment which strengthened the recession of 1966–7. In contrast, the resignation of de Gaulle in 1969 raised prospects for a new impetus to the European market and this had a positive impact on business expectations. Nevertheless the economic upturn of the late 1960s soon ran into substantial exogenous difficulties, notably the 1971 monetary crisis and the oil embargo in 1973. These external issues had the effect of breaking the European growth cycle.

THE GROWTH CYCLES IN JAPAN AND THE UNITED STATES

Japanese and American growth cycles did not differ markedly from the Western European pattern, although the chronology in the three areas did not always coincide.

In Japan, the first serious recession occurred during 1949. It was called the Dodge Recession because it followed from the stabilization measures taken according to the Dodge Plan mentioned earlier. Other Japanese recessions, particularly in 1954, 1957–8 and 1962, were closely related to economic downturns in the United States. [28] This parallelism with American cycles was not surprising in that during this period the United States became a vital market for Japanese exports. At the same time, domestic monetary policy, aimed at relieving balance-of-payments problems, also exercised a decisive influence on the Japanese economy. Monetary policy continued to be important, especially in regard to recessions in 1965 and 1970. Economic fluctuations in Japan were greater than in Western Europe. Even when comparison is restricted to European countries with high growth rates, such as West Germany and Italy, growth of Japanese GNP still appears less stable. Japan's annual growth rate varied between a minimum of about 3 per cent (in 1954 and 1958) and a maximum of about 17 per cent (in 1959). This highly unstable growth cycle consisted of expansionary phases with explosive growth occasionally interrupted by short periods of recession. [29]

In the United States and Canada the post-war economy performed even more fitfully than that of Japan, although the cyclical fluctuations were much less extreme. [30] The first recession came in 1948–9 as a reaction to the successful transition to a peacetime economy. [31] The tremendous industrial capacity of the United States was so quick to catch up with the increase in consumption and to replenish exhausted stocks that by 1948 signs of market saturation began to appear. Since the American economy could not fall back on a programme of reconstruction, as in Europe and Japan, there was a slowing-down of industrial activity. Economic recovery, however, soon followed and was generated not only by endogenous factors but by exogenous ones too. By means of the Marshall Plan, the American economy was plugged into the Western European recovery process. The outbreak of the conflict in Korea in 1950 and the intensification of the Cold War also had a major stimulus on industrial production. Of course, the other side of the coin was that the end of the Korean War and the consequent drastic reduction in the American defence budget were important elements in the recession of 1953–4.[32] Recovery from that recession was largely based on a boom in housing construction, which in turn can be seen as a result of the post-war 'baby boom'. The economy was also stimulated by a major increase in car sales, in part due to easier purchases on credit conditions. Both recovery factors went hand in hand, for housing construction implied more road traffic.

Research has shown that the American and Canadian business cycles between 1955 and 1965 were characterized by a gap between potential and actual production, the now famous diagnosis of 'demand slack'. Even during the first phases of economic upturns, the economy was still not working at full capacity and unemployment remained significant. In Western Europe, however, during the same period the gap between potential and actual production was smaller. Full employment was fairly well realized and excessive demand drove up prices. According to Lundberg, American investment demand fell short, so that private and government savings were not fully absorbed by the economy.[33]

Was the disinclination of American businessmen to invest in the domestic economy a consequence of better investment opportunities abroad because of the gradual overvaluation of the dollar? This is possible, but in any case President Dwight Eisenhower's administration (1953–61) had a very discouraging impact on investment in the United States.[34] The government was wary of going too far in supporting a strong growth policy and in particular feared the repercussions of more government intervention in the economy because this did not appeal to the political ideology of the Republican party. The administration was also worried that a policy of stimulating demand would soon lead to excessive inflation.

In 1957–8 a new recession hit the United States but again the Eisenhower administration refused to intervene. Instead, it remained faithful to the classical doctrine that business cycles were unavoidable and that the automatic stabilizers built into the fiscal system would be sufficient to iron out excessive fluctuations. At the same time, the administration devoted much attention to the need to balance the budget. Balanced budgets were seen as crucial factors in bringing about price stability, and on this issue the Eisenhower government did not hesitate to intervene actively. The serious recession brought stern measures to restore budget equilibrium. These were so successful that as early as 1960 a considerable budget surplus was recorded. The side-effect of this dramatic financial turnabout was a sudden contraction of about $15 billion in US net demand. At this point a policy of cheap money and credit expansion could have had a compensatory influence. Private investment might have increased, and this might have neutralized the fall in government demand. Instead a policy of high interest rates was introduced in order to bolster the international position of the dollar, which was now coming under pressure.

From December 1958, general acceptance of the gold-exchange standard gave the dollar a key role as international reserve currency just at the time that the United States began to run serious balance-of-payments deficits. The whole international monetary system depended on the firm belief that the dollar could be freely converted into gold at a fixed price, and it was felt that this confidence had to be maintained at whatever cost. But the fact that American monetary policy during the next decade was largely concerned with supporting the world position of the dollar was a heavy burden for the domestic economy to bear. Above all it was a major factor in the continued gap between potential and actual production. The result of all this was a new American recession in 1960–1. In the mean time, the Eisenhower administration was replaced by that of President John Kennedy (1961–3). From this point Keynesian principles and the 'New Economics' increasingly determined economic policy, although the transition was a gradual one.

Under Kennedy, economic growth became an important objective and the government was more willing to intervene actively in the economy so that production would stay as close as possible to the country's capacity.[35] It was nevertheless some time before Kennedy could be convinced that such a growth-orientated policy could only be realized by running major budget deficits and increasing the domestic money supply ('deficit spending').[36] No sooner was a consensus reached on this issue than a spirited disagreement broke out between fiscalists, who believed in tax reductions, and structuralists, who argued for more government expenditure. Fiscalists attributed the continued high unemployment demand slack to the gap between potential and realized production. Structuralists, on the other hand, stressed the structural nature of unemployment, for example the effects of the large-scale introduction of automation during the 1950s, and the problems of low education levels (particularly among the blacks) and youth unemployment. In the end a compromise was reached whereby the initial emphasis would be on raising public expenditure and thus expanding domestic money supply. As for tax cuts, their timing was thrown into doubt by a rapid improvement in economic conditions.

Only in January 1963, when recession again loomed, was Kennedy moved to present the necessary fiscal measures to Congress. The tax cuts finally became a reality in February 1964 with the Revenue Act, which was signed by President Lyndon Johnson, Kennedy's successor (1963-9). Its aim was to smooth away the 1963-4 recession.[37] The triumph of the New Economics was now complete. The tax cuts of 1964 were designed not only to expand total demand but at the same time to stop the automatic fiscal stabilizers from acting too soon in checking the economic upturn. Investors would thus be encouraged into a long-term expansion of investment. The Revenue Act completely satisfied expectations and unemployment fell to 5 per cent in 1964 and, after further tax cuts, to 4.4 per cent in 1965.[38] The gap between potential and actual production began to close visibly and the American economy started to move more in line with the other growth economies of the West. An expression of this was an acceleration of the American rate of growth.

The American growth policy was given further impulse with the escalation of the Vietnam War in July 1965. Normally one would look for the expansive effects of increased military expenditure to be neutralized by higher taxation, by a reduction in non-military spending, and by extreme caution in expanding the money supply. In reality, none of this came about because Johnson was unwilling to sacrifice the social aspects of his 'Great Society' programme. Instead the government attempted to moderate increases in prices and wages solely through direct contacts with management and the unions. This policy proved insufficient and new inflation resulted in 1965-6. At this juncture the autonomous Federal Reserve Board made use of its powers to introduce some monetary restrictions, which led to a slight downturn in 1966-7. It was only in January 1968 that taxes were actually increased, but this had little or no effect. The reason for this was that in the mean time 'demand-pull' inflation had developed increasingly into 'cost-push' inflation, against which the macro-techniques of the New Economics were powerless. Companies exploiting monopolistic tendencies found they could simply pass increased costs on to the consumer. Unions kept up with price increases by successfully demanding higher wages. Indeed, in their wage demands, unions even anticipated future price rises. As a result, monetary policy began to reassume its previous importance.[39]

President Richard Nixon's administration (1969–74) initially tried to combat inflation by the classical means of monetary and fiscal restrictions.[40] These served to slow down economic activity to the extent that a recession was under way by 1970. Nevertheless inflation continued at a significant level. Prices and unemployment rose simultaneously, the effects of the powerful new phenomenon which has become known as stagflation.

It was clear that post-war methods of economic management were proving more and more inadequate, and on 15 August 1971 Nixon launched a new policy. First he introduced international measures such as the suspension of dollar convertibility into gold, in order to restore the American balance of payments and give domestic monetary and fiscal policies more flexibility and influence. Secondly he clamped strict government controls over prices and wages to curb inflation. It was no use. Keynesian growth policy possessed a battery of macro-economic instruments to boost the economy from stagnation to a position of full employment and economic expansion, but in the long term was powerless to prevent the consequent inflation. Instead, temporary resort had to be made to classical deflationary measures which had the unavoidable effect of increasing unemployment. But changes that had taken place in social and institutional mentality prevented the deflation process from getting very far. There now existed a chaotic situation which would be exacerbated by further external shocks, such as the oil crisis.

EXPLANATIONS FOR THE REMAINING INSTABILITY OF THE WORLD ECONOMY, 1945–73

Although business cycles after the Second World War had transformed themselves into milder growth cycles, one still cannot talk of wholly stable economic activity in the West. Moreover, the degree of instability differed from area to area. The best example of instability in Europe was Britain, where Keynesian methods were fairly thoroughly applied and at an early stage. Nevertheless, in comparison with earlier cycles, post-war fluctuations of GNP in Britain were noticeably weaker and of shorter duration.[41] Employment cycles were milder still, largely because of the priority given by the British to full employment. This policy created in numerous sectors a labour shortage and raised the cost of hiring and firing workers. In consequence, many firms during recessions practised labour hoarding; that is, they held on to labour that was actually surplus to their requirements. In addition, some sectors with a chronic labour shortage saw recession periods as an opportunity to take on new workers that they had no immediate need for. What fluctuations remained in employment were chiefly the result of changes in the rates of participation of different population groups such as women.

When one disaggregates British GNP into components and compares the fluctuations of each of these with the aggregate cycles, further interesting conclusions can be drawn.[42] Fluctuations in the production of consumer durables appear to have had an important effect on the general economy; a very close parallelism between the two curves can be detected. Moreover, changes in the production cycle of consumer durables showed a systematic tendency to precede changes in other categories of consumption. Adjustments in inventory levels also had a clear direct impact on the British economy. These inventory cycles were mainly determined by psychological factors and were subject to constant and rapid change, thus helping to explain the short length of business cycles in Britain. The other component having a strong influence on the British economy was imports. Imports proved very sensitive to changes in growth rates. Higher growth had the effect of raising imports, which in turn weakened the balance of payments and forced the government to take corrective measures, thereby choking growth. It was the effect of rising imports, taken together with inventory investment, which was responsible for the short duration of post-war business cycles in Britain. It was also responsible for ironing out extreme cyclical fluctuations and generally for the slow rate of growth in Britain. To sum up, imports made a crucial contribution to the stop-go policy which characterized the British economy after the war.[43]

Imports and the balance of payments did not in themselves determine the stop-go policy. Instead they acted indirectly by affecting confidence in sterling. Sterling, unlike its European counterparts, was assigned the role of a key currency for the international monetary system. This meant that the British government had to intervene much sooner than other Western European governments when imports rose and the deterioration of the balance of payments endangered the value of the currency. This is not to say that such factors were unimportant in other European countries, but they did not restrain growth as much as in Britain. But another important conclusion drawn from the British case can be applied to all Western Europe. The greater stability of the European economy after the war, compared to the decades before 1940, was due not only to specific European factors but also, in large measure, to the remarkably stable expansion of international trade after 1945.[44]

In Japan, the pattern of economic development was determined by a combination of the balance of payments, inventory investment, and economic policy.[45] As in continental Europe, and in contrast to Britain, a stable growth pattern was not interrupted by long-term balance-of-payments difficulties. Instead, in the long term, the expansion of Japanese exports was more than sufficient to catch up with the initial rise in imports which accompanied higher growth. Between 1951 and 1960 Japan doubled its share of world trade and transformed a balance-of-payments deficit into a surplus. There were disturbances in the short term, however, and during periods of economic expansion imports indeed grew faster than exports.

As for inventory investment, its periodic accelerations put heavy pressure on the money market and particularly on the balance of payments. This was because in Japan business inventories, to the extent they involved raw materials and energy, could only be serviced by imports and were subject to speculation when the economy was growing. Increasing liquidity problems, however, pushed up interest rates and this worked as an automatic counter-effect. As for economic policy, restrictive measures by the government worsened the contraction in the economy, leading to a dramatic fall in the sums invested in inventories and to a weakening in total growth. Until 1965 the Japanese government relied solely on monetary policy to control the economy. The monetary measures proved to be both fast-working and effective. Bank credit played a highly influential role in Japanese investment. The broad sector of small- and medium-scale concerns in industry ensured a very large number of marginal borrowers, all very sensitive to any restrictive measures brought in by the government. Indeed, these smaller businesses reacted immediately to any credit restrictions, and their decisions showed much greater awareness of changes in economic conditions than those of the big *Zaibatsu* concerns.[46] At the same time, the rapid success of credit restrictions allowed the government speedily to remove them. Consequently recessions were short and government economic policy had no long-term adverse repercussions for growth.

Japan's growth also owed much to the evolution of prices and wages. Despite the huge increase in demand during the 1950s, inflation remained moderate.[47] To a great extent this was due to the flexibility of the economy. In the first place, there was a high degree of labour mobility, with workers moving from agriculture to industry, and within industry itself moving from low-productive to high-productive sectors. The impressive investment levels and technological innovation must be taken into account as well. A spectacular increase in labour productivity, up to 10 per cent annually in manufacturing, was the result. This made it possible for wages in manufacturing industry to rise on average by 6 to 8 per cent annually while consumer prices were rising only 2 per cent annually. After 1960 the flexibility of the Japanese economy declined somewhat. Labour shortages appeared and wages rose even more sharply. This was accompanied by a gradual acceleration in consumer prices until they were increasing by 6 per cent a year.

Business cycles in the United States were more frequent than those in Western Europe and Japan. But this instability did not spring from greater fluctuation in the components of its GNP, such as private consumption, exports, imports, fixed capital accumulation, inventory investment, and government expenditure. In reality the chief cause was that in the United States rather less was done to neutralize the effects of the cycles than elsewhere.[48] Federal government expenditure was considerable during the 1950s and 1960s but it was less a tool of growth and economic policy than was the case in Europe.[49] It was much more autonomous and more closely linked to military spending. The general effect of government expenditure was thus to stimulate the economy during upturns and depress it during downturns; in other words, it actually reinforced cyclical trends rather than neutralizing them. Naturally this ran counter to Keynesian principles. On the other hand, during the 1950s, the American government laid greater emphasis on fighting inflation than on economic growth. In this respect, a balanced budget became an important aspect of government policy; yet also crucial was the manipulation of what was later to be known as the Phillips Curve.[50] According to the theory expressed by this curve, inflation could only be moderated if wage increases were brought under control by maintaining sufficiently high rates of un-employment.[51] Federal government thus had no real commitment to raise the tempo of economic growth or to increase employment levels. Neither was it interested in fiscal measures to move towards a full-scale economic stabilization policy. In fact, the only stabilizing effects resulted from federal monetary policies, such as the influence of credit restrictions and credit expansions on the construction industry. Authorities at local and at state level, however, followed counter-cyclical policies through active intervention in the construction industry. Indeed, they went still further towards an economic stabilization policy by increasing their public expenditure during economic downturns and at the same time by implementing measures to encourage growth in the private sector.

After the breakthrough of the New Economics in 1962–3, American economic policy temporarily began to tread new ground. Federal government was no longer satisfied with relying merely on a few monetary counter-cyclical measures (leaning against the wind) but took an active interest in promoting full employment and in closing the gap between potential and actual production. As already stated, the fiscal policy of deficit spending came to the fore.[52] Instability increased as a consequence of accelerating inflation and evident overheating of the economy. The government would try to reverse this trend by new forms of monetary and fiscal policies.

EXPLANATIONS FOR THE MILD NATURE OF THE RECESSIONS, 1945–73

In the preceding section, some possible explanations were given for what economic instability remained in the West. Nevertheless the dominant characteristic of the post-war economy, namely its greater stability, must be highlighted and explained. The considerable supply potential that existed in the West in 1945, which afterwards was still further expanded to an impressive degree, could well have had an extremely destabilizing influence on the world economy. In fact such a distortion did not take place, and this can only be explained by the remarkable increase in demand, and by the specificity of the new institutional framework which supported that increase.

The first autonomous stimulus to demand resulted from the reconstruction and recovery process immediately after the war. Needs were particularly great in Europe and Japan but also existed in the United States.[53] The autonomous nature of this stimulus disappeared gradually after about 1950. Investment demand became no longer a function of recovery but of the current demand for goods and services as it then existed. As a demand factor influencing general growth, inventory investment also declined in importance. On the other hand it assumed greater significance in a few particular sectors of trade and industry and was even regarded by some as a strategic factor in economic cyclical instability.[54] A similar development took place in the capital goods sector. During the 1950s the coal, iron and steel, shipbuilding and timber industries in Western Europe were the first to show signs of overcapacity. From that moment capital investment in these sectors no longer contributed so substantially to general economic growth but became increasingly a function of current expectations about sales and profits.[55] In this respect, one might say that the investment situation in these sectors increased post-war economic instability. These destabilizing effects, however, were countered by a whole series of industries and services which maintained a tremendous autonomous demand for capital goods. This was chiefly due to the development of the post-war consumer society and here investment contributed substantially to both economic growth and cyclical stability since companies in these sectors continued to invest even during economic downturns.[56] Apart from autonomous demand factors, there were psychological ones as well and these too generally served to stabilize growth in the 1950s and 1960s. Lundberg has drawn attention to the vital importance of entrepreneurial behaviour.[57] Having expectations of continuous growth, entrepreneurs often maintained the level of their investment programmes even during temporary lapses in some of the components of demand, such as the demand for exports. These same expectations of future growth also ensured that consumers would continue to maintain their levels of consumption even when real incomes were temporarily reduced.

Nevertheless the most significant factor in explaining the constant upward pressure on post-war demand was undoubtedly of an institutional nature. Through various government measures, a network of economic and social institutions was set up in the West in order to guarantee greater economic stability. This framework saw to it that a slippage in one category of total expenditure would not spread to others; thus total demand would be maintained at a high level. On the international scene particular attention was paid to the need for co-operation in promoting world trade, and this is why post-war trade in the West underwent a powerful and almost uninterrupted expansion. Domestically, the main institutional change was the expansion of public welfare. Crucial in this respect were the automatic stabilizers which were built into the various systems of social security and progressive taxation. These helped to stabilize incomes, which in turn maintained consumption at a relatively stable level despite the periodic recessions. Another essential element was the considerable increase of government spending as a share of total national expenditure. This meant that a sizeable amount of consumption became independent of market fluctuations. Moreover, since rising government expenditure in the form of subsidies and investment in capital infrastructure was designed to support the extension of the consumer society, it also furthered the process of smooth economic growth. This comes out especially clearly in the permanent government preoccupation with reaching a position of full employment.[58] In consequence, during the 1950s unemployment levels in Western Europe averaged only 2.9 per cent of the working population and during the 1960s only 1.5 per cent.[59] These figures differ widely from those which existed before 1940, and they underline the impact that post-war employment policies must have had in causing greater cyclical stability during the 1950s and 1960s (Table 6). A last institutional aspect which helped to stabilize the working of the economy was the discretionary use by government of counter-cyclical measures, inspired by Keynesian principles.[60] Governments regularly intervened to make good any shortfall in demand. Alternatively they sought to restrain excessive demand when it threatened to cause problems for the balance of payments or for the labour market. During the inter-war period governments had also intervened regularly but on these occasions the effect had usually accentuated rather than diminished cyclical movements in the economy.[61]

When it is suggested that governments, by changes in institutional structure and by specific short-term measures, played a decisive role in stabilizing business cycles, this is not to reject the influence of the

Table 6 *Unemployment as a Proportion of the Labour Force, 1920–79*
(average per ten-year period)

	1920–9	1930–8	1950–9	1960–9	1970–9
Austria	6.0	13.4	3.9	1.9	1.4
Belgium	1.5	8.7	4.0	2.2	4.6
Denmark	4.2	6.6	4.3	1.2	4.6
France	1.8	3.3	1.3	1.4	4.1
West Germany	3.9	8.8	4.2	0.8	2.7
Italy	1.7	4.8	7.9	3.3	6.5
Netherlands	2.3	8.7	1.9	1.1	4.1
Sweden	3.2	5.6	1.7	1.7	2.1
Switzerland	0.4	3.0	0.2	0.0	0.4
United Kingdom	7.5	11.5	1.2	1.6	3.9
Norway			1.0	1.0	1.7
Europe (average)	3.3	7.5	2.9	1.5	4.2
United States	4.8	18.2	4.5	4.8	6.3
Canada	3.5	13.3	4.4	5.2	6.8
Japan	n.a.	n.a.	n.a.	1.3	1.8

Sources: For Europe: A. MADDISON, 'Performance in Europe', p. 452, p. 479
For US and Japan: 1920–60, A. MADDISON, *Growth in the West*, Appendix
For US and Japan: 1960–70, J. CORNWALL, *Modern Capitalism*, p. 206
For all countries, also: OECD, *Historical Statistics*, 1960–82

free-market economy. The tendency of the free-market system to react in an excessive and cumulative manner to exogenous developments continued to make its presence felt. Governments took account of this and so, when attempting to stimulate a sluggish economy, they usually introduced only indicative measures and left market forces to complete the economic recovery.[62] In some cases, signs of market saturation marked the beginnings of economic downturns and government action was limited to a consolidating role with the objective of giving special protection to the balance of payments.[63]

In principle, the influence of the free-market system on cyclical movements in the economy can be tested by analysing the synchronization of business cycles. Research on the existence of a world business cycle has been undertaken for the periods 1854–1938[64] and 1897–1959[65] in both of which the free-market system was a central feature. The results were positive and indicated the initiatory role of the United States during the inter-war years. Even before 1914, peaks in American cycles were preceding those in other countries, especially Britain. At that time American imports appeared to be a crucial variable. If these fell, the consequent decline in British exports was often sufficient to push Britain into recession. Between the two world wars, however, imports no longer appeared a decisive variable and their function was taken over by the American economy as a whole. The adage 'When America sneezes the rest of the world gets pneumonia' remained valid. Was the system of the free-market economy in the West after 1945 still sufficiently effective to maintain the hypothesis of a world business cycle? That is, did the growth cycles after the Second World War have a specifically international character?

As a point of departure, it can be argued that two opposing forces influenced the post-war economy. On one side, the priority given by national governments to domestic growth and to counter-cyclical policies must have had a desynchronizing effect. On the other, the increase in international co-operation under the system of fixed exchange rates and the interdependency of national economies were forces likely to strengthen the synchronization. Given free trade and unrestricted movement of capital, a world system of free-market economies linked by fixed exchange rates would ensure that changes in economic fortune would be transferred from one part of the world to another. This was, in principle, no longer the case when fixed exchange rates made way for floating ones. With floating exchange rates, governments can better insulate themselves economically from the rest of the world. Increasing desynchronization from the 1970s onwards might then be expected. Empirical research for the period 1952–74 with respect to twelve industrial countries in the West[66] has shown that there was a certain international synchronization of growth cycles, but this was chiefly due to the effects of exogenous shocks, such as the outbreak of the Cold War, the Korean conflict in 1950, and the oil crisis in 1973. Discounting these external elements, a tendency towards greater synchronization could be observed only amongst the Benelux countries, West Germany, Austria, and Britain. The other countries, notably the United States, Japan, and Italy, did not follow this pattern.

Important conclusions can be drawn from this. In the first place, the influence of the free-market system in the West after the war was still considerable. This was especially so within the great regional trading blocs, respectively Western Europe, North America, and East Asia. Under the influence of major external shocks, business cycles even in these three separate blocs converged. To some extent then, with reservations, one might well still talk of a world business cycle and even of international growth cycles. In addition, it is clear that the United States no longer had the initiatory influence it once had. Finally the fact that, discounting external shocks, the business cycles of the big trading blocs were less synchronized with one another (especially between 1950 and 1968) was a significant force working in favour of economic cyclical stability. Thus desynchronization too plays a part in explaining economic stability in the 1950s and 1960s.

2. FROM UNSTABLE GROWTH TO STAGFLATION: THE SEVENTIES

THE SEEDS OF CHANGE

During the 1960s the solid confidence in the operational growth of the mixed economy led most politicians and economists to judge that the problem of economic crises had been largely solved and that attention should be turned to the problem of social and economic welfare. The application of Keynesian macro-economic principles, it was believed, made it possible to 'fine tune' the economy. Planning and associated policy instruments seemed to guarantee a climate of long-term economic growth. So the consolidation of the modern welfare state became the central plank of government policy.

This shift in emphasis had the effect of switching creative attention away from the concept of technological efficiency and towards that of social efficiency. In some government circles it was considered more important to use additional factors of production to raise the level of public welfare than to use them simply in the most economically efficient way. But providing the resources for public welfare is very labour-intensive, and this had the effect of putting pressure on the labour market. At the same time the financing of higher levels of welfare caused taxation to be increased, and this squeezed private savings. This squeeze, taken in conjunction with greater government borrowing, pushed up interest rates.

The student protest movement at the end of the 1960s clouded optimism over the future of the Western welfare model. It undermined the growth ideology, an ideology that formed the very basis of the mixed economy. Furthermore, the hitherto sturdy framework of post-war international co-operation had already begun to show some serious cracks during the course of the 1960s. This development came precisely at a time when the interdependence among the industrial nations and also between the industrialized world and the Third World had reached a high level which appeared irreversible.[67] When American defeat in Vietnam became certain, the 'giant with feet of clay' began to totter and American political and economic leadership of the world lost a degree of its authority. Simultaneously, lack of confidence in the future of the dollar became another factor of disquiet. In so far as the Western welfare society relied on a liberalized world economy, oiled by a convertible dollar, the system was thus preparing its own downfall.[68]

Against this background of spiralling uncertainty, the final phase of post-war growth played itself out. In the United States, welfare demand increased considerably from the middle of the 1960s. The new economic policy that had been tentatively introduced by Kennedy was fully developed under the Johnson administration. Macro-economic, growth-orientated objectives were central to this. The government took an active role in stimulating demand in order to raise production, introduce full employment, and eliminate the possibility of economic crisis.[69] From 1966 full employment was nearly achieved.[70] At the same time, the rate of inflation increased, not only in absolute terms but also in comparison to other members of the Organization for Economic Co-operation and Development (OECD). The average yearly rise in American consumer prices grew from 1.3 per cent for the period 1960–3 to 3.3 per cent for the period 1965–8, 5.4 per cent in 1969, and 5.9 per cent in 1970.[71] Moreover, this was increasingly cost-push inflation. Johnson finally announced measures to restrain the economy in 1968, but they had no real effect. Keynesian New Economics began to lose credence, and in the great debate between Keynesians and monetarists, the monetarists, led by Milton Friedman and the 'Chicago School', began to take the upper hand.

The American balance of payments was also giving cause for concern, not just because of a deficit on capital account but, for the first time in the twentieth century, a deficit in trade as well. The overvaluation of the dollar was the main reason for this. World exchange rates had not undergone a thorough revision since September 1949, and meanwhile most countries had greatly improved their competitive position in relation to the United States. The overheating of the American economy at the end of the 1960s also undoubtedly contributed to the deterioration of the trade balance. A rising deficit in the American balance of payments implied significant surpluses in Japan and Europe, and these surpluses could be used to finance Japanese and European desires for improved growth rates and welfare.[72] In Japan this led to more deficit spending and an acceleration in inflation, and there was a similar effect in Europe,[73] which continued to maintain an expansionary policy until 1970. France too embarked on a bold expansion policy, but only after the dramatic *événements* – a sort of mini-revolution – in May 1968. Britain lagged behind because the overvalued pound obliged the government to stick with the stop-go policy. The British finally devalued sterling in 1967, but did so in order not to waste the restored balance-of-payments position. Accordingly, Britain lost touch with the general expansion programme in Western Europe, although the restrictions were not strong enough to stop inflation from increasing in Britain too. In fact, inflation picked up pace over the whole of Western Europe, yet not as rapidly as in the United States or Japan.[74]

THE WAGE EXPLOSIONS OF 1968–9 AND THE OVERHEATING OF THE WORLD ECONOMY

Although inflation in Europe up to the end of the 1960s was not as threatening as in the United States and Japan, the European labour market, on the other hand, reacted much more violently than that of the other areas. In France the disturbances of 1968 led to sharp wage increases, and so did the West German wildcat strikes of 1969. In Italy, the Netherlands, and elsewhere, the pace of wage increases quickened after 1969.

The European wage explosions of 1968 and 1969 have to be seen in the context of the general prosperity of the 1960s and the tendency towards full employment. Attempts to solve the resulting labour market problems by attracting foreign workers and expanding technical and higher education yielded increasingly meagre returns. During the 1960s nominal wages continually rose faster than productivity and prices; therefore various European governments felt themselves obliged to take corrective measures. The explosive nature of the wage increase of 1968–9 can thus be explained as a reaction by wage earners against those government efforts to moderate wage rises. In some countries, including France, the reaction came when economic restrictions were at their height. In others, such as West Germany, it occurred at a time when economic conditions were more favourable.

Other factors also influenced the general wage rises in the West. The new generation of workers, who had grown up in a world of Keynesian economics, regarded full employment as a natural phenomenon. They strove to protect their incomes by taking future inflation into account in any wage negotiations, a practice which received full support from the unions.[75] Governments even considered full employment as more important than stable prices and wages. Monetary authorities since the war, especially in Europe, had ceded much of their independence to political control and had adjusted their policies accordingly.[76] The implications were far-reaching.

During the 1950s, particularly in the United States, the conviction had grown, based on the Phillips Curve, that in every industrial nation there existed an inverse relationship between the unemployment rate and price-wage inflation. It was held, moreover, that reducing unemployment *too far* would lead to a rise in inflation that was more than proportional to the decrease in unemployment. The same disproportionality was also said to apply to a situation of too high unemployment. Between the extremes there was an area of equilibrium, with an inversely proportional elasticity between the rates of unemployment and inflation. Within the area of equilibrium, the government could manipulate this relationship; that is, it could choose any combination of unemployment and respective inflation which it regarded as optimal. The creeping inflation present in the West during the 1950s and at the beginning of the 1960s was accepted by governments as the price for pushing employment to as high a level as possible.[77] In the course of time, however, the relationship became distorted. For the seven major industrialized countries of the West, the decisive break took place between 1968 and 1970. Prices grew at a much faster rate than unemployment fell, as MacCracken revealed in his OECD report of 1977.

This break had much to do with the wage explosions and the severe shortages in the labour market.[78] In addition, the expansionary monetary policy, which was partly responsible for distorting the unemployment-inflation relationship, also began to threaten the working of the international monetary system. In several countries money creation started to outpace increases in currency reserves.[79] During the course of 1971, the United States government realized that the functioning of the then world monetary system made accelerating inflation and the overvaluation of the dollar inevitable. The US trade deficit accentuated the imbalance, and therefore, as already mentioned in connection with growth cycles, President Nixon ended dollar convertibility in August 1971. This single measure struck at the very heart of the world monetary system, which gradually broke up.

Fears of a consequent collapse of the world economy caused most national governments to continue their expansionary policies. This implied, in turn, a period of further monetary expansion and easy borrowing conditions. At the same time, pessimism about the future of the American currency stimulated heavy selling of the dollar. An immediate and catastrophic effect was wrought on the American balance of payments, which was already in deficit. The massive increase in international liquidity which stemmed from American deficits in 1971 and 1972 further fuelled the excessive growth in national money supplies. This generated still more inflation, although growth in money supplies was clearly also a function of previous inflation.[80] Meanwhile, expansionary policies and higher inflation led to a sharp rise in economic activity. In only twelve months, from 1 July 1972 to 30 June 1973, real GNP in OECD countries rose by 7.5 per cent and industrial production, again in real terms, by 10 per cent. Under these circumstances, overheating was unavoidable. For the first time since the 1950 Korean War, however, the overheating expressed itself not only in terms of labour supply but also in terms of raw materials and foodstuffs. Steep price rises followed. In the course of one year, 1972–3, prices of primary products (excluding energy) rose by 63 per cent, and over a three-year period, 1971–4, by 159 per cent. Speculation in real estate became widespread and the demand for gold rocketed.[81] Eventually, in 1973, national governments judged it advisable to adopt policies of economic restriction.

The rise in prices of raw materials and foodstuffs should not be seen purely in terms of the overheating of the world economy. Chance events, such as serious harvest failures in the Soviet Union, had the effect of abruptly raising the demand for primary products in the West. More important, though, was the concern for the future of the dollar. Those who received dollars in exchange for raw materials and foodstuffs on the world market were unsure of the real purchasing power of the dollar, should they, in turn, wish to buy. Finally, there was the deeper-lying question of the relative prices of primary products against those of industrial products.[82] The high prices of raw materials and foodstuffs during the Korean War had led to considerable input of technology and capital investment in the primary sector during the 1950s. The effect was a cycle of falling prices for primary products and rising prices for industrial ones. This development caused, in turn, an increasing switch of investment away from the primary sector and towards the industrial sector. And the effect of that was the eventual rise in raw material prices in the 1970s.

The quadrupling of oil prices was influenced by the same circumstances. High energy and transport prices during the 1950s stimulated significant investment in exploration for new oil and gas fields. After subsequent discoveries, there followed tremendous investment in transport and in adapting industry to the new energy sources. The consequent downward price movement for oil and gas reinforced the overheating of the world economy at the start of the 1970s. The Organization of Petroleum Exporting Countries (OPEC) cartel reacted in November 1973 with a dramatic increase in oil prices as a countermeasure against the general inflation trend and the depreciation of the dollar. The impact of the rise in oil prices on the world economy was heavy. The shock wave quickly aggravated the recession which had already been set in motion at the beginning of 1973 by restrictive national economic policies.

FROM RECESSION TO STAGFLATION

The rise in energy prices during a period of accelerated inflation considerably raised costs in the oil-importing countries, but these were largely passed on to the consumer. In nominal terms price increases raised national income, but at the same time desperate struggles broke out among various social and economic groups to get a share of this increased income. Accordingly, inflation was increasingly built into wage demands, business contracts, and financial agreements.[83] The Phillips Curve now seemed wholly obsolete. How could governments act to restrain the inflationary spiral without sacrificing their original goals of economic growth and full employment? By way of compromise, a stop-go policy was introduced which contributed to yet more instability everywhere.[84] On the other hand, the rise in oil prices had a braking effect on consumption in the industrial West. The sudden transfer of income to the oil-producing countries drastically reduced Western purchasing power. Consumer spending fell, especially on energy-intensive goods. In Japan and Western Europe the sectors most hit were precisely the ones whose expansion in the post-war period had been the greatest.[85] The fall in consumption in the West was not nearly compensated by a consumption increase in OPEC countries. There, the pattern of both consumption and income distribution was very different from that which existed in the West. The effect was similar in respect of price rises for other primary products.

The oil crisis and price increases in primary products generally, coming at a time when Western governments were already deflating the economy, had a grave effect. Confidence slumped, and from the second half of 1974 the West was in serious recession.[86] This time it was not just a question of a slowing in the rate of growth. This time GNP in OECD countries actually fell.[87] For industrial production, at a certain moment, the fall was 13 per cent. Everywhere stocks were run down and even the volume of foreign trade diminished. Unemployment in the OECD countries increased by 7 million in 1974–5, and this figure takes no account of the large numbers of guest workers who returned to their native lands. In real terms the loss of purchasing power in the OECD countries was double that which was transferred to the oil-exporting countries.[88] Nevertheless the recession did not immediately develop into a full-fledged crisis. World trade stagnated initially but certainly did not collapse as it had done during the 1930s. Improvements in productivity slowed in relation to the two previous decades but the pace was still clearly higher than it had been in the period 1870–1950.[89] The annual rate of inflation for OECD countries rose to 15 per cent in the spring of 1974, then fell during the recession, although it was still running at a high level of 10 per cent in mid 1975. Inflation was accompanied by stagnation in the economy. The phenomenon of stagflation had been born.[90]

A stringent deflationary policy could have pushed prices down but this seemed unacceptable from the point of view of the even higher unemployment which would result. Furthermore, in the context of the post-war growth economy, it was not acceptable for nominal wages to be reduced in line with the loss of real national income caused by the transfer of purchasing power to non-Western countries.

From the middle of 1975, Western governments once again started cautious expansionary policies. United States officials believed that the US money supply should be increased in order to support the rise in prices. They expected that in time the upward movement would be moderated by the growth in unemployment. High unemployment would give added leverage to efforts to keep wage increases below the rate of inflation and so the necessary fall in real income would be brought about.[91] The dollar would no longer be supported abroad, and its fall on foreign exchange markets would have a beneficial effect on the balances of trade and payments. European and Japanese governments were, however, much more cautious and tried to restrict the expansion of the money supply and to reduce budget deficits.[92] To the extent to which they succeeded, their exchange-rate position in relation to the dollar was strengthened and they attracted international reserves via either the balance of payments or the Eurodollar market. Thus, contrary to their best endeavours, they were still unable to control the size of increases in the money supply.

Economic recovery was perceptible from the second half of 1975 in the United States and Japan and, shortly afterwards, in most European countries. Yet this remained a fragile recovery. The end of the 1970s was characterized by relative stagnation.[93] Productive investment in the private sector remained weak. This lack of enthusiasm on the part of entrepreneurs was undeniably a function of the overcapacity and saturation now present in the former leading industrial sectors. Industrial production therefore grew only slowly. Unemployment continued at a high level, much higher than in the 1950s and 1960s. A tendency towards increased protectionism developed but was curbed by international consultation. The combined balance of payments for the OECD countries against the rest of the world improved considerably – an improvement due, among other things, to a flow of petro-dollars back to the West. This flow resulted partly from OPEC countries reinvesting in the West and partly from their placing orders for military hardware and capital infrastructure. The OECD improvement was very uneven, however, and countries with strong currencies and balance-of-payments surpluses, such as Japan and West Germany, stood in stark contrast to countries with serious deficits, notably the United States.[94]

Further oil price rises in 1979 and 1980 brought the problem of balance of payments and the problem of the international monetary system once again to the fore and triggered a new economic recession at the beginning of the 1980s. Simultaneously there was still more growth in international liquidity and thus further additions to national money supplies. Specific government measures to reduce unemployment also served to create more money as did social mechanisms to maintain levels of real income. These factors all helped to flame inflation against a background of economic stagnation. Average consumer prices in the OECD countries rose by 7.8 per cent in 1977, 6.8 per cent in 1978, and 8 per cent in 1979.[95]

STAGFLATION: CYCLICAL OR STRUCTURAL CRISIS?

Economists who have analysed the stagflation of the 1970s, have fallen into two main categories: those who regarded it as an integral part of the evolution of post-war business cycles and those who saw it as a manifestation of a deeper, structural crisis.[96]

According to the first group, the recessions of the 1970s, though displaying some new characteristics, constituted no real break with other post-war recessions. Some economists in this group believe that stagflation must be combated largely by use of the old, Keynesian, fiscal-orientated medicine. But the extent of the accelerating inflation has rather discredited those who preached demand management via government fiscal measures, and the monetarist school has gained the ascendancy. Fiscal measures are anathema to monetarists, who believe business cycles can only be effectively controlled if government intervention is limited to regulation of the money supply. Although the differences between monetarists and Keynesians may appear at first sight to be great, they agree that stagflation does not comprise a structural crisis. Both stress the need to adapt the level of demand, Keynesians looking to effective demand and monetarists to nominal demand.

To what extent can stagflation be integrated into the framework of the evolution of post-war business cycles? An analysis of price evolution can throw some light on that question. Fred Hirsch and Peter Oppenheimer examined price development over nearly two centuries.[97] Between 1815 and 1914, prices were largely stable. Hirsch and Oppenheimer argued that this stability matched the balanced use of the different factors of production at the time – that is, balanced growth. Between 1914 and 1939 the price movement was essentially downward and it reflected massive unemployment and under-utilization of capital equipment – that is, unbalanced growth. Between 1945 and 1980 the price movement was upward, in the form of inflation, first creeping and then galloping. This reflected full employment and intensive use of capital equipment – that is, forced economic growth. Angus Maddison[98] and Erik Lundberg[99] saw the Hirsch/Oppenheimer analysis as too simplistic and called for greater distinctions to be made in the form of subperiods and subsectors. They also argued that post-war inflation cannot be ascribed wholly to policies of economic growth and full employment; in other words it cannot be ascribed wholly to the pressure of effective demand.

Monetarists explained the phenomenon of post-war inflation exclusively in terms of excessive money creation by the government and the financial sector – that is, the pressure of *nominal* demand. John M. Fleming reacted against this with an argument emphasizing the significance of interdependence: inflation was not only a consequence of excessive money supply but also a cause of future money creation. Fleming judged inflation to be the result of a complex interaction of factors which do not all bring about the same effect at the same time.[100] Rostow ascribed the mild nature of inflation during the 1950s and at the start of the 1960s to the considerable increases in productivity in the primary sector (agriculture and mining) around the world and to comparable increases in the secondary (industry) and tertiary (services) sectors in the industrial economies. From the mid 1960s a first acceleration phase in inflation took place on a world scale. Rostow saw the pressure of effective demand, which at one time was closing, or even closed, the gap between potential and actual production, as the main factor involved. From the start of the 1970s, however, a second acceleration phase took place; and Rostow concluded that the former link between effective demand and inflation was now broken. Other elements instead appeared to play a crucial role, namely the relative scarcity of foodstuffs, raw materials, and energy, as well as domestic and international monetary policy.[101]

Some analysts of American business cycles studied the course of the business cycle itself rather than price evolution.[102] They expected that the synchronization of world business cycles would decrease during the 1970s. The system of floating exchange rates, which now prevailed, supposedly would have the effect of isolating national economies from each other more and more, thus reducing the international transmission of cycles and inflation.[103] But when the various hypotheses were tested against real data, the results were unexpected.[104] To general astonishment, the international synchronization of business cycles was greater in the 1970s than in the 1960s.[105]

External shocks, such as the oil crisis, were initially put forward as the main cause, but even when these were allowed for in the calculations, the figures still pointed towards greater synchronization. Some economists suggested that monetary factors were responsible since the system of freely floating exchange rates had quickly developed into *managed* floating. Others stressed the increasing co-ordination of government policy on a world scale through summit meetings, although the usefulness of such meetings has often been questioned.

In the end, increasing interdependence of the Western industrial economies appeared to be the most important factor. Cyclical synchronization was strongest in the case of heavily trade-dependent countries. Furthermore, in world terms, the relative share of international trade in the GNP of all industrial nations continued to grow during the 1970s. It is true that economic stagnation aroused some calls for protectionism, but interdependence still grew sufficiently to be a major force behind the increasing synchronization of production cycles.

Working from this conclusion, some economists came to believe that the solution to the stagflation problem lay in supplementing the business-cycle approach with structural reforms. The gradual process of the unintended socialization of the production system, within the framework of the mixed economy, had to be halted and reversed.[106] Government policy and the economic system should once more begin to move towards the ideal of the free market. At its extreme, this implied mainly limiting government action to regulating the money supply.

For other economists, historical reality consists of cumulative processes and any deliberate attempt to resurrect the previous system of the free-market economy must be regarded *a priori* as inappropriate for contemporary and future society. So these economists identified stagflation as a decisive downward phase in the long-run Kondratieff Cycle.[107] They rejected the concept of a rigid production structure and gave foremost attention to developments in the structure of supply. In this light Rostow and Van Duijn stressed the importance of the mutual relationships between the primary, secondary and tertiary sectors of the world economy. During the 1960s the enormous investment in the secondary and tertiary sectors in the West, the Eastern bloc, and the Third World, seen in connection with world population growth, held out the prospect of a shortage of foodstuffs, raw materials and energy. The turning of the terms of trade in favour of primary producers from the beginning of the 1970s came as a result of this growing imbalance. Rostow and Van Duijn argued that both the increase in inflation starting in the mid 1960s and the stagflation starting in the 1970s had to be seen in this context.[108] Both economists supplemented this concept of relative prices with the hypotheses of leading sectors within manufacturing industry and of chronological differences in the distribution of income and wealth.[109]

The catching-up movement in Europe and Japan *vis-à-vis* the United States led to tremendous overinvestment in the traditional industrial sectors of the modern consumption economy during the 1960s, causing massive overcapacity. This overinvestment and overcapacity in the West were accentuated by the industrialization process in the Eastern bloc and the Third World, a process which was often concentrated on identical sectors.[110] A crucial element in the saturation resulting from post-war growth and in the downward turn of the Kondratieff Cycle was, according to Rostow and Van Duijn, the exhaustion of innovation potential in the leading industrial sectors of the Western economy. Other factors had to do with the structural budget deficits caused by increased social expenditure as well as the general uncertainty regarding international monetary order. Finally the evaporation of expectations of further growth also made a significant contribution.

According to Rostow and Van Duijn, the downward phase of the Kondratieff Cycle explains why new private investment in the traditional sectors of the consumption economy, even when encouraged by government subsidy, was such a laborious process. The structural character of stagflation is the cause. Of course, the Kondratieff Cycle can turn upwards for the same structural reasons and the primary condition for this is the realization of a series of basic inventions and innovations in new branches of industry. Possible areas would be alternative energy technology, biochemistry, the exploitation of maritime resources, and the provision of advanced services as in modern banking. The restructuring of the Western economies, as envisaged here, is a difficult process, which can only be realized through the mixed economy. The principles of the market must be respected; yet at the same time the government has to play a decisive role in stimulating the development of new leading sectors, either in industry or in the tertiary (services) or quarternary (public goods) fields.

In fact the structural vision of Rostow and Van Duijn goes back to the hypothesis of Jacob M. Schmookler.[111] Economic growth is essentially the result of increasing technological knowledge. The direction taken by technological advances is determined by demand, and the pace is determined by the size of investment. According to Schmookler, input into technological progress yields proportional returns. That is, if expenditure on research and development doubles, so does the pace of technological progress. Nathan Rosenberg and Angus Maddison accepted this hypothesis, but only for countries which have technological ground to make up on others. They argue that as soon as the frontier of world technological knowledge is reached, further research to extend the frontiers in current leading sectors brings only diminishing returns. Moreover, it is not certain that transferring research programmes to other areas can reverse this process.[112]

Marxist-inspired economists have made extensive use of the Kondratieff Cycle but have tried to characterize the inflation and stagflation of the 1970s as a more fundamental, socio-political crisis. On this issue Ernest Mandel has referred not only to the social context of the Third World but also to that of the West itself.[113] He saw the economic situation of the 1970s as a typical overproduction crisis in the phase of late capitalism. It has had a less serious effect than the one between the wars because it was neutralized by systematic political action and the major expansion of bank credit. The 1970s, he argued, were also characterized by a crisis of the imperialistic system in which surplus value no longer exclusively accrued to Western industrial countries. Instead a redistribution took place between the dominant bourgeoisie of the imperialistic nations on one side and those of oil-producing and industrializing areas of the Third World on the other. This redistribution was the subject of much discussion at the Fifth United Nations Conference on Trade and Development (UNCTAD) at Manila in 1979. Within the inflation and stagflation of the 1970s Mandel sees a socio-political crisis, with dominant groups seeking to impose the costs of the Kondratieff downturn on the working classes. Mandel believes that this structural crisis can be solved through fundamental techno-logical innovation which would create additional surplus value for the benefit of the dominant classes. He also argues, however, that during one of the subsequent Kondratieff crises the working classes in the West and the Third World will refuse to accept the system in which they are expected to shoulder the burden of downturns in the Kondratieff Cycle while, on the other hand, the surplus value resulting from upturns is appropriated by the bourgeoisie; a revol-ution will change the entire social order and, in principle, will resolve the problem of income distribution; a centralized, imperative planning system will then eliminate the danger of overproduction so that structural crises will become a thing of the past.

Many ecologically-minded economists are very sceptical about Marxist utopianism. They believe that socialist state capitalism not only seeks a more thorough application of capital than bourgeois capitalism (by being more productive) but also, through its authori-tarian and centralized rationalism, is predisposed to realize its objective of massive accumulation regardless of social or economic cost. These ecological economists do not believe that overproduction and overcapacity will necessarily be solved by the change in social structure as recommended by Marxists. Both catastrophes can only be avoided if the organization of production is fundamentally changed. Ecologists regard the inflation and stagflation of the 1970s more as the manifestation of a crisis of business and state organization which has come about because the economic system has developed to a point beyond its optimum.[114] The functioning of the economic system in both East and West has become so complex that further growth in production goes towards maintaining the system itself rather than raising individual well-being. Increasing the economies of scale generates so much tension and inertia that it can only be managed by reinforcing control mechanisms, at both company and government level. The amount of goods and services produced by the community simply in order to keep this economic and political control structure in place grows even faster than total production. Consequently, a constantly diminishing share of total communal production is allocated for individual income, so that living stan-dards begin to fall despite continuously rising production.[115] Meanwhile, the economies of scale and technological progress make such savings in the need for labour that employment in industry falls rather than rises. The real danger, according to the ecologists, is that the increase in industrial unemployment will be absorbed by extending employment in the public sector, that is, in bureaucracy and the army.[116] The implications of this are obvious.

Ecologists therefore advocate a fundamental change in the organization of both the mixed economy and socialist state capitalism. A central pillar in their philosophy is that production should be organized on a smaller scale and that the economy should be run on a more human basis. The ecological approach to economics is, however, often too vague and idealistic. Moreover, it is too concerned with micro-economics and insufficiently embracing as a theory to offer a real alternative for present society. Because of tremendous population growth, combined with the influential demonstration effect of the Western modern consumer model, world society seems unlikely to give up voluntarily the products of large-scale technology. Finally, from a geopolitical viewpoint, a national policy to reduce the size of production units would only be a realistic option if an international consensus on this could be achieved. At the moment, the chances of any such development seem remote.

From the previous pages the following comment can be made. Different analyses of the inflation and stagflation of the 1970s have led to extremely divergent interpretations. In my opinion it would not be responsible to select one as giving *the* explanation. It would be better to try to integrate the various partial explanations into one multi-faceted whole.

CHAPTER III

THE MALTHUSIAN DIMENSION

The development of the Western economy during the nineteenth century and the beginning of the twentieth brought with it a large growth in population. This growth stabilized during the twentieth century when a high level of general prosperity was reached. But in the less-developed countries – the Third World – economic development led to a powerful population boom, and the imbalance between population and food supplies increased. A Second Agricultural Revolution in the West was able to cope with these difficulties until the start of the 1970s, when major problems arose. At this point a 'Green Revolution' got under way in the Third World. Meanwhile, following the Second World War, the prospering economies in the West increased their demands for natural resources, especially raw materials and energy. Initially this pressure could be relieved by technological innovation and by increases in supply from the Third World. In the end, however, this became a further source of imbalance between demand and supply. The need for technological innovation and for international co-operation in respect of raw materials and energy became greater than ever.

1. THE PROBLEM OF 'DEMOGRAPHIC TRANSITION'

POPULATION TRENDS IN THE WEST AFTER THE SECOND WORLD WAR

The astonishing increase in the rate of world population growth is a recent phenomenon. For centuries growth remained a very slow process and it was not until 1800 that world population exceeded the 1 billion mark. It took 130 years to double this figure. Less than thirty years were needed to reach the 3 billion mark, and less than fifteen years more to get a population of 4 billion people. In 1980 the world population totalled 4.5 billion people. By then, the total was increasing each year by about 75 million, that is, 1 million every five days.[1] Demographers predict that by the year 2000 total world population will be around 6.5 billion.

The demographic revolution which brought about this rapid acceleration broke out first in Western Europe during the course of the eighteenth century and then spread to North America, Eastern Europe, and Australia. It maintained its influence in these developed areas until the middle of the twentieth century and in the period 1850 to 1950 their population grew from about 300 million to 850 million. In the same period the rest of the world experienced population growth at a much lower rate. Only from the beginning of the twentieth century was it, too, gradually affected by the European demographic revolution. But by the 1950s and 1960s, a veritable population explosion was occurring. According to estimates, the population of the Third World between 1950 and 2000 will increase from about 1.6 billion to about 5 billion. On the other hand, population in Europe, North America, and Australia from the 1960s onwards has grown either very slowly or not at all.

According to demographic theory, the slow or zero population growth in the developed countries of the West is the consequence of a demographic transition. This transition represents a watershed in demographic development, characterized by low birth and death rates.[2] Until the eighteenth century, the world, including the West, had experienced high birth and death rates. After that century, in Western Europe, because of improvements in hygiene, food, and medicine, the death rate began to fall. Not so the birth rate. Indeed, in many areas the birth rate rose, influenced by a drop in the average age of marriage. Thus, during the nineteenth century, the fall in the death rate increased while the birth rate continued high. It was at this time that the demographic revolution, as a counterpart of the Industrial Revolution, had its greatest impact. Only from the end of the nineteenth century did the birth rate decline and even then this movement was not immediately widespread. The decline nevertheless gained speed generally in the West during the two world wars and the Great Depression of the 1930s. Although there was a renewed rise in Western birth rates after the Second World War, they fell back again to a low, stable level in the 1970s.[3] Against this background of an uneven birth rate, the death rate continued to fall sharply and constantly, down to a low level.

Again according to theory, the general decline in the birth rate from the end of the nineteenth century onwards caused the demographic transition of the West. This transition was a slow and delicate process, closely linked to Western social and economic development.[4] Paradoxically, the Industrial Revolution, which had brought about the great population speed-up of the nineteenth century, in the longer run can now be seen as the chief explanatory factor in the population slow-down of the twentieth. Industrialization set to work social, economic and psychological mechanisms which fundamentally altered the behaviour of individuals. It led to growing urbanization, modern education, and gradual increases in living standards. Over a period of time, these in turn led to a modern pattern of consumption, with a growing appetite for industrial goods and consumer durables, and a more materialistic and rationalistic way of life. All these elements changed public opinion regarding the ideal size of the family. Restricting the number of births and using family planning thus became more common. The Great Depression of the 1930s further accentuated this tendency.

According to the stagnation theories of Alvin Hansen and John Maynard Keynes, the pessimism and low birth rates of the 1930s helped to push the economy down to an equilibrium level of low activity with future consumption rates very much threatened. Those economists believed that only a drastic increase in government expenditure, a decrease in interest rates, and a policy to redistribute incomes, could break out of the impasse. Economists such as Henry Roy Forbes Harrod and a number of politicians thought that difficulties arising from unsatisfactory birth rates could be resolved by specific government policies. After the Second World War, a number of Western governments, influenced by this thinking, introduced policies to facilitate, or even stimulate, an increase in the birth rate. They found encouragement for this in the climate of powerful economic growth and great confidence in the future of the West which existed at the time. During the 1950s and the start of the 1960s, the increase in the number of births was striking. The new fall in the birth rate began in the second half of the 1960s, and in the 1970s this fall took on such proportions that in nearly all industrialized nations of the West fertility rates fell below the net reproduction rate; that is, below the equilibrium level for a stable population. From Table 7 it can be seen that fertility in the industrialized nations of the West in 1978 varied around 1.8, which is clearly lower than the equilibrium figure of 2. Population in absolute terms (excluding migration) fell in West Germany, East Germany, the United Kingdom, Luxemburg, and Austria. Similar falls were expected in Belgium, Sweden, Denmark, Norway, Hungary, and Czechoslovakia by the mid 1980s. It is also predicted that Italy, Switzerland, Finland, Greece, and Bulgaria will have declining populations from about 1990. In general terms, then, a decline in population in both Eastern and Western Europe is expected by the end of the twentieth century.[5]

Death rates in the West, including infant mortalities, continued to fall during the 1970s so that by 1980 the average life expectancy was about seventy years in most countries.[6] At this point, however, the fall could no longer be regarded as spectacular and in any case was not sufficient to compensate for the considerable decline in marital fertility.

On the other hand, in some Western countries migration brought about significant population growth. In six European countries, namely France, West Germany, Switzerland, Belgium, Sweden, and Luxemburg, immigration exceeded emigration for the period 1950 to 1970. And in the 1970s, immigration into these countries continued to grow. In time other European countries followed this trend.[7] In the United States, Canada, and Australia, too, immigration was an important factor in further population growth after the Second World War.[8] In fact, official statistics underestimate the importance of immigration in population growth. Immigrants are usually young men who still stick to the tradition of large families and thus have a more than proportionate impact on population growth in their land of settlement.[9]

The reasons why marital fertility fell sharply in the West from the

Table 7 Demographic and Fertility-Related Indicators, 1960–80

		Crude birth rate per thousand population		Crude death rate per thousand population		Percentage change in:		Total fertility rate
						Crude birth rate	Crude death rate	
		1960	1980	1960	1980	1960–80	1960–80	1980
Low-income economies	(1)	43	31	18	12	−28.3	−36.0	4.2
Ethiopia		51	49	28	24	−2.8	−14.8	6.7
India		44	36	22	14	−18.5	−37.6	4.9
China		40*	21	14*	8	−47.4	−42.6	2.9
Middle-income economies	(2)	43	35	17	11	−18.3	−36.4	4.8
Nigeria		52	50	25	17	−4.4	−32.8	6.9
Indonesia		46	35	23	13	−22.7	−40.9	4.5
Brazil		43	30	13	9	−30.8	−33.6	4.1
Industrial market economies	(3)	20	15	10	9	−27.9	−4.1	1.9
United Kingdom		17	14	12	12	−22.0	0.0	1.8
France		18	14	12	11	−22.5	−6.1	1.9
West Germany		17	11	11	12	−38.7	9.7	1.5
Belgium		17	13	12	12	−25.7	−4.1	1.8
Japan		18	14	8	6	−22.6	−17.3	1.8
United States		24	16	9	9	−33.3	−7.4	1.9
High-income oil exporters	(4)	49	42	21	12	−12.9	−43.8	6.8
Saudi Arabia		49	44	23	14	−11.0	−4.0	6.9
East European non-market economies	(5)	23	18	8	11	−20.5	−29.6	2.3
Soviet Union		24	18	8	10	−23.1	−38.7	2.3

Notes: Countries with populations of less than 1 million were excluded from this study.

* Figure for the year 1957

(1) Low-income economies: 33 countries with an income per capita of less than $415 in 1978, of which 3 were chosen which were significant for the group

(2) Middle-income economies: 63 countries with an income per capita of more than $415 in 1978, of which 3 were chosen which were significant for the group

(3) Industrial market economies: 19 countries of which 6 were chosen which were significant for the group

(4) High-income oil exporters: 5 oil-exporting countries with a balance-of-payments surplus on the capital account, of which one was selected

(5) East European non-market economies: 6 countries of which one was selected which was significant for the group

Source: WORLD BANK, *World Development Report, 1980*, pp. 144–5

mid 1960s fall into four main categories. First there was the growing fear of overpopulation. A psychological effect of the demographic explosion in the Third World was to turn Western public opinion against the traditional philoprogenitive mentality. A second series of explanations has to do with changes in moral and sexual behaviour. The widespread use of birth control and the legalizing of abortion in many countries had a direct effect in reducing the number of births. Third, there was the impact of the affluent society, as consolidated in the West. This new form of society promoted the ideal of the small family. It advanced the individualization and emancipation of young married couples, and it contributed to the increase in the number of working women. It also offered the prospect of a rapid increase in material welfare for parents and children alike on the condition that the number of children per family remained low. A final set of explanations is related to the performance of the economy. Undoubtedly the economic uncertainty and the high unemployment of the 1970s strengthened the tendency once more to restrict the number of births.

The falling birth and death rates in the West led not only to an ageing of the population but also, in the longer term, to a decline in the proportion of the total population classified as 'working'.[10] The relative decrease in the number of those economically active was accentuated by the raising of the school-leaving age, the growth of further education opportunities, and the lowering of the retirement age. Running counter to this was the larger percentage of women who joined the working population – a movement especially noteworthy in some countries, including the Netherlands and Spain.[11] The large-scale immigration of guest workers also occasionally concealed the economic effects of an ageing population. In both these cases problems arose regarding the quality of the labour force. Many women and guest workers had not had the same kind of training as the traditional male worker. Therefore an extra effort had to be made to raise the educational levels of both groups. The fall in the number of those who worked, in relation to those who did not, also necessitated important adjustments to the social security system. Greater burdens were now placed on a smaller number of working people and this demanded a reorganization of the various mechanisms to redistribute incomes.

The psychology of an ageing population had a series of economic effects. Empirical research in the United States has shown that the ageing of the population has had a disruptive effect on labour mobility.[12] More important still were the changes in the pattern of consumption in the West. The preponderance of the small family and the rising number of adults in the total population made for greater consumption of consumer durables and luxury products. The trend also increased the size of the family budget allocated for rest and recreation, and it stimulated the demand for all forms of adult education. Moreover, the conviction grew that the relative decrease in the working population could only be adequately compensated for in economic terms by substantially raising the quality of the education received by those still economically active.

THE DEMOGRAPHIC REVOLUTION IN THE DEVELOPING COUNTRIES

So the demographic revolution from explosive population growth to stability is closely related to social and economic development; and that is why its first manifestation was in the West, the birthplace of the Industrial Revolution. Meanwhile, population growth in the Third World continued to be held in check by Malthusian mechanisms. Malthus distinguished between preventive checks, which serve to reduce the number of births, and repressive checks, which increase the number of deaths. Both can be influenced by either natural elements or man-made ones. As a third check, Malthus recognized the effect of moral restraint, which he understood as the postponement of marriage until a couple has sufficient resources to set up house and start a family.

Economic development in the Third World during the twentieth century and especially after the Second World War was accompanied by a big drop in the death rate while the birth rate fell much less. Even more than in the West, the demographic revolution led to a complete breakdown of the traditional balancing mechanisms, and the unprecedented population blast followed. Table 7 shows the tempo at which the population in developing countries grew and has continued to grow in the second half of this century. The explosion took place all over the Third World but was greatest in Latin America and Asia – especially Asia. A group of only seven countries in both continents, namely India, Bangladesh, Indonesia, Pakistan, Brazil, Mexico, and China, together comprise 60 per cent of the total population of the developing world, that is, 2 billion people. The rapid and substantial growth will be maintained for some time yet in the developing countries, since population continues to grow for another fifty to sixty years after marital fertility has fallen to a figure of 2.0 – the equilibrium-inducing level.[13] As the table shows, most developing countries are a long way from achieving this equilibrium.

Western techniques to reduce deaths are more easily absorbed by the Third World than techniques to reduce births. This phenomenon is at the heart of the whole problem.

Medical care for the masses can be organized fairly cheaply with a relatively small number of highly specialized personnel. Moreover, it does not crucially depend on the active participation of the whole population but can even work effectively with merely a passive consensus to reduce or eliminate suffering from disease. As a result some developing countries with a very young population now have lower death rates than some already developed countries.[14] In addition, many medical advances are of recent origin and so the impact on population growth in developing nations has been more dramatic than the equivalent impact in the older industrialized ones during the nineteenth century. It took 150 years to raise life expectancy from thirty to sixty in industrial Europe. For the younger, developing countries it has taken scarcely 50 years.[15] In nineteenth-century Europe, economic circumstances such as better food and heating were crucial elements in new population trends whereas this is much less the case now in the Third World. This explains why in 1970 the average life expectancy in Latin America was about the same as that of Western Europe just before the Second World War, even though Latin American living standards in 1970 were only about half those of Western Europe in the 1930s. Asia achieved in 1970 an average life expectancy which matched that of Western Europe for 1938; yet Asian living standards around 1970 were only one-fifth those of Western Europe in 1900.[16]

The introduction of techniques to control marital fertility is a much more difficult matter. An efficient spreading and general application of control techniques demands the active participation of the population. Socio-cultural and socio-economic circumstances usually hinder such an active participation. Thus there is a repetition of the conditions of the earliest phase of the demographic transition, with a rapid fall in the death rate accompanied by high or even rising marital fertility. Urbanization, the erosion of family ties and the weakening of the village as a social unit, all undermine the institutional arrangements which traditionally held marital fertility in check. Tribal taboos which formerly exerted a restraining influence lose effect. Furthermore, in the towns women usually give up breast-feeding and go out to work at an earlier stage, thereby becoming more quickly prone to pregnancy.[17] On the other hand, certain ethical, social and spiritual traditions remain deep-rooted. In consequence abortion, sterilization and contraception are often resisted because they affect fertility and thus attack the very *raison d'être* of women in these societies. Economic conditions also exert an important influence. The pressure of population in rural areas of the Third World encourages migration to the towns. These people leave their rural homes because of the increasing poverty there and the illusion that incomes can be better in urban areas, thus holding out the prospect of social and material improvement.

In the long run, for the advantages of small families to be appreciated in primitive society, individual incomes must be increased in both town and country. Economic progress and a more balanced income distribution in the countryside can slow down migration to the towns and inhibit the development of an urban subproletariat. The creation of a substantial educational structure and improvements in income gradually bring about changes in mental attitude. Parents realize that limiting the size of the family would secure a better income for themselves and would give their children access to the education which would ensure them a better future.

Current statistics clearly illustrate the distortion of the population structure caused by the first phase of the demographic revolution in the Third World. Deaths fell to an average of 12 per thousand in 1978 while in the developed countries the rate fluctuated around 9 per thousand. Births in the Third World continued at a very high level and from 1960 to 1965 the yearly average was still about 42 per thousand, as against only 20 per thousand in the developed countries, and this figure of 20 was still being affected by the post-war baby boom in the West, though this was coming to an end. Furthermore, the birth rate for the developing countries as a whole between 1950 and 1970 was significantly higher than it had been for Western European countries during the nineteenth century.[18]

From the 1970s onwards, a fall in marital fertility took place in some areas of the Third World, and here and there the decline was accelerating. An important factor here was the postponement of marriage by women in the 15–24 age group.[19] But the main cause was government-inspired family planning. Governments deliberately increased the availability of contraceptives, carried on information campaigns, encouraged sterilization for men and women, and legalized abortion. Improvements in income and the general spreading of educational opportunities were also decisive elements in the successful introduction of family planning. As already suggested, controls over marital fertility in the developing countries will not be able fully to stop population growth for another fifty years or even longer.

Meanwhile the rapid population growth in the Third World has had economic effects some of which also influence the Western economies. The foremost effect has been the still more rapid increase in the *urban* population. This was especially so from the 1950s onwards in Asia and Latin America. It is expected that by the year 2000 75 per cent of the people in Latin America will be living in urban areas.[20] Urbanization in the developing countries differs fundamentally from that which took place in the West during the eighteenth and nineteenth centuries. This is because it is not balanced by local agricultural revolutions as Western development was. Instead, the hundreds of millions of town-dwellers must, in the short term, buy a substantial portion of their food requirements from the developed countries. These purchases depend on two conditions: (1) if Western agriculture can considerably increase its productivity, and (2) if the growing urban population in the Third World can in turn produce goods which can be sold abroad. These are no simple conditions, especially when one remembers the changes in mental attitude as well as social structure which would be necessary in both North and South.

Rising population has a second economic effect. In order to keep the quality of the labour force at a suitable level, investment, both private and public, has to be concentrated on extending education and health services, broadening capital infrastructure, and increasing house construction. When population is growing as fast as this, the most that can be achieved is to maintain the level of capital and infrastructure per worker. Investment thus remains limited to 'capital widening' (equipping additional workers although maintaining existing levels of capital and infrastructure per worker) rather than progressing to 'capital deepening' (equipping all workers with additional amounts of capital and infrastructure).[21] The implications of this are far-reaching. The gulf between rich and poor countries is thereby continued. Industrialized nations are able increasingly to centre their attention on capital deepening and through innovation and rising productivity can raise their income levels. On the other hand most developing countries are satisfied if they can maintain levels of capital per worker and thus hold incomes steady. In these circumstances, the increase in the number of people who are not in the working population has the effect of lowering total income per head.

Actually, in real life, the extreme pattern described in the last paragraph rarely holds. Usually some part of savings is used not only to widen the existing modern sector but also to develop it more intensively. This investment helps the modern sector to progress both in depth and width but largely at the expense of the traditional sector, where both farmers and artisans lag hopelessly behind. The modern sector can then develop into a formidable competitor to industry in the West, all the more so since the pressure of growing population keeps wages rather low despite rising productivity. At the same time the traditional sector stagnates and poverty often becomes even more grinding. Calculations by Simon Kuznets have shown that if average family incomes in the developing countries rise, incomes for the very poorest families rise much slower than the average. In many cases income per head for these poorest groups actually falls, because of the increase in the number of surviving children.[22]

2. WORLD FOOD SUPPLIES

THE MALTHUSIAN VISION

Since the Second World War, Malthusians have continually stressed the growing danger of world overpopulation.[23] They believe that food production, despite improvements in productivity and increases in the amount of land farmed, will be unable to keep pace with population growth. In the long run, the supply of food will become insufficient. For Malthusians, a rapid and drastic curbing of population growth provides the only possible solution. Much statistical material backs up their sombre outlook. In particular, extrapolations into the future based on current trends predict a serious imbalance between population and food supplies.[24] In addition, population growth will continue to be concentrated in Asia, Africa, and Latin America, areas which even now are unable to satisfy their own food needs. The situation is getting steadily worse. Food production per head in the developing countries rose by 1 per cent annually during the 1950s but during the next decade it remained almost constant and in the 1970s it fell (Table 8). Asia and the Middle East are backward in food production, but in some African countries the position is even more critical and tragic. Undernourishment and malnutrition are characteristic phenomena in the Third World. The Food and Agriculture Organization (FAO) estimates that in the 1970s they afflicted about 1 billion of the world's inhabitants, and this estimate is on the cautious side.[25] Animal protein is especially scarce. In its 1980 report, the FAO urged particular measures which would be necessary to expand food production in the Third World in the 1980s. The agency predicted dire consequences if no progress was made.

The threat to the provision of food for the world does not come solely from the population explosion. In the industrial world too the demand for food is growing, although in a different way. In socialist countries such as the Soviet Union, industrialization and urbanization were accompanied by a notable stagnation in agriculture, so that more and more grain had to be imported. In Japan, agriculture did expand but not enough to keep up with the effects of urbanization and the increased demand for food, and much had to be imported.

In the West as a whole, rapidly rising incomes led to higher demand for new sorts of agricultural products – a shift away from grain and towards meat. In the developed countries after the Second World War, direct per capita consumption of grain remained at a steady level. On the other hand indirect consumption – grain fed to livestock – increased significantly.[26] The consumption of particular animal fodders and vegetal oils also increased. This in turn caused new agricultural imports in several Western countries. It should not be forgotten that meat is an expensive way of taking in calories and protein, compared to grain. Many more agricultural inputs are necessary to produce a given amount of calories and proteins in meat than in grain. This explains why some countries which were practically self-sufficient in food as long as their consumption pattern was based on grain had to resort to imports when meat consumption went up.

Table 8 *Annual Rates of Growth in Aggregate and Per Capita Food Production, 1950–79*
(*per cent*)

| | | Food production | |
		Aggregate	Per capita
1950–9	World	3.27	1.32
	Developed countries	3.18	1.80
	Developing countries	3.39	1.02
	Latin America	3.18	0.30
	Near East (excl. Israel)	4.18	1.55
	Far East (excl. Japan)	3.44	1.30
	Africa (excl. South Africa)	2.86	1.02
1960–9	World	2.66	0.64
	Developed countries	2.61	1.53
	Developing countries	2.79	0.19
	Latin America	3.13	0.39
	Near East (id.)	2.88	0.09
	Far East (id.)	2.81	0.18
	Africa (id.)	2.22	0.19
1970–9	World	2.26	0.39
	Developed countries	1.75	0.87
	Developing countries	2.97	0.77
	Latin America	3.27	0.77
	Near East (id.)	3.27	0.39
	Far East (id.)	2.97	0.68
	Africa (id.)	1.75	− 1.05

Sources: T. KING (*et al.*), *Population Policies and Economic Development*, p. 38, p. 179, p. 180

FAO, *Production Yearbook, 1981*

The growing dependence on food imports has had the effect of increasing the value of international trade in agricultural produce.[27] Trade in grain, for human and animal consumption, was a major contributor to the increase. It accounted for over half the total of agricultural trade and, after oil, was the most important category in all world trade. The trade in grain, moreover, has a very special character: governments and private dealers operate independently in the same market.[28] The most important deals are bilateral agreements at a governmental level. The Soviet Union, China, India, and Iran have made such agreements with the United States and Canada. But there are also important open markets in several cities in the United States, Rotterdam, Hamburg, and London. In these places government agents, big multinational concerns, and

specialized import companies operate, each with its own criteria
and norms. The international grain market consequently differs
from the classical conception of a competitive market. The grain
policy of national governments is still mostly concerned with increasing the degree of self-sufficiency. Another characteristic of the world
grain trade is that it is limited to a relatively small part of total grain
production. During the 1950s only 6 to 7 per cent of total grain
production was traded internationally and at the end of the 1970s
this had not risen higher than 10 per cent.[29] Trade among the
OECD countries accounted for some 44 per cent of the total world
grain trade in 1971–2.[30] After this date some shifts within the
OECD took place. Japan increased its imports, whereas Western
Europe decreased its imports but remained the largest importer.
The Soviet Union and China imported increasing amounts.[31] It is
striking how little the Third World participated in the international
grain trade until the 1970s.

On the export side, the dominant position of Canada and,
especially, the United States was the main feature.[32] France, Argentina, and Australia also exported a large amount of grain but to
relatively limited areas – France and Argentina to the OECD
countries, and Australia to Asia. On the other hand Canada and
the United States exported to the whole world. The United States,
in addition, dominated the export trade of agricultural products
other than grain – for example, rice, soya beans, corn, and meat.
Strong competition on the part of Thailand in the rice market and
Brazil in the soya-bean market was unable to bring about any
notable change to this.[33] Consequently the American share of total
world agricultural trade fluctuated between 12 and 15 per cent in
the period 1950 to 1972 although it must be pointed out that during
the same period agricultural trade as a proportion of all world trade
fell from 33 per cent to 17 per cent.[34] Still, the fact that the United
States repeatedly threatened embargoes on its agricultural exports
at times of world political tension shows how strong the American
position in this market is.

How can these series of figures and statements be summarized?
Until the 1970s the developing countries were able to tackle their
food problems by reducing agricultural exports, extending the area
of land under cultivation, employing more intensive methods, and
introducing some technological advances. In various countries,
however, impoverishment and undernourishment increased.[35] In

socialist countries, the food problem was solved by extending the
area of cultivated land and importing more foodstuffs from Canada
and the United States.[36] But progress in agricultural techniques
remained rather weak. In the industrialized countries of the West
there was no food problem as such, but demand increased for some
products, particularly meat and products related to raising livestock.
These countries were able to satisfy the increased demand largely
by raising their own production, even while reducing sharply the
percentage of the population engaged in the agricultural sector.
Some were also able to increase agricultural exports to other Western
countries, socialist countries, and the Third World. This suggested
a very great rise in land and labour productivity in Western agriculture after the Second World War. Some historians rightly regard
this as a Second Agricultural Revolution.

THE SECOND AGRICULTURAL REVOLUTION

The United States was undoubtedly the standard-bearer of the
agricultural expansion which followed the Second World War. It
possessed sizeable reserves of agricultural land, a legacy of the
agricultural New Deal of Franklin D. Roosevelt. Between the wars,
millions of acres of arable land had been left to lie fallow as a
government measure to neutralize overproduction. After the Second
World War, the American government reintroduced the restrictive
measures.[37] Thus, between 1950 and 1970, nearly 45 million acres
of farmland were taken out of production. In 1956 the establishment
of a Soil Bank by Congress was an attempt to put the various land
limitations on a more coherent and systematic basis. Under this law
no less than 21.4 million acres were transferred to an acreage reserve
in 1959. Farmers who gave up arable land for the purposes of soil
conservation received special compensation from the Soil Bank. In
the mean time, steps such as the Food Stamp plan for the needy and
the School Lunch Program for children were taken in 1961 to raise
the consumption of agricultural products. Farmers who complied in
certain ways with the policy to limit farmland received government
subsidies. New quotas, price subsidies, and government measures
were regularly announced; but all these actions were merely slight
adjustments to the system which had originally been set up by the
Second Agricultural Adjustment Act of 1938. Only in 1973, when
the world food shortage suddenly pushed up the demand for Ameri-

can food exports, was there a fundamental revision of government policy.

The government control of farm acreage and the low world prices for agricultural products were undoubtedly major factors in stimulating the Second Agricultural Revolution in the United States from the 1950s onwards. Applying advanced techniques to the reduced area of cultivation was the only way farmers could effectively raise their incomes. Technical progress was made over a wide front.[38] Systems of integrated crop and stock farming were intensified and soil conservation practices were generalized. Pesticides, insecticides, and herbicides led to more efficient control over plant disease, harmful insects, and weeds. There was, in addition, an astonishing expansion in the use of artificial fertilizers. In 1950, an average of eight pounds of artificial fertilizers were used per acre, but in 1973–4, this had risen to over fifty pounds per acre.[39] The genetic manipulation of seeds also led to historic results. Special high-yielding varieties were developed for rice, wheat, and maize. Finally, the mechanization of agriculture took place on a large scale. Agricultural machines increased in quality as well as in number. The most eye-opening advance here was the cotton harvester. In 1949 only 10 per cent of cotton was mechanically harvested; yet in 1969 this had risen to 96 per cent. In 1948 the production of a bale of cotton still needed 140 man-hours, but in 1968 barely 25 man-hours were required.[40] There were similar developments for tobacco and other crops.[41]

The total number of workers employed in the agricultural sector – including self-employed farmers – fell from almost 10 million in 1950 to 4.3 million in 1973.[42] This smaller working population produced much more than before, not only because of higher labour productivity but also because of higher land productivity. Between 1950 and 1975, wheat yields per acre rose from 16.5 bushels to 32 bushels, maize yields from 23 to 90 bushels, and cotton from 269 pounds to 520 pounds.[43] Obviously the sharp decrease in the total amount of land under cultivation also helped greatly to increase land productivity. Certainly it was the least fertile land that was withdrawn from cultivation. At the same time, however, the rise of land productivity was also influenced by changes in the kinds of agricultural activities undertaken. The cultivated area for wheat, maize, oats, hay, and cotton declined, whereas that for soya beans, rice, and sugar beets expanded. The production of lamb made way for pork and beef, and the production of chickens and turkeys increased.[44] Texas, California, and the Mississippi delta grew in prominence while states to the east and south of the corn belt declined.[45]

Farmers got only part of the benefit from the increases in productivity. World prices for agricultural products stagnated or even fell. Besides, higher returns from crops and livestock also required higher inputs.[46] At the same time some products once produced by the farm itself, such as seeds, fodder and fertilizers, were now purchased from industry. Some of the savings on labour – for instance, in weeding and irrigation – were partly neutralized by extra capital expenditure on mechanical weeders and modern irrigation systems. Equipment, fencing, buildings and the like, formerly made on the spot, were now bought from specialized companies. On the output side, the farmer was only one link in the chain of agribusiness. Processing and marketing activities, once the prerogative of farmers, were in the hands of industrial concerns that made food products and of wholesalers that specialized in distribution. About two-thirds of every dollar the American consumer spends on food goes to these industrial and commercial sectors, which are very effectively organized and highly concentrated.[47] It was thus the consumer rather than the farmer who profited from the Second Agricultural Revolution. Therefore the American government continued to support farm incomes with guaranteed minimum prices. Small-scale farmers sought a supplementary income in industry and trade. The larger farming concerns tried to raise their incomes by expanding and thus exploiting the economies of scale. The total number of self-employed farmers slid from 5.6 million in 1950 to 2.6 million in 1975.[48]

In Western Europe and Japan the Second Agricultural Revolution was perhaps not as sweeping as in the United States, but it represented a fundamental change and was closely related to technological progress.[49] Its main thrust lay in mechanization, which up until the Second World War had been very limited owing to the predominance of small farms. Although the average area of farms increased significantly, farming in Western Europe and Japan even after the war remained characterized by its small scale. The introduction of more intensive systems of integrated crop and stock farming was therefore an important factor in agricultural progress. In addition the use of pesticides, herbicides, insecticides and artificial fertilizers became general. New high-yield crop varieties were introduced and major strides forward were taken in improving the quality of livestock and in combating various livestock diseases.

The results of the Second Agricultural Revolution in Western Europe and Japan were extremely satisfactory. While the total area of farmland in Western Europe declined by about 5 per cent between 1950 and 1971, because of urbanization, total production continued to rise. The European Economic Community (EEC) was able to become more nearly self-sufficient in grain, dairy produce, poultry, pork, and vegetal oils.[50] This could only be achieved by an impressive increase in land productivity. During the 1960s and especially the 1970s, yields per acre grew very rapidly. For example, taking all grains together, the average increases between 1956–60 and 1971–2 was more than 50 per cent, and for hard wheat and maize even as much as 100 per cent. This rise in land productivity was all the more remarkable in that it was accompanied by a steep decline in the number of agricultural workers in both Western Europe and Japan. In Western Europe this fell by 4 per cent per year on the average between 1960 and 1970, and production per worker rose annually by 8.1 per cent. This was a good deal better than the increase in production per worker in any other part of the economy. It was the small farms that disappeared the quickest. From an investigation made in 1966–7, it appeared that 64 per cent of farmers were older than fifty. The particular measures for early retirement taken under the Mansholt Plan in respect of this category of farmers has undoubtedly facilitated the reduction in numbers.[51]

The support policy operated by the EEC for agriculture was largely meant to raise low agricultural incomes to levels attained by other sectors of the economy. However, also influential was the desire to achieve a higher degree of self-sufficiency. This was possible for a whole series of products but certainly not for vegetables, fruit and beef. Meat production expanded greatly but was still unable to keep up with rising consumption; so the degree of self-sufficiency in this area declined. Agricultural imports from outside the Community after the Second World War remained considerable. Trade within the Community was also significant. Japan, despite great progress in this sector, became increasingly more reliant on imports of agricultural products, especially grains.

THE GREEN REVOLUTION IN THE DEVELOPING COUNTRIES

Until the beginning of the 1970s, the Second Agricultural Revolution had sufficient dynamism and momentum to cope with the rising demand for agricultural products in the West, Eastern Europe, and the developing countries. Prices were indeed strikingly low, which indicated a tendency towards overproduction on a world scale. Moreover, Western countries provided subsidies to developing countries which were prepared to buy up the West's surplus agricultural produce.

This situation was abruptly changed by the crisis of 1972–4. After some years of harvest failures it became clear that there was a fundamental disequilibrium between world agricultural consumption and production. In particular, consumption in developing countries was obviously growing faster than world production and it was evident that this trend would continue in the near future. World prices for grains and other agricultural products rose sharply, then weakened somewhat after the crisis but nevertheless continued high. Indeed, world grain prices doubled between 1972 and 1976. The rise in meat prices was less rapid but none the less substantial. A number of factors influenced these developments. The Soviet Union and China were particularly active in the world market as buyers. There was also the rise in energy prices, which raised agricultural costs, especially for fertilizers. In addition, population growth in the Third World increased still more its demand for food imports. Finally the American and Canadian governments decided to unload their agricultural stocks almost entirely and not to replenish them. Those stocks had been a buffer, and their disappearance caused an increase in the instability of world prices.[52]

In the West there was a speedy reaction. The Second Agricultural Revolution was given a new impetus which was soon expressed in the form of new rises in land productivity. Furthermore, in the United States, between 1973 and 1974, nearly 45 million acres of idle cropland were brought into active use again. The Agriculture and Consumer Act of 1973 emphasized the need once again to raise American agricultural production and also to reorganize the management of the total amount of farmland in line with this new expansion policy.[53] In the mean time, high grain prices led to a new shift in agricultural activities – from livestock to crop farming. Finally the rise in prices also held out the prospect of higher profits which encouraged further investment in agriculture. There was even general speculation in land prices, which rose by 131 per cent between 1970 and 1977.[54] The fact that agricultural prices continued at a high level seems to indicate that the further development of the Second Agricultural Revolution in the West and the resumed farming of formerly idle land were, in the short term, insufficient to match world food supplies with demand. Everything suggests that the developing countries themselves must take resolute action to reduce their dependence on imports.

In fact, developing countries have considerable potential in this respect. The possibilities of bringing new land into cultivation are certainly not yet exhausted. Experts have calculated that on the basis of current technology, the expansion potential for world farmland still totals nearly 2.4 billion acres, of which 82 per cent is in the Third World. If the problems associated with the desalination of sea water and the active cultivation of tropical areas can be solved, then this figure rises to about 11 billion acres.[55]

Of course, land reclamation is a costly affair and lack of capital in developing countries is often a huge and sometimes an insurmountable obstacle. Moreover, large-scale land reclamation often requires alterations in property rights and changes in century-old traditions and customs. These are usually very hard to bring about in the short term. Finally it must be remembered that governments have often discouraged land reclamation because it did not fit in with the policy of stabilizing food prices by importing low-priced agricultural produce from the West (often subsidized by the exporting country). The idea behind this was to keep urban labour costs low and thus attract industrial investment. Such a policy was preferred to increasing direct investment in agriculture at a time when agricultural prices were low and did not appear attractive.[56]

The current and future food problem can be effectively attacked not only by extending the amount of land under cultivation but also by technical and technological progress. Expectations in this respect were very high when, shortly after the Second World War, the Green Revolution was begun.[57] The ground for its first successes was prepared at the International Maize and Wheat Center, which was set up in Mexico in 1946 with support from the Rockefeller Foundation. Its development of new high-yielding varieties of wheat served to double Mexican yields in the 1950s and again in the 1960s. Starting in 1956 these new varieties were introduced into other countries, especially Pakistan, India, and Nepal. The success was so great that in 1959 an International Rice Research Institute was set up in the Philippines, with support from the Rockefeller and Ford Foundations. Here too, the results were excellent.[58] Around 1966 the first high-yield varieties of rice were introduced on a large scale. By 1969 the Philippines were already self-sufficient in rice. The demonstration effect was heartening and many developing countries set up comparable laboratories to develop applied varieties for their own lands.

Unfortunately, expectations that the Green Revolution would eliminate rural poverty in the Third World went unfulfilled.[59] The new varieties of rice and wheat demanded special irrigation systems and heavy fertilizing. This required major investment which could only be justified if production was on a large scale. In other words the new crops were best suited to big landowners, large-scale farmers who were more open to the idea of modernization, had better access to money and capital markets, were relatively limited in number, and were more easily approached by the government and international institutions.[60] And this all had the effect of making the social consequences of the Green Revolution somewhat unfavourable.[61] In fact, as it was actually organized in the 1960s, the Green Revolution increased income inequalities. Many peasants found themselves obliged to sell their pieces of land to the big landowners, who then hired the peasants as wage labourers to implement the improvements. Examples of this can be found in Central America, Pakistan, India, Sri Lanka, and the Philippines. Land reforms could have avoided this evil, but such reforms are never easy and usually incur high cultural costs. The Green Revolution ran into other obstacles too. Even in the large farming concerns, the initially excellent results were not as long-lasting as had been hoped. The low level of food prices until 1973 reduced government readiness to support these programmes.[62] The emphasis on one-crop farming and the massive use of herbicides and insecticides disturbed the ecological balance. In some areas, the use of artificial fertilizers exceeded the threshold of increasing returns. There were also cases of soil erosion.

The disappointments of the Green Revolution do not mean that all hope of the developing countries solving their agricultural difficulties should be given up. In a remarkable book, Ester Boserup has emphasized that population pressure in primitive communities has historically led to structural modifications in food provision.[63] When circumstances were unfavourable in respect of extending the area of land under cultivation, population growth always led to the intensification of agricultural production. Thus it was not a question of cultivating new, less fertile land but rather of attempting to make more productive use of the increasing amount of concealed unemployment by introducing new crops and more intensive systems of field rotation. The higher the population density, the greater was the intensification. Boserup's hypothesis raises optimism for the future of the Green Revolution in the developing countries, although only in the long term. Too many institutional inertias, too many psychological factors and too many problems in finding necessary capital stand in the way of a rapid and flexible solution to the problem of feeding the population of the Third World.[64] Meanwhile it is vital that governments in the developing countries try everything to force a breakthrough. They must centralize resources and create effective structures for planning, research, information, education, credit provision, and the use of market forces. Land reforms must also be implemented so that large numbers of peasants are equally able to benefit from the new technology. This is no simple task. The technology of the Green Revolution is labour-saving and this conflicts with the growing class-consciousness of the poorer peasants. The transition can thus cause serious social tension and it therefore requires from the government a very subtle and careful approach.

While awaiting positive results for the Green Revolution in the Third World, the West can help to bridge the gap between the levels of world population and food supplies. This can be done by further development of the Second Agricultural Revolution. Moreover, the currencies earned by the West through increased agricultural exports could be used to buy more manufactured products from the rising industries of the Third World. This would do much to correct unbalanced growth.

3. THE EXHAUSTION OF MINERALS

THE REPORT OF THE CLUB OF ROME

The growth of the modern consumer economy in the West after the Second World War, along with the industrialization process in many countries of the Third World, vastly increased the demand for minerals. Particular circumstances served to strengthen the rate of increase still more. In order to finance imports of the advanced machinery necessary for further industrialization, the developing countries needed more foreign currency. Accordingly, they increased their production of minerals, which many possessed in abundance. They either took this in hand themselves, using large-scale modern technology, or they entrusted it to big Western companies. On the basis of the abundant minerals and the consequent low prices, the Western economies built up a specific production model. They sought maximum production to satisfy the rapidly increasing modern consumer demand while economizing on expensive economic resources, namely labour and capital. This economizing was not applied to the same extent to the relatively cheaper minerals and energy. Therefore, during the booming 1950s and 1960s, the generous consumption of minerals and energy by the West gave extra stimulus to the production of these resources.

Indeed, the world's mineral consumption rose at a faster rate than even population, which itself showed exponential growth (Graph A). Production of metal ores grew fourteenfold between 1900 and 1970 and that of non-metallic minerals grew twentyfold.[65] Out of the total world demand for metals, the share of iron and steel was overwhelming. In 1974 iron and steel represented no less than 71.14 per cent of the total value of world demand for metals (91.79 per cent if measured quantitatively).[66] Copper, aluminium and zinc then followed, with respectively (in value terms) 7.53 per cent, 6.5 per cent and 4.01 per cent of the total. Iron therefore remained the pre-eminent basic metal of the post-war world economy. This was mainly due to its very high consumption per head in the industrialized countries and especially the United States. Nevertheless the developing countries also played an important role. These countries often started their industrialization with the establishment of a heavy industry based on iron and steel. The consumption of other minerals by the developing countries, starting from a low level, also grew steadily.[67]

The rapid growth in the world consumption of minerals alarmed some economists. In a report published by the Club of Rome in 1972, entitled *The Limits to Growth*, Dennis H. Meadows and others came to the conclusion that industrial society was too frivolous and wasteful with the world's natural resources and this would inevitably lead to their exhaustion.[68] Through a whole series of assumptions and extrapolations, the authors predicted future world needs and

Graph A   *Population and Raw Material Use in the United States, 1900–75*

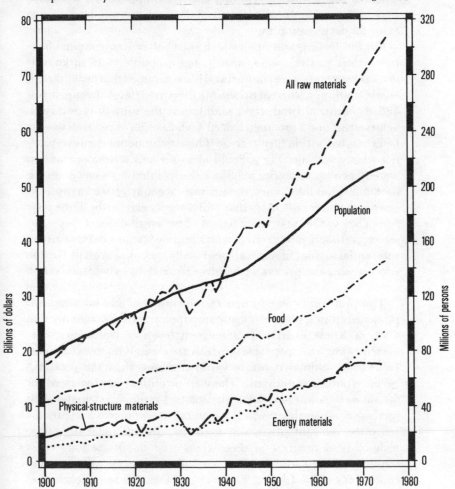

Source: C. W. HOWE, *Natural Resource Economics*, p. 27

matched them with current and expected supplies. Their results suggested grave imbalances between demand and supply and gave cause for deep pessimism.

But the assumptions upon which the Club of Rome experts had based their analysis were, in fact, too simplistic.[69] If all known workable reserves were counted and it was assumed that exploitation would continue at current prices with the current level of technology, and if industrial production maintained the growth rate it had achieved around 1970, then indeed a whole series of minerals would be exhausted within fifty years.[70] These assumptions, however, are not wholly realistic. They should allow for new technology which would open up to production the resources that are known but to date unexploitable. They should take account of the many still unknown sources of supply that undoubtedly exist on or in the sea-bed. They should also take account of the possibilities of recycling which, through new technological improvements, could lead to substantial savings in mineral use. Finally they should allow for the effect of rising cost prices and the fall in demand that would inevitably result.

The problem of exhaustion of minerals thus needs to be approached from a more economic standpoint than that used by the Club of Rome experts. If at current levels of technology, the presently known exploitable minerals are measured against a more realistically estimated future world demand, then the problem becomes much less dramatic. There are no critical shortages, except for silver.[71] Naturally, for some non-fuel minerals, demand will increase considerably towards the end of the century. In all probability the relevant prices will then rise, and this will stimulate technological progress in these areas, and so, in the long run, solutions will be found for those particular shortages. Although the conclusions of the Club of Rome report are open to criticism, the authors have in any case made a substantial contribution towards raising public awareness of the seriousness of the problem of the minerals.

THE POLITICIZATION OF THE MINERAL PROBLEM

Minerals are not distributed equally over the world. Some countries are exceedingly rich in minerals and others exceedingly poor. On the other hand, a geographical concentration of world industrial production has developed which, for historical or economic reasons, no longer (if it ever did) coincides with the geographical concentration of known reserves of minerals. In order to link the production of minerals with their consumption by industry, the world market for minerals came into being. Here, the forces of supply and demand interact and determine prices. Both producers and consumers attempt to build up their influence so as to be able to modify these prices to their own advantage. The raw materials problem thus becomes an issue in world politics as countries try to acquire control over the supply. Producers try to raise prices by creating relative scarcities and consumers try to lower them by creating a surplus.

When the geographical distribution of reserves is examined in detail, a number of interesting observations can be made. In most cases, reserves of a particular mineral are concentrated within just four countries (Table 9). In addition, the names of particular countries frequently reappear on the full list of mineral reserves. The United States, the Soviet Union, Canada, South Africa, and Australia are especially rich in mineral resources. On the other hand, Western Europe and Japan are very poor. The analysis of world trade in these resources also reveals interesting information.[72] As might be expected, there is a large deficit in the trade balance of Western Europe and Japan. Both areas export hardly any raw materials but import tremendous quantities. The United States produces mightily but its consumption is much greater still and so it too has a trade deficit. Africa, Latin America, and Australia export far more minerals than they import, especially to the United States, Western Europe, and Japan. Nevertheless this is still insufficient to satisfy all the needs of the West, and so the Eastern bloc, in particular the Soviet Union, also sells a large amount of minerals to the West.

All this serves to underline the vulnerability of Western industrial nations (including Japan). They have less than one-fifth of the world's population and yet account for almost two-thirds of world energy consumption and even more in respect of metals. On the other side of the coin, the developing countries have half of the world's population but their consumption of metals is less than 10 per cent of the world total and their energy consumption is only slightly higher. In a sense it can be seen that the two groups are clearly complementary, Western economies being heavily dependent on the developing countries. On the other hand the Eastern bloc is

Table 9 *Percentage of 1975 World Production and Reserves Shared by the Four Largest Producing Countries (selected mineral commodities)*

Mineral commodity	Share of world production (per cent)	Share of world reserves (per cent)	Countries
Bauxite	64	62	Australia, Jamaica, Guinea, Surinam
Chromium	70	96	Soviet Union, South Africa, Zimbabwe, Philippines
Cobalt	90	64	Zaïre, Zambia, Canada, Morocco
Copper	53	57	United States, Chile, Canada, Soviet Union
Fluorspar	51	42	Mexico, Soviet Union, Spain, Thailand
Gold	84	88	South Africa, Canada, United States, Australia
Iron ore	55	61	Soviet Union, Australia, United States, Brazil
Lead	59	77	United States, Australia, Canada, Mexico
Manganese	78	95	South Africa, Gabon, Brazil, Australia
Mercury	65	65	Spain, Soviet Union, China, Italy
Molybdenum	99	98	United States, Canada, Chile, Peru
Nickel	63	65	Canada, New Caledonia, United States
Phosphate rock	81	88	United States, Morocco, Spanish Sahara, Tunisia
Platinum group	99	99	South Africa, Soviet Union, Canada
Potash	90	95	Canada, West Germany, United States, France
Silver	53	60	Peru, Mexico, United States, Canada
Tin	65	48	Malaysia, Soviet Union, Indonesia, Bolivia
Vanadium	85	96	South Africa, United States, Soviet Union, Chile
Zinc	43	57	Canada, Australia, United States, Brazil

Source: J. F. TILTON, *Non-fuel Minerals*, p. 83

considerably less so and indeed, taken in general terms, is self-sufficient.

This vulnerability in the West is not confined to Western Europe and Japan. Of the sixteen most important metals, the United States in 1970 could satisfy its own needs in only four – gold, silver, molybdenum, and wolfram. It had to import at least part of its needs in all others.[73] The American outlook for future supplies is still more sombre. By the year 2000, if its economy continues to develop as it has during recent decades, the United States will have to import half of all its mineral needs. This prospect explains in large measure American policy towards the developing countries. The other world power, the Soviet Union, because of its high degree of self-sufficiency in minerals, is not nearly so vulnerable. Therefore until the 1970s, the Russians were not very active in the Third World. But this policy has changed because of studies in the late 1970s which forecast that the Soviet Union too would become increasingly dependent on the outside world for minerals. In the 1980s the Soviet Union's growing interest and activity in the Third World suggest that the Kremlin has taken these pessimistic studies seriously.

After the Second World War, raw material production in the Third World remained very much in private hands. It was controlled from Europe by colonial or post-colonial concerns and from the United States by the rapidly developing multinational companies. The multinationals, extremely dynamic, profited from decolonization and the political naïveté of the Third World to seize a major share of the international trade in raw materials. The success of the American multinational concerns was undeniably due in large measure to the efficiency of their company organization. The strategy of long-term planning created an excellent alternative to the former unstable competitive market for raw materials. Traditionally, this market was dominated by capriciously fluctuating prices, uncertainty, and speculation. The American multinational was able, via large-scale vertical integration, to internalize the demand for raw materials. By adopting a planned rationale for production, the multinationals were in a position to guarantee a steady stream of raw materials at constant prices to their integrated operations. For many resources, such as iron ore, bauxite, nickel, molybdenum, magnesium, and oil, world prices thus remained fairly stable.[74]

As soon as American and European concerns had taken over a dominant position in the world market for minerals, they set about consolidating it. They thus set up obstacles to prevent possible competitors from entering the market. They tried, by means of agreements with the relevant governments, to make the exploration for new reserves and the recovery of known ones the sole preserve of the few existing large companies. They also built up an exclusive network of sales markets and together formed oligopolies where production, prices, and market share were agreed. It would nevertheless be wrong to ascribe the characteristics of rigidity, conservatism and inefficiency to this oligopolistic structure. In fact, in the post-war world these oligopolies provided a very model of aggressive competition, dynamic action, and efficient organization. What were the causes of this? Despite endeavours by existing companies, the world market for minerals after the Second World War was not hermetically sealed and was ultimately open to new competitors. This was, of course, first demonstrated by the American multinationals themselves, which successfully penetrated territory that had been largely controlled by European colonial enterprises. Later, in the 1970s, the big Japanese concerns were also able to win a place for themselves in this market.

Actually, there was always room for newcomers who could capitalize on the recent political sovereignty of the developing countries. Many formulas were possible. For instance, newcomers, in consultation with the relevant governments, could set up joint-ventures with national companies. Sometimes this was a question of long-term delivery contracts with the state enterprises which governments of the Third World had set up to compete with the big multinationals. Developing countries were quick to express their resentment of the powerful influence the multinationals soon established in respect of the exploitation of raw materials. They forced the multinationals slowly to reduce their profits, often demanded participation, and even went as far as expropriation. With expropriation, however, contact had to be made with other multinationals or with newcomers in order to handle sales overseas. This was not always easy and generally a compromise solution was worked out. The developing countries thus sought with the multinationals a *modus vivendi* which kept the oligopolistic structure in place. Profits continued but were now shared and at the same time the national governments acquired more control over production.

Another strategy which made progress in the Third World was that of international cartelization at the government level.[75]

Governments controlling large reserves of a particular mineral tried to reach agreements concerning minimum prices and maximum production with the other producing lands. Sometimes these agreements even involved market sharing. The overall objective was continually to raise prices in order to increase profits. To be successful, the international cartels had to satisfy certain conditions. The participating countries had to control a large part of the production of the minerals in question and show sufficient solidarity to stick to any mutual agreements. On the other hand, the level of demand had to remain steady in the face of sharp price increases. Usually in the short term this was the case, but in the long term the danger that substitutes would take over part of the market was very real. In addition there was always the threat that outside countries possessing significant quantities of the minerals would increase their own production. Ideological divisions could also, in principle, be a complicating factor, but usually in practice these were conveniently blurred. For instance, one of the oldest and most stable cartels is that of diamond producers, in which the Soviet Union and South Africa sink their differences and co-operate closely. Even the free-market tradition of the United States was unable to prevent the Webb-Pomerance Act of 1976, by which Congress permitted American companies to join foreign cartels – i.e., government ones – provided these did not adversely affect the domestic market.[76]

The reserves of many metal ores are sufficiently concentrated for cartelization to be a practical option. International cartels – governmental as well as private ones – existed for copper, mercury, wolfram, tin, and phosphate.[77] Nevertheless these could not all be held together, for the condition of solidarity among the participants could not always be fulfilled. Some participants broke agreements regarding production levels or sold below the fixed price. Non-participants aggravated the situation. The difficulty of achieving effective control over these cartels led the developing countries into raising the raw material problem during international discussions on the world economic order which took place from the 1970s onwards. The Third World countries insisted that the prices of metals such as copper, bauxite and tin, which are very sensitive to economic fluctuations, should be stabilized by special intergovernmental arrangements.[78] Out of this notion was born, in 1975, the International Tin Agreement (ITA), which involved the most important tin-producing countries: Malaysia, Bolivia, Indonesia,

Nigeria and Zaïre. The agreement was a success and during the economic crisis of the late 1970s tin prices were held at a relatively stable level.[79] Agreements for other raw materials were discussed but because of conflicts of interest did not always bear fruit.[80] Experience of the tin agreement suggests that the stabilization of raw material prices works to the advantage of the exploiting companies as well as the producing countries. This fact was the cause of much frustration and criticism in the Third World. The big exploiting companies were identified with the most powerful industrial nations of the West, which were considered to be sufficiently advantaged already.

LONG-TERM SOLUTIONS

Increasing consciousness of the problem of minerals provision not only led to immediate short-term action but also caused private companies and national governments to take long-term measures. These can be split into three categories: (1) measures to accelerate technological progress in regard to the recovery and exploitation of metal ores; (2) measures to promote the replacement of scarce metals with more plentiful materials; and (3) measures for further exploitation of the metal-rich sea-bed.

In the first category, private companies, often with the support of governments, have intensified efforts everywhere to advance the technology used to recover and refine metals. It must be noted that the richest seams are always exploited first and that in later stages increasingly poorer seams must be worked. Working these lower-quality seams requires greater use of energy, and this, as an unavoidable by-product, increases pollution and disturbance of the environment. Around 1900, the copper ores being mined still contained, on average, 4 per cent metal; but by 1973 this figure had fallen to 0.53 per cent. For tin and some other metals, the decline in quality was even greater.[81] In addition, metal refining is in general energy-intensive and polluting. The example of aluminium, which makes use of fluoride, is well known. Major research programmes on metals are under way. The significant progress in the area of hydro-metallurgy and the use of micro-biology provide the best hopes.[82]

The second category, substitution for existing, traditional metals, is also in progress. Research is especially concentrated on finding substitutes – even artificial materials – for metals whose ores are already in short supply. Governments are also trying to reduce the need for specific raw materials by changing the pattern of consumption. Extending public transport at the expense of private vehicles, for example, not only saves on energy but also economizes on raw materials. In a similar way governments can stress the need for products to be more durable. Here and there, campaigns against the 'throw-away society' have already been mounted. Closely related are the increasing efforts in both the private and public sectors to recycle used materials. Certainly, in respect to metals, recycling is not new, especially in the United States, but it has greatly expanded. By 1974, 20 to 30 per cent of total consumption of iron, lead, copper, nickel, and tin, was already being supplied through recycling, and for antimony the figure was more than 50 per cent.[83]

The third series of measures is related to discussions held on the Law of the Sea.[84] Scientific research has shown that tremendous amounts of raw materials exist on the sea-bed. Magnesium is an outstanding example of the potential. Far from continental coastlines, deep under the oceans, lie vast quantities of manganese nodules which contain about 24 per cent magnesium, 14 per cent iron, and small amounts of copper, nickel, and cobalt. Given the current level of technology, it is already economically feasible to raise these nodules from depths of between 3,000 and 4,000 metres. American and Japanese companies have been carrying out this work. Many other minerals are also known to be on the sea-bed. Phosphate nodules exist and tin and diamonds have already been found, but present technology does not allow their economic exploitation.

The recovery of raw materials from the sea-bed raises thorny problems of property rights over those reserves which lie outside territorial waters. In the early 1980s international legislation on these matters was still entirely lacking. According to existing international law, by analogy with rules concerning salvage, the exploiting organization would become the owner of any recovered raw materials. Under these circumstances, Western industrial countries, which have made the most progress in the necessary technology, would stand to gain all the benefits. This reasoning has naturally come in for fierce criticism from countries of the Eastern bloc and the Third World.

Efforts to draft the Law of the Sea have taken place within the framework of the United Nations. The broad objective was to lay down accepted rules for international waters – not only on mineral rights but also on fishing and shipping and energy sources. By 1982 four international conferences had been held. The first, in 1958, concerned itself largely with fishing and shipping. The second, in 1960, set about tackling the problem of rights to the sea-bed but yielded no positive results. The bargainers could not even reach agreement on extending territorial waters beyond a three-mile zone. A sharp East–West confrontation gradually gave way to a North–South split, which dominated the third conference from 1974 to 1980.

The 'Group of Seventy-Seven', representing the Third World (see page 403), wanted to merge the problem of the sea-bed into a general discussion about a new international economic order. More specifically, they wanted the distribution of mineral rights in international waters to be managed in such a way as to discriminate more in favour of the poorer nations. At the third conference the Group of Seventy-Seven, especially influenced by Latin America and China, therefore proposed a territorial zone extending 200 miles offshore. According to this method, a large part of the world's maritime mineral reserves would fall under the control of individual nation-states. Western countries would stand to gain far less than if property rights simply accrued to those in a position to undertake exploitation.

The 200-mile proposal was not accepted by the industrial countries of the West and East.[85] Another proposal for the creation of a supranational organization, the International Sea-Bed Resources Agency, which would systematically control the exploitation of raw materials on the sea-bed, was also rejected. All that could be agreed on at that long conference, and this almost unanimously, was the extension of territorial waters to a twelve-mile zone. Yet there seemed no prospect of agreement on exploiting the sea-bed. Mutual standpoints remained diametrically opposed. The Third World countries demanded a political solution which would serve their interests in the long term and the industrial countries wanted a pragmatic solution which would allow them to capitalize on their stronger economic positions. The auguries were therefore not good when the fourth conference started in 1981 but in 1982 a compromise was hammered out. The US administration of Ronald Reagan, however, refused to approve it.

4. THE ENERGY QUESTION

THE EXPLOSION IN ENERGY CONSUMPTION

The post-war development of the world economy created a ravenous appetite for energy. In fact, energy consumption grew much faster than did world population. Even during the second quarter of the twentieth century, the average yearly increase in energy consumption had been 2.2 per cent while the population figure was 1.1 per cent. During the 1960s, the annual rate for population climbed to 1.9 per cent but the rate for energy consumption soared to 5.6 per cent.[86] If this rate of increase continued till the year 2000, total world energy consumption would then be four times the level recorded in the early 1970s. This is not an unrealistic estimate. Although mature industrial nations, such as the United States, increase their energy use more slowly than the world average, one must remember the catching-up movement in Western Europe and Japan after the war and take into account the probability of a similar catching-up movement for the Third World in relation to the West. Such a movement could bring still higher rates of world increase in the next few decades.

Differences in energy consumption among countries are not wholly determined by the level of industrial development. Cultural and institutional factors may also be important. For example, the United States and Sweden are both countries with high per capita production as well as a strongly developed modern consumer economy. Nevertheless the United States has a much higher per capita energy consumption.[87] There are a number of reasons. Sweden's urban population and energy-intensive industry are more concentrated geographically than those of the United States. Sweden, too, is noted for government and private initiatives which are energy-saving. For example, Sweden has a larger proportion of multiple-family homes with communal heating installations, and measures regarding the insulation of new buildings are considerably stricter. When the United States, Japan, and Western Europe are compared, other interesting differences in energy consumption come to light.[88] The United States appears to have a transport sector that is more energy-intensive or even energy-wasteful. On the other hand, in households and service sectors Western Europe uses the most energy. As for industry, that of Japan in general is more energy-intensive than that of the United States or Western Europe. Structural and cultural circumstances are responsible for these differences.

Finally, the explosion in world energy consumption after the war must also be seen in terms of changes in energy sources. Mankind traditionally employed two main kinds of source. One kind, consisting of sun, water, and wind, produces natural energy, which can be used directly to supply heat or turn wheels. The other kind relies on the conversion of non-fossil organic material such as wood, straw, and organic waste. Manpower and animal-power also belong to this category. Both of these main categories still contribute energy in industrial society but their relative share has fallen precipitously. At present much research is being done to increase the use of solar and wind energy. Water-power has become once again a significant source of energy in some industrialized countries like France, Italy, Japan, and the United States, through the use of hydroelectricity. On the other hand, application of water-power in the Third World has been very limited.[89]

But these traditional sources could not meet the energy needs of industrial society as it developed in the nineteenth and twentieth centuries. Hence the emergence of a third category, fossil fuels, namely coal, oil, and natural gas. Fossil fuels have the great advantage that they exist in huge quantities. The major disadvantage is that supplies are non-renewable.

Coal was *the* fossil fuel during the Industrial Revolution of the nineteenth century. Its production was organized on a large scale and rose continuously and rapidly. An added advantage of coal is its large number of by-products, including tar, ammonia, gas, coke, benzene, and sulphur. Nevertheless, after the Second World War, coal production was unable to maintain its level of dominance in the energy field. Indeed, coal production dwindled until it stabilized at its pre-war level. Its share in total world energy production fell from nearly 70 per cent in 1953 to 45 per cent in 1970.[90] In some areas, such as Western Europe and Japan, production ran up against depletion of reserves and the rising cost of exploitation. The extensive pollution associated with coal consumption had some effect as well, for the burning of coal gives off carbon dioxide and sulphur dioxide, adversely influencing the atmosphere and the climate. Britain in the 1950s provided a ghastly example. In the mean time other countries with very large coal reserves expanded their production, and the consequence was an increasing concentration in a few countries. In

1975, the Soviet Union, the United States and China together accounted for 75 per cent of total world production.[91] World coal reserves are so immense that their exhaustion poses no immediate problem.

The difficulties encountered in the production and consumption of coal have contributed to the rise in the use of a second fossil fuel, oil. Industrial production of crude oil first dates from the middle of the nineteenth century but large-scale production was only begun after the First World War and accentuated after the Second World War. In 1953 the share of oil in world energy production had already risen to 20 per cent and by 1970 it exceeded 40 per cent. Coal lost ground as oil gained. Indeed many industrial and transport sectors switched from coal to oil. In the United States the switch was already well under way during the inter-war period, and that, together with the rise of the automobile, explains the impressive level of US oil production before 1940. In Western Europe and Japan the switch did not really begin until after the Second World War. At present, the known reserves of crude oil are heavily concentrated in the Middle East, the Soviet Union, and North America. Table 10 shows how oil production after the war was concentrated in these same areas. Meanwhile, exploration technology made rapid strides; new fields were discovered; and during the 1960s the known oil reserves grew faster than oil production and consumption, though not in the United States. Furthermore, the potential for finding new reserves is still immense, with good prospects in the developing countries and in Siberia, as well as under the sea-bed.[92] Oil is already being obtained in large quantities near the sea-coasts on the continental shelves. Oil rigs and artificial islands make this exploitation possible. Yet this is just the beginning. Oilfields lying in deeper waters are still commercially beyond reach but they offer much hope for the future.

The increase in the use of oil has been fostered by the relative ease with which it can be recovered and by low exploitation costs. Nevertheless in the 1950s a problem did arise, not so much in production but rather in the long-distance transport of oil. Available shipping seemed unable to cope with the rapid expansion in oil production and world-wide consumption. The Suez crisis in 1956, which led to the closing of the Suez Canal, brought the problem of long-distance oil transport to a head. The consequent construction of supertankers and specially designed ports was a satisfactory

Table 10 *Production of Crude Petroleum in Selected Countries, 1960–80*

(*in thousand tons*)

	1960	1970	1972	1975	1980
Argentina	9,138	20,000	21,576	19,550	25,000[1]
Bahrain	2,256	3,800	3,761	3,100	2,500[1]
Canada	25,614	69,500	64,416	80,000	70,500
Colombia	7,674	11,000	11,127	8,000	6,500
India	445	6,800	7,185	8,300	11,500[1]
Indonesia	20,596	45,000	43,790	63,000	78,000
Iran	52,185	190,000	223,921	268,200	74,000
Iraq	47,460	75,600	83,775	111,300	130,000
Kuwait	81,867	138,000	146,786	93,200	85,000
Mexico	14,171	21,000	21,412	37,500	100,000
Saudi Arabia	62,068	175,500	223,412	337,300	496,000
Soviet Union	147,859	353,000	337,075	490,000	603,000
United States	347,975	534,000	446,704	485,000	424,000
Venezuela	152,364	193,000	185,776	124,000	114,000
World Total	1,056,700	2,334,000	2,399,400	2,702,000	3,086,000

Note: [1] Figures for 1978

Sources: A. DAS GUPTA, *Economic and Commercial Geography*, p. 200

UNITED NATIONS, *Statistical Yearbook, 1979–1980*

solution. Oil prices fell and so did the costs of international transport in general, and this, in turn, gave further impetus to oil consumption in the 1960s.[93]

Another factor in the success of oil in the post-war period was its many non-energy industrial applications. Oil not only is converted into direct energy when refined into various kinds of fuels but also provides the basis for a significant petrochemical industry. It is thus the raw material for the manufacture of plastics, synthetic fibres, synthetic rubber, detergents, artificial fertilizers, and many other products. Petrochemicals, since the 1960s, have become an extremely dynamic sector with an average yearly growth rate of about 15 per cent. Oil ports around the world have developed into major industrial growth centres. Where petrochemical concerns set up, others soon followed. Rotterdam, Antwerp, and Houston are striking examples of such ports.[94]

The 1973 oil crisis raised question marks regarding oil supplies from the traditional areas and turned attention towards the possibility of obtaining oil from oil shales and tar sands. Oil shales exist in great quantities in the Soviet Union, China, the United States, Sweden, and Scotland.[95] Exploitation, however, was not yet economical in the early 1980s; further technological progress was needed both in actual recovery and in minimizing disturbance of the environment.

More important and already fully viable, on the other hand, is the recovery of natural gas. This is the third great fossil fuel after oil and coal. Large amounts of natural gas exist in all continents of the world and can be readily obtained. Initially there were problems with storage and transport, but these have recently been solved by converting the gas into liquid form (LNG). As such, it can be more easily transported, by pipelines or refrigerated vessels, to the desired destination. The United States has won a leading position in the production of natural gas. The Soviet Union and Canada are now also major producers with potential for further growth.[96]

Nuclear fission can be considered a major new category of energy source, supplementing the traditional and fossil categories. In the aftermath of the oil crisis of 1973, nuclear energy attracted much attention. Although it had started out with mainly political and military significance, it came to be seen as a way in which the West could reduce its energy dependence on the rest of the world. Governments and private companies in Western Europe and the

United States decided to build more nuclear power stations. There are inevitable problems with pollution, and there is a real danger of radiation through technical defects in the reactors and through the disposal of nuclear waste. Consequently there has been much protest from environmental groups.

ENERGY AND WORLD POLITICS

The explosion of energy consumption in the economies of the West and in the industrializing areas of the Third World has created dangerous imbalances between energy production and consumption. Some countries have large energy surpluses but others large shortages.[97] In Western Europe it was already necessary to import energy sources before the Second World War. After the war this import dependence became much greater, and imports grew fivefold between 1955 and 1974. North America was more or less self-sufficient in energy until the Second World War but since then it too has had to rely increasingly on imports. In East and South Asia, with Japan as the largest consumer, the trade deficit in energy rose fifteenfold between 1955 and 1974, although this area remained still less dependent upon imports than Western Europe. Australia and the South American countries taken as a group have neither a surplus nor a shortage. The Soviet Union, Central America, Africa, and especially the Middle East, have a surplus.

The West's increasing reliance on outside sources for energy had much to do with the transfer of interest away from dearer coal and towards cheaper oil. And a dominant factor in the transfer was cheap oil from the Persian Gulf. Its influence was so great that even in the United States, for example in 1970–1, domestic production of oil and natural gas actually fell. Environmental factors already mentioned increased the West's hunger for oil, since these tended to restrict the production of pollutant coal and slowed the construction of new nuclear power stations.

Running parallel with such changes in demand were developments on the supply side. The big oil companies, especially the so-called 'seven sisters' – Exxon, Royal Dutch Shell, Socal (Chevron), Mobil, Texaco, British Petroleum, and Gulf Oil – had reacted to the increase in demand with technological innovation and large-scale exploration. In order to ensure future supplies they had made long-term contracts with oil-producing countries and had even organized profit-sharing schemes or sometimes joint-ventures. By these means, production increased enormously and supply outstripped demand, so that world oil prices fell by about 10 per cent between 1955 and 1967. Meanwhile the terms of trade for the oil-exporting countries fell by 23.5 per cent (Table 11) and frustration there grew.

Table 11 *Indices of World Export Prices for Oil in US Dollars and Evolution of the Terms of Trade in Oil-Producing Countries*
(*1970* = *100*)

	Export price	Terms of trade (export prices/ import prices)
1955	105	123.5
1960	101	112.5
1965	96	106.3
1967	95	102.7
1970	100	100.0
1971	125	119.0
1972	135	118.8
1973	169	125.2
1974	456	265.9
1975	476	257.4
1976	503	270.5
1977	556	275.1
1978	558	244.2
1979	782	317.9
1980	1,016	360.3
1981	1,179	375.5

Source: G. DANCET, 'De gevolgen van de olieprijsstijgingen', p. 3

In order to better defend their interests, thirteen countries with large oil reserves set up the Organization of Petroleum Exporting Countries (OPEC) in 1960. These countries were Algeria, Ecuador, Gabon, Indonesia, Iran, Iraq, Kuwait, Libya, Nigeria, Qatar, Saudi Arabia, Venezuela, and the United Arab Emirates. They hoped to form a cartel which would reduce the power of the big oil companies and raise the incomes of the member countries.[98] The first signs of OPEC's effectiveness came when the exporters won more favourable terms in their contracts with the oil companies. Yet there was much more. From the 1960s onwards the increase in world demand strengthened the oligopoly position of the OPEC countries. Thus they not only gained *vis-à-vis* the oil companies but also were able to intervene directly in the international price-forming mechanism. At the same time the report of the Club of Rome and other comparable publications served to heighten concern about an impending exhaustion of oil reserves.

The Yom Kippur War in the Middle East in November 1973 provided the occasion for a vigorous OPEC offensive. Embargoes were placed on countries suspected of supporting Israel and steep increases in the export prices of crude oil were pushed through. In the short term, the demand for oil appeared insensitive to changes in price so the world could do nothing but accept these increases. All round the world, balances of trade and payments were thrown into confusion. Oil-importing countries were not able immediately to pass on the higher oil prices but still had to pay immediately for any oil deliveries. On the other hand the exporting countries could not instantly convert their higher revenues into demand for Western industrial products. As a result, they began to build up substantial balance-of-payments surpluses. In the West, the increased energy costs undermined spending in other sectors and hit investment hard.[99]

In Western Europe and Japan, measures were taken at once to narrow the yawning deficit in energy balances and to reduce dependence on OPEC countries. Governments banned Sunday driving, reduced speed limits, economized on public lighting, lowered temperatures in public buildings, and above all announced drastic increases in domestic energy prices. Furthermore, with an eye to long-term developments, they stepped up their nuclear power programmes. They also reactivated interest in coal mining and stimulated research for more economical engines and for alternative energy sources. They encouraged further exploration for natural gas and even began negotiations with the Soviet Union about buying Siberian gas. These measures were not without effect. By 1977 the EEC countries and Japan were importing less oil (in volume terms) than before the oil boycott. Even during the economic revival which came at the end of the 1970s, France and Italy were still able to reduce their dependence on the OPEC countries.[100]

The United States, on the other hand, followed a rather lax policy after the 1973 oil crisis. It did take steps to boost the nuclear energy programme and to promote fuel-saving motor vehicles. President Jimmy Carter launched a major energy plan on 20 April 1977. Moreover, a large amount of government money was invested in research for alternative sources. Nevertheless during those years the government neglected a badly needed drastic rise in energy prices. On the contrary, it did all it could to minimize the effect of international oil prices on the domestic economy as a way to keep inflation down. In this sense, the government discouraged attempts to save energy and find new energy sources. The result was that oil imports continued to rise, and this further upset the US balances of trade and payments. Between 1973 and 1977, US oil imports (in volume terms) actually grew by 20 per cent.[101]

World inflation did not ease up but instead grew still faster. In 1978 the terms of trade of the OPEC countries against the rest of the world began to fall again. Against this, the increasing American dependence on oil imports strengthened the OPEC position. Therefore OPEC acted to raise oil prices once more, in real terms, during 1979 and 1980 (Table 11). Nor was OPEC alone; the big oil companies too profited from the rise in prices. They still controlled the technology for oil production and exploitation, and they also had a firm grip on transport and distribution. They were thus irreplaceable. They used some of their extra profits to speed up the rate of technological progress in oil exploration and recovery. In addition, they intensified research for alternative energy sources and introduced large-scale programmes for company diversification and integration. As a result, the oil concerns considerably strengthened their industrial position in the world during the 1970s. They became the most powerful group of companies in the West.[102]

Meanwhile some new uncertainties about the provision of energy developed around 1980. Western governments did not dare to restrict energy consumption too much, fearing that the level of economic activity would slump and raise unemployment still higher. At the same time war in the Persian Gulf threatened a new period of scarcity. Then the accession to power of the Reagan administration increased the possibility of military confrontation between West and East. Furthermore, the rise of the dollar on international money markets during 1981 meant a new increase in world prices.

Fortunately, the prospects for long-term energy provision are developing more favourably. All Western governments resolutely chose to make greater use of nuclear energy via nuclear fission. There were numerous programmes to accelerate the construction of new nuclear power stations.[103] Environmental groups stepped up pressure for improved safety measures and lower pollution levels but were unable to force governments to change their basic strategies.

Research also increased greatly. There is real prospect of meaningful, long-term progress in the area of energy technology. Energy from nuclear fusion is at present the subject of much research, as is geothermic energy (this makes use of the earth's internal heat), chemical energy, hydroelectricity, sun, wind and so on.

Malthusians have justly drawn attention to the dangers of the post-war world population explosion and the tremendous increases in demand for raw materials and energy by Western economies and Third World industrializing countries. The Malthusians have increased public consciousness of the need to seek adequate solutions and take effective measures. On the other hand, they have often made ill-considered extrapolations and irresponsibly sounded a premature death-knell for industrial society. The Second Agricultural Revolution in the West demonstrates the possibilities which exist to escape the problem of overpopulation once this revolution can be spread throughout the Third World. The influence of economic rent, which rises as scarcity increases, can, together with technological innovation, offer basic solutions to the problem of depletion of minerals and energy resources. Deep pessimism for the long term thus appears unwarranted.

Nevertheless problems in the short-term provision of supplies may well lead to serious political conflicts, and this is a greater reason for concern. Governments do not always optimally perform their role of preparing for the future.

CHAPTER IV

LABOUR AND CAPITAL
AS GROWTH FACTORS

Economic growth since the Second World War has been the result of a complex interaction of variables. Growth is not exclusively obtained by the greater application of the traditional factors of production, namely land, labour, and capital. Innovation, meaning technological and organizational progress, also plays a crucial role. The explanation of growth demands a broad and thorough statistical and theoretical analysis. One point of departure for such an analysis is the neo-classical one: that is, the acceptance of balanced growth as the guiding principle. Equally possible would be a structural viewpoint, in which unbalanced growth and the transformation of economic structure are central concepts. In this chapter the advantages and disadvantages of both approaches will be studied, as will the general influence of labour and capital, and in the next chapter innovation as a residual factor will be examined in all its diversity. When all these supply factors have been fully treated, attention will then be turned to demand factors, to see what influence they have had on the phenomenon of post-war growth.

1. MARGINAL EXPLANATION VERSUS STRUCTURAL ANALYSIS

THE GROWTH ACCOUNTING OF E. F. DENISON

The neo-classical school attempts to analyse economic growth via a marginal approach. Those who take this approach distinguish two factors of production, labour and capital, with possibly a third, land. For each factor they calculate the extent to which an additional application of the same factor will lead to an increase in total output.[1] If the percentage result of this calculation is equal to the rise in total national production, then it can be supposed that the economic growth can be imputed wholly to the increased input of the given factor. Investigations by many leading economists have shown, however, that usually the growth rate of total national production cannot be fully explained by a higher input of the combined physical factors of production.[2] John W. Kendrick even demonstrated that the added input of land, labour and capital explained less than half the growth of total production in the United States between 1869 and 1957.[3] The residual factor – that is, the part which cannot be imputed to the additional input of physical factors of production – can be considerable. In the post-war period this residual factor was indeed very important.

Edward F. Denison adopted the neo-classical explanation of economic growth and worked it out on a very detailed basis. He thus founded growth accounting. In a first major study, economic growth in nine Western countries between 1950 and 1962 was painstakingly clarified. A separate analysis of the United States from 1929 to 1969 followed and then another on Japan from 1953 to 1971. Finally, US growth in the 1970s was studied.[4] Denison concentrated exclusively on the growth of total productive capacity and took no account of the fact that in recessions this capacity was not fully used. He divided his explanatory factors into two categories: first, the physical factors of production, and second, the residual factor, which in turn was split into further subcategories.

Denison did not simply measure the contribution of the physical factors by a crude addition sum involving all employed manpower and capital goods. For measuring labour, he introduced all kinds of nuances and made use of qualitative corrections. He looked not only at the number of workers but also at the average number of hours worked and differences in the return on different kinds of worker, depending on age and sex.[5] He also took account of education and training levels in his general effort to measure the influence of 'human capital'.[6] For measuring capital, as distinguished from labour, only a few small qualitative corrections were made. Denison divided capital into four subgroups: housing, industrial building and equipment, inventories, and foreign investment. He then tried to ascertain the contribution of each to economic growth.

As for the residual factor, Denison ascribed to it the influence of advances in productivity and he distinguished four subcategories, as follows.[7]

(1) Gains in productivity can be made through general improvements in knowledge, either in technology or in business organization. More specifically, this kind of progress is made at the *frontier* of applied knowledge.

(2) Productivity gains can also be made by means of a catching-up movement relating to knowledge. Some countries which lag behind the leaders in applied knowledge have a special opportunity to close the gap and move closer to the then known optimum. The productivity gains in this case do not result from new advances made at the frontier of world knowledge, but merely from the application of already known techniques.

(3) Alternatively, increased productivity may result from the better allocation of the physical factors of production. According to the marginal doctrine, factors of production are only optimally used when they are applied to the sectors and regions where their return is the highest. In fact, for various reasons, actual allocation always deviates from the optimum. For example, social forces may hinder the transfer of economic resources from one sector or region to another: workers or employees may, for instance, choose work security or independence rather than higher incomes. Whenever the actual allocation of the physical factors of production moves closer to the optimum, productivity is raised. Denison suggested three kinds of possibility in this respect: one is that the agricultural sector may decline (surplus labour moves to other sectors, hidden unemployment is absorbed, and the supply of capital is better used); another is that the sector of small, independent producers outside agriculture may decline (with effects similar to a reduction of the agricultural sector); and the third is that restrictions on international trade may be lifted (a better international division of labour comes about).

(4) Denison regarded larger economies of scale as a fourth source of productivity gains. Economies of scale at the level of national markets are the most important. These develop alongside growth of the national economy, which promotes specialization and enables a more effective use of infrastructure. Economies of scale can also result from increases in the size of local markets, which are not necessarily linked to growth of the national economy. These local economies of scale are promoted by growing urbanization and motorization. Finally, economies of scale may be related to the consumption of specific goods. When incomes rise above a certain minimum welfare level, there results a more than proportionate increase in demand for consumer durables; in other words, demand for consumer durables shows a high income-elasticity. It is precisely these sorts of goods which are most suited to mass production, that is, to the application of efficient production techniques.

However wide-ranging Denison's growth accounting may be, it is still far from complete. For instance, in addition to the factors mentioned by Denison, the efficient allocation of resources may be obstructed by the action of unions, by entrepreneurial attitudes, and by government industrial policy. Denison does not deny the influence of these factors but since he regards them as unquantifiable he does not make explicit use of them in his findings. Besides, demand factors are only treated indirectly, supply factors being used as the principal point of departure. Moreover, Denison concerns himself with measurable national production and measurable national income. Changes in the *quality* of goods and services are thus ignored. The sometimes adverse effects that economic growth and increased material welfare exert upon the environment and individual well-being are also disregarded. These shortcomings take nothing away from Denison's achievement in specifying an impressive range of explanations for the post-war growth of the Western economies.

DENISON'S GENERAL CONCLUSIONS

Denison drew two separate forms of conclusions from his work, that is, explanations for two kinds of differences among Western countries – in growth rates and in income levels.

In respect to differences in economic growth rates, he established that Japan and Western Europe grew significantly faster than the

United States during the 1950s and 1960s. Between 1953 and 1971, the Japanese GNP grew at an average yearly rate of 8.81 per cent. Between 1950 and 1962 eight Western European countries (Britain, Belgium, Denmark, France, West Germany, the Netherlands, Norway, and Italy) taken together, achieved an average yearly growth rate of 4.78 per cent. This percentage would be considerably higher if the low British rates were excluded and if the period was extended to 1971; that is, if it included the 'golden sixties'. The American economy averaged only 3.32 per cent during that same period, 1950–62. This improved to 4 per cent when the period 1948–69 was chosen, again including the 'golden sixties', but fell to 3.87 per cent when the early 1970s were included, that is, taking the period 1948–73 (Table 12).

Between Western European growth and American, some striking differences can be noted. American growth was not only in general weaker but was also determined by different factors.

The growth which took place in the United States was to a considerable extent due to the use of additional amounts of labour and capital, rather than to better productivity. In five consecutive post-war subperiods, 1948–53, 1953–64, 1964–9, 1969–73 and 1973–6, the total contribution of productivity increases was less than that made by added physical factors of production. Moreover, between 1948 and 1973 this pattern of contribution was remarkably stable.[8] As for the American improvements in productivity, these were favourably influenced by an acceleration in technological progress after the Second World War. The contribution of technological progress to the rate of growth during 1929–41 had been only 0.23 per cent but during 1941–8 this rose to 0.80 per cent. Between 1948 and 1969, when the total annual growth was 4 per cent, the contribution of technological progress was about 1.05, and between 1969 and 1973 it was 1.24.[9] The technological frontier has thus been rolled back much faster since the Second World War than before. In contrast, other categories involved in Denison's concept of productivity declined in relative importance. Productivity gains through improved factor allocation and greater economies of scale yielded smaller and smaller contributions to growth. Finally, from the 1970s onwards, government measures to protect humanity and the environment have also helped to curb the rise in productivity. These last measures exerted a negative influence upon productivity and neutralized the favourable effect of technological progress, so

Table 12 *Sources of Growth of Total National Income and National Income per Person Employed in Selected Countries, 1950–76*
(contributions to growth rate in percentage points)

	United States				Canada	Japan
	1950–62	1948–69	1969–73	1973–6	1950–67	1953–71
RATE OF GROWTH = (1) + (2)	3.32	4.00	3.79	1.60	4.95	8.81
TOTAL FACTOR INPUT (1)	1.95	2.09	2.18	2.20	3.02	3.95
Labour	1.12	1.30	1.56	1.76	1.85	1.85
Employment	0.90	1.17	1.58	1.97	1.82	1.14
Hours of work	−0.17	−0.21	−0.28	−0.44	−0.20	−0.21
Age-sex composition	−0.10	−0.10	−0.41	−0.39	−0.13	0.14
Education	0.49	0.41	0.48	0.58	0.36	0.34
Residual	0.00	0.03	0.19	0.04	0.00	0.02
Capital	0.83	0.79	0.62	0.44	1.14	2.10
Inventories	0.10	0.12	0.08	0.03	0.10	0.73
Non-residential structures & equipment	0.43	0.36	0.31	0.23	0.87	1.07
Dwellings	0.25	0.28	0.18	0.21	0.30	0.30
International assets	0.05	0.03	0.05	−0.03	−0.12	0.00
Land	0.00	0.00	0.00	0.00	0.00	0.00
PRODUCTIVITY (2)	1.37	1.91	1.61	−0.60	1.96	4.85
Advances of knowledge	0.76	1.19	1.24	−0.56	0.66	1.97
Improved allocation of resources	0.29	0.30	0.15	0.11	0.64	0.95
Contraction of agricultural inputs	0.25	0.23	0.07	0.04	0.54	0.64
Contraction of non-agric. self-employment	0.04	0.07	0.08	0.07	0.10	0.30
Reduction of international trade barriers	0.00	0.00	—	—	0.00	0.01
Economies of scale	0.36	0.42	0.82	0.18	0.66	1.94
Growth of national and local markets	0.36	0.42	—	—	0.63	1.06
Income elasticity	0.00	0.00	—	—	0.03	0.88
Various	−0.04	0.00	−0.10	−0.31	0.00	0.00

Sources: E. F. DENISON, *Slower Economic Growth*
E. F. DENISON, *Why Growth Rates Differ*, p. 278, p. 299, p. 300
E. F. DENISON, W. K. CHUNG, *How Japan's Economy Grew*, pp. 41–2

Table 12 (*cont.*)

N.W. Europe	Belgium	Denmark	France	West Germany	Italy	Netherlands	Norway	United Kingdom
1950–62	1950–62	1950–62	1950–62	1950–62	1950–62	1950–62	1950–62	1950–62
4.78	3.03	3.63	4.70	6.27	5.60	4.07	3.43	2.38
1.69	1.17	1.55	1.24	2.78	1.66	1.91	1.04	1.11
0.83	0.76	0.59	0.45	1.37	0.96	0.87	0.15	0.60
0.71	0.40	0.70	0.08	1.49	0.42	0.78	0.13	0.50
−0.14	−0.15	−0.18	−0.02	−0.27	0.05	−0.16	−0.15	−0.15
0.03	0.08	−0.07	0.10	0.04	0.09	0.01	−0.07	−0.04
0.23	0.43	0.14	0.29	0.11	0.40	0.24	0.24	0.29
0.00	0.00	0.00	0.00	0.00	0.00	0.00	0.00	0.00
0.86	0.41	0.96	0.79	1.41	0.70	1.04	0.89	0.51
0.18	0.06	0.15	0.19	0.33	0.12	0.22	0.13	0.09
0.64	0.39	0.66	0.56	1.02	0.54	0.66	0.79	0.43
0.07	0.02	0.13	0.02	0.14	0.07	0.06	0.04	0.04
−0.03	−0.06	0.02	0.02	−0.08	−0.04	0.10	−0.07	−0.05
0.00	0.00	0.00	0.00	0.00	0.00	0.00	0.00	0.00
3.07	1.86	2.08	3.46	3.49	3.94	2.16	2.39	1.27
1.32	0.84	0.75	1.51	0.87	1.30	0.75	0.90	0.79
0.68	0.51	0.68	0.95	1.01	1.42	0.63	0.92	0.12
0.46	0.20	0.41	0.65	0.77	1.04	0.21	0.54	0.06
0.14	0.15	0.18	0.23	0.14	0.22	0.26	0.23	0.04
0.08	0.16	0.09	0.07	0.10	0.16	0.16	0.15	0.02
0.93	0.51	0.65	1.00	1.61	1.22	0.78	0.57	0.36
0.47	0.40	0.42	0.51	0.70	0.62	0.55	0.45	0.27
0.46	0.11	0.23	0.49	0.91	0.60	0.23	0.12	0.09
0.14	0.00	0.00	0.00	0.00	0.00	0.00	0.00	0.00

that productivity in general has had a somewhat meagre impact on American growth (Table 12).

In Western Europe the situation was reversed. With the notable exception of West Germany, the application of additional amounts of labour and capital was less important than in the United States. On the other hand, productivity gains had a dominant influence on the successful economic development of Western Europe after the war. About two-thirds of growth can be imputed to better productivity.

What were the chief factors in these productivity gains in Western Europe? Denison's work revealed no clear answer. But one would expect that Europe's catching-up process in relation to the United States was an important element.

The press and academic publications during the 1950s and 1960s continually pointed out the enormous gulf between the two geographical areas with respect to technological and managerial expertise. Nevertheless for the period 1950–62 Denison could find concrete evidence for this only in France and, to an extent, in Italy.[10] The determined measures the French took after the war to modernize economic structure are clearly reflected in Denison's growth accounting. European economies of scale, however, had a more widespread effect than modernizing. Economic recovery and increasing prosperity during the post-war years rapidly created a large market for consumer durables, which were suited to mass production and efficient American techniques. The expansion of this industrial sector in Western Europe was consequently an important source of productivity gains. Finally, Denison found evidence of a better allocation of the physical factors of production in various European countries, especially through the reduction of hidden unemployment in agriculture, with labour moving into other sectors. Italy, France, Norway, and West Germany boosted their productivity levels in this way. In contrast, Britain and Belgium, since both had a relatively small agricultural sector, enjoyed hardly any benefit from this at all. So the analysis of productivity gains helped to explain differences in growth rates not only between Western Europe and the United States but also among European countries.

The spectacular growth of the Japanese economy was not largely due to any single variable. All exerted influence. Additions of labour and capital were responsible for nearly one-half of Japanese growth, and gains in productivity for the rest. The expansion of capital goods stands out as the biggest single factor in Denison's growth accounting for Japan. Of the total annual growth of 8.81 per cent for the period 1953–71, the factor of capital equipment accounted for 2.1 of those percentage points. Such an expansion supposes a very large increase in gross investment, made possible by a rise in national production and savings together with a relative fall in the price of capital goods. As for the productivity gains, their single most important cause was advances in technology, particularly the absorption of the more modern American methods. Those advances accounted for 1.97 of the 8.81 percentage points in the annual growth figure. Economies of scale contributed 1.94 points and the better allocation of economic resources 0.94. The fall in agricultural employment, from 35.6 per cent of the total employment in 1953 to 14.6 per cent in 1971, gives an indication of the allocation possibilities open to the Japanese.

Denison's second series of conclusions related to differences in income levels. He calculated that in 1960 the income per employed worker in the eight Western European countries named in Table 12 was still only 59 per cent of that in the United States. This is all the more remarkable when one considers that the pressure of demand in the post-war years, certainly till the mid 1960s, was much stronger in Europe than in the United States. In other words, the evolution of demand in Europe was much more favourable for the expansion of production and thus the development of incomes. Denison ascribed 73 per cent of the European backwardness respecting income levels to the lower productivity of labour and capital in comparison to the United States. Post-war European productivity gains via the better allocation of production factors appeared to have very little effect in reducing the income differential between the United States and Western Europe. On the other hand, the catching-up movement in manufacturing did seem to offer further possibilities to close the gap, but it only began to have an effect from the 1960s onwards.

Japanese income per employed person even in 1970 was only 59.2 per cent of the American equivalent. According to Denison, 77 per cent of the gap was caused by lower productivity of labour and capital, an even greater proportion than in the case of Western Europe. Denison had difficulty in providing a solid explanation of differences in productivity levels between the United States on one side and Western Europe and Japan on the other. He did suggest some possible causes. He believed the managerial gap to be crucial. He also held institutional factors to be important, because these can give rise to differences in the intensity of competition and thus either stimulate or retard growth in productivity.[11]

Besides comparing growth rates and income per employed person, Denison examined the factors which have been responsible for the slowing of growth in the 1970s.[12] Between 1973 and 1976, the American growth rate averaged only 1.60 per cent. As before, the application of additional amounts of labour and capital continued to influence the rate of growth quite favourably; but factor productivity in this period ceased to contribute positively to growth and, indeed, had a negative impact. According to Denison, government regulations in the area of environmental control had an adverse effect on productivity. Other unfavourable influences were the slowing of technological progress and the ageing of the capital stock owing to lack of investment.

THE CRITICISM BY STRUCTURALISTS OF DENISON'S GROWTH ACCOUNTING

Denison's analysis is clear and methodical but it has major shortcomings. Criticism has been levelled at his methods of calculation, his use of some indirect indicators, and his application of weighting coefficients. More fundamental, though, was the criticism directed at the 'static nature' of Denison's growth accounting. His point of departure was that economic growth is a simple and balanced process which can be reduced to a series of determinant factors that can work in only one direction. During his investigations he himself found that his basic hypothesis was not entirely tenable. He therefore introduced some explanatory factors which referred to a catching-up movement. He supposed that actual, realized production could lag behind potential production if resources were not optimally used. The closing of this gap could be a source of growth and could imply a change in economic structure.[13] By the inclusion of this dynamic element, Denison was in fact introducing into his analysis the concept of unbalanced economic growth.[14]

The more structurally inclined economists see the idea of unbalanced growth as central to their reasoning. Ingmar Svennilson used this approach brilliantly in his study of the European economy during the inter-war period.[15] For such economists, economic growth is not a simple increase in national production, harmoniously linked with technological progress. On the contrary, growth consists of a process of permanent change in the composition of production: it is the expression of the rise and fall of different industrial sectors and the continuous redistribution of labour and capital over various industries and regions. Such a dynamic approach to growth entails a different point of departure for economic analysis. Growth becomes closely connected with the transformation of economic structure. Thus changes in the consumption needs of the population, in sectoral organization and in the production techniques of industry provide the sole impulse for growth. Moreover, the process of structural transformation is not one determined exclusively by technological improvement[16] since structural transformation is itself to a great extent a function of growth.[17] When economic growth raises income per head, shifts in the demand for particular goods also take place. For instance, rising incomes increase the demand for certain consumer goods more than for other kinds of goods. In this way economic growth, through the pressure of demand, leads to changes in the structure of production. Furthermore, technological progress and improved business administration are clearly advanced by the favourable psychological climate which accompanies growth and by the problems in the production process which growth inevitably throws up. In addition a growing market extends the area of application suitable for technical specialization, reduces the cost price of capital goods, and thus stimulates the structural transformation process.[18] The rising labour costs which often accompany growth also facilitate transformation.

According to the structuralists, growth does not depend solely on changes in economic structure. It is also linked, and in a very specific way, to new capital goods. New expanding industrial sectors have need of an extra amount of new capital goods which will incorporate the most modern technology available. The efficiency of new sectors will therefore increase in comparison to old ones. Economic growth thus becomes in large measure determined by the higher efficiency of the additional capital equipment in expanding sectors of the economy, and new additional investment in turn is determined by growth.[19] This set of interdependencies leads to a 'virtuous circle' of fast growth. Svennilson's study of inter-war Europe showed that the same interdependencies, during conditions of stagnation, work in the opposite way (a 'vicious circle'). During times of structural malaise, threatened sectors display much inertia when it comes to the renewal of capital. The equipment of the threatened sectors thus becomes technologically out of date. This means that these old sectors hold on to labour which could otherwise have been shifted into new expanding sectors. Structural transformation is thus restrained by stagnation and in turn this inertia exacerbates stagnation.[20]

Three important economists who studied post-war growth in the West from a structural, dynamic standpoint are John Cornwall, Angus Maddison and Gerhard Mensch.[21] The main question raised in a structural approach is as follows: to what extent do labour and capital display the mobility and flexibility that are necessary in order to promote, prolong, and possibly accelerate the transformation of economic structure? Such a question is of itself a direct attack on Denison's growth accounting, which presumes perfect mobility and flexibility of labour and capital. Both Cornwall and Maddison rejected this hypothesis by Denison and instead studied to what extent existing imperfections in the allocation of production factors in various countries can be alleviated.[22] In this respect they devoted much attention to the capital goods stock and the working population, and they argued that expansion of both facilitates the structural transformation process. In these circumstances, new sectors do not need to draw labour and capital away from traditional industrial sectors, which is usually a difficult process. Instead, they can make use of new reserves. Cornwall and Maddison also adopted the catching-up hypothesis as a way to help explain the rapid growth of Western Europe and Japan. When labour and capital are considered within the framework of unbalanced growth, then the catching-up hypothesis takes on a much more central role than in Denison's growth accounting.

Mensch introduced the Schumpeterian viewpoint. In his opinion mobility and flexibility of labour and capital can be enhanced by the growth-orientated actions of entrepreneurs. In addition the innovative role of dynamic entrepreneurs must be seen in the context of long waves. For example, a downward Kondratieff Cycle stimulates the search for fundamental technological innovation.[23] In the Mensch model, technological progress and entrepreneurs constitute the motor for the transformation of economic structure.

During the crisis of the 1970s attention was turned to the slowing down in the growth of total factor productivity and the deindustrialization process apparent in several OECD countries. Falling employment in manufacturing industry, at first relative but later absolute, and the extension of the services sector were seen as structural shifts and manifestations of unbalanced growth.[24] In an affluent society the demand for manufactured goods in general will grow less rapidly as soon as income per head exceeds certain limits. From this point the demand for services grows faster. Such considerations hardly figure, if at all, in Denison's growth accounting. The interdependencies of different factors are also neglected. They are, however, essential and therefore in the rest of this chapter, and in the next, a structural approach will be adopted.

2. THE FLEXIBILITY OF THE SUPPLY OF LABOUR

THE POST-WAR LABOUR SUPPLY, SEEN QUANTITATIVELY

The major growth achievements of most Western economies since the war imply a big input of labour. Denison's work contains a whole series of concrete indications for this. Structural economists, too, saw the availability of additional labour as an important factor in the acceleration of growth. In a quantitative sense the labour supply can increase in five ways: by a natural increase in population, by a surplus of immigration over emigration, by a change in the age-structure of the population, by an increase in the percentage of the population becoming economically active, and by the absorption of hidden unemployment from traditional agricultural or artisan sectors.

M. Macura produced an interesting overview of changes in the European populations (Table 13). From the figures it appears

Table 13 *Decennial Per Cent Change of Regional Population in Europe, 1920–80*

	1920s	1930s	1940s	1950s	1960s	1970s
Western Europe	7.1	4.2	8.1	9.9	10.2	4.3
Southern Europe	11.8	10.7	5.7	8.3	9.0	2.7
Eastern Europe	11.4	8.1	−6.8	8.1	7.3	7.8
Northern Europe	4.8	5.2	6.1	4.5	6.2	1.2
Soviet Union	15.3	8.9	−7.7	19.1	13.2	8.6

Sources: M. MACURA, *Population in Europe*, p. 8
UNITED NATIONS, *Statistical Yearbook*, 1979–80

Table 14 *Demographic Indicators of Various Western Countries, 1950–77*
(*percentages*)

	(1) Share of labour force in population 1950	(2) Share of women in labour force 1950	(3) Age composition of population 1950		
			− 15	15–64	65 +
Canada	38.0	21.8	29.7	62.6	7.7
United States	42.7[1]	29.4	26.8	65.1	8.1
Japan	46.0 (1953)	40.4 (1953)	34.3	1953 60.5	5.2
Austria	48.3 (1951)	38.8 (1951)	22.8	66.8	10.4
Belgium	41.0	28.7	20.9	68.1	11.0
Denmark	47.8 (1955)	34.6 (1955)	26.3	64.7	9.0
Finland	n.a.	n.a.		n.a.	
France	45.3	35.2 (1954)	22.7	65.9	11.4
West Germany	45.9	35.6	20.8	1956 69.0	10.2
Greece	37.2 (1951)	18.0 (1951)	28.3	1951 64.9	6.8
Republic of Ireland	43.0 (1951)	26.0 (1951)	28.9	1951 60.4	10.7
Italy	39.5 (1954)	23.7 (1954)	26.5	65.5	8.0
Luxemburg	n.a.	n.a.		n.a.	
Netherlands	38.7	24.6 (1954)	29.3	63.0	7.7
Norway	44.8	27.8	24.4	66.0	9.6
Portugal	39.0	23.0	29.5	63.5	7.0
Spain	38.7	16.1	26.2	66.5	7.3
Sweden	n.a.	n.a.	23.4	66.3	10.3
Switzerland	45.7	29.7	23.6	66.8	9.6
Turkey	n.a.	n.a.	38.3	58.3	3.4
United Kingdom	47.1 (1951)	32.6	22.5	1951 66.7	10.8

Notes: Col. (1)   [1] United States, excluding Alaska and Hawaii

Table 14 (cont.)

	(4) Yearly growth rate of population (incl. migration) 1950–60	(5) Share of migration in yearly population growth 1950–60	(6) Yearly growth rate of population group between 15 and 64 years 1950–60	(7) Age composition of population 1960		
				− 15	15–64	65 +
Canada	2.7	26	2.0	33.7	58.7	7.6
United States	1.7[1]	10.8	0.8[1]	31.0	59.7	9.3
Japan	1.2	0.4	1.8 (1953–60)	30.1	63.9	6.0
Austria	0.2	−85	0.1	22.0	65.7	12.3
Belgium	0.6	13.4	0.04	23.5	64.5	12.0
Denmark	0.7	−15.9	0.6	25.2	64.2	10.6
Finland	n.a.	n.a.	n.a.	30.4	62.3	7.3
France	0.9	23	0.3	26.4	62.0	11.6
West Germany	1.1	48.2		21.3	67.8	10.9
Greece	1.0	−25.5	1.1 (1951–60)	26.1	65.8	8.1
Republic of Ireland	−0.5	29.3	−0.8 (1951–60)	30.5	58.6	10.9
Italy	0.6	−36.9	0.7	23.4	67.6	9.0
Luxemburg	0.6	48	n.a.	21.4	67.9	10.7
Netherlands	1.3	−9.9	1.0	30.0	61.0	9.0
Norway	0.9	n.a.	0.5	25.9	63.2	10.9
Portugal	0.5	−161.2[s]	0.4	29.2	62.9	7.9
Spain	0.8	−32.0	0.5	27.3	64.5	8.2
Sweden	0.6	23.4	0.6	22.4	65.9	11.7
Switzerland	1.3	43.0[s]	1.1	23.7	66.0	10.3
Turkey	2.8	n.a.	2.3	41.2	55.1	3.7
United Kingdom	0.4 (1951–60)	−8.5[1]	0.2 (1951–60)	23.3	65.1	11.6

Notes: Col. (4) [1] United States 1950–8, excluding Alaska and Hawaii

Col. (5) [s] Migration and statistical adjustment taken together

[1] For the period 1950–60 the share of migration in yearly population growth in the United Kingdom is −9.6 per cent, but the figures for 1951–60 (−8.5 per cent) are more reliable.

Col. (6) [1] United States 1950–8, excluding Alaska and Hawaii

Table 14 (cont.)

	(8) Share of labour force in population 1960	(9) Yearly growth rate of labour force 1950–60	(10) Share of women in labour force (excl. military) 1959
Canada	36.5	2.3	25.7
United States	39.9	1.2 [1]	32.7
Japan	48.4	1.8 (1953–60)	40.9
Austria	47.9	0.3 (1951–61)	n.a.
Belgium	40.2	0.2	30.7 (1960)
Denmark	45.7	0.7 (1955–60)	31.8 (1960)
Finland	n.a.	n.a.	44.4
France	43.3	0.009 (1954–60)	n.a.
West Germany	47.8	1.5	37.6
Greece	43.2	2.7 (1951–60)	31.9 (1961)
Republic of Ireland	39.4	− 1.4 (1951–60)	n.a.
Italy	42.3	1.4 (1954–60)	31.2
Luxemburg	42.7	n.a.	n.a.
Netherlands	36.8	1.2	n.a.
Norway	40.6	0.2	28.9
Portugal	36.6	0.4	n.a.
Spain	39.0	0.7	n.a.
Sweden	47.9	n.a.	36.1 (1962)
Switzerland	49.0	1.5	n.a.
Turkey	47.2	n.a.	n.a.
United Kingdom	47.8	0.6	34.0

Notes: Col. (9) [1] United States 1950–9, excluding Alaska and Hawaii

Table 14 (*cont.*)

	(11)	(12)	(13)	(14)	(15)
	Share of agricultural sector in total labour force		Yearly growth rate of employment in non-agricultural sectors	Yearly growth rate of employment in manufacturing sector	Yearly growth rate of population (incl. migration)
	1950	1960	1950–60	1950–60	1960–70
Canada	22.9	13.2	3.0	1.5	1.8
United States	13.5	9.3	1.7	1.0	1.3
Japan	42.4 (1953)	32.5	4.1 (1953–60)	3.9 (1953–60)	1.1
Austria	33.0 (1951)	n.a.	1.2 (1951–60)	n.a.	0.5
Belgium	11.1	7.6	0.6	0.2	0.6
Denmark	24.9 (1955)	21.2	2.2 (1955–60)	n.a.	0.7
Finland	n.a.	36.4	n.a.	n.a.	0.4
France	28.2 (1954)	22.7	1.1 (1954–60)	1.0 (1954–60)	1.1
West Germany	24.7	14.4	3.4	3.5 (1950–9)	0.9
Greece	48.2	53.4 (1961)	− [1]	2.3 (1951–61)	0.5
Republic of Ireland	40.9	37.1	− 0 8 (1951–60)	n.a.	0.4
Italy	39.9 (1954)	31.1	4.6 (1954–60)	5.0 (1954–60)	0.9
Luxemburg	n.a.	n.a.	n.a.	n.a.	0.8
Netherlands	14.3	10.3	1.7	1.3	1.3
Norway	30.5	23.3	1.1	0.6	0.8
Portugal	49.7	44.2	1.4	2.1	0.9
Spain	49.8	41.9	2.3	3.2	1.1
Sweden	n.a.	n.a.	n.a.	n.a.	0.7
Switzerland	16.5	11.1	2.2	2.5	1.6
Turkey	77.4 (1955)	74.9	3.4 (1955–60)	4.8 (1955–60)	2.5
United Kingdom	5.6	4.4	0.8	0.3	0.6

Notes: Col. (13)   [1] Greece 1951–61: + 1.5 per cent according to OECD, *Labour Force Statistics, 1950–62*
1951–60: − 0.2 per cent according to OECD, *Labour Force Statistics, 1959–60*

Table 14 (*cont.*)

	(16) Share of migration in yearly population growth 1950–60	(17) Yearly growth rate of population group between 15 and 64 years 1960–70	(18) Age composition of population 1970		
			− 15	15–64	65 +
Canada	21.9[s]	2.4	30.3	61.9	7.8
United States	15.8	1.6	28.3	61.9	9.8
Japan	− 0.1	1.9	23.9	69.1	7.0
Austria	− 0.4	− 0.2	24.5	61.3	14.2
Belgium	37.0	0.3	23.7	63.0	13.3
Denmark	7.5	0.8	23.3	64.4	12.3
Finland	− 82.3	1.1	24.6	66.4	9.0
France	43.0	1.1	24.8	62.4	12.8
West Germany	54.3	0.3	23.2	63.6	13.2
Greece	− 59.4 (1960–9)[s]	0.5 (1960–9)	25.1	65.0	9.9
Republic of Ireland	− 159.1[s]	0.2	31.2	57.5	11.3
Italy	− 7.3[s]	0.7	23.0	66.4	10.6
Luxemburg	65.0	0.4	22.0	65.4	12.6
Netherlands	6.9	1.5	27.3	62.6	10.1
Norway	0.8[s]	0.7	24.5	62.6	12.9
Portugal	− 39.0 (1960–9)[s]	0.8	28.7	62.4	8.9
Spain	− 16.5[s]	0.7	28.0	62.5	9.5
Sweden	38.5	0.7	20.8	65.5	13.7
Switzerland	47.2[s]	1.5	23.4	65.2	11.4
Turkey	n.a.	2.4	41.5	54.2	4.3
United Kingdom	0.1	0.3	24.0	63.2	12.8

Note: Col. (16)   [s] Migration and statistical adjustment taken together

Table 14 *(cont.)*

	(19)	(20)	(21)	(22)
	Share of labour force in population 1970	Yearly growth rate of labour force 1960–70	Share of women in labour force (excl. military) 1970	Share of agricultural sector in total of labour force 1970
Canada	39.8	2.6	32.6	7.7
United States	41.9	1.8	37.7	4.4
Japan	49.8	1.3	39.3	17.4
Austria	40.6	−0.3	n.a.	18.3
Belgium	39.7	0.6	33.0	4.8
Denmark	48.3	1.3	39.4	11.5
Finland	n.a.	n.a.	45.0	2.27
France	42.2	0.7	n.a.	14.0
West Germany	44.2	0.3	36.2	8.6
		(1962–70)	(1971)	
Greece	37.2	−0.9	27.5	38.7
Republic of Ireland	37.9			27.1
Italy	38.5	−0.7	27.0	19.5
Luxemburg	39.7	n.a.	n.a.	11.1
Netherlands	36.5	1.1	n.a.	7.2
Norway	40.2	0.7	30.8	13.9
Portugal	40.1	−0.02	n.a.	31.7
Spain	38.7	0.7	n.a.	29.5
Sweden	48.6	0.9	39.4	8.1
Switzerland	49.1	1.5	n.a.	7.6
Turkey	42.8	1.1	n.a.	69.4
United Kingdom	45.6	0.2	36.9	2.8

Table 14 (cont.)

	(23) Yearly growth rate of employment in non-agricultural sectors 1960–70	(24) Yearly growth rate of employment in manufacturing sector 1960–70	(25) Yearly growth rate of population (incl. migration) 1970–7	(26) Share of migration in yearly population growth 1970–7
Canada	3.5	2.3	1.3	30.7[s]
United States	2.2	1.4	0.8	21.0
Japan	3.2	3.7	1.3	− 1.0
Austria	0.5	− 0.1	0.1 (1971–7)	108.0 (1971–7)[s]
Belgium	1.2	0.4	0.3	66.8
Denmark	2.3	1.6	0.4	66.0
Finland	n.a.	1.3	0.4	− 18.7
France	1.9	1.1	0.6	21.6
West Germany	0.8	0.6	0.2	156.2[1]
Greece	3.0	3.3	0.7	4.5[s2]
Republic of Ireland		2.5	1.1	− 1.0[s]
Italy	1.2	1.1	0.7	17.6[s]
Luxemburg	n.a.	1.3	0.7	109.9
Netherlands	1.7	0.9	0.9	26.7
Norway	1.6	1.2	0.6	18.3
Portugal	1.3	1.6	1.2	13.8[s]
Spain	2.8	2.3	1.2 (1971–7)	10.4 (1971–7)
Sweden	1.7	− 0.1[1]	0.4	29.8
Switzerland	2.0	1.4	0.06	− 37.4[s]
Turkey	3.7	2.4	2.4	n.a.
United Kingdom	0.3	− 0.3	0.1	− 92.4

Notes: Col. (24)   [1] According to more recent OECD *Labour Force Statistics*, the figure for Sweden is slightly positive.

Col. (26)   [s] Migration and statistical adjustment taken together

[1] For the years characterized by highest immigration (the period 1970–3) the figure stood at 193.7 per cent.

[2] After 1975 the migration balance for Greece is positive. This explains th small positive figure.

Table 14 (cont.)

	(27) Yearly growth rate of population group between 15 and 64 years 1970-7	(28) Age composition of population 1977			(29) Share of labour force in population 1977	(30) Yearly growth rate of labour force 1970-7
		− 15	15–64	65 +		
Canada	2.3	24.9	66.2	8.9	45.4	3.2
United States	1.6	23.8	65.4	10.8	45.9	2.1
Japan	1.0	24.2	67.5	8.3	47.9	0.8
Austria	0.4 (1971–7)	22.3	62.5	15.3	40.4	0.1
Belgium	0.6	21.4	64.6	14.0	41.3	0.8
Denmark	0.4	22.1	64.0	13.9	50.7	1.1
Finland	0.7	21.3	67.4	11.2	48.2	0.6
France	0.8	23.2	63.1	13.7	42.7	0.8
West Germany	0.4	20.3	64.7	15.0	42.4	− 0.4
Greece	0.6	23.8	63.8	12.7	n.a.	n.a.
Republic of Ireland	1.2	31.4	57.8	10.8	35.8	0.3
Italy	0.6	22.3	65.9	11.7	39.2	0.8
Luxemburg	1.3 (1970–6)	19.6	(1976) 67.2	13.2	41.5	1.2
Netherlands	1.4	24.2	64.8	11.1	35.2	0.4
Norway	0.6	23.3	62.6	14.1	45.8	2.0 (1972–7)
Portugal	1.2	27.9	62.2	9.9	45.6	1.0 (1974–7)
Spain	1.2 (1971–6)	27.5	(1976) 62.5	10.0	37.4	0.7
Sweden	0.02	20.5	63.9	15.6	50.6	0.9
Switzerland	0.1	21.3	65.5	13.2	44.9	− 1.2
Turkey	2.8	39.9	55.3	4.8	39.8	1.5
United Kingdom	0.2	22.5	63.2	14.3	47.1	0.6

Table 14 (*cont.*)

	(31)	(32)	(33)	(34)
	Yearly growth rate of the share of women in labour force (excl. military) 1970–7	Share of women in labour force (excl. military) 1977	Share of female unemployment in total unemployment 1970	Share of female unemployment in total unemployment 1977
Canada	2.9	37.5	34.4	44.3
United States	2.0	40.5	45.3	47.7
Japan	0.7	38.1	35.6	34.5
Austria	0.1	38.2	55.0	54.0
Belgium	0.2	34.7	40.5	60.3
Denmark	0.6	42.3	35.2	51.1
Finland	− 0.09	47.4	24.4	38.0
France	0.4	31.1 (1975)	62.2	60.0 (1976)
West Germany	− 0.9	37.9	37.6	49.7
Greece	n.a.	n.a.	34.3 (1971)	n.a.
Republic of Ireland	− 0.3	26.8 (1973)	13.8	19.4
Italy	0.5	30.6	51.0	56.4
Luxemburg	1.2	n.a.	n.a.	n.a.
Netherlands	− 0.09	n.a.	19.6	28.0
Norway	2.0 (1972–7)	39.3	46.4 (1972)	59.3
Portugal	0.1 (1974–7)	38.5	48.8 (1974)	54.6
Spain	0.04	29.3	12.9	33.2
Sweden	0.9	43.5	45.8	53.3
Switzerland	− 1.2	n.a.	n.a.	25.0
Turkey	1.0	35.6 (1975)	n.a.	n.a.
United Kingdom	0.1	36.3	14.4	27.5

Table 14 (*cont.*)

	(35)	(36)	(37)	(38)
	Share of agricultural sector in total labour force 1977	Yearly growth rate of employment in non-agricultural sectors 1970–7	Yearly growth rate of employment in manufacturing sector 1970–7	Yearly growth rate of employment in service sector 1970–7
Canada	5.7	3.2	1.8	3.8
United States	3.7	2.2	0.5	3.0
Japan	11.9	1.6	0.5	2.4
Austria	11.8	1.3	0.2	2.3
Belgium	3.3	0.4	− 1.7	1.9
Denmark	9.1	1.0	− 2.5	3.4
Finland	12.9	1.6 (1971–7)	− 0.3 (1971–7)	3.0 (1971–7)
France	9.7	1.1	− 0.3	2.3
West Germany	6.8	− 0.6	− 2.1	0.9
Greece	n.a.	n.a.	n.a.	n.a.
Republic of Ireland	23.1	0.4	− 0.09	0.8
Italy	15.9	1.3	0.1	2.4
Luxemburg	5.9	1.6	0.7	2.5
Netherlands	6.3	0.2	− 2.2	1.5
Norway	9.0	2.8 (1972–7)	0.9	3.9
Portugal	32.5	1.3 (1974–7)	− 1.2 (1974–7)	4.0 (1974–7)
Spain	20.7	1.1 (1972–7)	0.6 (1972–7)	1.7 (1972–7)
Sweden	6.1	1.2	− 0.7	2.3
Switzerland	8.5	− 1.2	− 2.9	0.4
Turkey	61.6	4.9	3.9	5.7
United Kingdom	2.7	0.2	− 1.5	1.5

Source: Own calculations

that Western European countries were still experiencing a sizeable population growth after the Second World War, certainly in comparison to the years before and during the war.[25] In Southern Europe the population clearly grew less quickly after the war than before it. This slowing was due to post-war emigration from this relatively overcrowded region. The same slowing occurs in Eastern Europe with the one difference that the war years witnessed a startling decline in population. In the Soviet Union the human loss during the 1940s was still more grave, but the demographic recovery after the war was very strong.

It appears that migration had a great effect on post-war labour supplies in various Western countries (Table 14). In Europe the pattern of migration underwent a structural change. Intracontinental migration replaced intercontinental migration and economic migration replaced the political migration of the years immediately before and after the war. The earlier stream of European migrants, which for centuries had been colonizing North America, Australia, New Zealand, and other overseas areas, had been curtailed during the 1920s and 1930s by means of quotas established by the recipient countries. At the same time, many political refugees from the Soviet Union, Nazi Germany, and the Balkan states began to move to Western Europe. This movement was even stronger immediately after the war. Between 1945 and 1947 the United Nations Relief and Rehabilitation Administration (UNRRA) repatriated no fewer than 30 million people, mostly European. Between 1947 and 1951, more than 1 million displaced persons who could not be repatriated in their native lands (700,000 Germans and 300,000 Poles) were settled in the West. During the 1950s the westward migration of Germans continued, mostly coming from East Germany and the Balkans.

From the 1950s onwards, Western European countries began to attract economic migrants, first from Southern and Eastern Europe, but gradually also from North Africa, especially Algeria and Morocco. Later Turkey became an important area of recruitment, and later still, although to a lesser extent, Iran and Pakistan (Table 15).[26]

The 1950s and 1960s witnessed an astonishing surge in the number of foreign workers in EEC countries. In France, Germany, Italy, and the Benelux countries (Europe of the Six) there were 1.5 million foreign workers in 1960 and more than 4.5 million in 1973. When

Table 15 *Trends of Immigration (+) and Emigration (−) in European Countries, 1950–80*
(net migration in crude figures rounded to the hundreds)

	Annual average 1950–4	Annual average 1955–9	Annual average 1960–4	Annual average 1965–9	Annual average 1970–4	Annual average 1975–80
Belgium	+ 3,200	+ 10,600	+ 19,200	+ 12,200	+ 17,200	+ 6,000
France	+ 27,800	+ 156,000	+ 316,000	+ 115,400	+ 112,600	+ 5,000
West Germany	+ 221,400	+ 297,200	+ 312,600	+ 229,800	+ 342,400	+ 72,500
Luxemburg	+ 900	+ 600	+ 2,100	+ 900	+ 3,800	+ 1,400
Netherlands	− 20,600	− 3,200	+ 6,400	+ 10,600	+ 26,200	+ 40,300
Sweden	+ 9,200	+ 9,800	+ 14,000	+ 25,600	+ 7,600	+ 16,300
Switzerland	+ 22,800	+ 32,000	+ 56,400	+ 17,000	+ 6,600	− 22,300
United Kingdom	− 33,600	− 1,300[a]	+ 27,000	− 72,200	− 58,600	− 23,600
Greece	− 13,800	− 25,000	− 44,200	− 23,800	− 30,700	+ 45,500
Republic of Ireland	− 34,800	− 44,400	− 22,200	− 15,200	+ 11,000	+ 5,000
Italy	− 100,800	− 127,400	− 113,200	− 123,800	+ 59,800	+ 54,100
Portugal	− 64,200	− 68,000	− 60,200	− 130,200	− 52,800	+ 39,000
Spain	− 51,800	− 104,000	− 80,600[b]	− 42,200	− 28,800	+ 29,400[c]
Turkey	n.a.	n.a.	+ 26,900[b]	n.a.	n.a.	n.a.
Yugoslavia	n.a.	n.a.	+ 34,000[b]	n.a.	n.a.	n.a.

Notes: [a] 1956–9
[b] Migrants out of Europe
[c] 1975–9

Sources: J. CORNWALL, *Postwar Growth*, p. 85
OECD, *Labour Force Statistics, 1969–1980*

Great Britain, Ireland, and Denmark (Europe of the Nine) are included the total number of foreign workers in 1973 was 6.4 million, of which nearly 2.5 million were in West Germany. When these numbers are compared with total population and total working population, remarkable percentages can be noted in some countries (Table 16).

As economic difficulties grew during the 1970s, most Western European governments decided, around 1973 and 1974, to stop the recruitment of guest workers. They succeeded to an extent,[27] but around 1977 numbers began to increase once again.[28] The problem of guest workers in Western Europe had developed into a paradox. Western European governments encouraged and organized large-scale immigration of foreign workers during economic booms in order to relieve temporary pressure on the labour market. Even the guest workers regarded themselves as 'temporary migrants'. In the end, things turned out differently. The 'temporary' immigrants found a permanent place in the economy and the recipient country developed a permanent need for foreign labour.[29] What can explain these reversals in attitude?

One part of the answer has to do with the policy of full employment and the great increase in prosperity levels after the Second World War. Industrial workers in Western Europe acquired the opportunity and the ambition to move up to more highly qualified categories of work and thus improve their material and social status. At the same time the demand for unskilled and semi-skilled labour, especially in the traditional sectors, did not fall but even increased. Consequently there developed a critical shortage of labour – for instance, in French and Belgian coal mines, the service sector in Switzerland, and German agriculture. Western European governments had three possible solutions: they could raise wages for low-esteemed jobs, introduce a policy of permanent migration or develop the idea of temporary migration.[30] They chose temporary migration because they could not radically change the domestic employment structure and because they were convinced that their labour market problems were short-term ones only and that migration could be easily put into reverse.

On this point they were making a serious mistake. The 'temporary' immigration of guest workers became a self-perpetuating process, once started. Immigration quickened the flow of native workers out of socially unpopular jobs. But this outflow did not remain limited

Table 16 Share of Immigrants in the Total Population and in the Labour Force of the EEC Countries, 1 January 1973

	Total Population	Immigrants	Percentage	Total Labour Force	Immigrants	Percentage
Belgium	9,695,400	775,632	8.00	3,176,000	220,000	6.92
France	51,487,400	3,608,400	7.00	16,443,000[1]	1,770,000[1]	10.76
West Germany	61,181,000	2,839,400	4.64	22,470,000	2,460,000	10.94
Italy	54,025,200	151,000	0.28	12,797,000	44,030	0.34
Luxemburg	345,000	90,900	26.35	122,500[3]	43,000	35.10
Netherlands	13,296,000	204,000	1.53	3,952,000	121,086	3.06
Denmark	4,953,500	54,000	1.09	1,923,000[1]	36,000[1]	1.87
Republic of Ireland	2,944,400	86,500	2.94	722,000[1]	32,120[1,2]	4.44
United Kingdom	55,812,000	2,579,000	4.62	23,008,000	1,665,005	7.23
Total	253,739,900	10,388,832	4.09	84,613,500	6,391,241	7.47

Notes: [1] Yearly average 1972
[2] Those with labour permits plus 30,000 Britons (estimate)
[3] Including military personnel

Source: F. MOULAERT, 'Gastarbeid', pp. 343-64.

to the original sectors where the labour shortages had been reported. On the contrary, as W. Böhning found in West Germany, the outflow of native workers broadened itself to include all sectors of industry.[31] Guest workers could no longer be considered as a marginal concern. The relative share of native workers in blue-collar jobs, particularly in unskilled and semi-skilled work, fell strikingly as guest workers took over these positions. Consequently, after a period of time, guest workers no longer comprised a labour reserve which could be drawn on during booms and got rid of during periods of crisis and rising domestic unemployment. They began to fulfil a structural need, permanently occupying low-esteemed and low-paid jobs in which Western European workers had no further interest. This explains why, at the beginning of the 1970s, guest workers were no more hit by unemployment than native workers. Towards the end of the 1970s the 'guests' were hit by more unemployment, but this was caused not so much by native workers taking over the jobs of guest workers as by the circumstance that the traditional sectors of the economy, where most guest workers were employed, were worst affected by the crisis.

The transition from temporary migration to permanent settlement resulted not only from the permanent need for foreign workers but also from a change in the behaviour pattern of the immigrants themselves.[32] Initially these migrant groups consisted of young, unmarried men who came on a temporary basis but quickly adopted the norms and values of their new surroundings. In a second phase of immigration the average age of guest workers rose and soon whole families came, speeding the process of permanent settlement. Meanwhile the Western governments introduced measures to improve the living conditions of guest workers. Family dependants were allowed to enter the country at the very time that the immigration of new guest workers began to slow down. Attempts were made to provide better accommodation and social infrastructure (such as education), in short, to help integrate the guest workers. Finally civil and religious leaders also took up residence and this too strengthened the tendency towards permanent settlement.

In broad outlines, immigration into the United States, Canada, Australia, and New Zealand followed the same pattern as in Europe. In these areas too immigration during the whole post-war period remained very important.

Between 1950 and 1959, immigration accounted for 10.8 per cent of the total growth in US population. This figure grew to 15.8 per cent in the 1960s and to 21 per cent in the 1970s. These figures become even more impressive when expressed in absolute form. For example, the 10.8 per cent figure for 1950–9 represents 2,420,000 immigrants. The lands of origin were mostly Mexico, Costa Rica, and other Central American countries, and the West Indies. Moreover, many American immigrants were initially clandestine seasonal workers who stayed on illegally, hoping to get official permits for residence and work later. Illegal immigrants are not included in the figures just given, but it is estimated that their numbers are very high. The number of illegal immigrants in Canada is probably negligible, but on the other hand the percentage of legal immigrants in relation to the total population growth is much higher than in the United States: for the 1950s 26 per cent, for the 1960s 21 per cent and for the 1970s 30.7 per cent (Table 14).

In Japan, the wave of immigration was limited to the period immediately after the Second World War, when about 5 million troops and civilians together with their families returned from overseas areas. Repatriation and natural population growth added some 8 million to the Japanese population by the end of 1948; that is, an increase of 11 per cent over the population at the end of the war. Immigration into Japan after the 1940s was negligible. Labour-market problems were solved by investing abroad. For instance, investment in South Korea made possible the use of an unskilled, cheap, local work-force.

Alongside natural population growth and migration, changes in the age-structure and in the percentage of the population becoming economically active also had significative effects on the post-war labour supply. As for the age-structure of the population, in all Western countries there was a trend towards a generally older population, although its extent has often been exaggerated (Table 14, columns 3, 7, 18 and 28). In the 1970s, the number of people younger than fifteen fell in relation to total population and the percentage of those between fifteen and sixty-five increased; in some countries this group even grew a good deal faster than total population.[33] As for the level of participation, the share of women in the labour force is the decisive factor. In countries with a high general level of participation, such as Denmark and Sweden, the share of females in the working population is high, whereas in countries with a low level of participation, such as Spain, Italy, and the Netherlands, relatively few women work. Immediately after the Second World War, countries still differed considerably in female participation. In 1950 Japan was still at the top of the league with women comprising 40 per cent of the total labour force. The equivalent figure for Britain was 32.6 per cent, for the United States 29.4 per cent, Canada 21.8 per cent and Spain only 16 per cent. Between 1950 and 1980 there was a certain convergence in these rates and also an upward trend. In 1950, American, Canadian, Western European, and Japanese women together comprised 28.5 per cent of the total working population in those countries. In 1959 this percentage had risen to 33.8, in 1970 to 35.4, and in 1977 to 37.4.[34] From these figures it is clear that the entrance of women into the working population after the war contributed much to the growth of the working population in the West. This development is a consequence of changes in social and mental attitudes regarding women, especially in the last few decades. Female liberation, the improvement and extension of education, and the falling birth rate have made it easier for women to join the labour market.

On the other hand, in recessions, such as in the 1970s, female unemployment rose disproportionately. There are two possible reasons for this discrepancy. Despite the female liberation movement, job opportunities for many women remained restricted to low-esteemed work. It is argued that this restrictiveness was due to high absenteeism and to lack of business training and of motivation. So women were often the first victims of dismissals in periods of recession. A second possible reason for the discrepancy may lie in the link between the rate of participation and age.[35] For men, the rate of participation in the labour force rises rapidly and regularly between the ages of fifteen and thirty and stabilizes itself at a high level of 98 per cent. After the age of fifty this rate slowly begins to fall. For women, however, the curve is much more irregular. Usually a first high point is reached between the ages of twenty and twenty-five; then there is a fall, followed by a new rise from the age of about thirty-five which reaches a second, although lower, high point between the ages of forty-five and fifty. The curve then falls definitively.[36] This irregularity in comparison with the male rate of participation may well adversely affect the employment of female labour.

The outflow of labour from agriculture is a final factor which influenced the flexibility of the post-war labour supply. Table 17 shows what changes have taken place in the structure of the labour force in Western countries during their industrialization. These figures confirm the conclusions of Colin Clark.[37] In some countries, including Britain and the United States, those changes were already close to completion in the 1950s. For example, around 1950 only 5 per cent of the economically active population in the United Kingdom was engaged in agriculture, by 1973 this had fallen still further to 2.9 per cent. For the United States the figures were respectively 12 per cent and 4.1 per cent. In countries with initially greater employment in agriculture the decrease was of greater magnitude. In Japan in 1950 the agricultural sector still comprised 49 per cent of the total working population but in 1973 this had fallen to only 13.4 per cent. In Italy the percentages for roughly the same years were respectively 41 per cent and 17.4 per cent, and in France 33 per cent and 12.2 per cent.

The decline of employment in agriculture in all Western countries was accompanied by a parallel rise in employment in the service sector. There was no uniform trend in the industrial sector. In most countries the absolute number of workers in industry rose during the 1950s and 1960s. The relative share of industrial, as against total, employment rose steadily during the same period in Japan and Italy but in West Germany and France it displayed a tendency towards stabilization. In the United States, Britain, Sweden, and the Benelux countries, the share of industrial employment fell from the 1960s onwards.

Three main factors determined the reduction of employment in the agricultural sector. In the first place, labour productivity in agriculture grew impressively both in absolute terms and in comparison to the industrial and service sectors. The growth rate of labour productivity in agriculture was usually higher than in each of the other sectors and always higher than all three sectors taken together.[38] Second, the demand for agricultural products in the West did not rise as strongly as that for other kinds of goods and services. The affluent society had developed beyond subsistence levels, and further increases in income did not lead to proportionate increases in demand for foodstuffs. The third main factor which contributed to the outward flow of labour from the agricultural sector was income. After the Second World War, except for countries where agriculture accounted for only a negligible amount of the total employment (Belgium and the United Kingdom), incomes in

Table 17 Percentage Composition of Total Employment between Agriculture, Industry, and Services, 1866–1980

	Italy		West Germany		France		United Kingdom		United States		Japan		Netherlands		Sweden	
Agriculture	1871	62.0	1882	42.0	1866	52.0	1911	12.0	1870	50.0	1877	83.0	1909	28.0	1910	46.0
	1954	41.0	1933	29.0	1950	33.0	1951	5.0	1950	12.0	1950	49.0	1947	19.0	1950	20.0
1957		35.6		16.3		24.6		4.4		9.3		34.3		12.8		16.5
1965		25.6		10.9		17.7		3.3		6.1		23.5		8.9		11.4
1973		17.4		7.5		12.2		2.9		4.1		13.4		6.8		7.1
1980		14.2		5.6		8.7		2.6		3.6		10.4		4.9		5.6
Industry	1871	24.0	1882	36.0	1866	29.0	1911	43.0	1870	25.0	1877	6.0	1909	35.0	1910	26.0
	1954	31.0	1933	41.0	1950	34.0	1951	47.0	1950	35.0	1950	21.0	1947	33.0	1950	41.0
1957		35.3		48.0		37.5		49.2		35.5		26.7		42.1		42.2
1965		41.6		50.4		39.4		48.1		33.4		32.4		40.9		43.0
1973		44.0		49.5		39.3		42.6		31.7		37.2		36.2		36.8
1980		37.8		44.2		36.0		37.8		30.5		35.3		31.4		32.2
Services	1871	14.0	1882	22.0	1866	20.0	1911	45.0	1870	25.0	1877	11.0	1909	37.0	1910	28.0
	1954	28.0	1933	30.0	1950	33.0	1951	48.0	1950	53.0	1950	30.0	1947	48.0	1950	39.0
1957		29.1		35.7		37.9		46.4		55.2		39.0		45.1		41.5
1965		32.8		38.7		42.9		48.7		60.5		44.1		50.2		45.6
1973		38.6		43.0		48.5		54.5		64.2		49.4		57.0		56.1
1980		47.9		50.3		55.3		59.6		65.9		54.2		64.6		62.2

Sources: J. CORNWALL, Modern Capitalism, p. 17
OECD, Historical Statistics, 1960–1982, pp. 46–7

the agricultural sector lagged far behind those in industry and in services (Table 18). Since this gap hardly closed at all during the post-war period, the flow of labour out of agriculture and towards other sectors continued on a large scale.[39]

Table 18 *Income and Employment in Agriculture in Various Western Countries between 1953–5, 1959–61, and 1965–7*

	1953–5		1959–61		1965–7	
	A %	B	A %	B	A %	B
Austria	41	920	42	798	39	662
Belgium	86	337	100	299	110	218
Canada	49	971	47	796	69	668
Denmark	70	338	62	365	57	315
France	n.a.	4,639	39	4,191	47	3,341
West Germany	40	4,182	47	3,630	45	2,768
Italy	50	7,453	46	6,540	49	4,656
Netherlands	86	521	90	465	91	376
Norway	45	330	43	300	40	242
Sweden	52	553	49	524	54	387
United Kingdom	104	1,045	95	1,002	106	818
United States	54	6,283	53	5,408	60	4,061

Notes: A: Income in agriculture as a percentage of average income in the rest of the economy per employed person
B: Employment in agriculture in thousands
Source: J. CORNWALL, *Modern Capitalism*, p. 51

THE POST-WAR LABOUR SUPPLY, SEEN QUALITATIVELY

The flexibility of the labour supply is determined not only by quantity but also by quality. Many economists, influenced by Theodore W. Schultz,[40] began during the 1960s to pay attention to efforts by various Western countries to improve the quality of the work-force. Research indicated that in the United States investment by the community in 'educational capital' had a very positive effect on economic growth. In Europe too, improvements in human capital made a substantial contribution to post-war growth (Table 12).

Such improvements do not represent a new phenomenon. It is generally accepted that education and training had a perceptible effect on the general economic development of the West from the 1920s onwards. Denison's calculations showed that during the period 1929–48 in the United States, education contributed 0.41

per cent to the general yearly growth rate of 2.49 per cent.[41] The statistics that Maddison published on the education of the working population in thirteen OECD countries point implicitly to a watershed occurring around the First World War. In 1870 the average length of education had been 3 to 4 years and many workers could neither read nor write. By 1950 the average duration had risen to 8.2 years.[42]

The significance of investment in education and training for economic growth appeared to increase after the Second World War. The contribution of education to the post-war American rate of growth was 0.36 per cent for the period 1948–53, 0.4 per cent for 1953–64, 0.37 per cent for 1964–9, 0.5 per cent for 1969–73 and 0.67 per cent for 1973–6.[43] Despite general improvements in education and training after the First World War and further improvements since the Second World War, there remain differences in the quality of human capital between different countries. It is precisely these differences which are regarded as a major explanation of the continuing lag in productivity of Western Europe and Japan in relation to the United States after the Second World War.[44] How real is this post-war 'educational gap' and has there been no catching-up movement in this field?

During the 1950s and the 1960s a general rise in expenditure on education took place in all Western countries. This rise was not only absolute but also relative, in the sense that the amount spent on education grew faster than GNP. This development is all the more impressive in the light of the huge increase in Western GNP during the same period (Table 19).

Again, during the same two decades, the United States continued to devote a greater proportion of its GNP to education than any other OECD country.[45] The United States maintained this lead despite the fact that all the other OECD countries increased their educational spending as a proportion of GNP. Western European countries and Japan extended their secondary education in depth and breadth and thereby created at this level a system of mass education. The United States had already largely achieved this and was extending its structure of higher education, a development that in Western Europe and Japan took place generally from the 1970s onwards. In 1976 the average length of education that Americans between the ages of twenty-five and sixty-four had received was still somewhat longer than in Western Europe and Japan. In the United

Table 19 *Total Expenditure on Education as a Proportion of GNP,*
1955–64
(percentages and indices)

	1955	1960	1964	Index of increase in expenditure 1955–64 (1955 = 100)	Index of real increase in GNP 1955–64 (1955 = 100)
	(1)	(2)	(3)	(4)	(5)
United States	4.1	5.3	6.2	151	138
Belgium[a]	3.0	4.5	4.3	143	139
France	2.9	3.4	4.3	148	156
West Germany	2.8	3.0	3.4	118	171
Italy	3.3	4.5	5.4[b]	164	161
Netherlands[a]	3.6	4.7	5.7	158	139
United Kingdom	3.2	4.1	4.9	153	133
Sweden[a]	4.4	5.0	5.7[c]	130	146
Canada	3.0	4.5	5.8	193	142
Japan[a]	4.4	4.1	5.3[d]	120	234

Notes: [a] Only public expenditure
       [b] Private expenditure: estimate based on 1960 figure
       [c] 1962
       [d] 1963

Source: OECD, *Gaps in Technology*, p. 32

States it had increased from 10.5 years in 1960–2 to 11.6 years in
1976. In that same year the comparable figure for Japan was 10.42
years, Britain 10.41, France 9.87, West Germany 9.36, and Sweden
9.33.[46]

The post-war lead of the United States in the area of higher
education can be deduced from still other statistical sources. Of the
total American population in 1963, 2.4 per cent had received higher
education, whereas the respective figure for Japan was 0.9 per cent,
France 0.8, West Germany and Sweden 0.7, and Italy 0.5.[47] The
gap was still not closed in 1976. The average duration of higher
education for the entire American population between the ages of
twenty-five and sixty-four comprised 1.05 years. In other Western
countries the equivalent figure was much less: in Sweden 0.65
years, Belgium 0.62, France 0.56, Japan 0.44, Italy 0.24 and West
Germany 0.23.[48] To look at it another way, at the beginning of the
1960s 17 per cent of the American labour force consisted of academic

and managerial personnel as against 10 per cent in 'Europe of the Six' (France, West Germany, Italy, and the Benelux countries) and 11 per cent in Britain.[49] The share of university graduates in this occupational group was significantly higher in the United States than in Western Europe or Japan. The proportion of managerial workers in the total labour force was also considerably higher. In contrast, the proportion of engineers and technical personnel in the working population was slightly lower in the United States than in Europe of the Six and in Britain. Nevertheless, in respect to manufacturing industry, the proportion of academics and management personnel was clearly higher in the United States than elsewhere and the number of engineers and higher technical personnel was also relatively greater.[50] In the American service sector these groups were relatively smaller. Research thus confirms the hypothesis that although Western Europe is richer than the United States in the field of technical personnel, the Americans make more efficient use of their resources.

Two other conclusions regarding higher education must be mentioned. During the 1960s about 12 per cent of American students in higher education attended a business school. At that time the teaching of business administration at university level in Western Europe and Japan was still rather primitive. This would help to explain the post-war managerial gap between the American and other Western economies. In addition, interest in the various branches of the natural sciences was not evenly spread in the West. In Europe and especially Britain there was a preference for university courses in the applied sciences leading to technological degrees. The United States, on the other hand, produced relatively more graduates in the pure sciences.[51] Thus Western European countries after the war began to close the gap between themselves and the Americans in the area of higher technological education but not in the area of pure science, where the American lead seemed to lengthen. These findings support the hypothesis that, in industrial terms, Western Europe and Japan found themselves lagging far behind American technology immediately after the Second World War and that the subsequent catching-up movement was the most dynamic source of their economic growth. But the necessary technological advances were not characterized by wholly new techniques and original innovations – that is, rolling back the frontier of world knowledge – but by concrete application and improvement of already existing knowledge, sometimes called 'improvement engineering'.[52]

Another aspect of the technological gap was the problem of the migration of highly educated personnel to the United States. How important was immigration into the United States of researchers and engineers from the rest of the world? Statistics for the period 1956–66 show that a yearly average of 135,000 economically active immigrants settled in the United States. In 1956 13 per cent of these had received higher education and by 1963 this figure had risen to 20 per cent, where it stabilized. Graduates in pure and applied sciences accounted for about one-quarter of this 20 per cent (4.6 per cent in 1966). Since in the United States at that time less than 2 per cent of the working population held degrees in pure or applied science, immigration had a positive impact on the level of education of the American work-force. A similar conclusion can be reached when one looks at recent engineering graduates during this period. In 1963 and 1964 the number of engineers that emigrated to the United States amounted to more than 10 per cent of the number of engineers domestically produced in the same years.[53]

During this period Europe provided about 40 per cent of these highly educated immigrants into the United States, the lion's share coming from Britain. Indeed Britain provided the Americans with an increasing proportion of its most qualified researchers. No less than 5.2 per cent of the Britons who took a doctorate in pure sciences in 1956 emigrated to the United States. In 1964 this had risen to 10.4 per cent. The phrase 'brain drain' was often heard, and the exodus was undoubtedly a real problem for Britain, although less so for other countries.[54] The emigration of highly qualified labour to the United States clearly made a positive contribution to American growth but its significance should not be exaggerated. Furthermore, Harry Johnson has justifiably pointed out that the international integration of the market for highly educated researchers and engineers has considerably improved the efficiency of world scientific research, either pure or applied.[55] The American contribution to the progress of education and research in the world has been vital.

Naturally the American lead in technology cannot be explained solely in terms of education, science, and the brain drain. Other factors must also be considered, especially the organization of management and the way industrial research was conducted. Moreover, education is not exclusively a managerial investment, independent of income and demand. As soon as general prosperity exceeds a certain level, a demand for higher education is created that is no longer closely related to the actual needs of the economy. During the 1970s the number of university students in social sciences grew more than proportionately, not because the economic need was greater but rather because students had a greater interest in the human and social aspects of society.

3. THE LABOUR RESERVE AS A BASIS FOR EXPLAINING GROWTH

THE LEWIS MODEL AND ITS APPLICATION FOR THE INDUSTRIAL WEST

Some scholars, in particular Charles P. Kindleberger, regard the flexibility of the labour force as the decisive variable in explaining the differences in international growth rates in the West during the 1950s and 1960s.[56]

This thesis is based on the dual-development models worked out by economic theorists, of which the one by Arthur Lewis, a Nobel prize-winner, is the best known.[57] The following analysis will be based on the Lewis model.

The Lewis model presupposes, in the first place, a high degree of labour flexibility. It assumes in addition that the industrial sector plays a critical role in the process of economic growth, and this implies that a considerable degree of importance should be attached to the influence of capital, technological advances and entrepreneurship. The model also stresses the unbalanced nature of growth. The phenomenon of economic development is thus explained by the fact that labour and capital are unequally rewarded in different sectors of the economy. It is precisely this unequal return on production factors that stimulates flexibility in the labour supply and sets dynamic growth in motion.

The Lewis model divides the economy into two main sections: agriculture, where land and labour are the dominant factors of production, and industry, where capital and labour are dominant. In the agricultural sector of the model a labour surplus exists and labour productivity is extremely low; indeed marginal product is zero, which means that one less worker does not reduce general production. Wages are thus also worryingly low and fluctuate around subsistence levels. In industry, by contrast, there is no labour surplus. The amount of employed labour is a function of available capital, the level of technology, and the demand for manufactured goods. The productivity of industrial labour is clearly higher than that of agricultural labour. Wages in industry remain low, owing to the relatively elastic supply of labour from the agricultural sector; but they are nevertheless higher than in agriculture, in order to attract labour off the farms and to compensate for the higher living costs in urban areas.

A favourable change in the industrial sector – for example, an increase in demand for a country's exports – will raise the demand for industrial workers. This brings no particular problems, since the elasticity of the supply of labour (out of the agricultural sector) ensures that industrial wages barely rise. Industrial profits do rise, owing to the stability of wages and the achievement of new economies of scale. These profits rise not only in absolute terms but also as a proportion of national income. On the other hand rising employment in the industrial sector enlarges the total volume of wage incomes, which increases the domestic demand for industry's products. The upward spiral develops further and companies invest part of their profits in extending capacity. Rising profits, then, have a dynamic effect on growth.

Meanwhile, back on the farm the departure of a large number of workers initially causes no difficulties; but ultimately the point will be reached when the marginal productivity of agricultural labour begins to go up. As soon as this marginal productivity becomes higher than the cost of subsistence wage levels, agricultural employers will be obliged to pay higher wages in order to restrict the outflow of labour. Then if industrial entrepreneurs wish to attract more labour out of rural areas they too must offer higher wages. Their profits are now reduced because their costs are increased through the higher wage bills. As a result, the industrial entrepreneur has less to spare on investment and the domestic supply of industrial products loses its earlier flexibility. In these circumstances, a further increase in exports will only be possible through wage rises and higher production costs which on one side stimulate imports of food and other products, and on the other gradually undermine exports. The effect on the balance of payments is disastrous and growth is accordingly checked.

The Lewis model makes a distinction between two types of growth.

In industry, growth is chiefly generated by the application of additional labour. In agriculture, growth is chiefly generated by an outflow of labour. The elimination of surplus labour from the agricultural sector leads to a rise in marginal productivity of the remaining work-force. Before long this rise brings wage increases which drive up the cost of agricultural labour and make its replacement with machines a more attractive proposition. Growth in the agricultural sector is now fully under way. The two types of growth also cover two different investment functions. For industry, investment largely consists of capital *widening*. The investment function is essentially Keynesian and depends on greater demand for end-products which, given constant wage levels, gives rise to higher profits and more investment. In contrast the investment function in agriculture is more Schumpeterian, investment being determined rather by lower profits than by higher ones. Higher wage costs reduce profits and so an investment decision is taken to replace men with machines – capital *deepening* – in order to lower costs and raise profits.

Lewis developed his model explicitly for primitive, underdeveloped economies where the assumption of an agricultural labour surplus can be regarded as realistic. According to Lewis himself this assumption is untenable in respect of the modern industrial economies of the West. Other economists, such as Kindleberger, believe it is tenable although they recognize that some of the concepts relating to the supply of labour must be adapted in order to enhance the relevance of the model.[58] Kindleberger outlines the five chief components which determine the flexibility of the labour supply. The first is the transfer of labour from one sector to another, according to the original Lewis conception. In other words, a modern industrial sector absorbs disguised unemployment in the agricultural and artisan sectors. The other components are the elimination of open unemployment in the towns, an increasing level of participation, such as an increase in the number of economically active women, a strong population growth, and immigration.

Kindleberger has significantly broadened the concept of the labour reserve and has undoubtedly made it better applicable to the Western economy. But can it give a clear insight into the flexibility of the post-war labour supply? Can it help to answer the question of whether flexibility of the labour supply has been a crucial factor in the structural changes so necessary for rapid economic growth?

KINDLEBERGER'S EXPLANATION OF WESTERN EUROPEAN
GROWTH

Kindleberger applied the Lewis model to the post-war economic development of Europe.[59] He calculated the rate of growth of GNP and of the employment of labour and capital in a number of European countries during part of the 1950s and also in the period 1959–63 (Table 20).

He found that a rapidly rising rate of production was usually accompanied by a marked increase in the working population and in capital and that a slowly rising rate of production was usually accompanied by a slowly rising rate in the working population and in capital. Kindleberger divided countries into four categories. There were countries which positively confirmed the relevance of the Lewis model, with high growth rates of GNP and a high additional input of labour and capital. Prime examples were West Germany, Italy, Switzerland, and the Netherlands. There were also countries which confirmed the Lewis model, but in the reverse sense; that is, they attained low rates of growth of GNP with a low additional input of labour and capital. Examples here were the United Kingdom, Belgium, Sweden, Norway, and Denmark. On the other hand, some countries which fulfilled the Lewis concept of a considerable labour surplus in agriculture had fairly high growth rates of GNP and high additional inputs of labour but the increase in investment remained strikingly low. Mediterranean countries (Spain, Portugal, Southern Italy, Greece, Yugoslavia, and Turkey) belonged to this category. These countries not only provided labour for their own industrial sectors but also for those of other European countries and they thus functioned as a labour reserve for all of Western Europe. Finally, France and Austria did not accord with the Lewis model. Although they grew fast, the additional input of labour was only slight. Both countries therefore appeared to be exceptions to the rule.

Kindleberger concluded that the Lewis dual-development model forms an adequate explanation for Western Europe's growth after the Second World War. In general, the additional input of labour provided a decisive explanatory variable. The West German 'economic miracle',[60] according to Kindleberger, gives the clearest confirmation of his hypothesis. Rapid population growth, the presence of huge numbers of unemployed workers, the arrival of millions

Table 20 *Annual Growth Rates of Gross Domestic Product, Labour Force, Labour Productivity, and Gross Investment Ratio, 1959–63 compared with 1954–9*
(percentages)

	GNP		Working population (average annual rate of growth)		Labour productivity (average annual rate of growth)		Gross investment quotient	
	1954–9	1959–63	1949–59	1959–63	1949–59	1959–63	1954–9	1959–63
West Germany	6.9	5.4	1.6	0.8	5.7	4.6	21.7	23.9
Italy	5.7	6.2	1.1	0.1	4.8	6.1	23.0	26.1
Netherlands	3.7	5.2	1.2	1.4	3.6	3.7	24.4	26.1
Austria	5.7	5.2	1.1	—	4.8	5.2	24.1	25.8
France	4.6	5.8	0.1	0.7	4.3	5.1	20.2	21.7
Sweden	3.1	3.8	0.5	1.2	2.9	2.6	22.2	24.3
Belgium	2.0	3.8	0.3	0.5	2.7	3.3	18.0	19.1
United Kingdom	2.0	2.8	0.6	0.9	1.8	1.7	16.7	19.3

Source: C. P. KINDLEBERGER, *Europe's Postwar Growth*, p. 27

of refugees, especially from East Germany, and later the mass immigration of workers from Mediterranean countries, all contributed to the existence of a big labour reserve which kept the labour supply elastic. West Germany could thus for a period of years respond to and absorb a powerful export demand for capital goods and consumer goods, without experiencing price and wage inflation. On the other hand, Kindleberger noted a reduction in West German growth during the period 1959–63. He ascribed this to a drying-up of the labour surplus. The fact that this development did not rapidly lead to sharp rises in wages and prices and to balance-of-payments problems was due to various circumstances. The unions had a moderating influence, and the propensity of wage and salary earners to save ensured that domestic demand did not rise too sharply and exert too great an upward pressure on prices. When profits did start to fall as a result of the gradual wage rises and increasing costs, investment financed out of own resources was indeed curbed. Yet the propensity of workers to save, among other factors, compensated for this and facilitated the capital deepening which was able to ease labour-market problems.

Kindleberger believed that the post-war development of Italy confirmed his hypothesis as well. In this respect, following the lead of Vera Lutz, he made a distinction between Northern and Southern Italy.[61] In the north the industrial sector predominated, and in the south it was the primitive agricultural sector. The south also held a sizeable labour surplus which could be drawn on not only by Northern Italy but also by other Western European countries. Kindleberger also distinguished among industries in the north. A first group comprised the more traditional industries, very labour-intensive and using somewhat limited technology. Growth there was fast, as was the increase in employment. The influence of the elastic labour supply was particularly important in this group of labour-intensive industries, especially between 1950 and 1959. The second group of industries made more use of advanced technology. During the same period this group grew considerably but employment developed slowly. Most firms in this group had worked below capacity during the war and their first objective was to eliminate their own internal concealed unemployment. Besides, their technology had become backward during the war and they hoped to catch up again via labour-saving investment. Both objectives had a negative influence on total employment in this second group of industries when the post-war recovery got under way. By about 1960, however, the influence of these factors came to an end and, to achieve further growth, even these advanced-technology sectors had to recruit additional labour. The engineering industries, for example, give a clear illustration of this evolution. In two years – 1960 and 1961 – they took on more workers than they had done in the previous eight years together, and during the period 1959–63 the Italian labour reserve was gradually exhausted. In contrast to German wage and salary earners, the Italians chose not to save their higher income but to spend it immediately. The explosive rise in consumption led directly to the overheating of the economy, the deterioration of the balance of payments, and a serious currency crisis.

In the Netherlands, the post-war labour surplus was primarily based on the powerful growth of the working population. This was countered by the government's policy on emigration, which was designed to get rid of surplus labour, and above all by the lack of capital deepening, which followed immediately after the war. In consequence, by the 1960s the labour reserve was totally exhausted. The wage and price inflation which followed, in 1962–3, led the government to introduce a new policy initiative to increase the elasticity of the labour supply. Accordingly the replacement of labour by capital was encouraged and the recruitment of foreign workers supported.[62]

Britain is the prime example of a country that conforms to the Lewis model in an inverse sense. Slow post-war growth was combined with a low additional input of labour and capital. Traditionally, most economists seeking to explain Britain's poor growth achievements have concentrated not on the labour reserve but on the Keynesian aspect of demand. Their analysis had many variants but all pointed to poor demand management by the government.[63] Some economists believed that the level of demand was insufficiently supported by the government. Others believed that demand, on the contrary, was too strong and that this caused balance-of-payments problems which could only be handled by a stop-go policy.[64] This pressure in demand was chiefly due to the government policy of full employment which had the effect of eliminating the tempering influence of the labour reserve. Therefore Britain's economic growth after the war cannot be explained solely by factors of demand. Labour has also to be taken into account. If growth in Britain could not be activated by a large labour reserve, replacing labour by capital would have been a solution. Through inertia and conservatism, industry did not respond with investment designed to promote the capital deepening which would have achieved this.[65] The unions were also seen to have constituted an obstacle, by artificially restricting the flexibility of the labour supply, that is, by hindering inter-sectoral mobility of labour and thus encouraging excessive wage rises. The high level of concealed unemployment in British Rail was usually held up as a case in point.[66] Some economists argued that the emigration of workers, especially the earlier mentioned brain drain, exacerbated the labour scarcity in the expanding sectors and thus hindered growth. The supporters of this hypothesis advocated a liberal government policy in respect to immigration into Britain from the Commonwealth countries. The vicious circle the British economy was in, it was held, could only be broken by attracting cheap overseas labour, skilled and unskilled, and by tax concessions for stimulating industrial research and encouraging capital deepening.

The low growth rate of the Belgian economy during the 1950s and at the start of the 1960s can only partly be explained by the labour supply. As a small country with a restricted domestic market, Belgium had geared itself towards the export market.[67] In order to take full advantage of the exports of its heavy industry, Belgium, among other things, had made a speciality of standardized, semi-finished goods produced according to the most modern technology. In this manner the country achieved economies of scale which lowered costs and made Belgian products competitive throughout the world. But further technological progress in these traditional heavy industries could not be easily attained in the short term, and further expansion of export demand could only be met through a greater labour input. The same limitations held for the traditional textile sector, where a defensive investment programme was carried out, emphasizing product differentiation and additional labour inputs. Although a sizeable labour reserve was available in Belgium, growth remained strikingly low. Kindleberger regarded structural factors and weak export demand as the main reasons for this in the 1950s, but he thought that the Lewis model was applicable in explaining the considerable improvement in growth during the period 1959–63. The creation of the EEC and the opening of its large market generated a dynamic export demand. Belgium was able to respond speedily to this by absorbing open and concealed unemployment and bringing in a large number of guest workers from Italy, Turkey, and the Iberian Peninsula.

The countries around the Mediterranean formed, immediately after the Second World War, an area of still relatively primitive economic development and held a considerable labour surplus.[68] Kindleberger thus counted the Iberian Peninsula, Southern Italy, Yugoslavia, Greece, Turkey and the North African countries as the equivalent of the primitive agricultural sector in the Lewis model. Apart from emigration to North-Western Europe, the labour surplus was employed domestically to build up the industrial and service sectors. Tourism from the 1960s onwards created a rising amount of employment, not only in hotels, bars, and the like but also in the extension of infrastructure. Even so, emigration out of the Mediterranean area continued, partly because necessary structural changes could not be realized immediately and partly because the development mechanism did not always work as the Lewis model suggested. The profits made by modern industry in the Mediterranean area and the savings sent home by expatriate workers often appeared to have been inefficiently invested. In the mean time demand rose for advanced consumer durables which could usually be supplied via imports only. Above all, emigration sapped the dynamism of these Mediterranean countries. The most skilled workers never came back; the less skilled did and often started their own small businesses but showed little interest in applying modern techniques. In contrast, the large agricultural concerns, which were very numerous around the Mediterranean, became so mechanized that the exit of workers from agriculture took on major proportions. A large part of the profits made from the increased productivity was not invested in modern industrial or commercial sectors in the region itself but rather in the shares of Western European or American companies or in the bonds of the foreign governments. Such factors had the effect of making economic development in the Mediterranean area much slower than theory had suggested it would be. One positive factor, nevertheless, was the psychological influence which resulted from the increasing contact between modern and primitive sectors. Migration to Western Europe, the development of domestic modern industry, and the growth of tourism gradually broke through the centuries-old isolationism and traditionalism.

This gave rise to a new attitude towards consumption and a new mentality regarding innovation and progress.

In France and Austria, Kindleberger found exceptions to his hypothesis. During the 1950s and 1960s France experienced rapid growth despite an initially stagnant working population.[69] Kindleberger pointed to the exertions of the goverment in the field of economic planning and the rising military budget due to wars in Indochina and Algeria as causes of France's successful development. Still, in my view, the influence of the flexibility of the labour supply cannot be disregarded. The total number of small agricultural and artisan enterprises fell by 1.25 million between 1954 and 1962. The rate of this fall continued afterwards. The immigration of guest workers, mostly from North Africa, was systematically encouraged by the government from 1956 onwards. Meanwhile the war in Algeria came to an end, reducing the number of troops by 600,000 and stimulating the return of 1 million Algerian French (*Pieds Noirs*) to the mainland. Many Algerians who feared the new regime also settled in France. Finally the increase in the birth rate gradually had a positive impact on the size of the French working population.

In the non-European countries of the industrialized West too, the employment of additional labour appears to have been important for post-war growth. Denison's calculations give the first clear indication. In Canada, Australia, and New Zealand, immigration remained substantial. In Japan, repatriation was initially very large and traditional agriculture formed an important labour reserve. The influence of these factors on growth was undoubtedly very positive. In the United States the situation is not so clear. Legal as well as illegal immigration was considerable, as brought out earlier, and there was also the open and concealed unemployment of the black community in addition to the natural growth of population. But this great flexibility of the American labour supply after the Second World War accompanied only slow growth, at least till the start of the 1960s.

The Lewis model then does not provide an exclusive explanatory framework for post-war growth in the West. There was also criticism of Kindleberger's model in respect to Europe. For one thing, as already mentioned, the slow growth in Belgium during the 1950s was not due to a scarcity of labour (indeed there was much open and concealed unemployment) but to the structure of investment.[70] In Britain the problem lay in faulty demand management rather

Table 21 *The Growth Rate of Employment in the Non-Agricultural Sector compared with the Growth Rate of Total Output, in Selected Western Countries, 1950–79* (percentages)

1950–9

	Yearly average percentage change	
	Civilian employment in non-agricultural activities	Total output
FAST-GROWING COUNTRIES		
Italy	4.6 (1954–60)	5.8
Japan	4.1 (1953–60)	9.5
Turkey	3.5 (1951–60)	n.a.
West Germany	3.4	7.8
Canada	3.0	3.9
Spain	2.3	5.2
Switzerland	2.2	4.4
Denmark	2.2 (1955–60)	3.3
MIDDLE GROUP		
United States	1.7	3.2
Netherlands	1.7	4.7
Portugal	1.4	3.9
Norway	1.1	3.2
France	1.1 (1954–60)	4.6
Austria	1.2 (1951–60)	5.8

1960–9

	Yearly average percentage change	
	Civilian employment in non-agricultural activities	Total output
FAST-GROWING COUNTRIES		
Turkey	3.7	n.a.
Japan	3.2	10.5
Canada	3.5	5.6
Spain	2.8	7.5
Denmark	2.3	4.8
United States	2.2	4.3
MIDDLE GROUP		
Switzerland	2.0	4.5
France	1.9	5.8
Netherlands	1.7	5.1
Sweden	1.7	4.6
Norway	1.6	5.0
Portugal	1.3	6.2
Italy	1.2	5.7
Belgium	1.2	4.9

1970–9

	Yearly average percentage change	
	Civilian employment in non-agricultural activities	Total output
FAST-GROWING COUNTRIES		
Turkey	3.5	5.7
Canada	3.5	4.2
United States	2.5	3.0
Norway	2.4[1]	4.7
Republic of Ireland	2.0	4.3
MIDDLE GROUP		
Portugal	1.8	4.9
Japan	1.7	4.9
Italy	1.4	3.2
Denmark	1.3	2.4
Austria	1.3	3.7
France	1.3	3.7

SLOW-GROWING
COUNTRIES

United Kingdom	0.8	2.7
Belgium	0.6	2.9
Republic of Ireland	−0.8 (1951–60)	1.7

SLOW-GROWING
COUNTRIES

Austria	0.5	4.7
West Germany	0.8	4.8
United Kingdom	0.3	2.8

SLOW-GROWING
COUNTRIES

Belgium	0.4	3.3
Spain	0.4	3.8
Netherlands	0.3	2.9
United Kingdom	0.0	1.8
West Germany	−0.1	2.8
Switzerland	−0.2	1.3

Note: [1] 1972–80
Sources: Own calculations
OECD, *Labour Force Statistics, 1969–1980*

than in labour supply problems. Furthermore, if a longer period (1950–70) is taken instead of the one Kindleberger himself used (1950–63), still more irreconcilable issues come to light. For example, both West Germany and Italy could no longer be included in the group of countries characterized by a flexible labour supply.[71]

A more fundamental criticism can be levelled at Kindleberger's point of departure. Was growth in Western Europe hindered by the exhaustion of labour supply in the course of the 1960s as it was stimulated by the surplus of labour in the course of the 1950s? Some analysts have radically disagreed. From the 1960s, according to them, labour flexibility was no longer a crucial factor in the economic growth of the industrialized nations of Western Europe. These countries now had the means to relieve their labour-market problems by technological innovation and by replacing labour with capital.[72] Difficulties with the labour supply were therefore solved by changing the ratio between labour and capital. West Germany and Japan were given as prototypes for this type of development.[73] Other economists, such as John Cornwall, were more moderate in their approach to Kindleberger's reasoning. The flexibility of the labour supply was an important growth factor, in the first as well as in the second decade after the Second World War (Table 21).[74] When entrepreneurs in manufacturing industry needed additional labour for expansion, they could recruit workers immediately, or relatively soon, from domestic agricultural, traditional or service sectors, from school-leavers, from women prepared to take on a job, or from abroad. As proof of this, it is demonstrated that wage differentials among various industrial sectors in the West after the war have hardly been reduced.[75] Hence a real tightening of the labour market did not take place.

THE MORE STRUCTURAL VISIONS OF J. CORNWALL AND G. VACIAGO

Just as Kindleberger broadened Lewis's concept of the labour reserve,[76] Cornwall broadened Kindleberger's. The primitive sector from which labour could be drawn by Western Europe was not limited to the domestic agricultural sector or the Mediterranean area. Instead, the potential source included all domestic sectors where low productivity and low wages were prominent features. If employment in more productive sectors grew faster than employment in the economy in general, then the transfer of surplus labour out of less productive sectors was an important explanation of international differences in growth rates.[77] Cornwall tested his hypothesis for twelve OECD countries and reached highly satisfactory results (Table 22). In Austria, Denmark, France, West Germany, Italy, Japan, and Norway during the period 1950 to 1970, employment in high-productivity sectors grew faster than total employment, and the general growth rate of the economy was high. In Belgium, Canada, the Netherlands, the United Kingdom, and the United States, by contrast, employment in the most productive areas did not grow as fast as total employment, and the general growth rate of the economy was low.

Essential for the application of this model is the assumption that significant wage differentials exist between various economic sectors. These differentials have a permanent character and indicate permanent differences in labour productivity. Expressed in these terms, a labour surplus exists when groups of workers in low-productive sectors, receiving low wages, are prepared to move to new sectors. It is necessary that the general inter-sectoral wage structure be so rigid as to be nearly unaffected by the mobility of the above-mentioned group of workers. In other words, the mechanism which serves to relocate labour among different economic sectors must not produce a general equalization of wages. In addition, the demand for labour in industrial sectors with high productivity and high wages must increase faster than that in the rest of the economy. The mechanism for transferring the labour surplus is thus more complex than would first appear.[78] It is closely linked to the problem of structural change. Will the labour reserve be employed in the most productive sectors of manufacturing industry or not?[79] Are there inertias which prevent the transfer of labour from less productive to more productive ones? Can these inertias be broken down by capital deepening and the large-scale replacement of labour by capital? Can structural changes give the flexibility of the labour supply a new dynamism?

Giacomo Vaciago tried to answer these questions through a synthesis of the quantitative and structural approaches to the labour supply.[80] In common with others, he started by looking at differences in growth rates in Western countries since the war. These differences were substantial during the 1950s, in any case more so than before the

Table 22 *Average Annual Rates of Growth of Total, Manufacturing and Industrial Employment in Selected Western Countries, 1951–73 (rates of growth respectively E_t, E_m, E_i) (percentages)*

	E_t	E_m	E_i
Austria			
1951–70	− 0.40[a]	0.80	0.05[a]
1951–73	− 0.55[a]	0.73	0.24[a]
Belgium			
1951–70	0.52	0.49	− 0.11[a]
1951–73	0.53	0.41	− 0.18[a]
Canada			
1951–69	2.36	2.20	1.78[a]
1951–73	2.45	2.13	1.85[a]
Denmark			
1957–69	1.33	2.27	1.84
1957–73	1.30	n.a.	0.95
France			
1951–69	0.50	1.01	0.81[a]
1951–73	0.51	1.06	0.96[a]
West Germany			
1951–70	1.18	2.84	0.88[b]
1951–73	1.01	2.38	0.62[b]
Italy			
1951–70	0.64	2.21	1.26[b]
1951–73	0.50	1.93	0.99[b]
Japan			
1953–69	1.56	4.62	3.70[a]
1953–73	1.46	4.02	3.39[a]
Netherlands			
1951–70	1.19	1.19	0.76[b]
1951–73	1.01	0.70	− 0.05[b]
Norway			
1951–60	0.38	0.89	0.76[b]
1951–73	0.79	0.65	0.64[b]
United Kingdom			
1951–69	0.38	0.39	− 0.04[a]
1951–73	0.25	− 0.25	− 0.70[a]
United States			
1951–69	1.44	1.16	1.20[a]
1951–73	1.53	0.97	1.02[a]

Notes: [a] 1957
[b] 1956
Source: J. CORNWALL, *Modern Capitalism*, p. 63

war. On the other hand, starting in the 1960s a certain convergence could be noted. How could these phenomena be used to explain growth? The high growth rates achieved in some countries were in the first place due to a catching-up movement. The reduction of the technological gap allowed these countries to benefit from the economies of scale in a whole series of areas which in turn facilitated spectacular rises in growth rates. The strength of this movement was determined by the initial technological development the respective countries had reached.

Vaciago took this idea still further. The transition to a more highly developed structure did not take place according to a fixed formula or to a predictable schema. Flexibility or inflexibility of the economic system could influence the transition to economic maturity in very different ways. An initial period of supergrowth, which took place simultaneously in a group of countries as a result of a catching-up movement, could, in any of these countries, generate specific forces leading to differences in later growth rates. Everything depended on the flexibility of the collective system which, in turn, was based on institutional, cultural, material and psychological factors. Some countries during the 1950s and the start of the 1960s accelerated their rates of growth by means of an elastic labour supply. This acceleration brought about an autonomous growth dynamic which, through technological progress, was able to neutralize the later exhaustion of labour reserves. Growth was therefore maintained, but now was due to rises in productivity achieved by capital deepening in leading sectors. Italy, West Germany, and Japan provide good illustrations of such institutional flexibility in the 1960s. Other supergrowers in the 1950s did not possess the same institutional resilience and their growth rates weakened. When the countries in this latter group found they could not permanently rely on an elastic labour supply for expanding sectors, their institutional flexibility proved unable to realize enough capital deepening. For mature economies such as the United States, during the 1950s and 1960s there was no question of a catching-up movement. An acceleration in the rate of growth could no longer be attained by transformations within the same technological structure; that is, by switching from capital widening to capital deepening but at the same time keeping within the traditional production system based on electro-mechanical technology. Instead, an acceleration could only be brought about by extending technological knowledge in the area of electronics and integrating this sufficiently into the economy. Such innovation, however, entails far greater structural flexibility than that shown by Western Europe and Japan in their post-war growth.

4. GROWTH AND THE EMPLOYMENT OF CAPITAL

THE IMPORTANCE OF GROSS INVESTMENT

That capital formation has a decisive influence on the process of economic development has long been accepted by everyone. But recent studies have stressed that this axiom covers a much more complex problem than was formerly suspected.[81] It is not enough simply to accumulate capital; that is, add capital to existing stocks. In order to stimulate economic development, capital formation must also be introduced into the production structure in an optimal manner. It cannot be uncoupled from the availability of labour; moreover, the relationship between the price of labour and the price of capital must always be in equilibrium. Finally, capital formation requires competent entrepreneurship, most notably regarding the decision to invest. Capital formation as such implies the 'embodiment' of technology and this assumes a responsible and correct choice in the application of relevant technology to well-specified sectors having a strong growth potential. Also important in this respect is that entrepreneurs adequately control the day-to-day running of the company, being able to supervise general affairs and to respond to short-term developments.

In terms of capital formation, the post-war growth in the West was determined by the extension of capital and by the replacement of existing equipment with new and better equipment. Through this, production increased, as did productivity – both labour productivity (production per hour of labour) and capital productivity (production per unit of capital). Moreover, Wilfred E. Salter showed that there is continuous tension between the constant advance of technological progress in general and the slow, jerky adaptation process in industry.[82] Machines are durable, with a long life-expectancy, so that the incessant stream of new technology is not immediately incorporated in the total capital stock of industry. There is always a perceptible gap between the potential technological optimum of the total stock of capital goods and the real technological level it actually embodies. Salter illustrated his case with the example of productivity in American blast furnaces. In 1911 the average quantity of crude steel produced in 'best-practice plants' amounted to 0.313 tons per man-hour, whereas the industry average was 0.140 tons. In 1926 the respective figures had risen to 0.573 and

0.296 tons. Thus in 1911 the average labour productivity in this branch of industry was not even half the level achieved in the most modern firms at the same date, and another fifteen years were necessary for the average firms to catch up to that level; in the mean time, of course, the most modern firms had almost doubled their labour productivity and were again well ahead.[83]

According to Salter's hypothesis, an acceleration in the rate of gross investment (extension and replacement of capital) would correspondingly spur the rise in average labour and capital productivity. Such an acceleration would certainly reduce the difference between the potential technical optimum of the total capital stock and the level it actually represents. How can an acceleration in the rate of gross investment in a given economy be realized? This amounts to the structural question: how can the application of capital be further stimulated and how will this greater flexibility in respect to the supply of capital facilitate the structural changes which are so necessary to *perpetuate* the acceleration in the rate of investment?

Empirical research has shown that in the real economy there is often a connection between rapid growth in production and rapid growth in productivity (known as Verdoorn's Law). Industrial sectors in a given economy which score the highest production increases tend also to be the sectors where productivity grows fastest.[84] According to the hypothesis which has just been elaborated above, this is entirely logical. An increase in production assumes an increase in gross investment, by which the share of companies with the most advanced technology in any given sector rises. Productivity therefore increases sharply.

The virtuous circle of rising gross investment, leading to rapid production growth, leading to rapid productivity growth, leading to more rise in gross investment, was best achieved in the post-war period by the crucial manufacturing sector. Only when the growth rate of manufacturing in a given country exceeded that of GNP was the overall rate of growth high. Alternatively, when the growth of manufacturing was lower than overall growth, the overall growth was low.[85] Why was the stimulating effect of the above-mentioned virtuous circle on manufacturing so crucial for the economy as a whole? An initial explanation must undoubtedly be sought in the multiplicity of forward and backward linkages characterized in manufacturing. They form the bridge that enables manufacturing to be a decisive factor in the growth of production and productivity in many other economic sectors. Furthermore, manufacturing is the sector *par excellence* for the application of new technological improvements. It thus has great potential for the dynamic use of economies of scale and attracts, by the pressure of demand, much industrial research and technological investment.

The virtuous circle of rapid growth in production and productivity in manufacturing also has a dynamic effect in generating the transformation of economic structure. The embodiment of technological innovation in physical capital stands central to this concept, but it does not act in all countries at the same time and to the same extent. Some countries are particularly forward-looking and modern. In their most progressive sectors, average productivity lies nearer to optimal productivity (nearer the technological frontier) than in other countries. For those lagging countries, of course, there is a greater potential catching-up dynamic, which may have a stimulating effect on growth. As soon as the catching-up is realized, both groups have to depend on the integration of new technology for the realization of further growth. But the extension of the technological frontier can come up against problems of increasing saturation, especially when the advances are limited to particular sectors of manufacturing industry. In those sectors new gross investment will gradually decline, with a slowing effect on the total rate of growth. A *vicious* circle then comes about.

When a third group of countries, technologically backward in respect to the two other groups, realizes an extra catching-up movement in the very same sectors of manufacturing, then the adverse effect on gross investment in the more developed countries is still stronger. Deindustrialization is then not out of the question. Verdoorn's Law consequently represents no stable or absolute relationship. The experience of growth during the 1960s and 1970s has indeed shown that turning-points can be reached and countries can move in virtuous and vicious circles.

INDUSTRIALIZATION AND DEINDUSTRIALIZATION IN THE POST-WAR WEST

The Salter theory, stressing the significance of gross investment, has been empirically tested by Maddison against post-war economic growth.[86] His point of departure is the following. From the industrial census of 1967, it appears that in numerous sectors of American industry a clear gap existed between productivity of the most modern firms in a given sector and the general average productivity of the sector concerned as a whole. For all investigated sectors taken together the productivity of the most modern firms was 60 per cent higher than the general average. When the gap between the most modern and least modern firms in every sector was measured, the difference was still much larger. Thus, even in the technologically advanced economy of the United States after the Second World War, there was plenty of opportunity to raise the total rate of growth by increasing gross investment. During the period 1950–70, in comparison to the pre-war period, there was indeed an acceleration of gross investment in the United States. Nevertheless this acceleration was far from spectacular and it weakened considerably after 1970. The slow rate of growth can therefore be partially explained by the low level of American gross investment.

Maddison also tested the hypothesis that gross investment was the decisive influence in the catching-up movement in Western Europe and Japan during the 1950s and 1960s. If this hypothesis is correct, then this would explain the higher growth rate of these countries in relation to the United States. When an international comparison of the rate and development of labour productivity in the period 1870–1977 is made, the supremacy of the United States over the other parts of the West during the twentieth century is evident. Britain and Belgium could only with difficulty hold on to their lead over the United States until the end of the nineteenth century, a lead which they owed to their preceding the United States in industrialization.[87] Between 1900 and 1950 the general lead of the United States in respect of labour productivity was undeniable. American labour productivity was the highest in the world and, over the half-century as a whole, grew faster than anywhere else. Furthermore, empirical research has shown that before the Second World War the United States led the world in productivity for all economic sectors.[88] During the third quarter of the century the United States maintained its leading position but its productivity growth was clearly no longer the fastest in the world. Many other countries were engaged in their great catching-up act.

Important conclusions spring from the foregoing comparison. The American lead in labour productivity and the regularity of the increase point to a powerful growth in American gross investment during the first half of the twentieth century. Graph B confirms this hypothesis to the full. Increases in capital stocks during the first half of the century were indeed clearly higher in the United States than in the other industrial countries shown. The graphs moreover suggest that the American economy in the twentieth century kept up with technological advances and that this was mirrored in the application of these advances in the stocks of capital goods. For European countries and Japan, the problem of incorporating technological progress in the capital goods stock was totally different. The approaching of the technological frontier took place after the Second World War and was not direct but indirect. These countries executed a catching-up movement and could thus limit themselves to imitation rather than innovation in order to raise labour productivity. Naturally imitation did demand a specific capacity to innovate: the imitating country had to adapt American technology to its own relative prices for labour and capital, to the preferences and tastes of its own consumers, to its export potential and so on. These imitators had to have a good information structure as well, in order to absorb the stream of new techniques and products. Most of all they had to be specialists in improvement engineering. On the other hand, they could avoid many of the risks and much of the expense involved in product development. This meant that because of the catching-up movement the increase in capital productivity also followed a more favourable evolution in the imitating countries than in the innovating country. The employment of capital in Western Europe and Japan during the 1950s and 1960s certainly led to faster growth of GNP in these geographical areas than did the application of the same amount of capital in the United States.[89] Other factors also played a role. After the Second World War the use of machinery in terms of man-hours was clearly lower in the United States than in Western Europe and Japan.[90] In addition, technological progress in the United States in respect to applications for manufacturing industry and the service sector had reached a structural frontier. Innovations within the limits of traditional technology yielded only meagre returns, and initial costs of breaking through technological barriers were very high.

In Western Europe and in Japan gross investment after the Second World War grew impressively. The share of gross investment in total GNP rose significantly from 1950 to 1972. During the 1960s it reached a level of 26 per cent in West Germany and even 35.1 per

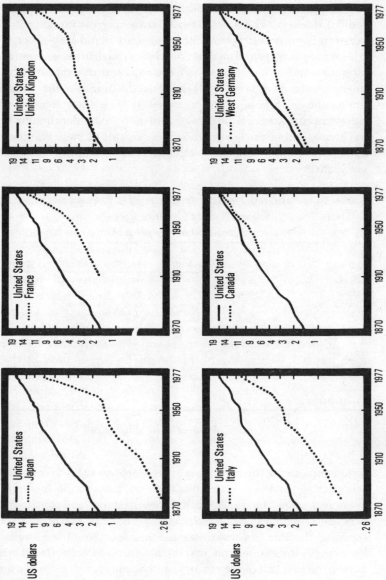

Graph B Gross Non-Residential Fixed Capital Stock per Man-Hour at 1970 US Prices, 1870–1977*

Note: *French and West German figures for years before 1950 based on movement in net stock
Source: A. MADDISON, 'Long Run Dynamics', p. 20

cent in Japan. In the United States, this share was barely 16.8 per cent (Table 23). The accelerated increase in gross investment in Western Europe and Japan had an obvious stimulating effect on labour productivity and on total economic growth in these countries after the war. Furthermore, when Cornwall compared the manufacturing growth of eleven OECD countries with that of the United States, the catching-up effect was very striking. Moreover, for all eleven countries the catching-up movement was considerable during the 1950s, and in the next decade there was still a clear statistical indicator of this influence, although its dynamism declined gradually.[91]

Table 23 *Total Gross Domestic Investment as a Proportion of GNP in Selected Western Countries, 1900–82*
(average annual percentage per subperiod)

| | Average for the periods | | | | |
	1900–13	1914–49	1950–60	1961–71	1972–82
Belgium	n.a.	n.a.	16.5	21.0	20.9
France	n.a.	n.a.	19.1	24.6	22.3
West Germany	n.a.	14.3	24.0	26.0	21.4
Italy	15.4	13.5	20.8	20.4	19.9
Japan	n.a.	n.a.	24.0	35.1	32.1
Netherlands	n.a.	n.a.	24.2	25.6	20.7
Norway	12.7	15.4	26.4	26.9	30.3
Sweden	12.3	15.5	21.3	23.0	20.4
United Kingdom	7.7	7.6	15.4	18.3	18.0
Canada	25.5	16.0	24.8	22.2	22.7
United States	20.6	14.7	19.1	16.8	18.2

Sources: J. CORNWALL, *Modern Capitalism*, p. 23
OECD, *Historical Statistics, 1960–1982*

The expansion of manufacturing in those eleven OECD countries was closely linked to the growth of the consumer-durable sector. In Western Europe, Japan, Australia, New Zealand, and some other Western economies after the Second World War, the market for consumer durables flourished owing to the rise of the affluent society. For the United States this market had already fully developed during the first half of the century, so that the growth dynamic for manufacturing had already burnt itself out. In the American post-war economy, emphasis shifted to the development of the service sector. At first no major productivity gains as a result of applying new technology were to be made here.[92] In consequence, American economic growth after the war, as far as manufacturing and services were concerned, appeared to be more labour-intensive than capital-intensive.

In agricultural development too there were also catching-up effects in the West. The American mechanization of agriculture was practically complete before the Second World War, but in Western Europe and Japan little progress had been made at this point. This meant that after the war Western Europe and Japan could achieve impressive gains in agricultural productivity, with a rate of growth far higher than in the United States, simply by mechanizing agriculture – that is, by an accelerated expansion of gross investment. The Second Agricultural Revolution was, of course, also very important but in this case the impact was as great in the United States as in the rest of the Western world.[93]

The expansion of gross investment in the West was financed to a large extent by national saving. Self-financing, by the reinvestment of profits, was an important source of investment. Fiscal incentives provided by the governments to encourage investment also made an important contribution. External financing was significant as well; capital markets in Western Europe and Japan flourished once again after the war. In addition, European firms borrowed in the capital market of New York.

Nevertheless, in time, much more important was American investment in Europe and, to an extent, in Japan too.[94] Previously, when it came to foreign investment, US companies had traditionally looked first to Canada and then to the developing countries of the American continent. During the 1960s and the early 1970s, however, the centre of gravity shifted to the EEC countries. Canada lost its primacy with respect to US foreign investment. The share of developing countries in US direct investment fell from about 50 per cent in 1950 to 25 per cent in 1975, although in absolute terms the size of this investment grew annually by about 10 per cent.[95]

The direct American investment in Western Europe, and to an extent in Japan, was largely centred on manufacturing, especially in petrochemicals. Also important, but later, was investment in banking, insurance, and accountancy. The marked preference for manufacturing was undoubtedly due to the monopolistic advantages which resulted from the technological lead that US companies held over their European counterparts.[96] The comparative advantages in manufacturing lay primarily in the area of production factors, especially in the application of new technology and in the field of management. In respect of the goods market, the advantage was largely to be found in product differentiation. Finally, the integration of the fast-growing European market for consumer durables enabled the American companies to make extensive use of internal economies of scale. Particular circumstances strengthened still further the explosion in foreign investment. American antitrust laws and measures to protect the balance of payments stimulated foreign investment, and the development of the European foreign-exchange market facilitated its financing. The overvaluation of the dollar threatened the exports of American companies and reduced the relative value of their shareholdings in European companies. So American enterprises, to strengthen their market positions abroad, increasingly bought European companies or set up subsidiaries on foreign soil.[97]

The rapid growth in foreign investment was not due entirely to American corporations. In the 1970s big Western European and Japanese companies joined the trend. By then, Western Europe was no longer the main attraction for foreign investment. Instead the capital largely flowed towards a group of newly industrialized developing countries such as Brazil, Mexico, Spain, Taiwan, South Korea, Hong Kong, and Singapore. The success of investment in these countries once again supported the catching-up theory and the Salter model. A substantial labour reserve, a low wage level, and a great catching-up potential accounted for this increase in gross investment. Western investors were seeking higher profits and were indeed able to achieve solid increases in labour productivity in newly industrialized countries in Asia, the Americas, and South-West Europe. In the 1970s, therefore, astonishingly high growth rates were recorded in those regions. The other side of the coin was the slowdown in growth in the United States and Western Europe from the mid 1970s onwards. In the United States this slackening was accompanied by falling gross investment and a more sluggish increase in productivity, even an actual fall in productivity around 1980. In Western Europe, gross investment remained at a high level during the 1970s. In several countries labour productivity rates continued to develop favourably also. Nevertheless even in those countries the rate of growth fell as a result of rapidly rising unemployment. Gross investment was thus not the only explanatory variable in the process of economic growth. Albert O. Hirschman has emphasized that if the West is to continue a high rate of growth, flexibility in the supply of labour and capital must be supplemented with a stream of basic innovations. [98]

CHAPTER V

INNOVATION AS A GROWTH FACTOR

Although the additional input of labour and capital made a substantial contribution to the economic growth of the West after the Second World War, these supply factors do not fully explain the phenomenon of post-war growth. Eventually they always run up against the law of diminishing returns. A third factor, namely innovation, can break through this inexorable law. As growth in productivity begins to approach the point of saturation, innovation can have the effect of opening up new vistas of expansion. In other words, it can transform periods of stagnating and falling efficiency into periods of increasing returns and rising efficiency. After the Second World War the pace of innovation was much faster than before. One reason for this was a revolution in industrial research and the startling technological advances that resulted. Another reason, no less important, was a revolution in business administration, which led to the development of so-called 'Managerial Capitalism'.

1. THE EXPLOSION IN INDUSTRIAL RESEARCH

PROFESSIONALIZING RESEARCH AND INSTITUTIONALIZING PROGRESS

The links between science, technological progress, and industrial innovation do not belong exclusively to our own modern industrial society. They have been an integral part of the Western economy since the Renaissance. The development of the steam engine in the seventeenth and eighteenth centuries and its successful industrial application in the eighteenth and nineteenth centuries owe much to the research of scientific institutions in France, Belgium, the Netherlands, Germany, and especially Britain.[1]

Although the industrial research of the twentieth century did not constitute a new phenomenon, it still represented a break with the past. Its scale, scientific nature, and professionalization all reached levels far in excess of anything that had gone before.

The increase in scale is made clear by some statistics. In 1921 in the United States, large-scale industry employed fewer than 20,000 workers in industrial research departments. By 1940 the number had already risen to 80,000. By 1960 it was 800,000, and by 1970 it was 1,500,000. The same sort of increase can be observed in the number of industrial research departments. In 1920 there were 307 such laboratories registered by the American National Research Council, but in 1960 the figure surpassed 5,400.[2] In Europe too, the number of industrial laboratories grew rapidly, especially after the Second World War. In 1963–4 some 460,000 graduates in the pure sciences and highly qualified technicians were involved in industrial research in Western Europe, and in 1970, to take just one country, Britain employed more than 250,000 workers in this sector.[3]

The scientific nature of industrial research reached a high level in universities and other academic institutions, as well as in business corporations. The impressive progress in scientific communication has greatly facilitated the flow of information from academic centres to industrial laboratories and vice versa so that one can talk increasingly in terms of 'science-related' technology.[4]

At the same time the point of emphasis has shifted away from pure scientific research centres towards industrial laboratories, especially those of big companies where research has undergone professionalization. In 1961 the 391 American companies which employed more than 5,000 workers accounted for no less than 86 per cent of total industrial research in the United States. Four giant concerns controlled nearly 25 per cent of this form of research.[5] The industrial laboratories invested their substantial budgets in hypermodern equipment and highly specialized personnel. The time of the individual inventor was now fading, as was the time when practical improvements were introduced on the spot by experienced workers during the production process. The increasing professionalization of industrial research is reflected in the number of patents applied for. In 1906 individual inventors in the United States still accounted for 78 per cent of all patents applied for. But in 1946 this share had shrunk to 50 per cent and in 1957 to 40 per cent. Their place was taken by big companies. The professionalization of industrial research was noted in a study by Jacob M. Schmookler, who found that in those American states where the number of engineers and graduates in the pure sciences rose sharply between 1900 and 1950, the number of patents applied for grew impressively too.[6]

Various factors explain this professionalization.[7] One is formal scientific education, without which modern technology cannot even be understood, still less improved upon.[8] Furthermore, machinery and equipment, particularly for continuous production, have become so capital-intensive that parts can no longer be taken out of the production system simply for experimental purposes. Consequently, research has been transferred to the company's laboratories or to small experimental concerns. Professional researchers, moreover, can benefit from the division of labour and specialization which Adam Smith described in his example of a pin factory. The process of discovery and innovation which resulted was no longer heavily dependent upon chance or accident – it had become more systematically organized and it continued more regularly. The systematic and large-scale organization of industrial research after the Second World War determined to a high degree the productivity of labour and capital in the West. Empirical studies have shown that the sectors recording the fastest increases in labour and capital productivity were those which spent the highest sums on industrial research or bought equipment from companies that based their production on intensive research. These sectors contributed decisively to general economic growth.[9]

INDUSTRIAL RESEARCH AND DEVELOPMENT COMPARED
INTERNATIONALLY AND SECTORALLY

A comparison of the amount spent on industrial research and development in various Western countries brings striking differences to light.[10] Especially during the first two decades after the Second World War, the predominance of the United States was enormous. For instance, from 1957 to 1966, no less than 157.7 billion dollars was spent on industrial research and development in the United States as against only 50 billion in Western Europe. Although this gap later narrowed, the American lead remained considerable. Of the total American expenditure on research and development during that period, 57 per cent went on projects concerning defence, atomic energy, and space exploration, 12 per cent went to universities and the like for projects concerning fundamental, pure research, and only 31 per cent directly involved implied research in the industrial sector.[11] Nearly two-thirds of American research expenditure was financed by the federal government, especially the Department of Defense, the National Aeronautics and Space Administration (NASA) and the Atomic Energy Commission,[12] because of the Cold War and the space race between the United States and the Soviet Union. However, one should beware of hasty conclusions. Although there was no direct link between the above-mentioned government expenditure and industrial technology,[13] government-subsidized research broadened and deepened the scientific base of industry and had a positive qualitative and quantitative impact on the technological lead of the United States over the rest of the world. On the other hand, for example, the source of the most important innovations in the field of micro-electronics lay in previous military expenditure. Moreover, in 1960 half of the American production of semiconductors was bought for military purposes. The same comments apply for space exploration and computer systems.

Between 1967 and 1975 the total annual expenditure on industrial research and development in the eleven most important OECD countries grew less rapidly than in the period 1957–66. The yearly growth of employment in industrial research and development was only 2 per cent, a departure from the past.[14] But within this general tendency towards stabilization there were glaring differences among countries. In the United States and Britain, total expenditure on industrial research fell. The United States' share in Western industrial research also fell, from about 60 per cent in 1960 to about 50 per cent in 1975 – still an impressive figure. In West Germany and Japan the expenditure increased, so that their shares climbed respectively to 12.1 per cent and 11.7 per cent of the world total in 1975. In fact Japan is the only country where the growth rate of expenditure on industrial research during the period 1959–67 was equalled in 1967–75.

The decline in expenditure on industrial research and development in the United States and Britain between 1967 and 1975 was largely due to a drastic decrease in government expenditure. In the other countries where the government played an important role in financing industrial research and development, namely France, Canada, and Norway, there was a comparable weakening in activity. In contrast, privately financed research expenditure in the eleven countries studied rose by 30 per cent although there was a certain faltering after the oil crisis of 1973. The general picture was thus one of a trend towards stabilization in the growth of industrial research although there was a certain redistribution of effort among countries.

In real terms the exertions of a given country in the field of industrial research and development can best be measured by comparing research expenditure and GNP or by looking at the number of researchers (defined as engineers, highly qualified technicians, and graduates in the pure sciences) per 10,000 inhabitants. On the basis of both criteria the United States held a huge lead over the rest of the Western world in the post-war years. American spending on industrial research and development still amounted to 3.13 per cent of GNP in 1967, and the number of researchers reached a record of 35.3 per 10,000 inhabitants (Table 24). For the United Kingdom, France, West Germany, Japan, the Netherlands, and Sweden, the percentages fluctuated between 2.37 per cent and 0.97 per cent of GNP and the number of researchers between 29.4 and 18 per 10,000 inhabitants. The statistics for Canada, Belgium and Norway were less favourable, and for Austria and Italy spurts occasionally took place. During the 1970s there was a clear convergence in the national rates of the above-mentioned countries. In 1975 American and British research expenditure sank respectively to 1.95 per cent and 1.75 per cent of GNP, whereas the West German, French, and Japanese percentages were more steady: German 1.59, French 1.37, Japanese 1.19.

Research expenditure differs considerably from sector to sector. Historically sectoral shifts take place, and countries do not always follow the same pattern. In the nineteenth century, for example, technological innovation was heavily concentrated in the metal sector, where a big potential for technological progress existed and, to a large extent, was realized. Between the two world wars the greatest possibilities for technological advance were in petrochemicals. In the 1950s and 1960s, attention was concentrated on sectors

Table 24 *Gross Expenditures on Research and Development by Principal Sources of Funds as Percentage of GNP, 1963–73*
(selected years)

	Business enterprises and abroad				Government and other national resources			
	1963	1967	1971	1973	1963	1967	1971	1973
Austria	0.16	0.34	0.33	n.a.	0.12	0.23	0.24	n.a.
Canada	0.34	0.44	0.43	0.39	0.62	0.87	0.89	0.85
Denmark	n.a.	0.30	n.a.	0.43	n.a.	0.44	n.a.	0.47
Finland	n.a.	0.32	0.35	0.47	n.a.	0.25	0.34	0.34
France	0.68	0.75	0.71	0.70	1.02	1.40	1.20	1.08
West Germany	0.79	0.98	1.04	1.15	0.58	0.71	0.68	0.91
Republic of Ireland	0.15	0.21	0.26	0.31	0.31	0.33	0.37	0.39
Italy	0.37	0.41	0.45	0.53	0.26	0.31	0.38	0.37
Japan	0.91	0.93	1.09	1.19	0.35	0.04	0.39	0.45
Netherlands	1.12	1.34	1.25	1.18	0.78	0.80	0.76	0.83
Norway	0.33	0.39	0.40	0.42	0.42	0.57	0.58	0.56
Sweden	0.67	0.79	0.78	0.90	0.61	0.62	0.56	0.68
United Kingdom	1.00	1.07	1.07	n.a.	1.31	1.30	1.24	n.a.
United States	0.85	1.08	1.07	1.01	1.86	2.05	1.72	1.54

Source: OECD, *Patterns of Resources devoted to Research and Experimental Development in the OECD Area, 1963–1971*

which, on the basis of intense scientific research, could generate a continual stream of new technology and new products. The most successful of these science-related, research-intensive industries after the war were space exploration, electronics, pharmaceuticals, chemicals, petrochemicals, and precision instruments.

It was precisely these high-technology sectors that achieved the highest growth rates. Moreover, by means of their technological predominance, they 'colonized' the more traditional industries. Textiles provide a good illustration. Research in the chemical sector led to an explosion in the production of synthetic fibres and research in electronics led to a far-reaching automation of textile machinery. Similar colonizations took place in many other sectors. The influence of research in the chemical industry on foodstuffs and construction materials is well known. The impact of electronics research on manufacturing industry, machine construction, and printing has also been extremely important.

All Western countries concentrated their industrial research on science-related sectors but there were national differences within this category (Table 25). In the United States the emphasis was on space exploration and in the sector of electronics and electricity. In Europe, on the other hand, greater attention was given to chemicals, basic metals and allied products, and to certain other sectors of manufacturing industry. In chemicals, Western European technology was not far behind that of the United States, although this was not the case in other high-technology sectors. This held equally for both pure and applied research. During the 1970s research expenditure on defence and space exploration declined everywhere. But this was compensated by a sharp rise in research expenditure on electronics and chemicals so that in general science-related sectors maintained their two-thirds share in the total industrial research of the OECD countries.[15] The privately financed research in electronics and electricity now made this sector the most important of the group of high-technology industries, the United States accounting for 57 per cent of research in 1975, the Common Market countries 30 per cent and Japan 10 per cent.

In 1975 chemical research was still being vigorously financed by private companies based in West Germany, the Netherlands, Belgium, and Switzerland. The energy crisis had the effect of raising research expenditure in the automobile sector and basic metals continued to receive special attention in Japan, Sweden, and Belgium. Increasing government measures to protect the environment stimulated greater research on pollution and the like. Finally, the deteriorating economic indicators during the 1970s also had an impact on the orientation of industrial research and development. Particularly striking in the United States, for example, was a reduction in the interval between invention and application. At the same time, research was less directed at the development of new products and more towards the improvement of already existing products. American expenditure on product-orientated research around 1970 was split about equally between the development of new products and the improvement of old. Around 1980 the relationship was one-third new to two-thirds old.[16] Does this change imply that economic upturns are largely determined by the introduction of new basic technologies, which stimulates production, which in turn creates new jobs? Are these upturns inevitably followed by phases of reduced growth, characterized by labour-saving innovations and by improvements to existing products? Do the 1950s and 1960s belong to the first sort of economic phase and the 1970s to the second? These questions will be dealt with later in the chapter.

Summary of the Trends in Expenditures on Research and Development in Selected Western Countries, 1967–75*

(percentage distribution)

	Period	High technological industries			Other metal and engineering industries			Chemical-linked industry***	Other manu-facturing industry****	Services
		Aerospace	Electricals and electronics	Chemicals**	Transport equipment excluding aerospace	Machinery and instruments	Basic metals and metal products			
United States	1967	34.6	27.3	11.6	8.3	7.7	2.5	2.6	2.2	3.4
	1975	23.6	30.3	14.2	10.1	8.9	3.2	3.5	3.2	2.9
Japan	1967	0.3	22.6	25.0	11.2	10.0	9.8	7.1	6.4	4.2
	1975	0.5	23.8	20.0	16.6	9.0	8.6	5.8	6.8	3.3
West Germany	1967	4.7	24.4	26.9	12.0	15.2	7.9	2.0	1.2	6.2
	1975	8.7	27.3	26.7	10.6	12.7	2.8	1.8	0.9	7.9
France	1967	26.6	22.6	17.5	7.9	5.2	4.1	5.6	2.6	6.5
	1975	18.8	29.5	17.9	10.2	4.8	3.8	5.7	2.1	5.6
United Kingdom	1967	23.7	22.6	13.8	7.9	11.0	4.7	6.3	3.7	5.6
	1975	21.8	23.7	17.9	7.8	7.1	3.5	6.5	2.7	7.8
Belgium	1967	0.4	22.8	35.9	0.8	8.9	14.8	4.6	8.4	1.9
	1975	0.2	19.9	40.1	1.1	5.1	12.4	8.4	9.0	8.1
Italy	1967	4.7	17.7	25.9	22.7	4.8	1.0	8.2	1.5	13.1
	1975	4.4	19.5	23.2	21.2	4.7	3.1	6.7	2.2	14.5
Canada	1967	12.4	32.1	19.6	1.1	3.1	9.2	6.0	9.1	3.5
	1975	7.1	28.0	17.0	2.1	6.6	10.5	5.1	6.0	11.5
Sweden	1967	11.8	21.6	8.7	5.2	17.0	12.7	3.9	6.5	10.5
	1975	7.7	20.6	8.5	13.6	15.2	8.6	4.7	6.8	7.8

Notes: * Industrial R & D expenditures refer to all private and public enterprises plus individual research institutes.

** 'Chemicals' group includes chemicals, drugs, and petroleum products.

*** 'Chemical-linked' group covers three manufacturing industries whose R & D activities are allied with those in the chemical group: food, drink, tobacco; textiles, clothing, leather; rubber and plastic products.

**** 'Other manufacturing' group covers: stone, glass, clay; paper, printing; wood, cork, furniture; miscellaneous manufacturing.

Source: Own calculations based on OECD, Trends in Industrial R & D, 1967–1975

INDUSTRIAL RESEARCH AND THE TECHNOLOGICAL GAP

Industrial research in the West after the Second World War led to numerous inventions and subsequent innovations. Inventions demonstrate a technological possibility to introduce a new product or production process and may give rise to an application for a patent. Innovations in the economy take place when a new product is manufactured or a new production process is brought into operation on a commercially viable basis. In Van Duijn's book on the long waves an overview is given of the most important inventions and innovations in the world economy from 1800 to 1971. Of the 111 mentioned innovations, 58 per cent were first successfully commercialized in the United States, 38 per cent in Europe, and barely 4 per cent in Japan. The predominance of American innovations was thus very considerable but far from absolute.[17] It is also noteworthy that American innovative capacity was better in new sectors than in traditional ones. In new sectors such as electronic computers, semiconductors, titanium, communication satellites, and scientific instruments, the Americans held an impressive technological lead. In traditional sectors which depended on older inventions and innovations, the position of the United States in relation to other Western countries was clearly less strong. In pharmaceuticals, synthetics, and bulk plastics, for instance, many important innovations had been made in the 1920s and 1930s, and in these sectors Western European countries continued to play a significant innovative role after the war. Western Europe showed a similar post-war innovative vitality in the generation and distribution of electricity and in traditional metal-working including copper and aluminium. Britain still made a considerable contribution to this Western European creativity.

Table 26 shows that American companies were particularly skilful at innovation based on pure research and at the commercial exploitation of their own and foreign inventions. The basic techniques for the production of titanium were discovered in Luxemburg. Much of the fundamental work that led to the development of modern computer technology was undertaken in Europe. The invention of the tunnel diode was based on Japanese research. But in these cases and many others American companies were able to convert invention into innovation. Europe and Japan were better at inventing than at innovating, whereas the United States proved

Table 26 *Export Performance of Ten OECD Countries in Research-Intensive Industries, 1963–5*
(*percentages*)

	Each country's share of total manufacturing exports	Each country's share of total world trade in research-intensive industries		Share of research-intensive industries in each country's manufacturing exports	
		Excluding aircraft and non-electrical machinery (1)	Including aircraft and non-electrical machinery (2)	Excluding aircraft and non-electrical machinery (1)	Including aircraft and non-electrical machinery (2)
United States	22.6	26.6	30.1	22.9	51.5
West Germany	18.1	21.8	22.1	23.6	47.2
United Kingdom	13.2	12.9	14.2	19.1	41.9
France	9.8	8.9	7.7	17.7	30.3
Japan	8.1	7.5	5.3	18.0	25.1
Italy	7.5	5.7	5.9	14.7	30.0
Netherlands	5.9	7.6	5.3	25.0	34.6
Belgium	5.8	3.5	3.2	11.7	20.8
Canada	5.5	3.3	3.4	11.6	23.9
Sweden	3.5	2.2	2.8	12.1	31.4
Total	100.0	100.0	100.0	19.5	39.0

Notes: (1) The sectors included are drugs, chemicals, electrical machinery, instruments.
(2) Same sectors as above but including aircraft and non-electrical machinery

Source: OECD, *Gaps in Technology*, p. 207

very creative in both fields.[18] Over the years there was little change to this pattern. In most research-intensive and high-technology sectors, American industry remained very dynamic and maintained its lead in innovation over the rest of the world. There was most probably an innovative catching-up movement for Japan but it was certainly not an overwhelming one. On the other hand the innovative lead of the United States in high-technology sectors was not absolute. For example, in the chemical sector Western European countries not only undertook much original research and made a whole series of inventions but also were able to convert these successfully into innovations. Japan made research advances in electronics and was able to exploit them in the production of electron microscopes and electronic consumer goods.

The concepts 'technological gap' and 'catching-up movement', as used by economists such as Cornwall and Maddison, must therefore be somewhat refined. In respect of discovery and invention, Western Europe and Japan were often very active at the technological frontier. In respect of innovation, the American position was much stronger, although in chemicals, for instance, Western Europe made a substantial contribution. A successful innovation is, after all, not simply a 'technological' phenomenon. Modern management techniques and market size play an important part as well. A number of innovations simply could not get off the ground in Europe, because of insufficient commercial opportunities and the relatively small number of big companies there. The American computer industry, for example, was during its initial growth phase supported by the demand potential of federal government and large private corporations, the number of which, certainly during the 1950s and 1960s, was higher in the United States than in Western Europe. The success of innovations in high-technology sectors, then, is not just a technological question since it also involves managerial and commercial factors. The interdependence of these three factors is of crucial importance in explaining the 'technological gap'.

RESEARCH AND DEVELOPMENT, THE TECHNOLOGICAL GAP, AND FOREIGN TRADE

Companies which have acquired a technological lead by industrial research and wish to make use of this in foreign markets can apply various methods. They can concentrate on the export of new products, they can invest abroad and serve local markets via subsidiaries, or they can license foreign companies to produce the new product for given markets. All three methods were applied on a large scale after the Second World War. The United States was the largest seller of patents and licences-to-produce. About half of the total amount of technology which French, British, West German, Italian, Japanese, and Canadian companies imported through patents and licences was of American origin. But those countries acquired as much technology from one another as from the United States. Sectoral studies confirm these conclusions. In electronics and electrical machinery, the sale of American patents and licences was far above the general average of all American sectors. On the other hand, in chemicals, basic metals, and metal products, sales of European patents and licences were clearly higher than the average of all European sectors. In these same sectors, sales of American patents and licences were plainly lower than the American average.[19]

If one analyses the export of the products themselves, the same patterns emerge with respect to the research-intensive sectors (Table 26). The relative share of these sectors in the total export value of a country's manufacturing accords fairly closely with the place that industrial research and development occupies in the country concerned. During the 1960s the share of research-intensive sectors in total exports fluctuated slightly above 50 per cent for the United States. For Britain and West Germany this share was about 40 to 45 per cent and it was also high for the Netherlands and Sweden, but for Belgium it only represented 20 per cent. If comparisons are made not sectorally (there may be non-research-intensive subsectors within the sectors deemed to be 'research-intensive') but based instead on the export of the fifty most research-intensive *products* in relation to total exports, then in the 1960s, once again, the highest percentages were in the United States, West Germany, Britain, the Netherlands, and Sweden.[20]

Nevertheless, the export performance of countries with a lead in high-technology sectors is more complex than the above-mentioned statistics would imply. Wassily Leontief contended that American exports were indeed successful in high-technology sectors, but more successful in labour-intensive than capital-intensive ones, and this at a time when American wages were the highest in the world.[21] The essential point here, however, is that the American labour input was of a higher quality than elsewhere. The large investment in educating and training in the United States meant that the labour force there had greater technological expertise. The labour represented in American products must thus be regarded as a sort of human capital. Once the significance of investment in this form is fully appreciated, then Leontief's paradox can be resolved.

The human capital represented in new, advanced products ensures for the producers a technological monopoly.[22] The innovating companies therefore enjoy a temporary lead in the world market. Even when the cost and price structure of the country where the innovation takes place is unfavourable, this lead is temporarily maintained. It is only in the second phase, when the new technology becomes available to competitors, that wage costs become a decisive variable in the manufacture of the new product. In most cases competitors will try to conquer a share of the market by producing in countries with low wage costs. The original innovative firm can protect its market by means of further innovations or by making comparable investments in low-wage countries. Other factors such as proximity of markets, and the provision of technical services etc., may also play a role.

Those are the essentials of the theory of the product life cycle. Various case studies confirm the theory.[23] American exports of high technology electronic capital goods and synthetic materials during the 1950s and 1960s followed the path mapped out by Michael V. Posner, Seev Hirsch and Raymond Vernon.[24] The American lead in the world market for the research-intensive sectors of electronic capital goods and synthetic materials was greatest during the 1950s and gradually wore away during the 1960s.[25] In contrast there was a gradual strengthening of the position of European Economic Community (EEC) countries and, later, Japan.[26] During the 1960s the American firms which had introduced the original innovations set up an increasing number of subsidiaries abroad. These subsidiaries were established first in EEC countries where there was a big demand for high technology goods and where wage costs still were lower than in the United States. In 1964 the amount of high-technology goods sold by European-based subsidiaries of American companies was four times the amount directly exported from the United States.[27]

This foreign investment in Europe represented a considerable injection of capital, and, just as important, a transfer of American technology and management techniques. It has been estimated that the tempo of the transfer of technology via direct foreign investment in Europe during the 1960s was much higher than the pace of innovation in the United States itself during the same period. It can thus be confidently asserted that American investment abroad in the 1960s effectively helped to close the technological gap between the United States and Europe. Statistics concerning American receipts from licences and patents paid by daughter companies or subsidiaries of American firms in foreign countries also confirm these conclusions. In 1957 these comprised 43 per cent of total receipts and in 1965 no less than 70 per cent.[28]

It is therefore difficult to overestimate the role played by American multinational corporations in reducing the technological gap between industrialized countries during the 1950s and especially the 1960s. Starting in the 1970s, however, such corporations began to invest increasingly in developing countries. Underdevelopment and a surplus of labour guaranteed a long period of low wages in these areas, in contrast to any part of the industrial West. Once again this investment led to a transfer of know-how, and technology and management techniques. By some developing countries these transfers were successfully assimilated.

2. THE 'MANAGERIAL REVOLUTION'

THE AMERICAN LEAD IN ORGANIZATION

On the supply side, the powerful growth of the world economy after the Second World War was not only influenced by the additional input of labour and capital and by spectacular technological advances. A further factor, as already hinted, was innovation in the field of business management. The importance of this factor has been shown by Alfred D. Chandler Jr. In order to realize the growth strategy of large modern companies in as efficient a way as possible, new forms of internal organization were devised. Basically the modern idea was a multidivisional structure, replacing the one-man operations and also the multi-unit firms. The multidivisional structure centralized supervisory and administrative systems. This notable organizational advance raised the potential for gains in productivity and was justly termed the 'Managerial Revolution'.

The Managerial Revolution was in the first instance an American phenomenon and only later, with a significant delay, was it taken up in Western Europe and Japan. The first innovations in internal business management had already taken place during the third quarter of the nineteenth century in American railways and telegraph services.[29] The changes in the technology of long-distance transport and communications made possible very great economies of scale. New market structures came about, and perspectives for new entrepreneurial activities were opened. Companies which sought to capitalize upon these developments and embarked on a growth strategy had to modify their management organization. A new organizational system was necessary in order to continue to execute efficiently the three fundamental functions of company management: co-ordination, supervision, and resource allocation. The spreading railway companies had necessarily organized themselves in geographical units, and each company had to establish a managerial hierarchy in order to co-ordinate transactions between the various units, to monitor their performance, and to distribute resources among them. In this way a functional distinction between top management, middle management, and lower management came about, a distinction which was sometimes supplemented with an additional set of linkages when the companies expanded still further.

This new form of organization quickly found wide application in the United States. The big distribution companies took up the idea of the multi-unit enterprise, and industrial companies that were engaged in refining and distillation, and in metal production and metal working, also divided up work into separate units. These were *functional* units, such as production, sales, purchases, raw materials, transport, finance, and research. Like the railways those large distribution and manufacturing firms built hierarchies. Middle management, based in a headquarters, supervised lower management, situated within the functional units, and reported to top management, again based in a headquarters, which was responsible for strategic decision-making. In sectors where high-value and complicated technology was intensively applied, the multi-unit organization appeared to provide a framework for a more efficient use of capacity.[30]

But the centralized multi-unit structure had major disadvantages, especially when the growth strategy was aimed at the diversification of production. Co-ordination among the different functional units or departments took place on a purely informal, *ad hoc* basis. Moreover, long-term investment strategy remained superficial, intuitive, and subjective. Top management was largely composed of those in charge of the units, and so it remained too dependent on the day-to-day management of those units and had too little time for long-term planning and strategic decision-making. The members of top management who were responsible for the various units were inclined to organize planning and resource allocation in terms of their own particular functional responsibilities and not in terms of the company as a whole.[31]

An inventory crisis of 1920–1 provided the impetus to improve the structure of multi-unit enterprise in those companies which were already fully engaged in diversification. Du Pont, General Motors, the Standard Oil Company of New Jersey, and Sears, Roebuck & Company, all formed themselves into multidivisional enterprises. They set up new autonomous divisions based on product lines or export areas. Each division was given its own multi-unit organization of the type which already existed. That is, it was controlled by a hierarchy of managers working in different functional units and in a headquarters. Over the various divisions was now spread a central, interconnecting organ which had two specific functions. It had to ensure co-ordination of functional activities across divisional lines and it had to execute long-term planning and accordingly distribute resources as efficiently as possible among the divisions (Graph C).

The setting-up of a multidivisional structure was a great step forward in the field of modern business management. The functional activities could now be more systematically and efficiently co-ordinated. Still more important was the improvement in resource allocation. The establishment of a central co-ordinating organ made it possible to follow closely the performance of different divisions and to evaluate objectively and precisely the return on employed capital. On the basis of these objective evaluations and of detailed projections and budgets, resources could now be efficiently allocated within the company as a whole. The danger of a subjective allocation of capital, influenced by those responsible for just a small part of the whole, was in this way averted. Middle management could concentrate wholly on administrative co-ordination, top management on supervising this co-ordination and on long-term planning and investment strategy.[32]

The advantages of this new system were so obvious that most

Graph C   *The Multidivisional Structure*

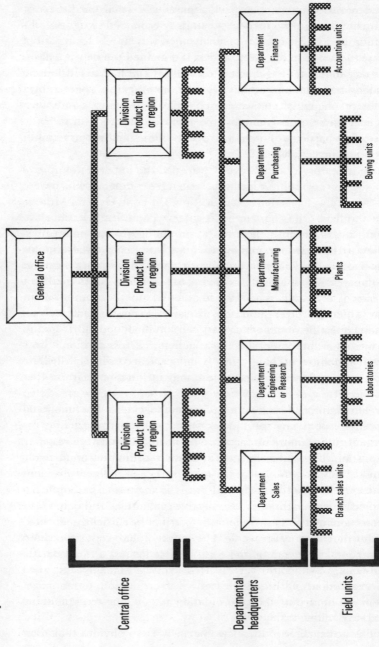

Central office

Departmental headquarters

Field units

Source: A. D. CHANDLER Jr, *Strategy and Structure*, p. 10

large American companies, which had hitherto adopted the form of a multi-unit enterprise, gradually took on the structure of a multidivisional firm after diversifying production. This transition came with a rush after the Second World War and was of decisive significance for the further successful development of American capitalism. The strategy of growth via diversification, a central pillar of the modern consumer economy, required a new, refined management organization which could adequately cope with the use of greater economies of scale. This was provided by the multi-divisional enterprise.[33]

THE EUROPEAN AND JAPANESE BACKWARDNESS

In the field of modern business management, the big European countries have consistently lagged behind their American counter-parts. In Europe during the nineteenth century, centralized adminis-trative control did not develop so strongly. European railway companies seldom created departments or units under the super-vision of a centralized headquarters. In European trade and indus-try, a hierarchical structure was rarely employed. Instead, a few top managers who mostly belonged to the family (or one of the families) which owned the company ran its affairs. They had under them a limited number of junior managers, and the relationships between top management and junior management were informal and per-sonal.

This European backwardness in adopting the system of central-ized, administrative supervision did not mean that the managerial organization of big European companies remained as it had always been. In Europe too, organizational innovations took place during the nineteenth century but these differed in nature and level from those in the United States. In Britain big companies had come into existence either through autonomous growth or through a long process of mergers and take-overs that had usually been going on for two or three generations.[34] Sometimes there were remarkable horizontal mergers of thirty to fifty enterprises. But neither auto-nomous growth nor mergers generated centralized administration. The autonomy of the subsidiaries was maintained and rationaliza-tion was limited to co-operation in the purchasing of raw materials and to dividing up markets. All in all, with a few exceptions, British industry developed along the lines of a sort of family capitalism.

France was not fundamentally different. The French really developed a variant of British family capitalism, except that in this case financial circles dominated the scene.[35]

Financial capitalism in its pure form existed in Belgium around the middle of the nineteenth century. The so-called 'mixed banks', that is, commercial banks which also made long-term investments, acquired control over heavy industry in Wallonia through their investment policies. They used this control to bring about horizontal integration and vertical integration both forward and backward. In addition, they set up holding companies, under their control, which specialized in particular industries or particular regions. In the same way the mixed banks were also able to organize their foreign investments into a strict supervisory framework.[36] German investment banks followed a similar strategy from the *Gründerzeit* (1871–3) onwards. The Belgian and German banking structure showed a clear resemblance to British and French family capitalism except that there was a more integrated organization. Decision-making on long-term investment strategy was transferred away from a number of decentralized points to one authoritative nucleus which had access to better information and better opportunities for supervision and co-ordination. This system created for each industrial group a well-organized and coherent mini-capital market, where resources were efficiently allocated by means of centralized decision-making. The system formed a sound framework for horizontal and vertical integration so that economies of scale and rationalization could be quickly realized.

Germany was the only European country that modernized its business management still further around the end of the nineteenth century. Even before 1900 numerous large companies had diversified and executed vertical integration. Some of them did adopt a multifunctional structure in common with their American counterparts. The German company Siemens even developed a multidivisional management organization before the First World War.[37]

Why did organizational advances in Europe develop mainly along the lines adopted by the big investment banks? Why was organizational progress largely restricted to the supervision of investment decisions, and why did it almost wholly neglect administrative centralization? The main reasons lay in the specific structure of the European market.[38] Because of low wages and dispersed markets, prospects for the mechanized mass production of textiles, food products, and consumer durables were less attractive than in the United States. These disadvantages did not apply to heavy industry. In the industrializing of Europe there was, in fact, a growing need for modern transport infrastructure. Such a modernization at home, and later in overseas areas, created a particular need for fixed capital. In continental Europe the capital market, in the proper sense of the word, was still too underdeveloped to be able to satisfy this demand. On the other hand the mixed banks and their holding companies were able to fill the gap perfectly. They made sizeable investments in the expanding railway companies and the basic industries linked with them.

The first major integrated firms in continental Europe were in the basic sectors of metallurgy, shipbuilding, chemicals, and heavy machinery.[39] They showed a tremendous growth potential that continued well into the twentieth century and, owing to colonial enterprise, took on a major, overseas dimension. Nevertheless, in an organizational sense, they stubbornly held on to the system of different financing companies with weak administrative centralization.[40]

After the Second World War a sudden change took place. The colonial empires disintegrated, and socialist and Third World countries began to develop their own basic industry in order to modernize infrastructure. At the same time Western European countries completed their transition into modern consumer economies, characterized by the extensive differentiation of industrial production and supported by the formation of the Common Market. For Europe the time had come to assimilate the American model of management organization. In order to build a diversified modern industry large enough to produce efficiently, European industry had to be restructured. A divisional reorganization and an administrative, hierarchical centralization thus had to be worked out. This indeed came about, partly through autonomous structural reforms and partly through mergers with, or take-overs by, American giants and the consequent introduction of American management techniques. The demonstration effect of the big American companies as they set up large-scale subsidiaries in Europe was also considerable.

In Britain the strategy of diversification got fully under way during the 1950s and especially the 1960s.[41] In 1970 only six of the 100 largest British companies based their growth strategy and product development on only one product. The modern, diversified companies now speedily changed their organization from a functional to a multidivisional structure. Chandler's basic theory of 'Structure follows Strategy' became reality. In 1950 only thirteen of the 100 largest British companies had a divisional organization, but by 1970 this had increased to seventy-two. There was a similar development in other European countries after the war.[42] West Germany had given promise of an earlier transition – diversification there had become general around 1900 – but the cartel movement had held back rapid administrative centralization.[43] So had the two world wars and the Great Depression. Consequently Germany likewise fully experienced the transition to multidivisional organization after the Second World War.

In Japan the *Zaibatsu* system, which to a considerable extent dominated business management in the larger companies before the war, had much in common with Western European family capitalism and especially Belgian financial capitalism. As mentioned in Chapters I and II, each *Zaibatsu* was a collection of diverse industrial, commercial and financial concerns directed by a central holding company which was, in turn, under the control of one or more rich families. The *Zaibatsu* had close links with heavy industry (mining, steel, and investment goods) as well as with banking and insurance companies. Those companies supplied the manufacturers with capital while specialized trading companies arranged transactions among subsidiaries and with foreign companies. Horizontal and, particularly, vertical integration were applied on a large scale but there was no question of strong hierarchical and administrative centralization. The main point of emphasis clearly lay in the centralization of investment decisions.[44]

After the Second World War the *Zaibatsu* were broken up. During the decade which followed the peace treaty of 1952, they did make a recovery but they never regained the position of power and coordinating influence that they had enjoyed during the 1930s and 1940s. At the same time the big Japanese companies, much like their European counterparts, brought in a strategy of diversification and differentiation. This was followed up with fundamental reforms in business organization.[45] From the 1950s onwards, American management techniques were systematically applied. The multidivisional form of business organization quickly won ground, and hierarchical centralizing of administration appeared. In 1959 no less than 107 of the 200 largest Japanese companies were already organized according to the system of modern management, and this development continued at a rapid pace.

Thus the lead which American companies had over the rest of the world in the field of modern business management presented Western Europe and Japan with a second catching-up potential. Their companies after the war could realize major productivity gains by closing not only the technological gap but also the management gap. Even small- and medium-sized concerns could assimilate part of the Managerial Revolution, for business schools trained numerous executives who were later able to take over the management of these small- and medium-sized companies and apply the new management techniques there.

Yet management techniques as developed by the Americans were at no time static. There was indeed a catching-up movement in Western Europe and Japan but at the same time American management techniques were refined still further and the technological progress in electronics, biology, chemistry, and air and space travel benefited from very important organizational support.

CHARACTERISTICS OF MODERN BUSINESS MANAGEMENT

The Managerial Revolution did more than address the technical issue of management reorganization. It also struck at fundamental price-forming mechanisms, and it influenced social relations not only within the company itself but also between the company and the outside world.[46] The development of the functional and multidivisional organization implied a revolutionary change in the use of human capital. The specialized labour or knowledge of one worker, or a few individuals, was systematically replaced by that of a massed body of workers. This extension of specialization was particularly necessary for complex technology. At the same time it offered great advantages. If a hierarchical supervisory and co-ordinating structure could be combined with specialized production, efficiency could reach new heights. It was in this way that the 'technostructure' and the 'managerial class', to use the terminology of John Kenneth Galbraith, came into existence. A body of specialized managers acquired hierarchical control and power over the complete production process in modern industry. Running the company was now the responsibility of the technostructure rather than individuals. Lower management monitored daily routine activity; middle management supervised and co-ordinated their decisions; and top management supervised and co-ordinated the company as a whole and decided long-term investment plans.

Naturally the power of the hierarchical technostructure was at its most evident in big companies, most of which adopted a multidivisional organizational structure after the Second World War. Small- and medium-sized concerns also took on many characteristics of technostructure, although the number of hierarchical co-ordinative groups was smaller and family capitalism largely remained intact. For instance, in smaller companies top management continued to maintain close contact with the owners.

On the other hand, some large companies developed into such giants and became so complex that even the multidivisional organizational structure had to be adapted. For example, many multinational companies which had organized their production for the domestic market on the basis of a department for each production line went on to set up a general international department (possibly subdivided by continent) to handle activities abroad.[47] Difficulties arose between the domestic and foreign departments, since they were differently organized, so that often an additional co-ordinating structure appeared necessary.[48] This difference in organization continued because both kinds of department had their own specific advantages. Departments based on product lines were most efficient when the application of complex technology made large economies of scale possible. General international departments were more practical when it came to operations in fragmented and diversified foreign markets. The combination of the functional and multidivisional form was termed a 'matrix organization' and was used particularly by multinationals heavily engaged abroad.[49]

The growing significance of the technostructure in modern business management also influenced the working of the economy. Galbraith even contended that in the world of large companies the technostructure replaced the market system with a planned system. The main objective of the company was no longer the maximizing of profit but instead constant growth. This change in objective was due to the increasing power of the technostructure and the diminishing influence of owners and investors. The greater the size of the company, the more numerous the number of shareholders and the more fragmented and weaker their power. According to Galbraith the technostructure adopted the stable and balanced growth of the company as the basic objective because such growth best served the aspirations of the managerial class ('affirmative purpose'). Growth perpetuated their own position of power, ensured eventual further promotion, and created room for new generations of managers. Growth was also the means by which the ambitions of the managerial class coincided with the welfare aspirations of the community as a whole. Finally, growth ensured that the independence of the technostructure from the outside world could be maintained or even extended. Profit nevertheless continued to be an important objective since it lent considerable support to the drive by the managerial class towards independence from owners and the outside world ('protective purpose'). In this sense, profit served to further growth. This meant that while short-term profit maximization grew less relevant, long-term profit maximization remained an important variable.

The technostructure sought to extend its power via consumers. The consumer industry had increased its potential to satisfy the need for a vast range of products. The technostructure adapted to this new situation. Through advertising, it tried to shape the behaviour of consumers to accord with its own planned system, that is, the scheme of production which it regarded as optimal. Galbraith argued that the planned system thus replaced the market system, even determining prices. In addition, pricing policy was based not on the maximization of profit (monopoly price) but on maximum sales (mass production), which guaranteed optimal growth for the company and for the managerial class.

The planned system of the technostructure also had the effect of reducing the traditional conflict between labour and capital. It made easier the integration of technological progress into the production process and made wage increases possible as a result of higher labour productivity. Even in areas where technological progress was no longer possible or could be realized only with difficulty, wage rises could still be granted since the technostructure was able to pass on costs to its consumers. The understanding between unions and big companies was often very good and this co-operation continued even during economic downturns when joint action, often with a conservative bias, was undertaken in order to ward off external threats.

The same spirit of understanding and co-operation was apparent in dealings with the government. After the Second World War the primary goal of all Western governments was the creation of an affluent society. The planned system which they introduced to achieve this goal fitted in very well with the planned system of big business. The state financed a large measure of industrial research, considerably extended technical and higher education, subsidized investment, and, through government orders, created lucrative markets. The big companies, on their side, were willing to step up investment and to take account of general economic guidelines set by governments. This co-operation between government and big business in the creation of the post-war affluent society thus formed a cornerstone in the building of the mixed economy.

The above-mentioned theories, formulated among others by Adolf A. Berle Jr, Peter Drucker and John K. Galbraith, have come under much criticism, the hypotheses being regarded as too extreme and general.[50] The actual share of big business in the total economy, either in terms of employment or capital, even in the United States, was not as large as suggested in these theories. After the Second World War there was still much room for small firms which remained closely linked to the market system. Indeed, big companies even made possible an increase in the number of small, independent firms – in supplementary manufacturing and service sectors.

It was also true that big companies never fully operated within the confines of the planned system, and a part of their activities continued to be integrated into the market system of the mixed economy. The divergent profit and growth figures of the big companies show that growth did not always completely follow the planned system. The market remained an uncertain and sensitive variable. For advanced and even traditional sectors a catching-up movement, brought about either by new firms or rising imports, remained a real threat. Even when a specific big company or group of big companies had acquired an overwhelming market share of a given product, this monopolistic or oligopolistic position was still vulnerable. Product substitution, made feasible through technological progress, remained a possibility and consumers could always reject a product. Furthermore, monopolies which were too flagrant became the focus of public opinion, and this was strongly anti-monopolistic.

Finally, the technostructure was never as homogeneous as the authors made it appear. Top management mostly formed a separate power group whose members used the technostructure and growth of the company to extend their personal ambition, either in the sense of power or status. This is precisely what the exponents of family capitalism had done, although by means of maximizing profits. In Western Europe and Japan top management was a much more aristocratic and closed group than in the United States and the influence of the great families continued after the Second World War. Within this family capitalism there existed a technocratic élite which, after its education in prestigious schools, received leading posts in big business.

Nevertheless, despite some reservations, the Managerial Revolution undoubtedly exercised a crucial influence on the development of the Western economic system and it helped give the modern state its typical social and economic outline.

3. INNOVATION AND GROWTH: CONVERGENCE OR DIVERGENCE?

THE KEYNESIAN DECADES

According to some economists, innovations tend to come up in clusters, appearing more frequently in some periods than in others. In the periods of higher frequency, there is a clear reduction of the time span between the moment of invention and that of innovation.[51] Such favourable periods have occurred repeatedly in the past, namely during the years 1760–70, 1825–40, 1880–95 and 1930–50. The wave of innovations between 1930 and 1950 was an impressive one and covered numerous sectors. In the area of transport one could mention, among others, the rocket (1935), the helicopter (1936), the diesel locomotive (1937) and the jet fighter (1942). For electricity and electronics there were the electron microscope (1933), radar (1935), the tape recorder (1935), television (1936), fluorescent lighting (1938), the long-playing record (1948), and the transistor (1948). In chemistry the most important innovations were plexiglass (1931), polyvinyl chloride (1932), cellophane (1933), colour film (1935), catalytic cracking (1935), nylon (1938), DDT (1942), and silicones (1943). In the field of pharmaceuticals, most notable were penicillin (1942) and streptomycin (1944). Other innovations that could be mentioned were the ballpoint pen (1945), continuous steel casting (1948), and xerography (1950).

It is very striking that most innovations in the 1930s and 1940s were made by German and American companies, especially American ones. Since the Second World War increasingly excluded Germany from the further application of the series of innovations of the 1930s and 1940s, the first phase of general application during the 1950s and 1960s was almost entirely concentrated in the United States. New markets were created and new growth sectors followed, so that innovations in the long term were of an expansive nature and generated new employment opportunities. During the 1950s and 1960s continental Europe and Japan gave evidence of greater growth potential than the United States, and, as already mentioned, the catching-up movement was the main element. This meant the assimilation not only of innovations made around the Second World War but also of those made in the previous period. The lead of the United States in the development of the modern economy was so great that the subsequent closing of the consumption gap exercised a spectacular and favourable influence on production and productivity, and thus on the general application of innovations. [52]

During the 1950s and 1960s as a whole, the emphasis was on capital widening. It was a period obviously influenced by John Maynard Keynes and thus one dominated by demand factors and by increasing investment designed to expand production in manufacturing industry. [53] Naturally the investment embodied many labour-saving and product-differentiating innovations but these were not the most characteristic feature of the time. Instead, stress was laid on the multiplication of new and existing techniques. So theorists who assigned a dominant role to this capital widening, downplayed the role of the entrepreneur. According to this interpretation, technological and organizational progress was mainly reduced to a simple process of capital formation, aimed at the mass production of consumer durables.

The advances of the 1950s and the 1960s were, however, more than that. Capital formation implied a justifiable choice as to which sectors should be allocated the extra capital. It implied, as well, a judicious choice as to what kind of capital should be used and how it could be most efficiently employed. In the Schumpeterian sense, then, there remained for entrepreneurs considerable opportunity for creative activity. Without their active engagement, capital formation would never have been converted into real prosperity growth.

It is also necessary to qualify the assumption concerning the closing of the gap between the United States and the rest of the world. Undoubtedly, during the 1950s and the 1960s, the dominant tendency in Western economic development was one of convergence, with the American rate of growth slower than that of Western Europe and Japan. Nevertheless it should be borne in mind that steady advances continued to be made at the technological and organizational frontier by the United States. In the new resultant growth sectors, the catching-up movement of Western Europe and Japan was much slower than in the traditional sectors of manufacturing industry. In broad terms, therefore, there was a real, general tendency towards convergence but in certain sectors the signs of a new divergence were perceptible.

THE REHABILITATION OF J. A. SCHUMPETER

The manufacturing advances of the 1950s and the 1960s – that is, the technological and organizational advances together with the investment-based growth in the West and afterwards in the Eastern bloc and some countries in the Third World – led to a situation of market saturation in the 1970s.[54] The expansion of industrial production in developing areas posed an immediate threat to manufacturing in older industrialized countries. The challenge was temporarily met by the diversification and rationalization of production. New products could be continually brought on to the market, either responding to existing needs or creating new ones. The demand for these new products still followed the pattern of a life cycle, initially rising but then leading to market saturation. When production was also begun in the new industrializing countries with lower wage costs, the traditional industrial countries were forced into further rationalization and diversification. Some economists, such as Gerard Mensch and Jaap J. Van Duijn, believed that the potential for further rationalization and diversification of manufacturing industry in the traditional industrial countries was exhausted in the 1970s. This exhaustion formed an inevitable link with the phenomenon of long-term structural change.[55] The preponderance of capital widening absorbed almost all the resources previously available for basic innovation and it was precisely these resources that could have made continued expansion possible. At the same time, in the technological field too, the emphasis was on extending and diversifying existing technology as much as possible. Innovations that *improved* the production process but did not *fundamentally change* it therefore gained the upper hand.

Mensch, agreeing with the ideas of Schumpeter, contended that the increasing rate of decline of basic innovations in favour of improvement innovations in all traditional sectors of manufacturing industry was bound to usher in a period of market saturation, long-term stagnation, and company rationalization. In a technological sense, the economy would stand at a position of stalemate (*'Das Technologische Patt'*). However, the tension resulting from the stalemate would pose such a fundamental challenge to traditional industrial countries faced with the possibility of relative economic decline that basic innovations would be given an extra stimulus and thus a new wave of innovations might be expected.[56] The 1980s and 1990s would thus comprise a period where the emphasis would no longer be on the widening of capital but on basic innovations. Brand-new products would be launched, and technological and organizational advances would bring a fundamental replacement of labour with capital, with basic changes in the macro-economic production function (capital deepening). It is clear that such large-scale innovations for both product and system would have to be supported by a well-organized research programme. For all this the new structure and consequent new long expansion phase would be born.

Experience of the 1960s and 1970s has shown that the products of manufacturing industry in the modern consumption economy indeed follow a life cycle and that their production regularly leads to market saturation. But Mensch and other neo-Schumpeterians give no argument as to why market saturation would necessarily take place in all important sectors of manufacturing industry at the same time in all countries. On the contrary, there is proof of desynchronization. The expansion phase of many consumer durables, such as the motor car, radio and refrigerator, made a start in the United States immediately after the First World War whereas in Europe and Japan it was only from the 1950s that lasting progress was made.[57] Ingmar Svennilson listed a series of innovations which could have transformed the European economy from the 1920s onwards and put it on a par with the American economy. But in fact the structural changes did not take place in Europe at that time but much later, after the Second World War.[58] The reasons for this delay were of a social, economic and institutional nature. The social context hindered a rapid development of the modern consumption economy, the labour surplus kept wages low, heavy industry used its dominant position to suck in much investment, and political institutions remained infused with conservative and aristocratic principles. The fact is that social, economic and institutional factors make it impossible to predict long-term structural changes in the Western economy according to the simple scheme of market saturation and innovation clusters as proposed by Mensch and other neo-Schumpeterians.

It is nevertheless undeniable that all the factors mentioned above have once more, during the 1970s, led to serious economic stagnation. It is also probable that stagnation will give greater impetus to the introduction of new basic innovations and will reduce the delay between discovery and innovation. What directions these basic innovations will take and in what country they will be introduced remains ultimately an open question. Development depends not only on the dynamic of the wave but also on the social, economic and institutional circumstances of different countries, as has already been indicated.

The direction taken by basic innovations will probably be determined by three main influences. The first is the micro-electronic revolution which, in an initial phase, has already had a considerable labour-creating effect since the Second World War. Even if this initial labour-creating effect should slow down, micro-electronics would still have a crucial innovative and expansive role not only in the manufacturing, service and public sectors, but also in individual and home-based consumption.[59] Labour-saving innovations and modernizations offered by advanced electronics are now being fully taken up. They ensure that electronics and machine industry, seen together, will remain at the forefront of technological progress in the next decades.[60] On the other hand, the spread of personal computers and the introduction of micro-electronics in all kinds of home-based consumption are creating new and fast-expanding markets. A second main influence will be the development of the demand for energy and mineral resources. If the relationship between the industrial countries and those Third World countries rich in energy and minerals deteriorates still further, much industrial research will be concentrated on basic innovations which provide substitutes for oil and traditional raw materials. The chemicals sector will thus continue to be an important source of technological progress. The third main influence will be exerted by the development of world population and the consequent food shortage. Further population growth and problems in the provision of food will undoubtedly stimulate basic innovations in the area of biology and biochemistry. The objective here will be to advance knowledge in respect of human, animal and plant life. In fact, in this third category a speeding-up in the rate of basic innovations is already taking place.

In the process of structural change, there is greater opportunity for a creative role to be played by the Schumpeterian entrepreneur. He is ultimately the one who must determine the new directions for industrial research, who must sense the social and economic potential of the cluster of new basic innovations, and who must convert these into expansive economic activity. He must, within the given institutional structure, seek new ways to expand the economy and realize any potential he finds.

Which countries are most likely to advance technological and organizational knowledge through basic innovations? On this issue K. Pavitt draws a comparison with European football, in which matches between different clubs are organized within a series of divisions, according to their qualifications in the field.[61] After a one-year competition the champions of a lower division step up to a higher division while the clubs with the poorest performances in the higher division move down to the lower division. Referring to this organizational pattern, Pavitt proposes to divide countries into four divisions, according to their performances in innovation.

In the first division are countries in which innovations are made at a high technological level. These are countries which operate very close to the technological and organizational frontier and are responsible for pushing it outwards. They react very creatively to this challenge, and the result is change in the use of technology and in relative costs. They also demonstrate intense activity in the area of basic innovations, especially in chemicals, petrochemicals, microelectronics, electronic machine industry and biology.

The second division includes industrialized countries which have some difficulties in changing and modernizing their industrial structure. Most of these countries, by means of a successful catching-up movement executed since the Second World War, have raised their manufacturing to a technological and organizational level close to that of countries in the first division. But they lack at present the economic and institutional infrastructure to achieve rapid restructuring and thereby to join the first division. Passage from the second to the first division seems to require overcoming a high structural threshold and is certainly no easy matter.

At the same time, countries in the second division are seriously threatened by those which, since the 1970s, have risen to higher positions within the third. Post-war experience suggests that promotion from the third to the second division does not encounter a high structural threshold and is not as difficult. This has been shown by Italy and Spain which, during the 1960s, were easily able to broaden their industrialization, originally based on the export of light industrial goods, to include the production of chemicals, steel, and consumer durables, and realizing by this a promotion from the third to the second division. At present it is the turn of the newly industrialized countries of Southern and Eastern Europe, Latin America, and South-East Asia. It is, however, much more difficult for a primitive economy to lift itself up to the development level of the third division. Here too a high structural threshold has to be overcome.

A closer study of the first division immediately reveals some particular characteristics. Around 1980 the role of the United States in advancing world technological and organizational knowledge was still extremely important and influential but no longer an exclusive one. Indeed, in some sectors of the capital goods industry and consumer durables industry, the United States has even been overtaken.[62] Some believe that the American lead has been lost in these sectors because of overconcentration on military technology, which cannot always be easily adapted for peaceful purposes.[63] In addition, the flight of capital in the form of foreign investment has removed resources which could have been used in furthering American industrial research in advanced sectors. All in all, however, the lead of the United States still remains an enormous one and in micro-electronics and biotechnology it appears to be growing rather than diminishing.[64] During the early 1980s, once again, the United States emerged as the most dynamic country of the world in introducing basic innovations.

A list of countries which, by means of an intense innovation activity, have worked themselves up to the first division, would include West Germany, Switzerland, and Sweden. Since the 1960s and 1970s, West Germany has shown a remarkable capacity to innovate in the areas of chemicals, machine industry, and motor manufacture. Switzerland plays a prominent role in innovations in chemicals and machine industry, Sweden is particularly dynamic in metal production and metal working. Japan in the early 1980s was on the point of stepping from the second into the first division. In electronics the number of Japanese innovations was increasing rapidly and the same could be said in the sectors of metal production and metal working (motor cars). The Netherlands (electronics) and Belgium (chemicals) were following the tracks made by Japan and were increasing their innovative activity. Nevertheless, neither of these countries as yet seemed to be able to push itself up into the first division, and the same could be said of Canada. Britain occupied a special position in that it provided an example of regression. As far as innovative capacity was concerned, Britain immediately after the Second World War could still be regarded as belonging to the first division; but following the 1970s there was a striking decline. In space and military technology Britain still held an important place but in all other sectors the British position had deteriorated visibly. The cause lies in severe technological competition – competition based not only on price but also on technological quality. British machines were sometimes more expensive than those of their competitors and they were lacking in a qualitative sense.[65]

The movement between divisions is based on numerous factors. The infeasibility of postulating a uniform development pattern proves definitively that the Kondratieff theory – that is, the theory of long waves – can no longer be accepted without modifications. Differences in social, economic and institutional circumstances mean that each country individually either accepts, modifies, or rejects the challenge of structural change. Furthermore, the creative role of the entrepreneur in the fundamental process of modification and structural modernization cannot be ignored. Seen in the perspective of world stagnation in the 1970s and 1980s, the diverse response to this challenge – ranging from innovative action to innovative passivity and innovative defencelessness – is laying the basis of a new divergence and imbalance in economic development. Just as there was a dominant trend towards convergence during the 1950s and 1960s when the catching-up movement was having its greatest impact, it is entirely possible that the structural challenges of the 1970s and 1980s will give rise to new divergences within the world economic system.

CHAPTER VI

THE IMPERATIVE OF DEMAND

Post-war growth and subsequent stagnation were not exclusively shaped by structural shifts in the area of supply and production. Structural shifts in the nature of demand and consumption wielded an important influence too. In most industrialized countries of the West, the Second World War marked a definitive watershed in the relationship between labour and capital. The benefits of the rapid rise in labour productivity now accrued overwhelmingly to the mass of wage and salary earners. At the same time their numbers increased. A first faltering step was made in the direction of a less unequal distribution of income. The economy adapted to this with new marketing techniques. The mass market was also considerably strengthened in that the liberalization of world trade and increasing economic interdependence had the effect of rapidly raising the export demand for consumer goods and investment goods.

1. THE FOUNDING OF THE MODERN CONSUMER SOCIETY

TURNING-POINTS IN THE RELATIONSHIP BETWEEN LABOUR AND CAPITAL

The rise of the modern consumer society in the industrialized countries of the West must be seen in a historical context. In the United States labour had traditionally been scarce, both at the time of the westward colonization and during the Industrial Revolution. Mechanization led to rising labour productivity but not to a surplus of labour. The potential for expansion of American agriculture and industry was immeasurable. The conditions thus existed for a high-wage economy based on farmers and skilled labour and for the flourishing of an American mass market in standardized consumer and investment goods. In the last quarter of the nineteenth century, the first signs of a modern consumer society were already apparent and its breakthrough and consolidation took place at the start of the twentieth century.[1]

For historical reasons, Europe lagged behind the United States. In Europe during the Industrial Revolution, the relationship between labour and capital was tilted much more in favour of capital. Overpopulation had always been latent, on the land as much as in the towns, and during the eighteenth century there was further population growth.[2] The surplus in the supply of labour held the incomes of industrial and agricultural workers ominously low. The beginnings of mechanization in urban industry brought no relief; on the contrary it led to technological unemployment which could not be immediately reabsorbed by the expansion of industry. In these circumstances, rising labour productivity was only partially reflected in increased industrial wages, and the surplus mostly accrued to the owners of capital and to consumers, particularly consumers of industrial products. The Industrial Revolution thus strengthened the conflict between labour and capital in European towns. Because of the greater vulnerability of industrial incomes, embitterment and militancy increased among the workers.

The European trade union movement and European workers' parties attempted to make the relationship between labour and capital more equal. Their objective was to make sure that salary and wage earners gained a greater share in the benefits of the higher productivity of labour which was resulting from increased mechanization and automation. The real breakthrough, neverthe-less, did not occur until after the Second World War, and then especially during the 1950s and the 1960s.

There are two main reasons for this delay. In the first place, during the depression of the 1930s unemployment in Europe was dramatically high. This had the effect of hindering and restraining the militancy of the unions and the workers' parties. It was only after the Second World War, when the structural labour surplus gave way to serious labour shortages in many sectors, that the union movement and social policy could be consolidated. More important still was the shift in economic ideology. Throughout the nineteenth century and deep into the twentieth the general economic ideology of the West remained based on the principle of economic efficiency. The provision of social services was still too often regarded as basically a form of charity which could either be granted on an individual basis by paternalistic entrepreneurs or else be compelled by union action or parliamentary legislation. One had to wait until after the Second World War for full acceptance of the principle of distributive justice. In this respect, Europe was in the forefront of change. Governments now were given the specific task of helping to increase labour productivity and ensuring that any gains were passed on to wage and salary earners. Growth, full employment, and a fairer distribution of income were all central pillars in governmental social economic policies after the war.[3]

For these reasons, demand management by governments was not restricted to the influencing of economic cycles but also took on a structural dimension. Social economic policy implied the stimulation of the demand for both consumer durables and public goods as well as the creation of adequate infrastructure and services to satisfy the stimulated demand.

In post-war Japan too, there was an acceleration in the development of the consumer society. In Japan just as in Europe, the historical circumstances of overpopulation and a labour surplus meant that initially the benefits of industrialization were largely monopolized by capital at the expense of labour. But post-war Japan differed from Europe in that neither a labour shortage nor union activity nor the growth of workers' parties constituted a decisive variable in the development of a broad domestic market for manufactures. Instead, the main factor was what one might call the paternalistic approach of big modern Japanese companies. The big companies integrated into their wage structure an elaborate system of seniority premiums, of bonuses and promotions. By doing so they created a periodic extra demand for consumer durables. This also had a demonstration effect for other categories of workers and employees in smaller firms and in the service sector.

THE RISING WAGE INCOME

The post-war consumer society of the West was primarily supported by an increase in the average level of wages and salaries, in nominal and in real terms. Table 27 compares some Western countries with respect to nominal and real wages during the period 1953 to 1982. The rise in nominal wages was already clear in the 1950s and the pace accelerated in the 1960s. In Europe wages in 1970 were generally about three times what they had been in 1953. In some cases the increase was nearly fourfold. Some countries started off with relatively low wage levels, either because of a low-wage policy as in the Netherlands or because of a greater labour surplus as in Italy, and so they could realize, after 1953, a catching-up movement. Other countries, France for example, followed a more lax monetary policy which led to greater inflationary pressure, and attempts were made to keep wages in line with the accelerating rate of price increases. In Japan and North America, wage evolution was somewhat different from that of Europe. In 1970, nominal wages in Japan were five times higher than in 1953. In the United States they only doubled. Japan started the immediate post-war period with a particularly low wage level and a weak currency; so the sharp rise in nominal wages can be partly ascribed to a catching-up movement. In the United States until 1970 the very opposite conditions prevailed, namely high wages and a strong currency policy.

From about 1970 to 1975 rises in nominal wages continued to accelerate considerably, due to high inflation and the booming world economy. Yet from this point onwards the tempo of wage increases slowed perceptibly. The Belgian figures are very illustrative for Europe as a whole. Nominal gross hourly earnings for Belgian workers rose from 1949 to 1958 at an average of 5.2 per cent annually. Then from 1958 to 1963 the annual average rise was 6.8 per cent; from 1963 to 1968 it was 8.5; from 1968 to 1973 it was 12.3; and from 1974 to 1975 it was 21. After 1975 the percentage rise fell rapidly to 11 in 1976 and to 9 in 1977, with further falls in later years. This latter development ran parallel to the decrease in inflation.[4]

Real wages did not rise as precipitously as nominal wages; nevertheless they did rise a good deal. In EEC countries, real wages increased on the average more than 40 per cent from 1964 to 1971. Once again taking Belgium as an example, gross hourly earnings

Table 27 *Nominal and Real Wages per Worker in Selected Western Countries, 1953–82*
(index-numbers: 1970 = 100)

		1953	1955	1960	1965	1970	1973	1976	1979	1982[a]
West Germany	nominal	27.0	30.7	44.0	66.5	100.0	139.0	181.1	215.9	253.0
	real	41.8	46.4	55.8	76.2	100.0	115.3	126.6	135.8	140.2
Italy	nominal	30.0	25.5	35.5	63.5	100.0	150.0	268.4	437.3	759.7
	real	37.5	41.3	52.5	74.0	100.0	118.6	126.3	134.8	139.7
Belgium	nominal	36.1	36.8	47.4	68.0	100.0	143.9	228.0	286.1	360.8
	real	53.5	54.4	64.3	78.8	100.0	123.8	144.7	156.5	168.3
Netherlands	nominal	21.9	26.1	36.5	59.5	100.0	147.4	214.4	264.5	304.9
	real	40.2	44.7	54.9	73.9	100.0	115.4	126.7	134.4	131.9
France	nominal	26.3	24.9	40.6	65.0	100.0	138.4	221.1	315.6	470.5
	real	55.5	51.2	61.9	81.7	100.0	116.0	133.8	146.2	154.4
United Kingdom	nominal	34.5	37.7	50.8	68.0	100.0	142.3	257.5	366.3	537.7
	real	61.1	63.4	75.3	85.2	100.0	113.3	121.8	123.1	126.2
United States	nominal	47.7	50.4	62.9	74.7	100.0	121.6	152.6	192.7	247.6
	real	69.0	72.0	81.0	89.5	100.0	106.7	105.9	105.8	106.9
Japan	nominal	19.3	21.6	29.4	52.9	100.0	158.5	261.3	325.1	383.3
	real	38.2	40.9	50.9	68.9	100.0	129.6	146.3	154.8	169.9

Notes: The *nominal wage figure* was calculated as follows: the total sum of wages paid during the year divided by the number of workers employed during the same period.

The *real wage figure* is the nominal wage figure deflated by the index of consumption prices.

[a] Provisional figures

Source: COMET-databank, based on the national accounts data, used in the EEC and OECD

for Belgian workers rose in real terms by 3.8 per cent on an annual average for the period 1949–58. Then for 1958–63 it was 3.9; for 1963–8 it was 4.7; for 1968–73 it was 7.1; for 1974–5 it was 8; and for 1976–7 and 1978–80 it was about 2. Seen as a whole, this represents a substantial raising of prosperity levels over the first three decades after the Second World War. Between 1948 and 1977 nominal hourly wages in Belgium rose fourteenfold while consumer prices less than tripled. In some countries, including West Germany, the evolution of hourly wages was even more favourable. In others it was less favourable: in Britain and especially in the United States inflation was only weakly compensated for by wage rises.

The above-mentioned rates of increase refer mostly to average *hourly* earnings of workers. In the course of the post-war period, however, the length of the working week was greatly reduced. In EEC countries this reduction between 1961 and 1976 was about 18 per cent in the industrial sector. Consequently, if wage earnings are calculated on a weekly rather than hourly basis, the percentage increases in wage incomes are not so high. In addition it should be noted that in general the wages and salaries of women rose more than those of men.[5] But the evolution of women's earnings started from a lower base; so it was only a question of a catching-up movement and even then often a rather limited one.

The increase in individual income was not exclusively confined to the increases in real wages and salaries. Reductions in the working week and social benefit payments also made an important contribution to enhancing individual well-being. Pensions and the benefits for sickness, disability, and unemployment were all extended. In Belgium the amount paid out in unemployment benefits in 1976 was nearly twelve times that of 1948. In other areas of social security, growth was still more remarkable. Alongside the systems of social payments, public services such as education, culture, tourism, sport, and transport improved prosperity levels too. These services were provided by governments either free of charge or at greatly reduced prices. Nevertheless the expansion of social benefits and other collective provisions also had negative effects. It depended in part on contributions deducted from workers' wages and on higher taxation. Therefore the above-mentioned gross wage incomes have to be reduced to net wage incomes to get a true picture of the real changes in disposable income. Naturally, any benefits actually received from social services must be added back on to the net result.

The expansion of the social services was additionally financed through employer contributions. As a result, total wage costs borne by employers rose higher than the gross hourly wage earnings of the employees. In Belgium the index figure for total hourly wage costs (gross hourly wage earnings plus employers' contributions per hour) stood at 1,137 in 1976 as against 100 in 1948, that of gross hourly wage earnings stood at 923.5. In some other EEC countries the difference was still more significant. When the development of total wage costs is compared with that of labour productivity, one is immediately struck by the sharp rise in wage costs per unit produced. The rise in costs was already apparent during the 1960s but it notably gained pace in the course of the following decade. It was reflected in the increase in the rate of price inflation; but the figures show that entrepreneurs were not able fully to pass on the increase in wage costs to the consumer via the process of inflation. Therefore, increasingly over the 1970s, entrepreneurs began to make savings in their use of labour. The high unemployment of that period and the outbreak of the micro-electronic revolution must be seen from this perspective.

THE RISING SHARE OF WAGES AND SALARIES IN THE NATIONAL INCOME

The post-war phenomenon of rising wages and salaries immediately raises questions concerning the functional distribution of national income. Should these rises be seen as an improvement of the average income position of hourly workers and other employees in relation to other income groups? That is, did the incomes of workers and employees increase more than those of the self-employed (farmers, retailers and others) and of entrepreneurs and the owners of capital? Moreover, did the increase in income of wage and salary earners affect the relative shares of the production factors of capital and labour in the composition of national income – that is, did it favour labour at the expense of capital?[6] It is not easy to give an answer to this question. For instance, for the self-employed and entrepreneurs that part of income derived from their own labour must be deducted and added to the income of wage and salary earners.

Simon Kuznets has traced the long-term development of the shares of labour and capital in the national income of Western countries (Table 28).[7] He found that during the nineteenth century

Table 28 Distribution of National Income among Factor Shares, Selected Countries, Long Period (underlying totals in current prices)

	Share in national income (per cent)			Percentage of entrepreneurs and self-employed in labour force
	Compensation of workers and employees	Income of entrepreneurs and self-employed	Income from assets	
United Kingdom				
(1) 1860–9	47	17	36	13
(2) 1905–14	47	16	37	13
(3) 1920–9	59	15	26	10
(4) 1954–60	70	9	21	6
France				
(5) 1853	36	46	18	36
(6) 1911	44	32	24	33
(7) 1912	44	31	26	33
(8) 1913	45	33	22	33
(9) 1920–9	50	29	21	30
(10) 1954–60	59	29	12	27
West Germany				
(11) 1895	39	45	16	26
(12) 1913	47	35	18	21
(13) 1913	48	33	19	21
(14) 1925–9	64	26	10	19
(15) 1954–60	60	22	18	16
Switzerland				
(16) 1913	66	n.a.	34	n.a.
(17) 1924	49	25	26	25
(18) 1954–60	50	18	22	19
Canada				
(19) 1926–9	59	25	16	28
(20) 1954–60	66	13	21	18
United States				
(21) 1899–1908	54	24	22	28.5
(22) 1919–28	58	18	24	21.5
(23) 1929	58	17	25	21
(24) 1954–60	69	12	19	15

Source: S. KUZNETS, *Modern Economic Growth*, pp. 168–70

the share of income from assets grew, albeit slightly, in all countries examined.[8] It was only in the United States that this rise continued during the 1920s; the share of assets actually declined in European countries, and in the crisis of the 1930s it declined in the United States too. After the Second World War there was a general fall in the West, including the United States, though Canada was an exception. When one studies the share of the income of the self-employed (as far as their income was derived from profit and capital), the conclusion is even more evident. In all countries examined this share has fallen almost without interruption from the nineteenth century on into the post-war era. In contrast, the share of salary and wage earners in the national income has generally increased from about 40 per cent in the nineteenth century to about 60 to 70 per cent in the post-war years.

Although the evolution of income from assets moved similarly in different countries – its share rising and then falling – the countries were not alike in the size of the percentages. In the United Kingdom, for example, the percentages until the First World War were remarkably high, and early in the twentieth century no less than 37 per cent of national income was derived from assets. From this point onwards the United Kingdom percentage, though declining, remained high in comparison with other countries. Its size goes a long way towards explaining the early development and militancy of union action in Britain, especially when one takes into account the large number of wage and salary earners present in the British economy, even as early as the nineteenth century. In France and Germany, the income from assets percentages evolved at a much lower level than in the United Kingdom. On the other hand, in both countries the relative share of self-employed incomes was higher than in the United Kingdom. Even so the income from assets percentages in France and Germany increased enough during the nineteenth century to provoke a fierce reaction from the unions.

The rise in the share of wages and salaries in the national income was already under way in the nineteenth century but it speeded up after the First World War and still more after the Second World War. When the percentages are closely examined, the trend must be primarily ascribed to the increasing dependence on wages, that is, the long-term steady rise in the number of wage and salary earners in relation to the total working population. This has taken place at the expense of the self-employed, including farmers, merchants, artisans, and entrepreneurs. In many countries the number involved in these occupational categories has fallen from 35 or 40 per cent of the total working population to less than 20 per cent. The question might be asked whether the share of wages and salaries in the national income still shows an upward trend when account is taken of the degree of wage-dependence, in other words when average income per wage and salary earner is compared with national income per capita. According to Kuznets, the general increase of the share of wages and salaries in national income since the Second World War is much less when the wage-dependency correction is applied. None the less, one can still incontestably talk in terms of a general increase. According to calculations by Herman Deleeck for Belgium, the share of private wages and salaries in national income between 1948 and 1975 rose from 36.9 per cent to 59.84 per cent. During the same period the number of wage and salary earners increased from 53.3 per cent to 74.43 per cent of the working population. Therefore almost two-thirds of the rise in the share of private wages and salaries in national income must be ascribed to an increase in the number of wage and salary earners and more than one-third to a relative improvement in their average income position.[9] In Belgium it appears that even the steep inflation of the 1970s has not led to an undermining of the average income position of wage and salary earners in the private sector. On the contrary, this position further improved, and Belgium was certainly not an exception. In most if not all Western countries after the Second World War, the share of capital in national income fell and that of labour rose.[10]

2. THE EFFECTS OF INCOME INCREASES ON DOMESTIC DEMAND

THE HIGHER PROPENSITY FOR CONSUMPTION AND INVESTMENT

Rising incomes after the Second World War and the spread of the American consumption model to all industrialized countries of the West led to an explosion in demand and a dynamic response by entrepreneurs in their investment strategy. Immediately after the war the chief motor of demand was the process of reconstruction and recovery. Countries had to make good the gross underconsumption of the war years, replenish exhausted stocks in households and businesses, and replace residential and industrial buildings, infrastructure, and outdated machinery and equipment. After the completion of the recovery process, the construction of the modern consumer economy became the driving force for demand – to be more precise, it was rather the extension of the consumer economy in the United States, and its construction in Western Europe and Japan. Increasing prosperity became a central objective in all government programmes.

The modern consumer economy was based on the mass introduction of all sorts of consumer durables, the rapid expansion of the leisure and fashion industries, the expansion and improvement of housing, the development of existing infrastructure, the creation of new public services, and the strongly increased demand for financial services, personal transport and tourism. The cause of all of this was the continuous rise in family incomes after the Second World War. As soon as necessities were taken care of, additional income was used to satisfy prosperity needs. Of course, saving increased too, but it was the greater affluence demand that implied higher production and a tremendous expansion in capacity. Demand thus promoted much additional investment in the form of capital deepening, and more important still in the form of capital widening. Governments were active in this process; not only did they themselves invest in order to satisfy the rapidly expanding demand for public services but they also encouraged investment in the private sector by means of subsidies and other measures. This is not to say, however, that the private sector was a laggard in the march; indeed it showed great dynamism in both extending and renewing capacity. The increase in investment worked as a powerful lever creating new employment, new incomes, and new consumer demand.

The imperative of demand also had an important psychological effect on the behaviour of entrepreneurs.[11] The post-war affluent economy initiated a long-term upward price movement and evened out economic cyclical fluctuations. For Western entrepreneurs this was a whole new experience, in sharp contrast to the depression and falling prices of the inter-war period. The variegated experiences of the first half of the twentieth century had created a climate of caution, since entrepreneurs felt uncertain of themselves, and reacted with a policy of manifest underinvestment. After the war, this climate of insecurity made way for one of certainty, notably in respect of demand and economic performance. High profit expectations became the rule. The macro-economic future seemed to be both plain sailing and full of promise. Investment now was made for preventive reasons; that is, entrepreneurs wished to avoid losing market shares and they appeared more concerned about the possibility of investing too little than too much. In addition, they wanted to neutralize rising wage costs via technological progress and rising labour productivity. They also sought ways within this favourable psychological climate to ensure the economic future of their companies.[12] They spent lavishly on advertising, as a way to manipulate the consumer. They took account of factors such as the growing purchasing power of youth, the ageing of the population, and changes in life-styles brought by motorization and increasing mobility, and they tried to integrate all of these into their market policy. By means of product differentiation, innovation, and advertising, they continuously created new needs, which generated demand for progressively more advanced products.

The management of consumption patterns and the creation of new consumer needs are only possible through a powerful growth in the size of companies. Affluence demand therefore stimulated first the expansion of oligopolistically inclined big business. The increase in consumption was accompanied by a tendency to concentrate purchasing of certain goods in large shopping centres, especially at particular times of the week. In these large shopping centres there was diversification of activity, customer self-service, and the like. At the same time affluence demand also promoted investment in small firms. In the selling of consumer durables guarantees and after-sales service are important factors. These maintenance services can usually be provided more efficiently by small, autonomous units. Moreover, creativity in fashion – clothing and footwear, for example – is usually more flexibly realized by smaller firms, in production as well as in distribution.[13] In 1966 the 500 largest concerns in the United States employed only 19 per cent of the total number of wage and salary earners, and this total does not include self-employed workers and entrepreneurs. Companies with fewer than fifty workers represented no less than 97 per cent of the total number of companies. In Europe the situation is the same. In Belgium in 1972, industrial companies employing no more than fifty workers and companies in the service sector employing no more than twenty together accounted for more than 40 per cent of the total number of wage and salary earners. These same companies represented 94.2 per cent of the total number of companies, and their production was more or less 40 per cent of GNP.[14]

For these reasons, affluence demand in the market economies of the post-war West in no way implied the end of the small firm. In this respect, the contrast with the centrally planned economies of the Eastern bloc is striking. In Eastern Europe the production of goods and services was centralized and differentiation took place more slowly than it did in the West. The enhancement of self-employed small business in the West also had an important political effect. It increased the number of self-employed with middle incomes and consequently strengthened their bargaining position in determining government economic policy. The post-war evolution of income distribution in favour of the affluent middle classes must also be seen from this viewpoint.

UNION ACTIVITY AT THE NATIONAL LEVEL

The integration of union activity into the modern consumer society in Western Europe took place on two levels: on a macro-economic level, where union activity became more centralized, and on a company level, where there was an increasing tendency towards decentralization. Both of these trends exhibited their own dynamism and generated specific effects.[15]

The increasing centralization of union activity on the macro-economic plane grew out of a historical development process that goes back to the nineteenth century, when the unions had to battle grimly for existence in a hostile climate. They campaigned to establish themselves permanently by winning concessions such as the freedom of association, legal recognition of the status of unions, the right to strike, political influence via universal suffrage, and so on. In various European countries workers' parties finally managed to break through into political power: during the First World War or shortly afterwards they got into government and then after the Second World War they sometimes even assumed complete governmental responsibility. Simultaneously, representatives of workers' parties were granted places in administration, on government committees and the like.

As the political influence of workers' parties rose, so the dynamism of the unions faded.[16] The unions institutionalized themselves as a pressure group within the framework of the mixed economy and became instruments in the integration of workers into the new structure of industrial society. The revolutionary union movement made way for a participative one which implicitly accepted the capitalistic organization of the Western economic system. In order to make this consensus operational, the 'consultative economy' was developed. The unions, employers' organizations, and government became the most important partners in a central deliberation on economic policy, especially on labour and wage policies. The new political development fundamentally changed the internal structure and organization of the European union movement in strengthening its cohesion nation-wide. The consultative economy functioned at the highest level of government[17] and this led to more centralizing and professionalizing of union federations. An extensive apparatus of specialized officials was established in order to draw up union demands and to ensure that the negotiation process was efficiently handled. Union demands now made full allowance for economic realities in a nation-wide sense and indeed became an integral part of the functioning of the total economy. In this respect the union movement co-operated in a moderate wage and labour policy. At the same time the centralization also brought with it increased bureaucracy, which broadened the gap between the union organization and its members. The unions replied that by gaining political power through the penetration by their representatives into the decision-making bodies of the system they strengthened the power of the working class as a whole.[18]

The post-war consultative economy introduced, in many European countries, a very active labour policy. In 1957 the Netherlands stood alone with its concrete and heavily controlled wage policy. Subsequently Britain and Austria attempted to introduce comparable wage planning and in the 1960s many other countries followed too. The first successful experiments in centralized wage negotiation were carried out in the Scandinavian countries, and, again in the 1960s, other European countries took the same path. Finally, there was an increasing number of government measures to extend legal controls over workers. In various countries laws were passed, often with the co-operation of workers' parties and unions, to regulate the right to strike, with the object of incorporating the workers into the system of the mixed economy.[19] To decide from this that union activity was now fully circumscribed and that the unions were no longer able to secure primary or secondary advantages for their members would, however, be a mistake. In fact the unions, in a reformist manner, continued to press for an increase and improvement in workers' wages. None the less, if aggression was indeed shown, its origin could mostly be traced back not to the centralization but rather the decentralization of union activity. This decentralization was the second characteristic of the post-war union movement.

UNION ACTIVITY AT THE COMPANY LEVEL

The centralization and bureaucracy of the European union movement instilled in many members a sense of alienation from their leadership. This generated a desire to intensify union activity at the level of the individual company where the original spirit of confrontation and the immediate involvement of the rank and file remained guaranteed. The development of the post-war economy also facilitated this trend.[20] In the modern, large concerns, individuals lost much of their significance. The amount they earned for their labour was less dependent on individual performance and more on the profitability of the company as a whole. In addition workers, through their particular professional training and specialized knowledge, became more closely attached to their own company since their career and promotion were increasingly determined by the company's growth. In the consultative economy, only the general criteria of wage policy were centrally laid down, and the discussion of ways to implement these guidelines was left to individual sectors and companies. At issue here were not just wage agreements as such but also many other problems such as the conditions of employment, shiftwork, the hiring of workers, dismissal procedures, overtime, safety, holidays, bonuses linked to profits, and so on.[21]

Because post-war production showed a high degree of differentiation, many specific systems of remuneration were introduced. Central wage negotiations therefore had to be completed by negotiations at a sectoral and even increasingly at a company level. Empirical wage studies concerning the post-war economy of the West bring to light very significant differences in wage levels by sector and by company. Sectors and companies are characterized by differences in labour productivity, unemployment levels, size, degree of concentration and organization. As the unions assimilated partially these differences within their demands, income differences between sectors and between companies came about.[22]

The decentralization of union activities led not only to differences in wage and income levels but also to increasing institutional evolution. The wartime co-operation between workers and employers (for the sake of productivity) opened the prospect of joint management when peace came. Thus the new concept of participation for the unions included not only a role in national consultation but also involvement in business management. All over Europe workplace committees were set up by law in order to realize the new ideal of co-operation.

The union movement attempted to gain control over these committees. Quite often the list of worker candidates had by law to be drawn up by the recognized unions. If the legislation did not go as far as that, then the union leaders made sure that their representatives played a prominent role in the electoral campaigns. Those elected became the official representatives of the workers; their task was to defend the interests of the workers in that particular company. They often received the privilege of immunity and their dismissal was impossible or, at the least, difficult. In Germany participation was still further extended and union representatives became *de jure* members of the board of directors and of the board of surveillance in companies involved in the steel and coal sectors. This particular form of participation became known as the '*Mitbestimmung*' system.

The institutionalizing of the union movement at the company level often weakened its aggressiveness. Empirical research shows that in the German coal and steel sector, despite close consultation, wage rises and other benefits were significantly lower than those reached in other industrial sectors.[23] The sense of responsibility for the general interest which the official labour representatives acquired as soon as they were involved in the management process had the effect of moderating union activity. Moderation was all the more necessary when the existence or profitability of a sector or company was threatened by structural changes or by foreign competition. The coal and steel sector, for example, was threatened by both.

The discipline of the official representatives often caused bitterness among the workers themselves, and the local union leaders, like the national ones, became more alienated from their members. In the lower reaches of the union organization, at company level, the authority of the union representatives was occasionally rejected and alternative leaders were elevated. Sometimes the local union representatives associated themselves with the rank and file, and this often led to a general revolt against the guidelines established by the union hierarchy. In these conditions wildcat strikes were more likely to occur. The decentralization of union activity at company level was therefore a far from harmonious process. It was often characterized more by conflict than by consensus.

By the start of the 1970s one could see that drastic structural changes in many industries were unavoidable. Dismissals and closures became a regular phenomenon. Structural reforms normally implied a complete transfer of resources from one industrial region or sector to another and the realization of a new pattern of economic activity. Such radical change was confronted not only by the conservatism of the endangered industrial sectors but also by the inertia of the traditional union leadership. Fears for the future shared by rank-and-file members combined with rigidity in the upper reaches of the union hierarchy converged into a movement for government protection and government subsidies, a movement supported in most cases by the managers and owners, while unions and workers alike not infrequently aimed at direct worker control at the company level; 'from co-determination to self-determination' was the new call.

Centralization and decentralization of union activity benefited all workers engaged in the production process, but some more than others. Many employed in the modern large-scale industry of the West managed to work themselves up to higher social and economic categories.[24] There has always been a 'workers' aristocracy'. In the nineteenth century machine personnel and technicians already belonged to this group. In the post-war period the workers' aristocracy expanded. As for the large numbers of less privileged workers employed in unskilled jobs or in sectors that faced increasing structural difficulties, their income levels were much better than previously but their job uncertainty and relatively low wages remained a handicap. During the difficult years of the 1970s, some cautious union measures were taken in various European countries to try to protect these less privileged groups.

The post-war history of American trade unionism was entirely different from the European experience.[25] The strong expansion of the American trade unions in the first half of the century, increasing union membership between 1910 and 1953 from 5.6 to 25.7 per cent of the total labour force, was not to be maintained. From the mid 1950s membership stagnated: in 1970 it stood at only 22.6 per cent. This levelling-off was due in large part to the dramatic increase of employment in the service sector: in the 1970s more than 60 per cent of the labour force was employed in service industries (against less than 30 per cent in 1920), and fewer than 10 per cent of workers in the service sector were unionized (against more than 40 per cent in the goods-producing sector).

The limited and stagnating character of the union membership clearly undermined the action of the unions. In fact, other factors too were weakening the impact of American trade unionism on the social and economic development of the country. The Taft-Hartley Labor-Management Relations Act of June 1947 imposed important restrictions and obligations upon the unions. Although the two largest trade union organizations, the American Federation of Labor (AFL) and the Congress of Industrial Organizations (CIO) merged in the mid 1950s, the power of the new federation was impeded by internal frictions and by revelations of corruption and improper practices in certain unions, resulting in the Landrun-Griffin Labor-Management Reporting and Disclosure Act of 1959. An important additional obstacle to successful action was undoubtedly the shift in public attitudes, which has increasingly criticized unions for growing bureaucratic and complacent. The AFL-CIO leaders, trying with the Carter administration to exert pressure for legislation favourable to the unions, therefore did not meet with success. With the Reagan administration the influence of the unions was still less.

Nevertheless, organized labour was not always a loser. It was able to broaden its scope as in the organization of federal employees, who in 1962 were given the right to unionize and to bargain collectively. Similar rights were received by state and municipal employees in most of the states. Moreover, with unemployment rising in the late 1970s, the labour movement worked with success for the passage in 1978 of the Humphrey-Hawkins Full Employment and Balanced Growth Act, aiming at reducing unemployment to 4 per cent by 1983 and designating the national government as the employer of last resort through the eventual creation of government work projects. From a general point of view, however, the contribution of trade unionism in shaping the American mixed economy in the post-war period was rather small.

Japan was also a special case in the area of union activity. On a nation-wide basis the union movement hardly existed, but it was very important within big companies, although rather co-operative in nature. Managers and union representatives jointly set themselves the goal of making their own particular company as profitable as possible. There was little dispute regarding the distribution of the results of this co-operation. The paternalistic solidarity measures taken by management were so institutionalized that there was almost an *a priori* consensus. Japanese union activity was thus an instrument of management rather than a source of obstruction.

INCOME DISTRIBUTION AND AFFLUENCE DEMAND

The shift in income distribution – the rise in the share of wages and salaries in the national income – and the general increase in incomes after the Second World War had a positive influence on the development of affluence demand. These mere facts cover, however, a very complex underlying reality. Changes in the distribution of income are slow processes which must be viewed in their historical context. So what is the long-term picture? In *primary* income distribution, that is, gross income before tax and before the payment of social security premiums, it is one of clear change. According to Kuznets' calculations,[26] primary income distribution in the United States and Europe from the end of the nineteenth century up to the First World War was highly skewed and showed little tendency towards change. Both the First and Second World Wars were turning-points; the skew spread of primary incomes diminished substantially immediately after both wars. Each time, however, after some years a tendency towards stabilization could be observed.

The long-term movement towards more normally distributed income in the West can be ascribed to various forces.[27] In general terms, differences in labour productivity among industrial sectors decreased. Furthermore, the number of those working in agriculture and in small independent units fell in relation to the total working population and it was in precisely these categories that low incomes were frequent. The proportion of income derived from assets also fell strikingly, as mentioned earlier: it lowered the earnings of the highest income groups. According to Kuznets, economic growth of itself facilitated a more normal distribution of incomes,[28] but this is not an opinion unanimously shared by economists.[29] Seen in the long term, there are undoubtedly connections between economic development and the tendency towards more normally distributed incomes, but in the medium term these connections seem less clear. For example, the tendency towards convergence of incomes in the West was much stronger during the war and the subsequent recovery period, when growth was decidedly weak, than during the 1950s, when growth began to increase spectacularly and the levelling process in incomes in some cases stopped altogether. There is thus no simple correlation between growth and converging incomes.

Changes in attitude towards the problem, however, have exercised a direct influence. Egalitarian philosophy, which goes back to the Enlightenment, first directed itself at the ideal of legal equality, then added political equality, and finally established economic equality as the goal of modern society. The chronology of the turning-points in the evolution of income distribution implies that the two world wars were of decisive importance in the change of general attitude. The wars and subsequent years of recovery destroyed many old customs and outdated conceptions, and gave governments greater control and more opportunity for initiatives and reform. Moreover, public opinion saw a chance to make a fresh start and build the consensus for a new, better society.

Changes in attitude also had an impact on the social stratification of the family, which affected income distribution by influencing per capita income.[30] The size of families in low-income groups in Europe fell appreciably around the middle of the twentieth century whereas family size in the highest income groups increased significantly in the same period. The same tendency could also be observed in the United States, although it was less apparent. Another point is that in the welfare economy it was easier for both young and older people to live in their own separate family units. The differentiated evolution of the family in the West had an important effect on income distribution. If income distribution is not calculated on the basis of family income but on income per capita, then the spread of incomes is less skewed. Jan Tinbergen calculated in this respect that the disparity between the highest and lowest income groups during the 1960s in countries such as West Germany and the Netherlands was reduced by about one-half.[31]

The change in mentality of the population also influenced the evolution of *secondary* income distribution, that is, the income distribution which results from conscious government intervention. Income redistribution became an important government objective immediately after the war, and indeed public opinion expected government to take concrete measures to build an equitable society.

In order to bring about this redistribution, the government could manipulate taxation and social security contributions. The introduction of progressive, direct taxation in the course of the twentieth century and especially after the Second World War was bound to hit the disposable income of higher income groups. Statistics on income distribution *after* taxation indeed show more tendency towards convergence than income distribution *before* taxation. Direct taxation has reduced practically everywhere the share of the highest income group (particularly the top 10 per cent in total income). It has also, although to a lesser extent, increased the share of the lowest income groups in total income.[32] On the other hand, indirect taxation, such as sales taxes, has not had the same income-equalizing effect. In many countries indirect taxation is collected on the most intensively used goods, and so the system works regressively, that is, it increases income inequalities.

Governments also brought about income redistribution through transfer payments which can be divided into two main categories, namely the payment of social benefits and the provision of public goods. After the war, both grew to represent enormous sums. In Europe government transfers in 1980 constituted between a third and a half of GNP, in the United States about a third. The intention was that the extra contributions of the socially advantaged should cover the income deficiencies of the socially disadvantaged and that the extra taxes paid by higher income groups should finance public services available to the whole population. Statistical research has shown that the welfare states of the West were only partially attaining this objective. The form of distribution studied is known as *tertiary* distribution and it takes into account the full effect of social benefit payments and the ultimate consumption of public goods. The calculations as worked out for Belgium by Deleeck[33] give a rather unfavourable result from the viewpoint of income equalization. Government transfer payments did not so much accrue to the lowest income groups as instead work largely to the benefit of higher and middle income groups. These groups made more use of the facilities offered by the social security system, for instance in the use of medical and paramedical services. Furthermore, the public goods are geared proportionately more towards the needs of high and middle income groups than to those with lower income. For example, college education and cultural opportunities are proportionately more exploited by the affluent than by the poor. The general figures must therefore be somewhat modified and corrected.

AN OVERVIEW OF INCOME DISTRIBUTION BY COUNTRY

The general characteristics of income distribution analysed above sometimes obscure important national differences. Some of these differences relating to the post-war period will now be examined.

In the United States, just as elsewhere, the Second World War marked an important turning-point, but, after that, income distribution remained remarkably stable. The improvement of general education and the Great Society programme of the 1960s seem to have had little effect. Detailed studies do show an improvement in the relative income position of blacks and other minority groups[34] but income differences within the global group of male wage and salary earners would appear to have somewhat increased during the 1960s.[35] The redistributive effect of taxation and social contributions in the United States remained also rather limited. The direct taxation is progressive, but indirect taxation and social security premiums are regressive.[36] Research in the early 1970s indicated that the greatest advantage from public goods and social benefit payments appeared to have been drawn by middle and higher income groups. Nearly a third of the amounts paid out in the form of unemployment benefits and government pensions in 1971, for example, had gone to families with incomes of $15,000 or more.[37]

Sweden stands at or near the top of the league when it comes to the reduction of income disparity. Direct and indirect taxation, together with social security premiums, comprised no less than 44–5 per cent of GNP at the start of the 1970s. Moreover, the tax system is steeply progressive in nature so that the distribution of after-tax income has a strong equalizing tendency. Finally the government has evolved a highly extensive system of transfer payments; and money transfers comprised about 18 per cent of total personal income. Alongside this, the government was subsidizing many services, including free education. Calculations have shown that in Sweden transfer payments accrue to lower income groups to a greater extent than anywhere else. In addition, this system benefits the non-economically active population in relation to the working population.[38] One negative effect of income levelling in Sweden is undoubtedly a decrease in private savings, which jeopardizes investment and might be an obstacle for the long-term economic growth.[39] This is a serious matter, especially in times of structural difficulties.

In terms of social policy, Britain lies very close to Sweden. The Labour government which came to power immediately after the war set itself the primary task of realizing the socially inspired welfare plan of Lord Beveridge. The Beveridge Plan implied a big redistribution of income by means of government transfer payments to lower income groups. The pension system worked in an especially redistributive fashion. On the other hand in public services the redistributive effects were weaker. Calculations showed that tertiary income distribution in Britain worked to the advantage of high and middle income groups. Direct taxation was steeply progressive but its income-equalizing effects were undermined by the somewhat regressive character of indirect taxation.[40] Whereas in Sweden the conflict between the ideal of income equality and economic growth was recognized as an impending threat, in Britain this conflict was already hard reality in the 1970s. This worrisome experience was an important factor in the defeat of Labour by the Conservatives in the general election of 1979.

In West Germany social policy was framed differently from that in Sweden and Britain. Immediately after the war the German government expressly laid emphasis on the market economy and on private initiative. The tariffs for direct taxation were even adjusted in order to promote savings and investment, and so direct taxation only became progressive at the very highest income levels. In this respect there is a certain similarity with the United States, but this is not the case for government transfer payments. In fact these had a rather redistributive effect in West Germany; they particularly benefited the non-working population, with the working population receiving proportionately much less. As for the government transfers which did accrue to the working population, waged workers were undoubtedly favoured. In this area, then, West Germany lay closer to Sweden and Britain.[41]

France, Italy and Belgium more or less followed the same line as West Germany, but Japan, again, is a case by itself.[42] The Japanese economy is much less 'mixed' in character. In structure it has remained fairly private-capitalist. Government expenditure on goods and services is very limited. So are government transfer payments (in 1970 comprising only 6 per cent of total personal income as against 20 per cent in France and 14 per cent in Sweden). The low government expenditure on social welfare in Japan can be explained by structural factors. Industrial companies there still exercise a very important social function, guaranteeing workers greater job security and providing them with all kinds of advantages in terms of money and goods (the yearly income of workers averages twice their basic wage). For the westerner such a structure appears paternalistic, but for the Japanese it is the expression of an elementary solidarity between employers and workers. After the war Japan laid a strong emphasis on savings and investment (private capital formation), and on economic growth. Tax receipts and social security premiums in 1970 amounted to only 21 per cent of GNP in Japan, compared with 43 per cent in Sweden and about 30 per cent in the United States. Direct taxation thus had a relatively slight equalizing effect on incomes, apart from those at the very upper end of the scale. In addition, income from assets rose from 9.5 per cent of national income in 1960 to 12.4 per cent in 1971. Nevertheless this structure did not lead to the very large differences in income levels that had existed before the war, when a few rich families controlled the *Zaibatsu* and land was possessed by a few large landowners. The reforms put through by the American occupation authorities after the Second World War undoubtedly represented a turning-point. Subsequent income evolution, despite the private capitalistic nature of the national economy, did not suggest a return to previous levels of inequality. Indeed, studies of the 1970s show that income distribution in Japan is more balanced than in West Germany and the United States.

What conclusion can be drawn from this short overview? Incomes in the industrialized countries of the West were more equitably distributed in 1950 than in 1939.[43] The Second World War was a general turning-point. During the 1950s the trend in the direction of equalization continued but the movement was an altogether weaker one. It continued nevertheless during the 1960s and the early 1970s in France, Italy, Japan, and the Netherlands. In West Germany and Britain the situation was more stable and in the United States disparity was even increasing somewhat. The general picture, however, is one of stability since the 1950s.[44]

Some additional comments must be made. Although the share of the highest 10 per cent in total income fell notably, that of lower income groups in some cases also fell, be it slightly, and in general stagnated. In contrast, the share of the middle income groups improved overall.[45] The social structure of the population is thus polarizing into two great blocks: on one side low income groups, strongly dominated by the relative increase in the number of pensioners and minority groups, and on the other side middle income groups, dominated by the relative increase in the number of wage and salary earners. Some statistical errors are concealed within these shifts. Formerly, for example, old people usually lived with their children and were not regarded as individual income earners. Nevertheless such statistical shortcomings do not affect the general conclusions.

Income relationships within the group of wage and salary earners can be seen as a reflection of the amount of education received. If a country wishes to move towards income equalization, an obvious policy is to democratize education. Studies have shown, however, that participation in higher education and the choice of study are socially determined and strongly influenced by family background. As a result the democratization of education does not lead to more income equalization, but rather the contrary.[46] Moreover, the education of the most able gives rise to increasingly higher specialization and technical qualifications and thus a new form of income disparity.[47] A final point is that post-war economy in the West tends to concentrate incomes in specific population categories. The increase in the amount of education received, the double incomes of man and wife, additional incomes, income from assets, and the like have a cumulative effect and, within the group of wage and salary earners, ensure that a distinction remains between the unskilled and low-skilled (including guest workers and minorities) on the one hand, and the better skilled and highly skilled on the other hand.[48] Even a system of high, steeply progressive taxation appears unable to change this very much (Table 29). There is a whole series of reasons for this. Tax exemptions for certain income groups, deduction of business expenses, the fact that not all family incomes are taxed jointly, the absence of capital gains taxes, fringe benefits, tax frauds, and other factors all reduce fiscal pressure on high and middle income groups.[49] These groups with higher incomes can thus easily maintain their position in the modern economy; indeed they form its very backbone. For this reason they have appeared to be the most dynamic and most stable element of post-war affluence demand. They have shown a great capacity to resist the structural crisis which has threatened the affluent society since the 1970s. In this sense they have been partly responsible for the appearance of the phenomenon of stagflation.

3. EXPORT AS A DYNAMIC DEMAND FACTOR

THE EXPLOSION OF WORLD TRADE

The decades which followed the Second World War were characterized not only by a notable increase in domestic demand, but also by an explosive boom in international demand. This boom is remarkable in two respects, first in the contrast with the pre-war situation and second in the fact that international demand grew faster than domestic demand.

In general, during the long period from 1914 to 1945, world trade stagnated. The First World War had come as a shattering break in the growth of world trade. Something like a recovery and even new growth took place in the 1920s but progress was obliterated during the world depression of the 1930s and the Second World War. From about 1950, however, world trade began a phenomenal rise which continued into the 1980s. The total nominal value of world exports, expressed in American dollars, increased nearly fifteenfold between 1953 and 1977 (Table 30). These statistics give a misleading impression since they are swollen by the inflation of the 1970s (on the other hand there are likewise no corrections for the many relative price reductions enabled by technological progress). In volume terms, world exports grew nearly fourfold between 1953 and 1977, still an impressive increase, all the more in that this figure surely underestimates the real development. Industrial goods played a big part in the growth of world exports, and an improvement in quality was an extremely significant factor. This improvement, of course, is not reflected in the volume statistics.

The development of post-war world trade did not just expand; there was an acceleration in the rate of expansion. This acceleration could first be observed in the 1950s and continued during the 1960s. From 1968 onwards the acceleration in volume terms began to falter. In value terms it continued, but this was rather the expression of inflation than of real export growth.[50] Around 1970, then, the first signs appeared that the dynamic trade growth was past its peak.

Table 29 *Size Distribution of Pre-Tax and After-Tax Income in Selected*
Western Countries
(double decile shares) (percentages)

	Year	Share of income of the 20 per cent lowest income earners before tax (1)	Share of income of the 20 per cent highest income earners before tax (2)	(2)/(1)
United States	1972	3.8	44.8	11.8
France	1970	4.3	47.0	10.9
Canada	1969	4.3	43.3	10.1
Norway	1970	4.9	40.9	8.3
West Germany	1973	5.9	46.8	7.9
Netherlands	1967	5.9	45.8	7.8
United Kingdom	1973	5.4	40.3	7.5
Sweden	1972	6.0	40.5	6.8
Australia	1966–7	6.6	38.9	5.9
Japan	1969	7.6	42.5	5.6
Average	—	5.5	42.9	7.8

	Year	Share of income of the 20 per cent lowest income earners after tax (1)	Share of income of the 20 per cent highest income earners after tax (2)	(2)/(1)
France	1970	4.3	46.9	10.9
United States	1972	4.5	42.9	9.5
Italy	1969	5.1	46.5	9.1
Canada	1969	5.0	41.0	8.2
Spain	1973–4	6.0	42.3	7.1
West Germany	1973	6.5	46.1	7.1
Netherlands	1967	6.5	42.9	6.6
United Kingdom	1973	6.3	38.7	6.1
Norway	1970	6.3	37.3	5.9
Australia	1966–7	6.6	38.8	5.9
Sweden	1972	6.6	37.0	5.6
Japan	1969	7.9	41.5	5.2
Average	—	5.9	41.8	7.1

Source: M. SAWYER, *Income Distribution in OECD Countries*, p. 14

The expansion of world trade after the Second World War must also be seen in comparison with the development of domestic demand. Again, the contrast with the pre-war situation is striking. From the start of the First World War until the end of the Second World War, the world economy was nationally rather than inter-

Table 30 Development of World Exports and Production, 1953–82

(world exports in billion dollars and in index-numbers, 1963 = 100; world production in index-numbers, 1963 = 100)

	1953	1958	1963	1968	1973	1977	1980	1982
WORLD EXPORTS								
– *Value (billion dollars)*								
Total	78	105	154	240	574	1,125	1,990	1,845
Primary goods: agricultural products	42	50	45	54	121	188	299	272
minerals			26	41	96	266	567	493
Manufactures	36	55	82	140	347	648	1,095	1,049
– *Unit value (1963 = 100)*								
Total	100	100	100	105	161	271	423	403
Primary goods: agricultural products	107	103	100	100	185	255	330	292
minerals			100	111	192	550	1,200	1,254
Manufactures	94	98	100	104	152	232	337	314
– *Volume (1963 = 100)*								
Total	52	70	100	149	231	269	305	300
Primary goods: agricultural products	60	74	100	121	147	166	203	209
minerals			100	144	195	188	185	153
Manufactures	44	66	100	166	280	344	400	410
WORLD COMMODITY OUTPUT								
– *Volume (1963 = 100)*								
All commodities	60	74	100	133	180	205	224	223
Primary goods: agricultural products	77	88	100	115	128	139	146	154
minerals			100	129	171	191	196	183
Manufactures	54	69	100	141	197	227	253	249

Source: GATT, *International Trade*, various issues, 1960–83

nationally based. The little economic growth during that time was largely in the area of world production – world trade lagged hopelessly behind. During the 1950s the position was precisely reversed. World trade as a whole grew faster, as well in value as in volume, than world production. When one considers solely industrial goods the contrast is still greater (Table 30).

From these statistics it can be argued that international demand exercised an important stimulative influence on the growth of world production in the post-war period. When world trade stagnated, as it did in the period 1914–50, world economic growth was languid and weak. When world trade exhibited powerful growth, as it did after the Second World War, the world economy suddenly took on an altogether more dynamic and expansive nature, characterized by a climate of hope and confidence in the future. If one compares growth in GNP and export performance on a national basis, the importance of international demand becomes even more evident. During the expansive period 1950–73, there was a remarkable parallelism between high general rates of growth and high export achievement.[51] The fastest-growing countries were precisely those which were the most export-orientated. In the 1950s, these were West Germany, France, Italy, Japan, the Netherlands, and Switzerland, with Belgium joining in the 1960s. The reverse was true as well, that is, slow-growing countries were rather weak performers in export markets. The most obvious examples were Britain and the United States (Belgium too during the 1950s).

The expansion of world trade, powerful though it was from the 1950s, was not totally stable. It followed a cyclical course, with the cycles being more pronounced than those of the various national production figures.[52] More specifically, the recovery of world production after the crises of 1958 and 1976 and after the recessions of 1961 and 1967 was accompanied by a more than proportional increase in world trade. International demand acted as an extra stimulus in the upturn.

The clear links that can be established between the expansion of world trade and economic growth after the war have led to a series of theories about exports as an initial motor in economic growth development ('export-led growth'). In these theories international demand is regarded as given, an exogenous variable which autonomously sets in motion a growth process. Against these theories stand others which stress domestic demand and see exports only as a derivative factor ('homespun growth'). Domestic demand is then considered the initial motor. Expansion of domestic demand leads to rationalization and improvement of production and facilitates a rapid development of exports. In this view, therefore, international demand merely fulfils a supplementary role.

Which of these approaches best fits post-war experience? This question is a difficult one, because both have an explanatory value. Moreover, domestic and international demand appear to be strongly influenced by each other and so it is impossible to draw a clear line between their impacts. However, a deeper analysis of the expansion of world trade by examining its geographical distribution and the kinds of products involved may provide some new insights on the significance of international demand. The two theories will be further examined at the end of this chapter.

THE GEOGRAPHICAL DISTRIBUTION AND THE COMPOSITION OF WORLD TRADE

One is immediately struck by the trade preponderance of the industrialized countries of the West, the countries with the highest incomes (Graph D). Between 1950 and 1970 the mutual imports and exports of these countries easily accounted for the bulk of international trade. After 1974 the developing countries somewhat improved their share as some of them built up their export industry. But even after 1974, the foreign trade of developing countries was heavily dependent on the industrial West. Almost 75 per cent of their exports went to industrialized Western economies and scarcely more than 20 per cent to other developing countries. The centrally planned economies of the Eastern bloc were only very slightly involved in trade with the rest of the world. Although they maintained trade relations within their own bloc, this mutual trade represented only a small fraction of world trade.

Within this general picture, some particular geographical shifts are worth noting. At the end of the Second World War, the relative position of the United States and Canada in total world trade was extremely strong; for example, together they accounted for more than one-third of the export of industrial products in 1950.[53] During the war the combatant or occupied European countries and Japan had seen their share of world trade diminish, especially to the benefit of North America. After the recovery of the European victors and

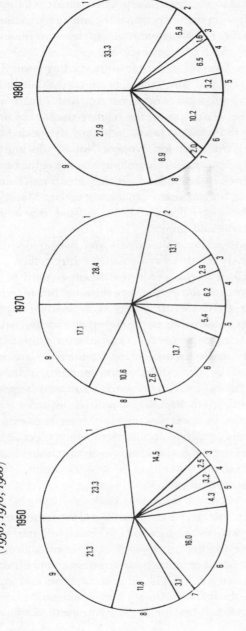

Graph D *Geographical Pattern of World Trade Exports from Major Areas as a Percentage of World Exports*
(*1950, 1970, 1980*)

1950

1: 14.5
2: 2.5
3: 3.2
4: 4.3
6: 16.0
7: 3.1
8: 11.8
9: 21.3
1 (EEC): 23.3

1970

1: 28.4
2: 13.1
3: 2.9
4: 6.2
5: 5.4
6: 13.7
7: 2.6
8: 10.6
9: 17.1

1980

1: 33.3
2: 5.8
3: 1.6
4: 6.5
5: 3.2
6: 10.2
7: 2.0
8: 8.9
9: 27.9

1 EEC
2 EFTA
3 Rest of Western Europe
4 Japan
5 Canada
6 United States
7 Australia, New Zealand, South Africa
8 Centrally planned economies
9 Developing countries

later of the defeated, the relative position of the United States and Canada in total world trade began slowly to deteriorate. The 1960s were characterized by a feverish growth in trade among the countries of the Common Market and an astonishing expansion in Japanese exports. Both Japan and EEC countries thus improved their positions in world trade (Graph D). Trade within the European Free Trade Association (EFTA) also grew substantially although the decline of British exports was a negative factor here (Table 31). After the crisis of the years 1974–6, the relative position of most European countries did weaken. Japan continued its rise and the United States won back some lost ground. Notable during the 1970s was the rapid improvement in position of some of the newly industrialized countries. In the Far East these included South Korea, Taiwan, Hong Kong, Singapore and, to a lesser extent, Malaysia. In Latin America there were Brazil and Mexico, and in Southern Europe Spain, Portugal, and Greece.

The further growth of Japanese exports and the rapid rise of exports from the newly industrialized countries during the 1970s must be partly ascribed to changes in the import pattern of the United States. At precisely this period American imports of industrial products from EEC countries were increasingly replaced by imports of comparable products from Japan and the newly industrialized countries.[54] Japan also established a foothold in Europe where the newly industrialized countries were not successful.[55] As a further point, all industrial countries, including the older ones in Europe and in North America, suddenly began to direct more of their exports to the rich oil countries. Japan seems to have been, once again, the most dynamic in this restructuring.[56] The energy crisis of the 1970s had another dampening effect on the future integration of international trade between the United States and the EEC countries: on both sides of the Atlantic the imports of industrial goods had to be cut back.[57]

The composition of world trade also changed. There was a decrease in the share of primary goods (agricultural products, energy resources, and minerals) and an increase in the share of industrial products. In 1955 the two groups were still roughly equal, but by 1970 the share of industrial products had risen to nearly two-thirds of total world trade (Graph E). The oil crisis of November 1973 changed all this and the share of primary products began to rise in value at the expense of industrial goods. Nevertheless the decline of

Table 31 *Geographical Distribution of World Exports of Manufactures*
(percentages)

	1963	1973	1976
Canada	2.61	4.16	3.32
United States	17.24	12.58	13.55
Japan	5.98	9.92	11.38
France	6.99	7.26	7.41
West Germany	15.53	16.98	15.81
Italy	4.73	5.30	5.49
United Kingdom	11.14	7.00	6.59
Spain	0.28	0.92	1.07
Portugal	0.30	0.35	0.21
Greece	0.04	0.15	0.22
Other OECD countries	15.65	17.63	17.71
Total OECD countries	80.49	82.25	82.76
Brazil	0.05	0.35	0.41
Mexico	0.17	0.64	0.51
Yugoslavia	0.40	0.55	0.60
Hong Kong	0.76	1.05	1.15
South Korea	0.05	0.78	1.20
Taiwan	0.16	1.04	1.23
Singapore	0.38	0.46	0.52
Total newly industrialized countries	2.59	6.29	7.12
Other developing countries among which:	2.70	2.34	1.55
India	0.85	0.45	0.49
Argentina	0.01	0.21	0.17
Eastern bloc	13.35	10.00	9.65
World Total	100.00	100.00	100.00

Source: OECD, *Newly Industrializing Countries*, p. 19

industrial goods in total world trade was slowed when the rich oil-exporting countries used their increased incomes to buy more of those goods.[58]

Within the general evolution of industrial products, there were also some important shifts between various subgroups. Seen in the long term, the export structure of manufactures followed the pattern of industrialization. The share of textiles and clothing in total world trade fell from 40 per cent in 1899 to 11 per cent in 1959 and during the same period the share of machinery and transportation products rose from 12 per cent to 40 per cent.[59] In the course of the 1960s,

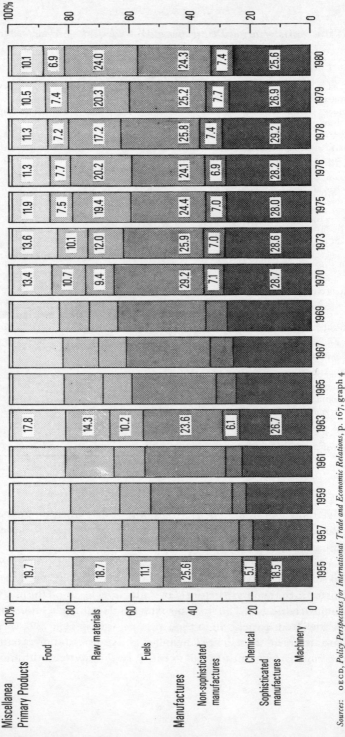

Graph E   *Commodity Structure of World Trade*
(share of world exports by major commodity classes) (percentages)

Sources: OECD, *Policy Perspectives for International Trade and Economic Relations,* p. 167, graph 4
UNITED NATIONS, *Statistical Yearbook,* various issues, 1974–83

textiles and clothing lost more ground but now the relative positions of iron and steel, non-ferrous metals and metal products also declined.[60] Chemical products made a slight improvement in the 1960s after keeping a fairly stable share ever since 1899. The percentages underestimate the real performance of the chemical industry because price reductions as a result of technological advances were much greater in chemicals than in other industrial products. During the 1970s, the share of chemicals in total world trade swelled again. Other advanced industrial products also increased their share of world trade, but chemicals became the leading sector of the decade, thereby pushing transportation products into second place. Iron and steel, non-ferrous metals, textiles, and paper all had to give further ground.[61]

These shifts within the general category of industrial products can be partly explained by the continued industrialization process. As industrialization reaches a higher level of development, the interdependence of industrialized countries becomes greater. This, in turn, is largely connected with the phenomenon of increasing cross-frontier vertical concentration and the consequent forward and backward linkages. It was in this way that the big companies acquired, on an international level, new sales markets for their advanced intermediate goods. This was facilitated by the reduction in transport costs and the increasing absolute differences in wage levels. The relative share of intermediate goods in world trade therefore rose considerably during the period 1950–70 and continued to rise in the 1970s. During the whole post-war period, Belgium, France, and Luxemburg were important producers of intermediate products. From the 1970s onwards the newly industrialized countries were also involved in this form of production.[62]

The years following the Second World War were also characterized by increasing international competition within certain industrial sectors producing finished products.[63] International competition came not only in the form of prices. Quality, style, appearance and after-sales service were all vital too. In advanced consumer goods, product differentiation could be carried out on a large scale. This in turn demanded the greater use of the economies of scale which were necessary for mass production, lower production costs, and lower sales prices. The capacity of the domestic market was in many countries too limited in relation to this mass production. Therefore attempts were made to export an increasing amount of the surplus of the highly differentiated and specialized products.

In order to understand fully the shifts in the trade of the various subgroups of industrial products, analysis cannot be restricted to the West. The developing countries also played a significant role. The relative decline of certain classes of products in world trade was not exclusively caused by the continued industrializing of the developed countries of the West, a process by which progressively more complicated and refined semi-finished and finished products were traded. The decline of some subgroups was also caused through import substitution by some developing countries. The decline in the world position of textiles and clothing, iron and steel, non-ferrous metals, and metal products in the 1950s and 1960s was partly due to some developing countries replacing imports of these goods as their own domestic economy industrialized. Soon, some even began to export industrial products, at first simple items but later more advanced goods. For these reasons the shares of the subgroups of clothing, machinery and transportation products in the total exports of the developing countries increased during the 1960s. In the 1970s the metal-working sector steadily assumed greater importance. Import substitution now clearly began to make way for the export of a wide range of goods. What were increasingly regarded in the industrialized West as traditional sectors were, in developing countries, outstanding growth sectors. Consequently the share of primary products, excluding oil, in the total foreign trade of the developing countries shrank, while that of industrial products rose.[64]

This increased export of manufactures by developing countries remained geographically very restricted. It was done by the few countries in Asia, Latin America, and Southern Europe which have already been mentioned (page 264). In 1974 more than 70 per cent of the export of the developing countries in clothing and footwear, electric and electronic machines, iron and steel, and transportation products was controlled by six of these newly industrialized countries.[65] Their success was largely due to a conscious government policy of switching from import substitution to a vigorous promotion of exports. The transfer of technological and development aid was also crucial. The World Bank and the United Nations Conference on Trade and Development (UNCTAD) were important in this, but no less important was private industry, particularly multinational companies. Those companies sought to get around the rising production costs in the West by means of massive direct investment in the newly industrialized countries. By this step they benefited simultaneously from the lower wage costs in the host countries, falling world transport costs, improved information and communication systems, and fiscal advantages provided by the local governments. The service sector profited remarkably from this shift in the geographical distribution of direct investment. From the 1970s onwards services in the areas of financial advice, transfer of technological know-how, and international freight were in especially heavy demand. It is thus not surprising that the share of services in total world trade from the 1970s onwards showed an upward trend.[66]

The economic expansion of the newly industrialized countries of the Third World is an impressive illustration of the decisive role that foreign trade in industrial products played in the process of growth and development during the 1970s. Indeed the same thing was going on in the West during the whole post-war period. The spectacular growth of the industrialized countries of the West cannot be fully understood without taking into account the dynamic influence of international demand.

EXPLANATIONS FOR THE STRUCTURE OF THE GROWTH IN WORLD TRADE

The time has come to reconsider the underlying mechanisms that have determined the burgeoning of post-war trade and its specific pattern.

The most prominent of these mechanisms is the relative availability of the factors of production. This forms the base of the neoclassical hypothesis, the Heckscher-Ohlin theorem, which is in fact a modern version of the Ricardian theory of comparative costs. If the production of certain goods requires production factors which are in relative surplus in a given country, this could well provide the basis for an export trade. Alternatively, if the production of certain goods requires factors which are relatively scarce in a given country, this would be a classic case for importing.[67] When one looks at the specific structure of world trade after the Second World War,[68] some general tendencies can be explained by this theorem, within certain limits. The increasing importance of the multinational company in the world economy meant that the labour component represented in certain products became more and more crucial in the choice of a production site for industrial goods. Multinationals gained increasing control over the geographical distribution of industrial production and organized this distribution on the basis of available labour and labour skills in different countries. They were particularly well suited to this role. Their structure was characterized by a sectoral and subsectoral planning system which knew no geographical boundaries. As such they could organize a world division of labour without great difficulty. They thus functioned much more efficiently than a national centralized planning system, irrespective of whether such a system was inspired by Keynesian macro-economic policy or by socialist planning principles.[69]

The concept of catching-up is often seen as a special explanatory factor for the rapid growth of foreign trade after the war.[70] Economic depression in the 1930s and during the war had so restricted world trade that a gaping opportunity had developed for a catching-up movement in trade. Simultaneously economic reconstruction in Europe also stimulated mutual trade. Though it should be admitted that reconstruction led at the same time to the replacement of imports by domestic industry, this was no real obstacle to the expansion of trade. Import substitution indeed implied the replacement of imported consumer durables destined for mass consumption, and so imports of parts and intermediate products were greatly increased instead. Reconstruction had a psychological effect too since European countries anticipated further recovery and further economic co-operation. Consequently, from the successful reconstruction of Europe, a natural movement towards economic integration resulted. Under the influence of this psychological factor, European industrialists began to make agreements with their counterparts in other European countries with an eye towards rationalization and specialization. Mergers took place and international specialization within industrial sectors became possible bringing significant economies of scale and price cuts.[71] Reconstruction and recovery also took place in Japan and elsewhere, but their impact on the development of trade was deepest in post-war Europe.

Events in the realm of economic policy can also be seen as important reasons for the expansive nature of international trade after the war.[72] In this respect the policy of economic integration must take pride of place. Economic integration as a movement could be found all over the world during the 1950s and 1960s but nowhere was it more successful and deep-rooted than in the realization of the European Economic Community (EEC). The European Free Trade Association (EFTA) was another example in Europe; it was later partly swallowed up by the EEC. Other government measures sought to liberalize trade and payments at a world level. The establishment of the International Monetary Fund (IMF) and the signing of the General Agreement on Tariffs and Trade (GATT) were the most important expressions of this. The Marshall Plan led to the setting-up of the Organization for European Economic Co-operation (OEEC), which was later formed into the Organization for Economic Co-operation and Development (OECD). The powerful influence of all these organizations in liberalizing trade and international payments was undeniably a contribution to the acceleration in the growth of international demand.

National governments were also very active in promoting their industrial exports. Goods destined for export were declared tax-free, and companies dynamically active in foreign markets could draw upon special government facilities for the discounting of bills and the allocation of export credits and credit insurance. Exporting companies were also granted accelerated depreciation allowances and were allowed to use different prices for home and export markets. Often national governments organized special promotional services for industrial exports. Finally, in some countries devaluation was used deliberately to undervalue the local currency in order to stimulate exports.[73]

Still other factors influenced the strong expansion of post-war trade. Technological progress in international transport, together with low, stable oil prices during the 1950s and 1960s, sharply reduced freight prices in comparison to the prices of industrial products.[74] In this way the share of transport costs in the total value of internationally traded goods was minimal. Some economists contend that big European and Japanese companies organized their post-war penetration of the world market through systematic discriminatory pricing and dumping. Part of the success of their exports of consumer durables is ascribed to these practices.[75]

The strategy of direct investment adopted by multinationals was another factor in the extension of foreign trade. Through the multinational corporations the planning of the production of raw materials and industrial goods took on a world dimension. The transport of raw materials, parts, and intermediate and finished products was now much more intensive throughout the world. From this, in turn, the international division of labour assumed a more dynamic character. It was largely the multinational companies that were able to exploit the enormous potential which could be realized by developing industrial skills in Europe and later in the newly industrialized countries of the Third World. Naturally the multinationals made use of the widened horizon of the post-war world: the circulation of people and ideas in the post-war West was far more rapid and intensive than ever before. Because of better information and communications and because the countries developed comparable patterns of consumption, the Western world was becoming more unified. The greater uniformity broadened the field of action for direct investment by multinational corporations and in general strengthened the growth of trade in the post-war period.[76]

During the 1950s some countries on the European continent had grown much faster than had Britain. To explain this A. Lamfalussy launched a model of export-led growth in which he applied the theory of virtuous and vicious circles.[77] Lamfalussy's empirical research showed that the difference in the rate of export growth was due neither to the structure of export industry nor to the structure of the export market but particularly to the competitive lead these continental European countries held over Britain.[78] Ultimately the origin of the difference could be found in the more rapid growth of labour productivity in continental Europe. High labour productivity and a high level of competitiveness in continental Europe stimulated a fast growth in exports, and this considerably raised the share of savings in the national income and the share of investment in GNP. From this resulted yet further growth in productivity and production. Inflationary tensions could thus be avoided and the competitive lead further increased so that the mechanism of the virtuous circle continued its action. In Britain the situation was precisely reversed: low labour productivity and the low level of competitiveness initiated the mechanism of a vicious circle.

S. B. Linder believed that post-war export growth was not primarily stimulated by the dynamic of international demand as such. He saw domestic production structure as the most important factor in the origin and growth of international demand.[79] The demand for industrial goods was largely determined by the level and structure of consumer incomes in specific regions of the home country. Naturally there were also sociological factors such as culture and religion, and chance factors too such as the weather, but income remained crucial. These factors in national demand thus shaped the structure of domestic industrial production. Entrepreneurs tried to optimize production of goods demanded by the domestic market as far as possible. Production could be optimized still further when foreign sales markets allowed the use of greater economies of scale. Countries with a comparable income structure were the best targets for these exports. The more the income and demand structure of different countries resembled that of one another, the more intensive was the exchange of goods, the more rapid was the growth of trade, and the more accurately this trade could be predicted.

The structural vision of A. Maizels has close links with Linder's hypothesis. In a remarkable book of 1963, Maizels postulated on the basis of extensive empirical research that industrialization, via an increase in incomes, brought about fundamental changes in the structure of demand.[80] Family expenditures on food and clothing grew only weakly in the industrialized countries of the West during the twentieth century, whereas the demand for consumer durables and chemical products soared. The demand for capital goods therefore soared too. Furthermore, countries which were in the same stage of industrialization began an increasing amount of trade in their consumer durables and in their capital goods and related intermediate goods. In addition, under the influence of the unions, they acquired the custom of converting productivity gains not into lower prices but into higher wages. Post-war prices of Western industrial products consequently no longer fell in the same way as they had done during the nineteenth century and even during the inter-war years.

Maizels argued that a new pattern of international trade thus developed after the Second World War, one in which the dominant position of primary goods in total world trade (in terms of value and volume) was taken over by industrial goods. This new trading pattern was not exclusively formed by the growth in trade between industrial countries. Developing countries were involved through their imports of consumer goods and capital goods. Moreover, technological progress in the primary sector also exercised a real influence on these structural changes. For instance, after the Second World War large-scale mechanization was introduced in the mines. The transport costs for raw materials fell dramatically. Furthermore, technology developed new ways to economize on the use of raw materials and made even greater progress in the production of synthetic raw materials. Finally the Second Agricultural Revolution forced down agricultural prices and raised autarkic tendencies in the agricultural sector. In the mean time the developing countries increased their supply of primary goods and the industrialized countries supported their own agricultural production with specific protectionist measures. These were just some of the many factors that reduced the share of primary goods in world trade in both value and volume terms.

Maizels was convinced that the structural changes he had outlined for the 1950s and 1960s were of a permanent nature. The more that countries industrialized, the greater would be the proportion of the higher incomes that would be spent on non-essentials and the more rapid would be the increase in the international demand for consumer durables and capital goods.

In the 1970s, however, it seemed that the structural changes were not as linear as Maizels had thought. First, the catching-up movement in the West was gradually exhausted. Second, industrialization, which after 1945 became more geographically spread and more thorough, generated fierce pressure on the provision of raw materials. The inevitable result was price increases. The demographic explosion in the Third World also had a perceptible upward effect on agricultural prices. Finally, industrial export demand was based on an infinite range of products, of which each had its own life cycle, its own rise and fall as part of the broad sweep of international trade. Therefore, to understand fully the nature of the structural changes, the product-life-cycle theory which was mentioned in Chapter V must also be duly considered.

The product-life-cycle theory[81] uses as a point of departure the Linder hypothesis that innovations occur where the demand for new products is highest. After the Second World War this was often the case in the United States, sometimes in Europe, and even in Japan. During the 'introductory phase', the new form of production was characterized by the use of highly skilled labour and labour-intensive production techniques. Patents protected the new production techniques so that marketing took on a monopolistic nature. Demand was not sensitive to price. At this stage the proximity of markets was important and a permanent adaptation of the product to the demand was still necessary. Gradually the product became sufficiently developed to be generally exported to countries with a comparable demand structure. At this point the introductory phase was replaced by a 'growth phase'. Both domestic and foreign demand grew. Greater rationalization and standardization of the production process became possible and prices fell. Abroad, local entrepreneurs via licences and imitations began to replace part of the imports. Often the original producers tried to protect their market shares abroad by means of direct investment. Nevertheless the rapid increase in production abroad of the product in question had more and more effect on the initial export markets of the innovating country. As a result the innovating country now began to direct its exports at countries where industrial infrastructure was still incomplete, if it existed at all. The 'maturing stage' was now entered. Production was fully standardized so that labour costs started to determine where production could best be undertaken. If the United States was the innovating country and the first imitating countries were in Europe and Japan (a situation which was often the case in the 1950s and 1960s), American exports now lost ground not only in the imitating countries but also gradually in other countries, with European and Japanese firms benefiting. During the fourth stage, the 'mature phase', technology became such common property that it could be transferred to the newly industrialized lands, especially in South and Central America and Asia, without too many problems. The United States now became a net importer and Japanese and European multinationals continued to produce under optimal circumstances, for a certain period. At the same time production in the newly industrialized countries developed with so much success that these very low-wage countries began to dominate production during the latter part of the mature stage. They gained a greater and greater share of exports to the rest of the world, usually under the control of American, European or Japanese multinational firms. The export trade of the newly industrialized countries now reached a high point but then in turn became threatened by new innovations from the advanced industrial powers of the West. This opened the way for a new life cycle. In many cases this new cycle had begun at an earlier stage and so the various cycles were interlaced.

The theory of the life cycle seems a very useful approach to help explain the complex dynamic of world trade after the Second World War.[82] Empirical tests indeed confirmed the theory when they were directed at the post-war growth sectors of the United States. Here many new products were developed which followed the growth pattern as predicted in the theory.

But the life-cycle theory is less suited to explain the slowdown in world trade which took place in the 1970s. There is not one single element in this theory that can offer an explanation for a *simultaneous* faltering in trade for a whole series of products and sectors. For this happening, the idea of structural change fits better. The structural break in the pattern of international trade is interpreted by many as being caused by the return to forms of protectionism.[83] O. Hieronymi sees world trade as a prisoner of an unavoidable oscillation between economic liberalism and economic nationalism.[84] The bankruptcy of economic nationalism revealed during the inter-war period, for example, rehabilitated economic liberalism as the possible key to the recovery of the world economy. The post-war economic system of the West was thus reconstructed on liberal foundations and principles. Nevertheless, at the same time, full employment became the central objective of national governments in the West. Conflict was thereby created between national and international objectives. When this uneasy combination encountered crisis, economic nationalism won the upper hand.

The *locus* of political power after the war still lay in the various nation-states and not in the international institutions. As long as the *locus* of political power does not shift – and there are no indications that this is going to happen in the near future – and as long as the structural crisis does not solve itself, economic nationalism will penetrate deeper into the political decision-making process. Monetary nationalism was a first flagrant expression of this tendency. By means of floating exchange rates, governments hoped to isolate the national economy from the rest of the world while at the same time not losing commercial advantages. They also tried to reach the same results through the undertaking of a whole range of neo-protectionist measures.

The new rise of protectionism in the 1970s is an undeniable development. It is equally clear that the rise is determined by the increasing conflict between national and international objectives of economic policy. There are, however, deeper causes for this phenomenon. They go back to the changes in the industrial structure of the world which have taken place since the Second World War. These changes cannot be isolated from the more general vision of the transformation of the economy which has been set out in the previous chapters. World trade has nevertheless played a decisive role. It has given the transformation a dimension and character it otherwise would not have had.

PART TWO

THE INSTITUTIONAL FRAMEWORK

CHAPTER VII

THE CONSTRUCTION
OF THE MIXED ECONOMY

The anxiety and confusion which had gripped the West during the Great Depression of the 1930s and the Second World War strengthened the belief that when peace came a new economic system should be set up, one which would take into account the lessons of the past. The mixed economy thus made its definitive appearance on the world stage. In micro-economic terms, the forces of the competitive free-market system continued to hold sway but, at the same time, in a wider sense, capitalism became humanized by means of systematic government intervention. Governments accepted a social responsibility and set about the organization of the modern welfare state. Success, even spectacular success, followed.

1. THE LESSONS OF THE PAST

The mixed economy did not come into being as a coherent system based on a specific ideology. Instead it grew out of the realization that the free-market economy had dramatically failed in the West during the inter-war period. The crisis of the 1930s with its massive unemployment and chaos clearly revealed to the world how far free-market capitalism had strayed from the path towards Utopia.

Indeed, even during the course of the nineteenth century, free-market capitalism had come under heavy pressure. On the domestic level the proletarianizing of the workers had led to violent reactions on the part of the unions. On the international scene, industrial countries had used capitalism as a means of strengthening the military power of the nation-state and armed conflicts were inevitable.[1] After the end of the First World War the bourgeois governments of the West once again turned to the ideal of free-market capitalism. The market economy was restored in full and the numerous measures to control the economy which had been introduced during the war were abandoned. The principles of free trade and the gold standard were once more adopted.[2]

When we look back at the 1920s, it appears that the gulf between dream and reality had never been so wide. There was no longer any international leadership to ensure the proper working of the market economy. Britain had emerged from the war too weak to continue this task and the United States fell back on its policy of isolationism.[3] Meanwhile domestically, new shortcomings of free-market capitalism were coming to light. National economies had expanded so much and grown so complex that the market ceased to work as smoothly as it had done in the past. Symptoms of overinvestment and market saturation appeared. Technological progress facilitated the development of monopolies and market manipulation. Economic power blocs were formed and no antitrust legislation seemed able to neutralize the distortions of the market system which resulted. In addition, the market economy showed little or no interest in providing public services and therefore social needs in the areas of housing, education, health and infrastructure remained neglected. Finally, the power of the unions led to new conflicts in free-market capitalism. The technological progress accentuated the differences in the growth rates of industrial sectors. In other words, a situation developed in which sectors with high labour productivity, able to afford higher wages, existed alongside older sectors with low labour productivity, where it would have seemed irresponsible to raise wages. The unions could hardly accept such a dichotomy, and they campaigned for more converging wages. But in doing so with successful results, they caused distortions on the labour market.

The tensions which had accumulated during the 1920s wrought their full effect during the world crisis in the following decade. The dislocation of the free-market economy was overwhelming. Financial and monetary chaos spread throughout the world, and international trade collapsed. Businesses started a concerted policy of retrenchment, ceasing investment altogether, and attempted to hold their market shares by means of cartelization and general protectionist measures. In the social sphere, corporatist tendencies emerged everywhere. The corrective mechanisms of the market on wages and prices, which according to classical theory would restore a new equilibrium in the national economy, were prevented from functioning properly. In other words, real behaviour on the micro-economic level no longer reflected true free-market principles and thus appeared not to be market-efficient enough to enable a return to a growth-orientated macro-economy.

The flood of bankruptcies and massive unemployment caused both entrepreneurs and workers to take an ideological stance that differed sharply from free-market capitalism. 'A necessitous man is not free', it was argued.[4] Governments had to intervene actively to reorganize the market system fundamentally and to ensure that profits and incomes were restored to orderly levels. Only thus could free choice regain its former efficiency in the free-market economy. So a wave of state intervention swept through the old capitalist free-market system. In this complete break with the past, Adam Smith's idea of 'the Invisible Hand' that regulated the market automatically and flexibly was rendered out of date.[5] State intervention could make use of examples which had been set either during or after the First World War but which in any case were far removed from the practices of pure market capitalism. In Germany during the First World War, Walter Rathenau, the Minister of War, had organized a state-controlled planned economy which could be used as a model.[6] In the Soviet Union the introduction of state-controlled five-year plans from 1928 onwards yielded positive results and the socialist economy appeared to benefit from the world depression rather than suffer.[7] Nevertheless most European governments did not throw themselves headlong into this new adventure; they contented themselves with greatly multiplying *ad hoc* measures taken to combat the crisis. These included measures to maintain monetary stability or restore the monetary situation, measures to protect domestic industry (extending loans, raising tariffs, restricting imports), measures to boost consumption (government-controlled minimum wages) and measures to tackle unemployment (reduction of the length of the working week).

In some European countries, especially Italy, Germany, Portugal and France, the governments, adopting a corporatist approach, went still further in the direction of systematized intervention. With a view to protecting certain industrial and agricultural sectors, cartel agreements were made under the watchful eye of government. Thus, by means of corporative or para-corporative structures, industrial and agricultural production in these countries and especially in Italy, Germany and Portugal, came under the indirect control of the state.[8] Direct government control also won ground in Europe. In France the Front Populaire (1936–8) carried out significant nationalizations, such as those of the railways, the Banque de France and certain branches of the war industry. In connection with a banking crisis the Italian government in 1933 set up the Istituto per la Ricostruzione Industriale (IRI) which gradually acquired a wide influence over industry. In Germany the Nazi government implemented a bold policy of deficit spending to improve infrastructure – the construction of *Autobahnen* for example. The rapid transition from a constitutional state to one based on coercion during the Nazi regime had an immediate impact on the economy. The introduction of four-year plans from 1933 and the gradual organization of a war economy strengthened government economic control. In the smaller European countries, too, the extension of government influence over economic life could be observed. In Belgium the *Plan De Man* was enthusiastically accepted as party programme by the Socialists in 1933. It proposed various structural economic reforms, with the government assuming overall control of the economy.[9] The De Man Plan was implemented on a partial basis after 1935 when the Socialists took over. In the Netherlands a comparable *Plan van de Arbeid* was outlined. In Sweden and Norway the same ideas were translated into general government policy measures when the 1932 and 1933 elections brought Social Democratic parties to power.[10]

The rapidly increasing influence of the government in the economic life of the 1930s was not purely the result of pragmatic political decisions taken in the context of a crisis-torn society. Thinkers with new theories tried to construct a rational basis to this reorientation of political decision-making. The Swedish Economic School, under the leadership of Knut Wicksell, emphasized the importance of money creation in the development of economic activity and refined the concept of deficit financing. In the United States the 'Brains Trust' of President Franklin Roosevelt attempted to provide a theoretical basis for the New Deal policy that was followed from 1933. The Brains Trust saw the collapse of agricultural incomes as the origin of the crisis. It held that only a far-reaching government intervention, designed to improve agricultural incomes and to reorganize agricultural debt, could restore the demand for industrial products. Only this kind of state intervention could remove the obstacles which stood in the way of the realization of a growth economy. Infrastructural projects in the areas of nature conservation, regional development, irrigation, traffic, public housing and education would certainly only be executed if the government intervened actively. Even basic expenditure for social welfare, for example on the blind, infirm, old, and unemployed, required an active role from the state.[11]

The British economist John Maynard Keynes with his book *The General Theory of Employment, Interest and Money* (1936) made the most important contribution to the theoretical foundation of the mixed economy. According to Keynes, market capitalism was by nature unstable and no automatic mechanism existed that would guarantee the harmonizing of production and consumption through full employment. Keynes believed that the government should apply its tremendous potential control in the field of taxation, expenditure, and monetary policy in order to temper this instability. Christian Democrats had already put forward powerful moral arguments for a more just income distribution and an extension of public services; Keynes provided the economic rationale. Where private investment fell short of providing full employment, increased government expenditure on education, on housing and on care for the poor and the sick would hold up the level of total effective demand. By means of corrective and guiding measures, the government would ensure that micro-economic decisions would conform to the proposed macro-economic objectives, namely full employment, price stability, social welfare, and an equilibrium in the balance of payments. Keynes continued to believe in the general principle of the free market but in his theory he supplemented it with a significant supervisory and corrective role for the government.[12]

Keynes's theory was fully confirmed in the Second World War. Increasing government expenditure in all countries involved in the war led to full employment.[13] And his theory remained in currency even after the war. Many agreed that Keynesian policy ought not to be merely regarded as a package of exceptional anti-crisis measures but that its essence should be integrated into the foundation of post-war society. The Labour movement saw in the broader role of the state an adequate means of curbing the evils of free-market capitalism. Industry counted on more co-operation and trust between the social partners and hoped that the favourable production climate which had existed during the war would continue afterwards.

The mixed economy thus came about as the result of the converging visions of different social groups during and after the Second World War and would on this basis gradually become institutionalized. It is true that free-market ideology, in its original and integral form, was abandoned only in terms of domestic policy and more so in Europe than in the United States. On the international scene the free-market ideology continued dominant for more than twenty-five years.

In ideological terms, seen as a whole, there was a clear break with what had gone before. The construction of the mixed economy marks a historic turning-point in the process of a weakening free-market system. The exclusive system of free-market organization which had been adhered to almost religiously for nearly two centuries was now, as a principle, renounced.

2. THE MIXED ECONOMY AS ECONOMIC SYSTEM

THE THEORETICAL STARTING-POINTS OF THE MIXED ECONOMY

On the resumption of peace, the social and political consensus to break with the traditional order and to build in harmony a new form of economic society presupposed a series of fundamental structural reforms. The spirit of co-operation in continental Europe after the liberation was expressed in governments of national unity in which left-wing, and in some cases even Communist, parties participated. For this a price had to be paid by the established order, namely the acceptance of a few essential points from the political programmes of these left-wing parties. The left-wing programmes were all orientated towards structural reforms of society and embodied deviations from the profit-based market economy. The principal demands were the nationalization of basic industry, the creation of planning organizations, the establishment of structures to facilitate worker participation in industry at the national, sectoral and even company level, government investment in reconstruction and infrastructure and, finally, legislation which would strip the market of its moral neutrality and thus impose a social conscience.

The new social system represented in the mixed economy was not, of course, purely the consequence of left-wing parties, however real their influence might have been. Right-wing and centre parties also defended the principle of a sizeable extension of government intervention into economic life, and they gained considerable support from industrialists, bankers, and intellectuals. In academic circles the discussion of Keynesian ideas led to a generally acceptable compromise, that is, a sort of practical recipe of concrete measures to avoid catastrophic economic fluctuations. The whole amounted to the government control of effective demand (demand management). Increasing the government expenditure through budget deficits would stimulate effective demand. Decreasing this expenditure would reduce the level of demand. Monetary measures would be especially effective in restraining the economy. During recessions the government would raise the level of investment. For example, it would increase spending on infrastructure or encourage housing construction. Fiscal measures too were envisaged, in the form of increases or cuts in taxation, the objective being either to curb or stimulate effective demand, depending on the economic circumstances. Fiscal policy, however, would have a less immediate effect than monetary policy.

The counter-cyclical government measures, as concretely formulated, did not fully satisfy Keynes's theoretical intentions but they did offer major advantages. Taken together they provided the government with a whole series of operational tools to avoid depressions. Although unions and management sought their own specific goals, both groups were willing, in a structural and cyclical sense, to accept each other's viewpoints. For instance, the counter-cyclical budgetary policy was favourably received by the unions, since it promised to lay the ghost of unemployment. At the same time the Keynesian theory of government intervention ended a series of taboos in the business world relating to direct government involvement in industry. The business world remained irritated that left-wing parties continued to press stubbornly for the principle of nationalization but it welcomed the fact that subtler techniques of government investment were being proposed and were considered acceptable. Finally businessmen much appreciated the active role that the government played in the reconstruction process. The postwar recovery was a difficult challenge for the private sector, and so direct help and support from the state were gratefully received.

The success of the reconstruction process confirmed the efficiency of a good co-operation between unions and management and the advantages of an active government economic policy. Therefore in most European countries the success soon led to the consolidation of this more positive conception of the role of government in economic life. European governments brought these objectives and instruments together into a new economic system which was termed the mixed economy. There were five main objectives: full employment, production at full capacity, price stability, rising incomes linked to higher labour productivity, and a balance-of-payments equilibrium. A consultative arrangement was worked out in order to achieve these goals. Its framework gave government, unions and management a voice in the choosing of the appropriate instruments.

Once the chief objectives and the basic tools to attain them were specified and accepted, and the accompanying institutional framework outlined to general satisfaction, the mixed economy offered great potential for growth. A further important step was made when the government extended its control over investment and investment strategy. Keynes had already shown irrefutably that investment in the private sector was the most sensitive spot in the free-market system. The technological revolution, which had picked up pace since the two world wars, considerably increased the risk of investment. It was in this way that the free-market system could be so wasteful – investment could be excessive and lead to overcapacity but, on the other hand, it could also be postponed for too long.[14] Therefore, in order to control cyclical economic fluctuations better, it seemed desirable that government should engage in short-term and long-term investment.

Government control over the flows of investment and over long-term investment strategy could only be adequately realized if the government had at its disposal enough statistical information to measure and predict the implications of state intervention. The Input-Output analysis of Wassily Leontief was used to measure interdependencies in the economic system. In this way forecasts could be made on the ultimate effect of the particular government counter-cyclical measure being considered. Out of this experience developed the macro-economic models for medium-term and long-term programming and planning, models designed for structural government policy. Government set itself the task of establishing quantitative targets for the future. It was then decided what form of government activity was required to attain the targets set. At that moment the structural policy of the government entered the realms of planning, the objective of which was to optimize economic growth. In this process the means which the government would apply in order to reach its targets were identified and coherently set out.

What the Keynesian Revolution did was to supplement the *micro*-static equilibrium of the free-market system with a system of *macro*-static equilibrium based on active government intervention. Furthermore, the combination of these two elements enabled the crossing of a new threshold in that a *dynamic* dimension was added to the double *static* efficiency. This was represented in the government policy designed to optimize growth. In consequence the mixed economy lifted itself to a higher plane. Growth became a target and as such was integrated into government policy.[15]

The shift in emphasis from a static counter-cyclical policy towards a more dynamic growth policy took place around the end of the 1950s. The Western economies had not experienced a crisis since the Second World War and had reached a position of full employment. It thus no longer appeared so necessary to concentrate all attention on avoiding depressions. Fine-tuning techniques could restrict the remaining economic fluctuations to a minimum.[16] Attention could now be switched to maintaining full employment in the years to come. For this a structural policy was necessary in order to ensure satisfactory levels of growth in the long term.[17] A government now had to make certain that pure and applied research at the technological frontier as well as the development of products and machines could guarantee long-run technological progress. Further-more, it was necessary for labour supply, by means of better education, to be prepared to meet the demands which technological innovation made on it. At the same time a government had to ensure that outdated industrial sectors were dismantled and replaced by new dynamic ones. In short, it was government's task not only to stimulate growth directly but also to remove the obstacles that stood in the way of long-term growth.

As soon as the objective of economic growth was accepted as a central pillar of government policy, there arose the problem of how to distribute the benefits of growth. Indeed, government intervention could not be restricted simply to measures to stimulate growth, for it also bore the responsibility of seeing that the cake was equitably shared by the whole population. By all kinds of direct and indirect measures, governments began to take steps to readjust the distribution of income through transfer payments. Alongside this they built up a considerable network of public services such as public housing, education, health, and infrastructure. Laws were also passed on minimum wages, capital taxation, and higher estate duties; and the income tax was made more progressive.[18]

Government policy on growth and income distribution pushed state intervention much further than Keynesian theory had originally contemplated. The mixed economy took on a totally new aspect, so that it would be wrong to consider it as purely an extension of the Keynesian Revolution. The dynamic of the 1950s gave the mixed economy an extra impulse, one which at first it did not possess.

THE NEO-COLLECTIVIST VARIANT

The realization of the mixed economy in the West after the Second World War was far from a uniform process. Some countries jumped in at the deep end, choosing an economic formula which was neo-collectivist in nature. Other countries chose initially a more socially adapted free-market course. A third group put more emphasis on social consultation and social planning. In the first group, collectively orientated, France undoubtedly took precedence.

Nationalizations came first on the French agenda. During the inter-war period, France had already developed a strong tradition of *entreprises mixtes* and take-overs of private companies. During the war, radical reforms were discussed in Resistance circles. After the war, a new wave of nationalizations was to be expected. The Socialist and Communist parties, which participated in the de Gaulle government of 1945, ensured that these nationalizations indeed came about. Thus the energy sector (electricity, gas and coal), the insurance sector (thirty-two insurance companies), the financial sector (the four largest deposit banks),[19] and some other companies including Renault, Berliet and Air France, all came under direct state control. The acquisitions amounted to one-fifth of total industrial production.[20]

According to the Socialist and Communist parties, the nationalization process in France should have been continued, but the departure from government of the Communists in 1947 and of the Socialists in 1949 hindered this development. In any case, state bureaucracy did not take over the *administration* of the nationalized sectors. Instead, most nationalized companies maintained their autonomy, and every one of them continued to function under the existing management.[21] So the direct influence of the state was rather marginal, but the wave of nationalizations still had a real impact on the development of French industry. In the energy sector, the only nationalized sector which was systematically integrated into the central planning process, investment programmes were on a larger scale. The numerous small concerns which had existed in this sector before the Second World War now all co-ordinated their management policies under centralized control.[22] In the financial sector, the state banks had to fall into line gradually with the policy of government supervision of industrial loans, a policy on which they had not been consulted.[23] In manufacturing industry, the state-owned companies were both a challenge and a stimulus to the private companies in the same field.

Government planning comprised the cornerstone and showpiece of the French mixed economy. In its initial phase it was based on the *Plan de Modernisation et d'Équipement*, launched in 1945 by Jean Monnet to buttress the national reconstruction process.[24] Monnet, in common with many of his compatriots, was convinced that the French economy was lagging behind the rest of the world. The conservative entrepreneurial structure, which was still closely based on the small-scale family concern, was seen as a chief cause of this. Critics such as Monnet held the basic belief that technological progress and the advantages of economies of scale could only be attained within a framework of large companies that to a certain extent enjoyed a monopoly position. This ran against a government decree of 30 June 1945, which had called for greater competition.[25] By adopting the Monnet Plan in 1946 the government raised the level of investment and production in the private sector by its active intervention and by stressing the need for closer co-operation.

The first French four-year plan covered the period from mid 1946 to mid 1950; it was later extended to 1952 and thus ended at the same time as the Marshall Plan. In concrete terms it conformed to the model of unbalanced growth.[26] Government planning concentrated on the rapid development of six key industrial sectors, namely coal, steel, cement, electricity, transport, and agricultural capital goods. Later, oil and fertilizers were added to the list. Government planning thus concentrated on sectors which were decisive for the reorientation of industrial structure and, initially, consciously neglected the consumer goods sector. The intention was to promote industrial innovation by avoiding the normal supply bottlenecks as a new industrial structure was developed.

The four-year plan was prepared by the Commissariat du Plan, which consisted of a small group of top civil servants; the group was directly answerable to the Prime Minister while also collaborating closely with the Ministry of Finance. The plan itself, an econometric model, was the first anywhere to make successful use of input-output techniques. The Commissariat du Plan got its information from the statistical service of the government. Through the well-organized Comités de Modernisation, in which civil servants, industrialists, union representatives, and independent experts exchanged information, the Commissariat informally consulted several thousand leading figures from business, labour and agriculture.[27] The Commissariat thus assumed a strategic function. It prepared a forecast of economic development for the government and the private sector, thereby reducing the risks associated with decision-making. It facilitated an optimal allocation of resources, organized an efficient framework for social consultation, and promoted better economic understanding in a wider section of the population.[28]

The second plan (1954–7) continued to adhere to the principle of unbalanced growth. Attention again was mainly limited to a number of key sectors, with some changes. In 1952 a parliamentary Commission des Comptes et des Budgets de la Nation was set up in order to give the deliberation over future plans a more open character. In addition, a decree was issued in 1955 that made particular provision for regional action programmes in an attempt to integrate regional development into government planning.

The French plan of the 1940s and 1950s was not compulsory. It could not be imposed. But it had a real influence. Its success was due to a number of factors. One was the *étatiste* and centralist tradition in France. The government took full account of the existing economic structure and the disposition towards cartels and mutual co-operation. Another important element was the understanding that existed between top civil servants and leading figures in the business world, many of whom had completed their education in the same *grandes écoles*.[29] The climate of consultation was further improved by the well-organized Comités de Modernisation, which discussed the coherence of the plan on a sectoral basis. No less crucial was the active support the Commissariat du Plan received from the Treasury. Government approval for loans and other financial benefits depended on this department of the Ministry of Finance. The close co-operation between the Treasury and the Commissariat du Plan therefore ensured that the influence of the Commissariat over sources of finance was real and effective. In this way the government exercised control over investment not only in nationalized sectors but also in private industry.[30] Besides, institutions with financial competence, such as the Conseil National du Crédit (1945) and the Fonds de Développement Économique et Social (1955), through a system of discriminatory subsidies, loans, and guarantees, could influence investment decisions and move industrial development in a given direction.[31]

The government planning mechanism in France did have its drawbacks. The near-exclusive attention to the removal of supply bottlenecks in key sectors certainly stimulated investment in heavy industry and the capital goods sector, but at the expense of investment in the consumer goods sector. In addition, the government's active investment policy, combined with its heavy military budget, meant that government expenditure rose rapidly. At the same time, successive weak administrations during the 1950s were unable to follow an effective policy on prices and incomes. The result was steep inflation, balance-of-payments problems, and a situation in which wages lagged behind prices with a consequent leap in the number of strikes. The union leaders were so annoyed that they withdrew from the Comités de Modernisation and thereby undermined the principle of consultation. On the other hand, the fragmented consumer goods sector profited from the inflationary climate in that it was able to keep prices artificially high, so that marginal firms stayed in business.[32] In this respect inflation worked completely counter to the objectives of government planning, which were to promote the rationalization of industry and improve production and productivity.

France was the best example of a post-war mixed economy in which an aggressive growth dynamic was added to Keynesian counter-cyclical government policy. Britain, in contrast, was the most representative type of a post-war mixed economy in which the application of Keynesian principles remained central. The Beveridge Report of 1942 (*Full Employment in a Free Society*) and the White Paper on Employment of 1944 had already shaped a post-war government policy orientated towards full employment and social welfare. The policy as developed was a search for a balance between freedom and equality in society.

Some essential fundamentals of the free-market economy would be maintained, but these would be subject overall to stringent government controls geared towards a more just distribution of income. A planned policy of prices and incomes to keep a grip on inflation was rejected for fear that this would entail excessive bureaucracy and inefficiency. Instead the government went for a strict application of monetary and budgetary measures along Keynesian lines. Prices and wages were thus to retain a certain flexibility. Monopolistic tendencies in the market and within labour and management were to be curbed by the state. In this manner the government would play an active role in avoiding depressions and crises.

The government would also ensure an equalizing distribution of income. This redistribution of the national income would take place by means of steeply progressive taxation on incomes, inheritances, and legacies, an equalization in holdings of real and personal estate, and a considerable expansion of transfer payments. Some people even proposed a weekly dividend, calculated according to the size of each family, which would guarantee everyone a minimum income. This scheme included a series of elementary public services such as health and education. It was also proposed that there should be strict controls on the environment, natural resources, and population growth. For these controls, structural planning was regarded as necessary.[33]

The only way to realize and maintain full employment, according to the Labour party, was the nationalization of industry. But the excesses of Stalinism caused British Socialists to abandon their original idea of complete, or virtually complete, nationalization, because overconcentration of power in the hands of the state could lead to the misuse of power even in Britain. They therefore chose a policy of selective nationalization which brought under state control all basic sectors such as energy, transport, coal, steel, and infrastructure.[34] When Labour was in power from 1945 to 1951 the programme went forward. In 1946 the coal industry was placed under the control of a National Coal Board, all railway companies under a British Railways Board, and all inland waterway companies under a British Waterways Board. In 1947 all companies producing and distributing electricity came under a British Electricity Authority. In 1948 the steel industry was nationalized and a National Steel Board formed. In total, more than 20 per cent of British industry came under direct state control.[35] Also nationalized were the Bank of England, the airline companies, the airports, and road haulage. Furthermore the government regularly bought shares in private companies, mostly because of particular circumstances, as much political as financial. The best-known companies with important state participation were British Petroleum, Rolls-Royce, and Upper Clyde Shipbuilders Ltd. Finally, mention should be made of the rather symbolic participations in a number of agricultural co-operatives and the shares that the nationalized companies held in all kinds of private concerns.[36]

In principle these nationalizations provided the British government with a powerful policy instrument. Control over investment created the conditions to avoid depressions, guarantee full employment, and rationalize the coal and steel sectors. But none of this actually resulted. The British Labour government which came to power immediately after the war was very suspicious of any form of central planning.[37] It is true that after the sterling crisis of 1947 the Chancellor of the Exchequer, Stafford Cripps, introduced an austerity policy. Government action, however, remained limited to a short-term Keynesian policy of squeezing the economy and regulating employment. Moreover, although Cripps set up an Economic Planning Board with an interdepartmental planning staff, still no general long-term industrial policy was established, even for the nationalized sectors, and no institutional co-ordination among the different nationalized sectors was arranged. At most, the companies of a specific sector were placed under the control of a special board which in turn was very loosely linked to a responsible ministry. In fact, the management of each company remained autonomous and free.

When the Conservative party came back into power (1951–64), there was initially little or no change in the situation; indeed they somewhat exacerbated it. The *dirigiste* policy of Cripps was changed so that rationing was gradually abandoned and the government control over prices, wages, and trade was relaxed.[38] As far as counter-cyclical policy was concerned, there were still more contradictions under the Conservatives than under Labour, for the Conservatives attached greater importance to a balanced budget but without giving up the objective of full employment. The stop-go policy which Labour had followed since the sterling crisis of 1947 was thus accentuated.[39] There was, in general, no question of adapting the business management of nationalized industry to a long-term policy. Initially the Conservatives were only interested in reducing state control and went as far as denationalizing road transport and part of the steel sector.

Around 1960 the conviction grew in both Conservative and Labour circles that profitability should be the crucial criterion in the public as well as the private sector and that returns from nationalized industries could only be increased if those industries were co-ordinated through national planning.[40] In the private sector too, the British stop-go policy came in for heavy criticism. The Federation of British Industries pointed out that the oscillation in government budgetary and trade policies threw the investment strategies of private firms into confusion.[41] Consequently the firms shied away from launching technologically innovative projects that required long periods before coming to fruition. Only a forceful, long-term, planned government policy could prevent the British economy from sinking into a structural morass. Economists too underlined the necessity of a dynamic growth policy that demanded active and systematic government planning.[42] From 1960 onwards employers' federations, academics, civil servants and research institutes began to study seriously the French experiences.

Prime Minister Harold Macmillan, himself never an enthusiastic supporter of the restrictive stop-go policy of the Treasury, introduced, during a remarkable volte-face in 1961, the idea of non-compulsory economic planning. To this end he set up in 1962 a National Economic Development Council (NEDC or 'Neddy'), composed of six employers, six union leaders, six government representatives and two experts. The chairman was Sir Robert Shone, who was sympathetic to the idea of a growth-orientated policy. Alongside the NEDC, a National Economic Development Office was established, with a staff of about forty experts, which worked out the actual plan, independent of the government. In 1964 sectoral Economic Development Committees ('little Neddies') were also set up.

That this had all been inspired by the French experience was obvious. Nevertheless the British government believed that only one of the two central objectives of the French planning model should be taken up, namely the publicity and action designed to favour growth. The other French objective, the mobilization of resources which would be distributed to industry under state supervision, was not seen as relevant for Britain. According to the British, the London capital market would be perfectly able to respond to this need.[43]

In a fairly arbitrary fashion the NEDC determined the desired rate of growth – 4 to 4.5 per cent annually for the period 1962–6 – expecting that the announcement would be sufficient to realize this growth rate. The NEDC was relying on a self-fulfilling effect. Once the plan was prepared and published, even though it was only indicative, companies presumably would draw up their investment programmes based on a probable growth rate of 4 to 4.5 per cent. Production would thus be given a boost. But in fact the various interest groups represented in the NEDC were a source of such rigidity that the government quickly found itself bogged down. To achieve the proposed rate of growth an improvement in the export position was vital; but higher exports implied stable prices and wages, and this could only be achieved within the framework of a coherent policy on prices and incomes. Both employers and workers immediately resisted such a framework. Moreover, an extension of government intervention and discriminatory measures on a company and sectoral level met resistance from the traditional civil service.[44] Still, the psychological planning policy did have some positive effects which favoured growth. The government gradually released more resources for use in stimulating technological innovations (Science and Technology Act, 1965, and Industrial Expansion Act, 1968). New business schools were established to undertake the training of modern, growth-orientated managers, and special attention was given to professional education and to retraining schemes.[45]

The Italian variant of the mixed economy was also neo-collectivist in inspiration. Its roots went back to the pre-war Mussolini government. On the insistence of the Fascist government, the Italian banks had accepted a considerable amount of shares to clear companies' debts. The banks had also frequently bought shares on the stock exchange in order to maintain the prices of the shares of these companies. As a consequence of both measures, the banks obtained control of numerous firms which had run into difficulties. When the banks themselves ran into financial problems, the state stepped in to save them from going bankrupt. In 1933 the state set up the

Istituto per la Ricostruzione Industriale (I R I) as mentioned earlier in this chapter, and this I R I provided the banks with liquid resources in exchange for the shares of the controlled business concerns. In this way the I R I acquired control of about 120 industrial companies and provided work for 280,000 employees.

After the Second World War the I R I developed into a successful state holding company with considerable independence from the government and a rapidly increasing co-ordination within its management structure. The need for a dynamic reconstruction policy in the north and for an active development policy in the poverty-ridden south furthered the expansion of the holding company. The I R I became the largest employer in the country, and it consciously accepted its industrial responsibility. It threw itself into an extremely dynamic policy of industrial expansion, and it financed this policy by reinvesting profits and by issuing bonds. The government itself also provided financial subsidies. The I R I tried to maintain employment levels in the companies under its control not through conservative measures but by labour-saving investment. It reasoned that technological progress would expand the demand for produced goods so rapidly that technological unemployment would be neutralized and additional employment prospects would be created.[46]

At first the I R I based its policy on export-led growth, because it judged that the need to import raw materials and energy as well as to attract foreign capital could only be met by means of a powerful export drive. Only when exports were at a level high enough to guarantee the desired inflows could attention be turned to stimulating domestic demand by a systematic improvement of domestic prosperity. The I R I hoped, moreover, that its dynamic policy would pull the rest of industry along with it. Indeed, this is what happened. Still more important was the effect on the government which, after the success of the I R I, was encouraged into setting up new state holding companies. The most dynamic of these was the E N I (Ente Nazionale Idrocarburi), created in 1953 with the objective of providing sufficient energy, especially gas and oil, for Italy's continued industrialization. As early as 1960 the E N I controlled more than 200 companies. It was managed by Enrico Mattei, a strong personality of the *condottiere* type, who until his death in 1962 used his independent position to build E N I into an international giant.

The I R I and later the E N I worked closely with the economic planning services in Italy. Immediately after the war the Prime Minister, Alcide de Gasperi, called for a new *Risorgimento* (resurrection) in order to overcome defeat, economic ruin, overpopulation and poverty, through a policy of industrial expansion. The Marshall Plan was an initial stimulus to industrial planning in 1948 and this was followed up in August 1950 with the publication of a ten-year plan for economic development in Southern Italy and the establishment of a Cassa per il Mezzogiorno, a government agency to finance this development. In the same year a land reform was carried out, the objective of which was to divide up the large, inefficient farms of the south and to encourage the modernization of agriculture.[47] Ultimately economic planning remained very much the business of the big state holding companies. These had already developed the practice of basing their growth on a long-term investment strategy and had thus gained significant experience in the field. They were responsible for getting industrial government going in the south by means of large-scale investment projects, first in chemicals, later in petrochemicals, steel and other manufacturing.[48]

Planning and industrial development in Italy would not have been so successful if the state holding companies had not received substantial support from the banking sector and the government. The governor of the central bank, the Banca d'Italia, was the only permanent expert member of the Interdepartmental Commission for Finance, a government agency that deliberated over all company issues of bonds and shares. The same commission also had the task of approving all bank loans to companies that exceeded a certain level. The Central Bank of Italy also controlled a sizeable share of short-term credit via its rediscounting operations. Moreover, most banks, as nationalized or government-controlled institutions, fell under the direct control of the Banca d'Italia. It was thus a very influential institution and, although its links with the government were obvious, it was still independent enough to work out and maintain its own strategy for long-term industrial expansion. It also allowed the commercial banks enough freedom to pursue their own investment policies. On the other hand it did insist that the commercial banks remain subject to its counter-cyclical policy so that in times of threatening economic crisis or overheating, the banks had to follow the central bank's guidelines.

Japan was the fourth and last representative example of countries which used a neo-collectivist system for economic planning.[49] Unlike the three countries mentioned above, Japan does not have an extensive nationalized sector, but there is far-reaching government intervention and economic planning. The Japanese planning system has a strong structural as well as cyclical influence. Its origin goes back to the occupation policy of SCAP (Supreme Commander of the Allied Powers) and the national reconstruction after the war. The breaking-up of the *Zaibatsu* by SCAP opened the possibility of government control over industry. A comparable effect came from the land reform which reduced the amount of land owned by large-scale landowners from 46 per cent of the total area to only 8 per cent. The fragmentation that resulted greatly increased the hold of the government on agriculture. [50]

At first the concrete results of government planning were not encouraging, because resources were insufficient to rebuild the economy after the destruction of the war. This all changed when hostilities broke out in Korea. The United States now reassessed its attitude concerning the recovery in Japan. Furthermore, United Nations troops used Japan as a recreation and supply base and this suddenly raised the inflow of foreign currency. [51] Consequently the government now had the necessary resources to implement a planned structural policy. In 1955 the government set up an Economic Planning Agency. Its task was to prepare forecasts for the future development of the economy and to lay down a desired rate of growth and long-term plans for government investment. Between 1955 and 1977 no less than seven plans were prepared, all of an indicative nature. [52]

In its structural policy for industry, the Japanese government initially gave priority to raising production in the key sectors of steel, chemicals, non-ferrous metals, oil, and shipbuilding. From the end of the 1950s onwards, attention was increasingly concentrated on rationalizing the steel sector and on creating and developing a petrochemical industry. At the same time greater economies of scale were stimulated by the government support for mergers and cartels. [53] The promotion of exports was also a central element. The Japanese variant of export-led growth did not depend on currency depreciation but rather on a panoply of material advantages allocated by the government to exporting companies. Japan joined various international organizations such as the International Monetary Fund (IMF) (1963), the Organization for Economic Co-operation and Development (OECD) (1964), and the Bank for

International Settlements (BIS) (1970). Relations were also opened with the Eastern bloc countries and with China.[54] Finally the Japanese government adopted a very dynamic policy in respect to industrial research and innovation.[55] The leading role here was played by the Ministry of International Trade and Industry (MITI) which, among other things, stimulated and organized the importing of foreign technology.

The ministry consistently tried to prevent the formation of industrial monopolies. For example, no company was allowed to buy foreign patents unless all other companies in the same sector could acquire a comparable patent. MITI itself was also very active in applying and developing imported technology. At the same time MITI exercised direct control on the export and import of finished products. Certain foreign goods could be bought only if the importer undertook to export Japanese goods of the same value (the so-called link system). MITI began by stimulating the importation of technology necessary for modernizing basic industry. As time passed more attention was given to expanding labour-intensive traditional export sectors, to nuclear energy, and to electronics.

The influence that government planning had on the structural development of Japanese industry was facilitated by the gradual recovery of the old *Zaibatsu* such as Mitsui, Mitsubishi, and Suminoto, supplemented by some newcomers such as Honda and Sony. Nevertheless, in political terms, the *Zaibatsu* never regained the political power they once had, and so they were more responsive to the government planning apparatus. They were also financially dependent on the Japanese banking system at a time when the capital market was still poorly organized. Because the Japanese banks, in turn, were dependent on the central bank for their supply of liquid resources, the government had a very efficient tool to execute a Keynesian counter-cyclical policy. Monetary policy therefore formed the backbone of Japan's successful management of demand. An increase in the discount and bank rate by the central bank tightly restricted the level of liquid resources the commercial banks had at their disposal. The banks were therefore immediately compelled to restrain their credit policies and industry, in turn, was forced to reduce investment and run down stocks.[56]

The success story of the Japanese post-war economy, even though no drastic nationalization was undertaken, still had much to do with the efficiency of government planning, in structural as well as counter-cyclical terms. In this respect, planning had a great impact on the post-war development of the mixed economy in Japan.

THE NEO-FREE-MARKET VARIANT

Opposite the neo-collectivist variant of the mixed economy stood the adapted free-market variant. The clearest examples of this category are the United States and West Germany, though both of them gradually evolved towards a more moderate position during the post-war era.

Even between the wars, the United States had gone far down the road towards a mixed economy with Roosevelt's New Deal policy. The Second World War had accentuated this development. At the end of the war, however, the traditional American mistrust of great federal power reasserted itself. Americans accepted the principle of the state's assuming special powers during emergency conditions but made sure that these powers were restricted again as soon as the special circumstances no longer existed. The back-to-normality policy was implemented and completed with astonishing alacrity. Nevertheless the New Deal and the war left their marks on the post-war mentality in regard to the relationship between state and community.

One expression of this changed mentality was the Employment Act of 1946, in which the government committed itself to work for a high rate of employment by means of counter-cyclical policy. In fact this was a response to the stagnation thesis of Alvin Hansen. According to Hansen's conception, the reaching of the final American frontier within the structure of market capitalism would inevitably lead to new depressions and high unemployment if the government did not intervene with a systematic demand-sustaining policy of the Keynesian type. In order to have a solid institutional framework for carrying out this policy, the 1946 act set up a Council of Economic Advisers to the President and required the submission of a President's Annual Economic Report to Congress. The Employment Act of 1946 was an important fundamental step by American legislation in the direction of the mixed economy. But it was not much more than this for at the same time concrete structural measures were taken to ensure the working of the market. The Taft-Hartley Act of 1947 was an attempt to break a potential monopoly position of labour organizations by means of a series of restrictive measures. At the same time a strict application of antitrust legislation attempted to block the forming of monopolies by big business.

The market mechanism thus continued to be regarded as the most efficient system of co-ordinating individual economic decisions. Only if it was a matter of protecting free competition could federal government intervene. Moreover, government intervention had to conform to the market, that is, not discriminate between industrial companies but instead take measures of general application. This executive power was divided among a number of federal bureaux as a safety device against the dangers of a concentration of power within a single federal office. The federal bureaux operated directly under the President and in their activities sought to out-compete each other, a state of affairs which Congress rather encouraged than discouraged.[57] Therefore, after the Second World War the American government continued to stick to the structure of the free market. As Arthur Okun put it, only good co-operation between state and market could realize the big trade-off between equality and efficiency.[58]

In the area of cyclical policy, governmental management of demand was introduced by the Revenue Acts of 1945 and 1948. Nevertheless the manipulation of demand remained constricted within a rather orthodox budgetary policy. The budget deficit resulting from the Cold War was covered during the Truman administration (1945–53) largely by higher taxes and during the Eisenhower administration (1953–61) by reductions in government expenditure.[59] The New Economics introduced by President Kennedy in 1961 changed all this.[60] The Keynesian principles of deficit spending were now systematically applied so that fiscal-based cyclical policy could take on an important role. From 1964 Congress also accepted tax increases and decreases as a counter-cyclical government instrument.

As regards structural policy, the free-market doctrine continued to hold the upper hand for a long time. Yet here too changes came about, especially under the pressure of the private sector. The enormous technological progress after the Second World War required progressively larger companies, and their increasing economies of scale could only be efficiently used by a highly developed organizational and supervisory apparatus. Big companies thus needed a long-term planning and investment strategy. From 1947 onwards private firms such as McGraw-Hill began to publish yearly overviews of the long-term projects of American business life. Gradually government institutions began to adopt the same practices. Five-year, ten-year and even twenty-year forecasts thus became available.

The introduction of planning in the private sector had a great influence on the development of state planning. When the Cold War broke out in the late 1940s and the government began to think again about large-scale rearmament, the contacts and co-operation between public and private sectors grew still closer. The development of new weapons demanded substantial research contracts and large government subsidies, as well as long-running accords with the private sector. The expansion of the space programme, with all the consequent development of new materials and instruments, also presupposed a period of intense co-operation between government and big business over a period of ten to twenty years. [61]

The United States government sector grew very large, and of course this growth was not exclusively due to rearmament and the space programme. In the United States as in other Western countries, there was agreement that the government had a certain responsibility in social welfare. Even President Eisenhower, who had decided to reduce the government sector once again and had made this clear during the election campaign of 1952, felt himself obliged to continue and even enlarge the system of governmental social provisions. [62] At the same time, the fragmentation of executive power over a very large number of federal bureaux was compensated for by the presidential Bureau of the Budget. This body had a co-ordinating competence in respect not only to the budget but also to legislation. It thus introduced a certain planning and programming element in the world of executive power. The planning and social policy brought in by John F. Kennedy from 1961 onwards was thus not wholly new, but it did constitute a clear acceleration.

The Kennedy administration began a systematic attempt to make government policy more planned. Defense Secretary Robert McNamara integrated all government bureaux and private companies which worked on defence projects into one homogeneous and standardized planning system. Among other things he established Program Evaluation and Review Technique (PERT), a system of full co-ordination for the development of new weapons so that overlapping could be avoided. McNamara also introduced systems to standardize equipment and parts and to rationalize supplies, enabling large-scale savings. Other departments followed McNamara's example. Starting in 1962 the Bureau of the Budget required that all federal agencies make five-year budget forecasts. The Bureau itself even made ten-year projections of federal expenditure.

Kennedy took the government planning policy even further. On the advice of the economists Wassily Leontief and J. K. Galbraith, he reintroduced the manpower planning of the immediate post-war period, only now gave it a broader perspective. In addition Kennedy introduced a federal policy of regional development (Area Redevelopment Act, 1961) and tried to make urbanization follow a more planned path. Through federal subsidies, he attempted to encourage co-operation among local authorities, state administrations, and the federal government. Much support was given to the construction of roads and highways, to urban renewal and the like, on the condition that the projects accorded with regional and federal planning. In this more planned approach to regional development, Kennedy even tried in 1962 to set up an overarching Department of Urban Affairs[63] but his proposal was blocked by Congress. Agriculture and mining had continued uninterrupted under government regulation since the New Deal, but here too the need developed for a more planned approach. Federal control over the area of land under cultivation was increasingly replaced by direct control over the quantity to be produced. For oil production the government assigned a monthly maximum quota to the state of Texas which served as basis for the other oil-producing states.

In general terms, then, it may be contended that during the 1960s in the United States a clear shift from the neo-free-market to the planned variant of the mixed economy took place. So there was an increasing convergence with the development in Western Europe.

West Germany, even more than the United States, was a typical example of the neo-free-market variant – but only in the beginning. As time went on, the trend was towards a system in which planning and consultation predominated.[64]

The first post-war years naturally saw a reaction to the far-reaching *dirigisme* of the Nazis. The structural policy of that time rested on the theories of the Freiburg School and in particular on Walter Eucken's principle that the greatest task of government was to ensure the maintenance and advance of the pure forces of the free-market economy.[65] Alongside this, the ideas of Karl Zwing concerning worker participation in management were clearly influential.[66] Ludwig Erhard, the West German Minister of Economic Affairs, modelled his structural policy on a social market economy, of which the break-up of cartels, denationalization, and worker participation were the chief characteristics. The antitrust policy led to the splitting-up of the big banks such as the Deutsche Bank, the Dresdner Bank and the Commerzbank into smaller regional banks, and the break-up of the big industrial concerns such as Vereinigte Stahlwerke, Krupp, Klockner, Flick, Hoesch, Otto Wolff, and I. G. Farben, among others. Vereinigte Stahlwerke, which once accounted for about 40 per cent of total German steel production, was thus split into thirteen metal and nine mining companies. There was also an active policy to help small and medium-sized companies and to strengthen the position of small shareholders in big companies (*Mittelstandspolitik*). Furthermore a stringent monetary policy was followed after the currency reform of 1948. Attempts in that same year and in 1953 to reduce personal and company taxation must also be seen in the light of the neo-free-market orientation of government policy.[67]

Post-war German legislation was active in the area of worker participation. As early as 1947 some states approved laws regarding so-called economic democratization. In the Ruhr, for example, some systems of participation came into force in 1947. In April 1951 the Bundestag passed federal legislation in respect of co-determination in the sectors of steel and coal. On the board of surveillance (*Aufsichtsrat*) of the steel and coal companies workers' representatives were to occupy five of the eleven seats, and on the board of directors there was to be a representative of the workers along with the technical and financial directors. The various denationalizations were organized in a way to promote worker participation. For instance, a number of large state companies, such as Preussag (denationalized in 1959), Volkswagen (denationalized in 1961) and Veba (denationalized in 1965), offered shares at specially reduced prices to employees on low incomes.[68]

As impressive as this German structural policy, inspired by the neo-free-market, initially appeared, in practice it was not so coherent. The forced reconstruction in Germany from 1948 onwards and the implementation of the Marshall Plan made far-reaching government intervention desirable, even necessary. At the same time the *dirigiste* tradition of the Nazi period lived on and the old hierarchical and corporatist structures of the past held their position

in economic life. An obvious illustration of this was the Bundes-
verband der Deutschen Industrie (BDI), a federal organization of
German industry, which was set up in 1949. The BDI organization
grouped together thirty-nine national industrial federations, subdivided into leading sectors and secondary sectors. It constituted a
statistical information centre for government and business, and an
important organ for negotiation with both the government and the
unions.[69]

In respect of the denationalizations and the measures against
trusts and monopolies, some qualification is required. First it must
not be forgotten that the government sector in West Germany
occupies a very important place. In the 1960s the federal government
owned no less than 40 per cent of the coal and iron ore sector, 62
per cent of electrical power stations, 72 per cent of the aluminium
industry, and 62 per cent of banking organizations as well as the
central bank. In addition, via shares in holding companies, it also
controlled a whole series of private companies.

In the banking legislation of 1952, the principle of deconcentration
among the big banks was abandoned, and it was only after ten years
of laborious negotiations that the anti-monopoly policy finally bore
fruit in the form of legislation – and even then numerous compromises
and exceptions were made at the request of the BDI. In fact, from
the 1960s onwards industrial concentration made substantial gains
in West Germany, largely because of the increase in competition in
the world and especially in the European Economic Community
(EEC). The government displayed growing tolerance of oligopolistic tendencies in the German chemical industry, the steel sector,
and other sectors.[70] Furthermore, under the auspices of the
Mittelstandspolitik, numerous discriminatory measures to support
small and medium-sized concerns in industry, agriculture, and trade
were implemented. This was in direct contravention of the principle
that government economic policy should conform to the existing
market, that is, policy measures should be *generally* applicable.

Planning was another important factor which ran counter to
the neo-free-market stance the government initially adopted. The
tendency towards concentration in German business life naturally
facilitated long-term planning. In a country where a tradition of
cartelization is very old and strong, threatened sectors such as coal
and steel quickly went over to a system of mutually agreed long-term
investment levels. In the coal industry these agreements included the

closing of some mining concerns and the modernizing of the rest, whereas in the steel sector the steel giants agreed to co-ordinate their long-term investment programmes.

Planning, of course, was not the sole preserve of threatened sectors. Companies in the growth areas of chemicals and electronics, such as Bayer, Hoechst, and Siemens, systematically based their investment programmes on long-term forecasts. Private institutions as well as the statistical department of the BDI published annual economic projections which companies could use to streamline their investment strategy. The German banks also facilitated planning in the private sector.[71] They had a tradition of controlling private companies and had long ago developed techniques to co-ordinate industrial management and investment on a flexible basis. Their role in the board of surveillance of large-scale industrial concerns was highly significant. Most private shareholders entrusted their banks with their voting rights in shareholders' meetings; so the banks could choose their own representatives on the board of surveillance. Moreover, the system of delegation of votes (*Stimmenleihe*) ensured that through a general exchange of voting rights particular banks acquired control of the board of surveillance in specific sectors, for instance the Deutsche Bank in the steel sector. In these circumstances, the co-ordination of investment and long-term planning became a common management practice. Thus in the field of big business there could be little, if any, talk of a free-market economy.

The government increasingly co-operated in the planning system of big business. Already in 1948, at the start of Marshall Aid, the federal government had set up a Kreditanstalt für Wiederaufbau (bank for reconstruction) which, on a planned basis, provided financial support to the commercial banks and to big business. In 1952 the federal government itself forced all German industry to extend a loan to be used by the government for completing economic recovery by means of a selective investment programme in a series of key sectors. In 1961 the Kreditanstalt für Wiederaufbau was converted into a permanent institution which, according to government guidelines, financed selective and long-term investment projects in sectors, regions, and companies that were neglected by the other banks.[72]

In cyclical policy the government also gradually drifted away from the neo-free-market paradigm. After the currency reform of 1948 orthodox monetary and budgetary policies were followed.

When, through certain circumstances,[73] large budget surpluses were recorded, these were not spent but simply saved and sterilized. The monetary instruments in the hands of the Bundesbank were used purely in a counter-cyclical sense. Owing to the domestic catching-up movement in consumption and, later, to the boom in exports, demand management was not necessary before 1960.[74] But the orthodox cyclical policy of the early post-war period was not to be continued. In the course of the 1950s the government decided to use its large budget surplus to finance the extension of social welfare and the provision of public services (including the 1957 increase in old age pensions, environmental protection and the like). From the 1958 recession onwards, Ludwig Erhard resolutely shifted his budgetary policy in the more Keynesian direction of deficit spending. In 1961 the government was even given the power to use fiscal measures to manage demand without first gaining the approval of the Bundestag. The triumph of Keynesian cyclical policy became complete with Karl Schiller's appointment as Minister of Economic Affairs at the end of 1966.

The new policy took its definitive form in the Law for Promoting Stability and Growth in the Economy, of June 1967. The law provided explicitly for influencing economic cycles through fiscal instruments and deficit spending. It also instituted a Council for Counter-Cyclical Policy (*Konjunkturrat*) and a counter-cyclical reserve fund. Furthermore, federal government and the governments of the states were now obliged to plan their current and investment budgets on a five-year basis. The law also gave the federal government a whole series of instructions concerning the management of the money supply and aggregate demand via concrete monetary measures.

The 1967 law represented the definitive breakthrough of the New Economics into the West German economic scene. It achieved much more than this, though, notably in integrating medium-term and long-term planning into government policy. In fact Erhard, as Minister of Economic Affairs, had tried to initiate some form of long-term government planning back in 1957 with his suggestion of a council for economic advisers, but this had been torpedoed by Chancellor Konrad Adenauer. When Erhard himself became Chancellor, with the same objective in mind, he set up a Council of Economic Experts in 1963. This council functioned as an independent body, although it had access to official papers. Its task was to draw up yearly reports with considerations of the economic past, present, and future. The council also made proposals to the government concerning its future cyclical and structural policies. The above-mentioned 1967 law integrated the activities of the Council of Economic Experts into the new policy of global state intervention. Apart from the five-year budgetary forecasts which the federal government and the governments of the states were required to make, the federal government also had to publish annually general economic forecasts and take these into account when executing future monetary and fiscal policy. The advice of the Council of Economic Experts was undoubtedly of great influence here. Also important was the establishment of a planned income policy. A special organ (Konzertierte Aktion) was set up in which government representatives, financiers, employers, workers and the central bank met to lay down future wage policy.

In the light of all this it is clear that the West German economy had abandoned its original neo-free-market point of departure in favour of a position closer to that of its Western counterparts.

THE CENTRAL CONSULTATION VARIANT

The smaller countries of Western Europe including Sweden, the Netherlands, Austria, and Belgium, have developed since the Second World War a form of mixed economy that can be classified neither as neo-collectivist nor as neo-free-market. In fact it is a specific type of mixed economy, a sort of intermediary form which promotes a central consultation between representatives of the various social partners as the most important foundation of economic order in the country. Co-operation between workers' and employers' organizations created a climate of social peace which greatly helped postwar reconstruction and recovery. Consequently this system was speedily institutionalized and it developed its own internal dynamism. Central advisory and discussion organs were established in order to contribute to national social and economic policy. Sometimes these organs were bipartite, in which case they were empowered to take certain decisions independently – for example, labour-management agreements. In other cases there was a tripartite structure in which the government participated alongside the social partners. The role of the government in the national discussion organs was a fairly major one in the countries concerned – Sweden, the Netherlands, Austria and Belgium.[75]

Sweden can be used as a model for the system of central consultation in Europe.[76] The Social Democrats were in unbroken power from the 1930s up to 1976, and at an early stage they systematically extended government intervention. Indeed during the 1930s Sweden experimented with a Keynesian-type cyclical policy even before Keynes had fully worked out his own ideas.[77] After the Second World War, the government went still further. By a special investment tax it sought to prevent the economy from overheating in periods of economic upturn, and in 1955 a reserve fund for investment was established with a counter-cyclical mandate. Every company that declared itself willing, during upturns, to transfer part of its profits to the central bank where they were then blocked, received in return certain forms of tax exemptions. When a company during economic downturns was willing to invest, it could receive its blocked savings and was permitted an extra writing-off on the investment. Budgetary policy followed a comparable counter-cyclical strategy. From 1955 onwards a special emergency fund was even set up. Local governments were encouraged to build up a reserve of investment projects for years when recession threatened. At such times municipalities implementing these projects could count on a subsidy of 50 per cent from central government. Finally the Labour Office was given the power to issue building permits. During upturns it could reduce the flow of permits and prevent the demand for construction workers from getting out of control. Alternatively, during downturns, it could issue more building permits.

The structural policy of the Swedish government was an innovative one both economically and socially. The contractual consultation among representatives of the workers' unions, employees' unions and the federation of employers served as the foundation for negotiating central collective labour contracts and for a smoothly working system of social planning. Based on the past and expected average productivity of labour and capital, national and sectoral agreements were negotiated on direct wage rises, on improvements in secondary incomes, and on the long-term development of production and labour. In accordance with this consultation the central government put into effect broad social legislation. It dramatically equalized income distribution by means of steeply progressive taxation and by transfer payments. It strengthened the workers' right to a subsistence income, stipulated far-reaching measures in the area of labour conditions and safety, extended the system of social security, and in general created a very large network of public services.

The Swedish government was also active at the level of structural policy. It followed a strict anti-monopoly policy designed to ensure healthy competition in business and thus favour Swedish exports. It sought to eliminate marginal firms and raised business efficiency by providing a good and flexible supply of capital for dynamic and creative entrepreneurs. In addition it encouraged labour mobility and built up a modern system of manpower training and retraining for workers and farmers.[78]

In the mixed economy of the Netherlands, fiscal measures of counter-cyclical policy were commonly used, such as measures to stimulate or restrain investment. More important was the Keynesian-inspired monetary policy formulated by a fairly autonomous central bank. As for structural policy, in the early post-war era it was largely based on low wages.[79] The Dutch wished to take advantage of the reconstruction process by a systematic restructuring of the economy in the direction of export-led growth and the practices of modern big business. To this end the government announced a low-wage policy, supported by bipartite consultation and closely supervised by the government. To the private body, an agency for labour relations (Stichting van de Arbeid) which had spontaneously developed in 1945 following the co-operation between employers and workers during the war, a new public social economic body was added in 1950. This was the Sociaal Economische Raad in which employers, unions, and government were represented by delegations of equal size. General wage rounds were discussed and approved in both institutions. The collective labour agreements which were negotiated and concluded here on a company or sectoral level also had to be validated by a board of official intermediaries which was controlled by the Ministry of Social Affairs.

In the long term, the Dutch low-wage policy was untenable. By 1953 the link between wage increases and the cost of living had already been replaced by one in which wages were tied to the evolution of average labour productivity. In 1959 even differentiated wage formation was permitted, on the basis of increases in labour productivity per industrial branch. From 1963, though in a zig-zag movement, there was a trend towards the complete liberalization of wage formation. Even the compulsory surveillance of the collective labour agreements was gradually abandoned.[80] The rise of European prosperity and the Dutch entry into the EEC were the chief reasons why the Dutch government could not maintain its tight wage policy. Instead, it shifted its social-economic policy to a control on prices and incomes. The Dutch also increasingly brought economic planning into government policy. Immediately after the Second World War a central planning bureau had been set up under the direction of Jan Tinbergen. Its initial tasks were to work out long-term projects for industrial and regional development and to prepare annual forecasts concerning economic activity in the public and private sectors. From 1963 the time scale of this planning bureau was lengthened and five-year plans were worked out. During that same era the Netherlands government, like other governments, was enlarging its role in the development of infrastructure, the broadening of public services, and the redistribution of income and wealth.

Austria and Belgium closely resemble the Swedish-Dutch model of social consultation. Government control in social planning gradually increased, and employers, unions, and central government came together to decide the share of prosperity growth over the coming years which would accrue to workers. The advantages of this were unmistakable: workers saw their share of the cake constantly grow bigger, and at the same time employers saw their social risks decreasing and could prepare long-term investment projects with a greater chance of execution. For the government, this form of consensus was a means of countering the danger of inflation.[81]

It would be incorrect to assign the different countries permanently and unreservedly to the above-mentioned categories of mixed economy. As time passed each country made use of techniques which had previously been characteristic of other categories. Moreover, in all countries adaptations took place which make classification still more difficult. Nevertheless it may be stated with certainty that the mixed economy after the Second World War was based on a combination of neo-collectivist, neo-free-market, and contractual conceptions, with the precise emphasis differing from country to country.

CHAPTER VIII

THE MIXED ECONOMY
UNDER PRESSURE

The successes achieved by the mixed economy during the 1950s and 1960s were not lasting ones. On the contrary they were the seeds of new, worrying disturbances in Western economic activity. The difficulties of the 1970s raised serious doubts concerning the efficiency of the mixed economy. Mainly at issue here were the inflationary implications of the post-war economic system. Keynesian theory too became the subject of serious criticism. All this led to modifications. Alternative systems were put forward, and the most dynamic force emerging in them was the idea of self-management.

1. THE CHANGE IN THE INSTITUTIONAL ENVIRONMENT

There were inner contradictions in the mixed economy: it was based on premises that lost their relevance as soon as the objectives of the system were realized. The first premise was that companies would always operate as large, planning-orientated organizations in a competitive environment and that they would remain subject to indirect and direct state control. The second premise was that the unions, once involved in consultation, would be prepared actively to co-operate in alterations to industrial structure. The final premise was that the government would demonstrate sufficient flexibility to keep the market mechanism in place. In fact the growth dynamic steered this whole institutional framework in a different direction.

There was a steadily increasing divergence between the basic assumptions and reality.

The development of the modern business company opened the first crack between theory and practice. The mixed economy was not hostile to big business; on the contrary the planning systems of modern business life fitted in perfectly with the government planning strategy. But the assumptions that this co-operation would continue to take place within a context of optimally sized firms, a competitive market, and a national policy were all seriously undermined by growth. Optimal firm size, upon which neo-classical theory rested,[1] was converted from a static to a dynamic concept after the Second World War. Apparently greater economies of scale, provided they were accompanied by improved hierarchical organization and adequate planning, constantly opened new perspectives for the increase of returns. Many new forms of co-operation, mergers, and take-overs thus saw the light of day in the post-war period. A powerful wave of new industrial concentration in the West was the result.[2] The newly realized economies of scale greatly increased the opportunities for monopoly and oligopoly. Of course, in many cases concentration actually increased competition: mergers undertaken for reasons of diversification could considerably strengthen the competitive position of the smaller firms which had been taken over as they now received financial and commercial support from the dominant large company. Despite a sharpening of competition in specific sectors and markets, however, one can still maintain that in general the monopoly power of modern big business grew.

This added power was used to reduce the enormously increased risks and uncertainty and to improve the aggregate efficiency of investment decisions. By means of self-financing, big companies were able to sidestep the competitive forces normally active in the traditional capital market. Even on the occasions when big companies did resort to external financing, through their multidivisional structure they continued to exercise a large amount of control over their investment strategy. The multidivisional form of organization gave every big company the opportunity to create its own efficient, autonomous, mini-capital market in which the allocation of investment capital remained subject to its own internal decisions.[3]

The influence of big business was also built up in other respects, and the position of the consumer in the market place grew weaker. Although association in consumer groups increased, individual consumers often suffered defeat in the face of the 'want creation' of big business.[4] Manipulation of demand by advertising and product differentiation dethroned the consumer as exclusive king of the market. The vertical integration of industrial companies also affected the buyer's market, because it introduced planning and control to the whole chain, that is, the buying and selling of raw materials and semi-finished and finished goods.[5]

The weakening of traditional competition in the post-war market of goods and services naturally brought counter-reactions. One was the development of the capital market into a mass market. This resulted from the rise of prosperous middle-class groups. A growing number of individuals from these groups participated directly in the financing of big business via the traditional capital market. They were also the main source of finance for institutional investors which began to play a dominant role in the capital market. The mass nature of the capital market had a real influence on the investment behaviour and development of big business, most notably on the monopoly power of the technostructure and top management. Those owners of capital that belonged to middle-class groups followed a specific strategy – they usually wanted a rapid and spectacular return, especially in the form of so-called capital gains (treated more favourably by the tax laws) and had little or no interest in the long-term growth strategy desired by the technostructure.[6]

Another attack on the monopoly power of the technostructure came from within. As education became more general, the number of technicians and intellectuals increased. Many of them took up management functions in large companies, attracted by the great opportunities those companies offered in the area of organization and planning because of the larger economies of scale. This growth in management personnel comprised a factor of potential protest against the strongly hierarchical structure of big business and was the source of a powerful demand for participation in the administrative control of the company.

Still another force standing against post-war monopolistic and oligopolistic tendencies was the affluent society, which was itself a product of growth. It offered good prospects for the expansion of the service sector and for the many small companies working in that sector. It is true that a number of these service companies were reliant on big business, but many others were independent and once more created possibilities for a market economy based on competition. The great post-war development of the communication media had a similar effect. It strengthened the hold of pressure groups on public opinion and thus on political decision-making. Through the communication media, the misuse of power by big business could be publicly criticized and the government forced to act.

Big business tried with some success to restrict the impact of these factors that worked for the restoration of market forces. Large American companies developed into multinationals during the 1960s and large European and Japanese companies followed this example in the 1970s. Big companies thus integrated themselves in a very dynamic fashion into the world economy that had reached maturity after the Second World War. Under the auspices of big business, technological progress, growth, economies of scale, and management all offered new potential. At the same time government control weakened. National governments continued to hold sovereignty over companies or divisions operating within their borders, but the crucial decision-making and the central investment strategy of multinationals remained largely independent of government control, especially as there was no real international political authority. Indeed in the smaller industrial countries and in the Third World, the relative influence of some companies was often so great that even the power of national governments was undermined.

However real the effect of market-restoring factors, the internationalization of large companies thus formed a new serious threat to the traditional market system. Multinationals took on such huge proportions, their organization became so world-wide and their hierarchical structure so efficient that eventually their plans no longer had to depend on national guardianship. By means of this autonomous power they could begin to control markets.[7]

It was not only big business that disrupted the balance of the market, for unions had a similar influence, both indirect and direct. Their indirect effect resulted from the strong support they gave to the growth strategy of big business during the post-war period. Greater economies of scale stimulated further technological progress, which in turn raised labour productivity and enabled higher wages and salaries to be paid. The unions consequently lent their full co-operation to the concentration and growth of big business in return for rapidly rising wages and a substantial improvement of other employment conditions. Simultaneously, however, they were also helping to increase the monopoly and oligopoly position of big business in the traditional market for intermediary and finished goods and for intermediary and advanced services. They thus contributed to the strengthening of the financial autonomy of big business.[8]

In direct terms the unions disturbed the free flow of market forces by themselves building up a monopoly-oligopoly position in the labour market. In most cases the unions were actively involved in national consultations organized by the government with the aim of implementing post-war policies of growth and welfare. The unions consequently developed into powerful organizations in the social, economic and political life of the West, being the official representatives of workers and employees. Their co-operation was nevertheless conditional: they demanded in exchange that workers' real incomes should steadily grow, and on this point, owing to their strong bargaining position, they often got their way. The upshot was that the normal working of the labour market was distorted. During the years of expansion, substantial wage rises took place in sectors where there were few, if any, increases in labour productivity. Wage evolution in backward sectors closely followed that in growth sectors, where improvements in labour productivity in fact justified the higher pay. These backward sectors made up the difference between higher wages and lagging labour productivity by increasing their prices and during the industrial stagnation of the 1970s, when structural changes were urgently necessary, the continuation of high wages in old and protected sectors with low labour productivity once more hindered the structural renewal of industry through the normal mechanisms of the labour market.

Not only big business and big unions but governments sometimes had a disturbing influence on markets. They did this indirectly through the support they lent to big business. Business was fostered by factors such as the co-operation between government and business in research and development, the harmonizing of the state and business planning, and the privileged position that companies enjoyed in selling goods and services to their governments. These kinds of co-operation were given not just to nationalized companies but also to large private ones. The Western governments which initially, after the war, had wanted to follow a neo-liberal policy, gradually changed their minds. Their attempts to hold back the concentration movement by means of antitrust legislation were put on the back burner; there were numerous examples of this in the United States, West Germany, and Belgium.[9]

Governments not only disturbed the working of the market by indirectly helping big business concerns to be monopolies or oligopolies, they also disturbed it by building up their own monopoly and monopsony positions. The first important step was the swelling of the nationalized sector after the Second World War. Countries often nationalized complete sectors such as banking, insurance, railway transport, postal services and telecommunications, steel and coal, thus creating a total monopoly. No less significant was the development of the post-war welfare economy. The rapid growth in government expenditure came not only from the extension of state controls and the broadening of counter-cyclical policy, but also from a huge expansion in the supply of public goods. As a result of all this, governments evolved into tremendous producers of services, often on a monopoly basis. At the same time the Western governments also became extremely important consumers; sometimes for particular items a government was the only buyer in the market place (monopsony). Defence expenditure and the resulting military-industrial complex provide the best illustration of market distortion by the government sector on the demand side.

The multiplying of state bureaucracy also disrupted normal market forces. The nationalizations, the public services, and the greater role of government in the management of the economy, had considerably increased the number of civil servants. The slow growth, stagnation, and even decline of employment in industry due to rapid technological advance were fortunately compensated by the expansion of employment in the services sector, which was precisely where governments occupied a very substantial place. As long as economic growth continued, the accompanying government expenditure could be financed by higher tax receipts; but when growth slowed or ceased there was no fiscal room available to extend state bureaucracy further. In order to keep the budget in balance it would have been necessary to slim down the state apparatus. This, however, did not happen. Through its monopoly position the government was able to extend state bureaucracy for some time still, even if it was just to keep down unemployment. Deficit spending thus took place on a large scale and the consequence was a fiscal crisis and an upward twist to the inflationary spiral.[10]

The mixed economy therefore came to function within an

institutional framework which differed fundamentally from the one originally set up. In order to cope with the increasing complexity of the economic process, new forms of organization came about in the fields of production, distribution and consumption. In this new context the original concept of the competition-based market was no longer fully relevant. The competitive market was not abolished, but the new centres of power which had developed in line with the evolution of economic organization modified its operation. A system came about in which there was no Invisible Hand to ensure automatically an equilibrium in the economy. Between the powerful interest groups only an uneasy truce was observed, one which was far removed from the overall equilibrium of the traditional market system.

2. THE FAILURE OF GOVERNMENT PLANNING AND OF CENTRAL CONSULTATION

The variants of the mixed economy that crystallized after the Second World War soon began increasingly to resemble each other. This trend continued up to the beginning of the 1970s, but the 1974–5 economic crisis radically changed the situation. Owing to the general disillusionment with the Keynesian-inspired New Economics, the enthusiasm for planning and central consultation waned and most governments turned back to the concepts of orthodox monetarism.

In the countries which had adopted a neo-free-market approach when building up their post-war economies, the introduction of planning and consultation took place at a relatively late stage. In West Germany it was only in 1967 that a legislative start was made on systematic government planning and concerted action between government, employers and employees (Konzertierte Aktion). Around 1972 there was still intensive discussion concerning the further extension of government planning and there were requests for a policy of direct government controls on private investment via a system of registration and government vetoes or permits. But the inflation of the 1970s reduced interest in demand management. Inflation was also the cause of the failure of the Konzertierte Aktion – the unions refused to co-operate further because they feared they would become trapped in a restrictive wage policy. The growth of social welfare was also curbed. The West German government laid more and more stress on the fight against inflation. To this end it started to follow a more monetarist line and gave the Bundesbank, especially from the mid 1970s onwards, greater competence to take autonomous, orthodox measures. From this strengthened position, the Bundesbank began to suggest target figures for the annual growth of the money supply. When these targets were not observed, the Bundesbank took unilateral measures which sometimes thwarted government policy.[11]

In the United States the pattern was very much the same, although developments took place still later than in West Germany. The expansion of social welfare which had been initiated during the 1960s by the growth policy of President Kennedy and above all by the Great Society programme of President Johnson, continued at full steam during the 1970s. This expansion was responsible for the third upward surge in government expenditure (the earlier two came as a result of the New Deal in the 1930s, and of the Second World War).[12] According to Charles L. Schultze, the rise in the share of social welfare provisions in aggregate GNP was due to three main factors: the introduction of new social aid programmes such as Medicare and the system of food stamps, the improvement of existing programmes, and the increase in the number of people taking up these services. The discussion about the introduction of a national health system (supported among others by Senator Edward Kennedy) comprised a closing chapter in this development.

Government planning was very slow to get off the ground in the United States. On a motion by Hubert Humphrey and Jacob Javits, the Balanced Growth and Economic Planning Act was approved in 1975; through this Act centralized government planning (indicative, not binding) was introduced. In 1974 the Congressional Budget Reform Act required the preparation of long-term budget forecasts. This work was to be undertaken from the start of 1975 by the Congressional Budget Office, under the direction of Alice M. Rivlin. The objective here was to bring more coherence to the often contradictory measures passed by the legislature.[13] This centralized planning initiative, however, had little effect.[14]

In countries where the mixed economy had been built according to neo-collectivist principles, the movement was in the opposite direction. The planning notion gradually weakened; denationalization was undertaken or management techniques from the private sector were adopted; and the concerted economy of the smaller Western countries was given more attention.

French government planning, which from the start had been an example for all the mixed economies of the West, finally began to lose its dynamism. There is no doubt that great improvements in planning technique were made between the Second and Seventh Plans, as the co-operative and somewhat improvised planning of the first years gradually made way for more refined plans based on econometric formulas.[15] Despite this the planning bureau visibly lost influence over economic development in France. The most obvious explanations for this loss of influence were the growing internationalization of economic life and the entry of France into the European Economic Community. The planning of domestic growth could no longer be seen in isolation.[16] A deeper cause lay in the strengthening of political authority during the Fifth Republic. Neither President de Gaulle nor the Minister of Finance, Valéry Giscard d'Estaing, was willing to accept the fact that an independent planning bureau could direct the French economy. The first attack came in 1963. The growth-orientated vision of the planning bureau, with its heavy emphasis on investment without a parallel effective control on incomes, had led to inflation, balance-of-payments problems, and devaluations. De Gaulle wanted to put an end to this and in 1963, via Giscard d'Estaing, began to restrict the influence of the planning bureau.[17] The *Plan de Stabilisation*, launched that year by Giscard d'Estaing, subordinated the execution of the French plan to the government's restrictive anti-inflation policy. Consequently from the 1960s onwards, French government planning switched from long-term planning to a short-term stabilization policy. In these circumstances the planning bureau now was closely bound to political reality. In the course of the 1970s a central planning council (Conseil Central de Planification) was set up, bringing together the President and his most senior ministers on a monthly basis to discuss problems concerning planning. In reality it was mainly the government's short-term stabilization policy that was discussed and this administrative framework became an instrument for the *dirigisme* of Giscard d'Estaing after he became President in 1974.[18] The stabilization policy resulted in the three plans drawn up by Prime Minister Raymond Barre: they show to what extent the government had itself taken over short-term planning and demoted the planning bureau to secondary status.

It was not the French government's intention to wind up the planning bureau completely, for it could still be helpful. It could be used to improve the coherence and consistency of government expenditure. It could function as a source of information and as a propaganda organ for the stabilization policy. Finally the government tried to use the planning bureau to integrate central consultation into the French policy-making process. The economic expansion begun after the war had created tensions which exploded in the riots of May 1968. The economic crisis of the 1970s threatened further social disorder, and more and more the government had to take account of the social implications of the stabilization policy. This was no easy task for a pronounced right-wing government, and so it tried to pass the problem to the central planning organs. In fact ever since the Fourth Plan (1962–5) the planning bureau had provided a social dimension to the government planning process by tackling the problems of regional development and collective provisions.[19] After the Fifth Plan (1965–9), the plans were no longer expressed in terms of production quantities but in terms of value. In this way the forecasts could now take account of financial circumstances and thus integrate the problems of incomes policies into the planning mechanism.[20] Ultimately, however, the government strategy of tackling social policy in this way did not succeed because the unions pulled out of the various planning organs. The planning bureau thus became a group of technocrats who regularly advised the government to introduce new social provisions and infrastructural programmes.

In Britain too, the experiment with government planning and central consultation was not particularly successful. The new Labour government which came to power in October 1964 immediately set about reorganizing the long-term government planning apparatus that had been established by Harold Macmillan and Selwyn Lloyd during the previous Conservative administration. All the functions of the National Economic Development Office and those of the Treasury relating to government planning were brought together under a brand-new ministry, the Department of Economic Affairs, headed by the energetic George Brown. Planning thus became a central part of the new government economic policy. At the same time the National Economic Development Office continued to function as a discussion forum for the social partners together with representatives of government and a group of independent experts. George Brown and his assistants immediately started work and prepared a new long-term plan to run until 1970 and designed to attain a yearly growth rate of 4 per cent.[21] But the Labour plan never really got off the ground.

Although the Labour government had made vague promises to adapt its policies to the plan, it never regarded itself as truly committed. On the contrary, the Labour government shared in the traditional belief that growth should be primarily determined by expected demand. The plan was to create a psychological climate that favoured growth expectations so that companies would be encouraged to expand their investment. It called for no direct intervention in either the nationalized or private sector. Moreover, as soon as growth generated too much demand and endangered the balance of payments, the short-term stop-go policy was reintroduced. In February 1966 a restrictive policy was announced and this was followed in July 1966 by a severe deflationary policy including tax increases, a six-month freeze on prices and wages, and drastic cuts in government investment. The devaluation of November 1967 came too late to breathe new life into the plan. The 1966 measures, then, signified the end of the Brown plan and in fact the end of long-term government planning in Britain.

The resumption of the stop-go policy meant that the objectives of planned growth were sacrificed for the sake of external equilibrium and to protect the international position of sterling. Although the Labour party adopted a radical programme of government planning when it was in opposition in 1973, nothing came of it when a new Labour government was formed in February 1974. On the contrary, with the approval of the union movement, the Labour government acceded to the Treasury demand of implementing a tight wage policy, easing price controls, reducing taxation on higher incomes, and cutting back on government expenditure. On the other hand Labour did pass an Industry Act in 1975 by which the National Enterprise Board was set up as a sort of state holding company. The same bill also introduced the Planning Agreements System which was designed to organize the management of state concerns and private companies on a more planned basis and to ensure better coordination all round. The bill had no effect, though, since the National Enterprise Board was given no powers and the Planning Agreements System was supposed to work on a voluntary basis. Disappointment in this respect undermined the policy of voluntary wage restraint and led to increasing confrontation between the

Labour government and the unions, that is, the breakdown of the concerted economy.[22]

The new Conservative government led by Margaret Thatcher in 1979 made a substantial change of course towards a more free-market-orientated policy. There was no longer any question of long-term planning and institutionalized consultation. The government put its faith in denationalization, reductions in direct taxation (especially favouring high incomes), increases in indirect taxation, drastic cuts in government expenditure, and an orthodox monetary policy. The new guiding philosophy was a monetarism inspired by Milton Friedman that sought a partial restoration of the market mechanism and turned its back on government *dirigisme*.

In Italy and Japan as well, long-term planning and government *dirigisme* weakened too. In Italy around the end of the 1960s there was a movement to increase the time-span of planning by linking the first five-year plan with a longer-term projection, in which structural changes would be dealt with. Nothing came of this. The second five-year plan (1971–5) was prepared but never approved. It ended up in the drawer, serving only limited use as a blueprint for an ideal development.[23]

In the mean time the economic policy of the Italian government became increasingly concerned with the problem of short-term instability. After the war the government had followed a policy very much based on export-led growth. To this end manufacturing industry was given special encouragement, the concentration of business enterprises was facilitated, and connections were sought with the European market. The result was spectacular growth but also greater vulnerability and more external dependence. The wage explosion, which even affected sectors with lagging labour productivity, led to a serious balance-of-payments crisis as early as 1963. A stream of further crises followed. These demanded an increasing amount of government attention, especially since the left-wing opposition was steadily gaining power.

Big business was the only group able to assimilate the wage explosion of the 1960s and 1970s. Using mechanized or automatized mass production, it was able to raise labour productivity to a level that kept pace with the wage rises or even outpaced them.[24] In consequence the power of large companies grew, in both state and private sectors. Moreover, these large Italian concerns became more internationalized, and even began to impose their long-term planning on the government rather than the other way around.[25] This factor, along with the series of crises, gradually undermined the dynamism of autonomous government planning in Italy.

Similar factors gradually eroded the government planning movement in Japan. As in Italy, post-war long-term government planning was primarily designed to stimulate export-led growth. As in Italy, the deterioration of the world economic situation during the 1970s caused attention to be switched to problems of the balance of payments and of inflation. In other words, policy became more aimed at correcting short-term instability.[26] By means of concentration and internationalization large Japanese companies had mushroomed and the long-term planning of the *Zaibatsu* began to overshadow that of the government. Running parallel to this was the liberalization of foreign investment in the Japanese economy. From 1963 the first cautious concession was made in this respect: foreign participation in Japanese companies could now be made on a fifty-fifty basis. During the following years, and especially after March 1969, an increasing number of industrial sectors in Japan were thrown completely open for foreign investment.[27] In the long term this was another factor which weakened the influence that the Japanese central planning bureau extended over big business.

The small industrial countries that had based their mixed economies on central consultation – and had later tried to integrate long-term planning into this consultation – also had to shorten sail during the 1970s. The Swedish system, which had served as a model for the whole world, came under heavy pressure. Indeed, during the great national strike of May 1980, it was even said that this model had outlived its usefulness.

The social consensus and the idea of class co-operation, on which the Swedish central consultation was based, had started to break down after wildcat strikes in the mining sector in 1969–70. These strikes were clearly directed against the principle of annual national wage rounds.[28] The strikers felt that the consultative system was too strongly institutionalized: the unions were over-organized and had reduced central consultation to a technical discussion in which an elite of ageing union leaders, together with the ruling elite of the Social Democratic Party, negotiated with business representatives. In this formula the rank-and-file workers and the younger generation had no say in proceedings.[29] Attempts to strengthen worker participation did not placate the workers. The obligation on every company to include two workers' representatives on the board of directors did nothing to counter the criticism that the unions were over-organized, because it was members of the union elite that occupied these new places on the board. A 1976 law under which employers no longer had the exclusive right to take on and dismiss workers, and the labour representatives on a board of directors were given a right to monitor such matters, again brought no improvement in relations. The same criticism still held, namely that only bureaucratized union executives were given power.

The difficult economic times of the 1970s brought further problems for the Swedish model, and much tension was generated on the domestic scene. In terms of social welfare, Sweden led the world. But Swedish social welfare was financed by taxation so high that it had reached an absolute maximum. The economic recession had the effect of exhausting this source of finance. The recourse to foreign loans and to deficit spending brought temporary relief but at the same time pushed up inflation and weakened the balance of payments. Thus the annual wage negotiations were conducted under difficulties. Sweden was highly dependent on exports, and inflation threatened the competitive position of Swedish industry in world markets. These external factors made the attitude of the employers during the wage negotiations firmer than it had ever been before. The 1978–9 increase in oil prices further stiffened the resolve of the employers and in May 1980 the wage negotiations broke down. The result was the catastrophic general strike mentioned above.

The difficulties with the balance of payments also hindered the manpower planning by which the Swedish government implemented its structural policy. The extent of the economic recession and the consequent rapid increase in unemployment made it no longer possible to rely on the restructuring of the labour market as a way to adapt the Swedish economy. Government retraining schemes no longer seemed sufficient to shift Swedish medium-term and long-term investment to new sectors with a higher labour productivity. An improvement in the world economy was a necessary condition. The fight against inflation, which had never been a central policy in Sweden, now began to receive more attention. Thus during the 1970s Sweden too turned to a monetarist-inspired economic policy that sacrificed long-term planning to the needs of the present.[30]

In the other small countries the same disruptive factors were at work. In economic terms, countries such as Belgium, the Netherlands, and Denmark were very reliant on export markets. In Belgium, exports represented more than 50 per cent of GNP. The reduction in trade within the OECD area after the difficult economic situation of the 1970s demanded in all of these countries that more attention be paid to immediate problems, and it dissipated interest in long-term planning. Their connection with the German mark area caused them explicitly or implicitly to adopt the monetarist anti-inflation policy of West Germany. This also raised interest in short-term solutions at the expense of long-term policy. In these countries the influence of multinationals in particular sectors caused government planning to appear less relevant. During the crisis years these large companies preferred to follow their own transnational strategy which to a large extent fell outside the control of national governments. Finally the regionalization of economic and political decision-making, which was a powerful movement in some countries including Belgium, also restricted the influence of central planning.

The central consultative process, which played such a key role in the mixed economies of the small industrialized countries of the West, grew increasingly dislocated, and not just in Sweden. In the Netherlands, Belgium, Denmark, and elsewhere a growing number of wildcat strikes and factory occupations took place during the 1970s. Workers resisted the incomes policy which the governments, in a centralized collaboration with the social partners, tried to operate as a key element of their monetarist attacks on inflation. The union leadership, in order not to alienate its own rank and file, felt compelled to abandon the concerted action economy and take a more aggressive line.

To summarize: the development of the post-war mixed economies of the West can be characterized by a growing convergence. In countries which had originally adopted a neo-liberal system, interest in long-term planning did increase at one point but it soon waned again in favour of a short-term pragmatic *dirigisme*. Countries with a more neo-collectivist approach gradually gave up their long-term vision of government planning and turned to short-term measures of a counter-cyclical and anti-inflation nature. In the smaller countries, the concerted action economy ended up with a major confrontation between those who feared for the breakdown of the welfare state and those who were more concerned with holding on to foreign markets or restructuring export industry. In all countries, therefore, the mixed economy degenerated into pragmatic *dirigisme*. It was increasingly determined by bureaucratized structures, *ad hoc* measures, and laboriously reached compromises between strong pressure groups. Corporatist tendencies gradually appeared. Naturally the deteriorating world economic conditions during the 1970s were a vital factor in the rapid crumbling of the mixed economy, but there were deeper causes which should not be overlooked.

3. DEEPER CAUSES FOR THE FAILURE OF THE MIXED ECONOMY

From comparative studies it seems that there is no great correlation between target growth figures, such as those laid down by the various national planning bureaux, and the growth rates which were actually recorded over the period.[31] The effect of planning on economic events thus appears to have been only slight. The real factors that influenced growth lay elsewhere. For example, West Germany, Japan and Italy were among the fastest-growing countries in the OECD in the post-war period. These were not the countries with the best-constructed government planning apparatus. They were, however, those which had been defeated in the Second World War. Among other things, therefore, reconstruction and the catching-up movement played an important role in boosting growth and modernizing capital accumulation.[32]

As already stated, government planning in the West was indicative rather than imperative. The recommended target growth figures represented at most a compulsory guideline for the public sector, usually not even that. For the private sector, government planning amounted to recommendations only. Furthermore the stimulative measures that were taken in order to realize these goals had adverse consequences which finally undermined the success of government planning. The government controls on borrowing and the selective decisions taken in this respect led to a discriminatory policy that facilitated the formation of oligopolies and other forms of market distortion. On the other hand the system of subsidies and fiscal exemptions was not discriminating enough, in that, with time, any firm could gain these concessions provided that it satisfied all the relevant criteria. Thus the whole objective of the exercise – that is, the encouragement of the most dynamic companies – was rendered meaningless. Moreover, subsidy and exemption schemes are often made law, and laws are seldom abrogated, which means that the system outlives its usefulness. The disadvantages of the special loans, subsidies and exemptions became apparent to all when the multinationals began to avail themselves of these incentives in the course of the 1960s. The attempts by various national governments to attract multinationals to their countries led to an absurd contest, with each government seeking to outbid the others in offering still greater incentives in the form of loans, subsidies and the like. It often happened that a multinational, at one time attracted to a certain country, abolished its subsidiary after a while, perhaps because it was looking for new subsidized investment possibilities elsewhere. Government planning that seeks to accommodate such an investment strategy by multinational companies via the provision of support and incentives can hardly be considered very efficient.

The theoretical point of departure for government planning and government growth policy contained fundamental contradictions. It was based on Keynesian counter-cyclical intervention policy, made dynamic by combination with the Harrod-Domar growth model.[33] In the first place the Keynesian approach was a purely national one, whereas economic development after the Second World War had a strong international element. A structural conflict thus came about between the national-based economic policy of governments and the economic reality of greater internationalization. Multinationals reconciled these irreconcilables but usually at the cost of the authority of the national government. In the second place Keynesian theory chiefly concerned the efficient generation of economic recovery during times of serious depression and high unemployment – it took little or no account of cost-push inflation.

The application of Keynesian techniques gave very good results during the period of post-war reconstruction, but their further application as a means of forcing long-term growth led to serious distortions. A monetary policy designed to expand investment and consumption can only remain non-inflationary as long as the increased demand for capital and consumer goods can be met by a surplus of resources, especially labour, raw materials, and know-how. Under conditions of full employment and an increasing relative scarcity of raw materials, there is a strong upward pressure on wages and raw material prices. If this pressure is released by additional monetary injections, a spiralling cost inflation is set in motion which is difficult or impossible to control. Full employment was gradually attained in Western industrial countries in the 1960s, and in the 1970s a relative scarcity of raw materials developed. Inflation thus began to accelerate at an alarming rate. This in turn threatened the balance of payments of those countries in which imports had increased because of rising domestic prices. Out of fear of devaluation or of weakening floating rates large speculative flows of money entered the international money and capital markets. These flows increased general economic instability.

Financing policies of long-term growth through deficit spending had a comparable effect. As long as growth raised government incomes, the budget deficits of previous years could always be made good. But certain obstacles stand in the path of permanent growth, no matter how good the planning is. There are limits to export capacity. There are limits to the supply of labour and raw materials. The ageing of industrial structure and the internationalizing of economic activity also constitute restrictions. When growth for any of these reasons slackened or ceased altogether, a process of cumulative budget deficits began, stimulating an inflationary spiral. Numerous illustrations of this appeared in the 1970s. Faced with rising inflation, governments felt themselves obliged to take severe deflationary measures, including attempts to curb the policy of deficit spending. These were counter-cyclical actions, designed to cool an overheated economy. Long-term growth policies were sacrificed for these shorter-term urgencies. Inflation seemed to pose an irreconcilable contradiction to full employment and long-term growth. This exploded the theory of the Phillips Curve: there seemed to be no fixed relationship between the level of prices and the number of unemployed, and control over both of these variables appeared to be more difficult than had first been thought. In short, the belief in Keynesianism and government planning, in the mixed economy, was pretty thoroughly undermined.

The mixed economy also failed in the area of prosperity and social welfare. Most certainly income per capita soared in the industrialized countries of the West after the Second World War, and this held for most groups in the population. Nevertheless no conclusive solution was found for the problem of poverty. Inequalities of income and wealth remained.[34] Studies even showed that government transfer payments had a tendency to favour middle-income rather than lower-income groups.[35] In addition, sociological inquiries showed that increasing prosperity does not reduce the social tension between income groups, let alone eliminate it. People were found to measure an increase in income not on its own terms but in relation to income evolution in other income groups. General increases in prosperity, then, left existing levels of frustration and social tension intact. Moreover, the mixed economy with its nationally based policies of growth and welfare further distorted the *world* distribution of income and wealth.[36] The relentless and sometimes aggressive exploitation of the reserves of cheap raw materials and labour overseas caused much frustration and bitterness there.

These shortcomings of the mixed economy's treatment of prosperity and social welfare were accentuated by inflation. Some income and wealth groups profited from it and others fell victim. In the case of zero growth an improvement in the position of one income group could only be attained at the expense of other groups. It was precisely this growing partiality that broke the social consensus upon which the concerted action economy was based. It also led to the ultimate failure of the new initiatives made during the 1970s. The problem of redistribution now presented itself again in its clearest form. If no growth was expected and yet investment must continue to expand, who should then surrender real income? This question set the various interest groups in conflict with each other and attacked the very foundations of the economy based on a concerted action. It raised discussion concerning the class struggle once again and led to a deterioration in social relations. Strikes and similar conflicts increased in number and all showed a tendency to develop into national confrontations between the unions and either government or employers.

There were also technical reasons for the failure of the concerted action economy. The attempts to harmonize consultation by applying objective criteria, such as the average increase in productivity, were not always successful. Improvements in productivity are not easy to measure. Moreover, there is the psychological effect caused by the higher-than-average wages paid in growth sectors where there is rapid technological progress and rapid productivity gains (the wage-leader effect).[37] Nevertheless from the late 1970s national governments tried to hold back from topping up wage levels in sectors with lower productivity growth because of the inflationary consequences. For the same reason national governments began to curtail expenditure on social policies from the mid 1970s onwards.

Most governments were convinced that their social policies had run out of control during the previous decades. Economic stagnation meant that, in future, government receipts would be lower and could not be compensated by an increase in direct taxation. This was because the taxation of income and profits at a higher rate would only hit savings and investment, both of which had to be encouraged in order to break through the economic stagnation.

Various countries including West Germany, Sweden, Britain, the United States and Belgium introduced policies to cut government expenditure on public services and social welfare and to raise the share of profits as a percentage of the national income. Furthermore, within the framework of an incomes policy, tax relief was granted to wage earners in exchange for moderate wage demands from the unions. Such fiscal concessions, however, entailed a further cut in government expenditure on social welfare and thus also undermined the founding principles of the concerted action economy.[38]

Finally, the foundations of the mixed economy were weakened by the growing world criticism of the policy of economic growth.[39] From the beginning, economists and sociologists had warned against the dangers of the modern consumer society. For example, David Riesman with his book *The Lonely Crowd* (1950) did much to affect public opinion in the United States.[40] In the political arena the words of Adlai Stevenson, 'The next frontier is the quality, the moral, intellectual and aesthetic standards of the free way of life', attracted much interest. John Kenneth Galbraith, in *The Affluent Society* (1958),[41] attacked the way big business manipulated consumers by means of advertising campaigns (want creation). He also pointed to the danger of public squalor and private affluence.

Moves were gradually taken to counter the threat to social equilibrium by providing more public services but they proved insufficient to silence the criticism – on the contrary. Daniel Bell and Irving Kristol pointed to the cultural contradictions that lay behind the concept of economic growth.[42] On the supply side the mixed economy ultimately rested on the Protestant ethos of hard work, frugality, dedication, seriousness, and self-control. On the demand side, in contrast, it relied on the principle of mass consumption of which extravagance, frivolity, more free time, less hard work, sensationalism and sexuality were the slogans and ultimately the driving force. Bell and Kristol believed that a lasting combination between these two opposing forces was impossible. In Britain, E. J.

Mishan wrote of the unbridgeable gulf between the growth of a developed technological society and the instinctive, inner needs of humankind.[43] Robert McNamara, using his position as chairman of the World Bank in the 1970s, tried to dethrone G N P as the central criterion for development policies and emphasized the importance of values other than physical production and material welfare.

A crusade against economic growth was also conducted by more revolutionary movements, culminating in the organization of the New Left. The first revolutionary reaction occurred in the form of an anti-culture of beatniks (and later hippies) which enjoyed great success in American universities. This developed into the student revolts of the 1960s, which also took place in Europe, leading to the Paris riots of 1968. The student revolts on both sides of the Atlantic were in essence directed against the American model of the consumer society. In the United States there was also the trauma of the Vietnam War. The European revolts were characterized by a certain anti-Americanism and so had a nationalistic flavour. The students also turned against the monolithic Marxist doctrine and thus against the authoritarian state system of Soviet communism. They refused to accept the Soviet Union as the undisputed leader of world radicalism and in this manner laid the foundations for a new left-wing ideology.

The theorists who had the greatest influence on the development of a New Left were those of the Sociological Research Institute of Frankfurt.[44] In its social criticism the Frankfurt School rejected the historical materialism of Marx. The conflicts and contradictions generated by the mixed economy, according to the Frankfurt School, lay more in the cultural than the material sphere. They acknowledged that the technical civilization which was supposed to achieve Utopia in socialist societies was in fact attained by the mixed economies during their post-war development into welfare states. Yet this technical welfare-civilization had little or no emancipatory potential and in fact tended to alienate rather than satisfy. Moreover, it integrated the working class totally into its value system, so that the traditional social basis for revolution was lost. Lastly it created an educated elite which, through the co-operation between the bureaucratic state apparatus and the technostructure of big business, was able to establish and perpetuate its own power. The same social and cultural criticism was applied to the socialist economies, especially to the blurring of the distinction between state and society and the resultant alienation and indirect manipulation. Herbert Marcuse[45] brought this message to the United States and Jürgen Habermas[46] to West Germany. In France, Louis Althusser presented similar ideas.[47] Many others followed in their footsteps. All were convinced that only good could result for the masses from radical and revolutionary action carried out by minority groups. The student risings of the 1960s in no case brought the result hoped for. Despite this, the ideology of the New Left did not die out. Instead the movement went in for still deeper analysis and adopted more reformist concepts, designed to breathe new life into the mixed economy.

A third group of critics of the mixed economy and its policy of economic growth were the ecologists. Action to conserve the environment and to economize in the use of natural resources was not new; indeed it had been systematically undertaken during the nineteenth century and still earlier. Nevertheless the policy of economic growth, which reigned supreme after the Second World War, gave rise to larger-scale ecological defence than ever seen before. From the moment that the first atom bomb was exploded in Hiroshima more attention was given to the disastrous effects that could accompany the nuclear era. When economic growth was at full steam during the 1960s, there was a parallel, increasing wave of protests against pollution and against other undesirable or dangerous side-effects of factories, mines, and automobiles – effects which were visible or tangible everywhere.

Also important was the criticism of bigness, that is the increasing economies of scale which the policy of economic growth gave rise to. Leopold Kohr[48] and E. F. Schumacher[49] campaigned for a reversal of this tendency. Simultaneously Malthusian-inspired books and periodicals appeared. Some writers, such as Paul Ehrlich in his book *The Population Bomb*,[50] predicted a rapid increase in world population and a tremendous famine – an eco-catastrophe that would assume world proportions. In connection with the policy of accelerated industrial growth, the Malthusian School gradually shifted its attention to the area of raw materials and energy. In 1972 Dennis H. Meadows *et al.*, at the request of the Club of Rome, published their much-discussed report, *The Limits to Growth*.[51] The authors extrapolated into the future the economic growth which had been realized in the previous decades. They came to the startling conclusion that, given constant supplies of raw materials and energy, further economic growth would speedily lead to the exhaustion of these resources. The world would thus in a short period find itself on the edge of the abyss.

The conclusions of the Club of Rome came in for severe methodological criticism. None the less, they still had a great psychological effect on public opinion and even on the political acts of government leaders. The success of the O P E C oil cartel and other agreements among raw-material-producing countries must also be seen in this context. The introduction of concepts such as zero growth and 'landing'[52] (as opposed to take-off) revealed the change in mentality. Governments and the governed gradually reconciled themselves to the thought that the mixed economy with its policy of traditional economic growth had had its day.

4. THE ALTERNATIVES

The disillusionment with the working of the mixed economy which steadily grew in the course of the 1970s led on to the open consideration of corrective actions or possible alternatives. For many, the mixed economy, with its particular emphasis on growth, had run totally out of control. To retrieve the situation, cyclical measures were now insufficient and structural reforms were urgently required. The proposed structural reforms can be divided into three main categories: (1) return to the market economy and free competition, (2) transition to a fully centralized planned economy, and (3) movement towards a system of decentralized planning and of self-management by workers.

Among the leading proponents of the free-market-economy category were the neo-classical economists Ludwig von Mises and Friedrich von Hayek. From the end of the 1960s figures such as Milton Friedman, Karl Brunner and A. H. Meltzer took over the leadership and they were termed monetarists.

The neo-classicists had already long criticized government mismanagement and had fought energetically against the concentration of economic power in the hands of the state.[53] In their eyes, the concerted economy masked a renaissance of corporatist and bureaucratic structures which fundamentally distorted the free flow and efficiency of economic forces. The introduction of ethical principles such as distributive justice into the working of the market economy, according to von Hayek, destroyed the objectivity of the economic process. Individuals thus were rewarded on the basis of the subjective criteria of good and evil, arbitrarily determined by an elitist democracy or authoritarian government. In contrast, freedom ensured that rewards for economic activity were decided objectively. In other words, the market is neutral and therefore, in principle, individuals are rewarded according to the objective criterion of success. This line of reasoning led the neo-classicists to appeal for a return to an applied form of free-market liberalism.

The monetarists followed the same path but were more pragmatic in their approach. They pressed directly for the dismantling of the Keynesian model.[54] They pointed to the destabilizing impact of an increase in government intervention, and they emphasized that the objectives of full employment and price stability could not both be realized. The mixed economy, they judged, must be shorn of over-extensive government influence. At the same time the private sector should be extended again and integrated into a system of free markets and pure competition. Under these conditions, the self-regulating mechanism of the market would make the economic system more balanced and price stability would be restored. If the government wished to follow a policy of stabilization, then it had to ensure that the money supply developed within fixed limits. It also had to keep to these guidelines itself and balance its budgets.

The monetarist vision was enthusiastically accepted during the 1970s when inflation and stagflation swept through the mixed economies of the West. As already mentioned, many governments adopted a monetarist strategy in their macro-economic policies. Some even tried to reduce the government sector and its relative share of GNP but actually such measures were very moderate ones which met heavy resistance and usually had little success. Consequently the neo-classicists had to be satisfied with a shift in macro-economic government policy towards a more monetarist approach. Their calls for a structural reform of the mixed economy along the lines of a return to a pure free-market economy went unanswered.

A second group of structural reformers advocated the abandonment of the mixed economy in favour of a fully centralized, imperatively planned economy. In practical terms this amounted to the further nationalization of industrial and service sectors, and to a strengthening of centralized control over the nationalized economy. Often appeals were made for the creation of state holding companies to control the top manufacturers. New measures to increase central control were also put forward: the state holding companies, nationalized companies, and large companies in the private sector were to be subject to a system of long-term planning which, according to the British formula, would be laid down by central government in consultation with the union movement. More extreme solutions were suggested by the traditional Communist parties in the West. The application of these solutions was possible, though only partially, in cases where the Communists participated in government or took over complete control as happened for a short time in Portugal immediately after the 1974 revolution. In France, the coalition of the leftist parties (Union de la Gauche) in the mid 1970s offered some prospects for experiments in this form of economic organization. In Britain, the radicalization of part of the Labour party brought this alternative into the political arena. In Italy too, the greater chances of a historic compromise between the Christian Democrats and the Communists pointed to a more radical development of the economic policy. Nevertheless, all in all, the significance of this second group of structural reformers remained limited. The supporters of centralized imperative planning did not come into effective political power during the 1970s. Moreover, their ideas were passionately opposed by neo-classicists, by monetarists, and in fact even by the younger generation of the New Left, which detested a centralized planned economy and an authoritarian, bureaucratic state as much as it detested the neo-free-market variant of the mixed economy.

The New Left formed the nucleus of the third group of reformers, favouring a system of decentralized planning and worker self-management. This third group resulted from the integration of the protest movement of the 1960s into the Socialist parties of the West. The protest movement had begun with revolutionary overtones, and Castro's Cuba and the Cultural Revolution in China served as models. However, as mentioned, a more reformist approach was adopted during the 1970s. The integration of the New Left into existing society and the political system caused it to set itself more attainable objectives. Simultaneously the New Left brought new blood into the antiquated traditional Socialist parties. 'Socialism with a human face' became the motto and the Yugoslavian model of worker self-management the prototype.[55]

As one point of departure the New Left held that the traditional political systems of Left and Right had no solution to the problem of economic democracy. When right-wing parties were in power, economic institutions served the interests of privileged private groups. When left-wing parties were in power or left-wing political systems controlled the state, economic institutions served the interests of a privileged state and party bureaucracy. In the eyes of the New Left, the union movement still constituted the most important means to fight successfully against the power held by the state and the owners of capital. The British variant of the New Left held that it was sufficient that the union movement should restrict the power of the state and party bureaucracy by exercising a legal right to monitor large companies in the private and public sectors. On the European mainland, left-wing radicals did not regard such a right as a satisfactory solution to the problem. In the first place, they felt that the unions themselves were so strongly institutionalized that the leadership had lost contact with the rank-and-file membership. In these circumstances the right to monitor would be no more than a fiction. Furthermore, because of the increased economies of scale and organizational progress, the power of big business and the state had become so great that the union movement was no longer in a position to compete. The relatively decreased significance of wages in total production costs was just another manifestation of this. The only way to restore a balance of power was to introduce a new concept: self-management. If workers, through a system of active self-management, could take over a part of economic decision-making, then the danger of the misuse of power by elite groups would be eliminated. The extension and application of these principles to decision-making in the cultural and political spheres would lead to a complete, humanist-inspired democracy, freed of distorting power relationships.[56]

As a second point of departure the New Left held that the extension of individual material welfare is not of itself a sufficient basis for the construction of a modern, humane society. Non-material values and collective needs also are essential components. Consequently, increases in GNP and physical production are not satisfactory criteria in the pursuit of general well-being. A new method of national accounting was seen as being necessary, a new system of cost-benefit analysis which could reflect non-material as well as material well-being indicators, individual well-being as well as social well-being.[57] The New Left thus came down in favour of a programme of socialist planning or, more specifically, decentralized planning. The defining of the nature of general well-being would take place primarily at the local community level, and the outlining of investment strategy and income distribution primarily at the company level. Ways to humanize the work process would also be discussed, defined, and organized at the company level.[58] The structure of decision-making everywhere should remain simple and basic so that after a debate, which would be as wide as possible, choice would be conscious and explicit. On the other hand, the rationality of the system would be guaranteed by the preparatory information which would be intensively distributed from the top level down to the grass roots. Alongside this, a supervisory group of elected representatives would ensure maximum efficiency and productivity. The decentralization of the fundamental decision-making process would thus be supplemented by a powerful centralized apparatus although its power would be restricted to preparation and implementation.[59] In this manner a balance would be reached between rationality and democracy, between efficiency and a just distribution of benefits.

In France some of these ideas were taken up in the programme of the Union de la Gauche in the mid 1970s.[60] The New Left had still greater influence in the electoral programme of François Mitterrand in 1980–1. In Italy in 1970–1 some ideas of the New Left were integrated into the second five-year plan.[61] In Britain a radical programme of the same inspiration was approved in 1973 by the National Executive Committee of the British Labour party.[62] In the smaller countries, such as Sweden, Belgium and the Netherlands, the programmes of the Socialist parties grew more radical and the ideas of the New Left gained more and more prominence. Yet few of these ideas were translated into political reality. Even in the countries where Socialist parties were in power or later came into power, such as West Germany and Britain, self-management as an alternative system never got off the ground. The difficult world economic conditions since 1974 and the influence of moderate and conservative elements within the Socialist parties of the West has hindered the breakthrough of innovative experiments.

The relevance of the three principal alternatives to the mixed economy can be judged on the basis of their chief characteristics. The centralized or decentralized nature of the proposed systems best lend themselves to this form of analysis. The intellectual emancipation had the effect of moving the debate on the democratization of decision-making in the post-war West to a very central position. For this reason, the centralized planning alternative, seen in the long term, offers little or nothing to countries which wish to continue to function primarily as parliamentary democracies. In theory, centralized planning optimalizes the rationality and therefore the efficiency of economic activity. All decisions are rationally taken in accordance with the desired objectives. But the authoritarian character of imperative centralized planning causes such resistance and distrust from all its economic subjects that in a parliamentary democracy a consensus for such a strict compulsory centralized planning system is difficult to imagine. Moreover, experience with centralized planning in totalitarian regimes during the inter-war period and also in the Eastern bloc since the Second World War has yielded rather negative results. Imperative planning leads to the alienation of the individual. Still worse, as the economic process has grown more complex, the centralized planning has been accompanied by such an extension of the state bureaucracy that the theoretical rationality and efficiency have given way to arbitrariness and chaos, to irrationality and inefficiency. The countries of the Eastern bloc have therefore tried to make the centralized character of their planning more supple rather than more rigid. If, in the West, conservative reactions to economic crises lead to more authoritarian regimes and thus to a stricter form of centralized planning, this will probably only be a temporary phenomenon. Given further intellectual emancipation, the fundamental movement will continue to be in the direction of democratized political and economic decision-making.

Seen in the above context, decentralized planning has a better future. It can be conceived in two ways. In the first place decentralized planning can signify a return to the sovereignty of the market and to free competition (our first category of structural alternatives to the post-war mixed economy). In the second place decentralized planning can be organized in the context of a socialist conception of self-management (our third structural alternative). The return-to-the-market conception means, in effect, the decentralization of economic decision-making down to the level of the individual. In this case the planning function is entrusted to the automatic balancing mechanism of the market system. A definitive and complete return to such a market system seems unlikely. The increasing size of companies in the public and private sectors is an irreversible process in a civilization where technological progress plays a central role. In a totally free-market economy this would inevitably lead to the formation of monopolies and to the distortion of the relationships between social groups. The income inequality which would result and the absence of corrective mechanisms would not be acceptable in a society so much based on distributive justice, on just economic rewards and the solidarity of the community. As long as society prefers a parliamentary or other form of participative democracy, a pure free-market system would generate unacceptable social situations.

The other concept of decentralized planning is that of economic self-management at the company level, accompanied by comparable forms of self-management in the cultural, political and social domains. Together these make up a system of direct participative democracy. Implicitly it is accepted that the system of self-management involves costs in the area of material welfare, since it does lack economic efficiency. This relative loss is nevertheless argued to be more than proportionately compensated by benefits in the political, cultural and social domains.

But does the majority of the population have the same value judgement regarding the cost-benefit analysis just mentioned? For many, of course, material advantages are extremely important as a basis of social status and as a source of self-respect. Political, cultural and social advantages have little or no meaning.[63] To be sure, these convictions can be changed by information and education, but objections might be raised on the grounds of manipulation and authoritarian indoctrination. In any case, it is unlikely that the general public would easily be persuaded to change its attitude concerning social status and material acquisitions. There is also the problem of financing political, cultural and social benefits. This assumes an economy as efficient as possible. From this standpoint economic growth would appear to have much to offer.[64]

Self-management can also be criticized on an institutional level. It is not sufficient that all workers and employees belong to institutions that are given the task of organizing self-management. The working of the institutions must be in accordance with all the objectives of self-management. This condition is a difficult one to fulfil. Experience with self-management in Yugoslavia has shown that decision-making within the organs of self-management does not accord with the principles of participative democracy. Investment strategy remains determined by a small elite of technocratic and political officials. Moreover, income is not decided on the basis of labour input but on the social power exercised by the various economic officials on the self-management regulatory bodies. Bitter strikes and social tension therefore continue within Yugoslavian society. This is proof that institutional change alone is not enough to realize the ideals of participative democracy. Power relationships within society, based on differences in technocratic knowledge and on the elitist structure of the party organization, continue to influence the functioning of economic self-management, and these differences are being consolidated rather than weakened.

Even assuming that economic and political self-management could be made to work effectively, problems would still remain. The effective decentralization of decision-making introduces a process of corporatization into the working of the national economy which not only strikes at the efficiency of the system but in the long run destroys it altogether. Just as corporatism in the Europe of the seventeenth and eighteenth centuries brought industrial decision-making under the control of local sectors, so would a system of self-management transfer economic and political decision-making to a more localized level. This local basis, however, would now be under the control of a few large companies or a few local or regional professional organizations. Decision-making would thus become highly fragmented and reached on the basis of local, or at most, sectoral, interest groups. The more effective this system became, the weaker would be the co-ordination of decision-making, from the point of view of the general interest and general welfare. Economic planning in its full sense would therefore become impossible. The rigidity of local or sectoral conservative and protectionist attitudes would increasingly gain the upper hand, as was the case in the corporatist society of the *Ancien Régime*.

To the extent that economic self-management was institutionalized and politicized, it would become a nationally based, more or less permanent fixture. Within this structure there would be little room for independently realized dynamic initiatives. In contrast, such opportunity existed in eighteenth-century Europe only in the non-corporatist sectors and in the countryside – indeed, the competition that resulted between these two systems was able to generate the Industrial Revolution. Nowadays the challenge would have to come from the international environment, in particular from countries that keep a dynamic economy, either through centralized planning or through a decentralized market economy. This raises the whole question of whether economic self-management of itself has its own dynamism and vitality.

There is no doubt that in the West the spirit of the age is moving in the direction of economic self-management and decentralized planning. The driving force for this is the democratization of education and the communications explosion which has led to the intellectual emancipation of mankind. The crucial question is to what degree this trend towards self-management and decentralization can be combined with the existing mixed economy. To the extent that this combination can achieve a new balance between efficiency, distributive justice, and the intellectual and spiritual development of humanity, the perspectives for further development of the mixed economy are favourable and hopeful. If, however, no creative consensus about such a combination can be found, the mixed economy is doomed to fossilization and decline. In that case the alternatives mentioned above will again come to the fore.

CHAPTER IX

THE LIBERALIZATION OF WORLD TRADE AFTER THE SECOND WORLD WAR

An international division of labour based on the comparative costs of different countries and areas can greatly improve the efficiency of a growing world economy. In order to optimize this efficiency, world trade must be served by a solid and relevant institutional framework. Immediately after the Second World War such a framework did not exist because the protectionism which had developed during the Great Depression still held sway. On American initiative, however, a consensus was reached on the need for a new system based on the market economy and multilateral free trade. Europe was an active participant in constructing the new system but had reservations over the leadership of the United States. Europe therefore took initiatives that gave a specifically European dimension to the concept of an open, liberal world economy.

1. THE 'PAX AMERICANA' AS CORNERSTONE OF THE POST-WAR LIBERAL WORLD ECONOMY

THE HISTORICAL BACKGROUND

The liberal world economy of the nineteenth century collapsed at the outbreak of the First World War. Nevertheless nostalgia for *la belle époque* lingered in Europe, and speedily after the war concrete measures were taken to return to the old structure. In 1925 Britain went back on the gold standard, re-establishing gold as the basic unit of value with unrestricted external convertibility of currency into gold at the old fixed rate – the pre-war gold parity. Numerous countries followed Britain's example, although some did modify their gold parities. At the same time attempts were made to liberalize international trade once more. Results, however, were disappointing: the old ideal of completely free trade could not be realized in the short term.[1]

The catastrophe of the world depression during the 1930s put an end to the attempts to restore the pre-war liberal economic system. In September 1931 Britain abandoned the gold standard and introduced a system of floating exchange rates. This amounted to a drastic devaluation of sterling and a whole series of associated currencies. The United States followed, and after some years the remaining countries of Western Europe found themselves obliged to carry out drastic devaluations. Protectionism, in old and new guises, reappeared on the world stage. In the United States the Smoot-Hawley Tariff was enacted in 1930 and import duties rose from an average of 38 per cent during the period 1922–9 to an average of 53 per cent during the period 1930–3. Import duties were raised in Europe as well. In addition, direct measures were taken to reduce imports: quotas were imposed, import licences introduced, and government subsidies given to domestically produced goods. Even Britain, the traditional bulwark of free trade, announced in 1932 the creation of the Imperial Preference System, under which Commonwealth countries enjoyed preferential treatment in their mutual trade relations.

International trade, which had been so slow to recover after the First World War, fell back sharply during the crisis. The movement to restore the liberal world system lost its significance. A nadir was reached in 1933. Britain no longer had the resources or authority to impose the rules of the liberal world system on other countries, and the United States, which did have the resources and authority, refused at the critical moment to accept the responsibility of world leadership.[2] Nevertheless, the free-market movement was not wholly dead. As early as 1934 in the United States, a first sign of its resurrection could be observed. The US Trade Agreements Act of that year gave President Franklin Roosevelt the power to reduce tariffs by as much as 50 per cent of the levels established by the Smoot-Hawley Act.[3] The new law applied only to non-agricultural products and could only be used if concessions were made by the country in question. Fortunately this law stipulated that the 'most-favoured-nation' clause should still be applied: so any trading advantages conceded to one 'favoured' nation were also conceded to others and thus gradually took on a multilateral character. In this fashion the 1934 Act made an effective contribution to the gradual rebirth of the commitment to free trade.[4] After the Second World War this use of presidential powers, no longer confined to non-agricultural products, became the driving force behind the continued liberalization of American trade with the world. In the Europe and Japan of the 1930s, however, there was no comparable development in favour of free trade; there protectionism and neo-mercantilism continued to hold the upper hand.

THE UNIVERSAL VISION OF HULL AND ROOSEVELT

The United States emerged from the war as the dominant world power and now seemed prepared to accept the responsibilities that this entailed. The Americans worked out a universal system for a new world order, one clearly based on traditional liberal principles. Some important differences excepted, it amounted to a renewal of the earlier, inter-war attempt by Britain to restore the economic liberalism of the nineteenth century. The *Pax Britannica* of that century, however, was replaced by a *Pax Americana*. The United States would now ensure that the rules of the game were followed by all and to this end it designed a specific institutional framework which would help to realize the building of a new liberal world order and guarantee its successful working. Under Roosevelt the founders of this system were Cordell Hull, Secretary of State from 1933 to 1944, Henry Morgenthau Jr, Secretary of the Treasury from 1934 to 1945, and Morgenthau's deputy Harry D. White.

On the political level the realization of the new world order was entrusted to the United Nations, 'the old dream of a Parliament of Man'.[5] During the Yalta Conference in February 1945, President Roosevelt was even prepared to make Stalin important concessions relating to Soviet territorial expansion in Europe and Asia, if, in return, the Soviet Union was prepared to participate in the creation and functioning of the United Nations.[6]

On the economic front, the new world order consisted of arrangements for orderly finance and trade. The financial system was established with the Bretton Woods Agreements of 1944. The countries represented at a mountain resort in Bretton Woods, New Hampshire, opted for an open world economy and for multilateral free trade, based on fixed exchange rates and the gold convertibility of the various national currencies. By way of support an International Monetary Fund was set up, supplemented by an International Bank for Reconstruction and Development (popularly known as the World Bank).

In 1945, the US Trade Agreements Act of 1934 was renewed for a further three years and altered to permit further reciprocal trade concessions. In keeping with the new free-market spirit, the President was empowered to cut tariffs by up to 50 per cent of the levels in force on 1 January 1945.[7] This was a significant step towards a liberal world order; and the United States made use of its leading position in the world to bring other countries into line with the new American commercial policy. In June 1945 the government brusquely terminated its Lend-Lease agreement with Britain. The British government, unable quickly to repay its war debts, was obliged to request an enormous loan. To this the US Congress acceded only partially and then on the condition that Britain promise to dismantle gradually the Imperial Preference System and resume general free trade.

President Harry Truman proposed that the Economic and Social Council of the United Nations call an international conference with a view to establishing an International Trade Organization (ITO) and discussing a charter that would enshrine the principles of the new liberal world order. The conference began work in 1947. At once disagreement arose between perfectionists and protectionists. The perfectionists desired a speedy realization of all the fundamental principles of multilateral free trade, namely the reduction and later abolition of all import duties, the ending of all preferential systems among particular countries, immediate generalization of the most-favoured-nation clause, and termination of all remaining trade restrictions. This met with fierce resistance from European countries which felt themselves so economically weakened by the war that they were not willing in the short term to give up their protectionist policies. Furthermore, after the war most of these countries had resolutely chosen the Keynesian policy of full employment. This implied a policy of active government intervention which ran counter to the idea of a restored liberal world order. European countries rejected any form of agreement that could hinder any existing or future preferential system. In view of the evolution of sterling during 1947, Britain even refused to carry out its former promise to end the Imperial Preference System. Finally in March 1948 a laborious compromise was reached and fifty-three countries signed the Havana Charter. The text differed fundamentally from the original American point of departure: a whole series of exceptions butchered the basic principle of multilateral free trade. The US Congress therefore refused to ratify it, and the ITO and the Charter sank together.[8]

Despite these conflicts and failures, negotiations on tariffs were held simultaneously and were successful. As early as November 1946 the US government announced that it wished to begin talks immediately concerning the reduction of import duties within the framework of the Trade Agreements Act and its resulting presidential powers. These talks, which took place in Geneva, involved twenty-three countries. Out of the talks came 123 bilateral trade agreements, some entailing significant tariff reductions. Through the most-favoured-nation clause, these trade concessions had worldwide ramifications. The Economic and Social Council of the United Nations, which had organized the Geneva discussions, proposed bringing the results together into a single document. The concessions were supplemented by some language from the Charter negotiations. And thus was born the highly important General Agreement on Tariffs and Trade (GATT).

In a Protocol of Provisional Application, signed in 1947, the twenty-three participating countries promised to apply the GATT pending the advent of the ITO, after which the GATT would be administered by an autonomous commission under ITO auspices.[9] Because the ITO never got off the ground, the GATT began an independent career. The GATT consisted of lists of tariff concessions the contracting partners had made to each other, an elementary code of behaviour relating to international trade policy, and a handful of rules laying down the procedures for future meetings and possible complaints.

The code was based on two main principles. The cornerstone was the principle of non-discriminatory action. The most-favoured-nation clause ensured the concrete application of this. If Country A reduced import tariffs on goods from Country B, then all other countries exporting an item to Country A could demand the same

favourable tariffs. The second basic principle related to the reciprocity; each party was expected to make concessions so that everybody
benefited. The code also contained some exception clauses. In the
first place, the Protocol of Provisional Application said that the
signatories were only committed to the agreement to the extent that
it did not contravene existing legislation in any of the participating
countries. Furthermore, in some cases, it was permissible to suspend
the most-favoured-nation clause – for example, in respect of customs
unions and free trade areas, and during phases of transition to such
systems. If any country for particular reasons, such as balance-of-
payments problems, was not able to respect its obligations, it could
introduce a waiver procedure so that it could be relieved of its
obligations at the next meeting. If necessary, emergency action
could even be undertaken on an immediate basis.

A General Secretariat was established in Geneva to organize
international bargaining sessions on import duties. In addition
to the bargaining, complaints which had been submitted to the
Secretariat regarding non-observation of agreements and infringe-
ments of generally accepted rules would be examined in open
discussion. The conferences would also form a discussion forum
through which new ideas and initiatives could be launched. The
GATT meetings ultimately became a great success. The GATT
with its Secretariat gradually became a substitute for the dreams of
an ITO and a formal Charter. Indeed, during the 1960s, a number
of supplementary protocols were approved which, for example, took
account of the problems of the developing countries. In this way,
the content of the agreement took on a universal significance. By
the end of the 1970s at the 'Tokyo Round' of negotiations, the
number of participating countries had increased from twenty-
three to eighty-three, with a further twenty-five involved as official
observers.

Between 1947 and 1962 there were five GATT meetings: in
Geneva (1947), Annecy (1949), Torquay (1950–1), Geneva (1955–
6) and again Geneva (1961–2), the last being known as the Dillon
Round. During the first meeting the United States and Canada
made important tariff reductions, which were of immediate significance to European industry. At the same time they declared
themselves ready to maintain quantitative restrictions on their
exports to European countries; so the tariff concessions made by the
Europeans were of no immediate importance but held promise

for the future. On the other hand, all participants accepted the quantitative import restrictions and support prices which operated in the American agricultural sector (the waiver procedure provided the official administrative framework for this deviation).[10]

The other meetings also brought mutual tariff concessions. These concessions were organized on a product basis between those countries most involved in the trade of a particular product, and were subsequently spread around by the application of the most-favoured-nation clause. Beginning with the sixth meeting (the so-called Kennedy Round, 1963–7), negotiations were no longer organized on a product basis but made more general: all tariffs would now be reduced by the same general percentage, which would be accomplished in a series of agreed phases. The seventh GATT meeting (the Tokyo Round, 1973–80) took a new tack, with the main emphasis being the elimination of non-tariff barriers rather than further reductions in tariff levels.

THE COMING OF THE COLD WAR

Developments on the political stage immediately after the Second World War had a rapid adverse effect on the universal trade vision of the American government. At the Casablanca Conference of January 1943, Winston Churchill had demanded the unconditional surrender of Germany, and this was obtained in 1945. But the German defeat created a serious power vacuum in Central Europe and facilitated the domination policy of the Soviet Union.[11] At the Potsdam Conference in July–August 1945, Stalin demanded that political authority over Germany be collectively exercised by the allied military commanders. In this manner, the political reunion of the various occupation zones would be prevented. Stalin also demanded the complete industrial dismantling of Germany, as had been proposed in the American Morgenthau Plan. Hereby Russian economic reconstruction would be accelerated and the recovery of German economic might would be hindered. The foundations were thus laid for Soviet political control over East and Central Europe.

In the Far East after the unconditional surrender of Japan in 1945, a second power vacuum was created. General Douglas MacArthur as Supreme Commander, entrusted with the administration of Japan, decided on drastic structural reforms. He purged the administration, the educational system, and the business world, of figures that had been closely connected with the war regime, announced a general land reform, broke up the *Zaibatsu*, and dismantled heavy industry. At the same time he imposed heavy reparation payments. Japan's former might was thus totally destroyed. The whole of East Asia became an open area in which the Soviet Union began to expand its sphere of influence.[12]

The United States quickly realized that the break-up of the political and economic power of Germany and Japan ultimately served the hegemonistic ambitions of the Soviet Union and undermined its own dominant position. A counter-reaction took shape and culminated in the Truman Doctrine. On 12 March 1947, President Truman, in a message to Congress, proposed that the time had come to block the expansion of Soviet domination through a determined and vigorous defence. The principles were thus established for the American containment strategy.[13]

The conflict between Soviet expansionism and American world leadership was not the only cause of the political reorientation of the United States. The economic recovery of Europe also demanded a new political approach. Recovery was a far slower process than had been expected. Europe had an agonizing need for raw materials, machines, and consumer durables from the United States but had neither the exports nor the currency to finance the purchases. Moreover, the bad harvest of 1947 obliged Europe to increase its imports of agricultural products from the United States, and this worsened Europe's balance-of-payments problem. Finally a huge German trade deficit resulted from the negative Allied attitude towards the recovery of the German economy.

Measures were urgently necessary to get Europe on its feet again. The United States initially hoped to solve Europe's difficulties by providing temporary, short-term loans.[14] The loans, however, took on such wild proportions that the situation soon appeared hopeless. The Americans believed that if European economic recovery was not attained within a short period, the Soviet Union would exploit the consequent social malaise to extend its hegemony over the whole continent. The same reasoning was applied to the special case of Germany: a strong German economy would shore up European recovery and help to counter the Soviet threat; if the Soviet Union refused to contribute to the rehabilitation of Germany, the Western Allies would go it alone in their own occupation zones. European economic reconstruction was also fully integrated into the strategy of American world policy. On 5 June 1947, General George C. Marshall, then Secretary of State, expounded the new economic policy in a speech at Harvard University.[15] The famous Marshall Plan came into being.

THE MARSHALL PLAN AND ITS SIGNIFICANCE

The Marshall Plan proposed that in respect of European recovery a temporary suspension should be made of the principles of the liberal world economy and the existing system of short-term loans. Instead, a massive emergency programme would make the European economy self-supporting within a period of four years. The programme would be concentrated on a few strategic objectives. These were the modernization of infrastructure; dramatic increases in total production (particularly in the key sectors of steel and energy); a more balanced distribution of heavy industry in place of the intense concentration in the Ruhr area; the rationalization of production in agricultural and manufacturing industry; and, lastly, mechanisms to ensure monetary and financial stability. It was planned that after four years the principles of the liberal world order would be reaffirmed. The United States would play an active role in the execution of the programme. American economic know-how and expert advisers were to be made available, but more important still was the huge financial help offered. The current and prospective deficit in the European balance of payments would be partly covered by long-term loans from the World Bank, the capital for which was largely provided by the United States. The loans would amount to $3 billion. The rest of the financing, by far the greatest part, would be American gifts. Truman proposed to Congress a gift of $20 billion to be made under the auspices of the Economic Co-operation Act, and ultimately $17 billion was granted.[16]

Marshall Aid was offered to all European countries including the Soviet Union. A guiding principle of the plan was that Europe itself should take the initiative in its concrete implementation. The various European countries had to bring their disparate recovery measures into one coherent programme. In this fashion they would have to take into account the needs of each other; that is, the recovery programme had to be European in conception and based on mutual co-operation and co-ordination.[17] To promote this European vision, the Marshall Plan proposed the creation of an Economic

Commission for Europe (ECE) which would operate as a regional suborganization of the United Nations. The commission was set up in Geneva in 1947 but in the end did not have a very important role. The Soviet Union rejected the offer of Marshall Aid and compelled all Eastern bloc countries to do the same. Poland and Czechoslovakia had to reverse their earlier favourable overtures. As a counter-move, the Soviet Union set up Cominform in Belgrade on 5 October 1947, an organization that would group all socialist countries. To facilitate recovery in the Eastern bloc the Molotov Plan was launched. Then in February and March 1948 came the seizure of power in Prague. In these circumstances, the Economic Commission for Europe was condemned to inactivity.

Sixteen European countries which were not under the influence of the Soviet Union reacted positively to the Marshall Plan and organized a conference in Paris in June 1947 to discuss its implications. A Committee on European Economic Recovery was set up and this prepared the Paris Convention, which was signed on 16 April 1948 by the sixteen countries plus West Germany. The Organization for European Economic Co-operation (OEEC) came into being as a result.[18] The OEEC rapidly developed into a very dynamic institution with Paul-Henri Spaak of Belgium as the first chairman of the Council of Ministers, and Robert Marjolin as Secretary General of the Executive Committee. The OEEC framed the programme for European recovery and ensured its coherent nature. On the basis of this programme, it formulated recommendations on allocating Marshall Aid to the countries involved. Finally it prepared the establishment of institutions which would help to liberalize intra-European payments and make them more multilateral in nature.

The OEEC was also an important stride in the progress towards a united Europe. During the preparatory discussion for setting up the organization, two divergent conceptions of its institutional structure were expressed.[19] The first was French-inspired and Europe-orientated. It proposed rapid integration and the immediate incorporation of a supranational authority into the various institutions. The French saw the Executive Committee as a supranational organ, vested with real decision-making powers. This fitted in with the view of the federalists, who supported a strong federal parliament and a strong federal government for the Europe of tomorrow. The other conception was British-inspired and was less positive towards the idea of integration. Those who favoured the British approach wanted decision-making to be left to the Council of Ministers, in which each member would have a right of veto. This faction was also against the Dutch proposal of a customs union for Europe. In addition, it agreed with the 'functionalist' wing of the European movement, which believed that the federal European parliament should be given a consultative and not legislative competence.

The British view prevailed. The institutional structure in which the OEEC was ultimately encapsulated followed the functionalist pattern. Moreover, the recovery programme, which the British submitted to the OEEC in 1948, was wholly nationally based and took little, if any, account of the objective of European co-operation. In contrast, the French recovery programme did, for the French government had modified the nationally based Monnet Plan to this end. The later division of Western Europe into two groups of countries, one which supported European integration and one which opposed it, can be traced back to this difference in attitude.

As the Marshall Plan took shape, the conflict between East and West grew still sharper. Those countries which worked together in the Marshall Plan evolved into the Western bloc and those which joined Cominform formed the Eastern bloc. When the Western allied powers decided unilaterally to restore the West German economy using the Marshall Plan for this purpose, the Cold War began. The announcement of monetary reform, a basic element for the recovery of the West German economy, gave rise to the Russian blockade of Berlin and the famous American airlift from 24 June 1948 to 12 May 1949. A parallel development was the Brussels Treaty Organization (1948), which was signed by Britain, France, and the Benelux countries. This was expanded in 1949 into the North Atlantic Treaty Organization (NATO), of which the United States, Canada, Denmark, Norway, Portugal, Iceland, and Italy were also members.

THE ATLANTIC AXIS

Hopes for the recovery of the European economy were threatened by the American inflation after the great strike wave of 1946 and 1947, the increase in the European cost of living after the major harvest failure in 1947, and the high raw-material prices at the start of the Korean War in 1950. Despite so many unfavourable circumstances, Marshall Aid and the OEEC were nevertheless crucial factors in the European reconstruction process. Even during the first phase of the Marshall Plan (1947–9), the results were conspicuous. The modernization of infrastructure was apparent everywhere, industrial production grew on average by 30 per cent and labour productivity rose to a level 10 per cent above that reached on the eve of the war. During the next phase (1949–51), more attention was paid to increasing intra-European co-operation. It was at this point that the OEEC took vigorous measures to liberalize European trade. The quota system underwent radical pruning: 50 per cent of the goods subject to import quotas were immediately relieved of this form of quantitative restriction, and gradually this figure rose to 90 per cent. For the remainder, restrictions remained temporarily in use. These naturally comprised the most controversial sorts of goods and the requirement for unanimous decisions within the OEEC was apparently the reason for the incomplete liberalization of trade. Alongside this, the OEEC achieved a rapid improvement in flexibility in intra-European payments. In July 1950 the European Payments Union was established, and it organized the monetary system of Western Europe on the basis of mutual co-operation.

The Marshall Plan envisaged during the second recovery phase a gradual reduction in the amount of help provided. If deficits in the European balance of payments continued at a significant level, then American private investment in Europe and in the European colonies would have to provide the corrective mechanism. The outbreak of the Korean War, however, ended this hope of the American government. The Gray Report, requested by the government in the summer of 1950, dealt with the impact of the Korean War on the European recovery. It recommended that aid be continued for an additional period of three to four years, not only to consolidate recovery but also to help finance European rearmament.

In the early 1950s the nature of American policy towards Europe was the subject of much debate within the government.[20] According to the Department of State, American aid should not be used just to help restore the European economy and then be cut off. It was believed that Europe should serve as a lasting buttress. European discrimination against American products and against the dollar, tolerated by GATT, should be regarded as a permanent necessary evil. In effect, the Department of State viewed the economic development of Europe in terms of American political interest. A strong European economy was a necessary condition, an essential foundation, for a strong, politically united Europe, which was the only way to form a sturdy bulwark against the Soviet threat.

The Treasury did not share this vision. For it, the purpose of American support for the European economy was not to serve the political strategy of the Cold War but rather to facilitate the construction of a liberal world order under American leadership. To this end the Treasury was in favour of American aid to Europe and it was also willing to accept European discrimination against American products and the dollar. But the Treasury conceived these as only temporary measures which were necessary to establish Europe as an equal partner to the United States. As soon as Europe had achieved this status, American support should be discontinued and the liberal world order without discrimination be reimposed. It was this vision which gradually gained the upper hand once the Cold War had passed its peak. Nevertheless the Secretary of the Treasury recognized that the inevitable consequences of the Cold War should be accepted. The world was now divided into two opposing blocs and it was clear that the Eastern bloc wanted nothing to do with an American-led liberal world order. The dream of a *universal* free-market economy was therefore abandoned in favour of a Western free-market economy. The idea of a *Pax Americana* continued but it now mainly had an Atlantic dimension.[21]

It was within these new limitations that the liberal world order was built. The representatives of the United States in the international organizations of the 'free world', such as GATT, the OEEC, and the International Monetary Fund (IMF), thus advocated not only the lifting of trade restrictions and obstacles but also a return to the gold standard, based on fixed exchange rates and convertible currencies.[22]

The new liberal world economy gained new branches outside its main Atlantic axis. First Australia and New Zealand sought links, and later, Japan. In 1949 the American government had decided to end the occupation regime in Japan and replace it with a special peace treaty and a military alliance. It had also decided to accelerate Japanese recovery through direct aid, as had been done in Europe. During the Korean War of the early 1950s the support for Japan was further increased and this considerably speeded up the integration of

Japan into the Western world economy. In addition, most Third World countries in Latin America, the Middle East, and Africa were integrated into this system. The Atlantic nucleus thus expanded once more into a free-market economy of world dimension. None the less the main axis remained Western and Atlantic.

2. THE EUROPEAN REACTION: LIBERALIZATION WITHIN DEFINED BLOCS

THE FIRST EUROPEAN ATTEMPTS AT INTEGRATION

Around the end of the Second World War, some initiatives were made in Europe in the direction of customs unions and economic integration, and these would have a decisive influence on the later European unification. In 1944 the governments of Belgium, the Netherlands, and Luxemburg, all still in exile in London, decided to set up a customs union beginning on 1 January 1948, to be known as Benelux. The intention was to extend this customs union later into a full economic union, such as existed already between Belgium and Luxemburg, the BLEU having been in operation since 1921. Import quotas on the movement of industrial products within the Benelux area were ended during 1949 and 1950. The free movement of labour and capital was attained around the middle of the 1950s. The agricultural protocol which had subjected Dutch agricultural exports to a system of minimum prices in Belgium expired in 1962. Meanwhile in 1960 a treaty with a view to the formation of an economic union was signed. In it the principles of mutual consultation and unanimous voting were established as the basis for joint decision-making. The idea of supranational authority was not employed, and this considerably weakened the dynamism of the integration movement.

The customs union as such was a great success. Mutual trade grew rapidly, even faster than trade with countries outside Benelux. Until 1960, exports of the BLEU to the Netherlands grew faster than Dutch exports to the BLEU, even though during this period Dutch wages were at a considerably lower level. The customs union also appeared to facilitate structural reforms in Benelux industry. The competitive pressures accompanying the expansion of the market stimulated rationalization, specialization, and industrial renewal in the country with the highest cost structure. This phenomenon ensured, within the Benelux area, a new international division of labour not so much between as within industrial sectors. Finally the Benelux formula stimulated other European countries to promote economic integration. In March 1948 France and Italy set up a customs union known as Francital which was fully attained around 1955.

Still more important than the customs unions was the foundation of the European Coal and Steel Community, a milestone in the integration movement. The occasion for this was the American and British decision to rebuild the West German economy. France and the Benelux countries were very distrustful about this decision,[23] and they demanded that international control be established over the development of German heavy industry and that deliveries of coal from the Ruhr area to their own basic industries be guaranteed. At the Conference of London, held in March 1948, these countries got what they wanted: an International Control Authority for the Ruhr was set up, its members being the United States, Britain, France, West Germany, and the Benelux countries. This turn of events vexed West Germany which felt itself placed under guardianship just at the time when the recovery of its economy and the restoration of its political sovereignty seemed assured. The French politician Robert Schuman realized that this new situation comprised a decisive turning-point in the development of post-war Europe. He looked for a means to smooth away the feelings of unease and mistrust which were raised by this issue, especially in France and West Germany, and replace it with a positive attitude of cooperation between equals. He believed he could achieve this within the framework of a common European market for coal and steel and proposed its creation on 9 May 1950.[24]

Schuman's main idea was no doubt politically inspired. The proposed community would normalize Franco-German relations and would fully integrate West Germany as a sovereign state into Western Europe. The solution to the troublesome problem of the Saar would thus be simplified. The institution of a supranational authority would, moreover, be an interesting experiment in political organization of the Europe of tomorrow.

Schuman believed that the economic advantages were also important. The post-war Monnet Plan, which sought to restructure the French economy by developing a modern heavy industry, gained large benefits from Schuman's proposals. The Monnet Plan presumed free access to the coal reserves in the Ruhr area, and only the integration of European heavy industry, along the lines proposed by Schuman, could guarantee this access. Furthermore, a supranational authority would make possible an effective supervision over the coal and steel sectors. The formation of oligopolistic cartels could thus be avoided, appeasing left-wing circles. There were also advantages in respect to sales abroad. The Third World was developing economically but could only become an attractive sales market for European heavy industry when specialization and greater economies of scale had raised the competitiveness of European companies to the level of their American and Russian counterparts. In respect to trade with the Third World, Europe had a trump card in that its economy, in comparison with that of the United States and the Soviet Union, was more complementary in nature, so that the Third World could finance its imports from Europe with its own exports.

On 18 April 1951 the Treaty of Paris was signed, according to which the European Coal and Steel Community (ECSC) was set into operation from 25 July 1952. Its membership was France, West Germany, Italy, and the Benelux countries. An attempt to attract Britain failed. Within the resultant community, all import and export duties, all quantitative restrictions, and all subsidies or other discriminatory measures relating to coal and steel were abolished. Control was entrusted to a supranational organ, the High Authority, staffed by independent members assigned by the countries involved. The High Authority had its own financial resources, obtained by a levy on coal and steel production in the Community. Its decisions were binding on all member countries and related companies. The High Authority was given the task of promoting the maximum production of coal and steel at a minimum cost. Moreover, this production was made available without any discrimination to all countries of the Community at common prices set by the Authority itself. An additional task was to stimulate and guide the modernization and restructuring of heavy industry, and for this purpose the High Authority was granted a special equalization fund. The High Authority also co-operated with a Consultative Committee and a Special Council of Ministers. Discussion and decision-making took place according to agreed procedures, including a right of veto. Finally the High Authority was politically responsible to a Common Assembly composed of members of the national parliaments.

Although the significance of the ECSC was tremendous, its effect was mainly psychological. On a practical, day-to-day level, the Community quickly ran into serious difficulties. In the first place the ECSC was conceived far too narrowly. The sectors of coal and steel comprised only a part of each country's national production and furthermore it was very difficult to isolate them from the rest of the economy. As early as 1954 a working party was set up to study to what extent the common market on coal and steel could be extended to other basic sectors. In addition, coal only supplied a part of Western Europe's energy needs and from 1950 promising alternative sources of energy began to attract attention.

The replacement of coal by other energy sources soon presented the Community with a fundamental structural problem. The High Authority did not shirk this challenge and to this end it commissioned the Tinbergen Report under the direction of the Dutch economist Jan Tinbergen, which was presented in 1953. This made an estimate of the ten-year demand for coal on the basis of the expected growth of total industrial production.[25] From the results it appeared that the total combined annual coal production would have to be substantially increased. The Tinbergen Report took into account the possible substitution of coal by nuclear energy, gas, and oil. Substitution by nuclear energy was considered unimportant, because of the still excessively high cost. The Tinbergen Report also predicted a constant rise in international freight prices for bulk goods and therefore the future substitution of coal by gas or oil did not seem to be of great significance. The High Authority accepted these conclusions and began an active structural policy designed to boost European coal production steeply over the next ten years.

The premises of the Tinbergen Report, however, were undermined by the developments of the 1950s and 1960s. Vast new reserves of oil and gas were discovered in the Middle East, North Africa and elsewhere. Production grew rapidly and the world prices of oil and gas fell. At the same time the Suez Crisis of 1956 gave rise to the construction of enormous oil tankers which ensured a cheap link between the Persian Gulf and Europe, via the Cape of Good Hope. The substitution of coal by oil and gas therefore gained rapidly. The share of coal in the total energy provisions of the Community fell from 74 per cent in 1950 to 31.3 per cent in 1967, the share of oil over the same period increasing from 10 to 51.5 per cent.[26] In consequence, the structural policy of the ECSC was thrown into confusion. In place of measures to boost coal production, steps had to be taken to prevent overproduction, such as closing pits and even whole mining areas. In this switch to a defensive policy, the ECSC was bound to lose much of its dynamism. Coal had become a problem sector and economically the ECSC was much weakened.

In psychological impact, though, the ECSC was a smashing success. An international kernel of heavy industry, concentrated around the Ruhr and the Saarland and in Limburg, Wallonia, Luxemburg, and Lorraine, was no longer subject to continual war and conquest but now formed a framework for co-operation and progress. The future of this area could now be seen optimistically.[27] The institutional innovation of the ECSC also had a positive effect. The international co-operation stimulated by the ECSC strengthened the hope that a unified Europe was a practical proposition and opened the way for a series of new initiatives in the area of European integration.

THE EUROPE OF THE SIX

The six countries of the ECSC – France, West Germany, Italy, Belgium, the Netherlands and Luxemburg – accepted a French plan (the Meyer Plan) that a European army should be established and to this end, on 27 May 1952, signed the treaty of the European Defence Community. This form of integrated defence implied a common foreign policy and, in the long term, full political integration. In recognition of this, a European Political Community was also proposed: a combination of the supranational organs of the ECSC and the European Defence Community. No further progress was made, however, because on 30 August 1954 the French parliament refused to ratify the European Defence Community. At this point the élan of the European movement collapsed.[28]

In order to restore the ailing European movement to health the Benelux countries in 1955, under the auspices of the ECSC, launched the Beyen Plan, introduced in 1952–3 by the Dutch Minister of Foreign Affairs Johan W. Beyen, to promote the *economic* unification of Europe. The Benelux countries employed the following reasoning: in the short term political integration was no longer feasible; economic integration, however, was feasible, and this might pave the way for political integration later on. During a meeting at

Messina in June 1955, the Council of Ministers of the Community accepted the Beyen Plan and nominated a committee of experts under the chairmanship of Paul-Henri Spaak to prepare concrete proposals. Britain was invited to participate but withdrew in November 1955. The British delegates could not reconcile themselves to the options formulated by the other countries. They were of the opinion that to realize the Beyen Plan no particular institutions were needed and the creation of a simple free trade area within the OEEC was more than sufficient. The British also had objections to the intention of giving special protection to European agriculture and were mistrustful of the idea of supranational organs with real decision-making power.

The Spaak Report, completed in 1956, proposed a common market and a common organization for the development of nuclear energy. In Spaak's view the creation of the Common Market was to be attained in three successive stages. First a real fusion of the six national markets was to be brought about, that is, a full customs union which implied not only the abolition of all customs duties among the six countries but also the lifting of all quantitative restrictions and other non-tariff barriers to trade within the group. In the second stage a common policy would be developed on agriculture and transport, and legislation on all other matters would be harmonized. In the third stage the free movement of labour, capital, and services within the Six would be instituted. To manage all this, four specific institutions were envisaged, of which two might function under the auspices of the ECSC.

Discussion of the Spaak Report led to serious conflict within the Six. France requested special transition measures and resisted the low external tariff that was suggested by the Benelux countries. In addition France demanded of its partners a promise to share its financial responsibility for overseas territories. The other five countries gave way. On 25 March 1957 the Treaty of Rome was signed, according to which a European Economic Community (EEC) and a European Community for Atomic Energy (Euratom) came into being from 1 January 1958.[29]

THE EUROPE OF THE SEVEN

In the mean time Britain had taken steps to achieve its own version of economic co-operation. As soon as the British had withdrawn from the Spaak Committee in November 1955, they had sought consideration within the OEEC of a less binding form of co-operation. In January 1957 they proposed a European industrial free trade area. The negotiations, however, dragged on and on in the OEEC. At the instigation of the French they were finally broken off at the end of 1958. In fact the whole issue was disrupted by the creation of the European Economic Community earlier that year. The United Kingdom nevertheless continued the talks with Norway, Sweden, Denmark, and Austria. Soon the group was joined by Switzerland and Portugal. The result of these negotiations was the Stockholm Convention of 4 January 1960 in which the seven countries established the European Free Trade Association (EFTA).[30]

EFTA was conceived in very pragmatic terms, involving only industrial goods among the Seven. Apart from a few exceptions all agricultural goods were excluded from the agreement. Members could consequently import agricultural goods from the rest of the world, for example from Commonwealth countries, at low prices, but were not allowed to re-export them to the other members at these prices. Moreover, the absence of a common external tariff for industrial goods made it necessary to determine the country of origin for all products exported by one of the Seven to another member state of the group. Products in transit were easy to identify. But the problem was more complicated when products in transit had undergone some processing in the exporting member state. In contrast to the institutional structure of the European Economic Community, that of the European Free Trade Association remained extremely limited. Just one institution, the Council of Ministers, was mentioned in the treaty. On the other hand there were a few permanent and temporary commissions to tackle concrete problems, such as the identification of the origin of products.

THE EUROPE OF THE NINE

Although the reduction of mutual tariffs between the United Kingdom and its partners took place very rapidly and some countries, including Finland, Iceland, Liechtenstein, Greenland, and the Faroe Islands, joined as associate members, EFTA was still not a great success. In the end the British Conservative government reassessed its position and began to make overtures to the Europe of the Six. There were various reasons for this. First there was the deterioration in Britain's position in the world. Its empire gradually disintegrated, its share in world trade dwindled; sterling declined in significance as a key currency; and the Commonwealth lost its former cohesion so that the idea of a multiracial community under British leadership gradually became meaningless. Domestically the situation was also worrying. Economic growth was slow, public finances unstable, unemployment high, and investment low. In contrast to this stood the powerful economic growth of the Europe of the Six. The formation of a common market seemed to have had a dynamic effect and even had external implications. For example, trade between the seven members of EFTA and the EEC grew faster than trade within EFTA itself.[31]

The British Prime Minister, Harold Macmillan, drew his own conclusions, and on 31 July 1961 the United Kingdom applied for full membership in the EEC. The Republic of Ireland, Denmark, and Norway followed its example. Austria, Sweden, Switzerland, and Portugal requested some sort of association with the Six. The negotiations dragged on. In January 1963 President de Gaulle at a press conference finally declared a veto on the UK entry. As a consequence all negotiations were formally broken off in February 1963. According to de Gaulle, the British did not intend to accept the Treaty of Rome as such since they demanded too many changes. Moreover, the French President judged British policy to be too Atlantic and insufficiently European in nature and felt this would disrupt the growth of a coherent European bloc on both an economic and a political level.[32] In effect the French believed that the British would function as a Trojan horse for the Americans, who wished to counter the anti-American policy that France had been following within the Community.

In 1967 a British Labour government, headed by Harold Wilson, renewed the application for membership. This time the requested modifications posed were few. Nevertheless de Gaulle issued a second veto, this time against even the opening of negotiations. In his stated opinion, the situation of the British economy and of sterling was at that moment still too uncertain for the EEC to contemplate British membership. During the summit at The Hague (1–2 December 1969) President Georges Pompidou withdrew the French veto on negotiations since the devaluation of sterling at the end of 1967 had improved Britain's financial situation. In 1970 the negotiations were begun by the new Conservative government led by Edward Heath. On 22 January 1972, the United Kingdom, the Republic of Ireland, Denmark, and Norway joined the EEC and a series of transitional measures and modifications were laid down.[33] Norway left after a referendum on 26 November 1972 came out against membership. Denmark and the United Kingdom withdrew from EFTA. Thus the Europe of the Six now was the Europe of the Nine.

A new British Labour government, again under Wilson, coming to power in 1974, was unhappy with the terms on which the country had joined and it demanded a renegotiation. The Labour experts believed that the European agricultural policy would have adverse effects on Britain. In effect, imports of efficiently produced foodstuffs from Commonwealth countries and elsewhere would be replaced by imports from EEC countries where production was protected and inefficient. This was a perfect example of trade diversion which would bring about higher living costs and higher wage costs, and make things more difficult for export industry. In other words, there would be further devaluations of sterling and a drop in living standards.[34]

The renegotiations were successfully concluded. Within the EEC there was now a general admission that the Common Agricultural Policy (to be described below; see page 369) was in need of radical reform. Furthermore, the EEC partners were willing to reduce the British contribution to the Community budget and to take into account Britain's relative economic decline. In addition, a timetable that had been written for the attainment of a European economic and monetary union was made more flexible and the deadline extended. A British referendum in 1975 approved the new terms and the United Kingdom remained in the Community.[35]

THE REALIZATION OF THE EUROPEAN CUSTOMS UNION

The Treaty of Rome, on its signing in 1957, was conceived as a sort of legislative outline which would take on a more concrete form as initiatives and decisions were made in the process of actually building the European Community. The Treaty itself consisted solely of a chronological schedule made up of three phases. The first was the establishment of a customs union accompanied by an initial harmonization of economic policies and the free movement of labour, services, and capital. The second was to be full economic integration. The third was to be political integration.

The first phase went very well. For the complete removal of mutual customs walls and the erection of a common external tariff, a time-scale of twelve years was proposed. But operations went so smoothly that in ten and a half years, that is by 1 July 1968, a complete customs union, in internal and external terms, was in existence. The free movement of labour, services, and capital was achieved by that same date. The harmonization of economic policy, aimed at eliminating all discrimination between member states, was difficult but substantial progress was made. Trade restrictions, as far as they existed, were terminated and an active policy of competition was introduced. For instance, measures were taken against cartels and mergers that would give certain large companies too great a monopoly power. In fiscal policy the harmonization consisted of replacing the various divergent systems of indirect taxation with a uniform value-added tax system. Other measures included attempts to standardize technical norms and to co-ordinate economic legislation, especially on company law. The efforts of the various national governments were insufficient to remove all discrimination, but steps were clearly being made in that direction.

The realization of the customs union was accompanied by the establishment of a series of specifically European institutions: in Brussels the European Commission[36] and the Council of Ministers; in Luxemburg the Court of Justice; and in Strasbourg the European Parliament.

The European Commission is conceived as a supranational organ, the staff of which, although nominated by the member governments, functions independently. The Commission has no power of decision but it must ensure that the objectives of the Treaty of Rome are realized, and to this end it formulates its own initiatives, over which the Council of Ministers makes the final decisions. The Commission is charged with the implementation of these decisions and it supervises to what extent individuals, companies, and governments in the Community carry out agreed policies. Exactly which ministers participate in the Council of Ministers depends on the subject under discussion. The Treaty of Rome provided that Council decisions must be unanimous but it envisaged a gradual transition to a system in which, on most occasions, decisions would be reached by the principle of a majority vote. The Council of Ministers was thus in time supposed to develop into a supranational authority. From 1965 onwards this ran into French resistance and so the custom based on unanimous voting continued.

The members of the European Parliament were initially chosen from the various national parliaments, but in 1979 a system of direct general elections was inaugurated. Despite this, the European Parliament remained limited in competence, being advisory rather than legislative. It can demand the resignation of the members of the European Commission and has a limited power of supervision over the Community budget. Alongside the four above-mentioned institutions, some consultative committees were set up, the most important being the Economic and Social Committee and the Monetary Committee.[37]

The Treaty of Rome also allowed for the possibility that non-European countries, by means of an association, would form a loose connection with the Community. In the preparatory negotiations France had demanded that this association format be automatically applied to the French overseas territories. The Belgian and Dutch colonies also became associate members. These associate members enjoyed a preferential status in that they were included in the free trade area inside the common external tariff. They therefore became privileged suppliers to European countries of goods whose origin lay outside the Community. On the other hand the principle of reciprocity applied; so EEC countries were privileged exporters to these associated countries, the exports consisting largely of industrial products. In addition, the creation of a European programme of financial and technical aid was planned – gifts from a European Development Fund, chiefly for infrastructural investment. Of the nineteen African countries that became politically independent between 1958 and 1962, all except Guinea chose to continue their association with the European Community.[38]

The terms of the associate membership of overseas territories required that the arrangement be reviewed every five years. By this means the EEC could take into account possible changes in the political situation and economic structure of the countries involved. Such a review took place at the first Yaoundé Conference in 1964. During the preparatory talks, differences emerged within the

European side. West Germany and the Netherlands adopted a 'world' approach and advocated the gradual removal of preferential status, whereas France and Belgium had a more African-orientated view and argued that existing preferences should be continued. It was this group which prevailed. Nevertheless at the second Yaoundé Conference in 1970 the world view won ground. Since the first Yaoundé meeting the United Nations Conference on Trade and Development (UNCTAD) had condemned strongly the discriminatory nature of nationally orientated economic systems.[39]

When the United Kingdom joined the EEC in 1972 a further review of the association of overseas areas was necessary. To this end, at the Lomé Conference in 1976, the number of associate members rose from eighteen to forty-six, the sums available for financial and technical aid were quadrupled, and it was agreed that these could now be used for effective industrial development – no longer concentrated on infrastructure. Furthermore, the reciprocity of the preferential status was abandoned: exports from associate members to EEC countries continued to enjoy preferential treatment but the reverse was no longer the case. Finally, for twelve Third World export products a stabilization system was worked out (STABEX). A common fund was set up to give financial support to the producers of these twelve staple goods should incomes fall below a set minimum level. All this constituted an important step towards a European development policy for the Third World.[40] The second Lomé Convention, signed in 1980, was a further step forward; it achieved results not attainable within the UNCTAD framework. Various non-tariff barriers which had been restricting the exports of associated countries to the EEC were taken down. Moreover, the STABEX system was extended to forty-four products. There was, however, little or no expansion of financial aid, because the European countries themselves had serious balance-of-payments difficulties.

THE COMMON AGRICULTURAL POLICY

After the realization of a customs union and the harmonization of policies in the economic sphere, the Treaty of Rome envisaged a second stage in which full economic integration would be attained. In this connection a Common Agricultural Policy (CAP) was worked out, and it was regarded as a cornerstone on which the whole integration movement rested.[41]

The reasons for this were of a historical nature. The crisis of the 1930s had caused all European countries to build up different systems of support to the agricultural sector: many countries supported small farmers by increasing agricultural prices and by reinforcing protectionism. As a result substantial price distortions were initiated and small farms were artificially maintained. A liberalization of intra-European agricultural trade would drastically reduce the large number of small farmers in these countries. This was politically unfeasible. But different agricultural prices implied differences in living costs and led to unequal wage levels among countries. And this was an inadmissible factor of cost price discrimination in the industrial and commercial sphere. An integrated agricultural policy that would ensure uniform prices in Europe was therefore a necessity. European agricultural prices would not follow those on the free world market but instead would be on a higher level, one chosen by the Community itself. The intention was to guarantee a satisfactory income for European farmers, that is, one equivalent to that paid to other sectors of the working population. The proposed system would include a control over imports of agricultural products from outside the Community (via special import duties) and a manipulation of the agricultural market within the Community (the buying of market surpluses at guaranteed minimum prices).

It was only in 1967, after a series of marathon sittings, that the Common Agricultural Policy, based on these principles, started to operate.[42] In the mean time the price structure had been further specified. Each year the Community determined, per product and per region, a 'target price' which ensured farmers incomes at the desired level. 'Intervention prices' would lie at a level 5 to 7 per cent lower and function as guaranteed minimum prices at which the Community bought any surpluses. Lastly the Community established a system of 'threshold prices' which was applicable to agricultural imports from outside the Community. If the price of an imported product was less than the threshold price, a duty was levied to make up the difference. The proceeds from these duties accrued to the Community.

The CAP was financed by a European Agricultural Guidance and Guarantee Fund, which had already been set up in 1962, in view of the further common policy. Initially the Fund received contributions from the member governments. In time, however, it was to find its own sources of income, from levies not just on agricultural imports, but on non-agricultural imports too. Concerning the non-agricultural levies the European Commission in 1965 worked out a timetable for their transfer from the various national treasuries to that of the Community. Nevertheless these incomes remained insufficient to finance the tremendous demands of the C A P. The first source of this high cost was the policy of price support for market surpluses. The system of guaranteed prices led to a huge overproduction of a whole series of goods, including butter, milk, grain, and sugar. The Fund was obliged to buy up these surpluses at the established intervention prices and sell them abroad at a great loss. The Fund also had to finance the Community structural policy for agriculture, for alongside the short-term price-support mechanism there was the important task of long-term structural development, with the specific objective of modernizing European agriculture.

The E E C Commissioner for Agriculture, Sicco L. Mansholt, saw in the distortions which resulted from the price-support system an argument for immediate attention to structural policy. In December 1968 he proposed a ten-year plan, known as *Agriculture 1980*, with the aim of an accelerated rise in the productivity of land, labour, and capital.[43] The increased returns would improve the competitive position of European agriculture on the world market so that the expensive price-support system could be gradually dismantled. To achieve this a drastic restructuring was necessary: the size of agricultural units would be raised to an efficient optimum, the total agricultural area would be slashed, the European farm population would be cut by 1980 to 6 per cent of the total working population, and agricultural education and training would be improved. The proposals of the Mansholt Plan appeared to be too radical for the Community to accept in their entirety. Instead in 1971 the Council of Ministers made a compromise decision. Some proposals were accepted, such as those relating to the outflow of farm labour and the enlargement of agricultural units. Others were rejected or watered down. At the same time it was decided to maintain the price-support system and further raise the intervention prices (now to be expressed in a common unit of account rather than dollars). These were unfortunate decisions.

The monetary chaos and resultant world inflation of the 1970s distorted the CAP still further. Neither monetary evolution nor inflation ran parallel in the various European countries; so a certain compartmentalization of the agricultural market took place. Greater use of price adjustments was necessary to keep real agricultural incomes steady and, still more, to reduce the increasing distortions between member countries. More and more criticism was made of the system of intervention prices, which held European prices at a higher level than world prices. Britain was an especially bitter critic. Later, other countries joined in. A complete revision of the CAP became necessary.

THE DIFFICULTIES ON THE ROAD TO FURTHER INTEGRATION

Apart from agricultural policy, attention was devoted to the integration of transport, and of fiscal and cyclical policies.

Concerning transport very little was achieved, owing to the major conflict of interest between member states. The Netherlands, for example, because of its geographical situation and its well-equipped merchant fleet, supported a system of free competition and market-determined freight prices. The other countries wanted the Community to set up a price structure which would take account of their relative handicaps. This view won out, and thus the transport market was regulated, minimum and maximum rates established, and transport itself subjected to a sort of quota system.[44] After Britain joined the EEC there was something like a trend towards liberalization, with free competition winning ground.

In the area of fiscal policy, substantial success was achieved with the introduction of the value-added tax (VAT), but no further progress was made through the 1970s. Normally, to apply such a tax, it would be necessary to replace the principle of destination (levying the tax in the consuming country) with the principle of origin (levying it in the producing country). Only then would the levy become an actual tax on added value rather than, in effect, a tax on consumption. The failure to move to the principle of origin was due to the different VAT rates applied across the Community. Neither did the various systems of company tax become more integrated, even though this was essential in order to eliminate discrimination in investment in different EEC countries.

Attempts to organize a Community budget made more headway.

By 1977 this had risen to 0.7 per cent of the GNP of EEC members.[45] Income was derived not only from import duties based on the common external tariff and particular levies of the CAP, but also from payments from member governments. This situation changed on 1 January 1979. After this date 1 per cent of total community VAT receipts was allocated to the Community budget. Through this, the role of the European Parliament in the preparation of the Community budget was considerably increased.[46]

Another kind of integration was aimed at a Community counter-cyclical policy and a joint tackling of balance-of-payments problems.[47] The first plan of the European Commission's vice-chairman, Raymond Barre, and the Commission's supplementary memorandum of February 1969, both stressed the real danger of inflation.[48] Since mutual import duties were now abolished it was more difficult for national economies to keep inflation from being imported.

The manipulation of interest rates lost significance too because companies could get resources on the world market. The need for particular monetary measures became obvious. For this reason it was decided at The Hague Summit of 1–2 December 1969 to go through with economic and monetary union. In January 1970 a procedure of mutual consultation was worked out in order to facilitate short-term measures. In the same month the central banks were instructed to set up a scheme according to which they could provide each other with short-term help. Finally the Werner Report of June and October 1970 specified the conditions and the timing of monetary union. The monetary difficulties of the 1970s prevented progress, and it was only in 1978 at the initiative of the European Commission that the idea of monetary union was relaunched, now in the form of a common European currency. Again little headway was made, largely because the national governments ultimately had no intention of immediately surrendering their monetary sovereignty.[49]

An integration policy on energy was very slow to get off the ground, for various reasons. The initial distribution of responsibility to three institutions was a severe handicap. The European Coal and Steel Community (ECSC) was in charge of coal, the European Community for Atomic Energy (Euratom) was in charge of nuclear energy, and the EEC bore responsibility for other energy sources. Nuclear energy turned out to be far more expensive than had been anticipated; so the Community construction programme for nuclear reactors was abandoned. Instead, activity was limited to research, spread over four centres. France, however, chose to go it alone and refused to integrate its own nuclear research into the Community effort. As for coal, the increasing competition of oil during the 1960s led to a consensus over the need for a stronger integration of coal policies. In 1964 the Council of Ministers signed a protocol by which support measures to European coal-mines were co-ordinated. Simultaneously, for reasons of European security, they decided against closing down coal production altogether. A system of subsidies was worked out for mines which delivered coke to European steel concerns and which were threatened by competition from Poland and the United States.[50]

The oil crisis that broke out in 1973 brought acute problems for Europe but still did not lead to an effective integration of energy policy.[51] At the Copenhagen Summit of December 1973, general policy options were discussed but nothing else resulted. The growth of total energy demand was to be reduced by economizing on the use of energy and by using it more efficiently. On the supply side it was determined to expand the use of nuclear energy and natural gas which by the year 2000 were supposed to be supplying respectively 50 per cent and 30 per cent of total European energy needs. The possibility of a more intensive use of coal was re-examined, especially through its conversion into gas. Finally research into unconventional sources of energy was encouraged. The dependence on oil would thus be reduced, though not eliminated, and various European countries began separate negotiations with gas and oil producers in the Middle East, North Africa, and the Soviet Union. There was no question of an integrated Community policy, still less of joint action with the United States, as proposed by Henry Kissinger with his idea of an Energy Action Group.

The integration of national policies on industrial and regional restructuring gradually became the main focus of attention during the 1970s. At first the emphasis was on regional policy, in particular on the distribution of aid to less developed areas such as the Italian Mezzogiorno and the south-west of France, and later to Scotland and the Republic of Ireland. Then it was decided at the Paris Summit of 1972, at the instigation of Britain, to set up a Committee for Regional Policy and a Regional Development Fund.[52] Disagreement between Britain and West Germany over the concrete organization of regional help delayed the Fund's operation until 1 January

1975. Meanwhile the European economy had entered its period of structural crisis, and attention switched to the problem of deindustrialization and the restructuring of areas that had fallen victim to this process.

The textile industry was one sector badly hit in the 1970s. For instance, demand for synthetic fibres fell back sharply and there was manifest overcapacity. At the same time there were important investment projects under way, for example in Sardinia and Sicily, in connection with the regional development policy. Prices slumped and heavy losses were recorded. In 1978 Étienne Davignon, a member of the European Commission responsible for industrial relations, was able to persuade eleven large groups to form a cartel to organize production quotas and a reduction of production capacity. Subsidiaries of American firms such as Monsanto and Du Pont had to withdraw, however, since participation would have exposed them to prosecution under the Sherman Act. Furthermore, the Commission itself decided in November 1978 that the cartel for synthetic fibres eliminated competition in this sector and was thus in conflict with Article 85 of the Treaty of Rome. Consequently the cartel had to be broken up and Davignon overruled.

The steel industry was in a still worse position than textiles. From 1976–7 onwards, the Commission took measures to protect European steel. First there was a Simonet Plan, conceived by Henri Simonet, Davignon's predecessor in the Commission, which set up supervision of the steel market based on statistical information. Delivery programmes of individual firms, via a voluntary and confidential consultation with the Commission, would be matched with expected demand. The Simonet Plan failed: imports from outside the Community had a disruptive effect, and within the Community some companies (including the so-called Bresciani in Italy) were unwilling to co-operate. Next there was a Davignon Plan on steel, which was an attempt to plug these gaps. It came into force in May 1977. For reinforced steel, compulsory minimum prices were imposed on all producers, and target prices were announced for five other sorts of steel. The system of voluntary limitations on deliveries remained in force. For steel imports from outside the Community a system of automatic import permits was announced, the objective of which was to track down dumping practices. At the start of 1978 the system of compulsory minimum prices was extended to other categories of steel. In addition temporary anti-dumping levies were imposed on imports. On this occasion the Commission supported Davignon's measures.

Nevertheless these measures still appeared insufficient. So in October 1980 Davignon invoked Article 58 of the Treaty of Paris, which permitted further action in case of a crisis related to the industrial structure. Davignon subjected the entire European Community steel output to a compulsory quota system. He also tightened controls on imports from outside the Community and gave extra financial support and extra guidance to the European steel sector, first to modernize production and second to help restructuring in the areas affected, especially in Wallonia, Lorraine and Luxemburg. These new measures came up against heavy resistance, from the West Germans in particular. The existing West German steel industry already made use of the most modern technology and thus hoped to be able to ride out the crisis on its own. It feared that in reducing its own production, it would ultimately be shouldering the main burden for the Community plan.[53]

According to the Treaty of Rome, after economic integration was attained, political integration should follow. Nothing at all came of this. In the first place the concept of economic integration had been brought into total discredit by the economic crisis of the 1970s and the subsequent national reactions. This being true, preparations for political integration also resulted in utter failure. De Gaulle had vetoed the original decision to phase out gradually the need for complete consensus within the Council of Ministers in favour of a decision-making process based on the principle of a majority vote and no European politician considered it useful to raise this question again. During the Paris Summit in 1974 the Belgian Prime Minister Leo Tindemans was given the task of finding a new formula for the realization of political and economic union. The Tindemans Report[54] of 1976 proposed dividing Community countries into groups which could follow the integration process at different speeds. The fast group would have an integrated defence force and a European Parliament with effective, legislative competence. Again, nothing concrete resulted. On the other hand, direct elections to the European Parliament were held in the spring of 1979, but this did not increase its actual powers. The further enlargement of the Community, with Greece joining in January 1981 and Spain and Portugal on the waiting list to join in January 1986, was not likely to change this situation.

THE SIGNIFICANCE OF THE EUROPEAN ECONOMIC
COMMUNITY

In the field of trade, the EEC was a great success. Trade between
EEC countries quadrupled from 1958 to 1969 and continued to
increase thereafter. Furthermore trade between member states grew
much more than their trade with non-member states. Table 32
shows this.

Table 32 *Total Intercommunity Trade as a Percentage of Total Exports,
1958–82*

	1958 (Six)	1969 (Six)	1979 (Nine)	1982 (Nine)
BLEU				
(Belgium &				
Luxemburg)	45 per cent	68 per cent	73 per cent	71 per cent
Netherlands	42	60	73	72
France	22	48	53	49
Italy	24	43	49	46
West Germany	27	40	48	48
EEC	32	48	54	52

Source: EEC, *European Economy*, No. 18, Statistical Appendix

The unification of the European market was undoubtedly an
important factor in the expansion of trade, that is, in *trade creation*.
Yet it must be appreciated that a series of other favourable circumstances at the same time contributed to trade creation. In the first
place, only economically developed countries were involved in the
EEC. This led to specialization, with different countries comp-
lementing each other. Also, at the start of the European experiment,
tariffs and other trade restrictions were still sufficiently high for
liberalization to have tangible results.

The advantages of the unification were not just static, in the sense
that higher productivity was achieved by a better international
division of labour. Dynamic advantages also resulted: market expansion led to greater economies of scale and company diversification; it
stimulated the modernization of management, created a favourable
climate of demand that promoted new investment and new initiatives, advanced technological progress and innovation, encouraged
new forms of co-operation in the industrial and service sectors,
and aided the development of the European money and capital
market.

The dynamic effect of the EEC was not limited to Europe but

also had an impact on the rest of the world. The expansion of the economy and of trade attracted a lot of foreign investment, especially from American companies.[55] The foreign investment stimulated the transfer of technology and of management techniques from the United States to Europe and thus helped to close the gap between the two regions in these fields. The transfer of knowledge opened the way for new applications in Europe, and stimulated investment and the growth of intra-European trade. At the same time this transfer prepared the ground for a catching-up movement by Europe in relation to the United States and thus led to a better geo-economic balance in the industrialized West.

It is obvious that not all of the post-war growth of the European economy can be attributed to the integration of the European market.[56] The growth of the European economy and of intra-European trade was already well under way in the 1950s, before the EEC was launched. This was a catching-up movement following the slump in trade during the Great Depression and the Second World War. Moreover, part of the later growth of trade in Europe was determined by the expansion of total world trade. For example, some industrial exports from Europe to the Third World were financed by American capital and development aid.

Besides, not all the aspects of the EEC were positive ones. In some cases integration hampered rather than promoted the expansion of trade and the term 'trade diversion' could justifiably be employed. The high external tariff was the first example and the Common Agricultural Policy the second. Both were protectionist-inspired and gave rise to the inefficient use of the factors of production. This protectionism meant extra costs for the consumer. It also raised wage costs and thus hindered production and exports.

The policy on agricultural incomes was a fiasco. It led to enormous production surpluses which were sold abroad at great loss. At the same time it did not achieve its objective. Large farms profited excessively from the artificially high intervention prices whereas small farms lost out. Consequently the CAP created more income distortions than it eliminated. It was also injurious to agriculture outside the Community. The high level of protectionism for Community agriculture entailed increasing autarky and thus hindered the integration of the developing countries into the world economy. Criticism was also directed at the preferential system implicit in the various association treaties. This system favoured some countries at the expense of others and thus ran counter to the concept of universal solidarity which lay at the heart of development co-operation.

On an institutional level too, the EEC did not fully meet its expectations. The transition from customs union to political community via economic integration, as had been set down in the Treaty of Rome, could not be realized. Neither could a real supranational authority be formed. In fact some earlier decisions relating to this were even reversed and each country's right of veto was maintained. Nevertheless it is not to be denied that the creation of numerous administrative agencies, especially in Brussels around the European Commission and the Council of Ministers, did give the Community a clear sense of identity. The Community standpoint can no longer be ignored in the economic life of European countries. In external relations as well, the attitude of the Community has become an essential factor, with European countries beginning to operate as a bloc.

The European Community served as a model for numerous countries in the Third World. In many areas, following the European pattern, initiatives were taken along European lines to promote economic co-operation and integration, for instance in Central and Latin America, West Africa, East Africa, Southern Africa, Equatorial Africa, and the Middle East. In most cases, however, the results were less than expected. In these regions the level of development was still too low, the production structure still insufficiently diversified, and the political regimes usually still too unstable, to undertake balanced co-operation and economic integration.

CHAPTER X

TOWARDS A NEW
INTERNATIONAL ECONOMIC ORDER

The liberal world economy that was conceived and built during the 1950s gradually broke up. President Kennedy tried to hold back the regionalizing effect of the European Economic Community and the European Free Trade Association, but without much success. The Tokyo Round could make no headway against the tide of neo-protectionism that resulted from the crisis of the 1970s. The developing countries demanded a better and more complete integration into the world economy. At the same time the Eastern bloc took advantage of détente to further its own integration into the world economy and thus participate in the technological advances of the West. Any new international economic order would therefore have to provide a system which could handle the demands of the Third World and establish a new basis for East-West trade as well as for trade relations within the Western world itself.

1. THE DISMANTLING OF THE FREE-MARKET WORLD ECONOMY

THE ATTITUDE OF THE AMERICAN CONGRESS TO ITS GOVERNMENT'S FREE-MARKET DOCTRINE

Although the establishment of a free-market economy was the official doctrine of the United States government after the Second World War, it would nevertheless be wrong to see the nation's foreign trade policy exclusively in this context. Congress exerted influence too and its vision was much less free-market-orientated than that of the executive branch. In concrete terms the foreign trade policy of the United States was a laborious search for a balance in the conflict between a free-market-orientated executive branch and a conservative, protectionist-minded Congress.

The policy of the government after the war brought immediate reactions from agricultural and industrial circles in the country. Pressure groups forced a whole series of protectionist acts in Congress.[1] The Trade Agreements Act of 1934, which empowered the President to lower import duties, was not given its three-year renewal in 1945 until the President had made certain concessions. In all American trade agreements an escape clause would now be included, according to which if a domestic sector found its competitive position undermined by the lower tariffs, these could be raised again. The 1948 renewal of the Act led to still further restrictions. In addition to the escape clause, future trade agreements had to include a peril-point clause. Negotiations on tariff reductions could only take place after a special panel, namely the US Tariff Commission, had set minimum tariffs. These were considered as the absolute lower limit, below which any further concessions would damage domestic industry. In 1955 Congress attached a third restrictive condition to the Act – the defence clause. In the context of the Cold War, the government was prohibited from making tariff reductions that would interfere with domestic industry's contribution to defence. In the 1958 renewal of the Act, the defence clause was extended to sectors other than the arms industry, and from this point on, a threat to national security was used as the criterion.

Meanwhile protectionism was very evident in relation to agriculture. As early as 1948 there were congressional protests that Section 22 of the Agricultural Adjustment Act of 1933 (an amendment that permitted import restrictions) was being too sparingly applied. And in 1951 Congress slapped import quotas on many farm products which had previously not been subject to them.

The protectionist reactions of Congress put a brake on the American government's policy of liberalizing world trade. The government's field of manoeuvre was progressively narrowed. The fourth round of negotiations held in Geneva in 1956 within the GATT framework yielded only small results. The fifth round (the so-called Dillon Round), which took place in Geneva in 1960–1, also failed to make any real progress. At that point Congress had given the President a mandate to reduce tariffs by only 20 per cent, in four yearly steps, each of 5 per cent. In addition the US Tariff Commission had invoked the peril-point clause for more than half of the concessions proposed by the President. The Dillon Round was therefore doomed to failure. Just one-quarter of the number of products which were initially considered for tariff reductions were discussed in the actual negotiations. The final result was an average tariff reduction of only 7 to 8 per cent.[2]

The dilution of the American liberalizing policy during the 1950s was not solely due to the protectionist actions of Congress. The administration itself was partly responsible. After 1952 power had fallen into Republican hands and protectionist tendencies now appeared in the executive branch too. Furthermore, the creation of the EEC gave rise to feelings of disquiet and distrust. The growth rate of the EEC was decidedly faster than that of the United States and this gap threatened to widen further. The EEC also exerted a powerful pull on American companies. Their investment in Europe increased fast, causing unemployment at home, an acceleration in the transfer of technological know-how, and a weakening of America's industrial lead. The protectionist agricultural policy adopted by the EEC, including the high external tariff and the preferential system with Africa and the Middle East, also caused frustration in the United States. The government therefore began to have serious doubts about the efficiency of the free-market policy which its predecessors had followed. The success of the EEC from the end of the 1950s onwards was no longer seen as a useful means of strengthening America's political hegemony but more as a threat to its industrial supremacy. Therefore Congress got more and more support from President Eisenhower's administration in the protection of American industry and agriculture.[3]

THE AMERICAN STRATEGY REGARDING THE EUROPEAN INTEGRATION PROCESS

John F. Kennedy, who became President at the start of 1961, once more turned to the idea of a liberal world economy under American leadership with obligations as well as rights for the leading nation. At the same time Kennedy was fully aware of the increasing success of the EEC and the political implications that accompanied this.

Yet in no way did he seek to check Europe's growing power by adopting an obviously negative attitude. On the contrary, he attempted to integrate this power into the new dynamic of American world policy. He proposed an Atlantic Partnership between the United States and an enlarged EEC. The two blocs would co-operate in the economic and military fields on an equal footing but in political terms the United States would continue as sole leader. The Kennedy administration believed that the United States still held a clear technological lead over Europe and that, in contrast to Europe, it still had considerable unused production capacity. In the light of this, it was considered that economic co-operation and liberalization would generate a powerful expansion of American exports to Europe, one which would outmatch the rise in European exports to the United States. At the same time, European competition would throw down a challenge to American industry and generate new technological progress. Kennedy and his advisers were convinced that in this way the poor export achievements of the United States during the 1950s and the related problem of balance-of-payments deficits could be resolved.[4]

Kennedy made two important initiatives designed to realize his free-market conceptions.

First, in 1961, he proposed the restructuring of the Organization for European Economic Co-operation (OEEC) into an Organization for Economic Co-operation and Development (OECD), in which the United States and Canada would be included as full members. The intention was to liberalize the international mobility of the production factors of labour, capital, and entrepreneurship. In this manner the production of the West would be further harmonized and a more efficient international division of labour would come about. As soon as the OECD began to function, it played an important role in the area of mutual consultation, applied research, and the distribution of information, but in actual policy-making it had little influence.[5]

Kennedy's second initiative was to present Congress with a new Bill in the field of foreign trade. The result was the Trade Expansion Act of 1962. By this the President was given the power to halve all existing tariffs (provided that the reduction was spread over a five-year period) and to lift completely all existing tariffs of 5 per cent or less. He could also, after negotiation with the EEC, abolish all higher tariffs on EEC exports to the United States if, for the products involved, joint trade between the EEC and the United States represented at least 80 per cent of the world total (the 'dominant-supplier' clause). The President also gained the power to negotiate a certain liberalization in agricultural trade. In addition, some of the more trade-restricting conditions relating to the escape clause and the peril-point clause were dropped.[6]

The dominant-supplier clause was based on the assumption that the EEC would be enlarged. In order to make the clause applicable for a wide range of goods, all the major European countries, including Britain, would have to be in the Community. It was thus clearly Kennedy's intention to co-operate in the creation of a great united Europe and in this fashion facilitate the further development of an open world economy. The new Act also underlined the attention the American government was devoting to the problem of the balance-of-payments deficit. Its solution was seen in the expansion of exports which would result from the liberalization of Western trade.

The reaction of the EEC, however, was a negative one. De Gaulle's veto in January 1963 on Britain's entry removed any practical meaning to Kennedy's new powers to apply the dominant-supplier clause, since the number of products which could now be considered was very limited. Furthermore, the EEC demanded that exception clauses be made for significant goods such as steel, aluminium, textile and chemical products. The EEC also refused to liberalize its agricultural policy, which favoured autarky over efficiency.[7]

The American-initiated Kennedy Round, the sixth meeting of GATT, which was held in Geneva from 1963 to 1967, brought no spectacular results. True, the mutual concessions related to 22 per cent of world trade in 1967, and the West moved a step closer to the realization of a free trade area for industrial products, but that was the sum total of the achievement.[8] The high expectations regarding the dominant-supplier clause came to nothing, and problem sectors in industry were left to one side. The tariff reductions thus amounted, on average, to only 35 to 40 per cent of what they might have been. For agricultural products too, little was achieved. A few special tariff reductions of 25 per cent by EEC countries were agreed in exchange for a rise in world agricultural prices. At the very last moment the EEC and the United States agreed a joint food aid programme for the Third World. The US government secretly cherished the hope that the EEC's co-operation in this programme would lead to a production shortage in Europe, one that could be made good by agricultural shipments from the United States.

So the Kennedy Round was a failure in the sense that it delivered only meagre results in the area of liberalization but perhaps an even bigger failing was its wholly anachronistic nature.[9] The 1962 Trade Expansion Act was conceived in the spirit of traditional liberalization, employing the technique of mutual tariff reductions and based on the most-favoured-nation principle. It implied the ultimate setting-up of a free trade area on a world dimension for industrial products. The industrialized countries of the West would be the main beneficiaries as they would be able to capitalize upon this arrangement by using their technological lead over the rest of the world. The infant industrial sectors of the developing world would be the main losers. Third World countries thus condemned the Kennedy Round as a Rich Man's Deal, which ignored the burning and fundamental problem of economic development. The problem of East-West trade was also left to one side and began to grow increasingly acute. Besides, the Kennedy Round could be seen as anachronistic even from the point of view of the Western economy itself. The policy of reducing tariffs in the West had simply stimulated a search for a new, parallel forms of protection: everywhere governments took measures to compensate the tariff reductions with non-tariff trade barriers. The emphasis on further tariff reductions was thus based on assumptions that no longer corresponded to the real nature of the world economy at the end of the 1960s.

The trade between Japan and the rest of the Western world followed a similar pattern. After the Second World War the United States had tried hard to integrate Japan once more into the liberal world economy. As early as 1949 the Americans had proposed that Japan be admitted to GATT, but because of British opposition the Japanese had to wait until 1955. In the mean time the American government had liberalized trade with Japan on a bilateral basis, even at the cost of far-reaching discrimination against the United States itself. The Americans hoped that once Japan had completed its economic recovery, it would gradually lift its import barriers. Such concessions, however, did not come about. Indeed, during the 1950s and 1960s Japanese protectionism was bolstered by new measures, such as import restrictions, export subsidies, and controls over currency dealings and direct investment from abroad. For

Japan too, therefore, the framework of a liberal world economy was becoming less and less applicable.

THE NEO-PROTECTIONISM OF THE SEVENTIES

The anachronism of the Kennedy Round was related to deeper-lying structural contradictions. Standing opposite to the liberal organization of world trade was the Keynesian, neo-mercantilist growth policy of the national governments. Above and around this conflict functioned the world-wide planning system of the multinationals; that is, a system of managed, interdependent world trade which either tried to free itself as much as possible from the market mechanisms of the world economy and nationally based *dirigisme* or attempted to use them for its own purposes. The growing neo-protectionism of national governments must be seen as their prime weapon to defend their national growth policies against the threat posed by a liberalized world trade and the multinationals.

A chief immediate cause of the reinforcement of neo-protectionist tendencies was undoubtedly the depreciation of the American dollar during the 1970s. The United States had based the post-war recovery of the liberal world economy on the stability of the dollar but in the course of the 1960s had run into problems through a manifest overvaluation of its currency. The measures Nixon took on 15 August 1971 established a system of floating exchange rates, and gradually relieved the situation, although at the cost of other currencies. In fact, the dollar became significantly undervalued. In these circumstances one might have expected the world-wide wave of neo-protectionism which resulted.[10] The fundamental achievements of the post-war liberalizing were not, however, wholly lost.

Neo-protectionism consisted first of a strengthening of non-tariff barriers. National governments showed an interest in these as soon as tariff reductions began to lead to an obvious liberalization of world trade.[11] These non-tariff barriers can be grouped into five main categories: pseudo-import duties, administrative import costs, demands in the area of product standardization, direct government intervention, and quantitative import restrictions.[12]

During the 1970s, quantitative restrictions on the trade of industrial products increased a good deal. In 1970 the Mills Bill was put to the American Congress, proposing automatic quotas when imports reached a certain percentage of domestic production. In

1971 the Burke-Hartke Bill was presented, this time proposing a general quota system for industrial products, with 1965–7 as the reference period. Neither Bill was approved but they reflected the growing protectionist sentiment of American public opinion. At the same time protectionism in Western countries was having much success within the GATT framework. As early as 1962 a Long-Term Cotton Textiles Agreement had been signed, a multilateral agreement relating to voluntary restraints by developing countries on their exports of cotton material to industrial countries.[13] This was extended in 1970 into the Multifibres Agreement, and still further into the Arrangement Regarding International Trade in Textiles that was signed in Geneva on 20 December 1973. The principle of voluntary export restraints was reaffirmed in the 1973 agreement, but the industrial countries agreed that the quotas should be increased each year by 6 per cent. Later agreements, especially those in the period 1978–82, were much more restrictive. They gave each industrial country the formal competence to open bilateral negotiations with developing countries with a view to reducing the annual increases below the 6 per cent norm.[14]

The effectiveness of the textile agreements encouraged the United States government to press for comparable bilateral arrangements on other manufactures. Two sorts of agreement were reached: voluntary export restraints and orderly-market agreements. The first related solely to restraints on export volume; the second was especially concerned with eliminating unfair competition. Voluntary export restraint agreements were reached in 1977 with Japan on colour television sets and with South Korea and Taiwan on footwear. Other agreements followed – on motor cars, for example. There was a similar trend in Europe. France and Britain took the most initiatives in this respect; West Germany and Italy were not far behind. Britain got other countries to sign agreements limiting their exports of textiles, footwear, leather goods, television sets, cars, ball bearings, pottery, tableware and other items. Japan was the country most affected by these voluntary restraints, but South Korea, Hong Kong, Taiwan, Singapore, India, and Pakistan were often involved. The quotas were transferable, so that gradually in the exporting countries a trade in quotas came about which led to serious distortions and abuses.[15]

The American Trade Act of January 1975 also reflected the general shift towards a stricter protectionism. All sectors and companies were given the right to apply for countervailing duties on imported goods when it could be shown that the exporter had received some form of government subsidy. The Treasury had to decide on the various applications within one year. At the same time the terms on which the escape clause could be applied were made wider once again. Action could be taken as soon as imports seriously damaged domestic production or threatened to do so. Any decisions the President took on foreign trade which were considered too liberal could be invalidated by the Senate and the House of Representatives working together. In this way a conservative spirit entered American commercial legislation.[16] Steel was the chief sector in which the neo-protectionist dynamic of the Trade Act made its presence felt. For this sector the government worked out the Solomon Plan, which came into operation in February 1978. This plan set trigger prices, which were based on assumed Japanese production costs plus transport costs. Countervailing duties were levied on any steel imports priced below these trigger prices.

The EEC went even further. As already mentioned, it established a special monitoring system in order to detect if any imports were in fact being dumped. Along lines similar to the Solomon Plan, it also introduced, in 1978, a system of anti-dumping levies. This, however, was seen as a purely temporary measure, being gradually replaced by a system of bilaterally negotiated voluntary export restraints.[17]

Non-tariff barriers were not the only means governments used to protect their policy of economic growth and high employment. Neo-protectionism also involved government subsidies to domestic industry. Even before the oil crisis, shipbuilding in the United States and Europe received significant subsidies, and this was also the case for regional development. After the 1974–5 world crisis the number of sectors and regions in need of aid increased, as did the subsidies. Alongside this direct government support, fiscal advantages and favourable credit terms were also provided. In some countries special payments were made to the temporarily unemployed. For example, in West Germany the government paid 75 to 90 per cent of the difference in income between full-time workers and those on half-time work. Similar support was provided in Britain, Sweden, and elsewhere. Even in Japan legislation was introduced in February 1978 which permitted government subsidies to companies and sectors in need of them, with aluminium, steel, shipbuilding, and synthetic fibres deriving particular benefit.[18] Finally, the payment of government subsidies to domestic industry was a useful means of putting certain sectors under pressure. The government could use its power to force troubled sectors to form national or international cartels. The intention was to reduce overcapacity by production quotas and to reduce losses by the use of minimum prices. The EEC co-operated with its national governments in order to achieve this goal. This co-ordination of national and Community support in order to restructure and modernize certain companies facilitated, for example, the formation of a European-wide steel cartel. On this basis even world cartels were attempted – in steel and shipbuilding, among other sectors.[19]

The advocates of an open world economy were worried by the increase in non-tariff barriers and direct government support to industry, and they managed to get these questions on to the agenda of the seventh meeting of GATT. The Tokyo Round, as it became known, was a lengthy one. It started in September 1973 in promising circumstances when representatives of about a hundred countries signed the Tokyo Declaration of Ministers. After this, negotiators were divided into seven groups to discuss the important problems of import duties, non-tariff barriers, agriculture, exception clauses, sectoral agreements, tropical products, and structural issues.[20] These negotiations, however, ran aground as a result of the world crisis and it was only after the London summit meeting of 1977 that a new impulse was given to the Tokyo affair. On 11 April 1979 the various agreements were finally signed. Tariff reductions of 33 per cent were agreed upon, spread over a period of eight years. This did not represent much progress. In respect of agriculture an agreement was made to liberalize trade in meat and dairy products. On the reduction of non-tariff barriers and government aid, some codes on fair competition were accepted. Similarly codes were established to reduce discrimination in the matter of government subsidies, government purchasing, standardization norms, and customs formalities. It was also decided to set up special committees to monitor whether these codes were being followed and the committees even had powers to arbitrate any disputes.

Particular attention was devoted to the specific problems of developing countries. The fundamental GATT principle of reciprocity in negotiations was abandoned. Developing countries were now able to take protectionist measures in order to stimulate their

industrialization and development: in other words they were officially allowed to discriminate against other nations. Preferential
systems were worked out in order to stimulate their exports of
tropical and industrial products.[21]

These agreements on non-tariff barriers, government support,
and Third World trade undeniably comprised important steps
towards a restructuring of world trade. In this sense the Tokyo
Round constituted a significant break with the past. But there was
little concrete achievement. The eight-year spread for implementation of measures weakened the effect. In addition the eventual
structural changes remained fairly limited. GATT continued as the
institutional framework within which the new organization of world
trade was to be established. Third World countries were very
dissatisfied with this, believing that the reorganization of world
trade thus remained under the control of the rich industrialized
countries of the West and that the problem of economic development
was still being seen from a paternalistic viewpoint. Finally, world
economic conditions developed so unfavourably at the end of the
1970s that in practical terms little was realized from the Tokyo
Round decisions relating to non-tariff barriers and co-operation
with the developing countries.

2. THE INTEGRATION OF THE EASTERN BLOC AND THE DEVELOPING COUNTRIES INTO THE WORLD ECONOMY

THE NATURE OF THE SOCIALIST ECONOMIES

The Stalinist development model, which immediately after the
Second World War was fairly generally applied in Eastern Europe,
was in essence based on an autarkic industrializing process. In the
context of this model, foreign trade was given little attention, being
regarded purely as a means of obtaining vital imports, especially
raw materials and possibly necessary capital goods. Exports were
simply the means of paying for these imports. This process was
regarded, moreover, in bilateral terms: each country sought to keep
the trade balance with all its trading partners in equilibrium, so that
for every country imports were covered by exports. In 1949 a
Council for Mutual Economic Aid (Comecon) was set up in Moscow
in order to stimulate economic co-operation and integration among

the socialist countries – as was stated officially. The six charter members were Bulgaria, Czechoslovakia, Hungary, Poland, Rumania, and the Soviet Union. They were quickly joined by Albania in 1949 and East Germany in 1950. During the 1950s, Yugoslavia, Mongolia, the People's Republic of China, North Korea, and North Vietnam were admitted as observers. Mongolia became a full member in 1962, Yugoslavia an associate member in 1964, Cuba a full member in 1972 and Vietnam in 1978.

In the first years, the foreign trade of Comecon countries remained as insignificant as before. In reality the creation of Comecon was purely a political move, a Soviet reaction to the American Marshall Plan. *De facto*, the autarkic development strategy of the Stalinist regime was continued unaltered. This was gradually changed after Stalin's death. The principle of an international division of labour was now officially recognized as useful and its application was recommended in the construction of the socialist welfare state. Furthermore, foreign trade would promote co-operation between socialist countries and thus strengthen their political ties.[22] Comecon now got a real chance, and it became the main instrument for organizing economic specialization and co-ordination between member countries. In 1956 the first sectoral committees of Comecon were set up and recommendations regarding specialization were approved, concerning, for example, more than 600 categories of machines. In 1958 it was decided to use world prices as a criterion for intra-Comecon transactions, as a way to make these more flexible. A uniform system of international commercial law was also agreed upon. In 1963 an agreement was made on a system of multilateral payments, and this was supplemented by an International Bank for Economic Co-operation, which started to function on 1 January 1964.[23] Trade between Comecon countries increased considerably – in the 1950s at an average annual rate of 12 per cent, in the 1960s by 9 per cent annually, and between 1970 and 1978 by 15 per cent annually. Furthermore, the share of mutual trade in the total international trade of the Comecon countries was fairly high, fluctuating around 60 per cent between 1955 and 1980. Nevertheless, seen in terms of the world economy, the significance of these figures should not be exaggerated. In 1977 intra-Comecon trade amounted to less than 5 per cent of total world trade, at a time when this area contributed about 30 per cent of world industrial production.[24]

It may thus be concluded that trade within the Eastern bloc

remained considerably below its potential during the whole of the post-war period. The fact is, trade remained the prisoner of traditional attitudes because, despite the developments listed above, the autarkic development model remained basically in place. Trade continued solely as a means of obtaining essential goods from abroad, rather than a way of optimizing economic production. In addition, foreign trade was still a state monopoly run by bureaucrats, which meant that it lacked flexibility and dynamism. Trade remained largely organized within the framework of national planning systems and as a rule was based on yearly bilateral agreements. Even when the number of long-term agreements began to increase, these still had to be integrated on a yearly basis into the planning system, and this had a restraining effect. The problem of pricing remained unsolved, even after 1958 when it was decided to use capitalistic world prices as a point of reference.[25] The use of world prices was a symbol of impotence, proof that the Eastern bloc's pricing system was unsuitable for an equitable exchange of goods. Moreover, the adopted procedure did not work well. For raw materials and agricultural produce more or less uniform world prices were employed, but for industrial products the situation was much more complex. Exporting countries in the bloc were always looking for *expensive* comparable products in the West as a price standard, whereas importing countries were looking for *cheap* ones. Arbitrary decisions were therefore frequently made. Finally the multilateral payments system that was started in 1964, according to which all transactions were to be settled in transferable roubles, functioned more in formal than in real terms. A country with a surplus of transferable roubles could in practice only use these with its former debtor. Bilateralism thus still determined trade relations within the Eastern bloc.

The matching of foreign trade with agreements relating to specialization did not get very far either. For key sectors such as energy, steel, chemicals, metal construction, and transport, some co-ordination of the national planning systems could be arranged. Out of this grew specialization agreements, eliminating duplication in some areas of investment. At the start of 1979 about a hundred of these were in operation on a multilateral basis and about a thousand on a bilateral basis. All in all, however, the Comecon trade which resulted from these agreements amounted to scarcely 10 per cent of the total trade between Comecon countries. Co-operation in the area of investment was more successful although the projects were mainly limited to energy and concentrated in the territory of the Soviet Union, the gas pipeline between the Urals and the western border of the German Federal Republic being the outstanding example. The integration of the socialist economies was therefore still not very advanced in 1980 at which time there was still no question of a common market.[26] The structures of autarkic development were not easy to break down.

THE EASTERN BLOC AND ITS SHARE IN WORLD TRADE

The structual factors that stood in the way of the internal integration of the Comecon market formed a still greater obstacle for the integration of the socialist economies into the flows of world trade. The international trade of the Comecon countries as a percentage of the world total was strikingly small and was declining. In 1963 it still constituted nearly 12 per cent, but by 1979 it had fallen to only about 9 per cent. Up until 1973 it was the Western industrialized countries which were able to capitalize on this fall. After that the oil-exporting countries benefited (see Table 33). In the 1970s the international trade of the Comecon countries with the industrial West constituted only 2 to 3 per cent of total world trade[27] and this figure was still favourably influenced by the noticeable increase in trade between the Comecon countries and the industrial West during the period 1970–5. At that time imports and exports between the two blocs increased faster than the average growth of total Comecon trade. The world economic crisis put an end to this, so that the growth rate of trade with the industrial West slowed down considerably, whereas that of intra-Comecon trade accelerated.[28]

The reasons why East-West trade after the Second World War developed so laboriously are of a political and technical-institutional nature. As a political factor the Cold War was a central element. Already in 1947–8 the United States was announcing embargo measures on the export and re-export of strategic products to Eastern Europe. In 1949 the Export Control Act was issued, supplementing and strengthening the former measures. The system of controls over strategic shipments came to embrace Western European countries that were receiving US aid, and this led to the establishment in 1950 of a Co-ordinating Committee (COCOM), based in Paris, of which all NATO countries and Japan were members. In 1952 a separate

Table 33 *Regional Composition of World Trade, 1963–81*
(percentage shares of each area in world exports (X) and imports (M))

		1963	1968	1973	1975	1977	1979	1981
Industrial areas	X	64.0	67.5	68.0	64.0	62.5	63.5	61.0
	M	64.5	67.5	69.5	64.5	66.0	67.0	63.5
Traditional oil-exporting	X	6.0	6.0	7.5	13.0	13.0	13.0	14.0
developing countries	M	3.0	3.0	3.5	6.5	7.5	6.0	8.0
Other developing	X	14.5	12.0	12.0	11.5	12.5	12.5	13.5
countries	M	18.0	16.0	14.5	16.0	15.5	16.0	17.5
Eastern trading area	X	12.0	11.5	10.0	10.0	9.5	9.0	9.5
	M	11.5	10.5	10.0	10.5	9.5	9.5	8.5
Residual	X	3.5	3.5	2.5	1.5	3.0	2.0	2.0
	M	3.5	3.0	5.5	2.5	1.5	1.5	2.5

Sources: GATT, *International Trade 1979/80*, p. 5
GATT, *International Trade 1982/83*, p. 5

body, the China Committee (CHICOM), was set up to co-ordinate the more sweeping controls applicable to the People's Republic of China. At that moment many internationally traded items fell under the Western embargo system. In fact this was the high point and thereafter a certain flexibility was introduced. The European allies did not interpret the conditions as strictly as the American government, certainly when they were offered major contracts such as the building of an industrial complex. Pleading discrimination, American manufacturers gradually gained concessions from their government. Henry Kissinger's policy of détente gave a new impulse to the break-up of the embargo system. The precedence of political objectives over economic ones was no longer maintained and by 1974 there were only 150 items on the embargo list, chiefly military equipment, high-technology products, and some strategic raw materials.[29]

The conference on European Security and Co-operation, which was held in Helsinki in 1975, carried still further the political and economic détente between East and West. The closing agreement, signed on 1 August 1975 by thirty-three Western and Eastern European states together with the United States and Canada, contained provisions not only for co-operation relating to European security and humanitarian purposes, but also for co-operation in the fields of the economy, science, technology, and the environment.

The need for a multilateralization of East-West trade was recognized in the final declaration. Furthermore, the most-favoured-nation clause was accepted in principle – precisely the clause that occupied a key position in GATT. A first link between the Eastern bloc and GATT was thus brought about.[30]

Although political circumstances during the 1970s were thus favourable for a gradual development of trade between the Eastern bloc and the industrial West, institutional and technical factors still constituted a serious obstacle. Until 1975 East-West trade was strictly bilateral in character. Initially it was based on contracts with private firms in the West, and after 1959 there was also a system of bilateral trade agreements between states. Agreements usually ran for a period of five years and were supplemented with yearly protocols which specified the goods to be traded. This bilateral trading system reached its zenith between 1966 and 1975. On 1 January 1973, however, the European Commission gained the exclusive right to negotiate trade agreements with countries outside the EEC. This meant that individual EEC countries could no longer make trade agreements with Eastern bloc countries: instead, trade agreements had to be expressed in terms of an integrated trade policy with a multilateral character. The Eastern bloc countries were nevertheless against any form of multilateralism. They got round this problem by systematically integrating the bilateral trade agreements into broader bilateral agreements on economic, industrial and technical co-operation. On 30 June 1978 there were 169 of these agreements in force which still fell outside the competence of the EEC. Some, such as the ten-year agreement between France and the Soviet Union (1971–81), dated from an earlier period but these now were supplemented by a complex network of special institutions.

The EEC did not leave it at this. In 1974 it introduced a sort of model trade agreement which could serve as a basis for discussion with any Eastern bloc country. Only the People's Republic of China took this up. After 1976 Comecon made overtures to negotiate with the EEC as an autonomous political entity and the first high-level contacts were established in view of setting up a framework for trade agreements between the two communities. Prospects for the multilateralization of East-West trade were finally opening up. The world crisis and the subsequent increase in political tension between East and West put an end to this.

In the mean time the gradual ending of the bilateral trade agreements had created a vacuum in the organization of East-West trade which could not be so easily filled by the co-operation agreements as was expected. Besides, the EEC had introduced in 1975 a Community-wide system of quotas for its members, restricting the importation of certain goods whose domestic producers were being seriously hit by the crisis, such as textiles and steel. The Eastern bloc countries exported substantial amounts of textiles. The EEC was able to convince some of those countries to sign agreements voluntarily restricting their exports of textiles to the EEC, an arrangement which ultimately proved more favourable for the Eastern bloc countries than the system of imposed quotas would have been. Rumania signed such an agreement in 1976, Hungary in 1978, Poland and Bulgaria in 1979.[31]

The overwhelmingly bilateral nature of East-West trade was in essence determined by the institutional structure of the socialist economies, in which foreign trade is a state monopoly and only governments are empowered to sign agreements with other countries. This bureaucratic structure is the reason why the export promotion of Comecon products is carried out in an extremely primitive and unsatisfactory manner. As for imports, between the wishes of Comecon consumers and the supply of foreign goods lies the bureaucratic screen of a central state bureau, which obscures the free flow of commercial forces. Once again it must be emphasized that the national planning system used in Comecon countries is in no way geared to foreign trade. Comecon countries, with some justification, claim that since the war the West has built up a trading system which discriminates against the Eastern bloc. Within the framework of GATT, the liberalization policy has moved the industrial countries of the West towards completely free trade for industrial products. In the EEC itself this is an accomplished fact.

In addition, the association treaties of the EEC have created preference systems for a whole series of developing countries. The Eastern bloc is excluded from all of this. Some Eastern European countries attempted to escape these disadvantages by becoming members of GATT. Czechoslovakia was a member from the very beginning, Yugoslavia joined in 1966, Poland in 1967, Rumania in 1971 and Hungary in 1973. This, however, brought no solution. Since 1977 the EEC has drastically extended its import quota system, especially for industrial products, which are the Eastern bloc's main exports. In addition, Western countries have not infrequently resorted to anti-dumping actions as a way of countering effective competition from the Eastern bloc.

The defensive reactions of the West in regard to Eastern bloc exports are due not to their volume but to the specific nature of the goods being offered. Apart from the Soviet Union and Poland, Eastern bloc countries increasingly export industrial products to the West. During the 1970s industrial products exported to the West represented approximately two-thirds of the total exports of East Germany, Czechoslovakia and Hungary, and approximately one-half of the total exports of Bulgaria and Rumania. The recent restrictive attitude of Western economies regarding imports from the Eastern bloc must be seen in this context (Table 34).

Eastern bloc countries, on their side, imported a great deal of modern technology from the West. They bought all kinds of machines and equipment, and they also organized the importation of technology in the form of industrial co-operation.[32] They obtained licences from Western companies to produce certain goods and they paid the royalties by the export of the product concerned. Sometimes they imported whole factory installations, which again they paid for in goods produced there. The Soviet Union and Poland tried by this method to modernize their chemical industry during the 1970s.

Increasingly co-operation also took the form of co-production: companies in the East and West collaborated on the same product, with each company specializing in particular parts or production phases. In these cases too, the know-how or equipment imported by the East was paid for in goods. Subcontracting was a frequent phenomenon. Hungarian clothing firms, for example, produced shirts for West German companies. The material and models were sent to Hungary, the production process was supervised by West German technicians, and the machines were largely imported from West Germany. Mixed enterprises also came about when Western capital was invested in Eastern firms. As early as 1967 Yugoslavia had passed legislation which introduced and regulated the system of mixed enterprises. Rumania, Hungary and Poland followed.

Western companies grew increasingly critical of the various forms of industrial co-operation between East and West. The system of payments in goods implied that, in time, products from the Eastern bloc would become formidable competitors in Western markets. Not only companies but governments and unions in the West felt

Table 34 Foreign Trade between the Eastern Bloc and the West

Eastern Bloc (selected countries and total) and the West (rest of the world), 1970, 1976, 1982; product composition in percentages

	Imports from the West									Exports to the West								
	Total			USSR			GDR			Total			USSR			GDR		
	1970	1976	1982	1970	1976	1982	1970	1976	1982	1970	1976	1982	1970	1976	1982	1970	1976	1982
(1)	11.4	17.0	21.2	8.8	20.1	24.3	16.0	19.1	26.4	19.3	9.5	4.8	7.2	2.2	0.9	9.3	13.6	2.5
(2)	9.4	5.5	7.9	6.7	3.2	6.2	12.8	9.2	6.8	40.7	53.0	67.7	65.8	76.7	87.7	11.6	12.4	35.7
(3)	17.0	12.9	5.0	21.7	11.5	4.9	11.0	14.9	3.9	11.5	14.4	5.6	3.7	7.2	0.3	25.6	25.4	12.2
(4)	24.8	27.7	37.8	21.9	27.4	37.0	21.0	25.7	32.5	19.2	13.0	16.1	18.3	8.8	8.7	28.9	22.8	33.6
(5)	36.9	36.9	26.9	40.8	37.7	26.7	39.2	31.1	30.0	8.5	9.3	5.3	3.9	4.4	1.8	24.3	25.3	15.5
(6)	0.5	0.0	1.2	0.1	0.1	0.9	0.0	0.0	0.4	0.8	0.8	0.5	1.1	0.7	0.6	0.3	0.5	0.5

Notes: (1) Food; (2) Primary Goods (incl. Fuel); (3) Various Manufactures; (4) Metals, Chemicals; (5) Machinery and Transport Material; (6) Statistical adjustments and errors

Sources: M. LAVIGNE, *Les économies socialistes*, p. 393
OECD, *Foreign Trade by Commodities*, 1982

threatened, and they pointed to the danger of unemployment which accompanied this system of industrial co-operation. Their resentment was increased in that multinationals were dealing directly with Eastern bloc governments, which meant that a form of co-operation existed over which they had no control whatsoever.

From the 1960s onwards, the Eastern bloc's imports could not be totally financed by exports of raw materials and industrial products. Increasing use was made of borrowing in order to close the gap. This was largely in the form of credit provided by the supplier to the buyer. The Western banks which took over this credit covered themselves through specialized insurance schemes, usually government-run, but sometimes in private hands. In this way favourable conditions could be granted to Eastern bloc countries (low interest rates, long repayment periods and so on). The Eastern countries did not limit themselves to requesting special trade credit in countries with which they did business. In the 1970s they also began to borrow on the Eurodollar market. Loans here were much more expensive but the borrower did have the advantage of a greater freedom of manoeuvre. Comecon banks borrowed exclusively on this market.

The extension of credit in East-West trade gave rise, in the course of the 1970s, to the build-up by socialist countries of heavy debt to the industrial West.[33] During the crisis of the mid 1970s this debt suddenly started to grow very fast. In 1975 alone it doubled. By 1979 the total debt of the Eastern bloc to the West had risen to $74.8 billion and the situation deteriorated still further. The Soviet Union and Poland were the main debtors, together accounting for 55 per cent of the total Eastern bloc debt in 1976. For the Soviet Union this high level of indebtedness is ultimately less important, because it is a huge country, is the world's second largest producer of gold, and is busy developing Siberian gas for export to the West. On the other hand, for Poland the high burden was a dramatic factor in its 1980–2 crisis. Measures to tackle the debt problem included a drastic reduction of imports, a lowering of consumption levels, and a cutback on investment. The reaction of the Polish workers has to be seen in this context. East Germany, Czechoslovakia and Hungary had to face balance-of-payments problems too, but by means of more rapid restrictive measures they were better able to keep the situation in hand. It is precisely these restrictive measures which have tended to reduce East-West trade. The new relative growth of intra-Comecon trade since the mid 1970s is the result. A new initiative seems necessary in order to stimulate Comecon trade with the rest of the world, thereby integrating the socialist economies into a new international economic order.

THE INDUSTRIAL EMANCIPATION OF THE THIRD WORLD

The political and economic emancipation of the Third World came with a rush during the post-war period. Colonial empires fell away and young national governments everywhere showed an explicit interest in economic development, so that industrialization expanded over a broad front of new countries. Nevertheless until the 1970s the results, in global terms, were not spectacular, especially when the increase in population is taken into account. Between 1950 and 1967 the GNP per capita in all developing countries together increased by a yearly average of only about 2.8 per cent. Naturally there were great differences among the various countries. The general picture, however, was one of weakness, in comparison with the achievements of the industrialized countries.[34]

In the growth of foreign trade, a comparison between the developing countries and the industrialized countries during the 1950s and 1960s gives the same disappointing picture. An investigation into the export achievements of a representative sample of twenty-two developing countries was very informative in this respect. During the period 1950 to 1967 the exports of these countries grew annually by just 4 per cent whereas during the same period the exports of the six largest industrial countries of the West (the United States, Britain, West Germany, France, Japan, and Italy) grew annually by 9 per cent.[35] Beginning in the 1970s the relative export position of both the newly industrialized and the oil-exporting countries sharply improved, but these comprised only part of the Third World.

The reasons for the relatively poor export achievements of most developing countries can be sorted into three main categories: (1) reasons of a structural nature, (2) inefficient economic management, and (3) the political and economic power of the industrial nations.

The structural reasons differ from case to case.[36] The Western demand for the products which many developing countries exported, such as coffee, tea, cocoa, or other foodstuffs, was characterized by a low income elasticity; that is, an increase in consumer income in the West led to a less than proportionate increase in the demand. This was in contrast to the Western demand for consumer durables, which was characterized by a high income elasticity. Other crucial exports of the developing countries included raw materials, the demand for which was undermined by the introduction of substitutes, the most obvious examples being synthetic fibres and plastic.

The difference in the income elasticities of demand between the products of the developing and the industrial countries led to a difference in the volume of the trade flows. In addition it also affected the respective terms of trade: until the mid 1970s the prices of raw materials exported by developing countries had a downward tendency while prices of the industrial products manufactured by the industrial West tended to rise. Other factors in this price behaviour were the rapid technological advances in the primary sector, the expanded production of primary goods in the developing countries, and the low wage costs there. Both demand and supply factors thus negatively influenced the development of the international trade of Third World countries. The return on export diminished while the cost of imports rose.[37]

Inefficient economic management – our second category of explanations for poor export performance – was all too evident. When political independence was granted or new regimes established, the resultant governments permitted rises in income that generated greater demand in the domestic market for products that previously were exported. At the same time the ill-considered development of import-substituting industries concerning consumer durables also had a negative effect. For most products of these industries the domestic market was still much too small, not just in the short term but in the medium term. The new plants were able to rely on special protection from national governments so that efficiency and the spirit of competition took a back seat.[38] Still another factor was the nationalistic complexion of many of the developing countries – a serious obstacle to the expansion of foreign trade. Often a policy of economic autarky was followed without consideration of the costs involved. Furthermore, little was done to promote effective economic co-operation even between neighbouring countries. Frequently the will to export simply did not exist.

The third set of explanatory factors for low exports has to do with the power relationship between the Third World and the industrialized nations.[39] The political and economic might of industrial countries made possible a very effective defensive policy against any import threat from the developing world. The GATT tariff reductions were largely on trade between industrial countries.[40] On the other hand, the quantitative restrictions that were imposed were largely directed against developing countries, an example being the Long-Term Cotton Textiles Agreement of 1962. For certain agricultural goods the United States, many European countries, and later the EEC, followed a highly protectionist policy, as already mentioned.

The relatively poor export achievements of the developing countries, and their conviction that the misuse of power by the West was the main cause of this, helped to stimulate within the Third World the belief that the world economic system should be reformed and restructured.[41] The United Nations seemed a good framework to provide this movement with concrete form. Decolonization had rapidly increased the number of developing nations in the United Nations and had thus strengthened their position in the General Assembly. The 1960s were declared 'Development Decade' by the United Nations and this meant that the problems of the Third World came to the fore within the General Assembly. In 1961 the Assembly fired the opening salvo. Resolution 1707 affirmed that international trade was the most important instrument for the promotion of economic development and would accordingly open the way towards world peace and stability. Resolution 917 in 1962 confirmed this decision with the formula 'not aid, but trade', which was accepted as the point of departure for future action.

The non-aligned states met at Cairo in 1964 and declared themselves in agreement with the principle that economic development should be promoted via United Nations channels.[42] The same year, from March to June, the United Nations sponsored a world gathering, the United Nations Conference on Trade and Development, known as UNCTAD. That first UNCTAD conference was held in Geneva. The basis for discussion was a paper by Raoul Prebisch, *Towards a New Trade Policy for Development*.[43] Prebisch emphasized the need for the developing countries to be less autarkic and to integrate themselves more into the expansive world economy of that time. A more outward-looking policy, he argued, would strongly stimulate development. To achieve this, the policy of import substitution had to be relaxed, export-led growth encouraged, and regional co-operation increased. In a spirit of world solidarity the richer industrial countries of the West also had to lend their support.

Indeed, the new development policy could only be meaningful if the industrial countries were willing to co-operate in the reorganization of the world economic system as proposed by Prebisch. The industrial countries had to accept a preferential system for importing industrial products from the Third World.[44] They had to be prepared to enter into agreements which guaranteed favourable prices for raw materials and agricultural goods produced by the developing countries. They had to be willing to pay subsidies to exporting Third World countries if the terms of trade moved against those countries. They also had to be prepared to reduce import duties on tropical and subtropical crops and, by special measures, to try to relieve the debt position of the developing countries. Finally they had to reorganize GATT so that it encouraged trade with the developing world. In fact the Prebisch Report advocated a new policy of international trade which would take full account of development policy.

THE GROUP OF SEVENTY-SEVEN

The first UNCTAD conference achieved few concrete results but still held out great promise. The non-industrialized countries organized themselves into the Group of Seventy-Seven and thus laid the foundation for an international front that would press for world economic development.[45] The negotiation process now was institutionalized, and this considerably enlarged the potential power of the developing countries. Numerous general measures and norms were accepted in principle, and these formed a good basis for later, concrete actions. Moreover, UNCTAD was transformed into a permanent consultative organ within which four permanent working parties were set up.

Nevertheless the limited nature of the concrete results had a frustrating effect on the developing countries. In 1967 the Group of Seventy-Seven met in Algiers. From this came the Algiers Charter which adopted a much more radical stance. The industrial countries were now the subject of much reproach, especially since they were refusing to sign raw material agreements and remained deaf to calls for a broadening of financial transfers to the developing countries in the form of aid and credits. The industrial countries did not see why they should make such unilateral concessions. Their trade policy was still based on the principle of reciprocity, and as long as the developing world had nothing to offer, the industrial countries did not feel obliged to make substantial concessions. The radicalization of the Group of Seventy-Seven remained, for the time being, a verbal offensive. The only achievement of the second UNCTAD conference in New Delhi in 1968 was that the industrial countries promised that they would try to transfer 1 per cent of their GNP to the Third World in the form of development aid. The third UNCTAD conference in Santiago, Chile, in 1972 did not attain much more. The industrial countries refused to start immediate discussions based on the radical programme of the Group of Seventy-Seven; instead they demanded a series of prior modifications and wanted to see the discussion organized within the broader framework of the UN General Assembly. The conference was only saved from fiasco by an agreement to establish a Charter of the Economic Rights and Obligations of States.

The failure of the Santiago Conference strengthened the consensus within the Group of Seventy-Seven that the radical demands should be supplemented with a confrontation strategy. The oil embargo of November 1973 proved the effectiveness of this. The industrial countries now were willing to discuss the joint action programme of the Group of Seventy-Seven under the slogan of a New International Economic Order, within the framework of the United Nations.[46] The discussion took place in the General Assembly during 1974. In December the Assembly also discussed the Charter of the Economic Rights and Obligations of States.

The action programme of the Group of Seventy-Seven envisaged a reorganization of international trade relations. It held that this was particularly important for staple goods. It went on to stress the need for expanding and diversifying Third World exports of finished and semi-finished goods, and for the transfer of technology from the industrial to the developing world. In addition, the Group of Seventy-Seven believed that a system should be set up to relieve the debt problem of the developing countries and that co-operation between developing countries should be improved. Trade between the developing countries and the Eastern bloc was to be better arranged. The organizational function of UNCTAD was to be reinforced. In concrete terms an Integrated Programme for Staple Products was put forward as an item for discussion. The programme envisaged a system of international buffer stocks, in case world supply exceeded world demand. A Common Fund would finance the system, and guarantee a regular flow of export earnings to the developing countries, exporters of staple products protected by the programme.

The Integrated Programme for Staple Products met with general approval during the two discussion rounds in the United Nations. The dialogue between the industrial and developing countries was back on the rails and the confrontation strategy was put to one side. The Integrated Programme for Staple Products was applied in the first Lomé convention (1975), which involved forty-six developing countries associated with the E E C. The system of stabilizing income from exports was, as already mentioned (page 369), introduced for twelve staple products (the STABEX system). During the fourth UNCTAD conference in Nairobi in 1976 the Integrated Programme for Staple Products was accepted as a system for all developing countries that were members of the United Nations. A timetable for negotiations on individual sorts of goods was drawn up with September 1976 as a starting point. Seventeen staple products were indicated as especially suitable for international arrangements, namely coffee, cocoa, tea, sugar, cotton, rubber, jute, hard textile fibres, copper, tin, wheat, rice, bananas, meat, wool, bauxite, and iron ore. The first international agreements for staple products were reached on cocoa, tin, and sugar.[47]

A stumbling-block was the financing of the Common Fund. The discussions held under the auspices of the UNCTAD were broken off in March 1977, resumed in November, suspended again on 1 December at the request of the developing countries, and then resumed again. The developing countries wanted the financing to be undertaken by the governments concerned in the buffer-stock agreements, with the possibility of supplementary loans. The industrial countries, in contrast, wanted the financing to be provided by the producers, consumers and distributors of the goods in question, not the national governments. Any supplementary loans would be provided by the same groups, possibly with a state guarantee. In addition the developing countries proposed that the Common Fund finance not only the buffer stocks but also the Third World drive towards product diversification, market research, market promotion and measures to raise productivity. There was sharp resistance to all of this from the industrial countries, and it was only in 1979 that an agreement was reached in Geneva.[48]

In the mean time the political and economic circumstances of the

1970s had given rise to serious disorder in the international system. New initiatives were made. The success of the oil boycott had caused the developing countries to consider to what extent a boycott strategy could be used for other raw materials and how far such a strategy could accelerate the industrializing of the Third World. A conference for industrial development was organized by the United Nations at Lima in 1975 to answer those questions but led to no definite conclusions. The European countries, under pressure from the increasing political power of the developing countries, launched on their side the idea of a special North-South dialogue in Paris. The first round in 1975 was fruitless because of the rigid attitude of the Group of Seventy-Seven. The second, in 1975–6, got little further.

The increase in oil prices widened the differences within the group of developing countries. The oil-rich nations greatly improved their trade balances and embarked upon an energetic programme of economic development. In contrast, the rest of the developing nations were faced with enormous balance-of-payments deficits, which at first they tried to cover with expensive loans. The debt position of many developing countries became so alarming that they had to clamp drastic restraints on their development. Consequently the heterogeneity of the Third World increased.[49] Multinationals also played a distorting role in this respect, for they preferred to make their large-scale investment in countries where economic development was already well under way. So the developing world now fell into three categories: oil-rich countries enjoying accelerated development; countries without oil where industrialization was fully under way; and countries without oil whose economy remained backward. This last category has been called 'the Fourth World'. The fifth UNCTAD conference in Manila in 1980 had to resign itself to this unavoidable evolution within the developing world. The Group of Seventy-Seven did not actually break up, but the discussions and conflicts were sharp and irreconcilable. Solidarity was lost and militancy declined. Simultaneously it became clear that the economic crisis of the West meant that there could be no rapid and complete realization of the New International Economic Order. The strategy therefore shifted towards the attainment of a few concrete conditions, especially a general agreement on world trade in raw materials and a linkage between raw materials prices and those of industrial products. Control over multinationals and the right to nationalize companies were also discussed. The time of reckless offensive action seemed past.

THE EASTERN BLOC AND THE NEGLECT OF THE DEVELOPING COUNTRIES

Trade between the Eastern bloc and the Third World was insignificant during the post-war period.[50] Its share in total world trade fluctuated between 1 and 2 per cent. There were no important changes in the nature of this trade. The Eastern bloc's imports from the developing countries were mainly primary goods – 90 per cent during the 1970s. Its exports to the developing countries consisted largely of manufactures, especially iron and steel products, textiles, machines and other industrial equipment.

The Eastern socialist countries have consistently taken an ideological position in favour of the economic development of the Third World but at the same time have expressly emphasized the principle of national independence. They have used that principle to explain their unwillingness to participate in international aid programmes for the Third World. At first they also did not want to invest there directly. If industry was to develop in the Third World, they reasoned, it must be national industry, autarkic and independent. In this respect the Eastern bloc countries were not notably positive towards the idea of an intensive industrialization. In their opinion, it was in the interest of the developing countries to specialize in agricultural and mining products, for which they had geographical or climatic advantages.

The developing countries themselves strongly resisted this conception and stressed the fact that they regarded the international division of labour dynamically and not statically. They did not want to be forced for centuries into a straitjacket of exporting agricultural products and raw materials. They accused the socialist countries of using the principle of national independence as an excuse for passiveness and demanded that they provide real and effective help to promote the development of export industry in the Third World. The developing countries also demanded that the Eastern bloc give up its principle of a bilateral equilibrium between imports and exports and introduce a multilateral trading system. Lastly the Third World disliked the long-term bilateral trade agreements which had held the prices of their raw-material exports stable even during the 1970s, when prices on the open market had rocketed.

The Eastern bloc countries branded direct investment by the West in the Third World as an expression of capitalist exploitation, but they themselves did not hesitate to set up numerous mixed companies in the developing regions, starting around 1970. At first these initiatives were confined to research and trade, but they were gradually extended to production, particularly in agriculture, and also to mining construction and forestry. During the 1970s about 200 such mixed companies began operations, with Rumania, Czechoslovakia, Hungary and Poland very active in this respect, and the Soviet Union somewhat less so.[51] Economic co-operation also often took the form of bilateral government loans. The recipient developing countries could use the loan to buy machines, other industrial equipment, and complete factory installations, from the lender country. The interest rates were usually low (2.5 to 3 per cent) and the repayment period spread over eight to twelve years. The Soviet Union initially accounted for a large part of these loans, but a smaller proportion as time went on.[52] The Russians have been very selective in economic co-operation, and political motives have played a role. Nearly half of the Soviet loans went to countries in the Middle East. Others went to India, Pakistan, Afghanistan, and later Vietnam. In South America the recipient countries included Chile, Cuba, Peru, and Argentina. Most of these projects related to industry or energy, some concerned transport, agriculture and geological exploration. Apart from the economic co-operation, there was technical assistance. On one hand, grants were given to young people in the Third World so that they could study at institutes of higher and technical education in the Eastern bloc. On the other, specialists from the Soviet Union and other Eastern bloc countries were sent to developing countries in order to train local workers and technicians, not just in industry but also in such sectors as education, health, and government administration.

As impressive as the direct investment, the economic co-operation, and the technical assistance may appear, taken together they represented less than 5 per cent of what the Third World was receiving in development aid around 1978. It is therefore not surprising that the developing countries were very critical of the Eastern bloc's contribution. During the UNCTAD conferences of Nairobi (1976) and Manila (1980) they demanded that the socialist countries, in common with the West, commit themselves to devoting 1 per cent of their GNP to development aid. Calculations showed that the aid the socialist countries gave to the Third World around 1978 represented only thirteen hundredths of 1 per cent of their GNP, and this was considered by the recipients as inadequate.[53] During the same UNCTAD conferences the developing countries also criticized the Eastern bloc for refusing to participate in the international organizations for multilateral development aid. If by chance the Eastern bloc countries did participate, it had always been on a bilateral basis. Moreover, the Eastern bloc did not have its own multilateral aid programme for the developing world within the Comecon set-up. The few multilateral agreements signed between Comecon and a group of developing countries during the 1970s were in their concrete execution wholly bilateral.

There were still other reasons why the Third World's criticism of the socialist countries sharpened during the 1970s. Third World countries wish to implement their development strategy according to their own vision, not that of the Eastern bloc. Tremendous dams, such as the Aswan Dam in Egypt, and gigantic steel plants, such as those at Bokharo and Bhilai in India and El Hadjar in Algeria, have been regarded as disastrous in their economic and environmental effects. Moreover, the Third World countries are increasingly seeing the Eastern bloc as direct competitors. Both areas produce a comparable range of industrial products which they wish to unload in the West. Furthermore, the pessimistic forecasts on energy provision by the Soviet Union raised the suspicion that the other Eastern bloc countries would increase their exports to the rest of the world in order to get their energy imports from non-Russian sources. For these ideological, institutional and practical reasons, the ties between the Third World and the Eastern bloc were weak. A new initiative, a New International Economic Order, was urgently required.

3 THE PROPOSALS FOR REFORM

THE MODEL OF EXPORT-LED GROWTH

The economic crisis of the 1970s increased the conviction held by many that the operating principles of the liberal world economy were no longer appropriate for its further development. The countries of the Third World had gained a lot in political maturity, and in

UNCTAD conferences and in the North-South dialogue they forcefully demanded a greater role in the world economy and a greater share of world income. Equally, the increasing integration of the socialist economies into world trade made a modification of the Western market system necessary. In the West itself an increasing contradiction had developed between the nationally based expansionist and protectionist policies followed by governments and the actual internationalization of economic activity. Besides, the international institutions which had been set up after the war to support the world order of the time did not seem able to keep pace with the structural changes which had taken place since their creation. GATT had laid down rules for the construction of a liberal world economy but the reality which confronted it was increasingly at variance with its principles. In most countries government intervention and protectionism were becoming more common and preferential arrangements more widespread. Trade with the developing countries and the Eastern bloc seemed irreconcilable with GATT principles.[54] Although it was more than desirable that the various international institutions such as GATT, UNCTAD, OECD, IMF, and the World Bank should co-ordinate their policies in the organization of world trade, nothing concrete had been achieved in this respect.

For these reasons, attempts were made in the West to work out a New International Economic Order that would correspond better to the current and future needs of the world. Academics and politicians of the centre-left and centre-right in Europe and liberals in the United States started to work together on outlining a new institutional framework for the world economy. At the close of the 1970s the best-known proposals were those of the Club of Rome under the leadership of Jan Tinbergen entitled *Reshaping the International Order* (the RIO Report)[55] and the report of the Brandt Commission headed by Willy Brandt.[56] Studies by Hans Singer and Javed Ansari, by B. Herman and by Gerald Helleiner should also be mentioned.[57] All these moderate reformers accepted the liberal world economy as a basic principle, owing to its efficiency, but none the less believed that important modifications were necessary. They thus held firm to the principle of the free movement of goods, capital, and technology, since they recognized the benefit of an international division of labour, but they wanted modifications for humanitarian reasons. Efficiency remained a criterion but no longer a central one.

Instead, attention was concentrated on a fair distribution of the benefits of economic endeavour. These reformers could mainly be seen as fervent supporters of a humanitarian socialism. Particular attention was devoted to the basic needs of the poor, the expansion of employment, and the participation of the lowest social classes in economic development. At the same time these reformers were Keynesian-inspired and internationalist-inspired. They wanted to reconcile the new ordering of world trade with the economic objectives of the nation-states in respect to growth and full employment. In other words they sought a new balance between the political autonomy of national governments and the economic integration which was taking place on a global scale. National governments would have to extend their authority over the domestic economy and ensure that private interests (including those of the multinationals) were kept in hand. At the same time they also had to take into account the interests of the world community.

Every one of these reformers believed that the industrialization of the Third World was a necessary condition for successfully combating world poverty. The industrialization would make use of the relative advantage enjoyed by the developing countries, namely the surplus of cheap labour. Each developing country would therefore generate a dual industrial structure, consisting of a traditional and a modern sector. The traditional sector would be directed towards the production of basic needs, that is, self-provision, aided by simple applied technology. The modern sector would be geared towards the production of export goods, relying on cheap labour. In order to make the international division of labour operational, labour-intensive industries would be transferred from the developed countries to the Third World. The multinationals would be able to play a positive role here, being in a position to contribute effectively to the stimulation of export-led growth in the developing countries. It was thus recognized that multinationals had their good side too.

This new world system presupposed a fundamental review of international trade, one that would allow Third World countries to enjoy the benefits of export-led growth. Consequently the existing tariff and non-tariff import barriers in the West were to be lifted. At the same time special mechanisms needed to be thought out, mechanisms better able to integrate the export industries of the developing countries into world trade flows. But West and East would have to grant unilateral preferences for industrial exports from the Third World, taking into account the degree of development of the countries in question. Simultaneously a system would be worked out which would guarantee all countries of the world an orderly access to markets for raw materials, energy supplies, and foodstuffs. Such a guarantee would, of course, entail limits to the controls of national states over their own natural resources. An international authority would control prices, flows and stocks of goods, and by doing so it would ensure a transfer of income from the richer to the poorer nations of the world. The new system would also integrate the Eastern bloc into world trade. The setting-up of a universally applicable money of account would eliminate price discrimination. Adaptations of the national planning systems would open the way for the necessary multilateralism.

As already mentioned, the proposers of these reforms believed that the private investment programmes of multinational companies could comprise channels for the transfer of technology from the industrial West to the developing countries. Naturally, conditions would have to be imposed to ensure that the cause of Third World industrialization was being effectively served and profits would have to be equitably distributed. Multinationals are increasing their influence in the global allocation of economic resources; they are exerting more and more control over the location of industrial production. Such power, it is argued, requires an international control if the principle of distributive justice is to keep pace with the principle of efficiency.[58] In fact the same remarks hold for governmental investment made by the West or the Eastern bloc in developing countries. Governmental investment has a largely bilateral character, and so the danger of the misuse of power exists. Once again, international control could avoid possible distortions in this respect.

Lastly, the new world order, as defined here, presupposed a review of the international monetary system. The abandonment of the gold standard and the introduction of floating exchange rates in the early 1970s had already created the first conditions for this reform. The system of floating exchange rates gave national governments a flexible tool with which to protect the domestic economy from external pressure. To what extent, however, can floating exchange rates guarantee a balance between the interest of the national economy and the demands of international co-operation? The answer to this is not a simple one. The danger certainly exists that the manipulation of floating exchange rates will too strongly favour national isolation at the expense of international integration. The same distortion can result from speculation on international money markets. Therefore, in the financial sphere, international control would be relied upon to counter possible disequilibria.

The numerous controls and corrections which these reformers built into the capitalist model of the liberal world economy implied management and planning on a global scale. There would have to be an institutional framework which could functionally organize world trade.[59] The reformers thought that the United Nations was by far the best institution to take on this supranational management task. They suggested that the existing international economic organizations, particularly GATT, UNCTAD, OECD, IMF, and the World Bank, should be given specific supervisory and management roles and that the United Nations should function as an overarching, co-ordinative, supranational body. The management of the world trade would thus be undertaken by a sort of federation of international economic organizations under UN authority. By transferring concrete management to economic organizations, it was hoped that the problem of development would be depoliticized. Economic management would be divorced from political ideology. The international economic organizations would ensure the application of the principles of efficiency and the United Nations would ensure those of fairness. A happy medium would thus be achieved between economic rationality and social ethics on a world scale.

THE MODEL OF ZONAL TRADE

The proposals as described in the previous section received much attention but also much criticism even from scholars and politicians close to the ideology of the reformers themselves. First, the point of departure was criticized. Some economists took the view that the above-mentioned proposals for reform largely accepted the traditional framework of the liberal world economy, merely suggesting a series of measures to accelerate a new international division of labour. In essence the reforms, it was contended, only sought to adapt the location of world production to the availability of economic resources. Labour-intensive industries would be established in areas where there was a relative surplus of semi-skilled labour, and capital-intensive industries would be concentrated in areas where there was a relative surplus of machines and the appropriate kinds of human capital. As soon as this restructuring was achieved, there would be an optimal allocation of the factors of production and this would raise the efficiency of the liberal world economy, thus promoting its rehabilitation. The international economic organizations, under the control of the United Nations, would continue to ensure that the free-market rules of the game were being followed but the management aspects of the transition phase would gradually disappear. In this light the New International Economic Order would not differ very much from the old world order.

These critics followed up their argument by stressing that the real future was more complex than the one supposed by Tinbergen, Brandt and others. The new static balance as envisaged by these reformers was in fact based on a continuing gap between a simpler industrial society in the Third World and a more complex one in the West and in the Eastern bloc. Such a gap, however, would be just as unacceptable and discriminatory to the Third World. The principle of distributive justice, which has become so fundamental in Western politics, requires that management of the world economy be organized in a more dynamic sense and that all countries of the world be raised to the level of a complex, post-industrial society.

This more dynamic approach to trade and development poses a towering challenge, implying unprecedented exertions in world-scale economic management. Even assuming that a homogenization of economic development throughout the world were to come about, new problems would arise. Some economies have so many natural resources that they could possibly exist in an autarkic framework, whereas others are so poor in resources that they have to rely on massive imports. Imports must be financed by exports and in order to guarantee these exports, a country must win and keep a lead in technology and innovation. Through technological superiority it is possible to overcome the disadvantages of poverty in natural resources. But this technological differentiation is likely to become more and more unacceptable, because the more dynamic approach to the organization of world trade is clearly directed at an increasing equalization of technological know-how and human capital. The principle of distributive justice then comes into conflict with itself.

Sharp criticism was also levelled at the model of export-led growth which took so central a place in the Tinbergen and Brandt reform proposals. The advantages of this model had been seen as twofold;

it would enable the developing countries to accelerate their industrialization, and the consequently improved international division
of labour would raise efficiency and therefore prosperity. Both
arguments quickly came under attack. Export-led growth in the
developing countries assumes a rapid adoption of the Western
industrial model, but, as Iran has shown, this can produce a hostile
reaction. Moreover, in this vision, the neo-colonialism which exists
for agriculture and raw materials, is simply shifted to the industrial
plane. The transfer of labour-intensive industries to the Third World
ultimately serves the interests of the leading industrial sectors of the
West. Moreover, export-led growth is a risky undertaking for the
developing countries, because it makes them vulnerable and wholly
dependent on importing countries which can always decide to buy
their goods elsewhere.[60]

Export-led growth cannot hope to solve the development problems of *all* countries of the Third World, since neither the West nor
the Eastern bloc would be able to absorb such massive production.
Furthermore, the industrialization as conceived by these reformers
would create a dual economy and widen the gap between rich and
poor.[61] Finally, the proposed strengthening of the international
division of labour would involve disadvantages for the West. The
expansion of world trade only promotes growth when the countries
involved have a comparable economic structure. The expansion of
trade between countries of very different economic structure, in
contrast, can have an extremely distorting effect. It can quickly ruin
the traditional sectors in the developed countries, destroying there
in a dramatic way physical and human capital. In any case, the re-
allocation of the production factors of labour and capital would not
be an easy matter and much damage could be done.

Those critics who emphasized the disadvantages of the export-
led growth model wish to found the New International Economic
Order more on the 'basic needs' model as worked out by the World
Bank and by the International Labour Organization[62] and on the
'domestic consumption' model of Staffan Linder.[63] This separate
school of reformers set up a model of zonal trade. They argued as
follows. If trade is largely limited to areas with a comparable
economic structure, then industry will show a tendency to develop
along the lines of satisfying the needs of the domestic economy.[64]
As the national economy gradually develops, so will industrial
production become more differentiated. In this way the conditions

will be created for a part of production to be allocated for exports. West Germany and Japan are good examples of how countries might operate within this model. Both countries built up their export industry after the war as a continuation of their domestic market. In Japan a tight protectionist policy was even used in order to achieve this goal. Nothing could be imported into Japan unless it met the basic needs for industrial growth and unless it could not be domestically produced at an economically feasible cost. This protectionism was organized not only by the state but also by the *Zaibatsu*, and the result was an expansion in domestic demand which gradually led to the development of a successful export industry. Moreover, by concentrating on exports to countries with a comparable economic structure, Japan assured stability in the expansion of exports.

This school of reformers – critics of export-led growth – wanted world trade to be provisionally organized within zones made up of countries with comparable economic structure. In the zone with a highly developed economy, which would include, for instance, Western Europe, Japan, the United States, Canada, Australia, and New Zealand, trade would be very intense and involve all sorts of goods. The international division of labour would be optimal here, based on free exchange between countries. The industrializing countries of the Third World would make up a separate trading zone, and the least developed areas, the so-called Fourth World, would make up another. The Eastern bloc too could comprise a separate zone. Within each zone a specific form of export trade would come about, as an extension to the domestic market of each member country. In the zone for the industrializing nations of the Third World, the export trade would be in labour-intensive industrial products; and in the zone of the Fourth World it would largely be artisan products. The exports of the developing countries would thus keep in step with the development of their economies. In this way the danger of distortion would be avoided.

Zonal development, as outlined above, does not imply a status quo for the Third and Fourth Worlds; on the contrary, it guarantees supple, balanced industrialization. It does not seek to prevent contacts between the different zones, including investment by one zone in another, but cross-zonal trade and co-operation would be subject to international control. This cross-zonal connection would ensure that the developing world would receive help from the West in order to accelerate its industrialization, the poorest receiving the most and the richest the least, while at the same time the West itself would not fall victim to disruptive competition. The control and management of trade between zones would be assigned to the international economic organizations. Foreign investment by multi-nationals would come under the same control. This would have the primary objective of encouraging the growth of the domestic market and promoting a substantial transfer of income to the developing countries. On the other hand, the international organizations would set up a system of inter-zonal protectionism. A code of fair competition would ensure that products from less-developed zones could only be exported to higher-developed zones as long as certain employment conditions were fulfilled. This would put an end to the exploitation of cheap labour by the richer industrial countries.

THE CRITICISM IN THE THIRD WORLD AND FROM RIGHT AND LEFT

Many moderate economists and politicians of the Third World accepted, in general, one or the other of the above-mentioned proposals – export-led and zonal – but from their own experience they added some refinements. The majority of these critics have served as experts in the various international economic organizations or were involved in the North-South dialogue, examples being M. ul Haq[65] and A. Tévoédjre.[66] A new International Economic Order based on the advantages of an international division of labour was considered acceptable but corrections were deemed necessary. Corrections concerning the relationship between the industrialized and industrializing countries and between the various zones were given special emphasis. For many representatives of the Third World the political factor was of central importance. The management of world trade was not seen as a purely economic or technical concern but rather as a political one. The Third World therefore had to become conscious of its own specific power based on numerical superiority. From this position of power the management of world trade should be politicized, with the developing countries gaining as much economic advantage as possible. In the same spirit, the 'basic needs' model proposed by the World Bank and by the International Labour Organization and integrated into the first set of proposals described, was also accepted. The basic needs model would increase the autonomy of the developing countries and thus improve their negotiating position in the world economy. The Third Worlders gave a special slant to the model of intra-zonal world trade, with the spreading of the idea of technical co-operation among developing countries. Under the auspices of the United Nations a development strategy along these lines would be outlined, independent of the industrial West. This autonomous industrial development would be an important bargaining element in discussions on the construction and management of the New International Economic Order.

Conservatives in the West and in the Third World remained faithful to the free-market doctrine. They unleashed a bitter attack on the managerial and bureaucratic aspects of the various proposals for a New International Economic Order and called for a return to more orthodox liberal thinking. Richard N. Cooper,[67] Jagdish N. Bhagwati,[68] Charles F. Diaz-Alejandro,[69] Wassily Leontief,[70] Herbert G. Grubel[71] and Milton Friedman are some of the well-known members of this group. Harry Johnson, M. Corden, and Bela Balassa also deserve mention because of their important work on the problem of protection. Studies in the same area were also undertaken by the OECD, the World Bank, and the Brookings Institution.[72] According to these experts, the free-market system should remain the foundation of the world economic order. Efficiency must be the primary criterion for economic activity, which can only be optimal in a free world market. Government interventions which distort this system and hinder the free movement of capital, labour technology, and goods should be rejected. This is because they reduce the efficiency of the market and therefore the level of general prosperity. If reforms are necessary, these should be primarily directed at the break-up of world protectionism. Countries in the West and in the Third World should dismantle their tariff barriers and other import controls, and remove restrictions on the movement of capital and labour. In addition the political, institutional and social structures which hinder the economic development of the Third World should be taken away. In this matter, governments would play an important role.

Under these conditions, progress towards a new international division of labour will run on optimal lines. The production of light industrial consumer products will in general be transferred to the developing countries, with multinationals ensuring a supple transfer of technology and capital. The consequent crisis for the industrial lands of the West is seen in purely cyclical terms and the market mechanism will provide the necessary restructuring. For one group of countries, however, the free-market proponents make an exception. The Fourth World, owing to its primitive structure, will neither attract investment from the West, nor be able to develop on its own. In this case, therefore, rich industrial and oil countries will have to step in and provide multilateral aid and loans. This aid would not need any kind of bureaucratic international organization since the sense of responsibility which accompanies leadership would suffice. If the United States would not be willing to bear this burden alone, then a collective responsibility shared by the richer industrial and oil countries would be a solution.

The conservatives did not just have an impact on economic philosophy; they also exerted a real influence in policy-making in the world. In various countries of the West around 1980, governments coming into power began to follow more traditional policies again. In some South American countries the theories of Milton Friedman and the 'Chicago School' made great advances. Even in the general meetings of the I M F and the World Bank, this rebirth of orthodoxy could be clearly detected. Protectionist tendencies were condemned and the freest possible trade advocated. In the area of domestic policy, the dangers of excessive government and state intervention were stressed. The need for the continuation of market mechanisms was particularly highlighted.[73]

Neo-Marxists also reacted critically to the proposals for a New International Economic Order. Their criticism was not *ad hoc* but rather an attempt to integrate reality into their own models of society. Some models were neo-mercantilist-inspired. Robert W. Tucker,[74] H. Hudson[75] and André Tiano[76] regarded the discussion of the New International Economic Order primarily as the expression of a new power struggle between states. The reduction of political and economic inequalities between states and blocs of states made a redistribution of world power unavoidable. The world rulers fought to maintain their former hegemony, which was now contested by emergent countries. Initially this process involved the destruction of American leadership and Soviet hegemony but now it was held to be more complex. These critics contended that an alliance was developing between the secondary countries of the industrial West, such as France and Italy, and the new industrial countries of the

Third World, such as Brazil and Mexico, against the industrial bulwark of the United States, West Germany, and Japan. A similar power struggle was developing within the Eastern bloc. The outcome of these conflicts would form the basis of the New International Economic Order.

Neo-Marxists such as Christian Palloix,[77] P. Rey,[78] Paul Sweezy,[79] H. Elsenhans,[80] Samir Amin,[81] Arfiri Emmanuel[82] and Norman Girvan[83] based their criticism on the structure of the production process. For them, any new economic order that remains founded on the private control of the means of production comprises only a transition phase towards an ultimately socialist development model. Some of them see this transition phase as useful and even necessary. They argue that the developing countries must first go through a capitalist phase before they can start on the successful construction of a socialist economy. Multinationals can help to intensify the capitalist phase and accordingly provide the developing countries with a strong industrial base. Some neo-Marxists even add an anthropological dimension to their analysis. The new world order based on the introduction of a capitalist industrialization model in the developing countries must, in time, destroy itself, not just through internal contradictions but also through its incompatibility with the primitive societies of the Third World.

During the 1970s the construction of a New International Economic Order became an urgent necessity. In the West, the free-market system of the post-war period was no longer adapted to the reality of economic bloc formation and the general raising of non-tariff barriers. In the Third World the old system was attacked because it discriminated in favour of the rich industrial countries. This same system also hindered the smooth integration of the Eastern bloc into the world economy. Nevertheless the alternatives which were proposed to adapt the world trading system to the needs of the present and future found no general consensus. The conflict of interests was too great to permit an operational compromise between the principles of justice and efficiency.

CHAPTER XI

THE GOLD-DOLLAR STANDARD AS WORLD SYSTEM, 1944–71

The post-war international monetary system has had a turbulent history. Its development has been along lines very different from those which had been mapped out by its original creators. The Americans had wanted to achieve a new international order by means of a multilateral monetary system, based on gold-convertible currencies led by the dollar, on fixed but adjustable exchange rates, and on liberalized world trade. The Bretton Woods Agreement of 1944 was the point of departure for the new policy but the reality turned out more difficult than the vision. When in 1958 the multilateral payments system could finally be organized on a world scale, it seemed unable to cope with the fluidity and complexity of the rapidly growing world economy. The increasing tension led President Richard Nixon in 1971 to announce measures that suspended the convertibility of the dollar. This marked the end of the Bretton Woods System.

1. THE LEGACY OF AMERICAN AND BRITISH DIRIGISME, 1944–5

THE HISTORICAL BACKGROUND

The post-war Bretton Woods System can only be understood in the context of the world monetary events of the first half of the twentieth century. Around 1900 faith in the gold standard was still total.

According to the theorists and politicians of the time, the development of the world economy would best be served by stable prices. A stable price level was regarded as a function of the money supply. It would best be guaranteed by an internationally accepted gold standard with fixed exchange rates and full convertibility of currencies into gold. Any disturbances in a country's *external* equilibrium would be automatically corrected by the interaction of the balance of payments, gold movements and consequent price adjustments. For example, if one country, say through a successful export drive, began to run a balance-of-payments surplus, that country would attract gold, and if its government followed 'the rules of the game' the domestic money supply would also be increased. It was reasoned that prices in that country would therefore rise, making it less competitive abroad so that its exports would fall, re-establishing international equilibrium. For a country in deficit, the reverse held. Disturbances in *internal* equilibrium, which could be caused by the amount of commercial bank lending, would be rectified by central banks. If, for certain circumstances, note issue was excessive, then the central bank could raise the discount rate in order to bring the issue down again to its normal level. [1] At the start of the twentieth century this system, under the leadership of Britain, was still working fairly smoothly. It was therefore not surprising that after the trauma and chaos of the First World War the pre-war principles of the gold standard were accepted by almost everybody as the basic conditions for economic recovery.

The modifications proposed during the international conference of Genoa in 1922 largely related to the economizing of gold reserves by means of a gold bullion standard and a system of reserve currencies. In reality this had already been applied *de facto* before the First World War[2] but it was only officially sanctioned in 1925 when Britain reintroduced the gold standard on the basis of the pre-war gold parity of the pound sterling. Reserves would now no longer exclusively consist of gold since gold-convertible currencies could also be included. Numerous countries followed the British example, either immediately or a few years later. But not all went as far as Britain in establishing pre-war gold parity. Some of them, such as France and Belgium, adopted a gold parity which was significantly lower than that which had existed before the First World War. The range between undervalued and overvalued currencies now became so wide that the mechanism to restore equilibrium via the level of domestic prices functioned with increasing difficulty. In countries with overvalued currencies, and primarily in Britain, price evolution was especially apt to run up against massive inertia. The delays which thus came about in the normal, equilibrium-restoring operation of the system gave rise to sizeable speculative flows of capital. The speculative fever was also fed by the big increase in world liquidity caused by the inflation during and after the First World War. The rise of the financial markets of New York and Paris, which began to compete with that of London, greatly facilitated transfers of this liquidity in the form of 'hot money', on an international scale. Governmental hopes that the restoration of the gold standard would be able to hold post-war speculation in check therefore seemed ill-founded.

As early as September 1931 the British government was forced to abandon the gold standard. As a result, the pound sterling was no longer convertible and, as a floating currency, lost its fixed link to gold. The exact exchange rate of sterling would now be determined by the demand and supply of sterling on foreign-exchange markets. Nevertheless the Bank of England did try to reduce the size of fluctuations in sterling value by means of an Exchange Equalization Account. At the same time it attempted to hold the exchange rate of sterling at the relatively low level to which it had fallen during the 1931 panic when the pound was detached from gold. The Bank of England, as an extension of this policy, neutralized any further fall in world prices for raw materials and industrial products during the Great Depression by pushing down the international value of sterling. In this way the domestic price level was kept stable while British exports grew progressively cheaper. This British tactic raised the suspicion abroad that economic recovery in Britain was being made at the expense of employment in the rest of the world and that the interventions of the Bank of England amounted to nothing more than a systematic policy of currency dumping. Seen in the long term, however, these British measures marked the beginning of the system of *managed* exchange rates. The most authoritative economist of the day in Britain, John Maynard Keynes, supported this development. He believed that an industrial country could only effectively combat depression when it isolated itself from any deflationary influence on the open world economy and simultaneously implemented a policy of powerful domestic expansion. Economic nationalism therefore took precedence over orthodox international liberalism.

The general uncertainty which resulted from these British measures had far-reaching consequences. Most other countries in their turn decided to abandon the gold standard as well. Even the United States bowed to this movement in April 1933 and took the dollar off gold. In spite of this a large number of governments outside Britain had reservations about a generalized or permanent system of fairly free-floating exchange rates. Some wanted to bring back fixed gold values and others pressed for the relative stability they believed would be brought by linkages to key currencies.

At this point, the world split into a whole series of monetary blocs, the most important of which was undoubtedly the sterling area. All countries and territories of the British Empire (apart from Canada and Newfoundland), most Scandinavian and Baltic countries, and a few others, including Portugal and the Republic of Ireland, linked their national currencies to the pound and also held their official reserves in sterling. Even Japan, which did not wish to become a formal member of the sterling area, *de facto* linked the yen to the pound. The nucleus of the second most important bloc was the dollar, which, since the First World War, had developed into a key currency. On 30 January 1934 President Roosevelt signed the Gold Reserve Act, through which the dollar was given a fixed gold valuation once more: specifically $35 per troy ounce of gold.[3] Many countries in North, Central and South America decided to tie their currency to the dollar. In time, this new fixed link to gold became a source of great confidence, especially when political uncertainty increased in Europe. This confidence stimulated a huge flow of gold into the United States, a flow that continued until the Second World War. Germany, on the other hand, built up a system of stringent exchange control and of multiple exchange rates which was also to an extent adopted by some states in South-East Europe. And in 1933 the so-called 'gold bloc' had been formed by France, Italy, Switzerland, the Netherlands, and Belgium/Luxemburg. The aim of this joint action was to maintain, even in the monetary chaos of the 1930s, the gold-convertibility and fixed parities of the 1920s, but the deflationary policies that were adopted led to serious unemployment and to financial difficulties. General mistrust led to a flight of capital and substantial losses of gold reserves. When Belgium was forced into devaluing its currency in March 1935 the days of the gold bloc were numbered. In September 1936 the rest of the members, including France, abandoned their existing gold parities and most of them suspended convertibility altogether.

The prospect of a floating-franc zone as an additional independent monetary bloc in the West had already begun causing much concern before the French devaluation of 1936. France, however, supported by the Americans, was trying to persuade Britain to collaborate in a definitive mutual stabilization of the franc, dollar, and pound. The result was negative at first, but ultimately the Tripartite Agreement of 25 September 1936 was signed, according to which the United States, Britain and France accepted joint responsibility for the management of their national currency markets.[4] This step was an important innovation.[5] The Tripartite Agreement for the first time gave an official character to the joint actions of central banks. This was a vital basis for the further development of international monetary co-operation.[6]

THE WHITE PLAN AND THE KEYNES PLAN

The Second World War brought historic changes to the international monetary system. More than ever before, the world departed from liberal orthodoxy in the management of public finances. Governments eagerly accepted the Keynesian principle that public finances should be used to serve the real needs of the economy, and accordingly they brought national money and capital markets under their control. Financial relations between the Allied powers were also made subject to government control via the Lend-Lease arrangements.[7] The dollar emerged immediately as the strongest reserve currency in the world. In contrast the sterling area lost all its European members, and a strong regulatory framework had to be introduced.[8]

Britain and the United States began to work out a new international monetary system which would be implemented after the war. In the summer of 1941 Keynes produced a first text which in September began circulating in the British Treasury as 'Proposals for an International Clearing Union'. In December 1941 the American government instructed Harry Dexter White and his colleagues in the US Treasury Department to draw up proposals for an inter-Allied stabilization fund that would provide war aid to the Allies and simultaneously serve as the foundation for a post-war international monetary system. During the summer of 1942 the Keynes Plan and the White Plan were exchanged and studied by the two governments. The plans were in agreement over certain basic points. The stability of the domestic economy was to be strengthened and so a certain element of government monetary control over national economic life was considered necessary. This particular attention to the national economy implied that the world economy would now be less open. It meant that a certain international control was necessary and a small part of national sovereignty in the area of monetary affairs would have to be conceded. The authors considered it undesirable that a particular country should assume this international sovereignty and instead proposed international co-operation within the framework of a supranational institution. [9]

Although both authors clearly used the idea of international co-operation as the point of departure for their proposals, in other essential questions their visions differed fundamentally. Keynes gave precedence to national over international objectives whereas White reversed this priority. But both men made modifications to their plans during the years of consideration.

Keynes's stubborn fight to give precedence to national objectives in the new international monetary system has to be seen in the light of his experience during the 1930s. He was concerned about the possibility of renewed high levels of unemployment after the war and therefore wanted each country to maintain a substantial degree of independence in developing and executing national economic policy so that it would be able to promote full employment. On this reasoning, the integration of Britain into an open world economy seemed ill-advised, and only a sterling area, under strict British control, could be tolerated.

This narrow economic-nationalistic position was gradually relaxed because of the special circumstances of world war. Britain became more ready to participate in a multilateral world order, for various reasons. Britain had sold all its foreign assets, and therefore after the war it would not have the yields from those assets to finance part of its imports of foodstuffs and raw materials. Instead imports would have to be covered exclusively by exports, and this meant that access to the largest possible world market was essential. In addition the British war debt, especially that owed to the United States, took on alarming proportions, implying a high level of economic dependence on the Americans. Indeed during the war most of the world grew increasingly dependent on the United States.

In these circumstances any post-war expansionary policy in Europe or elsewhere outside the United States would lead to serious balance-of-payments problems. Moreover, an economic depression in the United States, which was considered possible despite the huge increase in productive capacity there, would rapidly spread over the rest of the world. In order to counter these dangers, Keynes thought it advisable that the post-war economy be placed under the guardianship of a supranational institution. A supple mechanism of automatic credit via this institution would provide European governments with the means to continue expansionary policies in spite of balance-of-payments deficits. Simultaneously, surplus countries such as the United States would be pressed by the supranational authority to adjust their policies, either liberalizing imports or increasing the amount of money in circulation.[10]

White was influenced by the New Deal tradition and was consequently in principle an advocate of economic planning and control. This philosophy, when applied to an international monetary system, led him to propose two supranational institutions – a stabilization fund and a world bank. The fund would provide credit to countries with a balance-of-payments deficit and in this respect would have access to a sum up to $5 billion. The world bank would in fact have access to a greater amount than this because it would supplement its capital by borrowing and thereby creating money. It would thus be able to expand international liquidity with a view to raising world living standards. Both supranational organizations would acquire significant control over the domestic monetary policies of their member states, especially relating to adjustments in exchange parities and to international capital movements.[11]

On the other hand, with a view to getting his plan approved by the State Department and Congress, and under the influence of the Keynes Plan, White made important amendments. The stabilization fund was made the centre of attention and the role of the world bank was reduced to that of a very orthodox organization for foreign investment.

Even in this altered form the White Plan differed substantially from that of Keynes. Keynes proposed the creation of a new international currency, to be known as 'bancor' and to be expressed in terms of gold. National exchange rates would then be expressed in terms of bancor. A supranational clearing union would use bancor to settle accounts between the central banks. So bancor, as an international reserve currency, would replace the existing national currencies. The White Plan, in contrast, took the view that the function of international reserve currency could be fulfilled by a basket of national currencies linked to gold. Another facet of the Keynes Plan was the system of automatic credit facilities for countries with deficits on their balance of payments. In other words, deficit countries would no longer be forced to restore equilibrium in their balance of payments by deflationary measures which would undermine or destroy national expansion policies. The White Plan, on the other hand, required normal, commercial criteria to be applied in the provision of international credit. All countries would have to contribute to the system in the form of gold and national currencies, and subsequently any countries in difficulties could borrow currencies only temporarily from the group, and then on strict conditions.

The Keynes Plan sought to involve the surplus countries in the correction of balance-of-payments disequilibria. Keynes saw his clearing union as a sort of central bank for the central banks of the member countries, so that a whole range of measures could be taken to correct such imbalances, including alterations in rates of exchange. In the White Plan fundamental balance-of-payments disequilibria could *only* be corrected by parity adjustments, and this was only possible if a sizeable majority of the member states approved such action. In other words the responsibility for the restoration of equilibrium lay chiefly with the deficit countries (which would probably have to deflate) whereas those with a surplus were left a free hand.

Long negotiations resulted in a Joint Statement by Experts on the Establishment of an International Monetary Fund (4 April 1944). At the end of June 1944 a meeting was organized in Atlantic City to prepare for the Bretton Woods Conference which was to take place in New Hampshire the following July, attended by representatives of forty-four countries. Although amendments were possible at both meetings and were in fact submitted (especially relating to the quotas), the joint British-American plan was in reality presented to the delegates as a *fait accompli*. In it the American vision prevailed over that of the British and ultimately the joint agreement amounted to a modified version of the White Plan.[12]

THE BRETTON WOODS AGREEMENT

The Bretton Woods Agreement of July 1944 made provision for the creation of an international stabilization fund known as the International Monetary Fund (IMF), which started operating in March 1947. The international investment organization called the International Bank for Reconstruction and Development (or World Bank) was also approved, and it began work a few months before the IMF. The new system was intended to be a realistic compromise between the rigid gold standard of the nineteenth century and the uncertain floating exchange rates of the 1930s. During the nineteenth century *external* equilibrium had been paramount, and this had been brought about by domestic measures. During the 1930s, however, *internal* equilibrium had been given precedence, with governments using trade restrictions, exchange controls, exchange rate manipulation and the like to achieve this end. The Bretton Woods Agreement confirmed the importance of the domestic economic objectives of full employment and rising incomes, but rejected the idea that autonomous exchange-rate manipulations should be used as the main instrument to achieve them. In place of this the principle of relative rigidity was accepted. That is, exchange rates were in principle fixed but from time to time, under certain conditions, could be adjusted.[13]

The parities would be fixed in terms of a certain weight of gold, and all national governments would make their currency externally convertible into gold at that parity. It would also be possible for governments to express the parity of their national currency in terms of another currency which was convertible into gold. In this case there would be *indirect* gold-convertibility. Great use would be made of this provision. All the countries of the sterling area stabilized their currency in terms of the pound and many others in terms of the dollar, which still had a gold parity of $35 per troy ounce. In currency transactions national monetary authorities could allow their exchange rates to fluctuate by 1 per cent both below and above the official parity (a total maximum width of 2 per cent).[14] Changes in the official parities would only be permitted when there was a 'fundamental' disequilibrium in the balance of payments. If this condition was satisfied, proposed changes of up to 10 per cent in the parity would be automatically approved by the IMF. If the proposal was for more than 10 per cent, then the IMF would first have to set up an inquiry. Great difficulties arose regarding these issues. The term 'fundamental' was open to numerous interpretations. In addition there was no concrete mechanism by which the IMF could compel national governments within a certain time to correct an existing or potential balance-of-payments deficit or surplus with adequate cyclical or structural policies. Only when the situation had reached crisis proportions could an *ex post facto* devaluation or revaluation be approved as a correction.[15]

The Bretton Woods Agreement also determined that the world system of fixed exchange rates would be set in a framework of multilateral free trade in which all international payment restrictions relating to current transactions would be abandoned. This was an important point, which amounted to a formal prohibition on the correction of balance-of-payments disequilibria through direct control measures. Nevertheless, considering the circumstances at the time, a system of multilateral trade and payment could not be immediately applied and so special arrangements were made. Governments in financial difficulties as a result of the Second World War were allowed, as a transitional measure, to subject the payment of international trade to national control for a period then expected to last five years. No such time limit was set on national control over international capital movements; here control could be maintained.

Finally, at the insistence of Britain, a procedure was introduced which made it possible to exert pressure on surplus countries to take measures of their own to restore equilibrium. If the balance-of-payments surplus of a certain member state became too large, so that the demand for its currency could not be met by the IMF, then not only could the IMF provide itself with extra quantities of this particular currency through loans or its gold reserve but it could also invoke the 'scarce currency' clause. In that case it was permissible for the other member states to restrict payments in the declared 'scarce currency' and by use of discriminatory measures, reduce the exports of that surplus country.[16]

The realization of domestic economic objectives within a framework of relatively fixed exchange rates and of liberalized flows in international payments would undoubtedly, here and there, give rise to balance-of-payments difficulties. By way of help, the Bretton Woods Agreement envisaged a series of short-term and medium-term loans. Countries in temporary difficulties could call on the reserves of gold and international currencies which were available on the General Account of the I M F.

The origin of these reserves was the compulsory contribution by the member states. When the I M F was first set up there were 44 members and by 1980 this number had risen to 131. Each member was assigned its contributory quota, largely based on its G N P and its relative share of world trade, and paid at the beginning of its membership. One-quarter of the quota was paid in gold or convertible reserve currency and the rest in the national currency. Since the quotas determined the voting rights of the member states, the foundation of an asymmetrical power structure was laid, with the United States and Britain acquiring in fact the right of veto.[17] The quota system could be modified every five years.[18] At a later period the E E C would also gain its own right of veto, after its global quota had risen.[19]

The loan system mentioned above operated as follows. When a country was faced with a balance-of-payments deficit, it could submit an application to buy foreign currency from I M F reserves with its own national currency as a sort of deposit. From the I M F's point of view, this operation would amount to a loan transaction. The use of the loan was subject to I M F control and it had to be repaid within a period of five years. The I M F, depending on its own reserve position, decided which currencies the applicant could draw from its General Account. Naturally for all these conditions the wishes of the drawing country were taken into consideration. In any twelve-month period, a country could draw currency up to only 25 per cent of its original I M F quota. In total only five consecutive drawings of the full 25 per cent (five tranches) could be granted to any one country. In other words, the I M F could only hold any one national currency up to a value of 200 per cent of the initial quota (75 per cent of the initial quota, plus 125 per cent resulting from deposits in exchange for five 25-per-cent I M F tranches).[20] Requests for the first drawing of 25 per cent (the 'gold tranche'), were normally granted without question. Requests for the next four drawings (the 'credit tranches'), were subject to increasing control from the I M F. When a member's currency deposits were run down to a low level, that member was invited by the I M F to exercise a special drawing right. In doing so, it provided the I M F with its own national currency, and this process could continue until the I M F once again held 75 per cent of that country's original quota. Such loans were termed drawings from the 'super gold tranche'. They were automatically granted and not subject to repayment within a specified period.

The size of the I M F reserves, initially somewhat limited, and the careful procedure concerning drawing rights were not accidental. These were obstacles which the American founders and later managers of the I M F deliberately set up to ensure that member states pursued all possibilities in the field of domestic policy to combat their balance-of-payments deficit before approaching the I M F. This attitude reflected not only the orthodox conceptions of the U S government but also the strong pressure exerted from international banking circles.[21] In this way the Bretton Woods Agreement contradicted itself. The limitations on exchange-rate flexibility demanded as a counterbalance a generous availability of foreign financial resources in order to bridge what were possibly temporary balance-of-payments difficulties, but it was precisely this bridge that was subjected to drastic limitations.

Another problem was the enormous gulf between the normative, ideal system worked out in Bretton Woods and the chaotic situation that existed in the world in 1945. Trade and payment restrictions had been increased as a result of the crisis of the 1930s and the subsequent war, and no country was willing to lift these controls in a hurry. Indeed, this was the reason why the Havana Charter was never ratified and why the International Trade Organization (I T O) did not come into being.

The I M F, lacking a liberal world economy and finding that it could hardly (if at all) fulfil its central function as an international credit institution, turned its attention to filling the gap caused by the abortion of the I T O. During the first decade of its existence the I M F concentrated on spreading and generalizing the principles of the General Agreement on Tariffs and Trade (G A T T).[22] It was only the advance of the trade liberalizing process that enabled the I M F to devote its full energies to its initial monetary and financial function. In the mean time it had developed its contacts with member states to such an extent that it had already become a very important centre for the discussion of international monetary problems and the promotion of technical assistance to the developing countries.

2. THE AMERICAN WORLD VISION

THE ATTEMPT TO RESTORE STERLING CONVERTIBILITY

The death of President Roosevelt in April 1945 led to far-reaching changes in American foreign policy. The *dirigiste* New Deal tradition, which via Secretary Morgenthau and the Treasury Department had strongly influenced the foreign policy of the President, made way for the State Department's vision, which was more in favour of free trade. When the development of an open, multilateral world economy under the leadership of the United States became the foundation of the new government policy, monetary policy had to be modified as well.[23] The new administration wanted an international system that would closely resemble the gold standard because this seemed to be the only way an open free-market economy was feasible. In this respect the Bretton Woods Agreement did not provide sufficient guarantees: the principle of external monetary stability was made too relative and member states with a balance-of-payments deficit could not be forced into taking countervailing restrictive measures in their domestic economy.

The United States government under President Truman therefore looked for ways to set world monetary recovery in a framework which corresponded to its conceptions now favouring a more free-market approach. To this end the 'Key Currency Plan' of the Harvard economist John H. Williams was taken up. The dollar and sterling, as stable and convertible currencies, would so strongly determine the international monetary system that the American and British governments, in return for their financial help, would be able to impose monetary stability and market liberalism on the rest of the world. In these circumstances the support function of the IMF would be practically superfluous. The new ideas of the State Department depended on a system of strong key currencies. In 1945 this was naturally no problem for the dollar, but sterling had been much weakened by the war. Moreover, Britain was a debtor not only to the United States, but also to its colonies and dominions and to still other countries, all of which held claims on it in the form of sterling balances. This was the situation which the United States saw as a unique opportunity, in return for substantial aid, to integrate Britain and the entire sterling area into its plan for the construction of an open world economy. The end of the Second World War with the Japanese surrender provided the occasion to cancel Lend-Lease.[24] Britain could do nothing else but send Keynes over to Washington to negotiate a major loan. The conditions imposed by the American government could be easily accepted by the financial community in London, since those contributions gave sterling an active role in world finance. Other conservatives, however, were more wary. They were conscious of Britain's weakened position in the world and wanted to limit the international role of sterling to a sealed sterling area in which the pound could still effectively exercise a dominant role. Still more distrustful was the Labour party, which had come into power in July 1945 and wanted to use monetary policy to serve its domestic objectives of full employment and social welfare. The manipulation of domestic monetary policy which was required for this, ran directly counter to American thinking.[25]

Nevertheless the balance of power in the post-war years was such that the British Labour government was forced to make large concessions.[26] The Anglo-American Loan Agreement was thus signed on 6 December 1945. One of its conditions waived for Britain the five-year transitional period which was originally to follow the creation of the IMF, during which time the restriction of international payments would still have been permissible. For current transactions Britain was bound to restore sterling convertibility from 15 July 1947, one year after the start of the loan.[27] In order to guarantee the success of this convertibility, the problem of the sizeable sterling balances also had to be tackled. This was a delicate matter since the largest creditors, especially India, Egypt, and Argentina, were developing countries and some of them were members of the British Commonwealth. In the text of the agreement the British government formulated its intention, in mutual consultation with the countries in question, to write off one-third of the balance and convert 90 per cent of the rest into long-term debt. As far as the liberalization of trade was concerned, the British found the American conditions more favourable. Since the United States itself wished to make no concessions on import duties, Britain was permitted to keep its Imperial Preference System unaltered.

During the public debate on the Anglo-American Loan Agreement in the British Parliament considerable hostility was expressed but, in the end, the arguments of the government (and Keynes) were persuasive enough to get it ratified. Undeniably important assurances which had originally been given to Britain at Bretton

Woods had been removed, but it was argued that the greater vulnerability which resulted would be more than compensated by the American and Canadian loan, amounting to about $5 billion.[28] In addition the American government had committed itself to work for the restoration of a strong international monetary system, and it was much to Britain's advantage to support this.[29]

With a view to a rapid transition to sterling convertibility, the British government grouped the countries of the world into four categories: those in the sterling area, those in the American account area, those in the transferable account area, and other countries. Transferable account countries, unlike American account countries, in effect agreed to use *and hold* sterling as a key or reserve currency only. On the other hand, all current sterling transactions in favour of the American account area from the sterling area or from the transferable account area would, on request, be converted into gold or dollars. The government tried to arrange things so that countries in the transferable account area would not immediately transfer their sterling balances to the American account area but instead use them as much as possible as a reserve currency. Moreover, those countries would continue to accept sterling for current transactions, even involving third countries, and would keep it to finance imports from the sterling area or, if possible, from third countries. For the outstanding sterling balances – in July 1947 amounting to about $10 billion, mostly in the form of British treasury bills – no long-term solution could be found. Only half of this sum could be subjected to special agreements according to which, in the short term, the accounts could be blocked.[30]

In the event, the measures taken proved quite insufficient to ensure a successful transition to convertibility. As soon as sterling convertibility was formally introduced on 15 July 1947, there was a headlong rush to use sterling for transactions from the transferable account area to the American account area and then to exchange it for gold or dollars. The indirect sterling convertibility of the transferable account area thus led to heavy pressure on British gold and dollar reserves. Just over one month later, specifically on 20 August 1947, the British, after consulting the Americans, had to suspend sterling convertibility again. The sterling area once more subjected direct convertibility of transactions in favour of the American account area to stringent restrictions. The indirect convertibility of transactions in favour of the transferable account area was ended completely. Britain fell back to the position where it was allowed to subject the payment of international trade to restrictions for a period of five years, as was envisaged by the Bretton Woods Agreement. At the same time a series of measures was taken to improve the transferability of the pound within the sterling area itself, within the transferable account area, within the fourth group of countries (on the basis of bilateral agreements), and *between* those three areas as well. In addition better arrangements were made regarding the blocking of part of the sterling balances.[31] In general the failure of the 1947 attempt to introduce sterling convertibility was a setback to the restoration of the international monetary system as framed by the Truman administration.

THE INTERNATIONAL MONETARY FUND ON THE BACK BURNER

The Anglo-American Loan Agreement was not the only strategy used by the United States to neutralize the unorthodox provisions (that is, provisions which were not free-market), in the Bretton Woods Agreement. Other measures, direct and indirect, followed. During the inaugural meeting of the IMF at Savannah, Georgia, in March 1946, Keynes was unable to achieve what he hoped. White, who together with Keynes had worked out the Bretton Woods Agreement and also had a certain *dirigiste* approach, was not elected as chairman. Instead this function was fulfilled by the more orthodox Camille Gutt from Belgium. Furthermore, the IMF headquarters were not placed in New York, but in Washington DC, under the protective wing of the American government. The Executive Directors, who co-operated closely with the governments they represented, were full-time not part-time officials. In this way the administrative staff was prevented from taking a strong, independent, supranational position.[32]

On 18 December 1946 the IMF announced the new parities for most of its then member states. These were parities which the governments had proposed based on the exchange rates which then applied. The IMF itself had suggested national parities with the aim of international equilibrium but had made no effort to impose these on the member states.[33] It thus relinquished the initiative in the area of exchange rates and in the following years continued to play a passive role in this respect. The effect of this passiveness was that the originally planned system of *relative* exchange-rate stability gradually shifted towards the principle of *absolute* stability.[34]

In the providing of credit to the member states, even the original competence of the I M F was an extremely watered-down version of the clearing union as proposed by Keynes. That potential which did remain was further reduced by the American representative. Under the pretext of insufficient resources or a danger of inflation, only very limited drawings on the I M F were allowed.[35] Countries receiving Marshall Aid were refused the right to draw from the I M F as long as the aid programme lasted.[36] Moreover, the operative conditions were interpreted in an increasingly restrictive way; the controls over the use of loans grew more stringent, the periods within which repayment was required became shorter, and so on.[37] Thus the labours of White and Keynes were considerably undermined by the United States' new policy. The smallness of I M F resources must be seen in the same context. The I M F was condemned to play a very modest role in the international monetary system in the first decade of the post-war period. During this time the I M F made only a marginal contribution to the relief of balance-of-payments problems in the world (see Table 35).[38] On the other hand, under the watchful eye of the United States and in co-operation with GATT, it did work for the lifting of trade and monetary discrimination between member states, as described above. In this way the I M F reconciled itself to the post-war world vision of the American government, based on a free-market-orientated *Pax Americana*.

At the very time when the I M F was playing the subdued role in the field of credit provision, the nations wrestled with serious balance-of-payments problems. Despite financial assistance and American gifts in kind, the demand for American goods and for dollars continued to climb. Europe's glaring shortage of capital goods, coal, foodstuffs and other things could only be met with the aid of ample imports from the United States. The American export surplus amounted to $6.5 billion in 1946 and according to experts would rise to about $10 billion in 1947. Before the war Europe had compensated its deficit on visible trade with a surplus on invisibles such as shipping and tourism but in the initial post-war period Europe was in deficit on this account too. Imports in these two years would therefore have to be financed by gold and dollars, and this operation alone would cost one-quarter of Europe's reserves.[39] The conviction grew that in these circumstances an automatic realization of a multilateral

Table 35 *Balance-of-Payments Assistance by the International Monetary Fund, 1947–71*

(in millions of US dollars)

	Gross Drawings on the Fund by Member States			Stand-by Arrangements (Amounts available at the end of the year)
	In US dollars	In other currencies	Total	
1947	461	7	468	—
1948	197	11	208	—
1949	101	—	101	—
1950	—	—	—	—
1951	7	28	35	—
1952	85	—	85	55
1953	68	162	230	50
1954	62	—	62	90
1955	28	—	28	62
1956	678	14	692	1,117
1957	977	—	977	870
1958	252	86	338	911
1959	139	41	180	208
1960	148	132	280	383
1961	822	1,656	2,478	1,415
1962	109	475	584	1,567
1963	194	139	333	1,743
1964	282	1,668	1,950	685
1965	282	2,151	2,433	280
1966	159	1,289	1,448	365
1967	114	721	835	1,804
1968	806	2,746	3,552	339
1969	1,341	1,530	2,871	849
1970	589	1,250	1,839	171
1971	10	1,890	1,900	222

Source: IMF, *International Statistics,* June 1972, p. 12

open world economy was totally out of the question. The failure of the attempt to re-establish sterling convertibility in July–August 1947 further strengthened this conviction. The only solution lay in an active, dynamic American approach. Hence the Marshall Plan, which was described in Chapter IX.

The stage for the Marshall Plan was set also by political factors. During the first post-war years the European political barometer was clearly pointing to the left.[40] There was a general consensus in Christian Democrat and Social Democrat circles in Europe on the need for various social reforms designed to spread welfare as much as possible; many left-wing leaders had served in the Resistance during the Second World War and their popularity had risen. The same could not always be said of the political, financial and industrial leaders of the right. Many of these had adopted a neutral or passive role during the war and some had even openly collaborated. This left-wing orientation in Europe led to the construction of the mixed economy there. In other words the domestic objectives of full employment and social welfare were to be given absolute priority, and national governments would intervene increasingly to ensure the execution of their policies, even at the cost of international solidarity.[41] This *dirigiste* vision of welfare policy ran directly counter to the American desire to restore a world economy, including Europe, based on open multilateralism and an orthodox gold standard. Furthermore, since the declaration of the Truman Doctrine in March 1947 the Cold War was running at a level higher than ever before. In this political climate the American distrust of the left-wing policy of the European governments increased and this strengthened the conviction of the Truman administration that a rapid and impressive initiative was necessary in order to press America's own international policy on Europe.

The Marshall Plan, which was put into operation on 1 July 1948, was the embodiment of this spectacular initiative.[42] It was a great success. Rapid results were achieved in respect of the recovery of industrial production in Europe, the rebuilding of infrastructure, and the promotion of price stability. In the area of intra-European payments and the restoration of open multilateralism, however, considerably less was achieved in the first two years. Only with the setting-up of the European Payments Union in 1950 would changes be made on this front. Nevertheless the deeper meaning of the Marshall Plan did not lie in its contribution to recovery in Europe, as decisive as this was. Still more important was its influence in reorientating the principles upon which the post-war economic world order was to be constructed. The dominant role of Marshall Aid in post-war recovery and the reduced impact of the IMF prepared the way for the great change of course in world economic policy that came about. The result was an open international market economy under resolute American leadership rather than the originally planned world economic order under the leadership of a supranational authority. The fact is that this change of course brought a situation which corresponded better to the reality of the day. The original formula for a supranational organization presupposed a certain balance of power between the major Western countries, but in the immediate post-war years no such balance existed.

THE DEVALUATION OF STERLING, A NEW STEP TOWARDS MULTILATERALISM

An open, multilateral world economy with a system of *de facto* fixed exchange rates required a general equilibrium among the different currencies; but the manner in which the parities had been decided in December 1946 gave no guarantee in this respect – just the contrary. Most governments, taking account of their huge import requirements for recovery, had chosen overvalued parities, which the IMF had accepted. Seen in the short term, this was a rational policy. Governments naturally wanted to import their needs at the lowest possible cost.[43] They could easily stop unnecessary imports by employing discriminatory payment controls, the use of which had been officially sanctioned by the IMF until 1952. The level of export prices was of no significance because there was no international competition in the first years after the war. Every government was convinced that after a few years its own national economy would be increasingly able to provide its own supply of goods. Falling prices, it was reasoned, would make the overvaluation of the currency disappear without any official action.

Sadly, reality turned out to be different. Until 1949 the relative stability of exchange rates could only be attained by using stringent currency restrictions, which obscured much fundamental disequilibrium. Not all countries were able to combat post-war inflation with the same degree of success. Economic recovery was not realized in the same way or at the same time by all countries. Differences in purchasing power between countries continued and indeed increased.[44] In 1948 these differences in relative prices started to influence exports here and there. Alongside the problem of relative prices, domestic monetary difficulties arose. Some countries, such as West Germany in June 1948 and Japan in April 1949, undertook a fundamental monetary reform. Others stabilized their currency through revaluations or devaluations in relation to the dollar. Most measures taken were designed to counteract pressures in the domestic economy, but they had unfortunate side-effects on the international currency market. For instance, the Italian and French decisions, in 1947 and 1948 respectively, to introduce a free dollar rate alongside the official one led to very disruptive cross-rates. The official sterling-dollar rate was £1 = $4, but calculated in terms of the lira equivalent on the free exchange market in Italy the cross-rate was £1 = $2.60. Goods to be exported from the sterling area to the United States were thus not transported directly but sent via Italy.[45] Comparable dislocations came about when governments introduced multiple exchange rates. In 1949 multiple exchange rates were being operated by eighteen member states of the IMF, twelve of which were in South America.[46] The manipulation of the international monetary system in order to serve national interests was pushed to its extreme form there. Some countries, which possessed large non-convertible sterling balances, began to sell their holdings on the black market for dollars at prices below the official parity. In particular such transactions were undertaken by countries in the Middle East whose royalties from oil were paid in sterling. Some dealers who gained these pounds on very favourable terms used them to buy goods from the sterling area which they sold cheaply in the dollar area.

The chaos quickly brought the US government to the realization that the Marshall Plan could not achieve its multilateral objective without a general realignment of currencies which would correct the undervaluation of the dollar and the Swiss franc against sterling and eliminate the mutual imbalances between the other currencies.[47] Although officially it was the IMF that ought to have inspired and proposed such an operation, the agency made no initiatives to this effect. The supranational role of the IMF had already shrunk to such an extent that the agency was not moved to action until, at the start of 1949, the Americans pressed for talks with European countries on the exchange-rate problem and for the creation of an *ad hoc* committee.[48] During the sterling crisis of August–September 1949, the American Treasury itself, anxious to see more realistic parities, took matters in hand. The IMF would only approve retrospectively what its members, under American pressure, decided.

The nub of the operation was a devaluation of sterling on 18 September 1949 by approximately 30 per cent in relation to the dollar. The new rate was £1 = $2.80. The entire sterling area, except for Pakistan, followed the British example. Furthermore, the British devaluation started a chain reaction all over Western Europe,

Table 36 *Devaluations of World Currencies,*
18–31 December 1949
(devaluations in relation to the American dollar:
1 US dollar = 100)

Sterling area (excluding Pakistan)	30 per cent
European countries:	
Austria	53 per cent
Greece	33
Denmark	30
Finland	30
Netherlands	30
Norway	30
Sweden	30
France	22
West Germany	20
Belgium/Luxemburg	13
Portugal	13
Italy	8
Switzerland	0
Other countries	
Argentina	47 per cent
Egypt	30
Canada	9
Japan	0

Source: BIS, *Twentieth Report*, p. 154

except in Switzerland. Some non-sterling countries outside Europe devalued their currency too (see Table 36).

The American recession of 1948–9 had put the devaluation process of September 1949 in motion. It had led to a considerable decrease in shipments of raw materials from the sterling area to the dollar area and had brought about a serious fall in the prices of raw materials. The adverse effect of this on the shaky reserves of the sterling area was sufficient to cause panic and push governments into adjusting their exchange rates.

Contemporary observers such as Ralph George Hawtrey found this decision premature and even argued that sterling was not fundamentally but only temporarily overvalued. Another criticism was directed against the disastrous effect of the devaluation on the dollar incomes of the sterling area. Exports from the sterling to the dollar area would have to rise immediately by almost one-third in order to maintain dollar incomes at pre-devaluation levels. Critics drew attention to the irrelevance of the motive of seeking a drastic reduction in imports from the dollar area by means of devaluation. They thought the ability of the British government to restrict imports in other ways was already so extensive that a devaluation was unnecessary. They said the only effect of such a decision was thus to push up the prices of necessary imports, and consequently the cost of living. This latter point was not wholly correct. Certainly it was true for Britain but other countries of the sterling area with a more liberal import regime towards the dollar area such as Australia and New Zealand suddenly found their imports greatly reduced, which relieved the pressure on the reserves in the Exchange Equalization Account.

From certain other viewpoints, devaluation could be seen as an advantage. For example, it put an end to the speculative pressure on sterling. Many foreigners, anticipating the devaluation, had postponed their purchases from the sterling area and the exporters from the sterling area had not immediately converted their dollar (or other) earnings into pounds. Such speculation now lost all meaning. The disorderly cross-rates also disappeared.[49]

In the long term the effect of the general adjustment of exchange rates was positive. The better balance among parities that was achieved in 1949, together with an increasing supply elasticity in the European export industries, cleared the way for the recovery of international trade during the 1950s. By eliminating the undervaluation of the dollar it also stimulated a flow of private capital from the United States which helped to close the dollar gap. The outbreak of the Korean War in 1950, and the arms race that immediately followed it, temporarily disrupted the equilibrium that had been achieved by the devaluations. The boom in the sales and world prices of raw materials suddenly strengthened the reserve position of the sterling area so much that Hawtrey seemed to have been correct. Indeed the pound seemed not as overvalued as had originally been suspected. Nevertheless the devaluations of September 1949 were not reviewed,[50] and with reason. In the second half of 1951 world prices of raw materials began to fall again, which led to a shrinkage of sterling balances in the rest of the world. The 1949 adjustments then came into their own.

FROM BILATERAL TO MULTILATERAL SETTLEMENTS IN
EUROPE: THE EUROPEAN PAYMENTS UNION

In the American strategy for the restoration of an open world
economy, just one element now was missing, namely an institution
that would handle intra-European trade payments on a multilateral
basis. The European solidarity that the Marshall Plan had promoted
in economic policy had not been consolidated in the field of monetary
co-operation. A first attempt to broaden Europe's structure of
bilateral payments had already been discussed, on American insistence, in the Committee for European Economic Co-operation,
where the co-ordinated application of the Marshall Plan was hammered out.[51] This led to an Agreement on Multilateral Monetary
Compensation, signed by fourteen OEEC countries in November
1947. Six of these countries declared themselves as permanent
members: the rest were temporary members. The results were
disappointing, and the compensation agreement was replaced in
1948 by an Intra-European Payments Agreement. All OEEC
countries were active members, and the reserves to cope with
multilateral settlement were considerably expanded. Even so, little
was attained.[52] Then there was a second Intra-European Payments
Agreement, which ran from 1 July 1949 to 30 June 1950. Once
more, the results were unspectacular.

The American disillusionment with this state of affairs had a
direct impact on the efforts by the US Treasury Department to
bring about a realignment of international parities. As already
described, this took place in September 1949. The Treasury believed
that the new, more realistic parities were a sufficient condition to
complete the automatic 'multilateralization' of payments in Europe.
But the officials responsible for the execution of the Marshall Plan
were sceptical of the Treasury's optimism.[53] They had agreed on
the necessity for more balanced exchange rates but did not believe
that such an adjustment was sufficient in itself to attain multilateralism in international payments. More in touch with the actual
situation in Europe, the staff of the Marshall Plan was aware that
temporary American help was not enough to put the European
economy on an equal footing with that of the United States. This
balance was nevertheless vital to the success of a multilateral world
economy, for only then could the dollar gap be *naturally* closed. The
staff of the Marshall Plan saw just one adequate way to restore

Europe's competitive position in respect to the United States: co-operation and economic integration between European countries. Only a European bloc as such could generate enough economies of scale and enough dynamism to keep on accelerating its progress towards American levels of competitiveness after the end of Marshall Aid in 1952. Integration presumed a far more intensive monetary co-operation than had so far been the case. It implied a complete transition from bilateral to multilateral payments within Europe. The limited payments agreements of the years 1947–9 therefore had to be replaced with a stronger institutional framework. At the request of the US Economic Co-operation Administration, Robert Triffin worked out a concrete scheme. It took up the idea of a clearing union that had been put forward by Keynes during the preparations for the Bretton Woods Agreement.[54]

There was much criticism of Triffin's proposal, from both the American and the European sides. The British view was that a rapid transition to multilateral payments would stimulate the conversion of European sterling accounts into dollars and thereby weaken the pound.[55] The British also thought that the monetary aspect of European economic integration could not be reconciled with their responsibility for the sterling area. According to the US Treasury, a clearing union would have an inflationary effect. The clearing union would embody credit facilities, and the Treasury thought this would make it impossible to force Europe into deflationary action, that is, to subject it to the discipline of an open world economy. Still worse, the clearing union, being intended as the stimulus for the economic integration of Europe, could be used for the creation of a specifically European monetary and economic zone, isolated from the dollar area. Such a development seemed very likely in view of the prospect that by the end of 1952 Europe would still not be strong enough to cope with the competitive challenge of the American economy. In these circumstances, it was argued, the dream of an open world economy with multilateral payments could never be realized.

The problem solved itself when the US Department of State involved Europe in the American Cold War strategy. The trial explosion of the Russian nuclear bomb in September 1949 and the victory of Mao Tse-tung in the following month increased the West's distrust of the Communist bloc and the former allies in Western Europe began to close ranks with the United States. European rearmament would be dependent on American hardware, European security dependent on the American nuclear umbrella. Simultaneously the American support for the European arms programme would offer an opportunity to fill the dollar gap which would open again when Marshall Aid came to an end. So the objections against an institutional strengthening of intra-European monetary co-operation fell away. The United States government pressed for action. A new European Payments Agreement was signed on 19 September 1950, and this one created the important instrument called the European Payments Union (EPU).[56]

The EPU operated as follows. Each month it took over all the deficits and surpluses that its members incurred in their trade with one another. For each country the total of bilateral deficits was balanced with that of bilateral surpluses, and the monthly net figure of each country was recorded by the twenty-year-old Bank for International Settlements (BIS), which acted as agent for the EPU. All balances were expressed in an EPU unit of account, the parity of which was set at one US dollar. The monthly results were cumulative, which meant that at the end of each month every member had a cumulative net balance *vis-à-vis* the EPU. A cumulative debt position had to be settled partly by relinquishing gold or dollars and partly by EPU credits. In the case of a cumulative credit position the EPU paid over gold or dollars, or credited the country concerned accordingly. The relationship between gold/dollar payment and credit was determined by a formula which related the cumulative position of each country to a quota allocated to that member. In order to begin, the EPU received from the US Economic Co-operation Administration a collection of currencies to the amount of $350 million.

The EPU was a great success. It was the decisive institutional link in the American strategy to push the still overwhelmingly bilateral structure of intra-European payments towards a multilateral system of payments. As an initial consequence, the Western payments system developed along a binary pattern – that is, a dollar area and a non-dollar area.[57] Within the dollar area the dollar had long been used for multilateral payments. Outside, however, because the dollar was such a strong or hard currency, it continued to be used almost exclusively for bilateral payments with the dollar area. Now the system of multilateral payments began to make new progress in the non-dollar area. First of all there was the traditional transferability of the pound within the sterling area. The EPU, of which Britain was also a member, signified a new important step forward towards complete multilateralism outside the dollar area. Although payments in the EPU were effected in terms of a common unit of account, the role of the pound, as the weaker reserve currency, was still not insignificant. Britain was the largest deficit country in the EPU so that multilateral clearing within the EPU already implied a fairly large transferability of sterling. Furthermore Britain tried to finance its excessive accumulated deficit as much as possible with long-term settlements in sterling and this too promoted the transferability of the pound within Europe. Now there remained just one major monetary task. The multilateralism which had been achieved *within* each of the two great regions of the Western world, the dollar zone and the non-dollar zone, should gradually be expanded into a world-wide multilateralism, comprising both zones. This ideal would finally be realized at the end of the 1950s, at least as far as the Western world was concerned.

THE TRANSITION TO A GENERAL CONVERTIBILITY

The transition to a system of general convertibility presupposed a conscious policy on the part of the European powers. Under the stimulating influence of the OEEC, both the sterling area and the EPU took a series of measures to this end. The effect of these was not limited to Europe. The sterling area included the whole Commonwealth; and the French, Belgian, Dutch and Portuguese currencies all functioned as reserve currencies in the colonial territories which were dependent on these countries.

From October 1950 onwards authorized dealers in the sterling area were gradually permitted to deal in American and Canadian dollars.[58] On 18 May 1953 a similar relaxation was made in the sterling area for the handling of French, Swiss, Belgian, Dutch, West German and Scandinavian currencies. The currency market in London could now conduct its international arbitrage operations on a much broader basis than before.[59] In March 1954 the British government went a step further. The bilateral status for countries was scrapped as a category, and transferable account status was now granted to practically all countries that did not belong to the dollar or sterling areas. The transferability as such was liberalized[60] and the distinction between current and capital transactions was removed. On the same date the London gold market reopened. Residents of countries outside the sterling area could now legally buy gold for dollars in London, provided the government had allowed that gold could be offered for sale.[61] Outside the sterling area a free market had developed earlier where pounds from the transferable account area were sold for dollars at a discount. Because of the liberalizing measures of March 1954 this free-market price gradually moved towards a level that in December of the same year lay only slightly below par, specifically at $2.70 as against $2.80 per pound. In February 1955 the Exchange Equalization Account, which operated as the central till for all gold and foreign currency (mostly dollars), was given government permission to intervene, if necessary, to hold the free-market level steady. From that moment the discount of the free-market rate in relation to the official one was a maximum of 1 per cent, so that pounds originating from the transferable account area had now become *de facto* convertible (this was already official for pounds coming from the American account area).[62]

Within the E P U a similar liberalization process could be observed during the 1950s. Trade restrictions were being rapidly removed as a consequence of pressure from the O E E C, and the increasing trade flows enlarged the volume of multilateral settlements within the E P U. At the same time Western European countries managed to raise spectacularly their reserves of gold and dollars from $8.4 billion at the end of 1949 to $17.2 billion in June 1956.[63] The improvement of the European reserve position made it possible to stiffen the conditions relating to the monthly E P U settlements in gold or dollars and to continue the process of trade liberalization. The more stringent conditions were introduced in the renewal agreements of mid 1954 and mid 1955. From 1 July 1954 50 per cent at least of any deficit in the monthly settlements had to be paid in gold or dollars while credit facilities could be used for the remaining sum. From 1 August 1955 the proportion of gold (or dollars) was raised still higher, to 75 per cent. Simultaneously various bilateral agreements were made between *excessive* creditor and debtor nations as well: these excessive positions were removed from the E P U system or consolidated, with the understanding that they would be settled in gold or dollars.

Any fears that the automatic credit facilities within the E P U would be inflationary seemed ungrounded. In fact during the process of the monthly settlements the emphasis was much more on multilateral payments than on credit facilities: between 1950 and 1956, 75 per cent of the total value of the monthly deficits and surpluses was mutually cleared; of the remaining 25 per cent only one-third was settled by means of credit, the other two-thirds being paid off in gold or in dollars. On the other hand, the EPU did facilitate the development of a protected *weak* currency zone. The automatic aid to deficit countries could have a discriminatory impact on relationships with non-OEEC countries because it encouraged a preferential liberalization within the OEEC area.

The potential discriminatory effect of the EPU was, however, very limited. The EPU was only a temporary arrangement which was designed to accelerate the realization of multilateral payments on a global basis.[64] Indeed on 5 August 1955, in signing a new European Monetary Agreement, the members committed themselves to disband the EPU and continue mutual monetary co-operation, once it was officially decided to restore convertibility.[65] Such a time appeared to lie in the near future. Since 1953 authorized banks in eight member states of the EPU could apply their own arbitrage operations on spot rates and forward rates and thus avoid the more expensive EPU multilateral clearing.[66] Furthermore, since March 1954 the transferability of sterling had been considerably extended and the pound from the transferable account area was *de facto* convertible. At the end of 1958, fourteen EPU member states – eight on 27 December[67] and six others immediately thereafter[68] – requested the abandonment of the EPU, the reintroduction of general convertibility, and the implementation of the 1955 European Monetary Agreement. At the beginning of 1959 general convertibility on the gold-dollar standard was officially established by all the EPU members. At the same time fifteen non-EPU members took a similar decision. This implied an abolition of the still operative exchange controls on current international payments. The two great monetary zones of the Western world, the hard dollar area and the weaker European one (that is, the sterling area and the EPU with numerous mutual links), merged into one large area for multilateral payments on the basis of liberalized merchandise trade and general convertibility with fixed exchange rates.[69]

CONVERTIBILITY UNDER THE GOLD-DOLLAR STANDARD

The IMF played a fairly minor role in the transition to general convertibility during the 1950s. Nevertheless on 13 February 1952, in the context of the termination of Marshall Aid, a system of stand-by arrangements was introduced. According to this, countries in temporary need could draw on the IMF up to a certain limit and for a determined period, irrespective of the debt position of the country concerned.[70] There were strings attached, however. Each application would be considered separately. At first there was little or no demand for these stand-by credit arrangements and indeed the amount of ordinary credit provided by the IMF in order to settle international payments remained small at the start of the 1950s. It was only with the Suez Crisis in the autumn of 1956 that the situation changed. Both France and Britain requested stand-by arrangements and in the December of that year received loans. This signalled the start of an intervention policy by the IMF which became gradually more active (Table 35).

In contrast to the IMF the United States was actively involved in the restoration of general convertibility, regarding this as a vital condition for an open, stable world economy, under American leadership. On the other hand it was essential to keep the size of world liquidity under careful control.[71] Therefore the American government, as explained above, had limited the credit potential of the IMF while it continued to seek the ideal of a generally applied gold standard. Nevertheless the Americans were conscious that a too stringent policy would compel some countries to maintain bilateral arrangements or abandon multilateralism. The United States government was thus ready to provide dollar loans and also encouraged the American private sector to invest abroad, even though such investment might have adverse effects on domestic employment in the short term.[72] Although the trade deficit of the OEEC countries with the United States remained enormous throughout the 1950s, it ceased to grow and even began to decline slowly. Even more important was the evolution of the general balance of payments of the United States (see Table 37). Because of American invisible imports and military expenditure, OEEC countries ran increasing surpluses with the United States, which led to an inflow of gold and dollars. From 1949 to 1959 the United States' deficit in relation to the rest of the world ran on average to

$600 million a year.[73] The gold and gold-convertible currency reserves of Western Europe and Japan now grew rapidly. Between 1952 and 1959 they almost doubled and by the end of 1959 they had risen to $22 billion out of a world total of $57 billion.[74]

The gradual redistribution of the world reserves of gold and gold-convertible currencies was a decisive factor in the successful introduction of general convertibility in December 1958. Alongside the American measures the economic recovery of Europe and Japan, in particular that of West Germany, thus guaranteed equilibrium in the new multilateralized world economy. The devaluation of the French franc by 17.55 per cent in 1958, followed by a successful deflationary policy at the start of the de Gaulle government, should not be overlooked either.[75]

Despite the unfavourable evolution of the American balance of payments, the world still believed in a continuing dollar shortage. In 1957 Donald MacDougall even published a study in which the dollar shortage was seen as the central problem in the construction and maintenance of a multilateral world economy.[76] This still prevalent trust in the dollar, together with the active wielding of American hegemony, would ensure that the gold standard largely amounted to a gold-dollar standard. The fixed parities were all expressed in terms of gold-convertible dollars, the gold value of which had remained unchanged since 1934. The dollar functioned in this system as the dominant reserve currency. Sterling remained a reserve currency in the sterling area but its weak position diminished the size of reserves still held in pounds. The guardianship of the United States over the I M F was so strong that an extension of international liquidity via this channel was only possible with American consent, and this was difficult to get. It is therefore not surprising that about $7.5 billion of the increase of total world reserves during the period 1949–59, estimated at $8.5 billion, consisted of American dollar obligations to foreign central banks.[77] Thus the multilateralized world economy with fixed, convertible exchange rates fulfilled United States expectations. In effect the United States was operating as a central bank for the West, controlling international monetary policy through its influence on world liquidity reserves.

Table 37 The US Balance of Payments, Summary, 1956–82
(in billions of US dollars)

	1956	1957	1958	1959	1960	1961	1962	1963	1964	1965	1966	1967	1968	1969
1. Current account														
1.1. fob exports	17.6	14.6	16.4	16.5	19.7	20.1	20.8	22.3	25.5	26.5	29.3	30.7	33.6	36.4
1.2. fob imports	−12.8	−13.3	−13.0	−15.3	−14.8	−14.5	−16.3	−17.0	−18.7	−21.5	−25.5	−26.9	−33.0	−35.8
merchandise trade balance	4.8	6.3	3.5	1.1	4.9	5.6	4.5	5.2	6.8	5.0	3.8	3.8	0.6	0.6
1.3. netto services	−0.6	−0.4	−1.1	−0.8	−0.8	—	0.5	0.7	1.8	2.3	1.1	0.9	1.4	0.7
1.4. netto remittances, pensions, and other transfers	−0.7	−0.7	−0.7	−0.8	−0.6	−0.7	−0.7	−0.6	−0.9	−1.0	−1.0	−1.3	−1.2	−1.3
1.5. netto US government grants	−1.7	−1.6	−1.6	−1.6	−1.7	−1.9	−2.0	−2.2	−1.9	−1.8	−1.9	−1.8	−1.7	−1.6
(1) *Balance on current account*	1.7	3.6	0.0	−2.1	1.8	3.0	2.4	3.2	5.9	4.4	1.9	1.5	−0.9	−1.6
2. Capital flows														
2.1. long-term capital flows	n.a.	n.a.	n.a.	n.a.	−3.0	−3.0	−3.4	−4.8	−5.9	−5.8	−4.4	−4.8	−1.2	−1.9
2.2. short-term capital flows	n.a.	n.a.	n.a.	n.a.	−1.2	−0.3	−0.5	−0.2	−0.5	1.0	2.3	0.7	3.5	8.2
2.3. errors and omissions	0.4	1.0	0.4	0.3	−1.0	−1.0	−1.2	−0.5	−1.0	−0.5	0.1	−0.4	0.1	−1.8
(2) *Balance on capital account*	n.a.	n.a.	n.a.	n.a.	−5.2	−4.3	−5.1	−5.5	−7.4	−5.2	−2.1	−4.5	2.4	4.5
3. Reserves flows														
3.1. flows on reserves (+ = loss)	−0.9	−1.2	2.3	1.0	2.1	0.6	1.5	0.4	0.2	1.3	0.7	0.1	−0.9	−1.2
3.1.1. gold reserves	−0.3	−0.8	2.3	1.0	1.7	0.9	0.9	0.5	0.1	1.7	0.7	1.2	1.2	−1.0
3.1.2. currency reserves	—		—	—	—	−0.1	—	−0.1	−0.2	−0.3	−0.5	−1.0	−1.2	0.8
3.1.3. net balances in IMF and in SDRs	−0.6	−0.4	—	—	0.4	1.0	0.6	0.0	0.3	−0.1	0.5	−0.1	−0.9	−1.0
3.2. others than reserves (+ = gain)	n.a.	n.a.	n.a.	n.a.	1.3	0.7	1.2	1.9	1.3	−0.4	−0.6	2.9	−0.6	−1.6
(3) *Official reserves transaction balance*	n.a.	n.a.	n.a.	n.a.	3.4	1.3	2.7	2.3	1.5	0.9	0.1	3.0	−1.5	−2.8
4. Total (1) + (2) + (3)	0	0	0	0	0	0	0	0	0	0	0	0	0	0

Source: *Survey of Current Business*, various issues (based on data of US Department of Commerce, Bureau of Economic Analysis)

Table 37 (*cont.*)

	1970	1971	1972	1973	1974	1975	1976	1977	1978	1979	1980	1981	1982
1. *Current account*													
1.1. fob exports	41.9	42.8	48.8	71.4	98.3	107.1	114.7	120.8	142.1	184.5	224.0	236.2	211.2
1.2. fob imports	-39.8	-45.5	-55.8	-70.5	-103.6	-98.0	-124.1	-151.7	-175.8	-211.8	-249.3	-264.1	-247.6
merchandise trade balance	2.2	-2.7	-7.0	0.9	-5.3	9.0	-9.3	-30.9	-33.8	-27.3	-25.3	-27.9	-36.4
1.3. netto services	0.8	2.6	1.0	10.1	14.6	13.8	18.9	21.4	24.8	34.4	36.1	41.2	33.2
1.4. netto remittances, pensions, and other transfers	-1.5	-1.6	-1.6	-1.3	-1.0	-0.9	-0.9	-0.9	-0.8	-0.9	-1.1	-0.8	-1.1
1.5. netto US government grants	-1.7	-2.0	-2.2	-2.6	-3.4	-3.7	-4.1	-3.8	-4.3	-4.7	-6.0	-5.9	-6.9
(1) *Balance on current account*	-0.3	-3.8	-9.8	7.1	4.9	18.3	4.4	-14.1	-14.1	1.4	3.7	6.5	-11.2
2. *Capital flows*													
2.1. long-term capital flows	-3.7	-7.0	-1.6	-7.9	-9.2	-17.9	-13.2	-10.5	-8.3	-13.9	-6.8	10.4	7.6
2.2. short-term capital flows	-6.5	-10.1	2.0	-1.8	-2.5	-9.1	-10.3	-6.8	-19.8	5.6	-33.3	-40.4	-35.2
2.3. errors and omissions	-0.5	-9.8	-1.8	-2.7	-1.6	-5.8	-10.4	-2.3	11.4	21.1	29.6	24.2	41.4
(2) *Balance on capital account*	-10.6	-26.9	-1.4	-12.4	-13.3	-32.8	-33.8	-19.6	-16.8	12.8	-10.5	-6.1	13.8
3. *Reserves flows*													
3.1. flows on reserves (+ = loss)	2.9	3.0	0.7	0.2	-1.5	-0.8	-2.6	-0.4	0.7	0.0	-7.0	-4.1	5.0
3.1.1. gold reserves	0.3	0.8	0.5	—	—	—	—	-0.1	-0.1	-0.1	—	—	—
3.1.2. currency reserves	2.2	0.4	0.0	0.2	-0.0	-0.3	-0.3	0.2	-4.7	0.3	-6.5	-0.9	1.0
3.1.3. net balances in IMF and in SDRs	0.4	1.8	0.2	0.0	-1.4	-0.5	-2.3	0.2	5.5	-0.2	-2.8	-3.2	3.9
3.2. others than reserves (+ = gain)	8.1	27.7	10.5	5.1	9.9	3.9	11.3	34.0	30.1	-14.2	13.8	4.5	-2.3
(3) *Official reserves transaction balance*	11.0	30.7	11.2	5.2	8.5	3.0	8.7	33.7	30.8	-14.2	6.8	0.5	2.6
4. *Total* (1) + (2) + (3)	0	0	0	0	0	0	0	0	0	0	0	0	0

Source: Survey of Current Business, various issues (based on data of US Department of Commerce, Bureau of Economic Analysis)

3. THE CONTRADICTIONS OF THE GOLD-DOLLAR STANDARD, 1958-71

TRIFFIN'S WARNING

The return to a system of general convertibility created great expectations. Many believed that the Bretton Woods Agreement could now be brought into full operation. But under American influence the spirit of Bretton Woods had been fundamentally altered in the course of the years, and the Bretton Woods System had in practice gradually made way for a key currency system,[78] with the dollar as the strongest key currency. As a result, the dollar area had expanded vastly and included now the whole of the West. The United States had become the world's banker and even the Eastern bloc depended on the dollar for its trade with the West and its mutual trade.[79] Sterling occupied a secondary status, remaining of significance only in the actual sterling area.

The gold-dollar standard, as introduced in most countries at the end of 1958, offered many advantages which had a stimulating effect on the further growth of the world economy.[80] Owing to the liberalization of trade and the convertibility principle, private bankers and financiers around the world, without any interference from central bankers and other monetary authorities, could organize a huge multilateral currency market which knew no restrictions in respect to international payments and at the same time guaranteed very stable exchange rates. Central banks did play an active role in the system. They regularly dealt with each other or with financial institutions such as the IMF and the Bank for International Settlements (BIS). Using their dollar reserves, they also intervened in the market in order to maintain the dollar parity of the national currency within the permitted limits of 1 per cent below and above par.[81] In addition the gold-dollar standard had the effect of imposing the discipline of American price levels on the rest of the world. With fixed exchange rates, all countries had to base their domestic monetary policy on the then stable American prices, and this stabilized world price levels. Finally the gold-dollar standard generated a free international capital market, with New York as the centre. International savers and investors were able, under ideal conditions, to lend or borrow long-term capital. Even governments made use of this market to raise long-term loans, the proceeds of which they used for their short-term policies of monetary intervention. Foreign commercial banks were also very active in New York.[82]

Nevertheless, despite its advantages, the gold-dollar standard also had serious disadvantages. The success of the system depended on an uncertain premise: America's continued and undisputed leadership of the world. Indeed, in the course of the 1960s, shifts took place in the economic standing of the nations. The EEC, and above all West Germany, expanded at a spectacular rate; Japan became the third industrial power in the world; and the developing countries gradually strengthened their influence through their raw materials and nascent industrialization. This redistribution of world economic might was very much at the expense of the United States.

Normally the exchange parities ought to have been adjusted to reflect the changing economic balance of power, but this was hindered by the gold-dollar standard with its stubborn preference for rigid exchange rates and its fixed gold price of $35 per troy ounce. As a seemingly irreversible trend, the undervalued American dollar, which had been so characteristic of the 1940s and 1950s, now made way for an increasingly overvalued dollar. The difficulties which the sterling area had experienced towards the end of the 1920s could again be observed – only this time the United States was the sufferer. Rising unemployment, slower growth of productivity, an increase in investment abroad seeking lower-cost areas, destabilizing capital outflows, and a steadily growing external disequilibrium, all made their mark in the American economy.

The problems of the gold-dollar standard did not remain limited to inadequate parity modification and its consequences. A second series of difficulties affected confidence in the dollar and the problem of world liquidity.[83] Even before 1960 Robert Triffin had irrefutably shown that, as far as world liquidity was concerned, the gold-dollar standard was fundamentally unstable and consequently in the long term not tenable.[84] Because of previous American policy, the role of the IMF had been reduced to providing conditional, short-term advances in the case of temporary balance-of-payments disequilibria. The much-weakened Britain, under the system of general convertibility, was hardly in a position to increase the amount of sterling balances because its gold cover was simply not sufficient.[85] The expansion of world reserves therefore relied totally on increased gold production and dollar reserves. Since the price of gold was fixed at $35 per ounce, there was no mechanism by which gold reserves could be dramatically raised. The total gold reserves of IMF members rose only from $33.5 billion in 1951 to $38.7 billion in 1968.[86] It followed then that a further growth in international trade would have to be accompanied by a worrying increase in the share of dollar reserves in total world liquidity. Moreover, with fixed parities, the decreasing gold cover for dollar reserves would, in time, be bound to generate so much distrust that convertibility itself would come under pressure.

Triffin drew attention to the unavoidable dilemma. Drastic deflation could considerably reduce American dollar liabilities in the rest of the world, adjust the gold/dollar proportion in total world reserves in favour of gold, and thus restore faith in the dollar. The danger, however, was that this could also lead to a world crisis and eventually to the abandonment of liberalized, multilateral flows of trade and capital; that is, to the destruction of the very system the proposal was trying to protect. The alternative within the framework of the existing system was the further expansion of dollar reserves throughout the world. This would have to be accompanied by a series of agreements, which the United States, as leader, would have to elicit from the rest of the world, designed to minimize or avoid altogether the conversion of dollars into gold. This alternative was taken into consideration by the Americans, but it too would eventually undermine the whole system. A declining gold cover could do nothing else but gradually lessen confidence in the gold-dollar standard and thereby increase instability.[87]

Besides, the alternative of further increasing the world's dollar reserves collided with the problem of how those reserves were *created*. Their volume was not determined by the actual needs for world liquidity but by the evolution of the American balance of payments. This was a derived factor and, moreover, could only partly be influenced by the American government. In addition, the development into a *de facto* dollar standard had introduced into the international monetary system a serious asymmetry which was financially and politically untenable. The United States obtained a *privilège exorbitant*, to use the terminology of President de Gaulle, to ignore balance-of-payments deficits, which went unpunished, whereas the rest of the world had to accept this discipline. Another dimension of the asymmetry was the continued political leadership of the United States at a time when, as mentioned above, economic power in the world was being redistributed. This redistribution brought the

Japanese yen and a series of European currencies, notably the German mark, the Swiss franc and the Dutch guilder, to the foreground as hard currencies. New potential reserve currencies thus developed which stimulated a competitive interconvertibility with the dollar and sterling and consequently increased the instability of the system. Psychological factors also had a destabilizing impact. It was resentment of this asymmetry which caused de Gaulle in 1965 to decide to demand the conversion of French dollar reserves into gold, producing great confusion and raising distrust of the dollar.

Triffin, who had highlighted the contradictions of the gold-dollar standard from the very beginning, called for an immediate reform of the international monetary system.[88] The Triffin Plan envisaged the creation of a supranational bank. It would function as lender of last resort for the various central banks which would deposit their existing reserves there. The new bank would also issue its own international currency and this would function as the sole official reserve currency for the whole world. In this way the delicate and arbitrary connection between gold/dollar reserves and the total extent of world liquidity would be broken. Moreover, the creation of international reserves would be matched to the actual liquidity needs of the world. Triffin thought that the IMF could be transformed into such a central bank for central banks. To this end he formulated a whole range of concrete proposals. The structure of the Triffin Plan clearly owed much to the proposals Keynes had made during the war as preparation for the Bretton Woods Agreement and also much to Triffin's own spiritual child, the EPU. Triffin's ideas, however, were not accepted in political circles. He had reintroduced the principle of supranational authority and at the start of the 1960s this was still irreconcilable with the American vision of itself at the head of a free, multilateral world economy.[89]

Jacques Rueff, who as far back as the 1920s had been extolling the virtues of gold to a series of French prime ministers, managed to win over de Gaulle to his ideas.[90] The French President at his notorious press conference of 4 February 1965 argued for a return to a pure gold standard (rather than a gold-dollar standard). The extent of gold reserves could be adjusted to the rising liquidity needs of the world through a policy of successive gold revaluations, or to put it another way, through the simultaneous devaluation of all currencies in respect to gold.[91] Although gold reserves in the United States in 1965 were still large enough to have entailed much

American benefit from an upward valuation of gold (in terms of all currencies), de Gaulle's call was ignored by the American government. There were psychological reasons for this and it was also pointed out that South Africa and the Soviet Union as major gold producers would stand to gain financially from such a move. Nevertheless the main reason was that the application of the gold standard as suggested by the French, would considerably reduce the role of the dollar as a reserve currency and thus undermine America's financial leadership of the world.

THE 'ADHOCCERIES'

The introduction of a general gold-dollar standard at the end of 1958 immediately brought the problem of the American balance of payments under the spotlight. A great academic debate was generated over the significance of the deterioration of the American trade balance in 1958 and 1959, and over the effect that the consequent gold loss would have (Table 37). Was this a chance and passing phenomenon or did it represent a definitive turn-about in the world position of the dollar?

The American trade balance recovered satisfactorily until 1967 but the American gold loss continued because the overall balance of payments seemed in a permanent deficit. Sizeable interventions were necessary to keep the dollar on level parity with the main world currencies. American gold reserves thus fell from $22.9 billion in 1951 to $10.9 billion in 1968. During the same period dollar balances held by foreign commercial and central banks rose from $8.95 billion to $38.5 billion. [92] The American government was caught in a trap. Its policy of an open world economy led by the United States implied a permanent government deficit, with overseas military expenditure and development aid figuring prominently in this respect. The government deficit had to be compensated in the overall balance of payments by a trade surplus. In the past this had been the case, but the increasing competition from Europe and Japan, together with the formation of the E E C, was bound to undermine the position of the United States in world trade. Huge capital flows strengthened this development. The formation of a bloc in Europe encouraged American companies to set up subsidiaries within Europe. When European wage costs went up in the late 1960s, the low wages in the developing countries would exert a similar attraction. No less important was the gradual overvaluation of the dollar.[93]

Kennedy, who was elected President in November 1960, was aware of the acute nature of the American balance-of-payments problems. He was afraid of a dangerous rise in dollar reserves in the rest of the world which, in the long run, would weaken confidence in the American currency. Such a crisis would shake confidence in the gold standard, in the whole liberal world vision and the American hegemony which lay behind it. Either on the initiative or through the influence of the United States, numerous *ad hoc* measures (often called 'adhocceries') were taken, with the objective of countering the spread of mistrust in the dollar. These measures can be divided into three categories. Some were designed to strengthen the gold-dollar standard directly, others to incorporate the IMF into the American strategy, and still others to control the export of capital from the United States.

The creation of the Gold Pool in 1960 belonged to the first category. The deterioration of the American balance of payments at the end of the 1950s increased the demand for gold in countries where official dollar reserves had grown substantially. Still more significant in this respect was the demand for gold on the part of private speculators who expected a devaluation of the dollar and other currencies in relation to gold after the American presidential elections of 1960. On 20 October of that year the free gold price on the London gold market reached a record high of $40 per ounce.[94] In order to avoid future speculative crises, the United States and seven other countries began in November 1960, via the Bank of England, to intervene systematically on the London gold market. This co-ordinated official sale and purchase of gold from the end of 1960 to the end of 1967 was so successful that the price of gold on the free market at no point rose higher than $35.35 per ounce.[95]

On the instigation and under the leadership of R. V. Roosa, Under-Secretary of the US Treasury Department, a number of other practical arrangements were made with European countries in order to strengthen the gold-dollar standard. For example, agreements were made about the accelerated repayment of war loans, the issue of so-called 'Roosa bonds' (non-transferable US government bonds held by European central banks and expressed in the currency of the country in question) and the 'swap' arrangements.

The 'swap' arrangements began in the early 1960s. Pressure on the dollar brought about by West German and Dutch revaluations of March 1961 caused the American government to introduce short-term, mutual credit facilities with foreign central banks. In February 1962 the Federal Reserve System took over this movement and consolidated it into a network of swap lines. The Federal Reserve Bank of New York (as executing authority for the United States), nine foreign central banks, and the Bank for International Settlements (BIS) opened credit facilities for each other. If a loan was made, it had to be paid off within three months, at the same rate of exchange as had been used in the initial transaction. It was also possible to renew the loan. Swap lines were thus short-term loans with exchange-rate guarantees for the lender. They were customarily used for official interventions on the international exchange market in order to counter speculative movements of hot capital. This was a very successful arrangement. At the end of 1962 the American swap network already amounted to $900 million, and in 1976 it had grown to $20 billion.[96]

The success owed much to the remarkable post-war resurrection of the Bank for International Settlements in Basle. Originally created in 1930 in connection with an arrangement for German war reparations, the BIS soon became inactive as a consequence of the world's Great Depression. After the Second World War it managed to develop into the official agency for intra-European payment schemes and particularly the EPU. At the same time it became a meeting-point for the governors of the central banks of Britain, France, West Germany, Italy, Belgium, the Netherlands, Sweden, and Switzerland, and, beginning in the 1960s, also of the United States, Canada, and Japan. Out of this developed the Group of Ten, with Switzerland as an associate member.

The swap network of the Federal Reserve System came about within the framework of monthly Basle meetings. After the establishment of the American swap network, other *specific* Basle Agreements were made, including those designed to help sterling. The first sterling rescue operation took place immediately after the German and Dutch revaluations of March 1961, a second in 1963, and a third in 1964, followed by others. In 1964 help was given to Italy as well and in 1968 to France. All these specific Basle Agreements also related to short-term loans, usually for three months with a possibility of renewal. From 1966 onwards, long-term Basle Group Arrangements were also made, with Britain as the main recipient. These too could be renewed.[97]

In the second category of protective measures for the dollar the IMF played a central role. Although the American government around 1960 still believed that the United States, as leader of the free world, should also be its banker and remain so, it nevertheless began to see that a call on the loan facilities of the IMF was not irreconcilable with continued American leadership and indeed could possibly become a necessity. The government came to think it desirable that the lending competence of the IMF be extended and its resources increased. The first step was to use the IMF statutes regarding the periodic reviews of national quotas. In 1959 a general rise of 50 per cent was approved, in 1966 one of 25 per cent and in 1970 one of 30 per cent. These rises, together with the quota payments of new members, lifted the IMF General Account from $9.2 billion in 1958 to $14 billion in 1959, $20.6 billion in 1966 and $21.3 billion in 1970.[98]

Alongside this, new credit facilities were introduced within the IMF (Table 35). During the annual meeting of the IMF in September 1961[99] the General Arrangements to Borrow (GAB) were brought into discussion, and they were approved before the end of the year. Thereby the ten richest countries of the world, the Group of Ten, gave an assurance that in an emergency they would provide extra resources to the IMF amounting in total to $6 billion.[100] The intention here was to be able to respond to the sizeable drawings from the IMF by the United States and Britain (and from 1968 by other members of the Group of Ten). The discussion of the GAB reflected the growing economic power of the European countries which considered the IMF as too dependent on the United States. It was stipulated that the IMF would not automatically get these extra financial resources but that the prior unanimous approval of the Group of Ten was necessary.[101] The GAB scheme was used for the first time in December 1964 when Britain borrowed a huge sum from the IMF. Another method to widen the IMF field of operations was to make the repayment conditions more flexible. Initially IMF drawings had to be repaid with American or Canadian dollars. But after February 1961 it became also possible to repay loans in the currencies of a number of Western European countries. So IMF drawings in dollars declined and instead a much wider range of currencies was employed.[102]

The third category of measures to protect the dollar consisted of American government measures to restrict capital movements. Under the name of 'Operation Twist', the Treasury and the Federal Reserve organized a strategy to raise the interest rate on government short-term debt relative to that on long-term debt. The intention was to discourage the outflow of capital.[103] In July 1963 Congress approved an Interest Equalization Tax on the purchase of foreign bonds by American residents; the aim was to moderate foreign borrowing in New York.[104] In February 1965 the same tax was imposed on credits granted by American banks to customers outside the United States. At the same time a programme of voluntary restrictions on the purchase of foreign bonds was introduced, including concrete guidelines for commercial banks, other financial institutions such as insurance companies, pension funds, and industrial concerns with overseas subsidiaries.[105] As time passed, the guidelines were made more stringent and in January 1968 compulsory restrictions on American investment abroad were laid down. As impressive as all these measures were, they remained too defensive and too heterogeneous to resolve the contradictions entailed by the gold-dollar standard. The American government was aware of this and therefore sought a more substantial solution.

THE ATTEMPTS AT A MORE FUNDAMENTAL REFORM

One historic attempt to reform the international monetary system was the introduction in 1969 of Special Drawing Rights (SDRs) within the framework of the IMF. The historical background for this was long and complicated.

Political leaders in the United States and elsewhere had gradually become aware of the serious shortcomings of the Bretton Woods System as it was operating since the beginning of 1959. There was in fact no mechanism at hand which could organize an orderly increase in world reserves to match real needs. European countries in Working Party No. 3 of the OECD[106] started fiercely to criticize the continuing American balance-of-payments deficit. Kennedy tried to correct this in his balance-of-payments programme from 1961 to 1963 when concrete measures were taken to reduce the deficit. Nevertheless Kennedy simultaneously emphasized the unshakeability of American world leadership. Translated into economic terms this meant that the United States within the framework of the gold-dollar standard would continue to function as the main world banker. The conflict between the two objectives of world dominance and external equilibrium would be resolved by the *ad hoc* strengthening of the credit function of the I M F. Since the Suez Crisis this particular role of the I M F had been revived to the special benefit of France and Britain. It could now be further extended so that the United States could take advantage of it.[107]

The Brookings Report, which was prepared in 1962 at the Brookings Institution and published in July 1963, made a forecast up to the year 1968. The American balance-of-payments deficit of $850 million in 1961 would be speedily turned into a surplus which by 1968 was expected to reach $2,700 million.[108] As a result, and taking into consideration the growth of world trade, the Report predicted a severe liquidity shortage. More and more calls were made, now also from academic circles, for the I M F to play a new role in this respect. It would not only have to broaden its credit activities but also be given competence to create international reserves and thereby provide an efficient solution to the problem of liquidity shortage. This vision had much in common with the ideas that Triffin had consistently defended since 1959–60 and with a proposal by the British Chancellor of the Exchequer Reginald Maudling at the annual meeting of the I M F in September 1962.[109] At first, the reaction of the American government was negative. Although the Americans wanted to see the role of the I M F extended, they thought that this should only be realized through an increase in the I M F's quotas and a broadening of its credit function.[110] European countries were unenthusiastic as well but for totally different reasons. They feared that an extension of the competence of the I M F would be a device to keep the gold-dollar standard in place; that is, to perpetuate the hegemony of the American dollar over the reserve currency system.

Nevertheless both the Americans and the Europeans were concerned over the need for increasing world liquidity, and in September 1963 an American proposal to study the possibilities was officially entrusted to a Group of Deputies, under the auspices of the Group of Ten.[111] The support from European countries for this initiative was a notable expression of the change which had taken place in the economic and political structure of the world. European countries wanted the discussions to be conducted outside the I M F, because the I M F remained dominated by the United States and because the developing countries were also expected to exercise increasing political control over the agency. The European preference was for talks within the framework of the Group of Ten, where the European position was strong. In June 1964 the Group of Deputies advised the Ministers and Governors of the Group of Ten to take certain concrete measures[112] and also to consider two important issues: first the adjustment mechanism for balance-of-payments disequilibria and secondly the problem of world liquidity. The liquidity problem was discussed in a study group chaired by Ossola and led to the Ossola Report of May 1965, published under the title *Report of the Study Group on the Creation of Reserve Assets*.[113] On the basis of this report a commission was set up under the chairmanship of Otmar Emminger of the Deutsche Bundesbank, and was instructed to formulate a concrete proposal. The Emminger Report, published in July 1966, came out in favour of a new international reserve currency, the creation and use of which would remain under the control of a limited number of developed countries – in this instance, the Group of Ten. The intention was that the report should serve as basis for definitive discussions of the liquidity problem within the I M F.

From the very first talks within the Group of Deputies (October 1963 to June 1964) the French had openly revealed their discontent with the existing reserve currency system and made clear their own preference for a modified restoration of the classical gold standard. The French further amplified their view during discussions in the Ossola group, proposing the introduction of a Collective Reserve Unit (CRU). This new reserve currency would be collectively created and managed by a select group of rich industrial countries (i.e., the Group of Ten), and would be distributed according to the size of existing gold reserves in the world. The CRU would be transferable, again with a fixed link to gold. Finally the creation of CRUs would require the unanimous agreement of the members of the Group of Ten.[114] The accent here clearly lay on the extension of world reserves, since these would be increased by the creation of CRUs. De Gaulle's press conference of February 1965 on the gold standard, which has already been mentioned, laid heavy emphasis on the idea of the CRU. Indeed, the French CRU proposal amounted to a disguised increase in the general price of gold. Instead of expressing such a rise in terms of an extra number of dollars, the French expressed it in terms of new CRUs. Furthermore the proposed system would greatly magnify the function of gold as reserve. It would be in the interest of each country to increase its gold reserves in order to maximize its quantity of available CRUs. American gold reserves would thus come under heavy pressure. Lastly, behind the idea of CRU transferability was the intention to replace the dollar as reserve currency with the CRU, which would be controlled by the Group of Ten.

Naturally the United States rejected the French proposals of 1965. Initially the American government repeated its former judgement[115] that maintaining international liquidity did not require a new structure, only new credit facilities. By making the credit function of the IMF more flexible, the difficulty could be wholly resolved. The world liquidity problem, the Americans went on to argue, was a matter for the IMF, not for the Group of Ten. This reference to the central role of the IMF and this negative attitude towards the Group of Ten ensured the Americans the support of the developing world. Indeed, after the resignation of Secretary of the Treasury C. Douglas Dillon and Under-Secretary Roosa, at the end of 1964 and the start of 1965 respectively, this support from developing countries increased further. In consequence, the United States changed its strategy. Henry H. Fowler, the new Treasury Secretary, began, from the second half of 1965 onwards, to defend the idea of a new international reserve currency *on the condition* that this new reserve currency would be created under the auspices of the IMF, that it should be valid as a substitute for gold reserves and that all countries, including the developing countries, should receive a share.[116] As a result of this, during the annual meeting of the IMF in September 1966, a joint commission was set up composed of the Group of Deputies of the ten richest countries and all Executive Directors of the IMF. Taking up the idea of Robert Solomon, this commission developed a scheme for Reserve Drawing Rights, which was discussed and approved (with certain amendments) during the annual meeting of the IMF in September 1967 at Rio de Janeiro.[117] Still more amendments were introduced after heated discussion in the Stockholm meeting of the Ministers of the Group of Ten in March 1968. Unanimous agreement, however, was impossible since the French and American viewpoints seemed irreconcilable. Remarkably, both standpoints now appeared to be the reverse of what they had formerly been. The United States expressed a frank desire for a new international reserve currency, which it had hitherto regarded as superfluous. On the other hand, the French Minister Michel Debré, who had seen the proposal to replace the dollar with the C R U torpedoed, became a fierce opponent of the idea of creating a new universal currency which, in the long term, might usurp the role of gold. He now called for a simple restoration of the classical gold standard by means of a general rise in the price of gold. Pursuing this line, he even alienated himself from his European partners.

The Rio scheme of 1967 underwent a number of important changes due to European, and especially French, pressure. The term 'Reserve Drawing Rights' was replaced with that of 'Special Drawing Rights' (S D Rs). The S D Rs were to be considered as rights given to all member countries joining the scheme, for obtaining credits from other participating countries, with the provision that the credits obtained had to be repaid (the so-called 'reconstitution rule'), although the obligation of repayment was conceived on very broad and supple lines. Decisions over the creation of drawing rights were to be subject to an 85 per cent majority, which provided E E C countries (representing 17 per cent of the vote) with an effective veto. The French student revolt of May 1968 and the subsequent departure from power of President de Gaulle robbed the French opposition of its force. In the mean time the I M F presented the change in some articles of its Charter to its members for ratification. By 28 July 1969 the necessary number of approvals had been received. Accordingly the I M F, in addition to the management of the General Account, was also entrusted with a new Special Drawing Account.

Although the term 'drawing right' was used, in essence a new reserve currency came into existence.[118] Precisely for this reason the introduction of S D Rs was a decisive turning-point in the history of the I M F and the evolution of the international monetary system. The traditional credit function of the I M F was supplemented by a new task, namely the creation of new world reserves. The I M F's role as a supranational body to carry through the planned reorganization of the international monetary system was thereby much expanded. The governors of the I M F would determine, in principle every five years, the volume of S D Rs to be brought into circulation. The demand for international liquidity and the expected increase or decrease of other international reserves would serve as guide. At its meeting in September 1969 the I M F, impelled by the fear of liquidity shortage, voted to go ahead with the first issue of SDRs, amounting to $9.5 billion, spread over three years starting from 1 January 1970.[119]

SDRs can be defined as a limited competence by one country to acquire an international means of payment from a third country. They were distributed to all interested member states according to the size of each country's IMF quota. Although it was not made compulsory to join the scheme, 104 countries made it known by the end of 1969 that they wished to participate. In the event of a balance-of-payments deficit, the participating countries could make use of their allocated SDRs without prior consultation. They could then directly approach other participants, who were obliged to provide them with a convertible currency in exchange for the SDRs. It was also possible to request currency from the IMF itself, which would supply a participant's needs, again in exchange for the SDRs. The value of SDRs was linked to gold and fixed at one thirty-fifth of a troy ounce. The total amount of SDRs allocated to any participant was called the 'net cumulative allocation' of that country. No single participant could be obliged to accept SDRs from third-party countries (in exchange for national currencies) to a value three times higher than its own net cumulative allocation. A further restriction was that each participating country had to keep a portion of its SDRs in reserve. Over any five-year period this portion must average at least 30 per cent of the country's net cumulative allocation. If a country failed to meet this requirement the 'reconstitution' clause had to be applied and the country had to reconstitute through repayments the above-mentioned minimum of 30 per cent. The rule on five-year averaging made it permissible for a country to make use of more than 70 per cent of its net cumulative allocation, though only on a temporary basis.[120]

The timing of the first SDRs in the early 1970s could not have been worse chosen. The whole reform was subsequently overtaken by the dramatic suspension of dollar convertibility, by inflation, and by the oil crisis. The world then had to cope with a surplus rather than a deficit of international liquidity. Moreover, the great discussion, interest, and emotions raised by SDRs meant that attention was centred on the liquidity problem rather than the more important question of exchange-rate rigidity in the face of increasing balance-of-payments disequilibria. The introduction of SDRs unfortunately shifted the priorities of world opinion in the wrong direction. Nevertheless SDRs remained a significant innovation. They consolidated the orderly creation and management of world reserves in the framework of a supranational institution.

A second reform with important international implications also deserves mention, namely the attempt to create a European monetary union.[121] In the 1957 Treaty of Rome, little attention had been devoted to monetary aspects of European unification. During the first years of the EEC, monetary co-ordination was improved by the creation of a few committees, but the impact of this was still fairly superficial. The success of European co-operation and the simultaneous increase of tension in the international system of fixed, convertible exchange rates, however, brought the question of the monetary unification of Europe more into the foreground. Institutionalists thought that it would be sufficient to set up a common, supranational organ as the means to bring about European monetary union. On the other hand pragmatists believed that this alone would be insufficient and therefore demanded a series of monetary integrations. It was only at the December 1969 summit at The Hague that it was decided officially to start work on monetary union.[122] A working group set up by the Council of Ministers in February 1970 under the chairmanship of Pierre Werner, the Prime Minister of Luxemburg, produced a report in October of the same year. The Werner Report agreed with a plan of the European Commission, which wanted to see union achieved in three stages. In addition the Werner Report defended the system of unchanging exchange parities and the principle of mutual convertibility. The margin for fluctuations of exchange rates around parity would gradually be brought back to zero. The alternative of a common currency was also mentioned. The possibility of a common system of central banks along the lines of the American Federal Reserve System was proposed, as was the creation of a European money and capital market. Finally, the need for a common budgetary policy was underlined.

The Council of Ministers, meeting on 8–9 February 1971, accepted the basic principles of the Werner Report and scheduled the first phase for the realization of monetary union in the three calendar years 1971, 1972 and 1973. At the same time consultation within the Monetary Committee and the Committee for Central Bank Governors was broadened, the system of medium-term financial assistance was worked out, and the creation of a European Fund for

Monetary Co-operation in the course of 1972 was proposed. Finally, by way of a trial run, the Council of Ministers requested the central banks to hold exchange-rate fluctuations between currencies of the EEC countries within narrower limits than those between currencies of the EEC countries and the dollar.[123]

Unfortunately the recommendations of the Werner Report and the ministerial decisions of February 1971 came to nothing. The monetary difficulties which shook the world shortly afterwards and the 1973 oil crisis led to such general confusion and uncertainty that *ad hoc* measures to tackle day-to-day problems took absolute priority over structural reforms. Nevertheless it had not all been in vain. The foundations had been laid for extensive reforms of the monetary structure of Europe, reforms which would come under discussion in the late 1970s.

THE RISE OF THE EUROCURRENCY MARKET

The Eurocurrency market operates within the international banking system and specializes in the borrowing and lending of currencies outside their land of origin. Since the largest part of the market was originally in Europe and most transactions were made in dollars, it first came to be called the Eurodollar market.[124] Essentially it was nothing new. Between the world wars international banks based in London had held dollar balances outside the United States; and after 1945, during the Cold War, Communist governments had switched their dollar balances from the United States to London fearing that otherwise their assets might be frozen by the Americans. What *was* new, starting in the 1950s, was that the circumstances which created tension within the liberalized world system also gave a sudden, additional impulse to dollar dealings in Europe. When European governments put restrictions on capital transactions in national currencies, American banks and other American companies seeking investment opportunities abroad for their highly valued dollars made great use of the Eurodollar market.[125] After the sterling crisis that followed the Suez War of 1956, for example, the British government clamped strict controls on the international sterling transactions of British banks. Accordingly, in order to maintain their position in international money and capital markets, these banks began to deal in dollars instead of pounds.[126]

In December 1958 when most European countries restored the

external convertibility of their currencies, foreign investment via Europe became very easy because all European banks could freely buy and sell dollars and invest these in any way they wanted. In the liberalizing climate of the 1960s, the competitive position of European and especially London banks was strengthened in relation to their New York counterparts. The London banks were advantageously placed for investment linked to the expansion of the E E C. The London Eurodollar market was totally free from Federal Reserve restrictions, such as those that related to legal cover, or prohibited the payment of interest on sight deposits, or set a maximum rate of interest on long-term deposits (Regulation Q). Besides, the London Eurodollar market could specialize in wholesale banking and in large, even unsecured, loans to trustworthy borrowers. Bank costs were therefore minimal which meant that in relation to the New York financial market higher interest could be offered to depositors and lower interest charged on loans.

The American balance-of-payments deficits of the 1960s and the specific measures the American government took to reduce the capital outflow strengthened still further the position of the London Eurodollar market *vis-à-vis* New York.[127] The introduction in 1963 of the Interest Equalization Tax on foreign borrowing in the United States closed the New York capital market for many foreigners and thus benefited London. The Voluntary Foreign Credit Restraint programme which was announced in 1965, and which became compulsory in 1968, had a similar effect.[128] Since American bank loans to foreigners outside the United States were now restricted to a certain maximum, attention switched increasingly to the London Eurodollar market. At the same time direct foreign investment from the United States was subjected to government controls. Consequently, American multinationals that wanted to make new or supplementary investments abroad either sought capital themselves in London or had their subsidiaries raise money there. American banks reacted too. They established subsidiaries in London or elsewhere and transferred some of their international bank activities from New York over to these new financial centres. During the period of restrictive monetary policy pursued by the American government in 1968 and 1969, these foreign subsidiaries of American banks were extremely active and thus gave a tremendous impulse to the Eurodollar market.

The exuberant growth of the London Eurodollar market during

the 1960s continued in the 1970s, although its structure fundamentally changed. The position of the dollar weakened in favour of some European currencies, especially the German mark and the Swiss franc. In West Germany and in Switzerland non-residents were subject to increasing capital controls. As a result of these controls, the Luxemburg Eurocurrency market recorded rapid growth. Other financial centres outside Europe also flourished, for instance in the Bahamas, Singapore, Panama, and Beirut.[129] Not only dollars and European currencies but also others, including the Japanese yen, were handled in these markets so that the Eurodollar market had developed into a Eurocurrency market and even into a so-called 'xenocurrency' market.[130] None the less London remained the most important centre and the Eurocurrency market the dominant structure.[131] The Eurocurrency market remained free of controls, extremely competitive, and biased towards the large transactions that characteristically took place between banks. For external investment it turned increasingly to the format of medium-term bank consortia. Sometimes as many as ninety-five banks participated in these syndicates.[132] London subsidiaries of American banks, in order to raise the liquidity of their deposits, began successfully in 1966 to issue transferable dollar certificates of deposits. An efficient secondary market ensured the quasi-liquidity of these certificates.

The development of a free Eurodollar and Eurocurrency market during the 1960s undeniably gave international capital flows a big boost. The *dirigisme* which had hitherto characterized the world economy now made way for a system of free international capital transactions. At first American companies drew great benefit from this because it enabled them to extend their penetration of the world economy in an extremely flexible way. But their dominance in this field gradually ebbed in favour of investors from Europe, Japan, and oil-exporting areas.

The liberalizing of the international capital flows stimulated the international trend of business activity. The liberalizing had such a far-reaching impact that national exchange restrictions and capital controls were doomed to failure before they even started. Such official measures were not only undermined by the flourishing free Eurocurrency market but also caused increases in balance-of-payments deficits, as shown by the American example.[133] The Eurodollar market facilitated and multiplied speculative capital movements. On the other hand it allowed European countries to provide for themselves financial services which had previously been bought from the United States.[134] Still more important was the significance of the Eurocurrency market for future levels of world liquidity. The streamlining and expansion of international money and capital movements improved the efficiency of the available reserves to such an extent that the balance-of-payments problems of the 1970s could be more easily resolved.[135]

THE DEMISE OF THE GOLD-DOLLAR STANDARD

The *ad hoc* measures to protect the gold-dollar standard, the governmental attempts to reform the system, and the reactions of the market all continually interacted. At the same time they in turn were influenced by a network of hectic speculative movements which, in the long term, brought the whole structure under strain. The devaluation of sterling in November 1967 and the ending of the Gold Pool in March 1968 were the first symptoms of growing imbalance.

Ever since 1964 sterling had been under heavy pressure. The big war debts, sterling's responsibility of being a reserve currency (albeit limited to the sterling area), and above all the crushing unavoidable difficulties involved in the restructuring of the British national economy, led to a large overvaluation of the pound as long as the existing fixed parity was maintained.[136] Uncertainty over the 1964 elections gave rise to the first major attack on sterling. This sterling crisis only abated when Prime Minister Harold Wilson on 17 October 1964 made the decision to defend the then parity of sterling at whatever cost; the balance-of-payments disequilibrium was to be wholly corrected through domestic measures.[137] Wilson's decision was based on the idea of a special relationship between Britain and the United States, an idea that had been revived since de Gaulle's veto on British entry into the Common Market. If sterling was forced to give up its position as a secondary reserve currency, an attack on the dollar would quickly follow. Beginning in November 1964, in order to help Britain maintain its fixed parity, the American government organized large-scale loans, with supplementary help from the IMF. The inertia of the British economic system, however, hindered a fundamental domestic adjustment. The overvaluation of sterling continued and the pound came under new speculative assaults in 1965, 1966 and 1967. The *coup de grâce* was inflicted in

1967. The Six Day War in the Middle East in June of that year, the closure of the Suez Canal, the expected Arabian flight out of sterling and the huge British trade deficit created such panic that the British government on 18 November 1967 decided to devalue the pound by 14.3 per cent. In other words, the official sterling parity was reduced from $2.80 to $2.40.[138]

The 1967 devaluation of sterling confirmed the great advantage of international co-operation in monetary matters. In 1949 when such things were done in a more disorderly and crude manner, the pound had to be devalued by 30.6 per cent in order to improve Britain's competitive position in real terms by 8 per cent. In 1967, however, by means of international consultation, the same effect was achieved with a devaluation of only 14.3 per cent.[139] Britain's clinging to the $2.80 parity for so long meant heavy losses for its treasury. In addition the British 1967 devaluation highlighted the terrible power of international speculative capital movements. The vulnerability of countries with a reserve currency in the system of the gold-dollar standard was now made clear to all and doubts as to the viability of the whole international monetary structure drifted through world capitals like fog.

A large-scale attack on the dollar now seemed unavoidable. It started in the open gold market in London. France's gold policy after 1965 had a substantial influence on this development. Not only did de Gaulle publicly reject the gold-dollar standard in 1965, and France convert its dollar reserves into gold in 1965 and 1966, but also France withdrew from the Gold Pool in June 1967.[140] This became known after the devaluation of sterling, and it increased world consciousness that the dollar and the pound would have to yield ground as reserve currencies. In order to counter the disquiet, the United States government resolutely persisted with interventions by the Gold Pool which held the free price of gold in London close to the official rate. But if the free gold price were to rise too far above the official rate, then central banks would be all too willing to sell gold dear at the free price and buy it cheap from the Federal Reserve. The convertibility of the dollar would thus in the long run be undermined.[141]

After the devaluation of sterling the intervention of the Gold Pool on the free London market rapidly became untenable. In the early years a net buyer of gold, the Gold Pool now became a huge net seller. In order to beat off speculative attacks it sold $3 billion in gold between 18 November 1967 and mid March 1968. If one adds to this the sales of October and early November 1967, the Gold Pool countries are seen to have lost about one-eighth of their total gold supply during the crisis. In these circumstances the Gold Pool could no longer be continued. The selling of gold not only reduced the total reserves of the central banks involved but also dangerously altered the composition of these reserves. Moreover, the speculation entailed no risk at all because the stable gold price of $35 per ounce comprised an absolute bottom in price evolution.

On 15 March 1968 the free gold market in London was temporarily closed. At a meeting of central bank governors in Washington on 16–17 March, it was decided to scrap the Gold Pool. On a suggestion from the chairman of the Banca d'Italia, Guido Carli, a two-tier system was brought in. Governments would no longer sell gold on the free market but would use their supplies exclusively for mutual monetary transactions between themselves. A free market would exist alongside, but central banks would no longer intervene. The American government was simultaneously given a guarantee that central banks would considerably limit their demands for gold. In the short term the new system seemed to achieve a degree of success for after rising to $43 per ounce the free-market price of gold began to fall at the start of 1969 and by the end of that year was down again to about $35.[142]

The abating of the crisis in respect to the price of gold and the gold-dollar standard was connected with a hearty improvement in the American balance of payments; there were actual surpluses in 1968 and 1969. The easing of pressure on the dollar must also be seen in the context of the social disorder in France in May 1968 and the social and political unrest in Europe which resulted. In France itself the chaos was so serious and the trade-balance deficit so great that the Banque de France saw its monetary reserves fall from $6.9 billion in May to less than $4 billion in November. During the Group of Ten meeting in Bonn on 20–22 November 1968 and its aftermath, no agreement on parity adjustment could be reached. West Germany refused to revalue the mark and the French delegation, which under heavy pressure had agreed in principle to a devaluation of the franc, was disavowed by de Gaulle in his radio message of 25 November. The consequent speculation against the franc finally brought President Pompidou to devalue it on 8 August 1969 by 11.1 per cent in relation to the dollar. The West German government then decided, on the day after the elections of 28 September 1969, to let the mark float. On 24 October it was linked once more to the dollar at a parity which lay 9.3 per cent higher than its pre-election level.[143]

The world, however, seemed to be on a monetary see-saw. The recovery of the situation in Europe was quickly followed by a new, dramatic deterioration of the American balance of payments. For insiders this development came as no surprise. The surpluses of 1968 and 1969 had been more apparent than real, resulting largely from a massive inflow of capital that was due to borrowing by American bank subsidiaries on the London Eurodollar market. The simultaneous deterioration of the American *trade* balance made the future still more worrying. The background to this was the expansive budgetary policy which Kennedy had implemented in the United States and which the Johnson administration had continued in order to finance both the Great Society programme and the Vietnam War. The decision not to increase taxes inevitably generated inflation which, owing to the fixed gold price of the dollar, led to a progressively heavier overvaluation of the dollar and further deterioration of the balance of payments.[144]

Increasing awareness of the fundamental shortcomings of the gold-dollar standard as conceived by the United States led to specialist discussion of monetary reform from the end of 1968 onwards. The Deming Group in West Germany, the Haberler Group in the United States, Robert Solomon and his study group in the Federal Reserve, newspapers such as the *Wall Street Journal*, to name but a few, all began to examine in what way exchange-rate flexibility could be built into the existing system.[145] Ideas such as greater band-widths for fluctuations around parity or 'crawling pegs' were more and more discussed.[146] In European countries, however, there was much resistance to the idea of revaluing their currencies against the dollar.[147] In their eyes such a move would allow the United States to avoid implementing necessary corrective domestic measures. Fixed parities, in contrast, would compel the Americans to take concrete action. It is against this background around 1970 that the political will to form a European monetary union must be seen. This determination was an expression of the growing European preference for fixed parities and an attempt, by means of bloc-building, to exert more pressure on the Americans to restore balance-of-payments equilibrium.

Developing countries meanwhile did not share the monetary conceptions of Europe. They were *a priori* against the principle of fixed exchange rates. The idea of a balance-of-payments equilibrium did not attract them, because a static vision of external balance did not fit in with their fundamental need for development and change. They favoured currency restrictions through which infant industries could be protected and scarce currencies channelled by the government into regions and sectors with high investment needs.[148]

The events of 1970 and 1971 proved that the European conceptions of monetary rigidity were wholly out of date and that the line the American specialists were following corresponded more to the real needs of the time. A reduction of the rate of interest in the United States, which was designed to stimulate the domestic economy, accompanied by an increase in European interest rates to prevent the importing of American inflation, led to a massive repayment of loans by American banks on the Eurodollar market. The increasing trade deficit in the United States made the situation still more precarious. Furthermore, European central banks placed their increasing dollar reserves with the Bank for International Settlements which in turn invested them on the Eurodollar market. To the extent that these dollars were lent not to the United States but to other countries, world liquidity rose. The fast growth of dollar reserves revived speculation against the dollar, first in favour of the mark and yen and later in favour of other European currencies.[149] On 5 May 1971 the West German government refused to undertake any further intervention to maintain the existing dollar parity. Austria, Belgium, the Netherlands, and Switzerland immediately followed suit.[150] During the meeting of the European Council of Ministers on 8–9 May 1971, the West German Finance Minister, Karl Schiller, tried to force a joint decision to uncouple E E C currencies from the dollar. France, however, refused any upward valuation of the franc against the dollar. West Germany and the Netherlands therefore decided to go it alone and float their currencies, and Belgium opted for a system of two-tier exchange rates (fixed exchange rates for trade transactions and floating exchange rates for financial transactions).

The further deterioration of the American balance of payments during the first half of 1971 just added further fuel to the fire of speculation. A report of Working Party No. 3 of the OECD found that there was a fundamental disequilibrium in international balances which could only be resolved by exchange-rate adjustments. There was now general agreement that the dollar was significantly overvalued and that specific measures could no longer be avoided. The climax was reached in August 1971. The West German mark once more began a powerful rise relative to the dollar, the free-market price of gold increased to $44 per ounce, and the flight from the dollar took on frenzied proportions.

On 13 August 1971 President Nixon and his most senior advisers withdrew for a weekend at Camp David. The Treasury Secretary John B. Connally Jr, who considered domestic issues to be of paramount importance, dominated the discussions. Then came the electrifying policy reversal that has been mentioned in earlier chapters in other contexts. On 15 August 1971 Nixon made his decision known: gold convertibility of the dollar was suspended; a temporary extraordinary import tax of 10 per cent was introduced; and the I M F was requested to make new proposals regarding a new international monetary system. To combat inflation, wages and prices in the United States were frozen for ninety days and a Cost of Living Council was set up.

Nixon's announcement caused general astonishment in the world. Everyone was aware that something had to be done, but such a fundamental decision as the abolition of the gold-dollar standard, taken unilaterally by the United States and without any prior consultation with the rest of the world, was regarded as an arrogant expression of the American policy of domination. But the gold-dollar exchange standard, intended as a modification of the Bretton Woods Agreement in order to perpetuate and guarantee American economic and financial leadership of the world, had since become hopelessly overtaken by events. In the industrialized, interdependent, and emancipated world of the second half of the twentieth century, economic leadership could no longer be monopolized by only one country. The American government was no longer in a position to force surplus countries into the required adjustment of domestic policy under the existing system and indeed was unable to contemplate far-reaching changes in its own domestic policy. In the mean time politicians, monetary authorities and experts had been looking at the wrong problem. They were still devoting all their energy to the quest for a mechanism that could make possible an orderly expansion of world liquidity, a problem which had been extrapolated from the situation around 1950. They had not fully realized the implication of the growth policies of mixed economies around the world. The problems associated with those policies were of a totally different nature. They related rather to ways of *restricting* surplus reserves as a means of fighting inflation, and to the need of improving external equilibrium without disturbing employment and income levels. In these circumstances the attempt to maintain an international free-market system with fixed parities was doomed to failure.

CHAPTER XII

TOWARDS A NEW INTERNATIONAL MONETARY SYSTEM, 1971–80

Now that the Bretton Woods System no longer worked, there was increasing fear that monetary disorder would have a fatal effect on world economic development. A serious effort was therefore made, by means of joint consultation within the International Monetary Fund, to design a new system. The effort failed. The floating standard made way for a *de facto* dollar standard. To limit the disadvantages of this, attempts were made to modify the system of free-floating exchange rates into one based on managed floating. This too met with little success.

1. THE GENERAL ESTABLISHMENT OF FLOATING EXCHANGE RATES

THE DISCUSSION OF THE 'GRAND DESIGN'

The Nixon Measures of 15 August 1971 had a profound significance. They put an end to the gold-dollar standard and to the fiasco of the American attempt to institute an international monetary order. Nevertheless the measures did not in any way imply that the United States was ceding its monetary hegemony over the West. On the contrary, the intention was to strengthen this hegemony, though on new foundations. Treasury Secretary John B. Connally Jr held that the price the United States was paying for its monetary leadership had become too high. The Americans had fully honoured their

obligations to maintain the gold price of the dollar and as a result
found themselves in a position of fundamental external disequilibrium. Since the other countries refused to follow the rules of the
system as they did not want to revalue their currencies in relation
to the dollar, the American government was left with just one
alternative. This was a crude, unilateral initiative that would force
surplus countries to change their policies. The United States simply
exerted its leadership function with the objective of restoring economic symmetry in the world. Europe naturally thought differently.
European governments thought that the United States had for years
been misusing its monetary hegemony. Its 'golden dollars rolled off
the printing press' to finance its growing balance-of-payments deficit
and strengthen its political and economic domination of the Western
world.[1] The suspension of dollar convertibility in 1971 was regarded
as the high point of American misuse of power. The American
government now renounced the domestic deflationary policies
which had been called for by the existing international monetary
system and laid the full burden of adjustment on countries abroad.
Because of the dollar glut, the rest of the world could do nothing but
accept this unilateral decision.

The animosity surrounding the measures of August 1971 convinced the United States as well as the other Western countries of
the basic shortcomings of the gold-dollar standard. It had become
clear to everyone that the mechanism to adjust balance-of-payments
disequilibria no longer functioned. The tightening of the 1944
principle of managed flexibility into the more rigid system of adjustable pegs, applied from the 1950s onwards, seemed to have been a
source of major instability. In the first place the principle of rigid
exchange rates seemed irreconcilable with post-war national policies
of full employment. Moreover, it facilitated private and even professional speculation. In a system of fixed parities and exceptional
adjustments nothing can be lost but only won.[2] A further basic flaw
was the asymmetry of different countries in respect to their economic
and political power, something that was not neutralized by a
supranational authority. As for international liquidity, the world
became increasingly dependent on the American balance of payments. If there was too large a surplus, then the reserves available
in the world were insufficient and the level of trade was threatened
by a deflationary climate. If there was too large a deficit, then
world liquidity grew excessively, confidence was undermined and the

danger of inflation increased. Since the dollar was the dominant reserve currency, the United States, in comparison with other countries, was able to finance balance-of-payments deficits fairly cheaply. On the other hand the American government could not permit itself the luxury of introducing unpopular deflationary measures at home. Even when there was tension in the foreign-exchange markets, the Federal Reserve System could abstain from any intervention, so that the costs of maintaining exchange-rate stability were regularly borne by central banks abroad. For all these reasons, Europe, Japan, and the Third World all forcefully demanded a new international order which would end the monetary leadership of the United States and the dollar.

The British Chancellor of the Exchequer, Anthony Barber, was the first to call openly for a new monetary world order after the Nixon Measures of August 1971. During the annual meeting of the IMF in September he offered a set of concrete guidelines for reform. The principle of fixed parities was adhered to, but it would be now much easier to adjust them. The dollar would no longer function as a basis. Instead the basis would be an independent unit of account, namely the Special Drawing Right (which at that moment still represented a certain amount of gold). The interventions of central banks would no longer exclusively be made in dollars. Barber preferred a system of multicurrency intervention that had already been discussed in Europe with a view to the preparation of the so-called 'snake agreement' (see p. 490). Balance-of-payments deficits would be settled periodically by a transfer of SDRs, and sanctions would be imposed on surplus countries unwilling to shoulder their part of the burden of adjustment (that is, reflate their economies). Within the framework of the IMF, a scheme would be worked out to substitute SDRs for the large amount of the world's official dollar balances; this would be accomplished through additional issues of SDRs. The issuing of SDRs – now the basic source of liquidity – would also enable the IMF to control the growth of world reserves.[3]

The Barber Plan was clearly aiming at a more controllable world system. The hope was that the IMF would evolve into an effective and independent supranational institution. The American government, however, under the influence of Treasury Secretary Connally, totally ignored the British reform proposals. Only when Connally left office were some allusions made to the need for a general reform.[4] Indeed, after Connally's departure in May 1972, the climate changed rapidly. His successor, the economist George P. Shultz, was more open to the idea of a Grand Design for the reform of the 1944 Bretton Woods Agreement. The IMF was quick to react.[5] As early as July 1972 it appointed a Committee of Twenty, composed of finance ministers and central bank governors, to plan the reform of the international monetary system.[6] At the same time it also formed a Committee of Deputies to make concrete proposals. Jeremy Morse, chairman of the Bank of England, headed this Committee of Deputies. During the discussions, three main positions could be detected: the American vision, which developed into the Volcker Plan, the European vision, in which there was a distinct French influence, and the view of the developing countries, reflecting the resolutions made by the third UNCTAD conference in May 1972.

The Volcker Plan, as defended by Shultz at the annual meeting of the IMF in September 1972,[7] was largely modelled on the Barber Plan. It remained true to the principle of fixed central exchange rates but like the Barber Plan sought to provide the system with greater flexibility. A wider band around the pivotal exchange rates would provide this greater flexibility. As an alternative possibility, a controlled floating currency was proposed. The plan also opted for a return to convertibility for the dollar but under certain conditions. First the balance-of-payments position of the United States had to be strengthened considerably. Furthermore dollars could be converted into SDRs only, and each country would be allocated a maximum sum of dollars which it could present for conversion (Primary Asset Holding Limit). SDRs would thus serve as the basis for the new world system, replacing gold, and their reserve function would be much enlarged.

The Volcker Plan also dealt with the mechanisms for adjustment and clearing. Since the inadequate functioning of these mechanisms was regarded as the chief cause of the collapse of the gold-dollar standard, an improvement was essential. This implied a better equilibrium between the balance-of-payments deficits and surpluses of different countries. It also involved more symmetry in the resolution of these balance-of-payments problems. That is, surplus as well as deficit countries had to take corrective action. To achieve this double goal, objective Reserve Indicators were proposed. For each country a basic level would be determined for the holdings of international reserves. If a country's actual holdings differed significantly from this prescribed level, either upwards or downwards, then regulations would be applied automatically and with increasing intensity to compel the surplus or deficit country into necessary policy adjustments.[8]

As a final point the Volcker Plan proposed a system of multi-currency intervention which would replace the former system of dollar intervention. A surplus country whose exchange rate with a deficit country was at the upper limit of the permitted band would be obliged to buy the currency of that deficit country. This currency could then be either held or converted into SDRs. Just as in the Barber Plan, the institutional implications of the Volcker Plan were fundamental. The authority of the IMF would have to increase a good deal and at the same time be exercised in a less discriminatory way. In addition the co-operation between the IMF and the GATT structure would have to be better harmonized.

European countries and Japan were not particularly enthusiastic about the American proposal.[9] For them, the reforms should be directed not so much at achieving a better symmetry in the obligations of surplus and deficit countries but rather at achieving a better symmetry between countries with a key currency and those without it. There were three major objections to the Volcker Plan. First, France and the smaller European countries emphasized the importance and use of stable exchange rates and believed that the American proposal would bring too great a flexibility into the monetary system. They were also sharply critical of keeping the dollar as an important reserve currency. Together with West Germany they feared that any future balance-of-payments deficit in the United States would lead to further expansion of world liquidity and thus inflame inflation. There should therefore be no limit on the convertibility of the dollar into SDRs. France even wanted a general convertibility into gold. A second objection concerned the automatic adjustment mechanism on the basis of Reserve Indicators. West Germany and Japan, as strong exporting countries, suspected that they would have to pay by means of a revaluation of their currency whereas deficit countries would ultimately remain passive. The mechanism would thus not curb but boost world inflation. The Germans and Japanese also feared that speculative capital movements would substantially increase. Future parity adjustments could therefore be expected with greater certainty. The third objection to the Volcker Plan had to do with the continuation of dollar balances. As a means of reducing and eventually eliminating the dollar overhang, Italy proposed a creation of SDRs in place of dollars, through a substitution account in the IMF. The substitution operation would lead to an accumulation of dollars in the IMF. These dollars would be repaid by the United States over the years on the basis of a voluntary consolidation scheme.[10]

The developing countries on their side were suspicious of any form of key currency, since this could always evolve into an instrument of hegemony. They consequently thought the central element of any reform should be the promotion of SDRs as international reserve instrument. At the same time institutional changes would have to ensure that the Third World was given more rapid access to the newly created international reserves.[11] The power of decision within the IMF should no longer be determined by the relative size of quotas, an arrangement which worked very much to the advantage of highly industrialized countries. The developing countries, which during the 1970s had become the largest borrowers from the IMF,[12] should be given a greater influence in decision-making there. In this way a special link would be made between the creation of SDRs and development aid.[13] The developing countries were hostile towards the existing system of distributing new SDRs according to the size of quotas. As contributors of very small quotas, they stood to gain only a small part of any new creation of SDRs. In order to acquire additional international reserves they therefore had to make a surplus on their trade balance.[14] They proposed a mechanism by which new issues of SDRs would be distributed through international organizations such as the IMF, the World Bank, and associated establishments, where concrete development needs would figure as the key criterion for SDR distribution.[15] The developing countries also demanded privileged access to world capital markets as well as IMF facilities for financing the long-term balance-of-payments deficits which would result from a policy of economic development.

THE FAILURE

The varying approaches clashed in endless debates. Morse's Committee of Deputies met at Washington in March 1973 and again in July 1973. The Committee of Twenty examined the various proposals and, during the annual meeting of the IMF in Nairobi in September 1973, approved an Outline of Reform that in effect amounted to a recognition of the discord. Different models were presented which could serve as a possible compromise between the suggested systems of improved adjustment and improved convertibility.[16] The finance ministers and the central bank governors, making up the Committee of Twenty, accepted in principle that SDRs would increasingly fulfil the role of international reserve instrument. This, however, was linked to an agreement of demonetarizing gold. SDRs would thus not take the place of national reserve currencies such as the dollar but would only function as a substitute for gold. The principle of a connection between SDRs and development aid was rejected on the grounds that it would be inflationary.[17] A change in the decision-making structure of the IMF was also not undertaken. On the other hand a few special finance schemes that favoured the developing world were envisaged.[18]

It was agreed that a definitive decision would be taken before 31 July 1974 on the problem of exchange-rate adjustment and convertibility; but when the final text of the Outline of Reform was published on 14 June it contained no such decision.[19] In fact by the time the text had been published, it had already been overtaken by the oil crisis and the subsequent monetary confusion.[20]

The attempt at reform was doomed for other, deeper reasons too. In effect the reform plans of Barber, Volcker and the French amounted to an exhumed version of the Keynes Plan which had been rejected by the United States in the run-up to the Bretton Woods Agreement of 1944.[21] The SDRs could be read as bancor, the altered rules relating to the IMF could be seen as a reference to the Keynesian idea of a clearing union and the mechanisms to achieve greater symmetry and to improve flexibility in adjusting balance-of-payments disequilibria could be seen as an expression of Keynes's concern to involve both surplus and deficit countries in corrective measures.

But the Keynesian approach was no longer adequate for the economic problems of the 1970s.[22] In the preparations for Bretton Woods, Keynes had been anxious to avoid the deflationary implications of the American proposals, which made no allowance for an adequate expansion of international liquidity and sought to heap the burden of external disequilibria on deficit countries.[23] Now the world was confronted with the problem of inflation. Domestic government policy, in its quest for economic growth, full employment and rising prosperity levels, was largely responsible for domestic inflation, and in the structure of the mixed economy the governments found that they could not put a lid on world inflation. Deficit countries could not abandon their expansionary policies. On the other hand the reform proposals amounted to an encouragement to surplus countries for further expansion of *their* economies. World inflation fed on such conditions. The reform proposals therefore completely missed their goal. Above all, the proposals took no account of the substantial growth in capital movements. A restoration of fixed parities (even though adjustable) was no longer relevant in a world where capital mobility had considerably increased.

Still another fundamental reason for the failure was the irreconcilability of national interests, which had become all too evident during discussion of the reform plans.[24] European countries and Japan had with much success embarked on a policy of export-led growth and wanted to continue its acceleration in spite of the balance-of-payments surplus that this implied. On the other hand they no longer wished to be compelled to take vast quantities of dollars into their currency reserves. The United States, on its part, recognized that its whopping balance-of-payments deficit ultimately meant a loss in domestic employment. The Americans too wanted export-led growth and in essence believed that the surplus countries ought to create the conditions for this by revaluing their currency. At the same time they did not want to give up the supremacy of the dollar as an international reserve and intervention currency. As for the developing countries, they too had their interests to defend. Their attention was directed solely at the relationship between rich and poor. Seen from this viewpoint it was necessary that the reform should seek primarily to internationalize the functions of reserve instrument and intervention currency. This process, in turn, should be used to encourage the economic development of the Third World, thereby paving the road to a significant global redistribution of wealth. In the light of these divergent and even opposing interests, it is not surprising that a compromise was elusive.

According to Jeremy Morse, chairman of the Committee of Deputies, what was missing was the political will to reach a positive result. This accusation was not wholly justified in respect of European countries and Japan. With the exception of West Germany, these countries were willing to make concessions to the interests of the developing world. But they also expected the United States to show more flexibility in relation to the European and Japanese standpoint. This expectation was not very realistic. As soon as the United States, by the actual development of floating exchange rates, had got the adjustment it wanted, it demonstrated no further interest in a formal reform. The developing countries, on their side, held stubbornly to their demands but these did not really seem relevant to the essence of the reform debate.

The general atmosphere of the negotiations also undermined the possibility of reaching a successful conclusion. The negotiations which had preceded the Bretton Woods Agreement had been dominated by two countries and by two experts and had taken place in a climate of political harmony. This was not the case for the negotiations in the 1970s. There were now opposing standpoints. Western Europe and Japan were convinced that the Bretton Woods System had collapsed because the United States had neglected its responsibilities.

Finally, the negotiation process itself was poorly handled. The International Secretariat produced highly technical preparatory reports but appeared unable to give a sense of innovation and coherence to the formulated proposals. The negotiating ministers were thus presented with a series of complicated and opposing alternative solutions and never could see the forest for the trees. That too was an important explanation for the failure.[25]

THE TRANSITION FROM AN OFFICIAL TO A DE FACTO DOLLAR STANDARD

The termination of the gold-dollar standard on 15 August 1971 not only set in motion the cumbersome machine for reform; it also generated a battery of practical measures and initiatives designed to adapt the world economy to the new situation. These practical attempts to adapt took place during the same years when the nations were trying in vain to reform the system. The American government, which had exploded the bombshell of August 1971 as a way of wringing concessions from the rest of the world, immediately came up with a firm demand. It held that the United States had become the victim of a system that had led to an increasing overvaluation of the dollar. For this reason, exchange rates, import duties, and defence costs had to be adjusted to the greater advantage of the United States. These proposed changes intensified the trauma of the

Nixon measures. Apparently the other industrialized countries of the West would have to foot the bill.

In the following September, efforts began within the Group of Ten, a meeting platform of financial leaders of the wealthiest nations of the West, to moderate the American demands. It was claimed that a restoration of the American trade balance would bring confusion and stagnation to the Western European and Japanese economies. Instead, delegates called for measures such as the lifting of American controls on capital flows in order to facilitate the repatriation of American capital. The French stubbornly continued to argue that only convertibility on the basis of a pure gold standard could provide the world economy with the necessary stability; so they wanted to see a devaluation of the dollar in terms of gold. Numerous multilateral discussions were held in October and November 1971 in Rome and Paris regarding the upward valuation of various world currencies in relation to the dollar. These talks were based on OECD world trade statistics and future extrapolations from them.

On 13–14 December President Nixon and President Pompidou met in the Azores in order to find a compromise. Nixon agreed ultimately to devalue the dollar in terms of gold and Pompidou, on his side, dropped his demand for the immediate restoration of dollar convertibility. The Azores compromise was ratified by the Group of Ten in their Smithsonian Agreement, reached in Washington on 18 December 1971. Under this agreement the American extra import tax of 10 per cent was immediately scrapped in exchange for an extensive multilateral realignment of parities.[26] The currencies of the major industrial countries were revalued in relation to the dollar and then once more linked to the dollar at a fixed rate. From now on, fluctuations of 2.25 per cent above and 2.25 per cent below the official rates were to be tolerated. The widened band thus increased the flexibility of the system without affecting the principle of fixed parities.[27] The official price of gold was raised from $35 to $38 per ounce, but this was of no operational value since gold convertibility of the dollar was not restored.

The Smithsonian Agreement confirmed the arrival of the pure dollar standard. Many developing countries had already linked their currency to the dollar after August 1971. As a result of the Smithsonian Agreement, the currencies of the most important industrial countries were once more officially linked to the dollar and were, in fact, convertible into dollars. The dollar itself, however, was no longer convertible into gold. As for SDRs, they were still too limited in extent to play a significant role in world reserves, even in the medium term. The dollar was thus promoted *de facto* to the main reserve currency of the world and *de jure* to a universal and dominant key currency.[28]

Although the American government would later make full use of the dollar standard to finance large balance-of-payments deficits, there was none the less in the United States a feeling of failure and disappointment over the new situation. According to experts, the Smithsonian Agreement did not provide a sufficient adjustment in favour of the United States. The revaluations in respect to the dollar were considered as being much too little. The evolution of the American trade balance, even allowing for the effect of the J-curve,[29] seemed to confirm this interpretation. In addition, no repatriation of capital to the United States could be observed, and this accentuated the climate of uncertainty. There was thus little enthusiasm on the American side to hold the Smithsonian Agreement in place at whatever cost.

The other countries of the Group of Ten had at least some reason for satisfaction. The unilateral action of 15 August 1971 had been supplanted by a decision based on extended multilateral consultation. Moreover, the revaluations had been held to reasonable proportions. Nevertheless all this was meagre consolation, for it quickly became evident that the American government had considerably widened its field of manoeuvre. Supported by the general consensus over the ending of the gold convertibility of the dollar and protected by its right of veto regarding the creation of the new SDRs, the United States could allow itself to handle monetary questions with a policy of 'benign neglect'. The glut of dollars in the world was sufficient in the long run to bring about an automatic adjustment favouring the United States.

The resultant feeling of impotence largely explains the European decision to press on with the attainment of monetary union as formulated by the Werner Report of October 1970. On 7 March 1972 the six original members of the EEC decided to limit the fluctuation-band of their mutual exchange rates to one-half of that which had been determined in the Smithsonian Agreement. In specific terms, these European countries set limits 1.125 per cent above and below the official parity; that is, a total band of 2.25 per cent instead of the 4.5 per cent total band under the Smithsonian Agreement.[30] Thus the mutual exchange rates of the Six wriggled within a second band that was narrower than the first. In this way the famous 'snake in the tunnel' came about. To maintain parities within the stated margins a particular system of multicurrency intervention was worked out in which central-bank interventions took place exclusively in European currencies.[31] The monthly settlements would be made in a 'basket' of international reserve currencies, excluding the dollar. The composition of the basket was subject to periodic review. On 1 May 1972 the three new members of the E E C – the United Kingdom, the Republic of Ireland and Denmark – decided to join the snake.

Although psychological factors played an important role in the decision to establish the snake, technical arguments also had some effect.[32] The monetary chaos of the previous months and accelerating world inflation had substantially widened fluctuations of the various European parities and this had disrupted the functioning of the E E C. For the European agricultural policy, monetary union would have an immediate operational impact. In addition there was the idea of a European bloc. If Europe was to develop into a political and economic power to rival the United States, then monetary union was an essential condition.

The E E C countries, with their system of mutual fixed parities, were rowing against the tide. Their political cohesion was still much too weak to enable them to make headway against fundamental monetary tendencies in the world, which in fact were developing along the lines of increased rather than reduced exchange-rate flexibility. The American colossus now considered that the time had come to restore external equilibrium by means of extreme flexibility. Other industrial countries which considered themselves extremely vulnerable because of the open nature of their economy (including some in Europe), finally decided to adopt a flexible monetary policy provided that this would serve domestic policies of employment and welfare. Indeed, even the E E C countries differed in their norms respecting inflation, increase in the money supply, and government expenditure, because they were developing at different speeds. This was inevitably a source of difficulties for the snake. As early as June 1972 the United Kingdom, the Republic of Ireland, and Denmark left the European snake,[33] followed by Italy in February 1973 and France in January 1974.[34] In contrast two non-EEC countries, namely Norway and Sweden, joined the snake,[35] and Denmark rejoined in October 1972. In effect the snake thus developed into a German mark zone, with the Scandinavian and Benelux countries following the footsteps of West Germany.[36]

The failure of the European snake had important effects. It led to the definitive end of the sterling area. Of the sixty-five or so countries which had linked their currency to sterling, only a dozen remained after Britain left the snake and even this small number diminished further in time. All former members of the sterling area increasingly diversified their portfolios of international reserves, with the share of sterling declining visibly.[37] In 1974 the Basle Agreements of 9 September 1968 relating to the settlement of sterling balances were not renewed. On 10 January 1977 a new Basle Agreement was reached between the Bank of England and eight industrialized countries to arrange an orderly liquidation of foreign sterling balances and put an end to sterling's career as an international reserve currency.

Another important effect of the snake's failure was the rapid generalization of floating exchange rates in the world. Britain on 23 June 1972 left not only the European snake but also the Smithsonian tunnel – the fluctuation-band of 4.5 per cent. Thereupon sterling started to float against the dollar and other important world currencies as well as against the other EEC currencies. From that moment the last dikes of the system of fixed exchange rates yielded (see Graph F). Britain's decision to let the pound float, and the disintegration of the sterling area that followed, generated a voluminous speculative movement against the dollar. Now that the weak British currency had been withdrawn from the European snake, a depreciation of the dollar in relation to the consequently strengthened snake seemed unavoidable. Distrust of the dollar was also undoubtedly fed by specific American factors. It was generally known that the American government was very disappointed with the Smithsonian Agreement. It was also expected that Western European and Japanese central banks would not be willing to continue accepting unlimited amounts of dollar reserves and this meant that, in the context of a larger-than-expected American trade deficit, further parity adjustments could be envisaged. The floating of sterling made the future developments of the American trade balance still more uncertain.

Another speculative run on the dollar followed in January and February 1973.[38] Measures taken in Italy[39] caused Switzerland to

Graph F *Exchange Rates of Major Currencies against the US Dollar, 1967–83*
(percentage deviations in respect to dollar parities of October 1967: average daily figures)

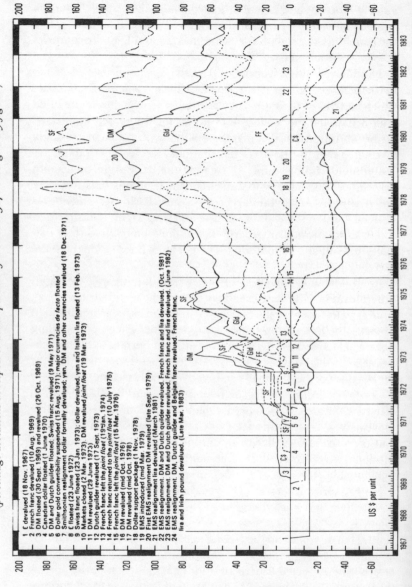

1 £ devalued (18 Nov. 1967)
2 French franc devalued (10 Aug. 1969)
3 DM floated (30 Sept. 1969) and revalued (26 Oct. 1969)
4 Canadian dollar floated (1 June 1970)
5 DM and Dutch guilder floated. Swiss franc revalued (9 May 1971)
6 Dollar gold convertibility suspended (15 Aug. 1971); major currencies *de facto* floated
7 Smithsonian realignment dollar formally devalued; yen, DM and other currencies revalued (18 Dec 1971)
8 £ floated (23 June 1972)
9 Swiss franc floated (23 Jan. 1973); dollar devalued, yen and Italian lira floated (13 Feb. 1973)
10 Markets closed (2 Mar. 1973) DM revalued *joint float* (19 Mar. 1973)
11 DM revalued (29 June 1973)
12 Dutch guilder revalued (17 Sept. 1973)
13 French franc left the *joint float* (19 Jan. 1974)
14 French franc returned to the *joint float* (10 July 1975)
15 French franc left the *joint float* (15 Mar. 1976)
16 DM revalued (mid Oct. 1976)
17 DM revalued (mid Oct. 1978)
18 Dollar support package (1 Nov. 1978)
19 EMS introduced (mid Mar. 1979)
20 First EMS realignment DM revalued (late Sept. 1979)
21 EMS realignment lira devalued (March 1981)
22 EMS realignment DM and Dutch guilder revalued. French franc and lira devalued. (Oct. 1981)
23 EMS realignment. DM and Dutch guilder revalued. French franc and lira devalued. (June 1982)
24 EMS realignment. DM, Dutch guilder and Belgian franc revalued. French franc,
    lira and Irish pound devalued. (Late Mar. 1983)

US $ per unit

panic and it decided to let its currency float. On 10 February the Japanese government closed its exchange market and also detached the yen from the dollar. On 12 February representatives of the United States, Britain, France, West Germany, and Italy met in Paris. It was decided to announce a new devaluation of the dollar in terms of gold. The official dollar price of gold was raised from $38 to $42.2 per ounce. Since the official gold parity of the other main currencies was maintained, this implied a series of new fixed exchange rates and an upward valuation of these currencies in relation to the dollar. In this way an improved version of the Smithsonian Agreement of 1971 was formally brought about. However, for sterling, the Italian lira, the Swiss franc, the Canadian dollar, and the Japanese yen, no new fixed parities were set. They remained or became floating currencies.

The new arrangement still could not put an end to the speculation against the dollar. On the contrary, at the end of February 1973 a new climax was reached so that on 1 March international currency markets had to be closed again, this time until 19 March. In the interim, on 11 March 1973, after discussions in Brussels and Paris, the E E C countries which still adhered to the snake (West Germany, France, the Benelux countries and Denmark) decided to maintain the 2.25 per cent total maximum fluctuation range for their mutual parities. At the same time they abandoned the fixed rates between the snake on one hand and the dollar and other important currencies on the other. This meant that the snake began to float against all other currencies. That is, the snake remained but the tunnel was taken away.[40] All world currencies were now floating. Nevertheless a great variety of specific arrangements were made with the aim of limiting the influence of these floating parities. Thus 1973 saw the beginning of an era of 'managed floating'. Indeed, the central bank governors of the Group of Ten, meeting at Basle in July 1973, made a conscious decision to practise managed floating in place of the system of free floating exchange rates.

In official terms the new situation signified the end of the dollar standard. In reality, however, the dollar held its ground and even extended its influence further. World reserves would increasingly be determined by the dollar. As an intervention currency too the dollar remained important. In practical terms most countries manipulated their floating currencies on the basis of the evolution of the dollar. The dollar also played a decisive role in the expansion of the international capital market. In June 1979 nearly 75 per cent of all transactions were still made in dollars.

2. THE ERA OF MANAGED FLOATING

THE MONETARY AND FINANCIAL IMPLICATIONS OF THE OIL CRISIS

The system of floating exchange rates – whether free or manipulated – worked better than expected. The fundamental realignment of the major currencies moved in the direction considered desirable to restore balance-of-payments equilibrium in the world.[41] Even the fact that the rate of the dollar showed an upward movement now and then (due among other things to a temporary improvement in the American trade balance) strengthened confidence.[42] For many, floating exchange rates initially seemed also to have positive aspects in the fight against inflation because they made it easier to control the divergent inflation rates around the world.[43] High inflation in a country would provoke a downward floating of its currency and thus prevent the automatic transfer of its high inflation to other countries. None the less, concern was felt over the inflation in the United States. Because of its leading economic position in the world it was possible that the downward floating of the dollar would be less than the domestic inflation rate. As a result the inflation could spread through the whole world.[44]

The oil-producing countries also had problems. Owing to the fact that oil prices were expressed in dollars, a falling international value of the dollar implied a decrease in income for these countries. At the same time the improving world economic position at the start of the 1970s pushed up the prices of foodstuffs and especially industrial products and this caused a serious deterioration in the terms of trade for oil-producing countries. The explosive quadrupling of oil prices in November 1973 must be seen against this background.

The raising of oil prices had important consequences for the world economy and the working of the international monetary system. In effect the price increase constituted a sizeable tax on the consumption of oil products in the industrialized world. It was inevitable that total demand in industrial countries would fall, and this largely explains the seriousness of the world recession of 1974–6.[45] The oil incomes of the OPEC countries rose from $33 billion in 1973 to

$108 billion in 1974 and this sudden transfer of income was not immediately compensated by increased purchases of Western industrial products by OPEC countries. Those countries therefore recorded increased balance-of-payments surpluses, reaching a total of $55 billion in 1974. The balance-of-payments deficits of oil-importing countries rose in the same proportions. These hard-hit importers were not only the industrial countries but also many Third World countries that had grown increasingly dependent on energy imports as they developed economically.[46] The national currencies of OPEC countries were nevertheless not important enough to function as international currencies. The suspension of gold convertibility meant that gold was removed from the scene and there were still not enough SDRs in existence. Only the dollar was available in sufficient supply to finance the huge balance-of-payments deficits in the world. In other words, the higher oil prices, together with the higher prices for raw materials and finished products, increased the dollar value of world imports stupendously and this development solved the problem of the dollar overhang almost overnight. This glut of dollars, which shortly before had been a cause of worry and annoyance, now suddenly became a valuable asset. The doubling of world reserves, which had come about at the start of the 1970s through the increase in dollar balances, thus greatly helped to satisfy the need for more international liquidity generated by world inflation and the oil crisis.[47]

Seen concretely, balance-of-payments deficits were financed largely through the transfer of existing dollar balances to the Middle East and through loans by OPEC countries to the industrial West. Part of the OPEC surpluses were siphoned back via credit facilities set up by the IMF in 1974 for oil-importing countries and by comparable arrangements in other international organizations (Table 38). Nevertheless most petrodollars found their way back to the West by means of OPEC deposits in the Eurocurrency market. Numerous Western governments borrowed large sums from European banks to cover their deficits. The London Eurocurrency market profited from this and flourished as never before. American banks, since January 1974 again able to lend freely to foreigners, also responded rapidly to the expansive demand for dollars. The market was thus more or less able to finance the world trade deficits of 1974 and the following years.[48] From 1976 uncertainty about the creditworthiness of some countries breathed new life into the old forms of official rescue operations such as those organized by the Bank for International Settlements and the IMF[49] (Table 38).

The flourishing of the Eurocurrency market in the course of the 1970s had its drawbacks as well as its advantages. For one thing it stimulated speculative capital movements and thus worsened instability in exchange rates between the main currencies of the world. Furthermore, it functioned largely beyond the control of national governments. The consequence of this was a decrease in the efficiency of national monetary policy. Finally, it increased the danger of a crisis in the international banking system. The Eurocurrency market worked without prescribed banking ratios and invested its deposits quite intensively, to a large degree through inter-bank operations. This intensification was greatly facilitated by the extraordinary progress of international communications. There exists, however, a serious discrepancy between the attitude of savers and that of investors. Most Eurocurrency deposits are short-term ones whereas most borrowers want medium-term or long-term loans. To even out this imbalance somewhat, European banks make use of the technique of roll-over credits, whereby short-term credit is transformed into long-term credit. Long-term loans are formally made on a medium-term basis only (for example, six or twelve months), but these can be regularly renewed over a period of three, five, or ten years. From the statistics it appears that these long-term loans on the Eurocurrency market are financed by sight deposits or quasi-sight deposits. As early as 1974 a serious banking crisis did take place, leading to the failure of the German bank Herstatt.

The instability of the Eurocurrency market was further increased by the structural weakness of some major borrowers. The debts of developing countries against industrial countries rose sharply, from $74 billion in 1970 to $264 billion in 1977. The further oil price rises of 1978–9 exacerbated this situation. In consequence, the developing countries were forced increasingly into extra borrowing on the Eurocurrency market. Between 1970 and 1978 the share represented by these loans in their total debt rose from 16.9 per cent to 38.5 per cent and continued to grow. Eastern bloc countries formed a second category of important but dubious debtors. Their total debts against OECD countries rose considerably during the 1970s and by the end of 1978 stood at almost $60 billion; and the Eastern bloc, like the Third World, began to borrow heavily from the Eurocurrency market. The political and economic difficulties in

Table 38 *Balance-of-Payments Assistance by, and Reserve Tranche Drawing on, the International Monetary Fund, 1972–82*
(in million of SDRs)

	Annual Amounts										
	1972	1973	1974	1975	1976	1977	1978	1979	1980	1981	1982
1. *Funds policies and facilities (drawings)*	1,612	733	4,053	4,658	7,010	3,425	3,744	1,843	3,753	7,082	8,784
Reserve tranche	962	391	966	723	991	80	2,536	147	359	310	1,336
Credit tranche (ordinary)	340	228	1,265	641	1,478	2,895	421	648	855	1,662	1,064
Compensatory financing (export shortfalls)	299	113	107	239	2,308	241	578	572	980	1,231	2,333
Compensatory financing (cereal import excesses)	—	—	—	—	—	—	—	—	—	12	295
Buffer stock financing	11	—	—	5	—	—	36	38	—	—	144
Extended fund facility (ordinary)	—	—	—	8	90	209	174	132	339	1,041	1,057
Oil facility	—	—	1,716	3,043	2,143	—	—	—	—	—	—
Supplementary financing	—	—	—	—	—	—	—	306	1,218	2,040	1,711
– Credit tranche	—	—	—	—	—	—	—	205	943	1,469	982
– Extended facility	—	—	—	—	—	—	—	101	275	571	728
Enlarged access policy	—	—	—	—	—	—	—	—	—	787	846
– Credit tranche	—	—	—	—	—	—	—	—	—	306	491
– Extended facility	—	—	—	—	—	—	—	—	—	481	354
2. *Fund-administered facilities*	—	—	—	—	14	181	713	546	1,284	441	54
Oil facility subsidy account (grants)	—	—	—	—	14	28	25	19	28	50	9
Trust fund (loans)	—	—	—	—	—	153	688	527	1,256	368	—
Supplementary financing	—	—	—	—	—	—	—	—	—	23	44

Source: IMF, *The International Monetary Fund: Its Evolution, Organization, and Activities*

Poland during 1980–1, however, made it clear that the creditworthiness of socialist countries could not be wholly trusted.

The danger of the overheating of the Eurocurrency market caused a number of safety measures to be taken. The Eurocurrency market itself tried to put its house in order by introducing more self-discipline. Stringent conditions of creditworthiness were laid down for participation in inter-bank operations. In 1978 the West German Eurobanks made an agreement with the government by which they voluntarily provided information about their foreign subsidiaries. Eurobanks also accepted greater supervision from the Bank for International Settlements (BIS) in Basle. In 1979 the BIS even began to examine ways in which the Eurobanks could be subjected to a system of compulsory reserves. In the same year the American government actually implemented concrete measures along the same lines. Finally, the Eurobanks themselves made overtures to the international institutions. By about 1980 they had extended themselves as far as they could in the financing of balance-of-payments deficits in the world. They therefore came to believe that official aid programmes had to be relaunched on a large scale; that is, closer co-operation between the public and private sectors was now desirable. This too offered the prospect of the Eurobanks revealing more of their operations to various authorities.

THE CONSOLIDATION OF THE DE FACTO DOLLAR STANDARD

The definitive reform proposal for the international monetary system that was made public in 1974 reflected, as already mentioned, no clear standpoint. It did not launch any new, promising ideas and it was quietly buried. The Committee of Twenty, which had been responsible for the preparation of the proposal, was replaced by an Interim Committee, which took a more practical line. At the same time a new shift of power took place within the IMF in favour of the five greatest industrial countries: the United States, Japan, West Germany, Britain, and France. These countries had already held a meeting during the IMF annual gathering in Nairobi in September 1973, and they continued to meet regularly in order to co-ordinate their strategies against the world recession. The fact is that after 1973 all major international economic decisions were prepared by this limited Group of Five before being presented for ratification to the Interim Committee.[50]

Within the Group of Five the United States wielded considerable power. This was partly due to the improvement in the American balance of payments and partly due to forecasts that Europe and Japan had more difficult economic times ahead than the United States because they were more dependent on energy imports.[51] The result was the orientation of the international monetary system towards the consolidation of a *de facto* dollar standard based on the conditions proposed by the American government. And this gave a new impulse to the leadership of the United States in the Western world.

The first important point of action in this respect was the strengthening of the dollar as dominant reserve currency. To this end the position of the two rivals, namely gold and SDRs, had to be weakened. At first sight the weakening of the position of gold seemed a difficult task, especially in view of the French reservations. In 1975, the Group of Five finally reached a compromise. The European countries and Japan accepted the demonetization of gold. They agreed that the IMF should eliminate all references to gold in its charter and in its transactions as well. They also agreed to a sale, within a two-year period, of one-third of the IMF's gold reserves. In return the United States consented that one-half of the proceeds of the sale should accrue to the member states in proportion to their paid-up quotas. The other half of the capital gain would be transferred to a Trust Fund. (According to America's original proposal all of the capital gain from the sale of gold would have gone to the Trust Fund and thereafter been used to help the developing countries.[52]) The decision was approved by the Interim Committee in Kingston, Jamaica, on 7–8 January 1976.[53]

The other rival of the dollar to be resisted was the system of the SDRs. If expanded too much, SDRs could eventually replace the dollar as reserve currency and raise the significance and power of the IMF. To counter the expansion of SDRs then, the proposal of the Third World to establish a direct link between SDR issue and development aid was rejected. Furthermore, to discourage such a link in the future the former 80 per cent voting majority necessary within the IMF was raised to 85 per cent.[54] This decision was taken to protect the American veto, but it satisfied Europe because it accorded veto power to the EEC too. To compensate the Third World for this disappointment, the credit facilities by the IMF for oil imports were renewed and expanded. The expansion was financed by an increase in the quotas of member states in 1976. On a suggestion from European countries in 1976, the joint quota of the OPEC countries was raised from 5 to 10 per cent of the total.[55] At the same time additional quota increases were agreed and came into operation on 1 April 1978 and 1 April 1980. The former obligation to pay one-quarter in gold was abandoned. The first increase was to be paid in the national currency and the second in SDRs.

The value of SDRs, originally set at 1 SDR = 1/35 of one troy ounce of gold, had become a serious problem after the suspension of gold convertibility for the dollar and the generalization of floating exchange rates. The Interim Committee had decided that, starting from 1 July 1974, the value of SDRs would be determined on the basis of a weighted average of the exchange rates of a basket of sixteen major currencies. The weighting was based on the value of foreign trade and on the political importance of the countries involved. The system would in principle be reviewed every five years. The first such review, which became effective on 1 January 1981, reduced the size of the basket to the five main currencies of the West: the American dollar (42 per cent), the German mark (19 per cent), the Japanese yen (13 per cent), the French franc (13 per cent) and the British pound (also 13 per cent). From this method of expressing the value of SDRs, it is clear how dominant the dollar remained in the world monetary system.[56]

The strategy of limiting the issue of SDRs was not restricted to the refusal to link SDR creation with development aid. Indeed, SDR issue *per se* was limited. After the emissions of 1970, 1971 and 1972, totalling $9.3 billion, no more were made for about six years. At the Kingston, Jamaica meeting of the Interim Committee in 1976 the restrictive policy was confirmed, and not until September 1978 did the IMF approve new emissions of SDRs of $4 billion a year, for 1979, 1980 and 1981. This brought the total to $21.3 billion. Although this sum constituted a sizeable supplement to international liquidity, it clearly could not be regarded as the genesis of a dollar substitute. Indeed, the idea of an IMF-organized substitute unit of account, with the objective of reducing the amount of dollar balances in the world, was put on ice. The question was raised at the Interim Committee in Hamburg in the autumn of 1979 but got no further. The United States still appeared unwilling to accept any kind of reduction in the international role of the dollar.

Apart from eliminating rivals to the dollar, American strategy also sought to maintain the system of floating exchange rates. With a *de facto* dollar standard and floating exchange rates, the American government would have its hands free to bring about the international parity adjustments which it wanted; that is, to the disadvantage of the rest of the world. It was for this reason that France continued its distrustful attitude regarding the system of floating exchange rates. A new Franco-American compromise, however, was reached during the summit meeting at Rambouillet, France, in November 1975, which involved the Group of Five plus Italy. Article IV of the IMF charter was changed to give France what it wanted, namely a declaration that, in principle, a system of fixed, though adjustable, exchange rates would be restored as soon as possible. The United States accepted this change because, at the same time, individual countries were given the right to maintain floating parities. In the context of the *de facto* dollar standard, this meant that the United States held a veto should the IMF want to restore fixed parities. The Americans also consented to the suggestion that the IMF should have the right of surveillance of the orderly evolution of exchange rate fluctuations in the world. This surveillance was to be applied pragmatically, via consultations with the countries concerned.[57] The IMF would be able to exercise real power over small countries but would be in a weaker position *vis-à-vis* the larger countries, most notably the United States itself. This principle of IMF surveillance, together with that of stable but adjustable exchange rates, was approved by the Interim Committee at that same meeting in Kingston, Jamaica, in January 1976. As already stated, the other decisions made during this meeting related to the demonetization of gold and the limitation of SDR issues.

All of these points were ratified by the Board of Governors of the IMF on 30 April 1976. The reform was known as the Second Amendment of the IMF Articles of Agreement and became effective from 1 April 1978. The Second Amendment thus confirmed and even strengthened the *de facto* dollar standard. It represented a great victory for the United States. By way of consolation, Western Europe and Japan received part of the proceeds of the public sale of IMF gold. The developing countries also received a part, via the Trust Fund.

The United States nevertheless had to pay a price for its victory. The Second Amendment stated the intention of the world's leading powers, in time, to allow SDRs to develop into the most important

reserve currency of the international monetary system. Indeed, to
this end, a number of concrete measures were immediately taken.[58]
The transfer of SDRs was made easier. Member states could now
transfer SDRs between themselves without the specific approval of
the IMF. In addition, the obligation in respect of reconstitution
was somewhat relaxed.

As already mentioned, these changes, seen in the short term, did
not threaten the supremacy of the dollar standard. The volume of
SDRs, in relation to total international liquidity, remained very
limited. Furthermore, SDR creation was subject to an American
veto. In the long term, however, the position of SDRs relative to
the dollar was strengthened. The future will show to what extent
this *de jure* increase in influence can translate itself into *de facto*
dominance.

The American attitude of benign neglect in relation to the
application of the floating exchange rates gradually became an
increasing bone of contention in the rest of the world, especially in
industrial countries. The United States did not wish to intervene on
foreign-exchange markets (despite the depreciating dollar) because
it wanted to carry through the external adjustment of its economy
as far as possible. But other countries found that this policy worked
to their disadvantage. First, the depreciation of the dollar caused
their dollar reserves, expressed in national currencies, to fall in value;
second, their export position relative to the dollar area continuously
deteriorated. They also protested against the considerable parity
fluctuations on the foreign exchanges. Therefore, in accordance
with the decision of July 1973 to replace the system of free-floating
exchange rates with one of managed floating, the interventions of
the central banks of Western Europe and Japan multiplied in order
to counter violent parity fluctuations and to slow the falling value
of the dollar. The United States, however, hardly acted at all; so the
dollar continued to fall, though with occasional mini-revivals.[59]

In 1974 the economists Wilfred Ethier and Arthur I. Bloomfield
launched a proposal to control floating parities by means of intervention according to an agreed pattern of interlinked exchange
rates, a pattern that would be regularly reviewed. In June of that
year, somewhat similar guidelines for central banks on the control
of floating exchange rates began to appear in IMF publications.
The intention here was to stop aggressive, discriminatory intervention: for example, intervention designed to bring about an

excessive depreciation of a national currency. On the other hand encouragement was lent to interventions which would contribute to the orderly evolution of foreign-exchange markets. In January 1975 the monetary authorities of Switzerland, West Germany and the United States decided to increase co-operation and make use of the IMF guidelines. A similar agreement was made during the Rambouillet Summit of November 1975, but until November 1978 the American monetary authorities continued to play a passive role and left the initiative with other countries.

On 1 November 1978 the administration of President Jimmy Carter took the initiative for positive co-operation with Switzerland, West Germany, and Japan in the field of exchange-rate stabilization.[60] The Americans also stressed the need for co-operation with the rest of the world.[61] The change in attitude came about because the United States was now convinced that floating exchange rates were inflationary.[62] A further fall of the dollar had to be avoided. At the same time the Americans thought that the depreciation of the dollar that had already occurred had brought external equilibrium. It was now desirable, therefore, to maintain the current rate of the dollar. The discount rate was raised from 8.5 per cent to 9.5 per cent, an historical high point at that time. Moreover, an intervention fund of $30 billion was set up to support the dollar. Its first source was a doubling of the swap arrangements with West Germany, Switzerland, and Japan. Other sources were provided by the issue of treasury paper, expressed in the currency of those three countries, by a drawing on the IMF within the credit tranche of the United States, and by sales of SDRs.[63] West Germany and Japan lent their support to this initiative because they judged that with their strong national currencies they could control domestic inflation. The action was successful. During 1979 and 1980 the dollar remained fairly stable. As a result, the United States abandoned the policy of benign neglect. Instead, with the co-operation of the other countries, a full system of managed floating was established in the spirit of the international decision of July 1973. This new American policy, however, did not remain in place for long. Ronald Reagan, who replaced Carter in January 1981, gave the fight against domestic inflation a still higher priority than Carter had done. Interest rates were consequently pushed up to a new record level and deflationary measures applied over a broad front. During the second quarter of 1981 the Federal Reserve refused to intervene, and the dollar shot up on the foreign exchange markets. The United States once again went its own way. It used monetary policy solely for domestic aims and ignored agreements relating to greater international co-operation and stable exchange rates.

It was with regret that EEC countries observed the success achieved by the *de facto* dollar standard from the beginning of the 1970s. On the one hand the United States functioned as the world's banker and, as such, wielded effective leadership in the formulation of international monetary policy. On the other hand it very actively manipulated the level of the dollar and, for its own domestic reasons, demand management. The dollar standard thus did not appear to guarantee monetary stability. European countries feared that unstable exchange rates between the dollar and other world currencies would stimulate speculation and put pressure on intra-European parities. The inflationary effect of the dollar standard also caused disquiet.[64] Besides, France and Britain were unhappy that the United States had sought contact with West Germany for they feared that the mark would be promoted as a sort of dollar-satellite with reserve currency status.[65]

To stop this, and to breathe new life into the idea of an independent and strong European bloc,[66] Roy Jenkins, President of the European Commission, launched a new formula for monetary unification in a speech at the European University Institute in Florence on 27 October 1977. He proposed that the EEC acquire a full-blown European Monetary System (EMS). The EMS plan was further elaborated at the Bremen Summit of 6–7 July 1978 and the meeting of the Council of Ministers in Brussels on 5 December 1978. It was supposed to commence on 1 January 1979.[67]

The European Monetary System had two main objectives: to strengthen monetary solidarity among the European countries and to make the mechanism for mutual exchange-rate adjustments more flexible.[68] Three new instruments were created to achieve those objectives: namely a European currency (the European Currency Unit or ECU);[69] a European system for the flexible adjustment of mutual exchange rates; and a European Monetary Fund.

The strengthening of monetary solidarity implied a more effective co-operation by the strong-currency countries with a view to stabilizing the snake. Up to now, responsibility for this matter had largely rested with countries with a weak currency, and their central banks were always drawing on their reserves. If speculation against a weak currency increased very much, the country hurriedly withdrew from the snake. This was the cause of the numerous crises of the snake in the course of the 1970s. The new EMS tried to tackle this problem by increasing the support that strong-currency countries lent to those with weak currencies. The immediate assistance from central banks was improved; the credit facilities which could be provided on a short-term basis were extended;[70] and the repayment schedules were made far more flexible. Moreover, in order to give this monetary aid programme a sturdier basis, it was decided to pool part of the reserves of the central banks into a supranational organization, the new European Monetary Fund. Each participating country contributed 20 per cent of its international reserves (dollars or gold) to that Fund. It was even decided later that national currencies could be deposited in exchange for European Currency Units, that is, ECUs. The Fund was a first step, it was hoped, towards the creation of a European central bank.

The other objective of the EMS was to smooth the process of mutual exchange-rate adjustment. The principle of mutual parities, with a 'central' or 'par' value, was retained. At the same time fluctuations within a limited band (2.25 per cent above and below the official parities) were still possible.[71] Flexibility was sought through an objective indicator that would register deviations between market rates and official rates. If these were excessive then measures would be taken to neutralize the deviation. If no such neutralization took place, then a joint decision would be made on whether or not an adjustment of parities was necessary.

Because of differences between France and Germany, the EMS did not start on 1 January 1979, as intended, but only on 13 March 1979. Even then difficulties remained.[72] Britain refused to participate. Italy joined on condition that the lira be allowed to fluctuate within a margin 6 per cent above and 6 per cent below the official rate. Determining the value of the ECU seemed particularly complicated and the value itself rather unstable. The functions of the ECU remained limited to those of an international unit of account, a reserve currency for central banks, and a means of payment for transactions between banks. The ECU could not be used as an intervention currency on international currency markets. For this reason, the ECU could not be considered still to be on an equal footing with other reserve currencies.

Therefore the EMS during the first years of its existence contributed little if anything to the effective monetary unification of Europe. In contrast, the mark, yen and Swiss franc were used more and more as reserve currencies. This pointed more in the direction of the possible establishment of a multipolar system based on national currencies. On the Eurocurrency market too, the significance of the mark, yen and Swiss franc grew. There was thus clearly a monetary diversification in the course of the 1970s but on the basis of several strong national currencies rather than one international one (Table 39).

Table 39 *Exchange Rate Regimes of I M F Members in June 1975*

		Number of currencies	Share in the total foreign trade of I M F members (percentages)
(1)	Independent floating currencies	11	46.4
(2)	Joint floating currencies	7	23.2
(3)	Currencies linked to another currency:		
	3.1. linked to the dollar	54	12.4
	3.2. linked to the French franc	13	0.4
	3.3. linked to sterling	10	1.6
	3.4. linked to the Spanish peseta	1	—
	3.5. linked to the South African rand	3	—
(4)	Currencies linked to a 'basket' of currencies:		
	4.1. linked to SDRs	5	5.0
	4.2. other	14	7.4
(5)	Currencies linked to another currency but according to an automatic adjustment formula	4	2.0
Total		122	98.4

Source: I M F, *Annual Report, 1975*, p. 24

THE UNCERTAIN FUTURE

The serious fluctuations in the mutual parities of the major industrial countries, especially the further fall of the dollar in the autumn of 1978 and its sharp rise in the spring of 1979, strengthened the impression that the system of floating exchange rates – even managed ones – could not serve as an exclusive foundation for the new international monetary order. Fluctuating exchange rates had a serious effect on the profit and loss calculations of the business world.

This provoked sharp words between companies and the fiscal authorities. Accountants no longer had any criteria to determine their companies' financial performance in real terms. Entrepreneurs complained that they had to spend much time and money on measures to protect themselves from losses caused by exchange-rate fluctuations. Lawyers specializing in international trade and business disputes were unable to quantify the damages involved. Moreover, some empirical studies seemed to demonstrate that floating exchange rates actually fuelled inflation, which was the very opposite of what had been initially believed.[73] Floating exchange rates promoted uncertainty on the foreign exchanges and caused import prices to fluctuate violently. This pushed up transaction costs and thereby boosted inflation.[74] Another effect was that governments were given a very free hand in dealing with inflation. This led to differing rates of inflation with the implicit threat that the openness and interdependence of the world economy would allow inflation to be spread from countries with a high inflation rate to countries with a low one.[75] There was general agreement that inflation had to be tackled using, among other measures, monetary policy. For this reason the reform of the international monetary system was once more seen as one of the highest priorities.[76] But what kind of reform? In any case the problems of exchange rates, international reserves, and capital movements would have to be solved first. In fact all three could be merged into one large problem: the control of the balance of payments on a global scale.

As far as exchange rates are concerned, many people still believe that the solution lies in a further strengthening of the system of managed floating parities. This would assume increasing intervention on the international exchange market. The intervention would be organized by national governments via their central banks but would involve international consultation and co-operation as well. It would also have to be based on objective criteria that would permit a distinction between incidental and fundamental exchange-rate fluctuations.[77] Finally, a joint intervention policy would only have a real and lasting effect if a power base could be formed with sufficient supranational authority to bring about equilibrium in the case of fundamental balance-of-payments problems.[78] According to official American thinking in January 1979,[79] the newly broadened I M F, now with its supervisory competence, would be able to have an innovatory impact in this area. The O E C D, the E E C, and the

Group of Seven (the Group of Five plus Italy and Canada) could play supplementary roles. The results which were achieved in the early 1980s, however, remained modest.

The development of a new international monetary order also implies a satisfactory solution for the problem of world reserves.[80] In the first place this requires the reorganization of the *de facto* dollar standard: the huge dollar balances have to be eliminated. They could be converted into SDRs or into other currencies that could be promoted into new reserve currencies, such as the mark, the yen, the Swiss franc or the ECU. Nevertheless, without attendant reforms, the idea of conversion into those other currencies is not tenable. In essence it would only be a holding operation because other currencies too can become the subject of uncertainty or irritation. Worse still, it would mean the reintroduction of a system of multiple, mutually convertible reserve currencies and all the dangers of speculation that accompany this.[81] At the time of writing the ECU was still too weak to be of much significance in the short and even medium term.

Conversion into SDRs is, for the moment, an unrealistic proposition as well. After a long pause it was decided in 1978 that $4 billion in SDRs would be issued in each of the next three years.[82] In comparison with the level of existing reserves, this increase in SDRs is of marginal significance and, in the short term, no solution to the dollar glut could be expected from this quarter.

There is an even more fundamental problem. The liquidation of dollar balances will ultimately have to take place via a considerable rise in the exports of American goods and services. Given the difficult economic climate of the early 1980s this would lead to much economic friction. Opposite the irritation resulting from the hegemony of the *de facto* dollar standard stands the friction that would be created by the liquidation of excessive dollar balances, and these two problems cannot be solved simultaneously.

According to some experts, a general and operational solution could only be found in a gradual expansion of the authority and functions of the IMF. Specifically this would mean the strengthening of its surveillance capacity and the extension of its function in the direction of a clearing union, such as had been originally conceived by Keynes.[83] A supranational authority would finally be able to bring fundamental movements of goods, services, and international capital into equilibrium. The extent of world liquidity could thus be efficiently matched with real needs. At the same time, the IMF, as clearing union, would be able to organize the distribution of available liquidity on a multilateral and systematic basis. Between 1978 and 1980 the United States government more or less supported this idea, as appears from its consent to the creation of new SDRs, its proposal to raise IMF quotas from 1980 by 50 per cent, and its suggestion to broaden the surveillance role of the IMF. The double problem of the dollar overhang and the *de facto* dollar standard would not immediately be resolved by this, but it is clear that liquidation would be both quicker and safer under IMF management than otherwise.[84]

Alongside exchange rates and world reserves, capital movements must also be subjected to more efficient international control. The management of the balance of payments cannot be streamlined unless capital is controlled along with current accounts. Indeed, attention is regularly drawn to the inflationary effects of speculative capital flows. In this, the Eurocurrency market is singled out, because the lack of any control there fosters credit creation and thus energizes inflation.[85] The United States government has wanted to exercise supervision over international capital flows, especially the Eurocurrency market, but at the minimum level necessary. It has pointed to its own painful experience when it tried to control capital exports in the 1960s and 1970s, and also to the still relatively small share that the Eurocurrency market has in total international credit. In addition, it stressed the useful role that the Eurocurrency market played in recycling petrodollars and the economic necessity of siphoning capital to regions and sectors where higher productivity gains could be realized. Finally, the United States government pointed to the existing national controls over banking institutions (including American banking subsidiaries abroad) and the growing information on international capital transfers, information to which the Bank for International Settlements had access. The Americans wanted this flow of information to be increased in the future. Again, reference was made to the new surveillance capacity the IMF possessed from 1978 onwards.[86]

The development of the international monetary system after the IMF Second Amendment on 1 April 1978 showed a definite trend towards the strengthening of IMF authority. As already mentioned, the issue of new SDRs was resumed in 1979. From 1 May 1981 full interest was granted to holders of SDRs.[87] Compulsory repayment (reconstitution), which had already been relaxed in the Second Amendment, was shortly afterwards completely abolished. SDRs could thus definitely be regarded as an important international currency. The Second Amendment also enabled the IMF to allow certain institutions to hold SDRs, a competence of which the IMF made effective use. At the end of 1980 nine important institutions were involved; for example, the Andean Reserve Fund, the Arab Monetary Fund, the Bank for International Settlements, the World Bank and the Swiss National Bank. The IMF also introduced SDRs as a unit of account in various international agreements. The World Bank accepted SDRs as a unit of account.

After 1978 the IMF surveillance of exchange-rate evolution underwent further practical development. Confidential consultations between the IMF and individual countries increased both in number and in substance. Through persuasion and flexibility the IMF attempted to strengthen its authority over monetary policy in the world. This was also clearly evident in the new discussion on gold. In 1980 and 1981 several proposals were made to the American Congress which, as a means of fighting inflation, sought to re-establish the role of gold in American monetary policy. A study commission, chaired by the Treasury Secretary, was set up to explore the possibilities. Its results, however, were negative and the IMF policy to demonetize gold must have had an influence.[88]

The promotion of the IMF to an institution with effective supranational authority to provide the basis for the management of a new monetary world order, can be seen as the logical end-point of postwar international monetary development. The system of a stringent code of behaviour and rigid exchange rates that was established after Bretton Woods inevitably had to give way as soon as there was no leader left to impose the rules upon itself and its partners. The collapse of gold convertibility in 1971 and the introduction of a system of extreme flexibility made necessary corrections in the short term; but in the long term they introduced instability and uncertainty. To counter this by supplementing the free floating exchange rates with a policy of complete national autarky would be irresponsible. The world economy has become so complex and interdependent that a policy of national autarky would imply a dismal loss of efficiency and world solidarity – an unacceptable regression. If one wants greater monetary stability and certainty within a growing world economy – that is, in an environment of increasing complexity and interdependence – one must make new organizational progress. A new form of regulatory authority is necessary. Without this, growth will inevitably lead to chaos and destroy itself. The only rational solution thus appears to be an ordering of the world economy by means of a supranational monetary body invested with effective authority. Through management and planning, this agency would try to find a satisfactory balance between efficiency and stability, between growth and equity.

However correct this reasoning may appear to be at first sight, there are two major drawbacks.

The first drawback is a theoretical one; it relates to the problem of diminishing returns that is inherent in any cycle of organizational or technological progress. Although it is quite conceivable that a well-established supranational monetary body could manage further growth of the world economy in an effective and socially acceptable way, this further growth would bring increasing complexity and interdependence. Let us assume that the supranational body would have a great potential for development, so that the growing economic complexity and interdependence could be assimilated by intensive monetary planning and new forms of monetary control. And let us also grant that the balance between efficiency and social justice would thus not be immediately undermined. Even so, the intensification of planning implies a strengthening of supranational authority, a progressively deeper penetration of monetary regulation in all sectors of economic life, a worrying bureaucratization of monetary control, and a gradual restriction of national and individual liberties. At a certain point in the development of this supranational body, bureaucratic sclerosis would therefore undermine any progress made in efficiency and equity.[89]

The second objection to a muscular regulatory authority is of a practical nature. The use of greater economies of scale in the world economy has strengthened the conviction that a policy of national autarky is no longer a realistic solution for the recovery of monetary stability and certainty. But on a world scale, between national autarky and strong supranational authority there lies the reality of large political and economic power groups. The United States and Canada, the E E C and its associated countries, Japan and its sphere of influence in East Asia, the Group of Seventy-Seven, and the Soviet Union with its satellites are real economic formations which possess sufficient scale to be able to tolerate some degree of autarky without great loss of efficiency. In the first place, these existing power groups might not accept a transfer of effective power to the supranational monetary authority. The world would then disintegrate into several large, powerful, autarkic, political and economic blocs with all the attendant dangers of mutual conflict. The developments of recent years undoubtedly show tendencies in this direction. In this scenario, of course, the supranational authority is quickly short-circuited. But even if the continental blocs joined in a decision to start co-operating within the framework of a strong supranational body – say the I M F – in the context of the present balance of power such co-operation is only conceivable if each bloc has a right of veto over all important I M F decisions. Under these conditions the authority of the I M F would only be operational to the extent that common ground could be discovered between the various power groups. As the world now appears, consensus exists on only a very limited number of fundamental points.[90]

EPILOGUE

Between 1945 and 1980 the world economy has traced a fascinating course. At first it was characterized by a specific pattern of unique achievement: successful growth, the results of which were distributed within the framework of the modern welfare society. Unfortunately, creative dynamism was not the sole characteristic of the post-war economy, for it was at the same time caught in the web of cyclical and structural developments. Upswings of limited duration and recessions followed each other incessantly. The whole period, moreover, can be reduced to one great cycle, spreading over several decades, in which the spectacular successes of the first decades led directly to the difficulties of the 1970s. In the previous chapters I have tried to untangle the complexity of post-war development. This has required an examination of the extent to which arbitrary events, personal interventions, and deeper-lying structural mechanisms have determined the path of the post-war economy – in other words, how the factors of 'chance, freedom, and necessity' have influenced our present reality. The intention throughout has been to explain as well as describe. The analysis of deeper-lying structural factors has occasionally demanded an extension of the chronological framework back to the Second World War, the inter-war period, and sometimes even further. It should be remembered, however, that structural factors form part of a historical background that stretches back over many centuries, and therefore they have to be seen in a very long perspective. For this reason I shall begin this epilogue with an attempt to integrate the structural analysis of post-war economic development into the history of Western capitalism since the late Middle Ages.

The merchant capitalism that prevailed in Europe between the eleventh and eighteenth centuries represented an important step forward from the more autarkic and agrarian subsistence economy of the early Middle Ages.[1] Individuals and urban authorities built with their own money and that of the community a new trading infrastructure, based on urban expansion. It was in this manner that the urban economy developed into a world-orientated open market system, one which, in the context of its time, may be regarded as revolutionary. In effect the towns and cities themselves were new fixed capital goods which the merchant-entrepreneurs were able to combine creatively with their own working capital. Indeed the dynamism of merchant capitalism lay precisely in this innovative combination between the new forms of fixed and working capital which made possible the expansionary development of new products and services. Towns allowed a more efficient division of labour and became dynamic centres of large-scale production, directed at export markets. They grew at the mouths and confluences of rivers or at the meeting-points of overland trade routes and formed a broad communications network along which agricultural staple goods and a whole range of hand-worked products could be distributed over the Western world.

The success of merchant capitalism also derived from the new balance between this urban efficiency and the distribution of the surplus value among different population groups. The gentry, the merchant-entrepreneurs, the farmers, artisans, labourers, all shared the benefits. Out of this sharing developed a social consensus and a solidarity which were crucial to the system. The merchant-entrepreneurs nevertheless profited from their strategic function in the system by gradually distorting the distribution pattern. To this end they also used political power, which they acquired through an increasing control over municipal authorities and later through a growing alliance with the mercantilistic state. Urban artisans and labourers reacted in two ways in an attempt to restore the balance. First, they improved their labour qualifications so that they could raise their physical and above all their economic productivity, and hence their own wages. Secondly, they combined into craft guilds. Initially these functioned as private organizations whose objective

was to improve wages and labour conditions; but later, as a result
of their great success, they acquired civil status. Corporations thus
became a driving force in the industrial development of the towns.
The basic principles were solidarity and participation. Within each
sector the craft guilds guaranteed equal, high wages for all their
members and full participation in the decision-making process.
Simultaneously, together with the merchant guilds and the government, they organized a consultative system within the framework
of the urban economy.

Gradually the urban economy concentrated on high-value products and services which permitted high wages for artisan masters
and journeymen. But in the continued effort to maintain the quality
of the goods and services, the number of trade and municipal
regulations grew to such an extent that innovation became highly
constricted. The guilds, in order to preserve the incomes of their
members, developed monopolistic and protectionistic tendencies so
strong that sectional interests began to dominate social-economic
and political decision-making in the towns and later in the mercantilistic states. At the same time the solidarity of artisans broke up into
a new polarization: artisan masters kept more money and power for
themselves and increasingly excluded journeymen and unskilled
workers. Rigidities and inefficiency became rife. The merchant-
entrepreneurs therefore sought new avenues for the maintenance of
efficiency. The production of standardized goods was transferred on
a large scale to the countryside, where there was much concealed
unemployment, where wages were low, and where no corporatist
structures existed. In rural industry great organizational progress
was made, for example, with the putting-out system. As a consequence, labour productivity in the countryside underwent an improvement from which rural workers were initially able to draw
benefit. A first form of modern industry spread through rural
Europe. Nowadays in specialized publications this has become
known as proto-industry.

On the other hand there were also many towns that picked up
the gauntlet with great resolution. The technological innovations
which enabled the mechanization of industrial production implied
an increasing concentration of the production process, that is, the
concentration of labour and a large amount of capital goods within
the walls of a large factory. Such concentration could most efficiently
be realized within the urban economy. Industrial entrepreneurs

therefore set up factories in the hearts of towns and cities, and these communities grew in the course of the nineteenth century into industrial growth centres. Mechanized factories and flourishing big cities were the essential foundations of industrial capitalism.

The new efficiency of industrial capitalism was thus not exclusively the result of technological advances. Organizational progress was also of crucial significance. Gradually the merchant-entrepreneur made way for the industrialist, the *homo novus* of the nineteenth century. Yet in addition to this there was a general reorganization along the lines of an open, liberal market economy. This new economic order was founded by national governments in conjunction with the industrial and financial bourgeoisie, which to an increasing extent controlled political power in the state. The rational planning system of the modern industrial concern now had the support of a rational free-market system, whose efficient working was supervised by government and the bourgeoisie. Industrial capitalism, as a result of its historic success in the twentieth century, began to grow into an extremely complex network of different activities. At that point rationalization was given a new impulse by the extended planning of the multidivisional firm and the development of centralized planning on a national level.

Industrial capitalism was also characterized by a new disruption in the balance between efficiency and equality. Industrial capitalism would never have been able to replace rural industry if it had not initially found support from the working classes, especially those which had suffered from the deindustrialization of the towns. For certain groups of skilled and unskilled workers, town-based mechanized industry meant both new employment and higher labour productivity, from which they could benefit. The industrial entrepreneurs, however, gradually acquired a position of economic and political power, and used this to monopolize surplus value, thus completely distorting its equitable distribution. Industrial workers were slow to react but ultimately they achieved success, first through private unions and later through official, state-recognized union bodies. In the industrial West the idea of communal solidarity and of equality once more gained acceptance. At a national level this development led, in the long term, to the concerted economy and the participation of labour organizations in the central planning and management of the state. The state was no longer just concerned with the smooth working of the market but instead was entrusted with a much wider competence. By means of centralized planning and under the watchful eye of the social partners, it sought to rationalize economic activity in order to maximize growth while at the same time redistributing income on a more equitable basis via government transfer payments.

The mixed economy has thus come to function in the West as a sort of neo-mercantilism. Undoubtedly it represents numerous elements of organizational progress: in principle, planning maximizes production by eliminating uncertainty on a macro-economic level. Nevertheless at the same time centralized planning generates bureaucracy and inertia, and this gradually undermines the advantages offered by the planning process. Sectional interests grow increasingly more influential, regulations more cumbersome and protectionist, and conservative tendencies more widespread. In order to compensate for the loss of efficiency which accompanies excessive centralization, the principles of the micro-economy are once again being called for. The conservatives want to slim down the size of the state and restore the working of the free market. What they fail to realize fully is that the clock cannot be turned back, that a return to the nineteenth-century market structure is for technical reasons unattainable, and that in any case the general acceptance of the principle of solidarity makes such a return impossible. Some left-wing economists and politicians, who had originally put their faith in centralized planning in their dream of rational utopianism, have likewise turned their attention to the micro-economy. They now press for decentralized planning; that is, for workers' participation in management or even for workers' self-management at the company and regional level. Rational utopianism thus makes way for poetic utopianism: if overtly centralized planning destroys freedom and creativity, then a decentralized model will maintain the rationality of planning while still guaranteeing creativity and freedom. [2]

There is, unfortunately, a tragic paradox concealed in poetic utopianism. In the simple industrialization model of the nineteenth century, workers' participation could have been possible in pure organizational terms but at that time authoritarianly managed companies were widespread. In the extremely complex technological industrial society of today, workers' participation or even workers' self-management is becoming politically realizable but for organizational reasons it is now no longer a practical proposition.

The only way around this latter problem would be to delegate a truly representative function to qualified union leaders and hierarchical, authoritarian businessmen. But under these conditions the concept of workers' participation or workers' self-management would become an empty shell, which is precisely what happened during the declining years of corporatism. Indeed, is not the whole trend towards decentralization in the framework of communal solidarity simply a return to the corporatism of the seventeenth and eighteenth centuries? The use of smaller economic units, on a national, regional, sectoral or company level, does offer a rich potential for efficient management and creativity. Yet when this reduction in the size of economic units is seen in conjunction with the principles of solidarity, the general outcome would be to facilitate the fragmentary effect of sectional interests and to strengthen the paralysing influence of the protectionism and conservatism inherent in the behaviour of relatively small groups. For this reason the optimism of left-wing economists and politicians in this respect is regarded very sceptically. The new priority for group interest creates in the West a certain *fin de régime* atmosphere. In democratic systems it leads inevitably to mutual envy, rivalry, and compromises – that is, to rigidity, protectionism, conservatism. Furthermore, this *fin de régime* atmosphere hangs over the whole industrial West and not just over urban industrial sectors as was the case in the eighteenth century. This makes the situation still more dramatic.

During the 1970s industrialists reacted aggressively to this increasing strangulation. Just as the merchant-entrepreneurs of the eighteenth century had shifted the *locus* of their industrial activity to the countryside, so multinationals began to look to the Third World, in particular to the newly industrialized countries. There the enormous unemployment, both open and concealed, meant that wages could be kept low, and at the same time foreign companies were made welcome because they created income and introduced modern production techniques. Unions were weak or non-existent in Third World countries and unable to confront the international nature of these companies. By and large the planning by multinationals also met with little interference from national governments in the Third World. Simultaneously multinationals escaped the control of Western governments. They were thus in a position to restore a liberal market system in the world economy. Under these conditions planning remained under the control of big business while remaining subject to the competitive stimulus of the market. For the multi-nationals this helped to improve the efficiency of their industrial production, although at the expense of the principle of solidarity within the boundaries of the national Western economies. The consequence of this trend was the threat of new deindustrialization in the West, now no longer limited to the towns but more generally spread, especially in the old industrial regions.

The strategy of multinationals to restore industrial efficiency constitutes a gigantic challenge for the traditional industrial areas of the West. Will this strategy entail the establishment of a new economic world order? Will it cause a transformation as sweeping as that of the eighteenth and nineteenth centuries? At that time the general spreading of rural industry opened the way for the Industrial Revolution and a free-market economy. Will the industrialization of the Third World give rise to a comparable change, this time based on a global balance between efficiency and equality?

This question has now become a blazing issue. If the West does not accept the challenge it simply has no future. The current strengthening of protectionism does suggest that it will not pick up the gauntlet. Excessive protective measures by the government strengthen defensive and conservative tendencies in the economy. If any further ground is ceded, the West as a whole, or a part of it, will gradually isolate itself from the dynamic forces that are now at work in the world, and economic decline will be the ultimate result. If the West tries to avoid the challenge by replacing national protectionism with international protectionism, that is, by withdrawing behind the walls of a few great continental power blocs, then the dangers are no less great. Through this process autarky acquires a broader dimension. The smaller scale of production which normally accompanies national protectionism would be avoided, and the dynamism of leading sectors would be maintained, but at the same time older, weaker sectors would be protected from the competition of the industrializing Third World. Such a strategy of protective bloc-formation would in essence mean a return to the structure of the mercantilism of the *Ancien Régime*, except for the fact that the political framework would not be a single nation-state but a group of nation-states. This neo-mercantilism would certainly not be any less dangerous for world security than the mercantilism of the seventeenth and eighteenth centuries. On the contrary, the greater size of units which would be possible under this system contains a potential for a concentration of power far beyond the scope of any nationalism.

If the West chooses to accept the challenge and to participate in the new economic revolution sweeping the world, it can marshal vast advantages and resources. How can the West assimilate the industrialization of the Third World into its own development? How can the West adapt this dynamism to a New International Economic Order? The solution exists on two levels; on the level of humanity's material needs and that of its existential needs.

At the level of material development, the New International Economic Order implies a transition from national to supranational planning. This centralized supranational planning is necessary to guarantee the efficiency and solidarity of the world system as a whole. Just as national governments in the nineteenth century contributed to the establishment and perpetuation of an open-market economy, so will an effective international authority have to organize the world economy as an open-market system (possibly in stages, as some have proposed). The international centralized planning mechanism will have no alternative but to incorporate this market dimension, because scarcity, in global terms, is still so great that the maximization of economic efficiency remains a necessity. In order to meet the world's needs satisfactorily, the world's resources will have to be carefully managed.

Before leaving the level of material needs, one must recognize that international planning assumes much more than the guaranteeing of maximum efficiency. The concept of solidarity can no longer be ignored in the world today; this too must be accorded a place in the New International Economic Order. The international authority will thus have to execute concrete policies in order to obtain a better distribution of wealth and income. The first priority in this respect will be the industrializing Third World. This means that the multinationals will have to be brought under the control of the international planning authority. The authority will also have to adopt a dynamic development strategy. It would not be sufficient to reorganize world-scale industrialization along the lines of a fixed pattern according to which the West would enjoy a monopoly of industrial innovation and growth sectors, and some Third World countries would be able to develop into intermediate industrial areas while others would mostly apply themselves to mechanized agricultural production, be it on a large or small scale. A truly dynamic policy would provide all countries with the long-term possibility of acquiring a post-industrial structure. The international planning authority will have to build sufficient flexibility into the system so that all countries that wish to continue to realize their development aspirations will be able to do so.

Is the establishment of such an international planning system utopian? In any case it poses extremely complex and diverse problems. The implementation of a dynamic development policy implies that the world economy, seen in the short term, will be functioning below its capacity for efficiency. On the other hand, again seen in global terms, the just distribution of economic gains would be facilitated by this and one could hope that in the long term efficiency could be restored and even improved. Granted, playing the future off against the present is by no means simple, and account must be taken of human factors which are in fact unpredictable. Even assuming that international planning does enable the construction of a New International Economic Order, and assuming too that technological knowledge as well as physical and human capital can be distributed equitably throughout the world, some countries will still have more difficulties than others. This is because all countries are not equally endowed with natural resources. Countries without energy sources or other raw materials will still have to import their needs in this area, and the only means of financing this will be through additional exports. This in turn would presuppose the perpetuation of innovative and technological leads by some countries over others. But this presupposition conflicts sharply with the new world vision based on the provision of equality for all.

As a final point on the level of satisfying material needs, one must consider whether the international planning system would in fact be able to respond adequately to all the demands made of it. Will not the growing complexity of the world economy, as described above, inevitably lead to the institutional rigidity of any international authority? If planning improves the balance between efficiency and equality it will simultaneously, through its increasing institutionalization, stifle individual and social creativity. Who can stop or slow down this process of institutionalization? Who will control the controllers? Totalitarian regimes are by nature conservative; that is, they show a strong inclination to bureaucratize control. They usually have no efficient means of controlling their controllers. The Western system of political democracy is in principle better suited to this task, but it too is not immune to the danger of institutional ossification. Professional organizations with large memberships have a good chance of influencing political power in their favour. They often belong to traditional economic sectors and as a consequence conservative tendencies multiply within the national political system and overflow into the international sphere.

The establishment of a New International Economic Order must take account not only of the satisfaction of material needs but also of other human aspirations – the existential level where dwell the freedom, responsibility, and subjective experience of individual human beings.

Fred Hirsch has already drawn attention to the conflicts that exist between the material and social aspects of growth.[3] The more that material scarcity is overcome, the more widespread social scarcity becomes and the more difficult it is for the individual fully to enjoy material welfare. People tend to see an increase in their living standards not in terms of itself but rather in the context of what is happening in their peer group. The result is a new sort of competition to move up the social ladder and, via a still higher income, to enjoy the welfare of a more privileged position. This leads to much waste because the infrastructure to cope with this form of competition requires continuous investment in the production of non-essential goods and services. It also involves the perpetuation of inequality. A solution can only be found when one looks beyond material aspirations, to a spiritual dimension or a religious philosophy of life.

There are similar conflicts in the field of knowledge. Even if a redistribution of income, based on a satisfactory compromise with the principle of efficiency, should prove able to eliminate or considerably reduce the conflict between the 'haves' and 'have-nots', problems will still remain. In the complex economy of the late twentieth century a new conflict is growing, one between the 'knows' and 'know-nots'. This is a new source of frustration and alienation, one that cannot be resolved by a better distribution of material gains.

Private capitalism or socialized capitalism, even if the latter manages to combine efficiency with 'socialism with a human face', will ultimately be unable to resolve the fundamental contradiction pointed out by Daniel Bell.[4] As long as both forms of capitalism seek to provide a universal and optimal system of social order and both continue to link this exclusively with material welfare, they will inevitably come up against an irreconcilable contradiction. In order to maximize the satisfaction of material needs they will have to appeal to the diligence, sobriety, and self-discipline of the active population – characteristics that the affluent society with its mass consumption and expenditure of leisure gradually attacks and destroys. For this reason systems of social order which are exclusively orientated to the maximization of material welfare and leave no room for the spiritual development or religious fulfilment of the individual cannot hope to relieve the psychological tensions they create.

Some supporters of the mixed economy or socialist economy claim that authoritarian planning by the company, by the state, or by an international authority will maximize efficiency and in that way will fully satisfy man's needs. But in fact this rational utopianism appears to lead inevitably to exploitation and misuse, not to mention bureaucratic inertia and alienation. Others argue that decentralized planning will bring about maximal freedom and dynamic creativity and in that way satisfy all man's aspirations. In fact this poetic utopianism in its extreme forms leads to chaos, egocentric group interests, and rigidity.

The solution to all the above-mentioned conflicts thus does not lie exclusively in the search for a workable compromise in the social sphere and for the full realization of material welfare. Much more is necessary. A new world society will not be built in the first instance by social *systems* but, in essence, by *people*. This means that it will not be created by external revolutions but rather by a general change in man's values and attitudes. The fusion of classical and Judaeo-Christian civilization in the so-called 'Dark Ages' managed to generate such a change and in so doing laid the foundations for our modern industrial society. Since that time, however, Western ideology has become something of a spent force. A new internal revolution is needed for the future, a new ideology to give renewed impulse to the development of the world. The West possesses the material and spiritual reserves to be able to play an innovative role in this respect. It can lead the way forward towards a new harmony in which rationality, equality, and creativity can be reconciled with one another. This is the ultimate challenge.

NOTES

Full bibliographical information on each book and article is given in the bibliography.

CHAPTER I

1. A. MADDISON, 'Performance in Europe', p. 470.
2. E.g., P. LEON (ed.), *Guerres et crises 1914–1947*, pp. 510ff., pp. 542ff., pp. 559ff.
3. P. ALPERT, *Economic History of Europe*, pp. 251–7.
4. A. MADDISON, *Growth in Japan and the USSR*, p. 11.
5. S. TSURU, *Japanese Economy*, vol. I.
6. A. GROSSER, *Colossus Again*, ch. 1; S. LIEBERMAN, *Mixed Economies*, p. 36.
7. P. LEON (ed.), *Guerres et crises 1914–1947*, p. 514, pp. 519ff.
8. E. F. DENISON, W. K. CHUNG, *How Japan's Economy Grew*, p. 11.
9. P. ALPERT, *Economic History of Europe*, pp. 245–50.
10. H. U. FAULKNER, *American Economic History*, pp. 696–725.
11. See Table 2.
12. See Table 2.
13. C. P. KINDLEBERGER, *World in Depression*.
14. C. P. KINDLEBERGER, *American Business Abroad*.
15. W. W. ROSTOW, *World Economy*, p. 231.
16. M. M. POSTAN, *Western Europe 1945–1964*, pp. 22–4; S. LIEBERMAN, *Mixed Economies*, pp. 35–6.
17. W. W. ROSTOW, *World Economy*, p. 232.
18. E. LUNDBERG, *Instability*, pp. 37–8.
19. For further information, see Chapters VII and VIII.
20. For further information, see Chapters IX to XII inclusive.
21. M. M. POSTAN, *Western Europe 1945–1964*, p. 28.

22. M. BRONFENBRENNER (ed.), *Business Cycle*.

23. In 1944 war production still represented 44 per cent of GNP; by 1946 this share had already fallen to 10 per cent and by the middle of 1947 the transition was virtually complete.

24. H. U. FAULKNER, *American Economic History*, p. 717.

25. F. C. MILLS, *Postwar Prices*, p. 66.

26. Using 1928–38 as a base-period, equal to 100, the index figures for wholesale prices, retail prices, and hourly wages in industry rose between June 1946 and February 1948 to 143, 128 and 119 respectively.

27. R. M. ROBERTSON, *American Economy*, pp. 671–3; H. U. FAULKNER, *American Economic History*, p. 718.

28. J. W. KENDRICK, *Postwar Productivity*.

29. P. ALPERT, *Economic History of Europe*, pp. 324–51.

30. Every civilian, in exchange for the old currency, received a sum of 2,000 francs in new notes. The rest was blocked: 90 per cent of all bank and savings deposits were blocked.

31. In 1944 the rate was fixed at $1 = 43.8 FF and after the devaluations of 1948 the rate was $1 = 265 FF: F. CARON, *Modern France*, pp. 275–6, 328.

32. J. C. R. DOW, *British Economy, 1945–1960, passim*; S. POLLARD, *British Economy, 1914–1967*, pp. 356–76.

33. The American government, which wanted to liberalize world trade as soon as possible, had attached to its long-term loan to Britain the condition that sterling had to become convertible by the end of the year (see Chapter XI).

34. OECD, *Premier et second rapport de l'OECE*.

35. P. BAFFI, 'Monetary Developments in Italy', p. 427.

36. For the German currency reform see: F. A. LUTZ, 'German Currency Reform', pp. 122–42.

37. On 1 October 1948 it was announced that of the currency blocked in June, 70 per cent should be regarded as destroyed, while 20 per cent was made freely available and 10 per cent remained blocked. Through this measure the effective rate of exchange of the money concerned was reduced from RM 10 = DM 1 to RM 10 = DM 0.6.

38. R. E. EMMER, 'West-German Monetary Policy, 1948–1951', p. 8.

39. P. BAFFI, 'Monetary Developments in Italy'; G. H. HILDEBRAND, *Growth and Structure*, pp. 15ff.

40. T. F. M. ADAMS, I. HOSHII, *Financial History*, pp. 15–77.

41. At that moment those countries which would later receive Marshall Aid derived 82 per cent of their energy needs from coal. In the United States coal supplied only 58 per cent of energy needs. P. ALPERT, *Economic History of Europe*, pp. 288–310.

42. W. W. ROSTOW, *World Economy*, p. 231.

43. P. ALPERT, *Economic History of Europe*, pp. 368–76.

44. On 15 August 1947 the total amount of outstanding loans made to European countries was $7,263 million.

45. All countries which received loans had to agree to promote a system of liberalized, multilateral world trade, once they had recovered from the effects of the war.
46. For further details on the Marshall Plan, see Chapter IX.
47. If Italy and Germany were excluded from the total, this figure would be much higher.
48. W. W. ROSTOW, *World Economy*, p. 236.
49. Later, under the influence of the Gray Report, Marshall Aid was supplemented with considerable military help which freed a substantial amount of European resources for non-military investment.
50. A. GROSSER, *Colossus Again*, pp. 87ff.
51. K. HARDACH, *Germany 1914–1970*, p. 213.
52. *Statistisches Jahrbuch*, 1952, p. 209.
53. A. MADDISON, *Growth in Japan and the USSR*, p. 46.
54. Ibid., pp. 46–9.
55. E. F. DENISON, W. K. CHUNG, *How Japan's Economy Grew*, p. 11, and the literature mentioned there.

CHAPTER II

1. In the Eastern bloc countries the post-war catching-up dynamic was also present. The Soviet Union had experienced the chaos of two world wars and the intervening Revolution. The other Eastern bloc countries had experienced both wars, the Great Depression and the transition to Soviet domination.
2. I. SVENNILSON, *Growth and Stagnation*, pp. 20ff.
3. F. JÁNOSSY, *La fin des miracles économiques*; E. LUNDBERG, *Instability*, p. 320.
4. The catching-up hypothesis also relates to the ideas of Alexander Gerschenkron (A. GERSCHENKRON, *Backwardness*): if the government of a country with a primitive economy decides to modernize and industrialize, then this country grows all the faster because its backwardness in respect to leading countries is greater.
5. On the one hand technological progress created a greater demand for highly qualified labour. On the other hand the production of consumer durables considerably increased the demand for semi-skilled labour too.
6. R. CAVES, M. UEKUSA, 'Industrial Organisation'.
7. A. MADDISON, *Growth in the West*, pp. 59–60.
8. The limited military expenditure was also indicated as a cause, especially for Japan and Germany.
9. 'If the United States were to raise her investment rate to Japanese levels, her rate of return would be lower than it is now, because she would have to explore new technologies much more intensively. This is less true in Europe, which lags behind the United States, and it is even less true in Japan, which has the biggest leeway to make up, and which, even at the very high rates of investment, is largely exploiting a technology which already exists': A. MADDI-

SON, *Growth in Japan and the USSR*, p. 60; id., *Growth in the West*, pp. 87–98.

10. Rostow has greatly expanded this concept: W. W. ROSTOW, *World Economy*, pp. 103ff., pp. 261–4. See also M. M. POSTAN, *Western Europe 1945–1964*, p. 128, pp. 163–6.

11. Third World and OPEC countries have, from the 1960s onwards, sharply criticized this development.

12. R. MUNTING, *The Economic Development of the USSR*, p. 92; A. MADDISON, *Growth in Japan and the USSR*, p. 36.

13. A. MADDISON, 'Performance in Europe', p. 478.

14. F. JÁNOSSY, *La fin des miracles économiques*, ch. 4.

15. WORLD BANK, *Development Report, 1978*, p. 3.

16. W. W. ROSTOW, *World Economy*, p. 55–7.

17. Ibid., pp. 58–9.

18. S. KUZNETS, *Economic Growth*, pp. 312–14.

19. WORLD BANK, *Development Report, 1979*.

20. E.g., B. BALASSA, 'Export Incentives'.

21. E. LUNDBERG, *Instability*, pp. 85ff.

22. E.g., R. A. GORDON, 'US Economy'; G. H. MOORE, 'International Business Cycle', pp. 21–8; P. A. KLEIN, *Business Cycles*.

23. One of the few economists who rejected the concept of the business cycle as outdated was Gilbert: M. GILBERT, 'Postwar Business Cycle'.

24. G. H. MOORE, 'International Business Cycle', p. 24.

25. M. GILBERT, 'Postwar Business Cycle'.

26. For the United States the delay was of the order of six to nine months: ibid.

27. F. CARON, *Modern France*, pp. 319–21; J. C. R. DOW, 'France, Germany and Italy'.

28. C. MORIGUCHI, *Japan's Economic Growth*; M. SHINOHARA, 'Postwar Business Cycles'.

29. E. LUNDBERG, *Instability*, p. 314.

30. W. W. ROSTOW, *World Economy*, pp. 346–67, Table IV–12.

31. For post-war American cycles see, among others: A. BURNS, *Business Cycle*; I. MINTZ, *Growth Cycles*; R. A. GORDON, 'US Economy'.

32. For the importance of military expenditure in post-war economic development see: A. MADDISON, *Growth in the West*, p. 104.

33. E. LUNDBERG, *Instability*, p. 357.

34. M. GILBERT, 'Postwar Business Cycle', pp. 107–8.

35. A. M. OKUN, *Prosperity*, p. 70.

36. S. E. HARRIS, *Kennedy Years*, p. 24.

37. J. E. SUNDQUIST, *Politics and Policy*; W. HELLER, *New Dimensions*; J. W. STIEBER (ed.), *Employment Problems*.

38. *Council of Economic Advisers, 1965*, p. 32.

39. A. M. OKUN, *Prosperity*, pp. 92–6.

40. On this question see, e.g.: R. J. MORRISON, *Expectations and Inflation*.

41. R. C. O. MATTHEWS, 'Postwar Business Cycles'.

42. Ibid., p. 106; W. W. ROSTOW, *World Economy*, pp. 338–41.

43. J. CORNWALL, *Growth and Stability*, pp. 230–70.
44. For the cycles in other Western European countries, see, e.g.: J. C. R. DOW, 'France, Germany and Italy'.
45. M. SHINOHARA, 'Postwar Business Cycles'.
46. Ibid., pp. 79–82.
47. From 1952 to 1960 the average GNP deflator did not grow more than 2 per cent annually.
48. E. LUNDBERG, 'Stabilization Policies', p. 482.
49. J. CORNWALL, *Growth and Stability*, pp. 147–50.
50. A. W. PHILLIPS, 'United Kingdom, 1861–1937'.
51. G. L. PERRY, 'Wages', pp. 897–904; M. FRIEDMAN, *Unemployment versus Inflation*.
52. The Federal Reserve followed a selective policy by which they took in more short-term than long-term credit. The interest rate for short-term money could thus be held at a high level to restrict the outflow of capital. The interest rate for long-term credit, on the other hand, could be held low so as not to discourage domestic industrial investment.
53. A. MADDISON, *Growth in the West*, p. 104.
54. This increasing importance of inventory investment in the course of post-war growth cycles was brought into doubt by Gordon: R. A. GORDON, 'US Economy'. Studying the American economy, Gordon pointed to the declining influence of inventory investment. Expressed as a percentage of GNP of the previous year (in constant 1958 prices): 1937–8, −3.9 per cent; 1948–9, −2.6 per cent; 1953–4, 0.7 per cent; 1957–8, −0.6 per cent; and 1960–1, −0.3 per cent.
55. E. LUNDBERG, *Instability*, p. 129, p. 130.
56. J. K. GALBRAITH, *Industrial State*, pp. 198–210.
57. E. LUNDBERG, *Instability*, p. 127.
58. J. CORNWALL, *Growth and Stability*, p. 231.
59. In the United States and Canada the figures were higher than in Western Europe and Japan. This had much to do with the non-expansionary policy of the Eisenhower administration during the 1950s and the success of the theory of the Phillips Curve. Some European countries also recorded high unemployment figures, e.g.: Italy (7 per cent between 1948 and 1961 because of structural unemployment in the south of the country); West Germany until 1957 because of the stream of immigrants from East Germany; Belgium and Denmark during the 1950s because of their unfavourable export structure at the time.
60. R. C. O. MATTHEWS, 'Postwar Business Cycles', p. 107.
61. A. MADDISON, *Growth in the West*, ch. 4; id., 'Performance in Europe', p. 479.
62. R. C. O. MATTHEWS, 'Postwar Business Cycles', p. 127.
63. J. CORNWALL, *Growth and Stability*, pp. 151–2.
64. P. A. KLEIN, *Business Cycles*.
65. G. H. MOORE, 'International Business Cycle'.
66. D. RIPLEY, 'Cyclical Fluctuations'. I would like to thank Ms Ripley

very much for the friendly co-operation which she gave to me on this work and for her invaluable comments during discussions of this problem.

67. R. N. COOPER, *Economics of Interdependence*.
68. R. TRIFFIN, *Gold and the Dollar Crisis*.
69. A. M. OKUN, *Prosperity*; J. E. SUNDQUIST, *Politics and Policy*; J. TOBIN, *New Economics*.
70. OECD, *Inflation*.
71. Unemployment fell gradually to a low of 4 per cent, or even lower, to 3.5 per cent, of the active population: W. W. ROSTOW, *World Economy*, p. 776.
72. Between 1964 and 1969 Japan and Europe each achieved a balance-of-payments surplus of respectively $2.5 billion and $6 billion (OECD, *Inflation*).
73. During the period 1960–5 the rate of inflation in Japan averaged 6 per cent annually; during the period 1965–8 the yearly average was 4.8 per cent; in 1969 it was 5.2 per cent, and in 1970 it even reached 7.7 per cent.
74. See the OECD reports of the period.
75. F. W. PAISH, 'Inflation', pp. 2ff.
76. For a broad overview of the concept of an accommodation policy concerning monetary activities in relation to wage demands or income expectations see: D. LAIDLER, J. M. PARKIN, 'Inflation'. See also: J. A. TREVITHICK, *Inflation, a Guide*, p. 97.
77. A. W. PHILLIPS, *United Kingdom, 1861–1937*; G. L. PERRY, 'Wages'; M. FRIEDMAN, *Unemployment versus Inflation*.
78. P. MACCRACKEN, *Towards Full Employment*, p. 42.
79. R. A. MUNDELL, *International Economics*, ch. 15; 'The International Disequilibrium System'.
80. J. M. FLEMING, *Inflation*.
81. R. N. COOPER, R. Z. LAWRENCE, 'Commodity Boom', p. 673 (see also the commentaries made on that paper by S. Houthakker and R. Solomon).
82. For the problem of relative prices and international terms of trade in historical perspective see: W. W. ROSTOW, *World Economy*, pp. 81–99.
83. R. L. Heilbroner even writes of an implicit agreement, a sort of silent conspiracy, between management and unions to pass on wage rises to the consumer via price increases; the government was then also implicated by making available the necessary liquidity (R. L. HEILBRONER, *Beyond Boom*, pp. 44–5).
84. Ibid., pp. 50–1.
85. W. W. ROSTOW, *World Economy*, pp. 358–62.
86. OECD, *Economic Outlook*.
87. Ibid.
88. W. W. ROSTOW, *World Economy*, p. 291.
89. According to calculations by Maddison, production per man-hour in 16 Western industrial countries averaged 3.8 per cent annually

during the period 1970–7, 4.4 per cent during the period 1950–70, 1.8 per cent during the period 1913–50 and 1.7 per cent during the period 1870–1913: A. MADDISON, 'Long Run Dynamics', pp. 4–5.

90. G. HABERLER, 'Stagflation', pp. 258–60.
91. Ibid., p. 251.
92. OECD, *Economic Outlook*, July 1977; W. M. BROWN, 'World Afloat'.
93. Compare the MacCracken Report, *Towards Full Employment*, and OECD, *Economic Outlook*, for the years 1977 and 1978.
94. OECD, *Economic Outlook*, July 1978, p. vii.
95. OECD, *Economic Outlook*, December 1979.
96. D. RIPLEY, 'Cyclical Fluctuations'.
97. F. HIRSCH, P. OPPENHEIMER, 'Managed Money', p. 672.
98. A. MADDISON, *Growth in the West*, pp. 134–42.
99. E. LUNDBERG, *Instability*, pp. 112–14.
100. J. M. FLEMING, *Inflation*.
101. W. W. ROSTOW, *World Economy*, p. 353.
102. G. H. MOORE, 'International Business Cycle', pp. 21–9; P. A. KLEIN, *Business Cycles*; D. RIPLEY, 'Cyclical Fluctuations', with supplement for the period 1952–75; G. PIGOTT, R. J. SWEENY, T. D. WILLETT, 'Aggregate Economic Fluctuations'.
103. G. H. MOORE, 'International Business Cycle', p. 22.
104. P. A. KLEIN, *Business Cycles*, pp. 27–39.
105. D. RIPLEY, 'Transmission of Fluctuations', *passim* (gratefully received from the author).
106. G. HABERLER, 'Stagflation', pp. 267–8.
107. W. W. ROSTOW, *World Economy*, pp. 359–67; L. H. DUPRIEZ, 'Long Waves'; J. J. VAN DUIJN, 'The Long Wave'; J. B. SHUNAN, D. F. ROSENAU, *Kondratieff Wave*; J. J. VAN DUIJN, *De Lange Golf*, pp. 95–150.
108. W. W. ROSTOW, *World Economy*, pp. 91–108.
109. Ibid., pp. 247–79; J. J. VAN DUIJN, *De Lange Golf*, pp. 95–114.
110. R. VERNON, 'International Investment'.
111. J. SCHMOOKLER, *Invention*.
112. N. ROSENBERG, *Perspectives*; A. MADDISON, 'Long Run Dynamics', pp. 14–18.
113. E. MANDEL, *Het Laatkapitalisme*, pp. 108–46; id., *La Crise 1974–1978*, pp. 179–208.
114. Among others: E. F. SCHUMACHER, *Small is Beautiful*; L. KOHR, *Overdeveloped Nations*.
115. L. KOHR, *Overdeveloped Nations*, pp. 33–41.
116. Ibid., pp. 111–12.

CHAPTER III

1. J. VAN DER TAK, C. HAUB, E. MURPHY, 'Trends in World Population', p. 51.
2. F. W. NOTESTEIN, 'Population: The Long View', p. 39.

3. E. ARNOLD (ed.), *Population Decline in Europe*, pp. 7–8.

4. S. E. BEAVER, *Demographic Transition Theory*, p. 10.

5. E. ARNOLD (ed.), *Population Decline in Europe*, pp. 14–16.

6. Ibid., pp. 10–12.

7. Ibid., p. 15.

8. T. J. ESPENSHADE, W. J. SEROW (eds), *Slowing Population Growth*, p. 233.

9. The share of immigrants in the natural population growth of Switzerland and Belgium in 1972 was 65 per cent and 72 per cent respectively: E. ARNOLD (ed.), *Population Decline in Europe*, p. 14.

10. E. ARNOLD (ed.), *Population Decline in Europe*, p. 5; V. CARVER, P. LIDDIARD (eds), *An Ageing Population*, p. 30.

11. For more details, see Chapter IV.

12. T. J. ESPENSHADE, 'Zero Population Growth', pp. 652–3.

13. The temporary further growth of the population after balance in marital fertility is reached is called 'Demographic Growth Momentum': R. LESTHAEGE, 'Bevolkingsproblemen en Ontwikkelingsbeleid', p. 6.

14. The World Bank records that in 1978 the average death rate in the industrialized countries was 9 per thousand; most of the richer developing countries in Asia and Latin America did better: WORLD BANK, *Development Report, 1980*, p. 144, Table 18.

15. WORLD BANK, *Development Report, 1980*, p. 65.

16. A. SAUVY, *Croissance Zéro?*, pp. 73–4.

17. G. MYRDAL, *Asian Drama*.

18. T. KING (*et al.*), *Population Policies*, p. 171.

19. Ibid., pp. 14–17.

20. There are good overviews of urbanization in the developing countries in: WORLD BANK, *Development Report, 1979*, pp. 72–3.

21. T. KING (*et al.*), *Population Policies*, p. 29.

22. S. KUZNETS, 'Growth and Income Inequality', pp. 1–28.

23. Among others: P. R. EHRLICH, A. H. EHRLICH, *Population, Resources, Environment*; P. VAN MOESEKE, K. TAVERNIER (eds), *Het huis staat in brand*.

24. R. F. HOPKINS, D. J. PUCHALA, 'International Relations of Food', pp. 581–616.

25. FAO, *Agriculture: Towards 2000*.

26. R. F. HOPKINS, D. J. PUCHALA, 'International Relations of Food', p. 599.

27. In relative terms this increase was less significant. Due to the expansion of trade in industrial products after the Second World War, the relative share of agricultural products in total international trade was almost halved. Naturally account must also be taken of the unfavourable terms of trade. Prices of agricultural products between 1950 and 1973 either fell or stagnated, those of industrial products and services rose.

28. See G. L. SEEVERS, 'Food Markets', pp. 721–43.

29. H. R. NAU, 'Diplomacy of World Food', p. 780.

30. Ibid., p. 789.
31. In 1950 Western European countries still accounted for almost two-thirds of the world grain trade, but by 1972–4 this share had fallen to less than one-third. During the same period the combined share of Japan, the Soviet Union and China rose from 7 per cent to more than 30 per cent: H. R. NAU, 'Diplomacy of World Food', pp. 780–2.
32. Ibid., p. 783.
33. R. F. HOPKINS, D. J. PUCHALA, 'International Relations of Food', p. 605.
34. Ibid.
35. On the deteriorating food situation in many developing countries, see: S. REUTLINGER, M. SELOWSKY, *Malnutrition and Poverty*.
36. A well-known example is the land reclamation undertaken by the Khrushchev government in the Asiatic areas of the Soviet Union.
37. W. D. RASMUSSEN, G. L. BAKER, J. S. WARD, *History of Agricultural Adjustment*.
38. W. D. RASMUSSEN, *Technology and American Agriculture* (an unpublished paper made available to me by the author, for which I am most grateful).
39. K. O. CAMPBELL, *Food in the Future*, quoted in: R. SELIM, 'United States World Granary', p. 15.
40. W. D. RASMUSSEN, *Technology and American Agriculture*, p. 11.
41. Ibid.
42. OECD, *Agricultural Policy in the US*.
43. W. D. RASMUSSEN, *Technology and American Agriculture*, p. 14.
44. OECD, *Agricultural Policy in the US*, pp. 11–14.
45. Ibid., pp. 10–12.
46. Ibid., pp. 19–29.
47. R. A. GOLDBERG, J. E. AUSTIN, *Multinational Agribusiness*.
48. W. D. RASMUSSEN, *Technology and American Agriculture*, p. 14.
49. For Western Europe see: OECD, *Agricultural Policy of the EEC*; for Japan see: OECD, *Agricultural Policy in Japan*.
50. OECD, *Agricultural Policy of the EEC*, p. 29.
51. For further details of the Mansholt Plan and other institutional aspects of the 'Common Agricultural Policy' of the European Economic Community, see Chapters IX and X.
52. R. F. HOPKINS, D. J. PUCHALA, 'International Relations of Food', p. 585.
53. W. D. RASMUSSEN, G. L. BAKER, J. S. WARD, *History of Agricultural Adjustment*, pp. 18–20.
54. G. E. BLANDOW, 'Agricultural Production', p. 84.
55. V. W. RUTTAN, 'Induced Innovation', pp. 196–216.
56. E. BOSERUP, 'Food Supply', pp. 164–76.
57. L. R. BROWN, *By Bread Alone*, pp. 133–46.
58. R. GHESQUIRE, *Tussen Eden en Utopia*, pp. 68–77.
59. There is an interesting empirical investigation into this failure in: K. GRIFFIN, *Agrarian Change*.

60. Taiwan is the only country where small concerns were actively engaged in the Green Revolution. The fact that many veterans of the Nationalist army were involved in the land reform undoubtedly facilitated the success in this area.

61. R. GHESQUIRE, *Tussen Eden en Utopia*, pp. 78–9.

62. K. A. DAHLBERG, *Beyond the Green Revolution*, pp. 76–86.

63. E. BOSERUP, *Évolution agraire*.

64. B. A. DATOO, 'Toward a Reformulation', pp. 135–44.

65. D. GABOR, V. COLOMBO, A. KING, R. GALLI, *Age of Waste*, p. 103.

66. H. E. GOELLER, 'Age of Substitutability', p. 150.

67. W. MALENBAUM, *World Demand for Raw Materials*, p. 7.

68. D. H. MEADOWS (*et al.*), *Limits to Growth*.

69. W. D. NORDHAUS, 'Constraint on Growth', pp. 22–6; G. M. BROWN, B. FIELD, 'Scarcity Measures', pp. 218–46; C. W. HOWE, *Natural Resource Economics*, pp. 108–28.

70. J. E. TILTON, *Non-fuel Minerals*, pp. 6–7.

71. T. BERTELMAN (*et al.*), *Resources, Society*, p. 68.

72. D. GABOR, V. COLOMBO, A. KING, R. GALLI, *Age of Waste*, p. 105.

73. A. R. DE SOUZA, B. FOUST, *World Space Economy*, p. 117.

74. C. F. DIAZ-ALEJANDRO, 'International Markets', pp. 269–311.

75. J. E. TILTON, *Non-fuel Minerals*, pp. 80–90.

76. Ibid., pp. 85–6.

77. Specific examples would be CIPEC (copper, 1974), IBA (bauxite, 1974), AIEC (iron ore, 1975). For raw material cartels, see: J. E. TILTON, *Non-fuel Minerals*, p. 81.

78. T. BERTELMAN (*et al.*), *Resources, Society*, pp. 132–3.

79. M. DESAI, 'Primary Product Prices', pp. 167–77.

80. C. P. BROWN, *Commodity Control*, pp. 11–19.

81. D. GABOR, V. COLOMBO, A. KING, R. GALLI, *Age of Waste*, p. 129.

82. Ibid. pp. 138–41.

83. A. R. DE SOUZA, B. FOUST, *World Space Economy*, p. 119.

84. R. N. COOPER (ed.), *A Reordered World*, pp. 153–67, pp. 241–62.

85. E. MILES (ed.), 'Restructuring Ocean Regimes', pp. 151–384.

86. W. W. ROSTOW, *World Economy*, p. 596.

87. L. SCHIPPER, A. D. LICHTENBERG, 'Efficient Energy Use', pp. 1001–13.

88. D. GABOR, V. COLOMBO, A. KING, R. GALLI, *Age of Waste*, p. 13.

89. Ibid., p. 70.

90. A. DAS GUPTA, *Economic and Commercial Geography*, p. 191.

91. Poland was the fourth largest producer, accounting in 1975 for about 7 per cent of world production.

92. D. GABOR, V. COLOMBO, A. KING, R. GALLI, *Age of Waste*, p. 31.

93. D. R. BOHI, M. RUSSELL, *Limiting Oil Imports*, pp. 21–44.

94. Y. KARMON, *Ports around the World*.

95. C. W. HOWE, *Natural Resource Economics*, p. 192.

96. Ibid., p. 194; A. DAS GUPTA, *Economic and Commercial Geography*, p. 210.

97. A. R. DE SOUZA, B. FOUST, *World Space Economy*, pp. 122–3.

98. DEUTSCHE BANK, *OPEC, Five Years after the Oil Price Increase.*
99. G. DANCET, 'De gevolgen van de olieprijsstijgingen', pp. 50–65.
100. OECD, *Economic Outlook*, No. 25, p. 63.
101. Ibid., pp. 63–4.
102. J. M. BLAIR., *Control of Oil*; R. VERNON, *Storm over the Multinationals*; J. H. DUNNING, R. D. PEARCE, *World's Largest Industrial Enterprises*; L. G. FRANKO, *European Multinationals.*
103. G. GREENHALGH, *Nuclear Power*, pp. 98–118.

CHAPTER IV

1. The neo-classical analysis of economic growth is based on the concept of the 'marginal productivity' of the different factors of production. With the aid of this concept, the marginal contribution of the different factors of production to total national production can be determined. The relevant question is as follows: when the amount of applied labour (capital) is raised (reduced) by 1 per cent, and all other circumstances remain unchanged, how great is the percentage increase (fall) in national production? (R. SOLOW, P. TEMIN, 'Introduction', p. 7).

2. A. MADDISON, 'Explaining Economic Growth', p. 213, footnote 6.

3. J. W. KENDRICK, *Productivity Trends.*

4. E. F. DENISON, *Why Growth Rates Differ*; id., *United States Growth 1929–1969*; E. F. DENISON, W. K. CHUNG, *How Japan's Economy Grew*; E. F. DENISON, *Slower Economic Growth.*

5. Denison also made allowances for differences in labour intensity but came under much criticism on this question from: A. MADDISON, 'Explaining Economic Growth', pp. 236ff.

6. On this issue see the works of T. W. SCHULTZ; see also M. J. BOWMAN, 'Schultz, Denison'.

7. The form of productivity which Denison studied was *output per unit of input* i.e. total factor productivity. Denison thus analysed neither labour productivity nor capital productivity separately.

8. It fluctuated between 1.58 per cent and 1.74 per cent: E. F. DENISON, *Slower Economic Growth*, p. 105.

9. Ibid., p. 105.

10. E. F. DENISON, *Why Growth Rates Differ*, p. 285.

11. Ibid., p. 292.

12. E. F. DENISON, *Slower Economic Growth, passim.*

13. Ibid., p. 279.

14. In the structural visions of Svennilson and Cornwall, great emphasis is laid on precisely these reallocations.

15. I. SVENNILSON, *Growth and Stagnation.*

16. In studying the contribution to growth of his different explanatory factors, Denison looked at each separately and in isolation. This hinders the application of any concept of interdependence and is a source of serious criticism. For example, the division into separate

categories of *Advances of knowledge: changes in the lag in the application of knowledge* and *Economies of scale: growth of markets and income elasticities* is wholly untenable because the interdependence between the two is clear and significant..

17. I. SVENNILSON, *Growth and Stagnation* , pp. 7–8.

18. The same circumstances can also lower the cost price of raw materials and energy and thus favour the transformation process as was the case in the 1950s and the 1960s. Experience, however, has shown that this effect can easily be neutralized.

19. I. SVENNILSON, *Growth and Stagnation*, p. 10. This vision runs very close to the later theory of Salter on technological progress: W. E. G. SALTER, *Productivity*.

20. I. SVENNILSON, *Growth and Stagnation*, pp. 10–11.

21. J. CORNWALL, *Modern Capitalism*; A. MADDISON, *Growth in the West*; id., 'Long Run Dynamics'; G. MENSCH, *Technologische Patt*.

22. See Cornwall's strong criticism of the neo-classical approach to growth in: J. CORNWALL, 'Postwar Growth'; id., *Modern Capitalism*, pp. 24–34.

23. J. CORNWALL, *Modern Capitalism*, p. 40.

24. Ibid., p. 96.

25. M. MACURA, 'Population in Europe'. p. 7.

26. M. LIVI-BACCI, *Report on the Demography*.

27. See in this respect the measures taken by West Germany, Switzerland, Belgium, the Netherlands, and France: OECD, *Reporting System on Migration, 1978*, p. 7.

28. OECD, *Reporting System on Migration, 1976*.

29. For this problem see the substantial and detailed studies of: W. BÖHNING, *Migration of Workers* (especially ch. 4); W. BÖHNING, D. MAILLAT, *Employment of Foreign Workers*.

30. W. BÖHNING, *Migration of Workers*, p. 56.

31. Ibid., pp. 59–61, Tables 4–1 and 4–2.

32. Ibid., pp. 63–71.

33. In Canada during the 1970s the population aged between fifteen and sixty-four grew annually by 2.3 per cent as against only 1.3 per cent for the population as a whole. In the United States the respective figures were 1.6 per cent and 0.8 per cent, in Belgium 0.6 per cent and 0.3 per cent and in the Netherlands 1.4 per cent and 0.9 per cent. See Table 14, columns 25 and 27.

34. See Table 14, columns 2, 10, 21, 32.

35. There is an interesting graphical comparison on this in: OECD, *Demographic Trends*, pp. 83–8.

36. Two other patterns can also be noted. In the Netherlands and to a lesser extent in Switzerland, the rate of female participation following marriage is strikingly low and the marital age is strikingly high, in comparison with other countries. In Finland and to an extent in Sweden too, the female curve describes the same pattern as that for men, but generally at a lower level.

37. C. CLARK, *Economic Progress*.

38. It must be emphasized that in most OECD countries the average level of productivity still remained considerably below that of industry.
39. It was only in Canada that agricultural incomes made distinct progress relative to other income levels: J. CORNWALL, *Growth and Stability*, p. 51.
40. T. W. SCHULTZ, 'Investment in Human Capital'. Schultz's theory has been worked out into very refined micro-economic models; for instance, see: G. BECKER, *Human Capital*.
41. E. F. DENISON, *Slower Economic Growth*, p. 104.
42. In 1976 the average length of education was 9.7 years: A. MADDISON, 'Long Run Dynamics', p. 25.
43. E. F. DENISON, *Slower Economic Growth*, p. 104.
44. J. J. SERVAN-SCHREIBER, *Le défi américain*.
45. Only Sweden and Japan were exceptions to this and then only before 1955. In later years the American lead was a general one.
46. A. MADDISON, 'Long Run Dynamics', p. 25.
47. OECD, *Gaps in Technology*. Account must be taken of the fact that university registration in the United States has a broader connotation than in Western Europe. When registrations in the specialized, non-university institutes in Western Europe are added to university registrations, however, the result is still only three-quarters of the American total.
48. A. MADDISON, 'Long Run Dynamics'.
49. OECD, *Gaps in Technology*, p. 18.
50. Only in Swedish manufacturing industry was the share of engineers and higher technical personnel as a percentage of the total work-force in this sector higher than in the United States, namely 8.5 per cent against 5 per cent: ibid., p. 22.
51. Ibid., p. 43.
52. West Germany records low scores in all statistics concerning education; for example, education expenditure in relation to GNP, the average length of education, and the number of academic and higher technical personnel. This is all the more surprising when one thinks that Germany's successful industrialization in the nineteenth century is partly ascribed to its lead in the area of education: D. LANDES, *The Unbound Prometheus*, p. 150. West Germany's current lag is attributed to the absence of statistics on part-time education, a form which appears to be particularly important in West Germany: OECD, *Gaps in Technology*, pp. 15–16.
53. Ibid., pp. 54–9.
54. Canada also experienced high emigration figures respecting the highly educated, although this essentially comprised only part of a wider picture of considerable inflows and outflows of labour. In fact Canada achieved a net surplus of *brain gain*: H. G. JOHNSON, *Technology*, pp. 106–7.
55. Ibid., ch. 6.
56. C. P. KINDLEBERGER, *Europe's Postwar Growth*.

57. W. A. LEWIS, 'Economic Development'. In connection with this see also: J. C. H. FEI, G. RANIS, *Labor Surplus Economy*.
58. C. P. KINDLEBERGER, *Europe's Postwar Growth*; N. KALDOR, *Strategic Factors*; V. LUTZ, *Italy*; R. MINAMI, *The Turning Point*.
59. C. P. KINDLEBERGER, *Europe's Postwar Growth*.
60. K. W. ROSKAMP, *Capital Formation*.
61. V. LUTZ, *Italy*; G. H. HILDEBRAND, *Growth and Structure*; G. VACIAGO, 'Alternative Theories of Growth'.
62. R. NOLEN, *Active Manpower Policy*.
63. J. C. R. DOW, *British Economy 1945–1960*; A. SHONFIELD, *British Economic Policy*; A. MADDISON, *Growth in the West*; S. POLLARD, *British Economy 1914–1967*.
64. See especially: F. W. PAISH, *Inflationary Economy*.
65. J. R. SARGENT, *Out of Stagnation*.
66. M. LIPTON, 'Manpower and Growth'.
67. A. LAMFALUSSY, *The Case of Belgium*.
68. For the specific characteristics of such zones with surplus labour consult especially: J. C. H. FEI, G. RANIS, *Labor Surplus Economy*.
69. See, among others: S. HOFFMANN (*et al.*), *In Search of France*.
70. A. LAMFALUSSY, *The Case of Belgium*.
71. If the calculation is refined by replacing the category 'increase in the active population' with the category 'growth of employment in the non-agricultural sector', the representativeness of Kindleberger's classification is substantially improved although it is still not perfect. If the calculation is still further refined and broken down into decades (i.e., growth of employment in the non-agricultural sector during the period 1950–9 and during the period 1960–9) the Lewis model appears to be fairly well applicable for the decade 1950–9. During this decade flexible labour supply undoubtedly played an important role in growth.
72. R. KRENGEL, 'Attempt at a Prognosis of Output'.
73. R. KRENGEL, 'Some Reasons for the Rapid Growth', pp. 134–5.
74. J. CORNWALL, *Modern Capitalism*, p. 95.
75. Ibid., p. 94.
76. Ibid., pp. 45–6; N. KALDOR, 'Productivity', p. 386.
77. Cornwall adds yet a second structural condition to his hypothesis. If the dual model is to be applicable, not only does *employment* in the most productive sectors of manufacturing industry have to grow faster than in the economy as a whole, the same has to apply for *production*.
78. R. D. SLEEPER, 'Manpower Redeployment'; L. C. HUNTER, G. I. REID, *Urban Workers' Mobility*; D. I. MACKAY, D. BODDY, J. BRACK, J. A. KIACK, N. JONES, *Wages and Labour Mobility*; id., *Labour Markets*.
79. For every 100 workers available for the non-agricultural sector of the economy, manufacturing industry employs 33 in West Germany, 28 in France, and 20 in Britain: J. CORNWALL, *Modern Capitalism*,

p. 91. See also: R. BACON, W. ELTIS, *Britain's Economic Problem*; J. WOLFF, 'Productivity and Growth'.

80. G. VACIAGO, 'Alternative Theories of Growth'.

81. F. CROUZET (ed.), *Capital Formation*.

82. W. E. G. SALTER, *Productivity*, p. 52.

83. Ibid., p. 48.

84. P. J. VERDOORN, 'Fattori che regolano'. Recent tests in: N. KALDOR, *Causes*, p. 12; J. CORNWALL, *Modern Capitalism*, p. 127.

85. T. F. CRIPPS, R. J. TARLING, *Growth*, p. 22; N. KALDOR, *Strategic Factors*, p. 8.

86. See the very interesting study of: A. MADDISON, 'Long Run Dynamics'.

87. During the last quarter of the nineteenth century Australia also led the United States in respect of productivity per man-hour. This was probably due to the combination there of relative underpopulation and labour-extensive livestock farming.

88. L. ROSTAS, *British and American Industry*; D. PAIGE, G. BOMBACH, *Comparison of National Output*.

89. The relationship between productive investment and output for the period 1950–60 was 4.1 in the United States, 4.3 in the United Kingdom, 3.1 in France, 2.3 in Italy, and 2.1 in West Germany. Thus in order to achieve the same increase in the annual rate of growth of GNP, the United States had to invest (gross) nearly twice as much as West Germany: A. MADDISON, *Growth in the West*.

90. Maddison calculated that in 1955 the real average number of hours worked per year by worker was 2,250 hours in Britain, 2,197 in West Germany, and 1,906 in the United States. He used this as an approximation of the number of hours of machine use: A. MADDISON, *Growth in the West*.

91. Around 1950 the catching-up movement contributed 8.08 per cent to the growth rate of Japanese manufacturing industry and 3.75 per cent to that in West Germany. By 1965 this influence had diminished to 4.29 per cent and 1.99 per cent respectively: J. CORNWALL, *Modern Capitalism*, pp. 141–3.

92. M. A. KATOUZIAN, 'Development of the Service Sector'; Y. SOBOLO, *Les Tertiaires*.

93. See Chapter III.

94. C. P. KINDLEBERGER, *American Business Abroad*.

95. A. DEVROYE, *Amerikaanse directe investeringen in Europa*.

96. S. HYMER, *International Operations of National Firms*.

97. J. H. MAKIN, 'Capital Flows and Exchange-rate Flexibility'.

98. A. O. HIRSCHMAN, *Strategy of Economic Development*.

CHAPTER V

1. B. M. HESSEN, *Newton's Principia*; A. MUSSON, E. ROBINSON, *Science and Technology*; J. JEWKES, D. SAWERS, B. STILLERMAN, *Sources of Invention*.

2. R. R. NELSON, M. J. PECK, E. D. KALACHEK, *Technology, Economic Growth*, p. 40.

3. OECD, *Gaps in Technology*.

4. M. GIBBONS, R. JOHNSTON, 'The Role of Science', pp. 220–41; NATIONAL SCIENCE FOUNDATION, *Interactions of Science and Technology*.

5. R. R. NELSON, M. J. PECK, E. D. KALACHEK, *Technology, Economic Growth*, p. 40.

6. J. SCHMOOKLER, 'Inventors, Past and Present'.

7. C. FREEMAN, *The Economics*, p. 25.

8. In mechanical engineering individual applications for patents are still fairly frequent. In the electronic and chemical sectors such applications are rather rare. In 1957 in the United States, 97 per cent of the chemical patents and 91 per cent of electronic patents were held by specific companies; for mechanical inventions the figure stood at only 12 per cent: R. R. NELSON, M. J. PECK, E. D. KALACHEK, *Technology, Economic Growth*, p. 73.

9. M. BROWN, A. CONRAD, 'The Influence of Research', F. RAINES, *The Impact of Applied Research*; N. TERLECKY, *The Effect of R & D*.

10. For the statistical problems encountered in international comparisons of R & D expenditure see: OECD, *Trends in Industrial R & D*, pp. 158–70.

11. OECD, *Gaps in Technology*.

12. It should be pointed out that European backwardness with respect to the use of highly qualified research workers was considerably less than its backwardness in the area of equipment and research budgets.

13. The OECD calculated that in American companies 40 per cent of all research expenditure produced results that were unsuitable for commercial development. In Britain, France, and Sweden, this figure fluctuated between 20 per cent and 30 per cent and for Canada and West Germany it was around 10 per cent.

14. OECD, *Trends in Industrial R & D*, pp. 15ff.

15. OECD, *Science and Technology*.

16. *Business Plans for Research and Development*, quoted in: OECD, *Science and Technology*.

17. OECD, *Gaps in Technology*.

18. J. BEN-DAVID, *Fundamental Research*. A concrete example is provided by the space industry: R. MILLER, D. SAWERS, *Modern Aviation*.

19. OECD, *Gaps in Technology*.

20. Ibid., p. 210.

21. W. LEONTIEF, 'Factor Proportions and the Structure of American Trade: Further Theoretical and Empirical Analysis', in *Review of Economics*, Vol. 38, (November 1956), pp. 392–7.

22. There is an overview in R. VERNON (ed.), *The Technology Factor*. See also: W. GRUBER, D. METHA, R. VERNON, 'The R & D Factor'.

23. C. FREEMAN (*et al.*), 'R & D in Electronic Capital Goods'; G. HUFBAUER, *Synthetic Materials*.

24. M. V. POSNER, 'International Trade', pp. 323–41; S. HIRSCH, 'United

States Electronic Industry'; R. VERNON, 'International Investment', pp. 190–207; S. HIRSCH, *Location of Industry*.

25. OECD, *Gaps in Technology*, p. 293.
26. For a statistical overview see: A. DEVROYE, *Amerikaanse directe investeringen in Europa*.
27. OECD, *Gaps in Technology*, p. 286.
28. Ibid., p. 262.
29. A. D. CHANDLER Jr, *The Visible Hand*.
30. O. E. WILLIAMSON, 'Emergence of the Visible Hand', pp. 182–202; H. DAEMS, 'Rise of the Modern Industrial Enterprise', pp. 203–23.
31. A. D. CHANDLER Jr, H. DAEMS, 'Administrative Coordination', pp. 28–54 (especially pp. 41–2).
32. A. D. CHANDLER Jr, *Strategy and Structure*. See also: O. E. WILLIAMSON, 'Managerial Discretion', pp. 343–86; id., *Markets and Hierarchies*, ch. 1.
33. A. D. CHANDLER Jr, *Strategy and Structure*, ch. 7.
34. A. D. CHANDLER Jr, 'Growth of the Transnational Industrial Firm', pp. 396–410; L. HANNAH, *The Corporate Economy*.
35. In France holding companies were predominant. These were linked to each other through mutual investments and thus formed a combination of family and financial capitalism: M. LEVY-LEBOYER, 'The Large Corporation', pp. 117–60. See also: D. GRANICK, *The European Executive*.
36. H. VAN DER WEE, 'Investment Strategy of Belgian Industrial Enterprise'.
37. Germany thus did not only take over some American management techniques, it also developed some of its own techniques: J. KOCKA, *The Modern Industrial Enterprise in Germany*, p. 102.
38. H. DAEMS, *The Holding Company*.
39. In Britain concentration and integration also took place in the food products and brewing industries. This was the only European country where the domestic market developed favourably in terms of size and income level: A. D. CHANDLER Jr, 'Growth of the Transnational Industrial Firm', pp. 404–7.
40. H. DAEMS, *The Holding Company*, pp. 65–91.
41. D. F. CHANNON, *British Enterprise*.
42. For a discussion and overview see: R. E. CAVES, 'Industrial Organization, Corporate Strategy', pp. 55–122.
43. J. KOCKA, H. SIEGRIST, 'Die hundert gröszten deutschen Industrieunternehmen', pp. 55–112.
44. E. M. HADLEY, *Antitrust in Japan*.
45. R. E. CAVES, M. UEKUSA, *Industrial Organization*, pp. 10–15.
46. A. A. BERLE Jr, *Capitalist Revolution*; P. F. DRUCKER, *The New Society*; J. K. GALBRAITH, *Industrial State*; id., *Economics and the Public Purpose*.
47. M. WILKINS, *Multinational Enterprise*.
48. R. E. CAVES, 'Industrial Organization, Corporate Strategy', p. 73.
49. S. T. DAVIS, P. R. LAWRENCE, *Matrix*.

50. For a summary of the criticism see: V. VAN ROMPUY, 'J. K. Galbraith', pp. 210–21.
51. G. MENSCH, *Technologische Patt* (translated and extended in G. MENSCH, *Stalemate in Technology*). See also: J. J. VAN DUIJN, *De Lange Golf*; D. LANDES, *The Unbound Prometheus*, p. 520.
52. For the influence of population growth on investment and on the assimilation of innovations: S. KUZNETS, *Growth and Structure*.
53. K. PAVITT, 'Technical Innovation: 1', p. 461.
54. G. MENSCH, *Technologische Patt*.
55. S. KUZNETS, 'Retardation of Industrial Growth', pp. 534–60.
56. G. MENSCH, R. SCHNOPP, *Stalemate in Technology, 1925–1935*, p. 12a.
57. D. LANDES, *The Unbound Prometheus*, pp. 423–39.
58. I. SVENNILSON, *Growth and Stagnation*, pp. 21–2.
59. C. FREEMAN, 'The Kondratiev Long Waves', p. 192.
60. Ibid., pp. 193–4.
61. K. PAVITT, 'Technical Innovation: 2'.
62. S. MELMAN, *Our Depleted Society*.
63. H. BROOKS, 'US-Lead in Technology', pp. 110–18.
64. R. GILPIN, *US Power*.
65. R. ROTHWELL, 'Technical Change in International Competitiveness'.

CHAPTER VI

1. S. KUZNETS, *Growth and Structure*, pp. 304–54.
2. H. J. HABAKKUK, *Population Growth*, ch. 2.
3. For further details, see Chapter VII.
4. BELGIUM: 'Het verloop van de bestaansvoorwaarden in België', pp. 3–25.
5. Ibid., p. 14.
6. There exists a great deal of literature on this problem, with conflicting conclusions. As early as 1939 Keynes pointed to a long-term stability of the macro-economic wage share (J. M. KEYNES, 'Relative Movements'). Other economists took issue with this, such as: R. M. SOLOW, 'Constancy of Relative Shares'. For a general overview of the discussion see: L. CUYVERS, W. MEEUSEN, 'Functionele inkomensverdeling'.
7. S. KUZNETS, *Modern Economic Growth*, pp. 172–7.
8. For other Western countries not mentioned in Table 28, for instance Belgium, Norway, Japan, Australia, and New Zealand, see: S. KUZNETS, 'Quantitative Aspects of the Economic Growth', IV, p. 48.
9. H. DELEECK, *Ongelijkheden in de Welvaartsstaat*, p. 125. For Belgium see: L. CUYVERS, W. MEEUSEN, 'Functionele inkomensverdeling'.
10. S. Kuznets' findings are sometimes disputed with statistical arguments. The average income position of wage and salary earners should not so much be compared with the evolution of national income but rather with the average income position of the working population.

In this way account is taken of structural changes of the composition of the working population in the countries concerned. The calculation of such a 'refined wage share' weakens Kuznets' conclusions that the share of labour in the national income rose significantly in the West after the Second World War. Instead the curves would show only a slight increase (J. KESENNE, 'De primaire inkomensverdeling in België'). But allowance should be made for the notable fall in the working week in the West. The share of labour in the national income could thus be maintained or even improved with far fewer hours worked than previously. In addition, there was an important distinction between the development of wages and salaries. In general, after the Second World War, the average income of workers (wages) rose perceptibly faster than that of employees (salaries).

11. H. DELEECK, *Ongelijkheden in de Welvaartsstaat*, pp. 128–9.
11. A. MADDISON, *Growth in the West*, pp. 49–56.
12. J. K. GALBRAITH, *Affluent Society*, pp. 89–120; id., *Industrial State*.
13. V. VAN ROMPUY, 'J. K. Galbraith', pp. 210–21.
14. G. EYSKENS (*et al.*), *Het land waarin wij werken*, pp. 70–1.
15. M. KIDRON, *Western Capitalism*, pp. 124–6.
16. S. MALLET, *La Nouvelle classe ouvrière*, pp. 47–103.
17. See also Chapter VII.
18. M. KIDRON, *Western Capitalism*, p. 124.
19. Ibid., pp. 86–97.
20. S. MALLET, *La Nouvelle classe ouvrière*, pp. 86–94.
21. M. KIDRON, *Western Capitalism*, p. 127.
22. D. VAN DER WEE, *Enkele theorieën over loonvorming*.
23. B. MARTENS, *De kollektivisering van de Industriële Besluitvorming*, pp. 154–68.
24. S. MALLET, *La Nouvelle classe ouvrière*, pp. 94–8.
25. S. RATNER, J. H. SOLTOW, R. SYLLA, *The American Economy*, pp. 476–93.
26. S. KUZNETS, 'Quantitative Aspects of the Economic Growth', Part IV, pp. 1–80; S. KUZNETS, *Modern Economic Growth*, pp. 206ff.; J. TINBERGEN, *Income Distribution Analysis*.
27. S. KUZNETS, *Modern Economic Growth*, pp. 214–15.
28. S. KUZNETS, 'Quantitative Aspects of the Economic Growth', Part IV.
29. A. BELIEN, *Inkomensongelijkheid in België*; A. BELIEN, J. KESENNE, K. TAVERNIER, *Inkomenshoogte en inkomensongelijkheid*.
30. J. TINBERGEN, *Income Distribution Analysis*, pp. 23–5.
31. Tinbergen's correction gives a too flattering picture. Some family expenditure, especially on consumer durables, is not proportional to family size. In addition, many tax systems and social security systems favour large families: M. SCHNITZER, *Income Distribution*, pp. 180–9.
32. J. TINBERGEN, *Income Distribution Analysis*, pp. 20–1.
33. H. DELEECK, *Ongelijkheden in de Welvaartsstaat*; H. DELEECK, *Maatschappelijke Zekerheid*.

34. M. SCHNITZER, *Income Distribution*, p. 41.
35. P. HENLE, 'Distribution of National Income'.
36. L. THUROW, *The Impact of Taxes*.
37. M. SCHNITZER, *Income Distribution*, pp. 46ff.
38. L. SODERSTROM, *Laginkomstproblemer*; L. SODERSTROM, *Svenska Kop-kraftsfordelningen*.
39. V. BERGSTROM, J. SODERSTEN, 'Industrial Growth and the Distribution of Incomes', pp. 98–108.
40. M. SCHNITZER, *Income Distribution*, pp. 184ff.
41. GERMANY: 'Einkomensverteilung und -schichtung'.
42. M. SCHNITZER, *Income Distribution*, pp. 224ff.
43. UNITED NATIONS, *Incomes in Post-War Europe*.
44. M. SAWYER, *Income Distribution in OECD Countries*.
45. On this issue in connection with Britain see: P. ROBERTI, 'U.K. Trend Towards Equality?', pp. 56–9.
46. L. VANDEKERCKHOVE, L. HUYSE, *In de buitenbaan*.
47. J. Tinbergen calls this factor the eternal competition between technological progress and educational achievement: J. TINBERGEN, *Income Distribution Analysis*.
48. W. DESAEYERE, K. TAVERNIER, E. VAN LOON, 'Personele inkomensverdeling in België', pp. 318ff.
49. According to calculations by M. Sawyer, Japan, Australia, Sweden, and Norway are countries closer to equality than France, the United States, Canada, and West Germay: M. SAWYER, *Income Distribution in OECD Countries*.
50. GATT, *Trends in International Trade*, 1957 to 1978.
51. For the 1950s see: A. MADDISON, *Growth in the West*, p. 166. For the 1960s and early 1970s see: J. CORNWALL, *Modern Capitalism*, p. 162.
52. OECD, *Policy Perspectives*, p. 177.
53. A. MAIZELS, *Growth and Trade*, p. 189.
54. R. BLACKHURST, N. MARIAN, J. TUMLIR, *Adjustment, Trade and Growth*, p. 35.
55. OECD, *Newly Industrializing Countries*, p. 29.
56. R. BLACKHURST, N. MARIAN, J. TUMLIR, *Adjustment, Trade and Growth*, p. 35.
57. IMF, *World Economic Outlook*, pp. 8–9.
58. WORLD BANK, *Commodity Trade, 1978 Edition*, p. 12.
59. A. MAIZELS, *Growth and Trade*, p. 163.
60. J. CORNWALL, *Modern Capitalism*, p. 177.
61. GATT, *Network of World Trade: 1955–1976*, p. 19.
62. R. BLACKHURST, N. MARIAN, J. TUMLIR, *Trade Liberalization*, p. 16.
63. H. G. GRUBEL, P. J. LLOYD, *Intra-industry Trade*, pp. 36–47.
64. D. B. KEESING, *World Trade and Output of Manufacturers*, p. 15.
65. Ibid., p. 29.
66. R. DICK, H. DICKE, 'Patterns of Trade', pp. 335–58.
67. For the Heckscher-Ohlin theorem see among others: R. J. CARBAUGH, *International Economics*, pp. 63–8.
68. Statistics are given in: BATTELLE, *Explor-Multitrade Data Bank*.

69. A. D. CHANDLER Jr, *Strategy and Structure*; A. D. CHANDLER Jr, H. DAEMS (eds), *Managerial Hierarchies*.

70. A. LAMFALUSSY, 'Europe's Progress', pp. 1–16; C. P. KINDLE-BERGER, *Europe's Postwar Growth*, pp. 113–15.

71. Naturally the tendency towards economic integration gained extra impetus when it was officially decided to set up a customs union.

72. For further information, see Chapters IX and XI.

73. A. MADDISON, *Growth in the West*, pp. 185–92.

74. R. N. COOPER, *Economics of Interdependence*, p. 65.

75. C. P. KINDLEBERGER, *Europe's Postwar Growth*, pp. 117–20.

76. R. N. COOPER, *Economics of Interdependence*, pp. 66–8.

77. A. LAMFALUSSY, *The United Kingdom and the Six*.

78. Ibid., p. 51.

79. S. B. LINDER, *An Essay on Trade*.

80. A. MAIZELS, *Industrial Growth*; id., *Exports and Economic Growth*; P. L. YATES, *Forty Years of Foreign Trade*.

81. R. VERNON, 'International Investment', pp. 190–207; L. T. WELLS, *International Trade*.

82. See Chapter V.

83. B. BALASSA, *World Trade*.

84. O. HIERONYMI, *New Economic Nationalism*.

CHAPTER VII

1. D. S. LANDES, *The Unbound Prometheus*.

2. S. S. TANGRI (ed.), *Command versus Demand*, p. vi.

3. C. P. KINDLEBERGER, A. SHONFIELD (eds), *North American and Western European Economic Policies*, pp. xiii–xv.

4. H. G. VATTER, 'The US Mixed Economy'.

5. A. D. CHANDLER Jr, *The Visible Hand*.

6. A. S. MILWARD, *War, Economy and Society*.

7. On this issue see the comparative table on economic performance published by A. MADDISON, (1913 = 100): *Growth in Japan and the USSR*, pp. 154, 155, 159, 164:

	Total Output in 1939 (1913 = 100)	Total Output per capita in 1938 (1913 = 100)	Industrial Production in 1938 (1913 = 100)
USSR	210.0	161.5	318.4
US	175.8	122.1	154.0
UK	138.3	119.2	151.7
Germany	165.9	132.2	149.3
France	124.0*	123.3	110.0
Italy	164.0	129.7	161.4

* 1938

8. For France see: F. CARON, *Modern France*, pp. 285–6; for Germany see: K. E. BORN, 'Government Action against the Great Depression', pp. 45–58.

9. H. DE MAN, *L'Exécution du Plan du Travail.*
10. J. DHONDT, 'Government, Labour and Trade Unions', pp. 253–62.
11. G. DALTON, *Economic Systems and Society*, pp. 97–101.
12. Ibid., pp. 101–5; S. S. TANGRI (ed.), *Command versus Demand*, p. vi.
13. For the United States see: H. G. VATTER, 'The U.S. Mixed Economy';
    P. A. SAMUELSON, *Economics*, p. 203.
14. G. R. DENTON, M. FORSYTH, M. MACLENNAN, *Economic Planning and Policies*, p. 152.
15. H. VAN DER WEE, P. JANSSENS, 'De overheidsinterventie', pp. 29–49.
16. P. A. SAMUELSON, *Economics*, pp. 470, 472.
17. A. SHONFIELD, *Modern Capitalism*, p. 63.
18. I. B. KRAVIS, 'Income Distribution', p. 142.
19. The banks involved were: Crédit Lyonnais, Société Générale, Comptoir National de l'Escompte, Banque Nationale pour le Commerce et l'Industrie.
20. S. LIEBERMAN, *Mixed Economies*, p. 5.
21. F. CARON, *Modern France*, pp. 299–300.
22. C. GRUSON, *La planification française*, p. 41.
23. At the start of the 1960s, 80 per cent of companies which had taken up industrial loans were paying interest set at a lower level than the normal free-market rate of interest: A. CHAZEL, H. POYET, *L'Économie mixte*, p. 102.
24. S. S. COHEN, *Modern Capitalist Planning*; P. PASCALLON, *L'Économie française.*
25. F. CARON, *Modern France*, p. 323.
26. COMMISSARIAT GENERAL DU PLAN DE MODERNISATION ET D'ÉQUIPEMENT, *Rapport général sur le Premier Plan*; see also: *Rapport sur la réalisation du Plan de Modernisation.*
27. G. DALTON, *Economic Systems and Society*, pp. 156–8.
28. J. DELORS, 'French Planning', pp. 9–12.
29. A. SHONFIELD, *Modern Capitalism*, pp. 71–87.
30. In this respect see S. LIEBERMAN, *Mixed Economies*, pp. 10–16; G. DALTON, *Economic Systems and Society*, pp. 157–60.
31. A. SHONFIELD, *Modern Capitalism*, pp. 128–30.
32. See the interesting conclusions in: W. C. BAUM, *The French Economy.*
33. For a summary and discussion of British policy see: J. MEADE, *The Mixed Economy.*
34. M. REES, *The Public Sector*, p. 125; H. A. CLEGG, T. E. CHESTER, *Nationalization*, ch. 1.
35. S. LIEBERMAN, *Mixed Economies*, p. 69.
36. M. REES, *The Public Sector*, pp. 204–15.
37. J. C. R. DOW, *British Economy 1945–1960*, pp. 33ff.
38. G. R. DENTON, M. FORSYTH, M. MACLENNAN, *Economic Planning and Policies*, p. 109. According to Balogh, the profit for the national income which was made as a result of a favourable evolution of the terms of trade after 1951, was neutralized by Butler's liberalization policy. Balogh argued that this profit should have been used to

finance a growth-orientated planning policy: T. BALOGH, 'Britain's planning problems', pp. 121–36.

39. The sizeable devaluation of September 1949 temporarily ended the overvaluation of sterling which removed the impending threat of a balance-of-payments crisis so that the stop-go policy could be somewhat relaxed. During the 1950s persistent overvaluation arose once more. During these years world opinion rapidly moved in the direction of a restoration of the gold standard and fixed exchange rates so that in the short term there was no longer any margin to adjust the sterling rate and a more stringent stop-go policy seemed the only solution left.

40. Interesting in this respect are the *White Paper on Financial and Economic Obligations of the National Industries* (1961) and the *White Paper on National Industries* (1967), in which five-year planning and financial returns are given full attention.

41. FEDERATION OF BRITISH INDUSTRIES, *Economic Planning in France.*

42. M. MACRAE, 'British Planning', pp. 140–2.

43. Ibid., pp. 143–5.

44. A. SHONFIELD, *Modern Capitalism*, p. 162.

45. S. POLLARD, *British Economy 1914–1967*, pp. 408–505.

46. V. LUTZ, *Italy*, ch. 12.

47. The land reform is often severely criticized. Many argue that the inefficient latifundia were mostly replaced by still less efficient minifundia and that this subsistence agriculture still further increased the poverty gap between north and south. On the other hand, it cannot be denied that the land reform had important social and psychological effects on the agricultural population of the south (G. G. D'ARAGONA, 'Land Reform in Italy', pp. 12–20).

48. V. LUTZ, *Italy*, pp. 279, 282–3.

49. For a general overview: N. JEQUIER, *Le défi industriel japonais*; O. KOMIYA, *Growth in Japan.*

50. G. C. ALLEN, *Economic History of Modern Japan*, pp. 170–205.

51. S. TSUNOYAMA, *History of Modern Japan*, pp. 96–101.

52. G. C. ALLEN, *Japan's Economic Expansion*, pp. 34–47.

53. The relaxation of antitrust legislation in order to stimulate rationalization and the use of greater economies of scale in industry is described in: R. CAVES, M. UEKUSA, 'Industrial Organization', pp. 482–9.

54. E. DOUGLAS, *Policies of Energy*, p. 127.

55. M. PECK, S. TAMURA, 'Technology', pp. 558–74.

56. H. T. PATRICK, 'Cyclical Instability', pp. 555–618.

57. A. SHONFIELD, *Modern Capitalism*, pp. 318–26.

58. A. O. OKUN, *Equality and Efficiency.*

59. S. E. HARRIS, *Economics of Political Parties.*

60. S. E. HARRIS, *Kennedy Years.* Harris writes that Kennedy initially believed in very traditional principles and only took up more modern conceptions under the influence of his personal advisers and the Council of Economic Advisors.

61. J. J. SERVAN-SCHREIBER, *Le défi américain.*
62. R. L. HEILBRONER, A. SINGER, *Economic Transformation of America*, p. 216.
63. The new Department of Urban Affairs was to co-ordinate forty or so programmes and thirteen different federal bureaux: A. SHONFIELD, *Modern Capitalism*, pp. 353–6.
64. K. HARDACH, 'Germany 1914–1970'.
65. W. EUCKEN, *Grundsätze der Wirtschaftspolitik.*
66. K. ZWING, *Soziologie der Gewerkschaftsbewegung.*
67. S. LIEBERMAN, *Mixed Economies*, pp. 54–6, pp. 196–201.
68. B. MARTENS, *De kollektivisering van de industriële besluitvorming.*
69. A. SHONFIELD, *Modern Capitalism*, pp. 242–6.
70. M. SCHNITZER, *East and West Germany*, pp. 38ff.; H. ARNDT, *Konzentration in der Wirtschaft.*
71. A. SHONFIELD, *Modern Capitalism*, pp. 246–54.
72. H. C. WALLICH, *The German Revival.*
73. The occupying Allies refused the German request to concede reductions in personal and company taxation. The lack of defence expenditure also had a favourable effect on the budget.
74. K. G. ZINN, 'Social Market in Crisis', p. 97.
75. In other countries too the role of the government was sometimes a dominant one, for example in sectoral consultative organs such as the French comités de modernisation or in the organs co-ordinated by the Japanese MITI.
76. OECD, *Labour Market Policy in Sweden*; J. COOPER, *Industrial Relations: Sweden.*
77. E. GINZBERG, 'Sweden', pp. 159–60.
78. OECD (Social Affairs Division), *Active Manpower Policy.*
79. J. DE VRIES, *The Netherlands Economy.*
80. From 1963 onwards the Stichting van de Arbeid was given the task of overseeing the collective labour agreements. After the wage explosion of 1963–4, the College van Rijksbemiddelaars temporarily took this task over but after 1969 it was scrapped. From that time onwards only the Ministry of Social Affairs could still intervene in collective labour agreements.
81. For Belgium see: H. DAEMS (et al.), *De Belgische industrie.*

CHAPTER VIII

1. J. K. GALBRAITH, *Economics and the Public Purpose.*
2. P. F. DRUCKER, 'The New Markets', pp. 44–9.
3. H. DAEMS, *The Holding Company.*
4. J. K. GALBRAITH, *Affluent Society*, pp. 132ff.
5. A. D. CHANDLER Jr, H. DAEMS, *Managerial Hierarchies.*
6. Peter Drucker writes that in take-overs/mergers, the number of which has multiplied since 1964–5, often new groups of managers come forward who, with the support of shareholders, are able to replace

the professional management with specialists in asset management: P. F. DRUCKER, 'The New Markets', pp. 46–8.

7. UNITED NATIONS, *Multinational Corporations*.
8. J. K. GALBRAITH, *Industrial State*.
9. For West Germany see: S. LIEBERMAN, *Mixed Economies*, pp. 199–200.
10. S. HOLLAND (ed.), *Beyond Capitalist Planning*, pp. 3–4.
11. A. SHONFIELD, *Western Capitalism*, pp. 13–14.
12. H. G. VATTER, 'The U.S. Mixed Economy', pp. 303–4.
13. A. SHONFIELD, *Western Capitalism*, pp. 32–3.
14. Chase Econometrics, the influential study department of the Chase Manhattan Bank, suggested a wage, prices and credit policy as the only adequate means of fighting inflation.
15. COMMUNAUTÉ ÉCONOMIQUE EUROPÉENNE, *Méthodes et procédures de programmation*; C. SEIBEL, 'Planning in France', p. 158.
16. J. BENARD, 'La planification française', pp. 756–84; B. BALASSA, 'French Planning?', pp. 537–54.
17. S. LIEBERMAN, *Mixed Economies*, p. 175.
18. J. DELORS, 'French Planning', pp. 25–7.
19. G. R. DENTON, M. FORSYTH, M. MACLENNAN, *Economic Planning and Policies*, pp. 86–91.
20. In this planning in value terms, account is taken of the present and expected prices of goods and services as well as of quantity.
21. W. BECKERMAN (ed.), *Labour Government's Economic Record*; DEPARTMENT OF ECONOMIC AFFAIRS, *The National Plan*.
22. S. HOLLAND, 'Planning Disagreements', pp. 138–52.
23. F. ARCHIBUGI, 'Capitalist Planning', pp. 53–4.
24. G. PODBIELSKI, *Italy: Development and Crisis*, p. 149.
25. Lieberman contends the opposite. The size and diversity of the state concerns ENI and IRI helped the penetration of the five-year plans into the economy and thus their realization. This was undoubtedly the case in the 1960s but not in the following decade, when the state concerns began to act increasingly autonomously and considerably diluted the influence of government planning: S. LIEBERMAN, *Mixed Economies*, pp. 268–9.
26. J. CLAEYS, *Ekonomische groei in Japan*; G. C. ALLEN, *Japan's Economic Expansion*.
27. A first step towards liberalization was taken by the Japanese government, coming into force on 1 July 1967, and a second series of measures came in March 1969: M. Y. YOSHINO, *Japan as Host*.
28. H. KNOOREN, *Het Zweeds ekonomisch systeem*, p. 17.
29. E. GINZBERG, 'Sweden', pp. 160–3.
30. H. KNOOREN, *Het Zweeds ekonomisch systeem*, pp. 47–59.
31. S. LIEBERMAN, *Mixed Economies*, passim.
32. E. MANDEL, *Het Laatkapitalisme*, ch. 5.
33. H. W. ARNDT, *Economic Growth* , pp. 33–4.
34. G. DALTON, *Economic Systems and Society*, p. 160.
35. H. DELEECK, *Ongelijkheden in de Welvaartsstaat*, pp. 185–235.
36. H. W. ARNDT, *Economic Growth*, pp. 154–5.

37. L. BAECK, *De westerse economie*, p. 57.
38. A. SHONFIELD, *Western Capitalism*, pp. 4–7.
39. H. W. ARNDT, *Economic Growth*, pp. 24–141.
40. D. RIESMAN, *The Lonely Crowd*.
41. J. K. GALBRAITH, *Affluent Society*, pp. 132ff.
42. D. BELL, I. KRISTOL (eds), *Capitalism Today*.
43. E. J. MISHAN, *Costs of Economic Growth*.
44. L. BAECK, *De westerse economie*, pp. 110–19.
45. H. MARCUSE, *One-Dimensional Man*.
46. J. HABERMAS, *Technik und Wissenschaft*.
47. L. ALTHUSSER (*et al.*), *Lire le capital*.
48. L. KOHR, *Overdeveloped Nations*.
49. E. F. SCHUMACHER, *Small is Beautiful*.
50. P. EHRLICH, *The Population Bomb*.
51. D. H. MEADOWS, D. L. MEADOWS, *Limits to Growth*.
52. H. W. ARNDT, *Economic Growth*, p. 134.
53. F. VON HAYEK, *The Road to Serfdom*.
54. M. FRIEDMAN, *Capitalism and Freedom*; M. FRIEDMAN, R. FRIEDMAN, *Free to Choose*.
55. M. MARKOVIC, *Van bureaucratie naar zelfbestuur*.
56. G. RUFFOLO, 'Socialist Planning', pp. 79–80; G. RUFFOLO, (*et al.*), *Progretto Socialista*.
57. F. ARCHIBUGI, 'A Method of Integrated Planning'.
58. Swedish companies such as Volvo made attempts to reorganize conveyor-belt work in more human terms.
59. J. ATTALI, *La parole et l'outil*.
60. PARTI SOCIALISTE (*et al.*), *Programme Commun*; J. BUYSE, *Het 'Programme Commun'*.
61. MINISTERIO DEL BILANCIO E DELLA PROGRAMMAZIONE ECONOMICO, *Programma Economica*.
62. THE LABOUR PARTY, *Labour's Programme*.
63. Research shows that an increase in material welfare has an important satisfying effect if it is greater than the material welfare increases in other population groups.
64. W. BECKERMAN, *Defence of Economic Growth*.

CHAPTER IX

1. D. E. MOGGRIDGE, *British Monetary Policy*; H. VAN DER WEE, K. TAVERNIER, *La Banque nationale de Belgique*, pp. 77–208.
2. C. P. KINDLEBERGER, *World in Depression*, pp. 199–231.
3. R. L. ALLEN, I. WALTER, 'U.S. Trade Policy'.
4. Between 1934 and 1945 the United States reached bilateral trade agreements with twenty-seven countries. The tariff reductions involved amounted to about 64 per cent of dutiable imports. Import tariffs were reduced on average to 44 per cent of the basic duties that applied in 1934 (J. W. EVANS, *The Kennedy Round*, ch. 1).

5. D. P. CALLEO, B. M. ROWLAND, *America and the World Political Economy*, ch. 2.
6. P. VAN DE MEERSSCHE, *De Europese integratie*, pp. 25–35.
7. D. P. CALLEO, B. M. ROWLAND, *America and the World Political Economy*, ch. 2.
8. R. VANES, *Buitenlandse handelspolitiek*, part III, pp. 87–91.
9. J. W. EVANS, *The Kennedy Round*, ch. 1.
10. During the first GATT meeting in Geneva (1947) tariff reductions of about 54 per cent of American dutiable imports were involved. The weighted average of tariff reductions was 35 per cent. American import duties as a whole were on average reduced by 18.9 per cent. The second meeting at Annecy (1949) and the third at Torquay (1950–1) achieved much less (J. W. EVANS, *The Kennedy Round*, ch. 1).
11. P. VAN DE MEERSSCHE, *De Europese integratie*, pp. 46–64.
12. J. B. COHEN, *Japan's Economy*.
13. It was George F. Kennan who first used this terminology in his famous X-article in the journal *Foreign Affairs* (July 1947). He drew attention to the absurdity of making unilateral concessions to the Russians as a price for Soviet co-operation in a new world order under American leadership (G. F. KENNAN, *Memoirs*, part I, pp. 354–67).
14. On 15 August 1947, short-term loans to France, Britain, Benelux and Italy had already risen to $7,263 million.
15. H. B. PRICE, *The Marshall Plan*; L. GORDON (ed.), *From Marshall Plan to Global Interdependence*.
16. M. MILLER, *Harry S. Truman*, pp. 262–5.
17. This latter point was explicitly emphasized by Kennan, head of the planning staff of the American State Department: G. F. KENNAN, *Memoirs*, part I, p. 343.
18. OECD, *European Recovery Program*.
19. H. BRUGMANS, *L'idée européenne*; H. W. CARTER, *Speaking European*, pp. 24–33.
20. D. P. CALLEO, B. M. ROWLAND, *America and the World Political Economy*, ch. 3.
21. B. SEMMEL, *Free Trade Imperialism*.
22. R. N. GARDNER, *Sterling-Dollar Diplomacy*.
23. P. GERBET, *La genèse du Plan Schuman*.
24. R. SCHUMAN, 'Plan Schuman'.
25. EUROPEAN ECONOMIC COMMUNITY, *EEG-Energiestatistiek*, 1972.
26. Ibid., 1972.
27. J. M. KEYNES, *Economic Consequences of the Peace*.
28. A. GROSSER, *La Quatrième République*.
29. For a good overview see: P. VAN DE MEERSSCHE, *De Europese integratie*.
30. M. CAMPS, *Britain and the European Community*.
31. Moreover, for each member state of EFTA, the EEC share of its foreign trade was larger than the combined share of its EFTA partners: M. SCHLOGEL, *Les relations économiques et financières*, pp. 114–16, 282–3.

32. In this respect, reference was made, for example, to the Nassau (Bahamas) Agreement on military facilities signed by Kennedy and Macmillan.

33. The annual tariff reductions would take place in five stages, each of 20 per cent, starting from 1 January 1973. The coming into line with the common external tariff would take place in four phases, each of 25 per cent, and the British share of the Community budget would gradually rise from 8.64 per cent in 1973 to 19.92 per cent in 1977.

34. The Tory leaders largely used the argument that the dynamic economic and political effects would be extremely positive ones for Britain. Critics on the Labour side replied that any such effects would be difficult or impossible to measure.

35. Turkey, Greece and Portugal also applied for full membership during the 1970s.

36. From 1 July 1967 onwards the High Authority of the ECSC, the Commission of Euratom and the Commission of the EEC were merged into one body, the Commission of the European Communities, more commonly known as the European Commission.

37. D. SWANN, *The Common Market*.

38. W. G. BARNES, *Europe and the Developing World*.

39. UNCTAD, *Global Strategy for Development*; R. S. WALTERS, 'UNCTAD Intervenes between Poor and Rich States', pp. 527–54.

40. P. COFFEY, 'Trade and Monetary Policy', pp. 102–3.

41. P. J. S. KAPTEYN, P. VERLOREN VAN THEMAAT, *The European Communities*.

42. T. K. WARLEY, 'European Agriculture', pp. 286–95; T. E. JOSLING, 'The Common Agricultural Policy', pp. 86–98; OECD, *Agricultural Policy*; J. VAN LIERDE, *Europese landbouwproblemen*.

43. S. MANSHOLT, *Memorandum inzake de hervorming van de landbouw*.

44. B. T. BAYLISS, *European Transport*; N. DESPICHT, *Transport Policy*.

45. In 1977 about 70 per cent of this amount went towards financing the CAP: A. R. PREST, 'Fiscal Policy', pp. 89–90.

46. In 1977 45 per cent of the budget was funded by the common external tariff, 12 per cent by special duties levied via the CAP and 43 per cent by contributions from national governments: ibid., pp. 90–1.

47. To this end various committees were set up; e.g., the Monetary Committee (1958), the Committee for Short-Term Economic Movements (1960), the Committee for Central Bank Governors (1964), the Committee for Medium-Term Economic Policy (1965) and the Budget Committee (1965).

48. P. COFFEY, J. R. PRESLEY, *European Monetary Integration*; H. J. N. ANSIAUX, M. DESSART, *L'Europe monétaire*.

49. See Chapter XI.

50. EUROPEAN COAL AND STEEL COMMUNITY, *Europe and Energy*.

51. G. BRONDEL, N. MORTON, 'Energy Policy', pp. 172–99.

52. L. LEVI-SANDRI, 'The Contribution of Regional Action'.

53. J. J. HEUSENS, R. DE HORN, 'Crisisbeleid Europese Staalindustrie',

pp. 299–326; R. JOLIET, 'Cartelization, Dirigism and Crisis', pp. 403–45.

54. L. TINDEMANS, *European Union Report*.
55. C. P. KINDLEBERGER, *Les investissements des Etats-Unis*, pp. 95–127; F. BRAUN, 'L'Inventaire statistique des investissements étrangers'.
56. F. JÁNOSSY, *La fin des miracles économiques*, pp. 63–113; A. LAMFALUSSY, *The United Kingdom and the Six*, pp. 121–35.

CHAPTER X

1. R. L. ALLEN, I. WALTER, 'U.S. Trade Policy', p. 64.
2. F. WEINER, *European Common Market*.
3. W. F. MONROE, *International Trade Policy*, pp. 15–19.
4. J. W. EVANS, *The Kennedy Round*, ch. 7.
5. P. VAN DE MEERSSCHE, *De Europese integratie*, pp. 196–9.
6. J. W. EVANS, *The Kennedy Round*, ch. 7; W. F. MONROE, *International Trade Policy*, pp. 17–22.
7. E. H. PREEG, *Traders and Diplomats*.
8. F. WEINER, *European Common Market*, p. 94; T. B. CURTIS, J. R. VASTINE, *Future of American Trade*, p. 228.
9. E. H. PREEG, *Traders and Diplomats*, ch. 16; K. KOCK, *International Trade Policy*, ch. 4; J. W. EVANS, *The Kennedy Round*, ch. 15.
10. More details in Chapter XI.
11. The relationship between the total income from import duties and the total value of dutiable imports can serve as a general indicator for the reduction of tariffs. In the United States this relationship averaged 38 per cent in the period 1922–9, 53 per cent in the period 1930–3, 25 per cent in 1957 and 8 per cent in 1974: B. BALASSA, 'World Trade and the International Economy'.
12. H. B. MALGREM, *Economic Peace-keeping*, pp. 82–118; G. CURZON, V. CURZON, *Barriers to Trade*; R. E. BALDWIN, *Non-Tariff Distortions*.
13. J. DE BANDT, H. C. BOS (*et al.*), *The World in Transition*, pp. 6–24.
14. B. BALASSA, 'World Trade and the International Economy', pp. 48–9.
15. B. HINDLEY, 'Voluntary Export Restraint', pp. 317–18.
16. B. BALASSA, 'World Trade and the International Economy', pp. 49–50.
17. R. JOLIET, 'Cartelization, Dirigism and Crisis', pp. 404, 426.
18. B. BALASSA, 'World Trade and the International Economy', pp. 52–4.
19. R. JOLIET, 'Cartelization, Dirigism and Crisis', pp. 426–37.
20. M. WASSELL, 'Current Trade Issues', pp. 18–19.
21. GATT, *The Tokyo Round*; W. VON DEWITZ, 'GATT Negotiations'.
22. W. N. TURPIN, *Soviet Foreign Trade*, p. 17.
23. For the creation and further development of Comecon see: M. KASER, *Comecon*; M. LAVIGNE, *Le Comecon*.

24. The following is largely based on: A. NOVE, *East-West Trade*; M. LAVIGNE, *Les économies socialistes*.
25. F. LEMOINE, 'Les prix des échanges', pp. 865–931.
26. M. LAVIGNE, *Les économies socialistes*, pp. 369–79.
27. M. M. KOSTECKI, *East-West Trade and the GATT-System*, pp. 9–11.
28. M. LAVIGNE, *Les économies socialistes*, p. 384.
29. W. KRAUSE, F. S. MATHIS, 'The U.S. Policy Shift'.
30. M. M. KOSTECKI, *East-West Trade and the GATT-System*.
31. M. LAVIGNE, *Les économies socialistes*, pp. 387–8.
32. W. BRAND, 'Het Oostblok', p. 654; M. LAVIGNE, *Les économies socialistes*, pp. 392–5.
33. A. NOVE, *East-West Trade*, pp. 211–31.
34. A. MADDISON, *Economic Progress*, p. 31.
35. Ibid., pp. 197–8. (There were, however, differences within the group of developing countries; e.g., Greece, Israel, South Korea, Taiwan, and Yugoslavia were already achieving good export results in the period 1950–67.)
36. A good overview in: A. MADDISON, *Economic Progress*, pp. 200–12.
37. The evolution of the post-war terms of trade as here described has recently been contested by some economists on empirical grounds, e.g. A. Krueger, J. Spraos, M. Michaely.
38. R. GHESQUIRE, *Tussen Eden en Utopia*, pp. 41–8.
39. G. MYRDAL, *World Poverty*.
40. From the 1970s onwards the newly industrialized countries of the Third World were able to benefit from the tariff reductions brought about under the auspices of GATT.
41. P. VAN DE MEERSSCHE, *De Noord-Zuid Confrontatie*.
42. The first important meeting of the group of non-aligned states was at the Bandung Conference in 1955. This was the first time that the Third World presented itself as an entity, separate from both the Western and Eastern blocs.
43. R. PREBISCH, *Towards a New Trade Policy*.
44. UNCTAD, *Implementation of the Generalized System of Preferences*; T. MURRAY, 'Preferential Tariffs', pp. 35–46.
45. By 1980 the original 'Group of Seventy-Seven' had already grown to a total membership of 114 countries.
46. W. F. MONROE, *International Trade Policy*, pp. 103–9.
47. M. WASSELL, 'Current Trade Issues', pp. 21–2.
48. Ibid., pp. 22–6.
49. H. W. SINGER, J. A. ANSARI, *Rich and Poor Countries*, p. 39.
50. GATT, *International Trade 1979/80*, p. 172.
51. M. LAVIGNE, *Les économies socialistes*, pp. 400–2.
52. W. BRAND, 'Het Oostblok', p. 652.
53. If the aid given by Eastern bloc countries to developing countries also within the Eastern bloc (Cuba, Vietnam and Mongolia) is included, the amount rises to 0.25 per cent of GNP: M. LAVIGNE, *Les économies socialistes*, p. 401.
54. THE ATLANTIC COUNCIL OF THE US, *GATT Plus*.

55. J. TINBERGEN (*et al.*), *Reshaping the International Order.*
56. W. BRANDT, *North-South: A Programme for Survival.*
57. H. W. SINGER, J. A. ANSARI, *Rich and Poor Countries*; B. HERMAN, *Division of Labour*; G. HELLEINER, *A World Divided.*
58. J. DE BANDT, H. C. BOS (*et al.*), *The World in Transition.*
59. H. B. MALGREM, *Economic Peace-keeping*, pp. 41–69; C. F. BERGSTEN, *Completing the GATT; Directions for World Trade.*
60. The advocates of the model of export-led growth reply that empirical evidence suggests the opposite: countries which are more autarkically biased, such as India, appeared to be much more vulnerable during the 1970s crisis than countries such as Taiwan and Brazil, where export-led growth was a central pillar of economic policy.
61. The advocates of the model of export-led growth contend the opposite. On this debate see, among others: D. MORAWETZ, *Economic Development.*
62. As early as 1972 and 1973 Robert McNamara, the chairman of the World Bank, was pointing to the urgent need of an economic growth model which would benefit the poorest 40 per cent of the population of the developing world: R. S. MCNAMARA, *Address*, 1972 and *Address*, 1973. The development of the basic needs model owes much to the International Labour Organization: BUREAU INTERNATIONAL DU TRAVAIL, *L'emploi, la croissance et les besoins essentiels.* The World Bank, in co-operation with the Institute of Development Studies of the University of Sussex, has published its own studies on the problem: H. CHENERY (*et al.*), *Redistribution with Growth.* In later papers of the World Bank and R. S. McNamara, this problem is again tackled: R. S. MCNAMARA, *Massachusetts Institute of Technology* and his speeches at the annual meetings of the World Bank later in the 1970s.
63. See Chapter VI.
64. For this model see: J. M. JEANNENEY, *Pour un nouveau protectionisme*; A. GRJEBINE, *La nouvelle économie internationale.*
65. M. UL HAQ, *The Poverty Curtain.*
66. A. TÉVOÉDJRE, *Poverty.*
67. R. N. COOPER (ed.), *Renovated International System.*
68. J. N. BHAGWATI (ed.), *The North-South Debate.*
69. A. FISHLOW, C. F. DIAZ-ALEJANDRO (*et al.*), *Rich and Poor Nations.*
70. W. LEONTIEF (*et al.*), *Future of the World Economy.*
71. H. G. GRUBEL, 'New International Economic Order', pp. 482–501.
72. P. STREETEN, 'Changing Perceptions of Development', p. 15.
73. WORLD BANK, *Development Report, 1980*; IMF, *Annual Report, 1980*, p. 36.
74. R. W. TUCKER, *Inequality of Nations.*
75. M. HUDSON, *Global Fracture.*
76. A. TIANO, *Dialectique de la dépendance.*
77. C. PALLOIX, *Travail et production.*
78. P. P. REY, *Alliances des classes.*
79. P. SWEEZY, 'Crisis of Capitalism', pp. 1–12.

80. H. ELSENHANS, 'Overcoming Underdevelopment', pp. 293–313.
81. S. AMIN, 'Self-reliance', pp. 1–21.
82. A. EMMANUEL, 'Multinational Corporations', pp. 754–72.
83. N. GIRVAN, *Corporate Imperialism*.

CHAPTER XI

1. R. S. SAYERS, 'Monetary Theory and Policy', pp. 487–94.
2. The gold exchange standard had already become *de facto* a gold-sterling standard by the second half of the nineteenth century: H. VAN DER WEE, K. TAVERNIER, *La Banque nationale de Belgique*, p. 17.
3. This price implied a devaluation of 41 per cent in relation to the former fixed gold value of the dollar.
4. The governments involved declared themselves willing to buy the currencies of their partners with gold at a fixed rate, valid for twenty-four hours.
5. R. S. SAYERS, 'Monetary Theory and Policy', p. 493.
6. The Netherlands, Switzerland and Belgium were very quick to join the Tripartite Agreement: F. DEHEM, *De l'étalon sterling à l'étalon dollar*, pp. 123–4. In 1937 the United States signed a bilateral stabilization agreement with Brazil. After the outbreak of the Second World War, Britain closed similar agreements with France and the Netherlands. In order to be able to use gold reserves for the purchase of war equipment from the United States, it was agreed to record mutual deficits in the currency of the other country (J. K. HORSEFIELD, *The International Monetary Fund*, p. 7).
7. F. HIRSCH, P. OPPENHEIMER, 'Managed Money', p. 622.
8. B. TEW, *International Monetary Cooperation*, pp. 170ff.
9. F. L. BLOCK, *Origins of International Economic Disorder*, p. 30.
10. Ibid., pp. 47–8.
11. Ibid., pp. 43–4.
12. W. F. MONROE, *International Monetary Reconstruction*, pp. 20–3.
13. W. M. SCAMMELL, *International Monetary Policy*, pp. 109–10.
14. Most parities were established at a fixed relation to the American dollar. The parity fluctuations between two currencies other than the dollar thus had a potential band-width of 4 per cent (B. TEW, *The International Monetary System*, pp. 110–11).
15. W. M. SCAMMELL, *International Monetary Policy*, p. 110.
16. Ibid., pp. 116–17.
17. H. M. VAN DER VALK, *Het Internationaal Monetair Stelsel*, p. 34; W. M. SCAMMELL, *International Monetary Policy*, p. 121.
18. J. K. HORSEFIELD, *The International Monetary Fund*, pp. 95–8; R. N. GARDNER, *Sterling-Dollar Diplomacy*; F. L. BLOCK, *Origins of International Economic Disorder*, p. 54.
19. R. SOLOMON, *International Monetary System*, pp. 144–8.
20. B. TEW, *The International Monetary System*, p. 104.
21. International bankers in the United States reacted violently against

the credit facilities contained in the IMF proposals and they mobilized opposition in Congress. They were afraid that governments would be able to get credit too easily from the IMF. The bankers therefore proposed an alternative plan, the Key Currency Plan of Harvard professor John H. Williams. The huge publicity campaign which accompanied the Williams Plan, supported by the international bankers, was considered by most authors to be the main reason why proposals relating to IMF credit facilities were so greatly watered down and, later, so restrictively applied (F. HIRSCH, P. OPPENHEIMER, 'Managed Money', p. 624; F. L. BLOCK, *Origins of International Economic Disorder*, pp. 52–5).

22. R. N. GARDNER, *Sterling-Dollar Diplomacy*.
23. F. L. BLOCK, *Origins of International Economic Disorder*, pp. 55–6.
24. R. N. GARDNER, *Sterling-Dollar Diplomacy*, pp. 181–7.
25. Ibid., pp. 24–35; F. L. BLOCK, *Origins of International Economic Disorder*, pp. 61–3.
26. G. DALTON, *High Tide and After*, pp. 68ff.
27. B. TEW, *International Monetary Cooperation*, pp. 174–7.
28. W. F. MONROE, *International Monetary Reconstruction*, p. 25.
29. F. HIRSCH, P. OPPENHEIMER, 'Managed Money', p. 625.
30. B. TEW, *International Monetary Cooperation*, pp. 175–7.
31. Ibid., pp. 177–83.
32. F. L. BLOCK, *Origins of International Economic Disorder*, p. 74.
33. C. GUTT, 'Exchange Rates and the IMF'.
34. W. M. SCAMMELL, *International Monetary Policy*, p. 129.
35. W. F. MONROE, *International Monetary Reconstruction*, pp. 30–1.
36. J. K. HORSEFIELD, *The International Monetary Fund*, ch. 8, ch. 9.
37. Ibid., pp. 129–35.
38. From 1 March 1947 to 30 April 1949 (termed the 'phase of dollar demand' because 88 per cent of all transactions took place in this currency), some activity could still be observed. From 1 May 1949 to the autumn of 1956, however, this activity became so minimal that the period became known as the 'phase of retirement'. Only afterwards came a 'phase of activity'. (W. M. SCAMMELL, *International Monetary Policy*, pp. 152–8).
39. R. SOLOMON, *International Monetary System*, p. 14.
40. F. L. BLOCK, *Origins of International Economic Disorder*, pp. 77–8.
41. H. VAN DER WEE, P. JANSSENS, 'De overheidsinterventie', pp. 41–9.
42. Details of the origins of the Marshall Plan are given in: G. F. KENNAN, *Memoirs*.
43. W. M. SCAMMELL, *International Monetary Policy*, p. 142.
44. P. A. SAMUELSON, 'Disparity in Postwar Exchange Rates'.
45. For more detailed information on the development of these cross-rates see: B. TEW, *International Monetary Cooperation*, pp. 90–2.
46. Ibid., p. 93, p. 221.
47. In its yearly report of 1948 the IMF had already noted that there was tension between the various currencies. An adjustment of

exchange rates, however, which was permissible according to its articles, was not proposed. The *ad hoc* committee presented a report emphasizing the urgency of a general adjustment of parities.

48. J. K. HORSEFIELD, *The International Monetary Fund*, p. 235.

49. T. W. KENT, 'Devaluation One Year After', pp. 22–37.

50. Canada, however, was an exception, reversing its decision in October 1950 and letting its currency float thereafter.

51. B. TEW, *International Monetary Cooperation*, pp. 138–65.

52. The first Intra-European Payments Agreement was in operation from 1 October 1948 to 30 June 1949.

53. An interesting overview of the discussion in: F. L. BLOCK, *Origins of International Economic Disorder*, pp. 96–198.

54. Ibid., p. 242, note 77.

55. R. TRIFFIN, *Europe and the Money Muddle*, p. 164, p. 167.

56. Ibid., pp. 168–88.

57. B. TEW, *The International Monetary System*, pp. 35–6.

58. B. TEW, *International Monetary Cooperation*, pp. 171ff.

59. At the end of June 1952 Britain had reached agreement to consolidate about £1 billion of blocked sterling balances out of a total of £3.4 billion.

60. Britain now demanded no more than that countries in the transferable account area should be willing to accept sterling from third countries by way of settling any current transactions.

61. Before this date such transactions could only take place in international free markets such as in Tangiers.

62. B. TEW, *International Monetary Cooperation*, pp. 186–7.

63. R. TRIFFIN, *Europe and the Money Muddle*, pp. 191–9.

64. Ibid., pp. 200–8.

65. The agreement provided for the creation of a European Fund with a capital of $600 million that would be able to lend short-term credit to countries in temporary balance-of-payments difficulties. In addition, a Multilateral System of Settlements was to be established which would organize multilateral compensations should this not take place via international exchange markets. The agreement remained a dead letter. (B. TEW, *International Monetary Cooperation*, pp. 161–2.)

66. The eight countries were Belgium, Luxemburg, Denmark, France, West Germany, the Netherlands, Switzerland, and the United Kingdom. Norway joined in December 1953 and Italy in December 1955. Initially the facilities remained limited to spot rates but from 5 October 1953 these were extended to forward rates. (R. TRIFFIN, *Europe and the Money Muddle*, pp. 212–13.)

67. Namely Belgium, Luxemburg, France, West Germany, Italy, the Netherlands, the United Kingdom, and the Republic of Ireland. It was usual to speak of only six countries making this request since Belgium and Luxemburg were linked monetarily in the BLEU agreement and the Republic of Ireland had a comparable connection with the United Kingdom.

68. Namely Austria, Denmark, Norway, Portugal, Sweden, and Switzerland.
69. B. TEW, *The International Monetary System*, p. 107.
70. J. GOLD, *Stand-by Arrangements*.
71. F. L. BLOCK, *Origins of International Economic Disorder*, p. 113.
72. The Commission of Foreign Economic Policy (Randall Commission) in its *Report to the President and the Congress* (January 1954) drew attention to the continuing dollar shortage. It recommended that government measures be taken to encourage American private investment abroad.
73. R. SOLOMON, *International Monetary System*, p. 131.
74. Ibid., p. 26.
75. In France a first devaluation had already taken place in 1957. Both devaluations together signified a decrease in value of 29 per cent relative to the dollar (E. S. FURNISS Jr, *France, Troubled Ally*, pp. 406–17).
76. D. MACDOUGALL, *The World Dollar Problem*.
77. R. SOLOMON, *International Monetary System*, p. 31.
78. This more or less amounted to the Key Currency Plan proposed by Williams during the 1940s as an alternative to the Bretton Woods Agreement. Williams originally accorded sterling a role of equal value to the dollar although at the start of the 1960s there was no longer any question of this. J. H. WILLIAMS, *Post-War Monetary Plans*.
79. The Comecon countries established the prices for their mutual trade in terms of current world prices, expressed in dollars.
80. R. I. MACKINNON, *Money in International Exchange*.
81. The characteristic of central bank market intervention was the use of dollars as intervention currency (there were only partial exceptions in the sterling zone and in the colonial zones).
82. C. P. KINDLEBERGER, *Balance of Payments Deficits*.
83. H. G. JOHNSON, *The World Economy*, pp. 24–5.
84. R. TRIFFIN, 'Return to Convertibility'; id., *Gold and the Dollar Crisis*.
85. The relationship between sterling balances and British gold and gold-currency reserves which in 1938 was fluctuating around 95 per cent, by 1958 had risen to 355 per cent. On the other hand this represented an improvement on the situation in 1947, when the relationship was 705 per cent.
86. R. I. MACKINNON, 'America's Role', p. 314.
87. F. HIRSCH, P. OPPENHEIMER, 'Managed Money'.
88. A first critique can be found in: R. TRIFFIN, 'Tomorrow's Convertibility'. See also: R. TRIFFIN, *Gold and the Dollar Crisis*; id., *The International Monetary System*.
89. Proposals along the same lines were made by E. M. Bernstein, Director of Research of the IMF: E. M. BERNSTEIN, 'The Gold Crisis', pp. 1–12.
90. J. RUEFF, 'The Rueff Approach', pp. 39–46; id., *Le péché monétaire*.
91. F. HIRSCH, *Money International*, pp. 385ff.

92. R. I. MACKINNON, 'America's Role', p. 315.

93. F. L. BLOCK, *Origins of International Economic Disorder*, pp 142–9.

94. Official declarations by the two presidential candidates that they were not considering devaluation caused the price to fall rapidly.

95. The agreement to undertake joint action was between the Federal Reserve of New York, as agent for the American Treasury, and the central banks of Belgium, France, West Germany, Italy, the Netherlands, Switzerland, and Britain: IMF, *Annual Report, 1963*, pp. 176–7, and *Annual Report, 1964*, pp. 31–2.

96. R. SOLOMON, *International Monetary System*, p. 41.

97. There are more details on this in the *Quarterly Bulletin* of the Bank of England.

98. Naturally there were national differences within these general increases.

99. President Kennedy in his Balance-of-Payments Message to Congress of 6 February 1961 declared that the United States was ready to call on the IMF if necessary in order to defend the gold-dollar standard. In April 1961 the Managing Director of the IMF, Per Jacobson, made public a scheme for additional resources.

100. The obligations were distributed as follows (in $ millions): the United States, 2,000; Britain, 1,000; West Germany, 1,000; France, 550; Italy, 550; Japan, 250; the Netherlands, 200; Canada, 200; Belgium, 150; Sweden, 100. From March 1963 Switzerland joined too with an obligation of $200 million.

101. Non-members of the Group of Ten, such as Australia and India, reacted very critically to the action, seeing the Group as a very exclusive club. R. SOLOMON, *International Monetary System*, pp. 43–4.

102. The deteriorating balance of payments of the United States of course played an important role here. There was also a conscious IMF policy to increase the number of currencies that could be drawn from the Fund.

103. R. SOLOMON, *International Monetary System*, p. 41.

104. The tax increased the cost of interest on long-term foreign loans by about 1 per cent per year.

105. Among other things the commercial banks were requested to restrict the increase in their foreign balances in the course of 1965 to a maximum of 5 per cent of the total at the end of 1964. American multinationals were asked to improve their individual balance of payments by 15 to 20 per cent.

106. During 1961 the Economic Policy Committee of the OECD set up the so-called Working Party No. 3 in order to study the monetary and fiscal policies of its members especially in the light of economic development and of possible balance-of-payments disequilibria.

107. The General Agreement to Borrow, as already mentioned, was the result of this change in American policy.

108. UNITED STATES, *United States Balance of Payments in 1968*.

109. Maudling proposed the creation of a Mutual Currency Account,

within the framework of the I M F. Surplus countries would be able to keep their surplus reserve currencies (dollars and sterling) there in exchange for another reserve. World liquidity could thus be extended. IMF, *Annual Meeting, 1962*, pp. 61–8.

110. R. V. ROOSA, *The Dollar and World Liquidity*, pp. 93–103.
111. R. SOLOMON, *International Monetary System*, p. 65.
112. The proposals in this respect were: (1) an increase in I M F quotas (this was discussed and approved in 1965), and (2) a system of control over the financing of balance-of-payments deficits. B. TEW, *The International Monetary System*, pp. 142–3.
113. The first study was published by the OECD in 1966 under the title of *The Balance-of-Payments Adjustment Process. A Report by Working Party No. 3 of the Economic Policy Committee.*
114. FEDERAL RESERVE SYSTEM, *Federal Reserve Bulletin* (August 1964), pp. 975–99; IMF, *The Creation of Reserve Assets*, pp. 26–9.
115. R. SOLOMON, *International Monetary System*, pp. 72–3.
116. Ibid., pp. 89–95.
117. Ibid., pp. 128–48. See also: B. TEW, *The International Monetary System*, p. 145.
118. FEDERAL OPEN MARKET COMMITTEE, *Minutes of the FO MC*, pp. 949–50. See also F. MACHLUP, *The Rio Agreement and Beyond*, pp. 8–12.
119. In January 1970 a first tranche of $3.5 billion was to be created, followed by a second of $3 billion in January 1971, and a third, also of $3 billion, in January 1972. The whole sum was equivalent to about 25 per cent of the total gold supply of the member states.
120. M. BARRET, M. L. GREENE, 'Special Drawing Rights', pp. 10–13.
121. F. BOLL, 'Le processus d'intégration monétaire'.
122. P. COFFEY, J. R. PRESLEY, *European Monetary Integration*; H. J. N. ANSIAUX, M. DESSART, *L'Europe monétaire.*
123. By way of a trial the Council of Ministers requested the central banks to reduce exchange-rate fluctuations between the currencies of member states to a total band-width of 1.2 per cent. According to the European Monetary Agreement of 1958 the total band-width with the dollar was set at 1.5 per cent (0.75 above and 0.75 below parity).
124. P. DE GRAUWE, 'The Euro-currency Market', p. 14.
125. E. W. CLENDENNING, *The Euro-Dollar Market*, pp. 21ff.
126. R. GHESQUIRE, 'Euro-currency Markets', p. 10.
127. Ibid., pp. 15–16.
128. B. TEW, *The International Monetary System*, pp. 117–21.
129. E. SAKAKIBARA, 'The Euro-currency Market', p. 13.
130. P. DE GRAUWE, 'The Euro-currency Market', pp. 14–15.
131. P. EINZIG, *The Euro-Dollar System*; G. BELL, *The Euro-dollar Market*; J. LITTLE, *Euro-dollars.*
132. For external investment a system of floating interest rates was often applied, being adjusted on a half-yearly basis to current interest rates on mutual bank transactions. The loans also often involved a

multicurrency clausule, according to which the choice of currency in which the loan was taken up was left free.

133. E. SAKAKIBARA, 'The Euro-currency Market', p. 13.

134. R. GHESQUIRE, 'Euro-currency Markets', pp. 13–15.

135. C. P. KINDLEBERGER, *Europe and the Dollar*, pp. 84–8.

136. F. L. BLOCK, *Origins of International Economic Disorder*, pp. 185–9.

137. R. SOLOMON, *International Monetary System*, pp. 87–8.

138. Ibid., pp. 89–95.

139. W. F. MONROE, *International Monetary Reconstruction*, p. 54.

140. FEDERAL OPEN MARKET COMMITTEE, *Minutes of the FOMC*, p. 1213.

141. With the objective of guaranteeing the working of the Gold Pool, the staff of the Federal Reserve Board, under the leadership of R. Solomon, developed a gold certificate plan. The plan became the official proposal of the American government but was rejected by the non-American central banks. R. SOLOMON, *International Monetary System*, pp. 115–16.

142. Ibid. pp. 119–24. For the deeper significance of the two-tier system see also H. G. JOHNSON, 'The Sterling Crisis of 1967' and R. TRIFFIN, 'International Monetary Collapse', pp. 375ff.

143. W. F. MONROE, *International Monetary Reconstruction*, p. 64.

144. R. I. MACKINNON, 'America's Role', pp. 316–20.

145. R. SOLOMON, *International Monetary System*, pp. 168–9.

146. Some American economists, such as L. Krause, showed that the existing gold-dollar standard, coupled to a passive American balance-of-payments strategy, would be of great benefit to the domestic economy of the United States. L. KRAUSE, 'Passive Balance of Payments Strategy', pp. 339–60.

147. G. HABERLER, T. D. WILLETT, *U.S. Balance of Payments Policy*, p. 15.

148. W. F. KRAUSE, *International Economics*, p. 371.

149. IMF, *Annual Report, 1971*, pp. 23–4.

150. For a more detailed description of events see especially: R. SOLOMON, *International Monetary System*, pp. 176–87.

CHAPTER XII

1. H. MAGDOFF, P. M. SWEEZY, *The End of Prosperity*, p. 1.

2. W. M. SCAMMELL, *International Monetary Policy*, pp. 238–47.

3. B. TEW, *The International Monetary System*, pp. 185–90.

4. R. SOLOMON, *International Monetary System*, pp. 219–20.

5. Ibid., p. 224.

6. To give the Committee as wide a base as possible so that the developing countries would be satisfied, for each of the twenty geographical areas entitled to appoint an Executive Director, a representative of ministerial rank was appointed, assisted by two associate members.

7. IMF, *Annual Meeting, 1972*. See also J. M. FLEMING, *International Monetary Reform*, and J. WILLIAMSON, *Failure of World Monetary Reform*.

8. For more details on this see *Council of Economic Advisers*, 1973, ch. 5, appendix.
9. w. f. monroe, *International Monetary Reconstruction*, pp. 90–7.
10. Ibid., pp. 101–12. See also imf, *International Monetary Reform*.
11. unctad, *Money, Finance and Development*.
12. The developing countries, which as a group represented 27.7 per cent of the total quota contributions at the end of 1971, accounted at that time for 53 per cent of the IMF loans. At the end of 1972 this had even risen to 92.3 per cent. m. osterrieth, *Système monétaire international*, p. 43.
13. cnuced, *La réforme monétaire internationale*; id., *Ressources financières pour le développement*.
14. h. g. grubel, 'Basic Methods for distributing SDRs', pp. 1009–22.
15. For a good overview, see: m. osterrieth, *Système monétaire international*, pp. 61–7 and 79–83.
16. r. solomon, *International Monetary System*, pp. 255–8.
17. g. haberler, 'The Case Against the Link', pp. 13–22; g. a. kessler, 'Should Development Aid be Linked', pp. 206–11.
18. Especially in relation to the oil crisis.
19. imf, *International Monetary Reform*.
20. p. simonnet, 'Après l'enterrement de la réforme monétaire'.
21. w. f. monroe, *International Monetary Reconstruction*, p. 91; r. solomon, *International Monetary System*, p. 242–3 and 253–4.
22. In this respect see the left-wing standpoint in h. magdoff, p. m. sweezy, *The End of Prosperity*, pp. 125–36.
23. w. f. monroe, *International Monetary Reconstruction*, p. 145.
24. h. b. van cleveland, 'International Economic Organization', pp. 9–14.
25. r. solomon, *International Monetary System*, pp. 191–2.
26. j. williamson, *Failure of World Monetary Reform*, pp. 53–60.
27. Indeed, if the rate of a particular currency in relation to the dollar fell from the top of the tunnel to the bottom and at the same time another currency made the reverse movement, then the change between both rates would be as much as 9 per cent.
28. However, the Federal Reserve made very little use of the dollar as intervention currency in the following years. The Federal Reserve Swap Network remained virtually unused from 15 August 1971 to the second half of 1973.
29. Immediately after devaluation the trade balance of the country involved usually continues to deteriorate. This is because the same export volume brings in less foreign currency than previously, while imports have to be bought by now dearer foreign currency. It is only later that cheaper exports begin to have an effect on the trade balance.
30. Acting on the advice of the Werner Plan, it was decided in March 1971 to reduce the common fluctuation band from 1.5 per cent to 1.2 per cent (0.6 per cent above and below parity). However, owing to

the monetary difficulties of 1971 this measure was not actually implemented.

31. If the band-width between two snake currencies threatened to stretch too far, then the stronger currency was used to buy the weaker (creditor intervention). Alternatively the weak-currency country borrowed from the strong and used this to buy up its own currency (debtor intervention).

32. F. HIRSCH, P. OPPENHEIMER, 'Managed Money', pp. 639–40.

33. For this see especially: E. VAN ROMPUY, *Groot-Brittannië.*

34. France rejoined the snake in July 1975 but left again in March 1976.

35. Norway joined the snake in May 1972 and Sweden in March 1973. Owing to the monetary crisis of October 1978 Sweden then left again.

36. Even between the members of the snake there were a few adjustments in mutual parities; for example, revaluations of the West German mark and Dutch guilder, and devaluations of the Danish krone.

37. In 1951 90 per cent of the official reserves of the sterling area still consisted of pounds. Just before the devaluation of 1967 the share had already fallen to 58 per cent and following the events of June 1972 this percentage fell still further. W. M. SCAMMELL, *International Monetary Policy*, p. 225.

38. TREASURY AND FEDERAL RESERVE FOREIGN EXCHANGE OPERATIONS, p. 758.

39. The Banca d'Italia decided to remove financial transactions from the parity system.

40. At the same time the German mark was revalued against the other currencies of the snake, while the Benelux countries for their part decided to narrow the band from 2.25 per cent to 1.5 per cent. They became the 'worm' in the snake.

41. M. V. M. WHITMAN, 'The Payments Adjustment Process', pp. 137–8.

42. IMF, *Annual Report 1975*, pp. 2–12.

43. G. HABERLER, 'The International Monetary System', pp. 115–23.

44. G. HABERLER, 'Inflation as a Worldwide Phenomenon'.

45. R. SOLOMON, *International Monetary System*, pp. 292–5.

46. E. R. FRIER, C. L. SCHULTZE (eds), *Higher Oil Prices.*

47. R. SOLOMON, *The Allocation of Oil Deficits.*

48. BANK FOR INTERNATIONAL SETTLEMENTS, *Annual Report, 1975*, pp. 139ff.

49. Similar credits were given to Britain and Italy in the course of 1976 and 1977.

50. P. A. VOLCKER, 'Priorities for the International Monetary System', p. 8.

51. The hope for a relative improvement of the American balance-of-payments position regarding Europe and Japan and the speculation on the consequent strengthening of the dollar was to end in disappointment and bring various banks into difficulties.

52. In 1974, on the suggestion of the American government, a Trust Fund

was set up to provide subsidized oil credit facilities to the hardest-hit developing countries.
53. R. SOLOMON, *International Monetary System*, pp. 302–7.
54. During the sixth general review of the quotas it appeared that the voting rights of the United States were going to fall below 20 per cent of the total voting rights. In order to secure the American veto, the necessary majority for certain decisions was raised to 85 per cent. J. GOLD, *Second Amendment*, pp. 16–17.
55. R. SOLOMON, *International Monetary System*, pp. 313–18.
56. For details of the calculation see: J. GOLD, *SDRs, Currencies and Gold*, pp. 1–11.
57. The guidelines that the IMF had given out in June 1974 relative to the achievement of a system of controlled floating exchange rates (see below) were abandoned. According to a decision on 29 April 1977, they were replaced by a system of surveillance over world exchange-rate policies. This new system was to come into operation at the same time as the Second Amendment, namely 1 April 1978. J. GOLD, *Second Amendment*, pp. 26–8.
58. Ibid., pp. 10–11.
59. A. HAYES, *Emerging Arrangements in International Payments*.
60. S. RAMSEY, 'Interview with Robert Solomon', pp. 38–41.
61. See the text of the speech by A. Solomon at the Royal Institute of International Affairs in London on 12 January 1979: INTERNATIONAL COMMUNICATIONS AGENCY, 'A. Solomon at the Royal Institute'.
62. W. S. SALANT, 'International Transmission of Inflation'.
63. INTERNATIONAL COMMUNICATIONS AGENCY, 'A. Solomon at an International Trade and Investment Conference'.
64. P. DE GRAUWE, T. PEETERS, *The European Monetary System*, pp. 8–11.
65. In this respect see: W. F. MONROE, W. KRAUSE, *The International Monetary System*, pp. 25–6.
66. E. H. PREEG, *Economic Blocs*.
67. As early as 1 November 1975 nine economists published 'the All Saints' Day Manifesto for European Monetary Union' in the *Economist*, proposing an indexed European parallel currency.
68. There is a good overview in: E. VAN ROMPUY, 'Relance van de Europese Monetaire Unie', pp. 1–6.
69. From 1 January 1978 the ECU was used for the EEC budget. International loans could also be expressed in ECUs.
70. These resources were extended to a total sum of 25 billion ECUs.
71. If other countries with a floating currency wished to join the snake it was possible for them to employ temporarily a wider band.
72. P. DE GRAUWE, T. PEETERS, *The European Monetary System*, pp. 14–22.
73. G. HABERLER, *Control over International Reserves?*, p. 23; W. R. CLINE, *International Monetary Reform*, p. 20 and pp. 46–7. The controversy over this problem still remains.

74. But see P. DE GRAUWE, *Floating Exchange Rates*, pp. 42–3. This study draws attention to the 'blessing in disguise for most LDCs'. Through the system of floating exchange rates industrial countries were able to tackle their balance-of-payments problems more efficiently, thus avoiding a world crisis and a return to protectionism which would have been even more disastrous for LDCs than the current situation.

75. E. SPITÄLLER, 'A Model of Inflation', pp. 254–77; P. HOOPER, B. LOUREY, *Impact of the Dollar Depreciation*; P. D. F. STRYDOM, D. MULLINS, T. W. VAN DER LINGEN, 'Exchange Rate Adjustment', pp. 213–24. To this it is often replied that in theory the spread of inflation from one country to another is facilitated more by fixed than floating exchange rates.

76. INTERNATIONAL COMMUNICATIONS AGENCY, *Carter: November 1, 1978*. See also: INTERNATIONAL COMMUNICATIONS AGENCY, 'A. Solomon at the Royal Institute'.

77. R. SOLOMON, *International Monetary System*, p. 324.

78. S. D. KRASNER, 'U.S. Commercial and Monetary Policy', pp. 635–71.

79. INTERNATIONAL COMMUNICATIONS AGENCY, 'A. Solomon at the Royal Institute'.

80. In this respect see: W. R. CLINE, *International Monetary Reform*, pp. 48–107.

81. W. F. MONROE, *International Monetary Reconstruction*, pp. 161–3.

82. G. HABERLER, *Control over International Reserves?*, p. 17.

83. W. M. SCAMMELL, *International Monetary Policy*, pp. 251–3.

84. According to W. F. MONROE, W. KRAUSE, 'The International Monetary System', the American government would be willing to accept SDRs as a unit of account in the new world system but would be less prepared to give up the dominant reserve function of the dollar.

85. However, there are also many who argue that the Eurocurrency market makes more efficient use of available world liquidity.

86. INTERNATIONAL COMMUNICATIONS AGENCY, 'A. Solomon at an International Trade and Investment Conference'.

87. The interest rate was calculated as a weighted average of market interest rates of 'basket' currencies used in working out SDRs. Until 1 May 1981 only 80 per cent of that average rate was accorded. After that date, the interest rate accorded went up to 100 per cent. J. GOLD, *SDRs, Currencies and Gold*, pp. 12–20.

88. Ibid., pp. 21–78.

89. For a more detailed analysis see Chapter X.

90. For example, convertibility between the various currencies in principle presents no problem but the question of what level or rate to use will always be a source of contention. Gold convertibility will remain suspended but European governments will never willingly accept a complete demonetarization of gold. In Europe there will always be reservations regarding the holding of too large a share of total reserves in the form of dollars or SDRs since there is scepticism over

the success of international co-operation. If this co-operation for any reason should break down and the I M F prove unmanageable then S D Rs will no longer be usable. No more need be said of the European distrust of the dollar. The nostalgia for gold as ultimate reserve value will therefore never totally disappear.

EPILOGUE

1. More details on this appear in: H. VAN DER WEE, 'Van middeleeuwen naar Nieuwe Tijd'.
2. J. LADRIÈRE, *Vie sociale*, pp. 211–25.
3. F. HIRSCH, *Social Limits to Growth*.
4. D. BELL, *Cultural Contradictions of Capitalism*, pp. 35–84.

BIBLIOGRAPHY

Note: short-form titles, used in the text and the notes, are given in parentheses at the end of entries.

ADAMS, J. (ed.): *The Contemporary International Economy: A Reader*. New York, St Martin's Press, 1979.

ADAMS, T. F. M., I. HOSHII: *A Financial History of the New Japan*. Tokyo, Kodansha, 1972. (*Financial History*.)

ADRIAANSEN, W. L. M.: *Overheid en multinationale onderneming*. Leiden, Stenfert Kroese, 1978. (*Overheid en multinationale onderneming*.)

ALLEN, G. C.: *Japan's Economic Expansion*. Oxford, Oxford UP, 1969 (3). (*Japan's Economic Expansion*.)

—— *A Short Economic History of Modern Japan, 1867–1937*. London, Allen & Unwin, 1972 (3). (*Economic History of Modern Japan*.)

ALLEN, R. L., I. WALTER: 'The Formation of U.S. Trade Policy: Retrospect and Prospect', in: *The Bulletin* (New York University, Graduate School of Business Administration, Institute of Finance), nos 70–1, February 1971. ('U.S. Trade Policy'.)

ALPERT, P.: *Twentieth Century Economic History of Europe*. New York, Schuman, 1951. (*Economic History of Europe*.)

ALTHUSSER, L. (*et al.*): *Lire le capital*. Paris, Maspero, 1965. (*Lire le capital*.)

AMACHER, R. C., HABERLER, G., T. D. WILLETT (eds): *Challenges to a Liberal International Economic Order*. Washington DC, AEI, 1979. (*Liberal International Economic Order*.)

AMERICAN ENTERPRISE INSTITUTE (ed.): *Food and Agricultural Policy*. Washington DC, AEI, 1977.

AMIN, S.: *Le développement inégal. Essai sur les formations sociales du capitalisme périphérique*. Paris, Minuit, 1973. (*Le développement inégal*.)

—— 'Self-reliance and the New International Economic Order', in: *Monthly Review*, vol. 29, no. 3, July–August 1977, pp. 1–21. ('Self-reliance'.)

568 *Prosperity and Upheaval*

ANDRIESSEN, J. E.: 'De economische groei in Nederland. Een terugblik over de jaren '50 en enig perspectief voor de jaren '60', in: *Maandbericht*, January 1962, Bankierskantoor Mendes Gans, Amsterdam. ('De economische groei in Nederland'.)

ANSIAUX, H. J. N., M. DESSART: *Dossier pour l'histoire de l'Europe monétaire, 1958–1973.* Paris/Brussels/Louvain, Vander–Nauwelaerts, 1975. (*L'Europe monétaire.*)

ARCHIBUGI, F.: 'A Progress Report: the "Quality of Life" in a Method of Integrated Planning', in: *Socio-Economic Planning Sciences*, vol. 8, no. 6, December 1974, pp. 339–45. ('A Method of Integrated Planning'.)

——— 'Capitalist Planning in Question', in: S. HOLLAND (ed.), *Beyond Capitalist Planning.* Oxford, Blackwell, 1978, pp. 49–68. ('Capitalist Planning'.)

ARNDT, H. W.: *Die Konzentration in der Wirtschaft* (Schriften des Vereins für Sozialpolitik, vol. 20, nos 1 & 2) Berlin/Munich, Duncker & Humblot, 1971. (*Konzentration in der Wirtschaft.*)

——— *The Rise and Fall of Economic Growth: a Study in Contemporary Thought.* Melbourne, Longman Cheshire, 1978. (*Economic Growth.*)

ARNOLD, E. (ed.): *Population Decline in Europe: Implications of a Declining or Stationary Population.* The Hague, Council of Europe, 1978. (*Population Decline in Europe.*)

ATLANTIC COUNCIL OF THE US, THE: *GATT Plus: A Proposal for Trade Reform* (Report of the Special Advisory Panel to the Trade Committee of the Atlantic Council of the US). Washington DC, 1975. (*GATT Plus.*)

ATTALI, J.: *La parole et l'outil.* Paris, PUF, 1975. (*La parole et l'outil.*)

BACON, R., W. ELTIS: *Britain's Economic Problem: Too Few Producers.* London, Macmillan, 1976. (*Britain's Economic Problem.*)

BAECK, L.: *De westerse economie in groei en crisis.* Antwerp, De Nederlandsche Boekhandel, 1979. (*De westerse economie.*)

BAFFI, P.: 'Monetary Developments in Italy from the War Economy to Limited Convertibility, 1935–1958', in: *Banca Nazionale del Lavoro Quarterly Review*, vol. 47, December 1958, pp. 399–483. ('Monetary Developments in Italy'.)

BAIROCH, P.: *Le Tiers Monde dans l'impasse. Le démarrage économique du XVIIIe au XXe siècle.* Paris, Gallimard, 1971. (*Le Tiers Monde dans l'impasse.*)

BALASSA, B.: 'Whiter French Planning?', in: *The Quarterly Journal of Economics*, vol. 79, no. 4, November 1965, pp. 537–54. ('French Planning?')

——— 'Export Incentives and Export Performances in Developing Countries: a Comparative Analysis', in: *Weltwirtschaftliches Archiv*, vol. 114, 1978, pp. 24–61. ('Export Incentives'.)

——— 'World Trade and the International Economy: Trends, Prospects and Policies', in: B. BALASSA (*et al.*), *World Trade: Constraints and Opportunities in the 80's.* Paris, The Atlantic Institute for International Affairs, 1979, pp. 43–70. ('World Trade and the International Economy'.)

BALDWIN, R. E.: *Non-Tariff Distortions of International Trade*. Washington DC, Brookings, 1970. (*Non-Tariff Distortions*.)

BALOGH, T.: 'Britain's Planning Problems', in: S. HOLLAND (ed.), *Beyond Capitalist Planning*. Oxford, Blackwell, 1978, pp. 121–36. ('Britain's Planning Problems'.)

BANDT, J. DE, H. C. BOS (*et al.*): *The World Economy in Transition. A Tripartite Report by Seventeen Economists from the European Community, Japan and North America*. Washington DC, Brookings, 1975. (*The World in Transition*.)

BANK FOR INTERNATIONAL SETTLEMENTS: *Annual Report, 1975*. Basle, BIS, 1975. (*Annual Report, 1975*.)

BARNES, W. G.: *Europe and the Developing World*. London, Chatham House, 1967. (*Europe and the Developing World*.)

BARRET, M., M. L. GREENE: 'Special Drawing Rights: a Major Step in the Evolution of the World's Monetary System', in: *Federal Reserve Bank of New York, Monthly Review*, vol. 50, no. 1, January 1968, pp. 10–13. ('Special Drawing Rights'.)

BATTELLE MEMORIAL INSTITUTE (ed.): *Explor-Multitrade Data Bank*. Columbus (Ohio), Columbus Laboratories, no date. (*Explor-Multitrade Data Bank*.)

BAUM, W. E.: *The French Economy and the State*. Princeton, Princeton UP, 1958. (*The French Economy*.)

BAYLISS, B. T.: *European Transport*. London, Ministry of Transport, 1965. (*European Transport*.)

BEAVER, S. E.: *Demographic Transition Theory Reinterpreted*. Lexington (Mass.), D. C. Heath & Co., 1975. (*Demographic Transition Theory*.)

BECKER, G. S.: *Human Capital. A Theoretical and Empirical Analysis with Special Reference to Education*. New York, National Bureau of Economic Research, distr. by Columbia UP, 1964. (*Human Capital*.)

BECKERMAN, W. (ed.): *The Labour Government's Economic Record, 1964–1970*. London, Duckworth, 1972. (*Labour Government's Economic Record*.)

—— *In Defence of Economic Growth*. London, Jonathan Cape, 1976. (*Defence of Economic Growth*.)

BELGIUM: 'Het verloop van de bestaansvoorwaarden in België sedert het einde van de tweede wereldoorlog', in: *Tijdschrift van de Nationale Bank van België*, 52, vol. 2, no. 4, October 1977, pp. 3–25. ('Het verloop van de bestaansvoorwaarden in België'.)

BELIEN, A.: *De invloed van de economische ontwikkeling op de inkomensongelijkheid in België*. (Mimeographed paper.) Louvain, CES, 1974. (*Inkomensongelijkheid in België*.)

BELIEN, A., KESENNE, J., K. TAVERNIER: *De relatie tussen inkomenshoogte en inkomensongelijkheid: een empirische verificatie van een hypothese op basis van de Franse en Duitse situatie*. (Mimeographed paper.) Louvain, CES, 1974. (*Inkomenshoogte en inkomensongelijkheid*.)

BELL, D.: *The Cultural Contradictions of Capitalism*. New York, Basic Books, 1976. (*Cultural Contradictions of Capitalism*.)

BELL, D., I. KRISTOL (eds): *Capitalism Today*. New York, Basic Books, 1971. (*Capitalism Today*.)

BELL, G.: *The Euro-dollar Market and the International Financial System.* London, Macmillan, 1973. (*The Euro-dollar Market.*)

BENARD, J.: 'Le Marché Commun Européen et l'avenir de la planification française', in: *Revue Économique,* vol. 15, no. 5, September 1964, pp. 756–84. ('La planification française'.)

BEN-DAVID, J.: *Fundamental Research and the Universities.* Paris, OECD, 1968. (*Fundamental Research.*)

BERGSTEN, C. F.: *Completing the GATT: Toward New International Rules to Govern Export Controls.* London, British–North American Committee, October 1974. (*Completing the GATT.*)

BERGSTROM, V., J. SODERSTEN: 'Industrial Growth and the Distribution of Incomes. A Conflict of Goals for Economic Policy', in: *Skandinaviska Enskilda Banken Quarterly Review,* no. 3, 1972, pp. 98–108. ('Industrial Growth and the Distribution of Incomes'.)

BERLE, A. A., Jr: *The 20th Century Capitalist Revolution.* New York, St Martin's Press, 1954. (*Capitalist Revolution.*)

BERNSTEIN, E. M.: 'The Gold Crisis and the New Gold Standard', in: *Quarterly Review and Investment Survey,* 1958, pp. 1–12. ('The Gold Crisis'.)

BERTELMAN, T. (*et al.*): *Resources, Society and the Future.* Stockholm, Secretariat for Future Studies, 1980. (*Resources, Society.*)

BHAGWATI, J. N. (ed.): *The New International Economic Order: the North-South Debate.* (MIT Bicentennial Studies.) Cambridge (Mass.), MIT Press, 1977. (*The North-South Debate.*)

BIS: *see* Bank for International Settlements.

BLACKHURST, R., MARIAN, N., J. TUMLIR: *Trade Liberalization, Protectionism and Interdependence.* Geneva, GATT, 1977. (*Trade Liberalization.*)

—— *Adjustment, Trade and Growth in Developed and Developing Countries.* Geneva, GATT, 1978. (*Adjustment, Trade and Growth.*)

BLAIR, J. M.: *The Control of Oil.* London, Macmillan, 1977. (*Control of Oil.*)

BLANDOW, G. E.: 'Agricultural Production, Prices and Costs: How have the farmers fared?', in: AMERICAN ENTERPRISE INSTITUTE, *Food and Agricultural Policy.* Washington DC, AEI, 1977. ('Agricultural Production'.)

BLOCK, F. L.: *The Origins of International Economic Disorder. A Study of United States International Monetary Policy from World War II to the Present.* Berkeley, Univ. of Calif. Press, 1977. (*Origins of International Economic Disorder.*)

BOHI, D. R., M. RUSSELL: *Limiting Oil Imports: An Economic History and Analysis.* Baltimore, Johns Hopkins UP, 1978. (*Limiting Oil Imports.*)

BÖHNING, W.: *The Migration of Workers in the United Kingdom and the European Community.* Oxford, Oxford UP, 1972. (*Migration of Workers.*)

BÖHNING, W., D. MAILLAT: *The Effects of the Employment of Foreign Workers.* Paris, OECD, 1974. (*Employment of Foreign Workers.*)

BOLL, F.: 'Le processus d'intégration monétaire des six: 1968–1972', in: *Civisme Européen,* vol. 2, no. 2, June 1972. ('Le processus d'intégration monétaire'.)

BORN, K. E.: 'Government Action against the Great Depression', in: H. VAN DER WEE (ed.), *The Great Depression Revisited. Essays on the Economics of the Thirties*. The Hague, Martinus Nijhoff, 1972, pp. 45–58. ('Government Action against the Great Depression'.)

BORNSTEIN, M. (ed.): *Economic Planning, East and West*. Cambridge (Mass.), Ballinger, 1975. (*Economic Planning*.)

BOSERUP, E.: *Évolution agraire et pression démographique*. Paris, Flammarion, 1970. (*Évolution agraire*.)

—— 'Food Supply and Population in Developing Countries. Present Status and Prospects', in: N. ISLAM (ed.), *Agricultural Policy in Developing Countries*. London, Macmillan, 1974, pp. 164–76. ('Food Supply'.)

BOWMAN, M. J.: 'Schultz, Denison and the Contribution of "eds" to National Income Growth', in: *Journal of Political Economy*, vol. 72, October 1964, pp. 450–64. ('Schultz, Denison'.)

BRAND, W.: 'Het Oostblok en de internationale economische orde', in: *Economische Statistische Berichten*, vol. 65, no. 3257, 4 June 1980, pp. 652–6. ('Het Oostblok'.)

BRANDT, W.: *North-South: A Programme for Survival. Report of the Independent Commission on International Development Issues under the Chairmanship of Willy Brandt*. London/Sydney, Pan Books, 1980. (*North-South: A Programme for Survival*.)

—— *Common Crisis, North-South: Co-operation for World Recovery. The Brandt Commission 1983*. London/Sydney, Pan Books, 1983. (*Common Crisis, North-South*.)

BRAUN, E., S. MCDONALD: *Revolution in Miniature: the History and Impact of Semiconductor Electronics*. Cambridge, Cambridge UP, 1978. (*Revolution in Miniature*.)

BRAUN, F.: 'L'Inventaire statistique des investissements étrangers en Europe', in: *Les investissements étrangers en Europe*. Paris, Dunod, Séminaire organisé par l'institut d'administration des entreprises de l'université de Paris et de gestion des entreprises, IX, 1968. ('L'Inventaire statistique des investissements étrangers'.)

BREEDVELD, D. C.: 'Nieuwe stappen op weg naar een vrij intra-Europees goederenverkeer', in: *De Economist*, 103, no. 9, 1955, pp. 597–619. ('Naar een vrij intra-Europees goederenverkeer'.)

BRITISH GOVERNMENT (ed.): *White Paper on Financial and Economic Obligations of the National Industries*. London, HMSO, 1961.

—— *White Paper on National Industries*. London, HMSO, 1967.

BRONDEL, G., N. MORTON: 'Energy Policy', in: P. COFFEY (ed.), *Economic Policies of the Common Market*. London, Macmillan, 1979. ('Energy Policy'.)

BRONFENBRENNER, M. (ed.): *Is the Business Cycle Obsolete?* (Based on a Conference of the Social Science Research Council Committee on Economic Stability.) New York, Wiley, 1969. (*Business Cycle*.)

BROOKINGS INSTITUTION (ed.): *Conference on World Inflation, Brookings Institution, November 21–23, 1974*. Washington DC, Brookings, 1974.

BROOKS, H.: 'What's Happening to the US-Lead in Technology?', in: *Harvard Business Review*, May–June 1972, pp. 110–18. ('U.S.-Lead in Technology'.)

BROWN, C. P.: *The Political and Social Economy of Commodity Control*. London, Macmillan, 1980. (*Commodity Control*.)

BROWN, G. M., B. FIELD: 'The Adequacy of Scarcity Measures for Signaling the Scarcity of Nation Resources', in: V. K. SMITH (ed.), *Scarcity and Growth Reconsidered*. Baltimore, Johns Hopkins UP, 1979, pp. 218–48. ('Scarcity Measures'.)

BROWN, L. R., E. P. ECKHOLM: *By Bread Alone*. Oxford, Pergamon Press, 1975. (*By Bread Alone*.)

BROWN, M. (ed.): *The Theory and Empirical Analysis of Production*. New York, National Bureau of Economic Research, distr. by Columbia UP, 1967.

BROWN, M., A. CONRAD: 'The Influence of Research and Education on CES Production Relations', in: M. BROWN (ed.), *The Theory and Empirical Analysis of Production*. New York, Columbia UP, 1967. ('The Influence of Research'.)

BROWN, W. M.: *World Afloat: National Policies Ruling the Waves* (Essays in International Finance, no. 116). Princeton, Princeton UP, 1976. (*World Afloat*.)

BRUGMANS, H.: *L'idée européenne, 1920–1970*. Bruges, De Tempel, 1970. (*L'idée européenne*.)

BUREAU INTERNATIONAL DU TRAVAIL: *L'emploi, la croissance et les besoins essentiels: Problème mondial. Conférence mondiale tripartite sur l'emploi, la répartition du revenu, le progrès social et la division internationale du travail*. Geneva, Bureau International du Travail, 1976. (*L'emploi, la croissance et les besoins essentiels*.)

BURNS, A. F.: *The Business Cycle in a Changing World*. New York, National Bureau of Economic Research, 1969. (*Business Cycle*.)

BUYSE, J.: *Het 'Programme Commun de gouvernement' en de theorie van het Staatsmonopoliekapitalisme*. (Unpublished thesis, K. U. Leuven, Department of Economics.) Louvain, 1977. (*Het 'Programme Commun'*.)

CALLEO, D. P. (ed.): *Money and the Coming World Order*. New York, New York UP, 1976.

CALLEO, D. P., B. M. ROWLAND: *America and the World Political Economy: Atlantic Dreams and National Realities*. Bloomington (Ind.), Indiana UP, 1973. (*America and the World Political Economy*.)

CAMPBELL, K. O.: *Food for the Future. How Agriculture can Meet the Challenge*. Lincoln, University of Nebraska Press, 1979. (*Food for the Future*.)

CAMPS, M.: *Britain and the European Community, 1955–1963*. Oxford, Oxford UP, 1964. (*Britain and the European Community*.)

CARBAUGH, R. J.: *International Economics*. Cambridge (Mass.), Winthrop, 1980. (*International Economics*.)

CARON, F.: *An Economic History of Modern France*. London, Methuen, 1979. (*Modern France*.)

CARTER, H. W.: *Speaking European: The Anglo-Continental Cleavage*. London, Allen & Unwin, 1966. (*Speaking European*.)

CARVER, V., P. LIDDIARD (eds): *An Ageing Population*. New York, Holmes & Meier, 1979. (*An Ageing Population*.)

CAVES, R. E.: 'Industrial Organization, Corporate Strategy and Structure', in: *The Journal of Economic Literature*, vol. 18, March 1980, pp. 64–89. ('Industrial Organization, Corporate Strategy'.)

CAVES, R. E., M. UEKUSA: 'Industrial organization in Japan', in: H. PATRICK, H. ROSOVSKY (eds), *Asia's New Giant. How the Japanese Economy Works*. Washington DC, Brookings, 1976. ('Industrial Organization'.)

CENTRAL BANK OF KOREA (ed.): *Proceedings of the Second Pacific Basin Central Bank Conference on Economic Modelling*. Seoul, Central Bank of Korea, 1976.

CHANDLER, A. D., Jr: *Strategy and Structure. Chapters in the History of Industrial Enterprise*. Cambridge (Mass.), MIT Press, 1962. (*Strategy and Structure*.)

—— *The Visible Hand. The Managerial Revolution in American Business*. Cambridge (Mass.), Belknap Press, 1977. (*The Visible Hand*.)

—— 'The Growth of the Transnational Industrial Firm in the United States and the United Kingdom: A Comparative Analysis', in: *The Economic History Review*, Second Series, vol. 23, no. 3, August 1980, pp. 396–410. ('Growth of the Transnational Industrial Firm'.)

CHANDLER, A. D., Jr, H. DAEMS: 'Administrative Coordination, Allocation and Monitoring: Concepts and Comparisons', in: N. HORN, J. KOCKA (eds), *Law and the Formation of the Big Enterprises in the 19th and Early 20th Centuries*. Göttingen, Vandenhoeck & Ruprecht, 1979, pp. 28–54. ('Administrative Coordination'.)

—— (eds): *Managerial Hierarchies. Comparative Perspectives on the Rise of the Modern Industrial Enterprise*. Cambridge (Mass.), Harvard UP, 1980. (*Managerial Hierarchies*.)

CHANNON, D. F.: *The Strategy and Structure of British Enterprise*. London, Macmillan, 1974. (*British Enterprise*.)

CHAZEL, A., H. POYET: *L'Économie mixte*. Paris, PUF, 1963. (*L'Économie mixte*.)

CHENERY, H., AHLUWALIA, M. S., BELL, C. L. G., DULOY, J. H., R. JOLLY: *Redistribution with Growth. Policies to improve income distribution in developing countries in the context of economic growth. A joint study by the World Bank's Development Research Center and the Institute of Development Studies at the University of Sussex*. Oxford, Oxford UP, 1974. (*Redistribution with Growth*.)

CIPOLLA, C. M. (ed.): *The Fontana Economic History of Europe* (vols 5 and 6). London, Collins Fontana, 1976. (*Fontana Economic History of Europe*.)

CLAEYS, J.: *Faktoren van ekonomische groei in Japan van 1950 tot 1970*. (Unpublished thesis, K. U. Leuven, Department of Economics.) Louvain, 1972. (*Ekonomische groei in Japan*.)

CLARK, C.: *The Conditions of Economic Progress*. London, Macmillan, 1957. (*Economic Progress*.)

CLEGG, H. A., T. E. CHESTER: *The Future of Nationalization*. Oxford, Blackwell, 1953. (*Nationalization*.)

CLENDENNING, E. W.: *The Euro-Dollar Market*. Oxford, Clarendon Press, 1970. (*The Euro-Dollar Market*.)

CLEVELAND, H. B. VAN: 'Modes of International Economic Organization: A Stalemate System', in: D. P. CALLEO (ed.), *Money and the Coming*

World Order. New York, New York U P, 1976, pp. 1–14. ('International Economic Organization'.)

CLINE, W. R.: *International Monetary Reform and the Developing Countries*. Washington D C, Brookings, 1976. (*International Monetary Reform*.)

CNUCED: *La réforme monétaire internationale et la coopération en vue du développement. Rapport du groupe d'experts*. New York, U N, 1969. (*La réforme monétaire internationale*.)

—— *Ressources financières pour le développement, le bien. Rapport du secrétariat*. Geneva, U N, 1971. (*Ressources financières pour le développement*.)

COFFEY, P. (ed.): *Economic Policies of the Common Market*. London, Macmillan, 1979.

—— 'Trade and Monetary Policy', in: P. COFFEY (ed.), *Economic Policies of the Common Market*. London, Macmillan, 1979, pp. 98–121. ('Trade and Monetary Policy'.)

COFFEY, P., J. R. PRESLEY: *European Monetary Integration*. London, Macmillan, 1971. (*European Monetary Integration*.)

COHEN, J. B.: *Japan's Economy in War and Reconstruction*. Minneapolis, University of Minnesota Press, 1949. (*Japan's Economy*.)

COHEN, S. S.: *Modern Capitalist Planning: the French Model*. Cambridge (Mass.), Harvard U P, 1969. (*Modern Capitalist Planning*.)

COMMISSARIAT GÉNÉRAL DU PLAN DE MODERNISATION ET D'ÉQUIPEMENT: *Rapport général sur le Premier Plan de Modernisation et d'Equipement*. Paris, A. COLIN, 1947. (*Rapport général sur le Premier Plan*.)

COMMUNAUTÉ ÉCONOMIQUE EUROPÉENNE: *Méthodes et procédures de programmation dans les pays membres de la Communauté* (Actes du Colloque de Nice, 19–23 Sept. 1977). Brussels, E E C, 1978. (*Méthodes et procédures de programmation*.)

COOPER, J.: *Industrial Relations: Sweden Shows the Way*. London, Fabian Research Series, 1963. (*Industrial Relations: Sweden*.)

COOPER, R. N.: *The Economics of Interdependence: Economic Policy in the Atlantic Community*. New York, McGraw-Hill, 1968. (*Economics of Interdependence*.)

—— (ed.): *A Reordered World: Emerging International Economic Problems*. Washington D C, Potomac, 1973. (*A Reordered World*.)

—— (*et al.*): *Towards a Renovated International System*. (*A Report of the Trilateral Integrators Task Force to the Trilateral Commission*.) New York, the Trilateral Commission, 1977. (*Renovated International System*.)

COOPER, R. N., R. Z. LAWRENCE: 'The 1972–1975 Commodity Boom', in: A. M. OKUN, G. L. PERRY (eds), *Brookings Papers on Economic Activity*, no. 3, pp. 671–713. Washington D C, Brookings, 1975. ('Commodity Boom'.)

CORNWALL, J.: 'Postwar Growth in Western Europe: a Re-evaluation', in: *Review of Economics and Statistics*, vol. 50, no. 3, August 1968, pp. 361–67. ('Postwar Growth'.)

—— *Growth and Stability in a Mature Economy*. London, Martin Robertson, 1972. (*Growth and Stability*.)

—— *Modern Capitalism. Its Growth and Transformation*. London, Martin Robertson, 1977. (*Modern Capitalism*.)

COUNCIL OF ECONOMIC ADVISERS: *1965, Annual Report of the Council of*

Economic Advisers. Washington DC, 1965. (*Council of Economic Advisers, 1965*.)
—— *1973, Annual Economic Report of the Council of Economic Advisers*. Washington DC, 1973. (*Council of Economic Advisers, 1973*.)
CRIPPS, T. F., R. J. TARLING: *Growth in Advanced Capitalist Economies, 1950–1970*. Cambridge, Cambridge UP, 1973. (*Growth*.)
CROUZET, F. (ed.): *Capital Formation in the Industrial Revolution*. London, Methuen, 1972. (*Capital Formation*.)
CURTIS, T. B., J. R. VASTINE: *The Kennedy Round and the Future of American Trade*. New York, Praeger, 1971. (*Future of American Trade*.)
CURZON, G., V. CURZON: *Hidden Barriers to Trade*. London, Trade Policy Research Centre, 1970. (*Barriers to Trade*.)
CUYVERS, L., W. MEEUSEN: 'Determinanten der functionele inkomensverdeling', in: *Inkomens-en Vermogensverdeling (14e Vlaams Wetenschappelijk Economisch Congres, Brussel, 1979)*. Brussels, VUB, 1979. ('Functionele inkomensverdeling'.)

DAEMS, H.: *The Holding Company and Corporate Control*. Amsterdam, North Holland, 1978. (*The Holding Company*.)
—— 'The Rise of the Modern Industrial Enterprise: A New Perspective', in: A. D. CHANDLER Jr, H. DAEMS (eds), *Managerial Hierarchies. Comparative Perspectives on the Rise of the Modern Industrial Enterprise*. Cambridge (Mass.), Harvard UP, 1980, pp. 203–23. ('Rise of the Modern Industrial Enterprise'.)
—— (*et al.*): *De Belgische industrie. Een profielbeeld*. Antwerp, De Nederlandsche Boekhandel, 1981. (*De Belgische industrie*.)
DAHLBERGH, K. A.: *Beyond the Green Revolution*. New York, Plenum Press, 1979. (*Beyond the Green Revolution*.)
DALTON, G.: *High Tide and After*. London, Muller, 1962. (*High Tide and After*.)
—— *Economic Systems and Society. Capitalism, Communism and the Third World*. Harmondsworth, Penguin, 1974. (*Economic Systems and Society*.)
DANCET, G.: 'De gevolgen van de olieprijsstijgingen voor België en zijn belangrijkste handelspartners', in: POLEKAR (ed.), *Krisis en werkgelegenheid*. Louvain, Polekar, 1981, pp. 50–65. ('De gevolgen van de olieprijsstijgingen'.)
D'ARAGONA, G. G.: 'A Critical Evaluation of Land Reform in Italy', in: *Land Economics*, vol. 30, February 1954, pp. 12–20. ('Land Reform in Italy'.)
DAS GUPTA, A. K.: *Economic and Commercial Geography*. Calcutta, Allied Bank Agency, 1978. (*Economic and Commercial Geography*.)
DATOO, B. A.: 'Toward a Reformulation of Boserup's Theory of Agricultural Change', in: *Economic Geography*, vol. 54, April 1978, pp. 135–44. ('Toward a Reformulation'.)
DAVIS, S. M., P. R. LAWRENCE: *Matrix*. Reading (Mass.), Addison-Wesley, 1977. (*Matrix*.)
DEHEM, R.: *De l'étalon sterling à l'étalon dollar*. Paris, Calmann-Lévy, 1972. (*De l'étalon sterling à l'étalon dollar*.)

DELEECK, H.: *Maatschappelijke Zekerheid en inkomensherverdeling in België.* Antwerp, Standaard, 1966. (*Maatschappelijke Zekerheid.*)
—— *Ongelijkheden in de Welvaartsstaat* (Opstellen over sociaal beleid, 2). Antwerp, De Nederlandsche Boekhandel, 1977. (*Ongelijkheden in de Welvaartsstaat.*)
DELFGAAUW, G. T.: 'Enkele vraagstukken van economische groei in Nederland', in: *De Economist*, 104, no. 3, 1956, pp. 161–75. ('Economische groei in Nederland'.)
DELORS, J.: 'The Decline in French Planning', in: S. HOLLAND (ed.), *Beyond Capitalist Planning.* Oxford, Blackwell, 1978, pp. 9–33. ('French Planning'.)
DENISON, E. F.: *Why Growth Rates Differ. Postwar Experience in Nine Western Countries.* Washington DC, Brookings, 1967. (*Why Growth Rates Differ.*)
—— *Accounting for United States Growth 1929–1969.* Washington DC, Brookings, 1974. (*United States Growth 1929–1969.*)
—— *Accounting for Slower Economic Growth. The United States in the 1970s.* Washington DC, Brookings, 1979. (*Slower Economic Growth.*)
DENISON, E. F., W. K. CHUNG: *How Japan's Economy Grew So Fast. The Sources of Post-war Expansion.* Washington DC, Brookings, 1976. (*How Japan's Economy Grew.*)
DENTON, G. R. (ed.): *Economic Integration in Europe.* London, Weidenfeld & Nicolson, 1969.
DENTON, G. R., FORSYTH, M., M. MACLENNAN: *Economic Planning and Policies in Britain, France and Germany.* London, Allen & Unwin, 1968. (*Economic Planning and Policies.*)
DEPARTMENT OF ECONOMIC AFFAIRS: *The National Plan.* London, 1964. (*The National Plan.*)
DESAEYERE, W., TAVERNIER, K., E. VAN LOON: 'Meten en verklaren van de personele inkomensverdeling in België', in: *De overheid in de gemengde economie.* (*11e Vlaams Wetenschappelijk Economisch Congres, Leuven, 1973*). Louvain, K. U. Leuven UP, 1973, pp. 285–320. ('Personele inkomensverdeling in België'.)
DESAI, M.: 'Stabilization of Primary Product Prices: the Lessons of the International Tin Agreement', in: A. SENGUPTA (ed.), *Commodities Finance and Trade. Issues in North-South Negotiations.* London, F. Pinter, 1980. ('Primary Product Prices'.)
DESPICHT, N. S.: *The Transport Policy of the European Communities.* London, Chatham House, 1969. (*Transport Policy.*)
DEUTSCHE BANK: *OPEC, Five Years after the Oil Price Increase: Facts, Figures and Analysis.* Frankfurt am Main, Deutsche Bank, 1978. (*OPEC, Five Years after the Oil Price Increase.*)
DEVROYE, A.: *Amerikaanse directe investeringen in Europa en in België na 1945: een synthese.* (Unpublished thesis, K. U. Leuven, Department of Economics.) Louvain, 1979. (*Amerikaanse directe investeringen in Europa.*)
DEWITZ, W. VON: 'The Multilateral GATT Negotiations', in: *Inter-Economics*, vol. 14, no. 4, July–August 1979, pp. 202–7. ('GATT Negotiations'.)
DHONDT, J.: 'Government, Labour and Trade Unions', in: H. VAN DER

WEE (ed.), *The Great Depression Revisited. Essays on the Economics of the Thirties.* The Hague, Martinus Nijhoff, 1972, pp. 249–57. ('Government, Labour and Trade Unions'.)

DIAZ-ALEJANDRO, C. F.: 'International Markets for Exhaustible Resources, Less Developed Countries and Multinational Corporations', in: *Research in International Business and Finance*, vol. I, 1979, pp. 269–98. ('International Markets'.)

DICK, R., H. DICKE: 'Patterns of Trade in Knowledge', in: H. GIERSCH (ed.), *International Economic Development and Resource Transfer* (Kieler Workshop, 1978). Tübingen, Mohr, 1979. ('Patterns of Trade'.)

DOUGLAS, E.: *The Policies of Energy. The Emergence of the Superstate.* London, Macmillan, 1976. (*Policies of Energy*.)

DOW, J. C. R.: *The Management of the British Economy 1945–1960.* Cambridge, Cambridge UP, 1968. (*British Economy 1945–1960*.)

—— 'Cyclical Developments in France, Germany and Italy since the Early Fifties', in: M. BRONFENBRENNER (ed.), *Is the Business Cycle Obsolete?*, ch. 5. New York, Wiley, 1969, pp. 140–96. ('France, Germany and Italy'.)

DRÈZE, J.: 'Quelques réflexions sereines sur l'adaptation de l'industrie belge au Marché Commun', in: *Comptes Rendus de la Société d'Économie Politique de Belgique*, no. 275, 1960, pp. 3–37. ('Quelques réflexions sereines'.)

DRUCKER, P. F.: *The New Society. The Anatomy of Industrial Order.* New York, Harper & Row, 1962. (*The New Society*.)

—— 'The New Markets and the New Capitalism', in: D. BELL, I. KRISTOL (eds), *Capitalism Today.* New York, Basic Books, 1971, pp. 44–79. ('The New Markets'.)

DUIJN, J. J. VAN: 'The Long Wave in Economic Life', in: *De Economist*, 125, no. 4, 1977, pp. 543–76. ('The Long Wave'.)

—— 'Dating Postwar Business Cycles in The Netherlands 1948–1976', in: *De Economist*, 126, no. 4, 1978, pp. 474–504. ('Postwar Business Cycles'.)

—— *De Lange Golf in de Economie. Kan innovatie ons uit het dal helpen?* Assen, Van Gorcum, 1979. (*De Lange Golf*.)

DUNNING, J. H., R. D. PEARCE: *The World's Largest Industrial Enterprises.* Farnborough, Gower, 1981. (*World's Largest Industrial Enterprises*.)

DUPRIEZ, L. H.: *The Long Waves confirmed by the Present Crisis.* (Discussion paper, Centrum voor Economische Studiën, 1978). Louvain, CES, 1978. (*Long Waves*.)

EEC: *see* European Economic Community.

EHRLICH, P.: *The Population Bomb.* New York, Ballantine, 1968. (*The Population Bomb*.)

EHRLICH, P. R., A. H. EHRLICH: *Population, Resources, Environment: Issues in Human Ecology.* San Francisco, W. H. Freeman & Co., 1972 (2). (*Population, Resources, Environment*.)

EINZIG, P.: *The Euro-dollar System.* London, Macmillan, 1970. (*The Euro-dollar System*.)

ELSENHANS, H.: 'Overcoming Underdevelopment. A Research Paradigm', in: _Journal of Peace Research_, vol. 12, no. 4, 1975, pp. 293–313. ('Overcoming Underdevelopment'.)

EMMANUEL, A.: 'The Multinational Corporations and Inequality of Development', in: _International Social Science Journal_, vol. 28, no. 4, 1976, pp. 754–72. ('Multinational Corporations'.)

EMMER, R. E.: 'West-German Monetary Policy, 1948–1951', in: _Journal of Political Economy_, vol. 63, February 1955, pp. 52–69. ('West-German Monetary Policy'.)

ESPENSHADE, T. J.: 'Zero Population Growth and the Economics of Developed Nations', in: _Population and Development Review_, vol. 4, no. 4, 1978, pp. 645–80. ('Zero Population Growth'.)

ESPENSHADE, T. J., W. J. SEROW (eds): _The Economic Consequences of Slowing Population Growth_. New York, Academic Press, 1978. (_Slowing Population Growth_.)

EUCKEN, W.: _Grundsätze der Wirtschaftspolitik_. Tübingen, Mohr, 1952. (_Grundsätze der Wirtschaftspolitik_.)

EUROPEAN COAL AND STEEL COMMUNITY: _Europe and Energy_. Brussels, EEC, 1967. (_Europe and Energy_.)

EUROPEAN ECONOMIC COMMUNITY: _EEG-Energiestatistiek_, Jaarboek 1972. Brussels, EEC, 1972. (_EEG-Energiestatistiek_, 1972.)

—— _European Economy_. Brussels, EEC, various issues. (_European Economy_.)

EUROPEAN TRADE UNION INSTITUTE: _The Impact of Micro-Electronics on Employment in Western Europe in the 1980s_. Brussels, 1979. (_The Impact of Micro-Electronics_.)

EVANS, D. (ed.): _Britain in the EEC_. London, Gollancz, 1973. (_Britain_.)

EVANS, J. W.: _The Kennedy Round in American Trade Policy: the Twilight of the GATT?_ Cambridge (Mass.), Harvard U P, 1971. (_The Kennedy Round_.)

EYSKENS, G. (et al.): _Het land waarin wij werken. Een doorlichting van het Belgisch economisch systeem_. Antwerp, Standaard, 1974. (_Het land waarin wij werken_.)

FAO: _see_ FOOD AND AGRICULTURE ORGANIZATION.

FAULKNER, H. U.: _American Economic History_. New York, Harper & Row, 1960 (8). (_American Economic History_.)

FEDERAL OPEN MARKET COMMITTEE: _Minutes of the FOMC_. New York, 1967. (_Minutes of the FOMC_.)

FEDERAL RESERVE SYSTEM: 'Ministerial Statement of the Group of Ten and Annex Prepared by Deputies', in: _Federal Reserve Bulletin_, vol. 50, no. 8, August 1964, pp. 975–99. ('Statement of the Group of Ten'.)

—— 'Treasury and Federal Reserve Foreign Exchange Operations', in: _Federal Reserve Bulletin_, vol. 58, no. 9, September 1972, pp. 757–82. ('Treasury and Federal Reserve Foreign Exchange Operations'.)

FEDERATION OF BRITISH INDUSTRIES: _Economic Planning in France. Report on the Brighton Conference of the Federation of British Industries, January 1961_ (P.E.P. Planning Paper no. 454.) London, Federation of British Industries, 1961. (_Economic Planning in France_.)

FEI, J. C. H., G. RANIS: _Development of the Labor Surplus Economy: Theory and Policy_. Homewood (Illinois), Irwin, 1964. (_Labor Surplus Economy_.)

FISHLOW, A., DIAZ-ALEJANDRO, C. F., RAGEN, R. F., R. D. HANSEN: *Rich and Poor Nations in the World Economy (1980s' Project)*. New York, McGraw-Hill, 1978. (*Rich and Poor Nations*.)

FLEMING, J. M.: *Reflections on the International Monetary Reform*. (Essays in International Finance, no. 107.) Princeton, Princeton UP, 1974. (*International Monetary Reform*.)

—— *International Aspects of Inflation*. (Paper presented at the IEA conference on Inflation Theory and Anti-Inflation Policy, Saltsjäbaden (Sweden), August 28–September 3, 1975.) Washington DC, IMF, 1975. (*Inflation*.)

FOOD AND AGRICULTURE ORGANIZATION: *Agriculture: Towards 2000*. Rome, FAO, 1980. (*Agriculture: Towards 2000*.)

FRANKEN, N.: *De betekenis van de Algemene Overeenkomst inzake Tarieven en Handel (GATT) in het internationale handelspolitieke overleg*. The Hague, Govers, 1956. (*GATT*.)

FRANKO, L. G.: *The European Multinationals: a Renewed Challenge to American and British Big Business*. London, Harper & Row, 1976. (*European Multinationals*.)

FREEMAN, C.: *The Economics of Industrial Innovation*. Harmondsworth, Penguin, 1974. (*The Economics*.)

—— 'The Kondratiev Long Waves, Technical Change and Unemployment', in: OECD, *Structural Determinants of Employment and Unemployment*, vol II. Paris, OECD, 1979, pp. 181–96. ('The Kondratiev Long Waves'.)

—— (*et al.*): 'Research and Innovation in Electronic Capital Goods', in: *National Institute Economic Review*, no. 34, November 1965, pp. 40–91. ('R & D in Electronic Capital Goods'.)

FRIEDMAN, M.: *Capitalism and Freedom*. Chicago, Univ. of Chicago Press, 1967. (*Capitalism and Freedom*.)

—— *Unemployment versus Inflation? An Evaluation of the Phillips Curve*. Washington DC, Institute of Economic Affairs, 1975. (*Unemployment versus Inflation*.)

FRIEDMAN, M., R. FRIEDMAN: *Free to Choose. A Personal Statement*. London, Secker & Warburg, 1980. (*Free to Choose*.)

FRIER, E. R., C. L. SHULTZE (eds): *Higher Oil Prices and the World Economy*. Washington DC, Brookings, 1975. (*Higher Oil Prices*.)

FURNISS, E. S., Jr: *France, Troubled Ally*. New York, Harper & Row, 1960. (*France, Troubled Ally*.)

GABOR, D., COLOMBO, V., KING, A., R. GALLI: *Beyond the Age of Waste*. Oxford, Pergamon Press, 1978. (*Age of Waste*.)

GALBRAITH, J. K.: *The Affluent Society*. Harmondsworth, Penguin, 1962. (*Affluent Society*.)

—— *The New Industrial State*. Boston, Houghton Mifflin, 1967. (*Industrial State*.)

—— *Economics and the Public Purpose*. Boston, Houghton Mifflin, 1973. (*Economics and the Public Purpose*.)

GARDNER, R. N.: *Sterling-Dollar Diplomacy: The Origins and the Prospects of our International Economic Order*. Oxford, Oxford UP, 1956. (*Sterling-Dollar Diplomacy*.)

GAREY, R. C. (ed.): *Europe's Future in Figures.* Amsterdam, North Holland, 1962. (*Europe's Future in Figures.*)

GATT: *see* GENERAL AGREEMENT ON TARIFFS AND TRADE.

GENERAL AGREEMENT ON TARIFFS AND TRADE: *Networks of World Trade by Areas and Commodity Classes: 1955–1976.* Geneva, GATT, 1978. (*Network of World Trade: 1955–1976.*)

—— *The Tokyo Round of Multilateral Trade Negotiations* (2 vols). Geneva, GATT, 1979–1980. (*The Tokyo Round.*)

—— *International Trade: 1979/80.* Geneva, GATT, 1980. (*International Trade: 1979/80.*)

—— *Trends in International Trade, 1957 to 1978.* Geneva, GATT, 1980. (*Trends in International Trade, 1957 to 1978.*)

—— *International Trade: 1982/3.* Geneva, GATT, 1983. (*International Trade: 1982/3.*)

GERBET, P.: *La genèse du Plan Schuman: des origines à la déclaration du 9 mai 1950.* (Centre de Recherches Européennes.) Lausanne, 1962. (*La genèse du Plan Schuman.*)

GERMANY: 'Einkomensverteilung und -schichtung der privaten Haushalte in der Bundesrepublik Deutschland, 1950 bis 1970', in: *Deutsches Institut für Wirtschaftsforschung: Wochenbericht 25,* vol. 40, 21 June 1973, pp. 217–26. ('Einkomensverteilung und -schichtung'.)

GERSCHENKRON, A.: *Economic Backwardness in Historical Perspective. A Book of Essays.* New York, Praeger, 1965. (*Backwardness.*)

GHESQUIRE, R.: *Tussen Eden en Utopia. Ontwikkeling in Zuidoost-Azië.* Louvain, Davidsfonds, 1976. (*Tussen Eden en Utopia.*)

—— 'Euro-currency Markets: A Critical Survey', in: *Tijdschrift voor Economie en Management,* vol. 22, no. 1, 1977, pp. 9–49. ('Euro-currency Markets'.)

GIBBONS, M., R. JOHNSTON: 'The Role of Science in Technological Innovation', in: *Research Policy,* vol. 3, London, 1975. ('The Role of Science'.)

GIERSCH, H. (ed.): *International Economic Development and Resource Transfer.* (Kieler Workshop, 1978.) Tübingen, Mohr, 1979. (*Economic Development.*)

GILBERT, M.: 'The Postwar Business Cycle in Western Europe', in: *American Economic Review,* vol. 52, no. 2, May 1962, pp. 93–109. ('Postwar Business Cycle'.)

GILPIN, R.: *U.S. Power and the Multinational Corporation.* London, Macmillan, 1976. (*U.S. Power.*)

GINZBERG, E.: 'Sweden: Some Unanswered Questions', in: D. BELL, I. KRISTOL (eds), *Capitalism Today.* New York, Basic Books, 1971, pp. 158–66. ('Sweden'.)

GIRVAN, N.: *Corporate Imperialism: Conflict and Expropriation. Transnational Corporations and Economic Nationalism in the Third World.* New York, Sharpe, 1976. (*Corporate Imperialism.*)

GOELLER, H. E.: 'The Age of Substitutability: A Scientific Appraisal of Natural Resource Adequacy', in: V. K. SMITH (ed.), *Scarcity and Growth Reconsidered.* Baltimore, Johns Hopkins UP, 1979. ('Age of Substitutability'.)

GOLD, J.: *The Stand-By Arrangements of the International Monetary Fund.* Washington DC, IMF, 1970. (*Stand-By Arrangements.*)
— *The Second Amendment of the Fund's Articles of Agreement.* (Pamphlet Series, no. 25.) Washington DC, IMF, 1978. (*Second Amendment.*)
— *SDRs, Currencies, and Gold. Fifth Survey of New Legal Developments.* (Pamphlet Series, no. 36.) Washington DC, IMF, 1981. (*SDRs, Currencies and Gold.*)
GOLDBERG, R. A., J. E. AUSTIN: *Multinational Agribusiness and Global Food Problems.* (Mimeographed paper.) Chicago, 1976. (*Multinational Agribusiness.*)
GORDON, L. (ed.): *From Marshall Plan to Global Interdependence. New Challenges for the Industrialized Nations.* Paris, OECD, 1978. (*From Marshall Plan to Global Interdependence.*)
GORDON, R. A.: 'The Stability of the US Economy', in: M. BRONFEN-BRENNER (ed.), *Is the Business Cycle Obsolete?* New York, Wiley, 1969, pp. 3–34. ('US Economy'.)
GRANICK, D.: *The European Executive.* New York, Doubleday, 1962. (*The European Executive.*)
GRAUWE, P. DE: 'The Development of the Euro-currency Market', in: *Finance and Development,* vol. 12, no. 3, September 1975, pp. 14–17. ('The Euro-currency Market'.)
— *Floating Exchange Rates: Current Experiences and Policies of LDC's.* (International Economics Research Paper no. 14.) Louvain, CES, 1978. (*Floating Exchange Rates.*)
GRAUWE, P. DE, T. PEETERS: *The European Monetary System. A Step towards Monetary Stability?* (International Economics Research Paper no. 21.) Louvain, CES, 1978. (*The European Monetary System.*)
GREENHALGH, G.: *The Necessity for Nuclear Power.* London, Graham & Trotman, 1980. (*Nuclear Power.*)
GRIFFIN, K.: *The Political Economy of Agrarian Change: An Essay on the Green Revolution.* London, Macmillan, 1974. (*Agrarian Change.*)
GRJEBINE, A.: *La nouvelle économie internationale.* Paris, PUF, 1980. (*La nouvelle économie internationale.*)
GROSSER, A.: *The Colossus Again. Western Germany from Defeat to Rearmament.* New York, Praeger, 1955. (*Colossus Again.*)
— *La Quatrième République et sa politique extérieure.* Paris, A. Colin, 1961. (*La Quatrième République.*)
GRUBEL, H. G.: 'Basic Methods for Distributing SDR's and the Problem of International Aid', in: *Journal of Finance* (Chicago), vol. 27, no. 5, December 1972, pp. 1009–22. ('Basic Methods for Distributing SDR's'.)
— 'The Case Against the New International Economic Order', in: J. ADAMS (ed.), *The Contemporary International Economy: A Reader.* New York, St Martin's Press, 1979, pp. 482–501. ('New International Economic Order'.)
GRUBEL, H. G., P. J. LLOYD: *Intra-industry Trade. The Theory and Measurement of International Trade in Differentiated Products.* London, Macmillan, 1975. (*Intra-industry Trade.*)
GRUBER, W., METHA, D., R. VERNON: 'The R & D Factor in Inter-

national Trade and International Investment of United States Indus-tries', in: *Journal of Political Economy*, vol. 75, no. 1, February 1967, pp. 20–37. ('The R & D Factor'.)

GRUSON, C.:*Origine et espoirs de la planification française*. Paris, Dunod, 1968. (*La planification française*.)

GUTT, C.: 'Exchange Rates and the International Monetary Fund', in: S. HARRIS (ed.), *Foreign Economic Policy for the United States*. Cambridge (Mass.), Harvard UP, 1948, pp. 217–35. ('Exchange Rates and the IMF'.)

HABAKKUK, H. J.: *American and British Technology in the 19th Century*. Cambridge, Cambridge UP, 1962. (*American and British Technology*.)
—— *Population Growth and Economic Development since 1750*. Leicester, Leicester UP, 1972. (*Population Growth*.)

HABERLER, G.: 'The International Monetary System: Some Recent Developments and Discussions', in: G. N. HALM (ed.), *Approaches to Greater Flexibility of Exchange Rates*. Princeton, Princeton UP, 1970, pp. 115–23. ('The International Monetary System'.)
—— 'The Case Against the Link', in: *Banca Nazionale del Lavoro Quarterly Review* (Rome), vol. 24, no. 96, March 1971, pp. 13–22. ('The Case Against the Link'.)
—— 'Inflation as a Worldwide Phenomenon. An Overview', in: *Weltwirt-schaftliches Archiv*, vol. 110, no. 2, 1974, pp. 179–93. ('Inflation as a Worldwide Phenomenon'.)
—— *How Important is Control over International Reserves?* (J. Marcus Fleming Memorial Conference on 'The New International Monetary System', IMF, November 11–12, 1976.) Washington DC, IMF, 1976. (*Control over International Reserves?*)
—— 'Stagflation. An Analysis of its Causes and Cures', in: B. BALASSA, R. NELSON (eds), *Economic Progress, Private Values and Public Policy. Essays in Honor of William Fellner*. Amsterdam, North Holland, 1977, pp. 311–29. ('Stagflation'.)

HABERLER, G., T. D. WILLET: *A Strategy for U.S. Balance of Payments Policy*. Washington DC, AEI, 1971. (*U.S. Balance of Payments Policy*.)

HABERMAS, J.: *Technik und Wissenschaft als 'Ideologie'*. Frankfurt am Main, Suhrkamp, 1971. (*Technik und Wissenschaft*.)

HADLEY, E. M.: *Antitrust in Japan*. Princeton, Princeton UP, 1970. (*Antitrust in Japan*.)

HALM, G. N. (ed.): *Approaches to Greater Flexibility of Exchange Rates*. Prince-ton, Princeton UP, 1970.

HANNAH, L.: *The Rise of the Corporate Economy. The British Experience*. Baltimore, Johns Hopkins UP, 1976. (*The Corporate Economy*.)

HARDACH, K.: 'Germany 1914–1970', in: C. M. CIPOLLA (ed.), *The Fontana Economic History of Europe: Contemporary Economics*, vol. 6, part 1. London, Collins Fontana, 1976, pp. 180–265. ('Germany 1914–1970'.)

HARRIS, S. (ed.): *Foreign Economic Policy for the United States*. Cambridge (Mass.), Harvard UP, 1948.

HARRIS, S. E.: *The Economics of Political Parties, with special attention to the*

Presidents Eisenhower and Kennedy. New York, Macmillan, 1962. (*Economics of Political Parties.*)

—— *Economics of the Kennedy Years and a Look Ahead.* New York, Harper & Row, 1964. (*Kennedy Years.*)

HAYEK, F. VON: *The Road to Serfdom.* London, Routledge & Kegan Paul, 1944. (*The Road to Serfdom.*)

HAYES, A.: *Emerging Arrangements in International Payments.* (*The Twelfth Per Jacobsson Foundation Lecture, 31 August 1975.*) Washington DC, IMF, 1975. (*Emerging Arrangements in International Payments.*)

HEERE, W. R.: 'De tegenwoordige en toekomstige demografische situatie in Nederland', in: *De Economist,* 97, no. 1, 1949, pp. 1–35. ('De demografische situatie in Nederland'.)

HEILBRONER, R. L.: *Beyond Boom and Crash.* New York, Norton, 1978. (*Beyond Boom.*)

HEILBRONER, R. L., A. SINGER: *The Economic Transformation of America.* New York, Harcourt, 1977. (*Economic Transformation of America.*)

HELLEINER, G.: *A World Divided. The Less Developed Countries in the International Economy.* Cambridge, Cambridge UP, 1976. (*A World Divided.*)

HELLER, W.: *New Dimensions of Political Economy.* Cambridge (Mass.), Harvard UP, 1967. (*New Dimensions.*)

HENLE, P.: 'Exploring the Distribution of National Earned Income', in: *Monthly Labor Review,* vol. 95, no. 12, December 1972, pp. 16–27. ('Distribution of National Income'.)

HERMAN, B.: *The Optimal International Division of Labour.* Geneva, ILO, 1975. (*Division of Labour.*)

HESSEN, B. M.: *The Social and Economic Roots of Newton's Principia.* New York, Fertig, 1971. (*Newton's Principia.*)

HEUSENS, J. J., R. DE HORN: 'Crisisbeleid Europese Staalindustrie in het licht van het EGKS-verdrag', in: *Sociaal-Economische Wetgeving. Tijdschrift voor Europees en economisch recht,* 27, no. 5, May 1979, pp. 299–335. ('Crisisbeleid Europese Staalindustrie'.)

HIERONYMI, O.: *The New Economic Nationalism.* London, Macmillan, 1980. (*New Economic Nationalism.*)

HILDEBRAND, G. H.: *Growth and Structure in the Economy of Modern Italy.* Cambridge (Mass.), Harvard UP, 1965. (*Growth and Structure.*)

HINDLEY, B.: 'Voluntary Export Restraint and the GATT's Main Escape Clause', in: *The World Economy. A Quarterly Journal on International Economic Affairs,* vol. 3, no. 3, November 1980, pp. 313–42. ('Voluntary Export Restraint'.)

HINSHAW, B. (ed.): *Monetary Reform and the Price of Gold.* Baltimore, Johns Hopkins UP, 1967.

HIRSCH, F.: *Money International.* Harmondsworth, Penguin, 1969. (*Money International.*)

—— *Social Limits to Growth.* Cambridge (Mass.), Harvard UP, 1976. (*Social Limits to Growth.*)

HIRSCH, F., J. H. GOLDTHORPE: *The Political Economy of Inflation.* London, Robertson, 1978. (*Political Economy.*)

HIRSCH, F., P. OPPENHEIMER: 'The Trial of Managed Money: Currency, Credit and Prices 1920–1970', in: C. M. CIPOLLA (ed.), *The Fontana Economic History of Europe: The Twentieth Century*, vol. 5, part 2. London, Collins Fontana, 1976, pp. 603–97. ('Managed Money'.)

HIRSCH, S.: 'United States Electronic Industry in International Trade', in: *National Institute Economic Review*, vol. 34, November 1965, pp. 92–7. ('United States Electronic'.)

—— *Location of Industry and International Competitiveness*. Oxford, Oxford UP, 1967. (*Location of Industry*.)

HIRSCHMAN, A. O.: *The Strategy of Economic Development*. New Haven, Yale UP, 1958. (*Strategy of Economic Development*.)

HMSO: *Agreement for Intra-European Payments and Compensations*. London, 1948. (*Intra-European Payments, 1948*.)

HOEFNAGELS, H.: *Een eeuw sociale problematiek. Van sociaal conflict naar strategische samenwerking*. Assen, Van Gorcum, 1957. (*Sociale problematiek*.)

HOELEN, H.: 'Critische beschouwingen over de loon- en prijspolitiek der Nederlandse regering sinds 1954', in: *De Economist*, 110, nos 10/11, 1962, pp. 698–739. ('Loon- en prijspolitiek'.)

HOFFMANN, S. H. (*et al.*): *In Search of France. The Postwar Resurgence of the French Economy*. Cambridge (Mass.), Harvard UP, 1963. (*In Search of France*.)

HOLLAND, S. (ed.): *Beyond Capitalist Planning*. Oxford, Blackwell, 1978. (*Beyond Capitalist Planning*.)

—— 'Planning Disagreements', in: S. HOLLAND (ed.), *Beyond Capitalist Planning*, Oxford, Blackwell, 1978, pp. 137–61. ('Planning Disagreements'.)

HOLTROP, M. W.: 'Monetaire problematiek in Benelux en E.E.G.', in: *De Economist*, 111, nos 1/2, 1963, pp. 1–25. ('Monetaire problematiek'.)

HOOPER, P., B. LOUREY: *Impact of the Dollar Depreciation on the U.S. Price Level: an Analytical Survey of Empirical Estimates*. (International Discussion Paper, no. 128.) Washington DC, FED, 1979. (*Impact of the Dollar Depreciation*.)

HOPKINS, R. F., D. J. PUCHALA: 'Perspectives on the International Relations of Food', in: *International Organization*, vol. 32, no. 3, 1978, pp. 581–616. ('International Relations of Food'.)

HORN, N., J. KOCKA (eds): *Law and the Formation of the Big Enterprises in the 19th and Early 20th Centuries*. Göttingen, Vandenhoeck & Ruprecht, 1979. (*Big Enterprises*.)

HORSEFIELD, J. K.: *The International Monetary Fund, 1945–1965*. Washington DC, IMF, 1969. (*The International Monetary Fund*.)

HOWE, C. W.: *Natural Resource Economics*. New York, Wiley, 1979. (*Natural Resource Economics*.)

HUDSON, M.: *Global Fracture. The New International Economic Order*. New York, Harper & Row, 1977. (*Global Fracture*.)

HUFBAUER, G.: *Synthetic Materials and the Theory of International Trade*. Cambridge (Mass.), Harvard UP, 1966. (*Synthetic Materials*.)

HUNTER, L. C., G. L. REID: *Urban Workers' Mobility*. Paris, OESO, 1967. (*Urban Workers' Mobility*.)

HYMER, S. H.: *The International Operations of National Firms: A Study of Direct Foreign Investment.* Cambridge (Mass.), MIT Press, 1976. (*International Operations of National Firms.*)

IMF: *see* INTERNATIONAL MONETARY FUND.

INTERNATIONAL BANK FOR RECONSTRUCTION AND DEVELOPMENT: *see* WORLD BANK.

INTERNATIONAL COMMUNICATIONS AGENCY (ed.): *Official Text of President J. Carter's Address of November 1, 1978.* Brussels, US Embassy, 1978. (*Carter: November 1, 1978.*)

—— 'A. Solomon at the Royal Institute of International Affairs, London, on January 12, 1979' (text excerpts). Brussels, US Embassy, 1979. ('A. Solomon at the Royal Institute'.)

—— 'A. Solomon at an International Trade and Investment Conference on May 11, 1979, sponsored by the National Journal' (text excerpts). Brussels, US Embassy, 1979. ('A. Solomon at an International Trade and Investment Conference'.)

INTERNATIONAL MONETARY FUND: *Summary Proceedings. Annual Meeting, 1962.* Washington DC, IMF, 1962. (*Annual Meeting, 1962.*)

—— *Annual Report, 1963.* Washington DC, IMF, 1963. (*Annual Report, 1963.*)

—— *Annual Report, 1964.* Washington DC, IMF, 1964. (*Annual Report, 1964.*)

—— *Report of the Study Group on the Creation of Reserve Assets, Rome 1965.* Washington DC, IMF, 1965. (*The Creation of Reserve Assets.*)

—— *Annual Report, 1971.* Washington DC, IMF, 1971. (*Annual Report, 1971.*)

—— *Summary Proceedings, Annual Meeting, 1972.* Washington DC, IMF, 1972. (*Annual Meeting, 1972.*)

—— *International Monetary Reform: Documents of the Committee of Twenty.* Washington DC, IMF, 1974. (*International Monetary Reform.*)

—— *Annual Report, 1975.* Washington DC, IMF, 1975. (*Annual Report, 1975.*)

—— *Annual Report, 1980.* Washington DC, IMF, 1980. (*Annual Report, 1980.*)

—— *World Economic Outlook.* Washington DC, IMF, 1980. (*World Economic Outlook.*)

ISLAM, N. (ed.): *Agricultural Policy in Developing Countries.* London, Macmillan, 1974.

JAIN, S.: *Size Distribution of Income. A Compilation of Data.* Washington DC, World Bank, 1975. (*Distribution of Income.*)

JÁNOSSY, F.: *La fin des miracles économiques. Apparences de réalité du développement économique.* Paris, Seuil, 1972. (*La fin des miracles économiques.*)

JEANNENEY, J. M.: *Pour un nouveau protectionisme.* Paris, Seuil, 1978. (*Pour un nouveau protectionisme.*)

JEQUIER, N.: *Le défi industriel japonais.* Lausanne, Centre de Rercherches Européennes, 1970. (*Le défi industriel japonais.*)

JEWKES, J., SAWERS, D., R. STILLERMAN: *The Sources of Invention.* London, Macmillan, 1958. (*Sources of Invention.*)

JOHNSON, H. G.: *The World Economy at the Crossroads.* Oxford, Oxford UP, 1965. (*The World Economy.*)

—— 'The Sterling Crisis of 1967' (the C. Woody Thompson Lecture), in:

Annual Meeting of Midwest Economic Association, 18 April 1968. ('The Sterling Crisis of 1967'.)
—— *Technology and Economic Interdependence*. London, Macmillan, 1975. (*Technology*.)
JOLIET, R.: 'Cartelization, Dirigism and Crisis in the European Community', in: *The World Economy. A Quarterly Journal on International Economic Affairs*, vol. 3, no. 4, January 1981, pp. 403–46. ('Cartelization, Dirigism and Crisis'.)
JOSLING, T. E.: 'The Reform of the Common Agricultural Policy', in: D. EVANS (ed.), *Britain in the EEC*. London, Gollancz, 1973, pp. 86–98. ('The Common Agricultural Policy'.)

KALDOR, N.: *Causes of the Slow Rate of Economic Growth of the United Kingdom*. Cambridge, Cambridge UP, 1966. (*Causes*.)
—— *Strategic Factors in Economic Development*. Ithaca (New York), Cornell UP, 1967. (*Strategic Factors*.)
—— 'Productivity and Growth in Manufacturing Industry: a Reply', in: *Economica*, vol. 35, no. 140, November 1968, pp. 385–91. ('Productivity'.)
KAPTEYN, P. J. G., P. VERLOREN VAN THEMAAT: *Introduction to the Law of the European Communities after the Accession of the New Member States*. London, Sweet & Maxwell, 1973. (*The European Communities*.)
KARMON, Y.: *Ports around the World*. New York, Crown, 1980. (*Ports Around the World*.)
KASER, M.: *Comecon. Integration Problems of the Planned Economies*. Oxford, Oxford UP, 1968 (2). (*Comecon*.)
KATOUZIAN, M. A.: 'The Development of the Service Sector: A New Approach', in: *Oxford Economic Papers*, vol. 22, no. 3, November 1970, pp. 362–82. ('Development of the Service Sector'.)
KEESING, D. B.: *World Trade and Output of Manufacturers: Structural Trends and Developing Countries' Exports*. (World Bank Staff Working Paper, no. 316.) Washington DC, World Bank, 1979. (*World Trade and Output of Manufacturers*.)
KEESING, F. A. G.: *De Europese Betalingsunie*. Amsterdam, North Holland, 1950. (*De Europese Betalingsunie*.)
KENDRICK, J. W.: *Productivity Trends in the United States*. Princeton, Princeton UP, 1961. (*Productivity Trends*.)
—— *Postwar Productivity Trends in the United States, 1948–1969*. New York, National Bureau of Economic Research, 1973. (*Postwar Productivity*.)
KENNAN, G. F.: *Memoirs. Part I. 1925–1950*. Boston, Little, Brown & Co., 1967. (*Memoirs, Pt I*.)
KENT, T. W.: 'Devaluation One Year After', in: *Lloyds Bank Review*, New Series, no. 18, October 1950, pp. 22–37. ('Devaluation One Year After'.)
KESENNE, J.: 'De ontwikkeling van de primaire inkomensverdeling in België', in: *De Gids op Maatschappelijk Gebied*, vol. 68, no. 12, December 1977, pp. 941–54. ('De primaire inkomensverdeling in België'.)
KESSLER, G. A.: 'Should Development Aid be Linked to SDR-Creation', in: *De Economist*, 119, no. 2, 1971, pp. 206–11. ('Should Development Aid be Linked'.)

KEYNES, J. M.: *The Economic Consequences of the Peace.* London, Macmillan, 1920. (*Economic Consequences of the Peace.*)

—— 'Relative Movements of Real Wages and Output', in: *Economic Journal*, vol. 49, no. 193, March 1939, pp. 34–51. ('Relative Movements'.)

KIDRON, M.: *Western Capitalism since the War.* Harmondsworth, Penguin, 1970 (revised edition). (*Western Capitalism.*)

KINDLEBERGER, C. P.: *Balance of Payments Deficits and the International Market for Liquidity.* (Princeton Essays in International Finance, no. 46.) Princeton, Princeton UP, 1965. (*Balance of Payments Deficits.*)

—— *Europe and the Dollar.* Cambridge (Mass.), MIT Press, 1966. (*Europe and the Dollar.*)

—— *Europe's Postwar Growth. The Role of Labor Supply.* Cambridge (Mass.), Harvard UP, 1967. (*Europe's Postwar Growth.*)

—— *American Business Abroad. Six Lectures on Direct Investment.* New Haven, Yale UP, 1969. (*American Business Abroad.*)

—— *Les investissements des États-Unis dans le monde.* Paris, Calmann-Lévy, 1971. (*Les investissements des États-Unis.*)

—— *The World in Depression, 1929–1939.* Harmondsworth, Penguin, 1973. (*World in Depression.*)

KINDLEBERGER, C. P., A. SHONFIELD (eds): *North American and Western European Economic Policies.* (Proceedings of a Conference held by the International Economic Association.) London, Macmillan, 1971. (*North American and Western European Economic Policies.*)

KING, T. (*et al.*): *Population Policies and Economic Development.* (A World Bank Staff Report.) Baltimore, Johns Hopkins UP, 1974. (*Population Policies.*)

KLEIN, P. A.: *Business Cycles in the Postwar World. Some Reflections on Recent Research.* Washington DC, AEI, 1976. (*Business Cycles.*)

KNAAPEN, A. L. M.: *De ondernemingsraden en de ontwikkeling van het medezeggenschap in de particuliere onderneming in Nederland en België.* Assen, Van Gorcum, 1952. (*Ondernemingsraden.*)

KNOOREN, H.: *Het Zweeds ekonomisch systeem. Mode of model?* Brussels, E. Vandervelde-instituut, 1979. (*Het Zweeds ekonomisch systeem.*)

KOCK, K.: *International Trade Policy and the GATT, 1947–1967.* Stockholm, Almqvist & Wiksell, 1969. (*International Trade Policy.*)

KOCKA, J.: 'The Modern Industrial Enterprise in Germany', in: A. D. CHANDLER Jr, H. DAEMS (eds), *Managerial Hierarchies. Comparative Perspectives on the Rise of the Modern Industrial Enterprise.* Cambridge (Mass.), Harvard UP, 1980.

KOCKA, J., H. SIEGRIST: 'Die hundert gröszten deutschen Industrieunternehmen im späten 19. und frühen 20. Jahrhundert', in: N. HORN, J. KOCKA (eds), *Law and the Formation of the Big Enterprises in the 19th and Early 20th Centuries.* Göttingen, Vandenhoeck & Ruprecht, 1979. ('Die hundert gröszten deutschen Industrieunternehmen'.)

KOHR, L.: *The Overdeveloped Nations. The Diseconomies of Scale.* New York, Schocken Books, 1978. (*Overdeveloped Nations.*)

KOMIYA, O.: *Postwar Economic Growth in Japan.* Berkeley, Univ. of Calif. Press, 1970. (*Growth in Japan.*)

KOSTECKI, M. M.: *East-West Trade and the GATT-system*. New York, St Martin's Press, 1978. (*East-West Trade and the GATT-system*.)

KRASNER, S. D.: 'U.S. Commercial and Monetary Policy: Unraveling the Paradox of External Strength and Internal Weakness', in: *Industrial Organization*, 1978. ('U.S. Commercial and Monetary Policy'.)

KRAUSE, L.: 'A Passive Balance of Payments Strategy for the United States', in: *Brookings Papers on Economic Activity*, vol. 3, 1974. ('Passive Balance of Payments Strategy'.)

KRAUSE, W. F., J. M. MATHIS (eds): *International Economics and Business, Selected Readings*. Boston, Houghton Mifflin, 1968. (*International Economics*.)

—— 'The U.S. Policy Shift on East-West Trade', in: *Journal of International Affairs*, 28, no. 1, 1974, pp. 25–37. ('The U.S. Policy Shift'.)

KRAVIS, I. B.: *An International Comparison of National Products and the Purchasing Power of Currencies*. Paris, OESO, 1953. (*National Products*.)

—— 'Income Distribution Functional Share', in: *International Encyclopaedia of the Social Sciences*, New York, Crowell Collier & Macmillan, vol. 7, 1968, pp. 132–45. ('Income Distribution'.)

—— *A System of International Comparison of Gross Product and Purchasing Power*. Baltimore, Johns Hopkins UP, 1975. (*A System of International Comparison*.)

KRENGEL, R.: 'Attempt at a Prognosis of Output and Factors of Production of Industry in the Federal Republic of Germany, 1965 and 1970', in: R. C. GAREY (ed.), *Europe's Future in Figures*. Amsterdam, North Holland, 1962. ('Attempt at a Prognosis of Output'.)

—— 'Some Reasons for the Rapid Growth of the German Federal Republic', in: *Banca Nazionale del Lavoro Quarterly Review*, no. 64, March 1963, pp. 121–44. ('Some Reasons for the Rapid Growth'.)

KUZNETS, S.: 'Economic Growth and Income Inequality', in: *American Economic Review*, vol. 45, 1955, pp. 1–28. ('Growth and Income Inequality'.)

—— 'Retardation of Industrial Growth', in: *Journal of Economic and Business History*, vol. 1, no. 4, August 1959, pp. 534–60. ('Retardation of Industrial Growth'.)

—— 'Quantitative Aspects of the Economic Growth of Nations, vol. IV: Distribution of National Income by Factor Shares', in: *Economic Development and Cultural Change*, no. 2, part 2, 1959. ('Quantitative Aspects of the Economic Growth, IV'.)

—— 'Quantitative Aspects of the Economic Growth of Nations, vol. VIII: Distribution of Income by Size', in: *Economic Development and Cultural Change*, no. 2, part 2, 1963. ('Quantitative Aspects of the Economic Growth, VIII'.)

—— *Economic Growth and Structure. Selected Essays*. London, Heinemann, 1966. (*Growth and Structure*.)

—— *Modern Economic Growth. Rate, Structure and Spread*. New Haven, Yale UP, 1966. (*Modern Economic Growth*.)

—— *Economic Growth of Nations: Total Output and Production Structure*. Cambridge (Mass.), Harvard UP, 1974 (2). (*Economic Growth*.)

LABOUR PARTY, THE: *Labour's Programme*. London, Labour Party, 1973. (*Labour's Programme*.)

LADRIÈRE, J.: *Vie sociale et destinée*. Gembloux, Duculot, 1973. (*Vie sociale*.)

LAIDLER, D. E. W., J. M. PARKIN: 'Inflation. A Survey', in: *Economic Journal*, vol. 85, no. 340, December 1975, pp. 741–809. ('Inflation'.)

LAMFALUSSY, A.: *Investment and Growth in Mature Economies. The Case of Belgium*. London, Macmillan, 1961. (*The Case of Belgium*.)

—— 'Europe's Progress: Due to the Common Market?', in: *Lloyds Bank Review*, no. 62, October 1961, pp. 1–16. ('Europe's Progress'.)

—— *The United Kingdom and the Six. An Essay on Economic Growth in Western Europe*. London, Macmillan, 1963. (*The United Kingdom and the Six*.)

LANDES, D.: *The Unbound Prometheus. Technological Change and Industrial Development in Western Europe from 1750 to the Present*. Cambridge, Cambridge UP, 1969. (*The Unbound Prometheus*.)

LAVIGNE, M.: *Le programme du Comecon et l'intégration socialiste*. Paris, Cujas, 1973. (*Le Comecon*.)

—— *Les économies socialistes soviétiques et européennes*. Paris, A. Colin, 1979 (3). (*Les économies socialistes*.)

LEMOINE, F.: 'Les prix des échanges à l'intérieur du CAEM', in: *Économies et Sociétés*, Série G, no. 35, vol. 12, nos 3-4-5, March–May 1978, pp. 865–931. ('Les prix des échanges'.)

LEON, P. (ed.): *Guerres et crises 1914–1947*. (*Histoire économique et sociale du monde*, vol. 5.) Paris, A. Colin, 1977. (*Guerres et crises 1914–1947*.)

—— *Le second XXe siècle: 1947 à nos jours*. (*Histoire économique et sociale du monde*, vol. 6.) Paris, A. Colin, 1977. (*1947 à nos jours*.)

LEONTIEF, W. (*et al.*): *The Future of the World Economy*. Oxford, Oxford UP, 1977. (*Future of the World Economy*.)

LESTHAEGE, R.: 'Bevolkingsproblemen en Ontwikkelingsbeleid', in: *Inter-university programme in Demography*, University of Brussels. (Mimeographed paper.) Brussels, VUB, no date. ('Bevolkingsproblemen en Ontwikkelingsbeleid'.)

LEVI-SANDRI, L.: 'The Contribution of Regional Action to the Construction of Europe', in: *Proceedings of the Third International Congress on Regional Economics*. Rome, 1965. ('The Contribution of Regional Action'.)

LEVY-LEBOYER, M.: 'The Large Corporation in Modern France', in: A. D. CHANDLER, Jr, H. DAEMS (eds), *Managerial Hierarchies. Comparative Perspectives on the Rise of the Modern Industrial Enterprise*. Cambridge (Mass.), Harvard UP, 1980, pp. 117–60. ('The Large Corporation'.)

LEWIS, W. A.: 'Economic Development with Unlimited Supplies of Labor', in: *The Manchester School*, May 1954, pp. 139–91. ('Economic Development'.)

LIEBERMAN, S.: *The Growth of European Mixed Economies, 1945–1970. A Concise Study of the Economic Evolution of Six Countries*. New York, Schenman-Wiley, 1977. (*Mixed Economies*.)

LIEFTINCK, P.: 'Europese economische integratie', in: *De Economist*, 98, no. 4, 1950, pp. 241–61. ('Europese economische integratie'.)

—— 'Nieuwe tendenzen in de monetaire politiek', in: *De Economist*, 109, nos 3/4, 1961, pp. 145–86. ('Monetaire politiek'.)

LIERDE, J. VAN: *Europese landbouwproblemen en Europese landbouwpolitiek.* Antwerp, Standaard, 1967. (*Europese landbouwproblemen.*)

LINDER, S. B.: *An Essay on Trade and Transformation.* Stockholm, Almqvist & Wiksell, 1961. (*An Essay on Trade.*)

LINDERT, P.: *Key Currencies and Gold, 1900–1913.* Princeton, Princeton UP, 1969. (*Key Currencies and Gold.*)

LIPTON, M.: 'Manpower and Growth', in: *Aspect,* no. 11 (London), December 1963. ('Manpower and Growth'.)

LITTLE, J. S.: *Euro-dollars. The Money Market Gypsies.* New York, Harper & Row, 1975. (*Euro-dollars.*)

LIVI-BACCI, M.: *Report on the Demography and Social Pattern of Migrants in Europe, especially with Regard to International Migrations.* (Second European Population Conference organized by the Council of Europe, Strasbourg, August 31–September 7, 1971.) (*Report on the Demography.*)

LLOYDS BANK: *Lloyds Bank Review,* October 1975, April 1976, July 1976. (*Lloyds Bank Review.*)

LOCKWOOD, W. W. (ed.): *The State and Economic Enterprise in Japan.* Princeton, Princeton UP, 1965. (*The State and Economic Enterprise.*)

LUNDBERG, E.: *Instability and Economic Growth.* New Haven, Yale UP, 1968. (*Instability.*)

—— 'Postwar Stabilization Policies', in: M. BRONFENBRENNER (ed.), *Is the Business Cycle Obsolete?,* New York, Wiley, 1969, pp. 478–98. ('Stabilization Policies'.)

LUTZ, F. A.: 'The German Currency Reform and the Revival of the German Economy', in: *Economica* (*N.S.*), vol. 16, May 1949, pp. 122–42. ('German Currency Reform'.)

LUTZ, V.: *Italy: a Study in Economic Development.* Oxford, Oxford UP, 1962. (*Italy.*)

MACCRACKEN, P. (*et al.*): *Towards Full Employment and Price Stability.* Paris, OECD, 1977. (*Towards Full Employment.*)

MACDOUGALL, D.: *The World Dollar Problem. A Study in International Economics.* New York, St Martin's Press, 1957. (*The World Dollar Problem.*)

MCGRAW-HILL: *Business Plans for Research and Development Expenditures.* New York, McGraw-Hill, 1979. (*Business Plans for Research and Development.*)

MACHLUP, F.: *Remaking the International Monetary System: The Rio Agreement and Beyond.* Baltimore, Johns Hopkins UP, 1968. (*The Rio Agreement and Beyond.*)

MACKAY, D. I., BODDY, D., BRACK, J., KIACK, J. A., N. JONES: *Wages and Labour Mobility.* Paris, OECD, 1965. (*Wages and Labour Mobility.*)

—— *Labour Markets under Different Labour Conditions.* London, Allen & Unwin, 1971. (*Labour Markets.*)

MACKINNON, R. I.: 'A New Tripartite Monetary Agreement or a Limping Dollar-standard?' (Essays in International Finance, 106.) Princeton, Princeton UP, VIII-23 p., 1974. ('America's Role'.)

—— *Money in International Exchange: the Convertible Currency System.* New York, Oxford UP, 1979. (*Money in International Exchange.*)

MACLEAN, J. M., H. J. RUSH: *The Impact of Micro-Electronics on the U.K.:*

A Suggested Classification and Illustrative Case Study. (SPRU, Occasional Paper Series, no. 7, June 1978.) (*Micro-Electronics on the U.K.*)

MCNAMARA, R. S.: *Address to the Board of Governors (of the) World Bank.* Washington DC, World Bank, 1972. (*Address, 1972.*)

—— *Address to the Board of Governors (of the) World Bank.* Nairobi, World Bank, 1973. (*Address, 1973.*)

—— *Address to the Massachusetts Institute of Technology.* Washington DC, World Bank, 1977. (*Massachusetts Institute of Technology.*)

MACRAE, M.: 'Whatever Happened to British Planning', in: D. BELL, I. KRISTOL (eds), *Capitalism Today.* New York, Basic Books, 1971, pp. 140–8. ('British Planning'.)

MACURA, M.: 'Population in Europe, 1920–1970', in: C. M. CIPOLLA (ed.), *The Fontana Economic History of Europe*, vol. 5. London, Collins Fontana, 1976, pp. 1–88. ('Population in Europe'.)

MADDISON, A.: *Economic Growth in the West. Comparative Experience in Europe and North America.* London, Allen & Unwin, 1964. (*Growth in the West.*)

—— *Economic Growth in Japan and the USSR.* London, Allen & Unwin, 1969. (*Growth in Japan and the USSR.*)

—— *Economic Progress and Policy in Developing Countries.* London, Allen & Unwin, 1970. (*Economic Progress.*)

—— 'Explaining Economic Growth', in: *Banca Nazionale Del Lavoro Quarterly Review*, no. 102, September 1972, pp. 211–62. ('Explaining Economic Growth'.)

—— 'Economic Policy and Performance in Europe', in: C. M. CIPOLLA (ed.), *The Fontana Economic History of Europe*, vol. 5. London, Collins Fontana, 1976, pp. 442–508. ('Performance in Europe'.)

—— 'Long Run Dynamics of Productivity Growth', in: *Banco Nazionale del Lavoro Quarterly Review*, no. 128, March 1979, pp. 3–43. ('Long Run Dynamics'.)

MAGDOFF, H., P. M. SWEEZY: *The End of Prosperity: the American Economy in the 1970s.* New York, Monthly Review Press, 1977. (*The End of Prosperity.*)

MAIZELS, A.: *Industrial Growth and World Trade.* Cambridge, Cambridge UP, 1963. (*Industrial Growth.*)

—— *Exports and Economic Growth of Developing Countries.* Cambridge, Cambridge UP, 1968. (*Exports and Economic Growth.*)

—— *Growth and Trade.* Cambridge, Cambridge UP, 1970. (*Growth and Trade.*)

MAKIN, J. H.: *Capital Flows and Exchange-rate Flexibility in the Post-Bretton Woods Era.* (Essays in International Finance, no. 103.) Princeton, Princeton UP, 1974. (*Capital Flows and Exchange-rate Flexibility.*)

MALENBAUM, W.: *World Demand for Raw Materials in 1985 and 2000.* New York, McGraw-Hill, 1978. (*World Demand for Raw Materials.*)

MALGREM, H. B.: *International Economic Peace-keeping in Phase II.* New York, Quadrangle Press, 1973. (*Economic Peace-keeping.*)

MALLET, S.: *La Nouvelle classe ouvrière.* Paris, Seuil, 1969. (*La Nouvelle classe ouvrière.*)

MAN, H. DE: *L'Exécution du Plan du Travail par le Bureau d'Études Sociales.* Antwerp, De Sikkel, 1935. (*L'Exécution du Plan du Travail.*)

MANDEL, E.: *Het Laatkapitalisme.* Amsterdam, Van Gennep, 1976. (*Het Laatkapitalisme.*)

—— *La Crise 1974–1978. Les faits, leur interprétation marxiste.* Paris, Flammarion, 1978. (*La Crise 1974–1978.*)

MANSHOLT, S.: *Memorandum inzake de hervorming van de landbouw in de Europese Economische Gemeenschap.* (Commissie van de Europese Gemeenschappen, Brussel, 18 December 1968.) Brussels, EEC, 1968. (*Memorandum inzake de hervorming van de landbouw.*)

MARCUSE, H.: *One-Dimensional Man.* London, Routledge & Kegan Paul, 1964. (*One-Dimensional Man.*)

MARKOVIC, M.: *De revolutionaire weg van bureaukratie naar zelfbestuur.* (Euroboekje 1972/3–4.) Groningen, Wolters-Noordhoff, 1972. (*Van bureaukratie naar zelfbestuur.*)

MARRIS, R., A. WOOD (eds): *The Corporate Economy. Growth, Competition and Innovative Potential.* Cambridge (Mass.), Harvard UP, 1971.

MARTENS, B.: *De kollektivisering van de industriële besluitvorming in West-Duitsland na de Tweede Wereldoorlog.* (Unpublished thesis, K. U. Leuven, Department of Economics.) Louvain, 1971. (*De kollektivisering van de industriële besluitvorming.*)

MATHIAS, P., M. M. POSTAN (eds): *The Cambridge Economic History of Europe*, vol. 7, part 1. Cambridge, Cambridge UP, 1978. (*Cambridge Economic History of Europe.*)

MATTHEWS, R. C. O.: 'Postwar Business Cycles in the United Kingdom', in: M. BRONFENBRENNER (ed.), *Is the Business Cycle Obsolete?*, ch. 4. New York, Wiley, 1969, pp. 99–135. ('Postwar Business Cycles'.)

MEADE, J.: *The Intelligent Radical's Guide to Economic Policy. The Mixed Economy.* London, Allen & Unwin, 1975. (*The Mixed Economy.*)

MEADOWS, D. H., D. L. MEADOWS: *The Limits to Growth.* New York, Universe Books, 1972. (*Limits to Growth.*)

MEERHAEGHE, M. A. G. VAN (ed.): *Economics: Britain and the EEC.* London, Longmans, Green & Co., 1969. (*Britain and the EEC.*)

MEERSSCHE, P. VAN DE: *De Europese integratie, 1945–1970.* Antwerp, Standaard, 1971. (*De Europese integratie.*)

—— *De Noord-Zuid Confrontatie en de Nieuwe Internationale Economische Orde. Een historische-thematische-kritische inleiding.* The Hague, Martinus Nijhoff, 1981 (2). (*De Noord-Zuid Confrontatie.*)

MEESTER, G.: *Prijs- en inkomensbeleid van de landbouw in de E.G.: alternatieven en hun effecten.* The Hague, Landbouw Economisch Instituut, 1979. (*Landbouw in de E.G.*)

MEIER, E. W.: *De Europese economische integratie. Aspecten der economische groei.* Leiden, Stenfert Kroese, 1958. (*De Europese economische integratie.*)

MELMAN, S.: *Our Depleted Society.* New York, Holt, Rinehart & Winston, 1965. (*Our Depleted Society.*)

MENSCH, G.: *Das Technologische Patt. Innovationen überwinden die Depression.* Frankfurt am Main, Umschau Verlag, 1975. (*Technologische Patt.*)

—— *Stalemate in Technology. Innovations overcome Depression.* Cambridge (Mass.), Ballinger, 1978. (*Stalemate in Technology.*)

MENSCH, G., R. SCHNOPP: *Stalemate in Technology, 1925–1935: The Interplay of Stagnation and Technology.* (Discussion paper for the Annual Meeting of the American Economic History Association.) New Orleans, 1977. (*Stalemate in Technology, 1925–1935.*)

MILES, E. (ed.): 'Restructuring Ocean Regimes: Implications of the third United Nations Conference on the Law of the Sea', in: *International Organization*, vol. 31, no. 2, 1977, pp. 151–384. ('Restructuring Ocean Regimes'.)

MILLER, M.: *Plain Speaking. An Oral Biography of Harry S. Truman.* New York, Berkeley Publishing Corporation, distr. by G. P. Putnam's Sons, 1974. (*Harry S. Truman.*)

MILLER, R. E., D. SAWERS: *The Technical Development of Modern Aviation.* London, Routledge & Kegan Paul, 1968. (*Modern Aviation.*)

MILLS, F. C.: *The Structure of Postwar Prices.* (Occasional Paper no. 27.) New York, National Bureau of Economic Research, 1948. (*Postwar Prices.*)

MILWARD, A. S.: *War, Economy and Society, 1939–1945.* Berkeley, Univ. of Calif. Press, 1977. (*War, Economy and Society.*)

MINAMI, R.: *The Turning Point in Economic Development. Japan's Experience.* Tokyo, Kimokumiya, 1973. (*The Turning Point.*)

MINISTERIO DEL BILANCIO E DELLA PROGRAMMAZIONE ECONOMICO: *Programma Economica Nazionale 1971–1975.* Rome, 1972. (*Programma Economica.*)

MINTZ, I.: *Dating the United States Growth Cycles.* New York, National Bureau of Economic Research, 1974. (*Growth Cycles.*)

MISHAN, E. J.: *The Costs of Economic Growth.* London, Staples, 1967. (*Costs of Economic Growth.*)

MOESEKE, P. VAN, K. TAVERNIER (eds): *Het huis staat in brand. Ecoloquium over bevolking en vervuiling.* Antwerp, Standaard, 1975. (*Het huis staat in brand.*)

MOGGRIDGE, D. E.: *British Monetary Policy, 1924–1931.* Cambridge, Cambridge UP, 1972. (*British Monetary Policy.*)

MONROE, W. F.: *International Monetary Reconstruction. Problems and Issues.* Lexington (Mass.), D. C. Heath & Co., 1974. (*International Monetary Reconstruction.*)

—— *International Trade Policy in Transition.* Lexington (Mass.), D. C. Heath & Co., 1975. (*International Trade Policy.*)

MONROE, W.F., W. KRAUSE: *The International Monetary System in Transition.* (Paper delivered before the Southwest Economic Association Meeting, Dallas, April 8, 1977.) (*The International Monetary System.*)

—— 'The International Monetary System in Transition', in: *Journal of Inter-American Studies and World Affairs*, summer issue, 1977. ('The International Monetary System'.)

MOORE, G. H.: 'The State of the International Business Cycle', in: *Business Economics*, vol. 9, no. 4, September 1974, pp. 21–8. ('International Business Cycle'.)

MORAWETZ, D.: *Twenty-Five Years of Economic Development.* Washington DC, World Bank, 1977. (*Economic Development.*)

MORIGUCHI, C.: *Japan's Economic Growth and Business Cycles in Twenty Years: an Econometric Presentation.* (Kieler Discussion Paper, February 1967.) (*Japan's Economic Growth.*)

MORRISON, R. J.: *Expectations and Inflation. Nixon, Politics and Economics.* Lexington (Mass.), D. C. Heath & Co., 1973. (*Expectations and Inflation.*)

MOULAERT, F.: 'De Gastarbeid in de Europese Gemeenschap (I)', in: *Tydschrift voor Diplomatie,* vol. I, no. 9, May 1975, pp. 343–64. ('Gastarbeid'.)

MUNDELL, R. A.: *International Economics.* London, Macmillan, 1968. (*International Economics.*)

MUNTING, R.: *The Economic Development of the USSR.* London, Croom Helm, 1982. (*The Economic Development of the USSR.*)

MURRAY, T.: 'Preferential Tariffs for the Less Developed Countries', in: *Southern Economic Journal,* vol. 40, no. 1, July 1973, pp. 35–46. ('Preferential Tariffs'.)

MUSSON, A., E. ROBINSON: *Science and Technology in the Industrial Revolution.* Manchester, Manchester UP, 1969. (*Science and Technology.*)

MYRDAL, G.: *Asian Drama: an Inquiry into the Poverty of Nations.* (Random House for the Twentieth Century Fund.) New York, Pantheon Books, 1968, vol. 3. (*Asian Drama.*)

—— *The Challenge of World Poverty.* New York, Pantheon Books, 1970. (*World Poverty.*)

NATIONAL SCIENCE FOUNDATION: *Interactions of Science and Technology in the Innovation Process (Final Report from the Battelle Memorial Institute, Columbus, Ohio, Columbus Laboratories).* Washington DC, National Science Foundation, no. 667, 1976.

NAU, H. R.: 'The Diplomacy of World Food: Goals, Capabilities, Issues and Arenas', in: *International Organization,* vol. 32, no. 3, 1978, pp. 775–810. ('Diplomacy of World Food'.)

NELSON, R. R., PECK, M. J., E. D. KALACHEK: *Technology, Economic Growth and Public Policy.* Washington DC, Brookings, 1967. (*Technology, Economic Growth.*)

NOLEN, R.: *Active Manpower Policy in the Netherlands.* (Report, no. 6.) Paris, OECD, 1965. (*Active Manpower Policy.*)

NORDHAUS, W. D.: 'Resources as a Constraint on Growth', in: *American Economic Review,* vol. 64, no. 2, May 1974, pp. 22–6. ('Constraint on Growth'.)

NOTESTEIN, F. W.: 'Population: The Long View', in: T. W. SCHULTZ (ed.), *Food for the World.* Chicago, Univ. of Chicago Press, 1945. ('Population: The Long View'.)

NOVE, A.: *East-West Trade: Problems, Prospects, Issues.* London, Sage Publications, 1978. (*East-West Trade.*)

OECD: see ORGANIZATION FOR ECONOMIC CO-OPERATION AND DEVELOPMENT.

OKUN, A. M.: 'Potential G.N.P.: Its Measurement and Significance', in: *Proceedings of the Business and Economic Statistics Section of the American Statistical Society*, 1962. ('Potential G.N.P.'.)

—— *The Political Economy of Prosperity*. Washington DC, Brookings, 1970. (*Prosperity*.)

—— *Upward Mobility in a High Pressure Economy*. (Brookings Papers on Economic Activity, no. 1.) Washington DC, Brookings, 1973. (*Upward Mobility*.)

—— *Equality and Efficiency. The Big Trade-off*. Washington DC, Brookings, 1975. (*Equality and Efficiency*.)

ORGANIZATION FOR ECONOMIC CO-OPERATION AND DEVELOPMENT: *Labour Market Policy in Sweden*. Paris, OECD, 1963. (*Labour Market Policy in Sweden*.)

—— *Seminar on Active Manpower Policy. Reports (Brussels, 1964)*. Paris, OECD, 1964. (*Active Manpower Policy*.)

—— *The Balance of Payments Adjustment Process. A Report by Working Party No. 3 of the Economic Policy Committee of the OECD*. Paris, OECD, 1966.

—— *Inflation: the Present Problem*. Paris, OECD, 1970. (*Inflation*.)

—— *The Growth of Output 1960–1980. Retrospect, prospects and problems of policy*. Paris, OECD, 1970. (*Growth of Output 1960–1980*.)

—— *Gaps in Technology: Analytical Report*. Paris, OECD, 1970. (*Gaps in Technology*.)

—— *Policy Perspectives for International Trade and Economic Relations*. Paris, OECD, 1972. (*Policy Perspectives*.)

—— *Agricultural Policy in Japan*. Paris, OECD, 1974. (*Agricultural Policy in Japan*.)

—— *Agricultural Policy in the United States*. Paris, OECD, 1974. (*Agricultural Policy in the US*.)

—— *Agricultural Policy of the European Economic Community*. Paris, OECD, 1974. (*Agricultural Policy of the EEC*.)

—— *Demographic Trends 1970–1985 in OECD Member Countries*. Paris, OECD, 1974. (*Demographic Trends*.)

—— *Continuous Reporting System on Migration*. Paris, OECD, 1976. (*Reporting System on Migration, 1976*.)

—— *Trends in Industrial R & D, 1967–1975*. Paris, OECD, 1978. (*Trends in Industrial R & D*.)

—— *Continuous Reporting System on Migration*. Paris, OECD, 1978. (*Reporting System on Migration, 1978*.)

—— *The Impact of Newly Industrializing Countries*. Paris, OECD, 1979. (*Newly Industrializing Countries*.)

—— *Science and Technology in the New Economic Context*. Paris, OECD, 1980. (*Science and Technology*.)

—— *Economic Outlook*. Paris, OECD, 1980. (*Economic Outlook*.)

—— *Manpower Statistics, 1950–1962*. Paris, OECD, 1963. (*Manpower Statistics, 1950–1962*.)

—— *Labour Force Statistics, 1969–1980*. Paris, OECD, 1981. (*Labour Force Statistics, 1969–1980*.)

—— *Economic Outlook. Historical Statistics*. Paris, OECD, various issues.

—— *Patterns of Resources Devoted to Research and Experimental Development in the OECD area, 1963–1971.* Paris, OECD, 1975. (*Patterns of Resources Devoted to R & D.*)

—— *Foreign Trade by Commodities, 1982.* Paris, OECD, 1984. (*Foreign Trade by Commodities.*)

—— *Main Economic Indicators and Historical Statistics, 1964–1983.* Paris, OECD, 1984. (*Historical Statistics, 1964–1983.*)

ORGANIZATION FOR EUROPEAN ECONOMIC CO-OPERATION: *Interim Report on the European Recovery Program.* Paris, OEEC, 1948. (*European Recovery Program.*)

—— *Premier et second rapport de l'OECE.* Paris, OEEC, 1949, 1950. (*Premier et second rapport de l'OECE.*)

OSTERRIETH, M.: *Système monétaire international et sous-développement. Aide et droits de tirage spéciaux.* Brussels, ULB, 1975. (*Système monétaire international.*)

PAIGE, D., G. BOMBACH: *A Comparison of National Output and Productivity.* Paris, OECD, 1959. (*Comparison of National Output.*)

PAISH, F. W.: *Studies in an Inflationary Economy. The United Kingdom, 1948–1961.* London, Macmillan, 1962. (*Inflationary Economy.*)

—— 'Inflation, Personal Incomes and Taxation', in: *Lloyds Bank Review*, no. 116, April 1975, pp. 1–20. ('Inflation'.)

PALLOIX, C.: *L'économie mondiale capitaliste et les firmes multinationales*, vol. I. Paris, Maspero, 1977. (*Travail et production.*)

PARTI SOCIALISTE (*et al.*): *Programme commun de gouvernement.* Paris, Flammarion, 1973. (*Programme commun.*)

PASCALLON, P.: *La planification de l'économie française.* Paris, Masson, 1974. (*L'économie française.*)

PATRICK, H. T.: 'Cyclical Instability and Fiscal-Monetary Policy in Postwar Japan', in: W. W. LOCKWOOD (ed.), *The State and Economic Enterprise in Japan.* Princeton, Princeton UP, 1965, pp. 555–618. ('Cyclical Instability'.)

PATRICK, H. T., H. ROSOVSKY (eds): *Asia's New Giant.* Washington DC, Brookings, 1976.

PAVITT, K.: 'Technical Innovation and Industrial Development. 1. The New Causality', in: *Futures*, December 1979, pp. 458–70. ('Technical Innovation. 1'.)

—— 'Technical Innovation and Industrial Development. 2. The Dangers of Divergence', in: *Futures*, February 1980, pp. 35–44. ('Technical Innovation. 2'.)

PECK, M., J. TAMURA: 'Technology', in: H. PATRICK, H. ROSOVSKY (eds), *Asia's New Giant.* Washington DC, Brookings, 1976, pp. 525–85. ('Technology'.)

PERRY, G. L.: 'Wages and Guideposts', in: *American Economic Review*, September 1967, pp. 897–905. ('Wages'.)

PHILLIPS, A. W.: 'The Relation Between Unemployment and the Rate of Change of Money Wage Rates in the United Kingdom, 1861–1937', in: *Economica*, vol. 25, no. 100, November 1958, pp. 283–99. ('United Kingdom 1861–1937'.)

PIGOTT, C., SWEENY, R. J., T. D. WILLET: 'Aggregate Economic Fluctuations and the Synchronization of Economic Conditions among Industrial Countries', in: *Rivista Internazionale di Scienze Economiche e Commerciale*, vol. 25, no. 5, May 1978, pp. 413–34. ('Aggregate Economic Fluctuations'.)

PLAN DE MODERNISATION: *Rapport sur la réalisation du Plan de Modernisation et d'Equipement de l'Union Française*. Paris, A. Colin, 1953. (*Rapport sur la réalisation du Plan de Modernisation.*)

PODBIELSKI, G.: *Italy: Development and Crisis in the Post-War Economy*. Oxford, Oxford UP, 1974. (*Italy: Development and Crisis.*)

POLEKAR (ed.): *Krisis en werkgelegenheid*. Louvain, Polekar, 1981.

POLLARD, S.: *The Development of the British Economy, 1914–1967*. London, Arnold, 1969 (2). (*British Economy, 1914–1967.*)

POPPER, K.: *The Open Society and Its Enemies*. London, Routledge & Kegan Paul, 1962 (2 vols). (*The Open Society.*)

POSNER, M. V.: 'International Trade and Technical Change', in: *Oxford Economic Papers*, vol. 13, no. 3, October 1961, pp. 323–41. ('International Trade'.)

POSTAN, M. M.: *An Economic History of Western Europe 1945–1964*. London, Methuen, 1967. (*Western Europe 1945–1964.*)

POSTHUMA, S.: 'Monetair economische verhoudingen tussen West-Europa en de Verenigde Staten van Noord-Amerika', in: *De Economist*, 113, no. 9, 1965, pp. 517–91. ('Monetair economische verhoudingen'.)

PREBISCH, R.: *Towards a New Trade Policy for Development*. New York, UN, 1964. (*Towards a New Trade Policy.*)

PREEG, E. H.: *Traders and Diplomats*. Washington DC, Brookings, 1970. (*Traders and Diplomats.*)

—— *Economic Blocs and U.S. Foreign Policy* (National Planning Association Report, no. 135). Washington DC, NPA, 1974. (*Economic Blocs.*)

PREST, A.R.: 'Fiscal Policy', in: P. COFFEY (ed.), *Economic Policies of the Common Market*. London, Macmillan, 1979, pp. 69–97. ('Fiscal Policy'.)

PRICE, H. B.: *The Marshall Plan and its Meaning*. Ithaca (New York), Cornell UP, 1955. (*The Marshall Plan.*)

RADA, J. F.: *Micro-Electronics, Information Technology and its Effects on Developing Countries*. (European Co-ordination Centre for Research and Documentation in Social Sciences, July 1979.) (*Micro-Electronics.*)

RAINES, F.: *The Impact of Applied Research and Development on Productivity*. Seattle, Washington UP, 1968. (*The Impact of Applied Research.*)

RAMSEY, S.: 'An Interview with Robert Solomon', in: *Economic Impact. A Quarterly Review of World Economics*, vol. 26, no. 2, 1972. ('Interview with Robert Solomon'.)

RASMUSSEN, W. D.: *Technology and American Agriculture: A Historical View*. (Mimeographed paper, US Department of Agriculture.) Washington DC, no date. (*Technology and American Agriculture.*)

RASMUSSEN, W. D., BAKER, G. L., J. S. WARD: *A Short History of Agricultural Adjustment, 1933–1975*. (US Department of Agriculture, Economic Research Service: Agriculture Information Bulletin, no. 391.) Washington DC, 1975. (*History of Agricultural Adjustment.*)

RATNER, S., SOLTOW, J. H., R. SYLLA: *The Evolution of the American Economy. Growth, Welfare and Decision Making.* New York, Basic Books, 1979. (*The American Economy.*)

REES, M.: *The Public Sector in the Mixed Economy.* London, Batsford, 1973. (*The Public Sector.*)

REITSMA, A. J.: 'De monetaire crisis, het vraagstuk van het optimale valuta-arsenaal en de Europese monetaire unie', in: *De Economist*, 120, no. 2, 1972, pp. 134–52. ('De monetaire crisis'.)

REUTLINGER, S., M. SELOWSKY: *Malnutrition and Poverty: Magnitude and Policy Options.* (World Bank Staff Paper.) Baltimore, Johns Hopkins UP, 1978. (*Malnutrition and Poverty.*)

REY, P. P.: *Les alliances des classes.* Paris, Maspéro, 1973. (*Alliances des classes.*)

RIESMAN, D.: *The Lonely Crowd.* New Haven, Yale UP, 1950. (*The Lonely Crowd.*)

RIPLEY, D.: 'Cyclical Fluctuations in Industrial Countries, 1952–1975', in: *Proceedings of the Second Pacific Basin Central Bank Conference on Econometric Modelling* (with later supplements, period 1952–1975, 1979). Seoul, Central Bank of Korea, 1976. ('Cyclical Fluctuations'.)

—— *The Transmissions of Fluctuations in Economic Activity: Some Recent Evidence.* (Mimeographed paper.) Washington DC, IMF, 1979. (*Transmissions of Fluctuations.*)

ROBERTI, P.: 'Did the U.K. Trend Towards Equality Really Come to an End by 1957?', in: *International Journal of Social Economics*, vol. 2, no. 1, 1975, pp. 52–9. ('U.K. Trend Towards Equality?')

ROBERTSON, R. M.: *History of the American Economy.* New York, Harcourt Brace Jovanovich, 1973 (3). (*American Economy.*)

ROMPUY, E. VAN: *Groot-Brittannië en de Europese monetaire integratie.* Louvain, Acco, 1975. (*Groot-Brittannië.*)

—— 'De relance van de Europese Monetaire Unie', in: *Kredietbank Weekberichten*, vol. 33, no. 29, 11 August 1978. ('Relance van de Europese Monetaire Unie'.)

—— 'The New Industrial State door J. K. Galbraith', in: *Tijdschrift voor Economie*, vol. 13, no. 2, 1968, pp. 193–224. ('J. K. Galbraith'.)

ROOS, F. DE: 'Zwevende wisselkoersen', in: *De Economist*, 121, no. 1, 1973, pp. 1–28. ('Zwevende wisselkoersen'.)

ROOSA, R. V.: *The Dollar and World Liquidity.* New York, Random House, 1967. (*The Dollar and World Liquidity.*)

ROSENBERG, N.: *Perspectives on Technology.* Cambridge, Cambridge UP, 1976. (*Perspectives.*)

ROSKAMP, K. W.: *Capital Formation in West Germany.* Detroit, Wayne State UP, 1965. (*Capital Formation.*)

ROSTAS, L.: *Comparative Productivity in British and American Industry.* Cambridge, Cambridge UP, 1948. (*British and American Industry.*)

ROSTOW, W. W.: *The World Economy. History and Prospect.* Austin, Texas UP, 1978. (*World Economy.*)

ROTHWELL, R.: 'The Role of Technical Change in International Competitiveness: the Case of the Textile Machinery Industry', in: *Management Decision*, vol. 15, no. 3, 1977, pp. 542–9. ('Technical Change in International Competitiveness'.)

ROTHWELL, R., W. ZEGVELD: *Technical Change and Employment*. New York, St Martin's Press, 1979. (*Technical Change*.)

RUEFF, J.: *Le péché monétaire de l'Occident*. Paris, Plon, 1971. (*Le péché monétaire*.)

—— 'The Rueff Approach', in: R. W. HINSHAW (ed.), *Monetary Reform and the Price of Gold. Alternative Approaches*. Baltimore, Johns Hopkins UP, 1977, pp. 37–46.

RUFFOLO, G. (*et al.*): *Progretto Socialista*. Rome-Bari, Laterga, 1976. (*Progretto Socialista*.)

RUFFOLO, G.: 'Project for Socialist Planning', in: S. HOLLAND (ed.), *Beyond Capitalist Planning*. Oxford, Blackwell, 1978, pp. 69–81. ('Socialist Planning'.)

RUTTAN, V. W.: 'Induced Innovation and Agricultural Development', in: *Food Policy*, August 1977. ('Induced Innovation'.)

SAKAKIBARA, E.: 'The Euro-currency Market Perspective', in: *Finance and Development*, vol. 12, no. 3, September 1975, pp. 11–13. ('The Euro-currency Market'.)

SALANT, W. S.: 'International Transmission of Inflation', in: L. B. KRAUSE, W. S. SALANT (eds), *World Wide Inflation. Theory and Experience*. Washington DC, Brookings, 1977, pp. 176–227.

SALTER, W. E. G.: *Productivity and Technical Change (second edition with an addendum by W. B. REDDAWAY)*. Cambridge, Cambridge UP, 1969 (2). (*Productivity*.)

SAMUELSON, P. A.: 'Disparity in Postwar Exchange Rates', in: S. HARRIS (ed.), *Foreign Economic Policy for the United States*. Cambridge (Mass.), Harvard UP, 1948, pp. 397–412.

—— *Economics*. New York, McGraw-Hill, 1973 (9). (*Economics*.)

SARGENT, J. R.: *Out of Stagnation: A Policy for Growth*. (Fabian Tract no. 343.) London, Fabian Society, 1963. (*Out of Stagnation*.)

SAUVY, A.: *Croissance Zéro?* Paris, Calman-Lévy, 1973. (*Croissance Zéro?*)

SAWYER, M.: *Income Distribution in OECD Countries*. (OECD Economic Outlook. Occasional Studies.) Paris, OESO, 1976. (*Income Distribution in OECD Countries*.)

SAYERS, R. S.: 'Monetary Theory and Policy in the 20th Century', in: *Seventh International Economic History Congress, Edinburgh 1978, Theme B10*. Edinburgh, Edinburgh UP, 1978, pp. 486–94. ('Monetary Theory and Policy'.)

SCAMMELL, W. M.: *International Monetary Policy. Bretton Woods and After*. London, Macmillan, 1975. (*International Monetary Policy*.)

SCHIPPER, L., A. D. LICHTENBERG: 'Efficient Energy Use and Well Being: the Swedish Example', in: *Science*, vol. 194, no. 4269, December 1976, pp. 1001–12. ('Efficient Energy Use'.)

SCHLOGEL, M.: *Les relations économiques et financières internationales.* Paris, Masson, 1972. (*Les relations économiques et financières.*)

SCHMOOKLER, J.: 'Inventors, Past and Present', in: *Review of Economics and Statistics*, vol. 39, no. 3, August 1957, pp. 321–33. ('Inventors, Past and Present'.)

—— *Invention and Economic Growth.* Cambridge (Mass.), Harvard UP, 1966. (*Invention.*)

SCHNITZER, M.: *East and West Germany: a Comparative Economic Analysis.* New York, Praeger, 1972. (*East and West Germany.*)

—— *Income Distribution. A Comparative Study of the United States, Sweden, West Germany, East Germany, the United Kingdom and Japan.* (Praeger Special Studies in International Economics and Development.) New York, Praeger, 1974. (*Income Distribution.*)

SCHULTZ, T. W. (ed.): *Food for the World.* Chicago, Univ. of Chicago Press, 1945. (*Food for the World.*)

—— 'Investment in Human Capital', in: *American Economic Review*, vol. 51, no. 1, March 1961, pp. 1–17. ('Investment in Human Capital'.)

SCHUMACHER, E. F.: *Small is Beautiful. Economics as if People Mattered.* New York, Harper & Row, 1973. (*Small is Beautiful.*)

SCHUMAN, R.: 'Origines et élaboration du Plan Schuman', in: *Les Cahiers de Bruges* (Collège d'Europe, no. 4). Bruges, 1953. ('Plan Schuman'.)

SEEVERS, G. L.: 'Food Markets and their Regulations', in: *International Organization*, vol. 32, no. 3, 1978, pp. 721–44. ('Food Markets'.)

SEIBEL, C.: 'Planning in France', in: M. BORNSTEIN (ed.), *Economic Planning, East and West.* Cambridge (Mass.), Ballinger, 1975, pp. 153–88. ('Planning in France'.)

SELIM, R.: 'The United States World Granary', in: *Economic Impact*, no. 32, 1980, pp. 14–19. ('United States World Granary'.)

SEMMEL, B.: *The Rise of Free Trade Imperialism.* Cambridge, Cambridge UP, 1970. (*Free Trade Imperialism.*)

SERVAN-SCHREIBER, J. J.: *Le défi américain.* Paris, Denoël, 1967. (*Le défi américain.*)

SHINOHARA, M.: 'Postwar Business Cycles in Japan', in: M. BRONFEN-BRENNER (ed.), *Is the Business Cycle Obsolete?*, ch. 3. New York, Wiley, 1969, pp. 73–95. ('Postwar Business Cycle'.)

SHONFIELD, A.: *British Economic Policy Since the War.* Harmondsworth, Penguin, 1958. (*British Economic Policy.*)

—— *Modern Capitalism. The Changing Balance of Public and Private Power.* Oxford, Oxford UP, 1965. (*Modern Capitalism.*)

—— *Western Capitalism in the 1970s: A New Balance between Public and Private Power?* (Colloquium paper, Dec. 1976, W. Wilson International Center for Scholars.) Washington DC, 1976. (*Western Capitalism.*)

SHUNAN, J. B., D. F. ROSENAU: *The Kondratieff Wave.* New York, 1972. (*Kondratieff Wave.*)

SIMONNET, P.: 'Après l'enterrement de la réforme monétaire: M. Jeremy Morse et sa momie', in: *Le Monde*, 18 June 1974, p. 38. ('Après l'enterrement de la réforme monétaire'.)

SINGER, H. W., J. A. ANSARI: *Rich and Poor Countries.* London, Allen & Unwin, 1977. (*Rich and Poor Countries.*)

SLEEPER, R. D.: 'Manpower Redevelopment and the Selective Employment Tax', in: *Bulletin of the Oxford University Institute of Economics and Statistics*, vol. 32, no. 4, 1970, pp. 273–99. ('Manpower Redevelopment'.)

SMITH, V. K. (ed.): *Scarcity and Growth Reconsidered.* Baltimore, Johns Hopkins UP, 1979.

SMULDERS, J. A.: 'Een vergelijking van de industriële loonkosten en de reële lonen in Nederland en enige andere landen', in: *De Economist*, 106, no. 11, 1958, pp. 776–96. ('Loonkosten en reële lonen'.)

SOBOLO, Y.: *Les Tertiaires.* 1974. (*Les Tertiaires.*)

SODERSTROM, L.: *Den Svenska Kopkraftsfordelningen: 1967.* Stockholm, Statens Offentlige Utredningar, 1971. (*Svenska Kopkraftsfordelningen.*)

—— *Laginkomstproblemer.* Stockholm, Statens Offentlige Utredningar, 1972. (*Laginkomstproblemer.*)

SOLOMON, R.: *The Allocation of Oil Deficits.* (Mimeographed paper.) Washington DC, FED, 1975. (*The Allocation of Oil Deficits.*)

—— *The International Monetary System, 1945–1976. An Insider's View.* New York, Harper & Row, 1977. (*International Monetary System.*)

SOLOW, R. M.: 'A Skeptical Note on the Constancy of Relative Shares', in: *American Economic Review*, vol. 48, no. 4, September 1958, pp. 618–31. ('Constancy of Relative Shares'.)

SOLOW, R., P. TEMIN: 'Introduction', in: P. MATHIAS, M. M. POSTAN (eds.), *The Cambridge Economic History of Europe*, vol. 7. Cambridge, Cambridge UP, 1978, pp. 1–27. ('Introduction'.)

SOUZA, A. R. DE, B. FOUST: *World Space Economy.* Columbus (Ohio), Bell & Howell Co., 1979. (*World Space Economy.*)

SOZIALISTISCHE PARTEI DEUTSCHLANDS: *Ökonomisch-politischer Orientierungsrahmen für die Jahre 1975–1985 (Mannheim, 14 November 1975).* Bonn, SPD, 1975. (*Ökonomisch-politischer Orientierungsrahmen.*)

SPITÄLLER, E.: 'A Model of Inflation and its Performance in the Seven Main Industrial Countries, 1958–1976', in: *IMF Staff Papers*, vol. 25, no. 2, June 1978, pp. 254–77. ('A Model of Inflation'.)

STATISTISCHES JAHRBUCH: *Statistisches Jahrbuch.* Wiesbaden, Statistisches Bundesamt, 1952. (*Statistisches Jahrbuch.*)

STIEBER, J. W. (ed.): *Employment Problems of Automation and Advanced Technology. An International Perspective.* London, Macmillan, 1966. (*Employment Problems.*)

STREETEN, P.: 'Changing Perceptions of Development', in: *Finance and Development*, vol. 14, no. 3, September 1977, pp. 14–46.

STRYDOM, P. D. F., MULLINS, D., T. W. VAN DER LINGEN: 'Exchange Rate Adjustment with Traded and Non-Traded Goods', in: *South African Journal of Economics*, vol. 46, no. 3, 1978, pp. 213–24. ('Exchange Rate Adjustment'.)

SUNDQUIST, J. E.: *Politics and Policy: the Eisenhower, Kennedy and Johnson Years.* Washington DC, Brookings, 1968. (*Politics and Policy.*)

SVENNILSON, I.: *Growth and Stagnation in the European Economy.* Geneva, UN, 1954. (*Growth and Stagnation.*)

swann, d.: *The Economics of the Common Market*. Harmondsworth, Penguin, 1975 (3). (*The Common Market*.)

sweezy, p. m.: 'The Present Global Crisis of Capitalism', in: *Monthly Review*, vol. 29, no. 11, April 1979, pp. 1–12. ('Crisis of Capitalism'.)

tak, j. van der, haub, c., e. murphy: 'Trends in World Population', in: *Economic Impact*, no. 32, 1980, pp. 51–8. ('Trends in World Population'.)

tangri, s. s. (ed.): *Command versus Demand. Systems for Economic Growth*. Boston, Heath & Co., 1967. (*Command versus Demand*.)

tavernier, k., c. clemer: *Tewerkstelling en Inkomensmatiging in België: een onvermijdelijke keuze*. (Leuvense Economische Standpunten, no. 16.) Louvain, ces, 1979. (*Tewerkstelling en Inkomensmatiging*.)

terlecky, n.: *The Effect of R & D on Productivity Growth in Industries*. Washington dc, National Planning Association, 1974. (*The Effect of R & D*.)

tévoédjre, a.: *Poverty, Wealth of Mankind*. Oxford/New York, Pergamon, 1979. (*Poverty*.)

tew, b.: *International Monetary Cooperation, 1945–1970*. New York, Wiley, 1970. (*International Monetary Cooperation*.)

—— *The Evolution of the International Monetary System, 1945–1977*. New York, Wiley, 1977. (*The International Monetary System*.)

thurow, l. c.: *The Impact of Taxes on the American Economy*. New York, Praeger, 1970. (*The Impact of Taxes*.)

tiano, a.: *La dialectique de la dépendance. Analyse des relations économiques et financières internationales*. Paris, puf, 1977. (*Dialectique de la dépendance*.)

tilton, j.: *International Diffusion of Technology. The Case of Semi-Conductors*. Washington dc, Brookings, 1971. (*International Diffusion*.)

—— *The Future of Non-fuel Minerals*. Washington dc, Brookings, 1977. (*Non-fuel Minerals*.)

tinbergen, j.: 'Nationale en internationale maatregelen ten behoeve van de volledige werkgelegenheid', in: *De Economist*, 98, no. 5, 1950, pp. 338–51. ('Volledige werkgelegenheid'.)

—— 'Do Communists and Free Societies show a Converging Pattern?', in: *Soviet Studies*, vol. 12, no. 4, April 1961, pp. 333–41. ('Communists and Free Societies'.)

—— 'De Toenaderingstheorie', in: *Maandschrift Economie*, vol. 30, no. 2, 1966, pp. 618–31. ('De Toenaderingstheorie'.)

—— *Naar een nieuwe wereldeconomie*. Rotterdam, Rotterdam up, 1965. (*Nieuwe wereldeconomie*.)

—— *Income Distribution. Analysis and Policies*. Amsterdam, North Holland, 1975. (*Income Distribution Analysis*.)

tinbergen, j. (et al.): *Reshaping the International Order. A Report to the Club of Rome*. New York, Dutton, 1976. (*Reshaping the International Order*.)

tindemans, l.: *European Union. Report*. Brussels, Ministerie van Buitenlandse Zaken, External Trade and Co-operation in Development, 1976. (*European Union. Report*.)

TOBIN, J.: *The New Economics One Decade Older*. Princeton, Princeton UP, 1972. (*New Economics*.)

Treasury and Federal Reserve Foreign Exchange Operations: see FEDERAL RESERVE SYSTEM.

TREVITHICK, J. A.: *Inflation, a Guide to the Crisis in Economics*. Harmondsworth, Penguin, 1977. (*Inflation, a Guide*.)

TRIFFIN, R.: *Europe and the Money Muddle. From Bilateralism to Near-Convertibility, 1947–1956*. New Haven, Yale UP, 1957. (*Europe and the Money Muddle*.)

—— 'The Return to Convertibility: 1926–1931 and 1958–?', in: *Banca Nazionale del Lavoro Quarterly Review*, vol. 48, March 1959, pp. 3–57. ('The Return to Convertibility'.)

—— 'Tomorrow's Convertibility: Aims and Means of International Monetary Policy', in: *Banca Nazionale del Lavoro Quarterly Review*, vol. 49, June 1959, pp. 131–200. ('Tomorrow's Convertibility'.)

—— *Gold and the Dollar Crisis*. New Haven, Yale UP, 1960. (*Gold and the Dollar Crisis*.)

—— *The Evolution of the International Monetary System*. (Princeton Essays in International Finance.) Princeton, Princeton UP, 1964. (*The International Monetary System*.)

—— 'International Monetary Collapse and Reconstruction in April 1972', in: *Journal of International Economics*, vol. 2, no. 4, September 1972, pp. 375–400. ('International Monetary Collapse'.)

TRILATERAL COMMISSION: *Directions for World Trade in the Nineteen-Seventies*. New York, the Trilateral Commission, 1974. (*Directions for World Trade*.)

TSUNOYAMA, S.: *A Concise Economic History of Modern Japan*. Bombay, Vora, 1965. (*History of Modern Japan*.)

TSURU, S.: *Essays on the Japanese Economy*, vol. 1. Tokyo, Kinokuniya Bookstore Co., 1958. (*Japanese Economy*.)

TUCKER, R. W.: *The Inequality of Nations*. London, Robertson, 1977. (*Inequality of Nations*.)

TURPIN, W. N.: *Soviet Foreign Trade: Purpose and Performance*. Lexington (Mass.), D. C. Heath & Co., 1977. (*Soviet Foreign Trade*.)

UL HAQ, M.: *The Poverty Curtain. Choices for the Third World*. New York, Columbia UP, 1976. (*The Poverty Curtain*.)

UNCTAD: see UNITED NATIONS CONFERENCE ON TRADE AND DEVELOPMENT.

UNITED NATIONS: *Economic Survey of Europe since the War*. Geneva, UN, 1953. (*Economic Survey of Europe*.)

—— *Incomes in Post-War Europe. A Study of Policies, Growth and Distribution*. Geneva, UN, 1967. (*Incomes in Post-War Europe*.)

—— *Multinational Corporations in World Development*. New York, UN, 1973. (*Multinational Corporations*.)

UNITED NATIONS CONFERENCE ON TRADE AND DEVELOPMENT: *Towards a Global Strategy for Development. Report by the Secretary General of* the United Nations Conference on Trade and Development. New York, UN, 1968. (*Global Strategy for Development.*)

—— *General Report on the Implementation of the Generalized System of Preferences.* New York, UN, 1973. (*Implementation of the Generalized System of Preferences.*)

—— *Money, Finance and Development: Papers on International Monetary Reform.* New York, UN, 1974. (*Money, Finance and Development.*)

—— *Statistical Yearbook.* New York, UN, various issues. (*Statistical Yearbook.*)

UNITED STATES: *The United States Balance of Payments in 1968.* Washington DC, Brookings, 1963. (*United States Balance of Payments in 1968.*)

VACIAGO, G.: 'Alternative Theories of Growth and the Italian Case', in: *Banca Nazionale del Lavoro Quarterly Review*, no. 93, June 1970, pp. 130–211. ('Alternative Theories of Growth'.)

VALK, H. M. VAN DER: 'Het Amerikaanse onderwijs I'; 'Het Amerikaanse onderwijs II'; 'De betekenis van het Amerikaanse onderwijs voor Nederland III'; in: *De Economist*, 106, no. 3–4–5, 1958, pp. 171–90/225–60/338–61. ('Het Amerikaanse onderwijs'.)

—— *Het Internationaal Monetair Stelsel in een vernieuwingsfaze.* Deventer, Kluwer, 1972. (*Het Internationaal Monetair Stelsel.*)

VANDEKERCKHOVE, L., L. HUYSE: *In de buitenbaan.* Antwerp, Standaard, 1976. (*In de buitenbaan.*)

VANES, R.: *Buitenlandse handelspolitiek.* Louvain, Acco, 1971. (*Buitenlandse handelspolitiek.*)

VATTER, H. G.: 'Perspectives on the Forty-Sixth Anniversary of the U.S. Mixed Economy', in: *Explorations of Economic History*, vol. 16, no. 3, July 1979, pp. 297–330. ('The U.S. Mixed Economy'.)

VERDOORN, P. J.: 'Fattori che regolano lo sviluppo della produttivita del lavoro', in: *L'industria*, vol. 1, 1949, pp. 45–53. ('Fattori che regolano'.)

VERNON, R.: 'International Investment and International Trade in the Product Cycle', in: *Quarterly Journal of Economics*, vol. 80, no. 2, May 1966, pp. 190–207. ('International Investment'.)

—— (ed.): *The Technology Factor in International Trade.* New York, Columbia UP, 1970. (*The Technology Factor.*)

—— *Storm over the Multinationals: the Real Issues.* Cambridge (Mass.), Harvard UP, 1977. (*Storm over the Multinationals.*)

VISSER, H.: *Economische groei en de structuur van de internationale handel.* Assen, Van Gorcum, 1970. (*Structuur van de internationale handel.*)

VOLCKER, P.A.: 'Priorities for the International Monetary System', in: *Federal Reserve Bank of New York. Monthly Review*, vol. 58, no. 1, January 1976, pp. 3–9. ('Priorities for the International Monetary System'.)

VRIES, J. DE: *The Netherlands Economy in the Twentieth Century.* Assen, Van Gorcum, 1978. (*The Netherlands Economy.*)

VRIJE UNIVERSITEIT BRUSSEL (ed.): *Veertiende Vlaams Wetenschappelijk Economisch Congres. Brussel 1979. Referaten. Inkomens- en vermogensverdeling.* Brussels, VUB, 1979.

WALLICH, H. C.: *The Mainsprings of the German Revival.* New Haven, Yale UP, 1955. (*The German Revival.*)

—— 'The World Monetary System after Postponement of the Substitution Account', in: *Intereconomics*, July–August 1980, pp. 163–7. ('Postponement of the Substitution Account'.)

WALTERS, R. S.: 'UNCTAD Intervenes between Poor and Rich States', in: *Journal of World Trade Law*, vol. 7, no. 5, September–October 1973, pp. 527–54. ('UNCTAD Intervenes between Poor and Rich States'.)

WARLEY, T. K.: 'Economic Integration of European Agriculture', in: G. R. DENTON (ed.), *Economic Integration in Europe*. London, Weidenfeld & Nicolson, 1969. ('European Agriculture'.)

WASSELL, M.: 'Background to Current Trade Issues', in: B. BALASSA (*et al.*), *World Trade: Constraints and Opportunities in the 80s*, pp. 12–27. ('Current Trade Issues'.)

WEE, D. VAN DER: *Enkele theorieën over loonvorming en de verklaring van de sectoriële loonverschillen in België in 1970*. (Unpublished thesis, K. U. Leuven, Department of Economics.) Louvain, 1978. (*Enkele theorieën over loonvorming*.)

WEE, H. VAN DER (ed.): *The Great Depression Revisited. The Economics of the Thirties*. The Hague, Martinus Nijhoff, 1972. (*The Great Depression*.)

—— 'De overgang van middeleeuwen naar Nieuwe Tijd', and 'Van commerciële economie naar industriële maatschappij', in: I. SCHÖFFER, H. VAN DER WEE, J. A. BORNEWASSER, (eds), *De lage landen van 1500 tot 1780*. Amsterdam/Brussels, Elsevier, 1978, pp. 11–37, 425–38. ('Van middeleeuwen naar Nieuwe Tijd'.)

—— 'The Investment Strategy of Belgian Industrial Enterprise between 1830 and 1980 and its Influence on the Economic Development of Europe', in: *Belgium and Europe: Proceedings of the International Francqui-Colloquium Brussels-Gent, 12–14 Nov. 1980*. Brussels, Koninklijke Academie, 1981, pp. 75–94.

WEE, H. VAN DER, P. JANSSENS: 'Historiek en oorzaken van de overheidsinterventie', in: *Elfde Vlaams Wetenschappelijk Economisch Congres: 'De overheid in de gemengde ekonomie', Leuven, 4–5 mei 1973*. Louvain, K. U. Leuven UP, 1973. ('De overheidsinterventie'.)

WEE, H. VAN DER, K. TAVERNIER: *La Banque nationale de Belgique et l'histoire monétaire entre les deux guerres mondiales*. Brussels, Nationale Bank van België, 1975. (*La Banque nationale de Belgique*.)

WEINER, F.: *The European Common Market and the World*. New York, Prentice Hall, 1967. (*European Common Market*.)

WELLS, L. T. (ed.): *The Product Life Cycle and International Trade*. Boston, Harvard University Business School (Division of Research), 1972. (*International Trade*.)

WHITMAN, M. V. N.: 'The Payments Adjustment Process and the Exchange Rate Regime: What have we learned?', in: *American Economic Review*, vol. 65, no. 2, March 1975, pp. 133–46. ('The Payments Adjustment Process'.)

WILKINS, M.: *The Maturing of Multinational Enterprise*. Cambridge (Mass.), Harvard UP, 1974. (*Multinational Enterprise*.)

WILLIAMS, J. H.: *Post-War Monetary Plans and Other Essays*. New York, Knopf, 1947 (3).

WILLIAMSON, J.: *The Failure of World Monetary Reform, 1971–1974.* Sunbury-on-Thames, Nelson, 1977. (*Failure of World Monetary Reform.*)

WILLIAMSON, O. E.: 'Managerial Discretion, Organization Form and the Multidivision Hypothesis', in: R. MARRIS, A. WOOD (eds), *The Corporate Economy. Growth and Innovative Potential.* Cambridge (Mass.), Harvard UP, 1971. ('Managerial Discretion'.)

—— *Markets and Hierarchies: Analysis and Antitrust Implications.* New York, Free Press, 1975. (*Markets and Hierarchies.*)

—— 'Emergence of the Visible Hand: Implications for Industrial Organization', in: A. D. CHANDLER Jr, H. DAEMS (eds), *Managerial Hierarchies. Comparative Perspectives on the Rise of the Modern Industrial Enterprise.* Cambridge (Mass.), Harvard UP, 1980, pp. 182–202. ('Emergence of the Visible Hand'.)

WITTEVEEN, H. J.: 'Vrijheid en internationale samenwerking', in: *De Economist*, 96, no. 11, 1948, pp. 742–67. ('Internationale samenwerking'.)

—— *Conjunctuurtheorie en conjunctuurpolitiek. De huidige ontwikkeling der conjunctuurtheorie en de crisis der conjunctuurpolitiek.* Haarlem, Bohn, 1952. (*Conjunctuurtheorie en conjunctuurpolitiek.*)

WOODWARD, V.: *The Impact of Electronic Technology on U.K. Employment.* (Paper prepared for IDS/SSRC Conference on U.K. Employment, University of Sussex, 24–5 May, 1979.) (*The Impact of Electronic Technology.*)

WOLFE, J. N.: 'Productivity and Growth in Manufacturing Industry: Some Reflections on Professor Kaldor's Inaugural Lecture', in: *Economica*, May 1968, pp. 117–226. ('Productivity and Growth'.)

WORLD BANK: *World Development Report, 1978.* Washington DC, World Bank, 1978. (*Development Report, 1978.*)

—— *Commodity Trade and Price Trends* (*1978 Edition.*) (Document of the World Bank. Report no. EC-166/78.) Washington DC, World Bank, 1978. (*Commodity Trade, 1978 Edition.*)

—— *World Development Report, 1979.* Washington DC, World Bank, 1979. (*Development Report, 1979.*)

—— *World Development Report, 1980.* Washington DC, World Bank, 1980. (*Development Report, 1980.*)

YATES, P. L.: *Forty Years of Foreign Trade.* London, Allen & Unwin, 1959. (*Forty Years of Foreign Trade.*)

YOSHINO, M. Y.: 'Japan as Host to the International Corporation', in: I. FRANK (ed.), *Japan's Economy in International Perspective.* Baltimore, Johns Hopkins UP, 1975, pp. 273–90. ('Japan as Host'.)

YOUNGSON, J. A.: 'Great Britain, 1920–1970', in: C. M. CIPOLLA (ed.), *The Fontana Economic History of Europe*, vol. 6. London, Collins Fontana, 1976. ('Great Britain, 1920–1970'.)

ZIJLSTRA, J.: 'Reflections on international economic and monetary problems', in: *De Economist*, 122, no. 3, 1974, pp. 193–203. ('International and monetary problems'.)

ZINN, K. G.: 'The Social Market in Crisis', in: S. HOLLAND (ed.), *Beyond Capitalist Planning*, Oxford, Blackwell, 1978, pp. 85–105. ('Social Market in Crisis'.)

ZWING, K.: *Soziologie der Gewerkschaftsbewegung*. Jena, Gewerkschafts-Archiv, 1925. (*Soziologie der Gewerkschaftsbewegung*.)

INDEX